PC Interfacing, Communications and Windows Programming

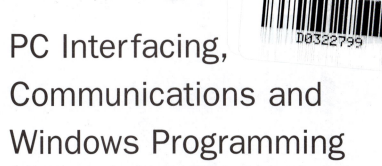

PC Interfacing, Communications and Windows Programming

William Buchanan

 ADDISON-WESLEY

Harlow, England • Reading, Massachusetts • Menlo Park, California
New York • Don Mills, Ontario • Amsterdam • Bonn • Sydney • Singapore
Tokyo • Madrid • San Juan • Milan • Mexico City • Seoul • Taipei

Addison Wesley Longman Limited
Edinburgh Gate
Harlow
Essex CM20 2JE
England

and Associated Companies throughout the World.

Typeset in Great Britain by William and Julie Buchanan
Printed and bound in Great Britain by Biddles Ltd, Guildford and King's Lynn.

First printed 1999

ISBN 0-201-17818-4

British Library Cataloguing-in-Publication Data
A catalogue record for this book is available from the British Library

Library of Congress Cataloging–in–Publication Data
Buchanan, William.
  PC interfacing : communications and Windows programming / William Buchanan.
  p. cm.
Includes bibliographical references and index.
ISBN 0-201-17818-4
1. Computer interfaces. 2. Communications software. 3. Microsoft Windows (Computer file)
I. Title.
TK7887.5.B85 1998
005.7'1—dc21
                                                    98-29435
                                                    CIP

Contents

Preface   *xiii*

1   8086 Processor   1
    1.1   Introduction   1
    1.2   8088 microprocessor   2
    1.3   Memory segmentation   5
    1.4   View inside the processor   8
    1.5   Machine code and assembly language   9
    1.6   Exercises   9
    1.7   Memory address reference   10

2   8086/8088 Instructions   11
    2.1   Assembly language mnemonics   11
    2.2   Characters and numbers   16
    2.3   Comments   16
    2.4   Move (MOV)   16
    2.5   Addressing memory   17
    2.6   Addition and subtraction (ADD and SUB)   18
    2.7   Compare (CMP)   19
    2.8   Unary operations (INC, DEC and NEG)   19
    2.9   Boolean bitwise instructions (AND, OR, XOR and NOT)   19
    2.10 Shift/rotate instructions   20
    2.11 Unconditional jump (JMP)   21
    2.12 Conditional jumps   22
    2.13 Subroutine calls (CALL and RET)   22
    2.14 PUSH and POP   23
    2.15 Moving around data in memory   23
    2.16 Assembler directives   24
    2.17 Data definition   25
    2.18 Equates (EQU)   26
    2.19 Exercises   26

3   80386/80486   31
    3.1   Introduction   31
    3.2   80486 pin out   31
    3.3   80386/80486 registers   35
    3.4   Memory cache   36
    3.5   Direct memory access (DMA)   41

4   Pentium/Pentium Pro   42
    4.1   Introduction   42
    4.2   Intel processor development   42
    4.3   Terms   44
    4.4   Pentium II and Pentium Pro   45
    4.5   System overview   45
    4.6   MMX technology   49

5   8086 Interfacing and Timing   50
    5.1   Introduction   50
    5.2   Interfacing with memory   50
    5.3   Memory mapped I/O   51
    5.4   Isolated I/O   51
    5.5   Timing   56

6   UART and PIC   59
        6.1   Introduction   59
        6.2   Universal Asynchronous Receiver Transmitter (8250)   59
        6.3   Programmable Interrupt Controller (8259)   67
7   PPI and PTC   69
        7.1   Introduction   69
        7.2   Programmable Peripheral Interface (8255)   69
        7.3   Programmable Timer Controller (8254)   77
        7.4   Exercises   85
8   Interrupts and BIOS   88
        8.1   Introduction   88
        8.2   BIOS and the operating system   89
        8.3   Interrupt vectors   90
        8.4   Processor interrupts   92
        8.5   Hardware interrupts   92
        8.6   Generating software interrupts   98
        8.7   Exercises   102
9   Interfacing Standards   104
        9.1   Introduction   104
        9.2   PC bus   104
        9.3   ISA bus   106
        9.4   MCA bus   110
        9.5   EISA bus   110
        9.6   Comparison of different types   111
        9.7   Exercises   112
10   Local Bus   114
        10.1   Introduction   114
        10.2   VESA VL-local bus   114
        10.3   PCI bus   115
        10.4   Exercises   125
        10.5   Example manufacturer and Plug-and-Play IDs   125
11   Motherboard Design   126
        11.1   Introduction   126
        11.2   Pentium processor   126
        11.3   82371SB PCI ISA Xcelerator (PIIX3)   128
        11.4   82438 System Controller (TXC)   130
        11.5   Error detection and correction   130
        11.6   PCI interface   132
        11.7   82091AA (AIP)   132
        11.8   DRAM interface   134
        11.9   Clock rates   135
        11.10   ISA/IDE interface   135
        11.11   DMA interface   135
        11.12   Interval timer   136
        11.13   Interrupt controller   137
        11.14   Mouse function   137
        11.15   Power management   137
        11.16   Universal serial bus   137
        11.17   Mouse and keyboard interface   138
        11.18   Example ATX motherboard   138
        11.19   Exercises   140
12   IDE and Mass Storage   141
        12.1   Introduction   141
        12.2   Tracks and sectors   141
        12.3   Floppy disks   142
        12.4   Fixed disks   142
        12.5   Drive specifications   143
        12.6   Hard disk/CD-ROM interfaces   144
        12.7   IDE interface   145

	12.8	IDE communication	146
	12.9	File systems	152
	12.10	Coping with disk errors	155
	12.11	Optical storage	156
	12.12	Magnetic tape	160
	12.13	Exercises	161

13   SCSI   163

	13.1	Introduction	163
	13.2	SCSI types	163
	13.3	SCSI Interface	165
	13.4	SCSI operation	167
	13.5	SCSI pointers	170
	13.6	Message system description	170
	13.7	SCSI commands	172
	13.8	Status	174
	13.9	Exercises	174

14   PCMCIA   176

	14.1	Introduction	176
	14.2	PCMCIA connections	176
	14.3	PCMCIA signals	176
	14.4	PCMCIA registers	178
	14.5	Exercises	182

15   RS-232   183

	15.1	Introduction	183
	15.2	Electrical characteristics	183
	15.3	Frame format	185
	15.4	Communications between two nodes	185
	15.5	Programming RS-232	190
	15.6	RS-232 programs	190
	15.7	Standard Windows serial communications programs	193
	15.8	Exercises	198

16   Interrupt-driven RS-232   201

	16.1	Interrupt-driven RS-232	201
	16.2	Win32 programs	201
	16.3	DOS-based RS-232 program	201
	16.4	Exercises	208

17   Parallel Port   210

	17.1	Introduction	210
	17.2	Data handshaking	210
	17.3	I/O addressing	213
	17.4	Exercises	218

18   Interrupt-driven Parallel Port   221

	18.1	Introduction	221
	18.2	Interrupts	221
	18.3	Example program	221
	18.4	Program explanation	223
	18.5	Exercises	225

19   Enhanced Parallel Port   226

	19.1	Introduction	226
	19.2	IEEE 1284 Data Transfer Modes	226
	19.3	Compatibility mode	226
	19.4	Nibble mode	227
	19.5	Byte mode	229
	19.6	EPP	230
	19.7	ECP	231
	19.8	1284 Negotiation	234
	19.9	Exercises	236

20   Modems   237

| | 20.1 | Introduction | 237 |

20.2	RS-232 communications	238
20.3	Modem standards	239
20.4	Modem commands	240
20.5	Modem setups	242
20.6	Modem indicators	244
20.7	Profile viewing	244
20.8	Test modes	245
20.9	Digital modulation	247
20.10	Typical modems	249
20.11	Fax transmission	250
20.12	Exercises	252
21	**VB (Introduction)**	**253**
21.1	Introduction	253
21.2	Event-driven programming	253
21.3	Visual Basic files	253
21.4	Other terms	255
21.5	Main screen	255
21.6	Properties window	261
21.7	Controls and Event	263
21.8	Programming language	264
21.9	Entering a program	265
21.10	Language reference	266
21.11	Exercises	278
22	**VB (Forms)**	**281**
22.1	Introduction	281
22.2	Setting properties	281
22.3	Forms and code	281
22.4	Temperature conversion program	289
22.5	Quadratic roots program	291
22.6	Resistance calculation with slider controls program	294
22.7	Exercises	298
23	**VB (Menus)**	**299**
23.1	Introduction	299
23.2	Menu editor	299
23.3	Common dialog control	305
23.4	Running an application program	311
23.5	Exercises	312
24	**VB (Events)**	**313**
24.1	Introduction	313
24.2	Program events	313
24.3	Exercises	320
25	**VB (Graphics and Timer)**	**322**
25.1	Introduction	322
25.2	Loading graphics files	322
25.3	Colours	324
25.4	Drawing	325
25.5	Timer	329
25.6	Exercises	331
26	**VB (Serial Comms)**	**332**
26.1	Introduction	332
26.2	Communications control	332
26.3	Properties	333
26.4	Events	339
26.5	Example program	340
26.6	Error messages	342
26.7	RS-232 polling	342
26.8	Exercises	343
27	**Windows 95/98/NT (Introduction)**	**344**
27.1	Introduction	344

27.2	Architecture	345
27.3	Windows registry	345
27.4	Device drivers	347
27.5	Configuration Manager	348
27.6	Virtual Machine Manager (VMM)	350
27.7	Multiple file systems	352
27.8	Core system components	354
27.9	Multitasking and threading	356
27.10	Plug-and-Play process	358
27.11	Windows NT architecture	359
27.12	Exercises	361

28 Windows Registry **362**

28.1	Introduction	362
28.2	Windows 95/98 and the Registry	362
28.3	Windows NT and the Registry	367
28.4	INF files	369
28.5	Exercises	373
28.6	Sample INF file	373

29 Win32 Introduction **376**

29.1	Introduction	376
29.2	Win32s and Windows 3.x	377
29.3	Exceptions	377

30 Win32 Basics **379**

30.1	Introduction	379
30.2	Main program	379
30.3	Creating windows	381
30.4	Sample application	391
30.5	Other Windows support functions	396
30.6	Exercises	398

31 Windows Messaging **400**

31.1	Introduction	400
31.2	Message structure	400
31.3	Message functions	401
31.4	Messages	403
31.5	Exercises	413

32 Windows Output **414**

32.1	Introduction	414
32.2	Device context	414
32.3	Text output	415
32.4	Various GDI functions	416
32.5	Exercises	421

33 Drawing and Painting **422**

33.1	Introduction	422
33.2	Colours	422
33.3	Painting and drawing functions	423
33.4	Structures	436
33.5	Exercises	437

34 Networking **439**

34.1	Introduction	439
34.2	OSI model	440
34.3	Communications standards and the OSI model	442
34.4	Standards agencies	443
34.5	Network cable types	444
34.6	LAN topology	445
34.7	Internetworking connections	446
34.8	Internet routing protocols	450
34.9	Network topologies	453
34.10	Exercises	456

35   Ethernet   457
35.1   Introduction   457
35.2   IEEE standards   458
35.3   Ethernet – media access control (MAC) layer   458
35.4   IEEE 802.2 and Ethernet SNAP   459
35.5   OSI and the IEEE 802.3 standard   461
35.6   Ethernet transceivers   463
35.7   NIC   464
35.8   Standard Ethernet limitations   468
35.9   Ethernet types   469
35.10   Twisted-pair hubs   470
35.11   100 Mbps Ethernet   472
35.12   Switches and switching hubs   477
35.13   Comparison of Fast Ethernet   479
35.14   Exercises   480

36   TCP/IP   482
36.1   Introduction   482
36.2   TCP/IP gateways and hosts   483
36.3   Function of the IP protocol   483
36.4   Internet datagram   484
36.5   ICMP   485
36.6   TCP/IP internets   486
36.7   Domain name system   491
36.8   Internet naming structure   491
36.9   Domain name server   492
36.10   Bootp protocol   493
36.11   Example network   495
36.12   IP Ver6   497
36.13   Transmission control protocol   499
36.14   TCP/IP commands   501
36.15   Exercises   506

37   WinSock Programming   507
37.1   Introduction   507
37.2   Windows Sockets   507
37.3   Practical Win32 program   516
37.4   Exercises   516

38   Java (Introduction)   517
38.1   Introduction   517
38.2   Standalone programs   519
38.3   Data types   520
38.4   Characters and strings   521
38.5   Java operators   523
38.6   Selection statements   527
38.7   Loops   530
38.8   Classes   532
38.9   Constructors   535
38.10   Method overloading   536
38.11   Static methods   538
38.12   Constants   539
38.13   Package statements   541
38.14   Import statements   541
38.15   Mathematical operations   543
38.16   Arrays   545
38.17   Exercises   548

39   Java (Events and Windows)   553
39.1   Introduction   553
39.2   Applet tag   553
39.3   Creating an applet   554
39.4   Applet basics   555
39.5   The paint() object   556

39.6	Java events	556
39.7	Java 1.0 and Java 1.1	557
39.8	Initialization and exit methods	558
39.9	Mouse events in Java 1.0	559
39.10	Mouse event handling in Java 1.1	560
39.11	Mouse selection in Java 1.0	562
39.12	Keyboard input in Java 1.0	564
39.13	Keyboard events in Java 1.1	566
39.14	Buttons and events	568
39.15	Action with Java 1.0	568
39.16	Action listener in Java 1.1	571
39.17	Checkboxes	574
39.18	Item listener in Java 1.1	574
39.19	Radio buttons	576
39.20	Pop-up menu choices	577
39.21	Other pop-up menu options	579
39.22	Multiple menus	581
39.23	Menu bar	582
39.24	List box	584
39.25	File dialog	587
39.26	Exercises	588
40	**Java (Networking)**	**590**
40.1	Introduction	590
40.2	HTTP protocol	590
40.3	Java networking functions	592
40.4	Connecting to a WWW site	598
40.5	Socket programming	602
40.6	Creating a socket	604
40.7	Client-server program	607
40.8	Exercises	608
A	**RS-232/Parallel Port**	**609**
A.1	RS-232	609
A.2	Parallel port	610
A.3	PC connections	613
A.4	Parallel port connection	613
B	**ASCII Character Codes**	**615**
C	**Win32**	**618**
C.1	Window classes	618
C.2	WNDCLASS	626
C.3	Messages	627
C.4	Win32 functions	628
D	**Modem Codes**	**648**
D.1	AT commands	648
D.2	Result codes	651
D.3	S-registers	652
E	**Quick Reference**	**656**
Index		658

Preface

This book is a follow-up to *Applied PC Interfacing, Graphics and Interrupts* and it is intended to provide a much deeper understanding of computer systems. Over the past few years, I have received a great number of emails from students and academics around the world. The main questions that I have been asked (in order of the number of times I have been asked it) are:

- *How do I communicate using the serial port?*
- *How do I communicate using the parallel port?*
- *How do I write interrupt-driven software?*
- *How do I communicate over a network?*
- *How do I program in Microsoft Windows?*
- *What is the best bus for connection to this peripheral (serial or parallel)?*
- *How do I program using Win32?*
- *How do I create a menu?*
- *Which is better for my application, C++ or Visual Basic?*
- *What devices does a PC use?*

I think there is thus a need for a book that covers all the different aspects of computer systems. From low-level hardware (such as processors and interface devices) to high-level software (such as Win32 programming). Gone are the days when a Software Engineer did not have to bother about the hardware and, by the same argument, Hardware Engineers did not need to understand the software.

This book is split into eight main sections; these are:

- Hardware. 8086 Processor, 8086 Instructions, 80386/80486/Pentium, Interfacing, UART, PIC, PPI, PTC, Interrupts, BIOS.
- Interfaces. Standards, PC/ISA, Local Bus, PCI, Motherboard Design, IDE, SCSI, PCMCIA.
- RS-232/Parallel Port. RS-232, Interrupt-driven RS-232, Parallel Port, Interrupt-driven Parallel Port, ECP/EPP mode, Modems.
- Windows Programming. VB Programming, Forms, Menus, Events, Graphics, Timer, Serial Comms.
- Windows Interfacing. Registry, Architecture.
- Win32 Programming. Messaging, Output, Drawing and Painting, Dialog Boxes and User Input, Networking.
- Networking. TCP/IP, Ethernet, WinSock.
- Java. Applets/Programs, Events and Actions, Networking.

Finally, I would personally like to thank Elaine Richardson (Senior Production Editor) and Karen Mossman (Acquisitions Editor) at Addison Wesley Longman for their hard work and their continued support. Also, I would like to thank my family, Julie, Billy, Jamie and David for their love and understanding.

Further information and source code can be found on the Addison Wesley Longman WWW site, or at:

```
http://www.eece.napier.ac.uk/~bill_b/ad_pc.html
```

Help can be sought using the email address:

```
w.buchanan@napier.ac.uk
```

Dr William Buchanan
Senior Lecturer
Napier University
219 Colinton Road
Edinburgh

Trademarks

Intel™, Pentium™ and Pentium Pro™ are registered trademarks of Intel Corporation. CompuServe is a registered trademark of CompuServe Incorporated. IBM, PS/2 and PC/XT are trademarks of International Business Machines. Microsoft® is a registered trademark. Win32™, Win32s™, DOS™, MS-DOS™, Windows™, Windows 95™, Windows 98™, Windows NT™, Internet Explorer™, Visual Basic™ , and Visual C++™ are trademarks of Microsoft Corporation. Turbo Pascal™ , Turbo Debugger™ and Borland C++™ are trademarks of Borland International Incorporated. Unix™, Novell™ and NetWare™ are trademarks of Novell Incorporated. Java™ is a trademark of Sun Microsystems Incorporated. ANSI™ is a trademark of American National Standards Institute. Netscape Communicator™ is a trademark of Netscape Communications Incorporated.

1 | 8086 Processor

1.1 Introduction

Intel marketed the first microprocessor, named the 4004. This device caused a revolution in the electronics industry because previous electronic systems had a fixed functionality. With this processor the functionality could be programmed by software. Amazingly, by today's standards, it could only handle four bits of data at a time (a nibble), contained 2000 transistors, had 46 instructions and allowed 4 kB of program code and 1 kB of data. From this humble start the PC has since evolved using Intel microprocessors (Intel is a contraction of *Int*egrated *El*ectronics).

The second generation of Intel microprocessors began in 1974. These could handle 8 bits (a byte) of data at a time and were named the 8008, 8080 and the 8085. They were much more powerful than the previous 4-bit devices and were used in many early micro-computers and in applications such as electronic instruments and printers. The 8008 has a 14-bit address bus and can thus address up to 16 kB of memory (the 8080 has a 16-bit address bus giving it a 64 kB limit).

The third generation of microprocessors began with the launch of the 16-bit processors. Intel released the 8086 microprocessor which was mainly an extension to the original 8080 processor and thus retained a degree of software compatibility. IBM's designers realized the power of the 8086 and used it in the original IBM PC and IBM XT (eXtended Technology). It has a 16-bit data bus and a 20-bit address bus, and thus has a maximum addressable capacity of 1 MB. The 8086 could handle either 8 or 16 bits of data at a time (although in a messy way).

A stripped-down, 8-bit external data bus, version called the 8088 is also available. This stripped-down processor allowed designers to produce less complex (and cheaper) computer systems. An improved architecture version, called the 80286, was launched in 1982, and was used in the IBM AT (Advanced Technology).

In 1985, Intel introduced its first 32-bit microprocessor, the 80386DX. This device was compatible with the previous 8088/8086/80286 (80×86) processors and gave excellent performance, handling 8, 16 or 32 bits at a time. It has a full 32-bit data and address buses and can thus address up to 4 GB of physical memory. A stripped-down 16-bit external data bus and 24-bit address bus version called the 80386SX was released in 1988. This stripped-down processor can thus only access up to 16 MB of physical memory.

In 1989, Intel introduced the 80486DX which is basically an improved 80386DX with a memory cache and math co-processor integrated onto the chip. It had an improved internal structure making it around 50% faster with a comparable 80386. The 80486SX was also introduced, which is merely an 80486DX with the link to the math co-processor broken. Clock doubler/trebler 80486 processors were also released. In these the processor runs at a higher speed than the system clock. Typically, systems with clock doubler processors are around 75% faster than the comparable non-doubled processors. Typical clock doubler processors are DX2-66 and DX2-50 which run from 33 MHz and 25 MHz clocks, respectively. Intel have also produced a range of 80486 microprocessors which run at three or four times the system clock speed and are referred to as DX4 processors. These include the Intel DX4-100 (25 MHz clock) and Intel DX4-75 (25 MHz clock).

The Pentium (or P-5) is a 64-bit 'superscalar' processor. It can execute more than one instruction at a time and has a full 64-bit (8-byte) data bus and a 32-bit address bus. In terms of performance, it operates almost twice as fast as the equivalent 80486. It also has improved floating-point operations (roughly three times faster) and is fully compatible with previous 80×86 processors.

The Pentium II (or P-6) is an enhancement of the P-5 and has a bus that supports up to four processors on the same bus without extra supporting logic, with clock multiplying speeds of over 300 MHz. It also has major savings of electrical power and the minimization of electromagnetic interference (EMI). A great enhancement of the P-6 bus is that it detects and corrects all single-bit data bus errors and also detects multiple-bit errors on the data bus.

1.2 8088 microprocessor

The great revolution in processing power arrived with the 16-bit 8086 processor. This has a 20-bit address bus and a 16-bit address bus, while the 8088 has an 8-bit external data bus. Figure 1.1 shows the pin connections of the 8088 and also the main connections to the processor. Many of the 40 pins of the 8086 have dual functions. For example, the lines AD0–AD7 act either as the lower 8 bits of the address bus (A0–A7) or as the lower 8 bits of the data bus (D0–D7). The lines A16/S3–A19/S6 also have a dual function, S3–S6 are normally not used by the PC and thus they are used as the 4 upper bits of the address bus. The latching of the address is achieved when the ALE (address latch enable) goes from a high to a low.

The bus controller (8288) generates the required control signals from the 8088 status lines $\overline{S0} - \overline{S1}$. For example, if $\overline{S0}$ is high, $\overline{S1}$ is low and $\overline{S2}$ is low then the $\overline{\text{MEMR}}$ line goes low. The main control signals are:

- $\overline{\text{IOR}}$ (I/O read) which means that the processor is reading from the contents of the address which is on the I/O bus.
- $\overline{\text{IOW}}$ (I/O write) which means that the processor is writing the contents of the data bus to the address which is on the I/O bus.
- $\overline{\text{MEMR}}$ (memory read) which means that the processor is reading from the contents of the address which is on the address bus.
- $\overline{\text{MEMW}}$ (memory write) which means that the processor is writing the contents of the data bust to the address which is on the address bus.
- $\overline{\text{INTA}}$ (interrupt acknowledgement) which is used by the processor to acknowledge an interrupt ($\overline{S0}$, $\overline{S1}$ and $\overline{S2}$ all go low). When a peripheral wants the attention of the processor it sends an interrupt request to the 8259 which, if it is allowed, sets INTR high.

The processor either communicates directly with memory (with $\overline{\text{MEMW}}$ and $\overline{\text{MEMR}}$) or communicates with peripherals through isolated I/O ports (with $\overline{\text{IOR}}$ and $\overline{\text{IOW}}$).

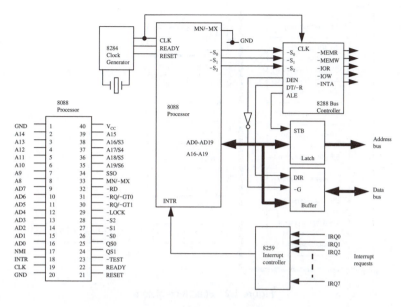

Figure 1.1 8088 connections.

1.2.1 Registers

Each of the PC-based Intel microprocessors is compatible with the original 8086 processor and is normally backwardly compatible. Thus, for example, a Pentium can run 8086, 80386 and 80486 code. Microprocessors use registers to perform their operations. These registers are basically special memory locations within the processor that have special names. The 8086/88 has 14 registers which are grouped into four categories, as illustrated in Figure 1.2.

General-purpose registers

There are four general-purpose registers that are AX, BX, CX and DX. Each can be used to manipulate a whole 16-bit word or with two separate 8-bit bytes. These bytes are called the lower and upper order bytes. Each of these registers can be used as two 8-bit registers, for example, AL represents an 8-bit register that is the lower half of AX and AH represents the upper half of AX.

The AX register is the most general purpose of the four registers and is normally used for all types of operations. Each of the other registers has one or more implied extra functions. These are:

- AX is the accumulator. It is used for all input/output operations and some arithmetic operations. For example, multiply, divide and translate instructions assume the use of AX.
- BX is the base register. It can be used as an address register.
- CX is the count register. It is used by instructions which require to count. Typically is it is used for controlling the number of times a loop is repeated and in bit-shift operations.
- DX is the data register. It is used for some input/output and also when multiplying and dividing.

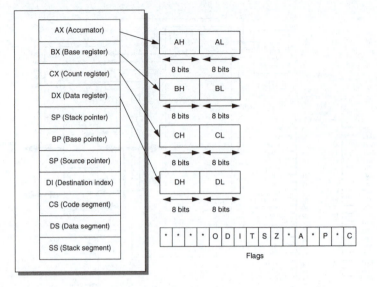

Figure 1.2   8086/88 registers.

Addressing registers

The addressing registers are used in memory addressing operations, such as holding the source address of the memory and the destination address. These address registers are named BP, SP, SI and DI, which are:

- SI is the source index and is used with extended addressing commands.
- DI is the destination index and is used in some addressing modes.
- BP is the base pointer.
- SP is the stack pointer.

Status registers

Status registers are used to test for various conditions in an operations, such as 'is the result negative', 'is the result zero', and so on. The two status registers have 16 bits and are called the instruction pointer (IP) and the flag register (F):

- IP is the instruction pointer and contains the address of the next instruction of the program.
- Flag register holds a collection of 16 different conditions. Table 1.1 outlines the most used flags.

Segments registers

There are four areas of memory called segments, each of which are 16 bits and can thus address up to 64 kB (from 0000h to FFFFh). These segments are:

- Code segment (cs register). This defines the memory location where the program code (or instructions) is stored.
- Data segment (ds register). This defines where data from the program will be stored (ds stands for data segment register).

- Stack segment (ss register). This defines where the stack is stored.
- Extra segment (es).

All addresses are with reference to the segment registers.

The 8086 has a segmented memory, the segment registers are used to manipulate memory within these segments. Each segment provides 64 kB of memory, this area of memory is known as the current segment. Segmented memory will be discussed in more detail in Section 1.3.

Table 1.1 Processor flags.

Bit	Flag position	Name	Description
C	0	Set on carry	Contains the carry from the most significant bit (left-hand bit) following a shift, rotate or arithmetic operation.
A	4	Set on 1/2 carry	
S	7	Set on negative result	Contains the sign of an arithmetic operation (0 for positive, 1 for negative).
Z	6	Set on zero result	Contains results of last arithmetic or compare result (0 for nonzero, 1 for zero).
O	11	Set on overflow	Indicates that an overflow has occurred in the most significant bit from an arithmetic operation.
P	2	Set on even parity	
D	10	Direction	
I	9	Interrupt enable	Indicates whether the interrupt has been disabled.
T	8	Trap	

Memory addressing

There are several methods of accessing memory locations, these are:

- Implied addressing which uses an instruction in which it is known which registers are used.
- Immediate (or literal) addressing uses a simple constant number to define the address location.
- Register addressing which uses the address registers for the addressing (such as AX, BX, and so on).
- Memory addressing which is used to read or write to a specified memory location.

1.3 Memory segmentation

The 80386, 80486 and Pentium processors run in one of two modes, either virtual or real. In virtual mode they act as a pseudo-8086 16-bit processor, known as the protected mode. In real-mode they can use the full capabilities of their address and data bus. This mode normally depends on the addressing capabilities of the operating system. All DOS-based programs use the virtual mode.

The 8086 has a 20-bit address bus so that when the PC is running 8086-compatible code it can only address up to 1 MB of physical memory. It also has a segmented memory architecture and can only directly address 64 kB of data at a time. A chunk of memory is known as a segment and hence the phrase 'segmented memory architecture'.

Memory addresses are normally defined by their hexadecimal address. A 4-bit address bus can address 16 locations from 0000b to 1111b. This can be represented in hexadecimal as 0h to Fh. An 8-bit bus can address up to 256 locations from 00h to FFh. Section 1.7 outlines the addressing capabilities for a given address bus size.

Two important addressing capabilities for the PC relate to a 16- and a 20-bit address bus. A 16-bit address bus addresses up to 64 kB of memory from 0000h to FFFFh and a 20-bit address bus addresses up to 1 MB from 00000h to FFFFFh. The 80386/80486/Pentium processors have a 32-bit address bus and can address from 00000000h to FFFFFFFFh.

A segmented memory address location is identified with a segment and an offset address. The standard notation is segment:offset. A segment address is a 4-digit hexadecimal address which points to the start of a 64 kB chunk of data. The offset is also a 4-digit hexadecimal address which defines the address offset from the segment base pointer. This is illustrated in Figure 1.3.

The segment:offset address is defined as the logical address, the actual physical address is calculated by shifting the segment address 4 bits to the left and adding the offset. The example given next shows that the actual address of 2F84:0532 is 2FD72h.

Segment (2F84):	0010	1111	1000	0100	0000
Offset (0532):		0000	0101	0011	0010
Actual address:	0010	1111	1101	0111	0010

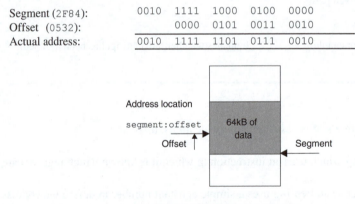

Figure 1.3   Memory addressing.

1.3.1 Accessing memory using C and Pascal

In C the address 1234:9876h is specified as 0x12349876. Turbo Pascal accesses a memory location using the predefined array mem[] (to access a byte), memw[] (a word) or memw[] (a long integer). The general format is mem[segment:offset].

1.3.2 Near and far pointers

A near pointer is a 16-bit pointer which can only be used to address up to 64 kB of data whereas a far pointer is a 20-bit pointer which can address up to 1 MB of data. A far pointer can be declared using the `far` data type modifier, as shown next.

```
char    far *ptr;      /* declare a far pointer          */
ptr=(char far *) 0x1234567;  /*initialize far pointer  */
```

In the program shown in Figure 1.4 a near pointer `ptr1` and a far pointer `ptr2` have been declared. In the bottom part of the screen the actual addresses stored in these pointers is displayed. In this case `ptr1` is `DS:1234h` and `ptr2` is `0000:1234h`. Notice that the address notation of `ptr1` is limited to a 4-digit hexadecimal address, whereas `ptr2` has a `segment:offset` address. The address of `ptr1` is in the form `DS:XXXX` where `DS` (the data segment) is a fixed address in memory and `XXXX` is the offset.

There are several modes in which the compiler operates. In the small model the compiler declares all memory addresses as near pointers and in the large model they are declared as far pointers. Figure 1.5 shows how the large memory model is selected in Borland C (`Options → Compiler → Model → Large`). The large model allows a program to store up to 1 MB of data and code. Normally, for DOS-based program, the small model is the default and only allows a maximum of 64 kB for data and 64 kB for code.

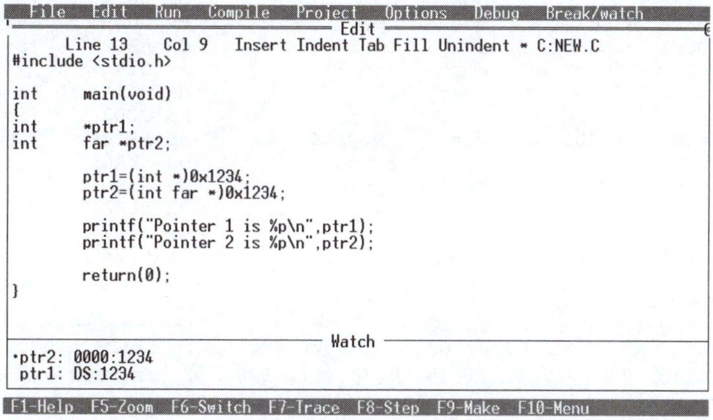

```
 File  Edit  Run  Compile  Project  Options  Debug  Break/watch
┌──────────────────────────── Edit ────────────────────────────┐
│      Line 13    Col 9    Insert Indent Tab Fill Unindent * C:NEW.C
│#include <stdio.h>
│
│int     main(void)
│{
│int     *ptr1;
│int     far *ptr2;
│
│        ptr1=(int *)0x1234;
│        ptr2=(int far *)0x1234;
│
│        printf("Pointer 1 is %p\n",ptr1);
│        printf("Pointer 2 is %p\n",ptr2);
│
│        return(0);
│}
│
│
├──────────────────────────── Watch ────────────────────────────
│•ptr2: 0000:1234
│ ptr1: DS:1234
└───────────────────────────────────────────────────────────────
 F1-Help  F5-Zoom  F6-Switch  F7-Trace  F8-Step  F9-Make  F10-Menu
```

Figure 1.4 Near and far pointers.

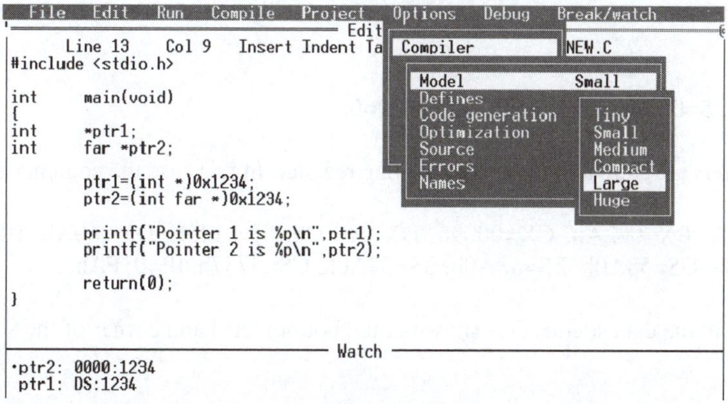

```
 File  Edit  Run  Compile  Project  Options  Debug  Break/watch
┌──────────────────────────── Edit ─┌─────────────────────────┐
│      Line 13    Col 9    Insert Indent Ta│ Compiler    │NEW.C
│#include <stdio.h>                          ├──────────────┬─────────┐
│                                            │ Model        │ Small   │
│int     main(void)                          │ Defines
│{                                           │ Code generation│ Tiny
│int     *ptr1;                              │ Optimization   │ Small
│int     far *ptr2;                          │ Source         │ Medium
│                                            │ Errors         │ Compact
│        ptr1=(int *)0x1234;                 │ Names          │ Large
│        ptr2=(int far *)0x1234;             │                │ Huge
│
│        printf("Pointer 1 is %p\n",ptr1);
│        printf("Pointer 2 is %p\n",ptr2);
│
│        return(0);
│}
│
├──────────────────────────── Watch ────────────────────────────
│•ptr2: 0000:1234
│ ptr1: DS:1234
└───────────────────────────────────────────────────────────────
```

Figure 1.5 Compiling a program in the large model.

1.4 View inside the processor

To be able to view the processor the user must use a debugging program. Figure 1.6 shows an example of Turbo Debugger which is available with many of the Borland software development products and can be used to view the operation of a program. It can be seen that the machine code and equivalent assembly language macro appears in the top left-hand window. A sample code line is:

```
cs:01FA→55                  push    bp
```

which specifies that the memory location is 01FA in the code segment (cs:01FA). The machine code at this location is 55 (0101 0101) and the equivalent Assembly Language instruction is push bp. Note that the cs segment address in this case is 5757h, thus the actual physical address will be with reference to the address 57570h.

```
+-[_]-CPU 80486---------------------------------Ð-------1-[□][□]---+
¦                                             _   ax 0000    ¦c=0¦
¦   cs:01FA→55            push   bp           _   bx 062A    ¦z=1¦
¦   cs:01FB  8BEC         mov    bp,sp        _   cx 0009    ¦s=0¦
¦   cs:01FD  83EC08       sub    sp,0008      _   dx AB02    ¦o=0¦
¦   cs:0200  56           push   si           _   si 0145    ¦p=1¦
¦   cs:0201  57           push   di           _   di 060A    ¦a=0¦
¦                                             _   bp FFD2    ¦i=1¦
¦   cs:0202  B89401       mov    ax,0194      _   sp FFC8    ¦d=0¦
¦   cs:0205  50           push   ax           _   ds 58A0    ¦   ¦
¦   cs:0206  E8D40B       call   _puts        _   es 58A0    ¦   ¦
¦   cs:0209  59           pop    cx           _   ss 58A0    ¦   ¦
¦                                                 cs 5757    ¦   ¦
¦   cs:020A  B8B501       mov    ax,01B5          ip 01FA    ¦   ¦
Ã□                                            □¦            ¦   ¦
¦  ds:0000 00 00 00 00 54 75 72 62       Turb ¦            ¦   ¦
¦  ds:0008 6F 2D 43 20 2D 20 43 6F o-C - Co   +------------------Â
¦  ds:0010 70 79 72 69 67 68 74 20 pyright    ¦  ss:FFCA 0001   ¦
¦  ds:0018 28 63 29 20 31 39 38 38 (c) 1988   ¦  ss:FFC8→011D ¦
+---------------------------------------------¤-------------------+
```

Figure 1.6   Example screen from Turbo Debugger.

The contents of the flag register is shown on the right-hand side. In this case the flags are:

C=0, Z=1, S=0, O=0, P=1, A=0, I=1 and D=0.

The registers are shown to the left of the flag register. In this case the contents are:

AX=0000h, BX=062Ah, CX=0009h, DX=AB02h, SI=0145h, DI=060Ah, BP=FFD2h, SP=FFC8h, DS=58A0h, ES=58A0h, SS=58A0h, CS=5757h, IP=01FAh.

The data (in the data segment) is shown at the bottom left-hand corner of the screen. The first line:

```
ds:0000 00 00 00 00 54 75 72 62       Turb
```

shows the first 8 bytes in memory (from DS:0000 to DS:0007). The first byte in memory is 00h (0000 0000) and the next is also 00h. After the 8 bytes are defined the 8 equivalent ASCII characters are shown. In this case, these are:

```
Turb
```

The ASCII equivalent character for 5A (1001 1010) is 'T' and for 75 (0111 0101) it is 'u'. Note that, in this case, the data segment register has 58A0h. Thus the location of the data will be referenced to the address 58A00h.

The bottom right-hand window shows the contents of the stack.

1.5 Machine code and assembly language

An important differentiation is between machine code and assembly language. The actual code that runs on the processor is machine code. These are made up to unique bit sequences which identify the command and other values which these commands operate on. For example, for the debugger screen from Figure 1.6, the assembly language line to move a value into the AX register is:

```
mov    ax,0194
```

the equivalent machine code is:

```
B8 94 01
```

where the code B8h (1011 1000b) identifies the instruction to move a 16-bit value into the AX register and the value to be loaded is 0194h (0000 0001 1001 0100b). Note that the reason that the 94h value is stored before the 01h value is that on the PC the least significant byte is stored in the first memory location and the most significant byte in the highest memory location. Figure 1.7 gives an example of storage within the code segment. In this case the two instructions are mov and push. In machine code these are B8h and 50h, respectively.

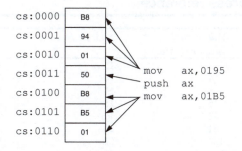

Figure 1.7   Example memory storage for code segment.

1.6 Exercises

1.6.1   How much memory can a 16-bit address bus address?

1.6.2   Outline how the 8086 differs from the 8088. Also, outline how the 80386DX differed from the 80386SX.

1.6.3   For the debug screen given in Figure 1.8 determine the following:

(i)   Contents of AX, BX, CX, DX, SI, DI.

(ii)   Contents of AH, AL, BH and BL.

(iii)   The first assembly language command.

(iv)   The physical memory address of the first line of code (Hint: the `cs:02C2` and the value in the `cs` register need to be used).

(v)   The physical memory address of the data (Hint: the `ds:0000` and the value in the `ds` register need to be used).

```
+-[_]-CPU 80486--------------------------------Đ-------1-[□][□]-+
¦                                              -  ax 0100  ¦c=0¦
¦  cs:02C2>55            push   bp             _  bx 02CE  ¦z=1¦
¦  cs:02C3 8BEC          mov    bp,sp             cx 0001  ¦s=0¦
¦                                              _  dx 02CE  ¦o=0¦
¦  cs:02C5 B8AA00        mov    ax,00AA        _  si 02C8  ¦p=1¦
¦  cs:02C8 50            push   ax             _  di 02CE  ¦a=0¦
¦  cs:02C9 E8F609        call   _puts             bp 0000  ¦i=1¦
¦  cs:02CC 59            pop    cx             _  sp FFF8  ¦d=0¦
¦                                              _  ds 5846  ¦   ¦
¦  cs:02CD 33C0          xor    ax,ax          _  es 5846  ¦   ¦
¦  cs:02CF EB00          jmp    #PROG1_1#10 (_    ss 5846  ¦   ¦
¦                                                 cs 5751  ¦   ¦
¦  cs:02D1 5D            pop    bp                ip 02C2  ¦   ¦
Ã□                                            □¦            ¦   ¦
¦  ds:0000 00 00 00 00 42 6F 72 6C      Borl  ¦            ¦   ¦
¦  ds:0008 61 6E 64 20 43 2B 2B 20 and C++    +---------------Â
¦  ds:0010 2D 20 43 6F 70 79 72 69 - Copyri   ¦ ss:FFFA 0000  ¦
¦  ds:0018 67 68 74 20 31 39 39 31 ght 1991   ¦ ss:FFF8□015B  ¦
+---------------------------------------------¤---------------+
```

Figure 1.8   Example screen from Turbo Debugger.

1.7 Memory address reference

Address bus size	Addressable memory (bytes)	Address bus size	Addressable memory (bytes)
1	2	15	32k
2	4	16	64k
3	8	17	128k
4	16	18	256k
5	32	19	512k
6	64	20	1M†
7	128	21	2M
8	256	22	4M
9	512	23	8M
10	1k*	24	16M
11	2k	25	32M
12	4k	26	64M
13	8k	32	4G‡
14	16k	64	16GG

* 1k represents 1024   † 1M represents 1 048 576 (1024 k)
‡ 1G represents 1 073 741 824 (1024 M)

2 8086/8088 Instructions

2.1 Assembly language mnemonics

Table 2.1 outlines the Assembly Language mnemonics (in column 1) and the equivalent encoded bit values (in column 3). It also shows the number of cycles for a 8086 processor and a 80386 processor (columns 4 and 5). The explanation of the encoded bit values is given after the table.

Table 2.1   Assembly Language reference.

Mnemonic	Description	Encoding	8086	386
AAA	Adjust after addition	00110111	8	4
AAD	Adjust before division	11010101 00001010	60	19
ADC accum,immed	Add immediate with carry to accumulator	0001010w mod,reg,r/m	4	2
ADC r/m,immed	Add immediate with carry to operand	100000sw mod,reg,r/m	4	2
ADC r/m,reg	Add register with carry to operand	000100dw mod,reg,r/m	3	2
ADC reg,r/m	Add operand with carry to register	000100dw mod,reg,r/m	3	2
ADD accum,immed	Add immediate to accumulator	0000010w	4	2
ADD r/m,immed	Add immediate to operand	100000sw mod,000,r/m	4	3
ADD r/m,reg	Add register to operand	0000010w mod,reg,r/m	4	2
ADD reg,r/m	Add operand to register	0000010w mod,reg,r/m	9	6
AND accum,immed	Bitwise AND immediate with operand	0010010w	4	2
AND r/m,immed	Bitwise AND register with operand	100000sw mod,100,r/m	4	2
AND r/m,reg	Bitwise AND operand with register	001000dw mod,reg,r/m	3	2
CALL label	Call instruction at label	11101000	19	7
CALL r/m	Call instruction indirect	11111111	16	7
CBW	Convert byte to word	10011000	2	3
CLC	Clear carry flag	11111000	2	2
CLD	Clear direction flag	11111100	2	2
CLI	Clear interrupt flag	11111010	2	3
CMC	Complement carry flag	11110101	2	2
CMP accum, immed	Compare immediate with accumulator	0011110w	4	2
CMP r/m,immed	Compare immediate with operand	100000sw	4	2
CMP reg,r/m	Compare register with operand	001110dw	3	2
CMPS arc,dest	Compare strings	1010011w	22	10
CMPSW	Compare strings word by word	1010011w	22	10
CMPSB	Compare string byte by byte	1010011w	22	10
CWD	Convert word to double word	10011001	5	2
DAA	Decimal adjust for addition	00100111	4	4
DAS	Decimal adjust for subtraction	00101111	4	4

DEC *r/m*	Decrement operand	1111111w	3	2
DEC *reg*	Decrement 16-bit register	01001 *reg*	3	2
DIV *r/m*	Divide accumulator by operand	1111011w	80	14
HLT	Halt	11110100	2	5
IDIV	Integer divide accumulator by operand	1111011w		
IMUL	Integer multiply accumulator by operand	1111011w		
IN *accum,immed*	Input from port	1110010w	10	12
IN *accum*,DX	Input form port given by DX	1110110w	8	13
INC *r/m*	Increment operand	1111111w *mod*,000,*r/m*	3	2
INC *reg*	Increment 16-bit register	01000 *reg*	3	2
INT *immed*	Software interrupt	11001101	51	37
INTO	Interrupt on overflow	11001110	53	35
IRET	Return from interrupt	11001111	32	22
JA *label*	Jump on above	01110111	4	3
JAE *label*	Jump on above or equal	01110011	4	3
JBE *label*	Jump on below	01110110	4	3
JC *label*	Jump on carry	01110010	4	3
JCXZ *label*	Jump on CX zero	11100011	4	3
JE *label*	Jump on equal	01110100	4	3
JG *label*	Jump on greater	01111111	4	3
JGE *label*	Jump on greater or equal	01111101	4	3
JL *label*	Jump on less than	01111100	4	3
JLE *label*	Jump on less than or equal	01111110	4	3
JMP *label*	Jump to label	11101011	15	7
JMP *r/m*	Jump to instruction directly	111111 *mod*,110,*r/m*	11	7
JNA *label*	Jump on not above	01110110	4	3
JNAE *label*	Jump on note above or equal	01110010	4	3
JNB *label*	Jump on not below	01110011	4	3
JNBE *label*	Jump on not below or equal	01110111	4	3
JNC *label*	Jump on no carry	01110011	4	3
JNE *label*	Jump on not equal	01110101	4	3
JNG *label*	Jump on not greater	01111110	4	3
JNGE *label*	Jump on not greater or equal	01111100	4	3
JNO *label*	Jump on not overflow	01110111	4	3
JNP *label*	Jump on not parity	01111011	4	3
JNS *label*	Jump on not sign	01111001	4	3
JNZ *label*	Jump on not zero	01110101	4	3
JO *label*	Jump on overflow	01110000	4	3
JP *label*	Jump on parity	01111010	4	3
JPE *label*	Jump on parity even	01111010	4	3
JPO *label*	Jump on parity odd	01111011	4	3
JS *label*	Jump on sign	01111000	4	3
JZ *label*	Jump on zero	01110100	4	3
LAHF	Load AH with flags	10011111	4	2
LOOP *label*	Loop	11100010	17	11
MOV *accum*,mem	Move memory to accumulator	101000dw	10	4

MOV mem, *accum*	Move accumulator to memory	101000dw	10	3
MOV *r/m,immed*	Move immediate to operand	1100011w *mod,*000,*r/m*	10	2
MOV *r/m,reg*	Move register to operand	100010dw *mod,reg,r/m*	2	2
MOV *r/m,segreg*	Move segment *register* to operand	100011d0 *mod,sreg,r/m*	2	2
MOV *reg,immed*	Move immediate to register	1011w *reg*	4	2
MOV *segreg,r/m*	Move operand to segment register	100011d0 *mod,sreg,r/m*	2	2
MOVS dest,src	Move string	1010010w	18	7
MOVSB	Move string byte by byte	1010010w	18	7
MOVSW	Move string word by word	1010010w	18	7
MUL *r/m*	Multiply accumulator by operand	1111011w *mod,*100,*r/m*	70	9
NEG *r/m*	Negate operand	1111011w *mod,*011,*r/m*	3	2
NOP	No operation	10010000	3	3
NOT *r/m*	Invert bits	1111011w *mod,*010,*r/m*	3	2
OR *accum,accum*	Bitwise OR immediate with accumulator	000010dw *mod,reg,r/m*	3	2
OR *r/m,immed*	Bitwise OR immediate with operand	100000sw	4	2
OR *r/m,reg*	Bitwise OR register with operand	000010dw *mod,reg,r/m*	3	2
OR *reg,r/m*	Bitwise OR operand with register	000010dw *mod,reg,r/m*	3	2
OUT DX,*accum*	Output to port given by DX	1110111w	8	11
OUT *immed,accum*	Output to port	1110011w	10	10
POP *r/m*	Pop 16-bit operand	10001111 *mod,* 000,*r/m*	17	5
POP *reg*	Pop 16-bit register from stack	01011 *reg*	8	4
POPF	Pop flags	10011101	8	5
PUSH *r/m*	Push 16-bit operand	11111111 mem,110,*r/m*	16	5
PUSH *reg*	Push 16-bit register onto stack	010101 *reg*	11	2
PUSHF	Push flags	10011100	10	4
RCL *r/m*,1	Rotate left through carry by 1 bit	1101000w *mod,*010,*r/m*	2	3
RCL *r/m,*CL	Rotate left through carry by CL bits	1101001w *mod,*010,*r/m*	8+4n	3
RCR *r/m*,1	Rotate right through carry by 1 bit	1101000w *mod,*011,*r/m*	2	3
RCR *r/m,*CL	Rotate right through carry by CL bits	1101001w *mod,*011,*r/m*	8+4n	3
REP	Repeat	11110010	9	8
REPE	Repeat if equal	11110011		
REPNE	Repeat if not equal	11110011		
REPNZ	Repeat if not zero	11110011		
RET [*immed*]	Return after popping bytes from stack	11000010		
ROL *r/m*,1	Rotate left by 1 bit	1101000w *mod,*000,*r/m*	2	3
ROL *r/m,*CL	Rotate left by CL bits	1101001w *mod,*000,*r/m*	8+4n	3
ROR *r/m*,1	Rotate right by 1 bit	1101000w *mod,*001,*r/m*	2	3
ROR *r/m,*CL	Rotate right by CL bits	1101001w *mod,*001,*r/m*	8+4n	3
SAHF	Store AH into flags	10011110	4	3
SAL *r/m*,1	Shift arithmetic left by 1 bit	1101000w *mod,*100,*r/m*	2	3
SAL *r/m,*CL	Shift arithmetic left by CL bits	1100000w *mod,*100,*r/m*	8+4n	3
SAR *r/m*,1	Shift arithmetic right by 1 bit	1101000w *mod,*101,*r/m*	2	3
SAR *r/m,*CL	Shift arithmetic right by CL bits	1100000w *mod,*101,*r/m*	8+4n	3
SBB *accum,immed*	Subtract immediate and carry flag	0001110w	4	2
SBB *r/m,immed*	Subtract immediate and carry flag	100000sw *mod,*011,*r/m*	4	2
SBB *r/m,reg*	Subtract register and carry flag	000110dw *mod,reg,r/m*	3	2

SBB *reg,r/m*	Subtract operand and carry flag	000110dw *mod,reg,r/m*	3	2
SCAS dest	Scan string	1010111w	15	7
SCASB	Scan string for byte in AL	1010111w	15	7
SCASW	Scan string for word in AX	1010111w	15	7
SHL *r/m*,1	Shift left by 1 bit	1101000w *mod,100,r/m*	2	3
SHL *r/m*,CL	Shift left by CL bits	1100000w *mod,100,r/m*	8+4n	3
SHR *r/m*,1	Shift right by 1 bit	1101000w *mod,101,r/m*	2	3
SHR *r/m*,CL	Shift right by CL bits	1100000w *mod,101,r/m*	8+4n	3
STC	Set carry flag	11111001	2	2
STD	Set direction flag	11111101	2	2
STI	Set interrupt flag	11111011	2	3
STOS dest	Store string	1010101w	11	4
STOSB	Store byte in AL at string	1010101w	11	4
STOSW	Store word in AX at string	1010101w	11	4
SUB *accum,immed*	Subtract immediate from accumulator	0010110w	4	2
SUB *r/m,immed*	Subtract immediate from operand	100000sw *mod,101,r/m*	4	2
SUB *r/m,reg*	Subtract register from operand	001010dw *mod,reg,r/m*	3	2
SUB *reg,r/m*	Subtract operand from register	001010dw *mod,reg,r/m*	3	2
TEST *accum,immed*	Compare immediate bits with accumulator	1010100w	4	2
TEST *r/m,immed*	Compare immediate bits with operand	1111011w *mod,000,r/m*	5	2
TEST *reg,r/m*	Compare register bits with operand	1000011w *mod,reg,r/m*	3	2
WAIT	Wait	10011011	4	6
XCHG *accum,reg*	Exchange accumulator with register	100011w *mod,reg,r/m*	4	3
XCHG *r/m,reg*	Exchange operand with register	100011w *mod,reg,r/m*	17	5
XCHG *reg,accum*	Exchange register with accumulator	100011w *mod,reg,r/m*	4	3
XCHG *reg,r/m*	Exchange register with operand	100011w *mod,reg,r/m*	17	5
XOR *accum,immed*	Bitwise XOR immediate with accumulator	001110dw *mod,reg,r/m*	4	2
XOR *r/m,immed*	Bitwise XOR immediate with operand	001100dw *mod,reg,r/m*	4	2
XOR *r/m,reg*	Bitwise XOR register with operand	001100dw *mod,reg,r/m*	3	2
XOR *reg,r/m*	Bitwise XOR operand with register	001100dw *mod,reg,r/m*	3	2

Syntax:

reg   A general-purpose register of any size.

segreg   A segment registers, such as DS, ES, SS or CS.

accum   An accumulator of any size: AL or AX (or EAX on 386/486).

m   A direct or indirect memory operand of any size.

label   A labelled memory location in the code segment.

src,dest A source of destination memory operand used in a string operand.

immed   A constant operand.

and the bits are specified by:

d   **direction bit**. If set (1) then the transfer is from memory to register or register to register, and the destination is a *reg* field. If not set then the source is a register field and the transfer is from register to memory.

w   **word/byte bit**. If set the 16-bit operands are used, else 8-bit operands are used.

s   **sign-bit**. If set then the operand has a sign-bit.

mod   **mode**. Identifies the register/memory mode. These are:

         00   If r/m is 110 then direct memory is used, else the displacement is 0 and an indirect memory operand is used.

         01   An indirect memory operand is used with an 8-bit displacement.

         10   An indirect memory operand is used with a 16-bit displacement.

         11   A two-register instruction is used; the reg field specifies the destination and the r/m field specifies the source.

reg   **register**. Specifies one of the general-purpose registers. These are:

reg	16-bit, if w=1	8-bit, if w=0
000	AX	AL
001	CX	CL
010	DX	DL
011	BX	BL
100	SP	AH
101	BP	CH
110	SI	DH
111	DI	BH

r/m   **register/memory**. Specifies a memory of register operand. If the mod file is 11 then the register is specified with the *reg* field (as given above), else it has the following settings:

reg	Operand address
000	**DS**:[**BX+SI**+*disp*]
001	**DS**:[**BX+DI**+*disp*]
010	**SS**:[**BP+SI**+*disp*]
011	**SS**:[**BP+DI**+*disp*]
100	**DS**:[**SI**+*disp*]
101	**DS**:[**DI**+*disp*]
110	**DS**:[**BP**+*disp*]
111	**DS**:[**BX**+*disp*]

The instruction encoding has the form:

OPCODE   *mod,reg,r/m*   *disp*   *immed*
(1–2 bytes)   (0–1 byte)   (0–2 bytes)   (0–2 bytes)

where:

disp   **displacement**. Specifies the offset for memory operands.

immed   **register/memory**. Specifies the actual values for constant values.

2.2 Characters and numbers

Integers can be represented as binary, octal, decimal, or hexadecimal numbers; 8086 Assembly Language represents these with a preceding B, O, D or H, respectively. A decimal integer is assumed if there is no letter. Examples of numeric constants are:

```
01001100b   3eh   10b   ffffh   17o
```

Character constants are enclosed with single quotes when they have a fixed number of characters (such as 'b', 'fred', and so on), or if they have a variable number of characters they are enclosed with double quotes (such as "a", "fred", and so on).
    For example:

```
'c'                'Press ENTER'
"Input Value> "    "x"
```

2.3 Comments

Assembly Language programs probably need more comments than high-level language as some of the operations give little information on their purpose. The character used to signify a comment is the semi-colon (;) and all comments within a program are ignored by the assembler. For example, the following lines have comments:

```
          ; This is a comment
mov ax,1  ; move instruction will be discussed next
```

2.4 Move (MOV)

The move instruction (mov) moves either a byte (8 bits) or a word (16 bits) from one place to another. There are three possible methods:

- Moving data from a register to a memory location.
- Moving data from a memory location to a register.
- Moving data from one register to another.

Note that in 8086/88 it is not possible to move data directly from one memory location to another using a single instruction. To move data from one memory location to another then first the data is moved from the memory location into a register, next it is moved from the register to the destination address.
    Examples of moving a constant value into registers are:

```
mov   cx,20          ; moves decimal 20 into cx
mov   ax,10h         ; moves 10 hex into ax
mov   ax,01110110b   ; moves binary 01110110 into ax
```

An address location is identified within square bracket ([]). Then to move data into a specified address the address location must be loaded into a register. For example, to load the value of 50h (0101 0000) into address location 200h the following lines are used:

```
mov   bx,200h
mov   [bx],50h    ; load 50 hex into memory location 200h
```

The general format of the mov instruction is:

```
mov r/m , r/m/d        or
mov sr , r16/m16       or
mov r16/m16 , sr
```

Where r/m stands for register (such as AH, AL, BH, BL, CH, CL, DH, DL, AX, BX, CX, DX, BP, SI, DI) or memory location. And r/m/d stands for a register, memory or a constant value. The register sr stands for any of the segment registers (CS, DS, ES, SS) and r16/m16 stand for any 16-bit register (AX, BX, CX, SP, BP, SI, DI) and 16-bit memory address.

2.5 Addressing memory

An address location can be specified with the BX, BP, SI or DI register. Examples are:

```
[BP]
[SI]
30 [BX]        ; which specifies the address BX+30
[BP+DI]
40 [BX+SI]     ; which specifies the address BX+SI+40
```

Program 2.1 gives an Assembly Language; it loads 1234h into address DS:0000h, 5678h into address DS:0002h and 22h into address DS:0005h.

📖 Program 2.1
code segment

```
mov bx,0
mov [bx],1234h
mov 2[bx],5678h
mov 5[bx],1122h
mov  ah,4ch
int  21h

code ends
end
```

Figure 2.1 shows a sample run of Program 2.1. It can be seen that the mov [bx],1234 operation loads the value 34h into address location DS:0000h and 12h into address DS:0001h. This is because the processor loads the least significant byte into the lower address location.

Figure 2.1 shows that the associated machine code for the instructions is:

```
BB    0000        mov    bx,0000
C707  3412        mov    word ptr [bx],1234
C747  02 7856     mov    word ptr [bx+02],5678
C747  05 2211     mov    word ptr [bx+05],1122
B4    4C          mov    ah,4C
```

Thus BBh is the machine code to load a value into the BX register, C707h loads a value into the address pointed to and C747h loads an offset value into an address location.

```
+-[_]-CPU 80486-------------------------------------Đ-------1-[□][□]-+
¦  cs:0000 BB0000          mov    bx,0000          -  ax 0000  ¦c=0¦
¦  cs:0003 C7073412        mov    word ptr [bx],1234  _  bx 0000  ¦z=0¦
¦  cs:0007 C747027856      mov    word ptr [bx+02],5678_  cx 0000  ¦s=0¦
¦  cs:000C C747052211      mov    word ptr [bx+05],1122_  dx 0000  ¦o=0¦
¦  cs:0011>B44C            mov    ah,4C            _  si 0000  ¦p=0¦
¦  cs:0013 CD21            int    21               _  di 0000  ¦a=0¦
¦  cs:0015 B253            mov    dl,53            _  bp 0000  ¦i=1¦
¦  cs:0017 018B7424        add    [bp+di+2474],cx  _  sp 0100  ¦d=0¦
¦  cs:001B 108B7C24        adc    [bp+di+247C],cl  _  ds 5707  ¦   ¦
¦  cs:001F 1483            adc    al,83            _  es 5707  ¦   ¦
¦  cs:0021 C404            les    ax,[si]          _  ss 5719  ¦   ¦
¦  cs:0023 56              push   si               _  cs 5717  ¦   ¦
¦  cs:0024 E85337          call   377A             _  ip 0011  ¦   ¦
Ã□                                                  □¦          ¦   ¦
¦  ds:0000 34 12 78 56 00 22 11 FE 4□xV "  _          +---------------Â
¦  ds:0008 1D F0 E0 01 21 24 AA 01 □-6□!$¬□            ¦  ss:0104 0000   ¦
¦  ds:0010 21 24 89 02 7C 1E EE 0F !$ĕ□|-‾¤            ¦  ss:0102 3D08   ¦
¦  ds:0018 01 01 01 00 02 FF FF FF □□□ □              ¦  ss:0100>C483   ¦
+---------------------------------------------------□---------------+
```

Figure 2.1 Sample run of Program 2.1

2.6 Addition and subtraction (ADD and SUB)

As they imply, the ADD and SUB perform addition and subtraction of two words or bytes. The ADD and SUB instructions operate on two operands and put the result into the first operand. The source or destination can be a register or address. Examples are:

```
mov ax,100
add ax,20    ;adds 20 onto the contents of ax
sub ax,12    ;subtracts 12 from ax and puts result into ax

mov bx,10    ;moves 10 into bx
add ax,bx    ;adds ax and bx and puts result into ax
```

The standard format of the add instruction is:

```
add r/m , r/m/d
```

where r is any register, m is memory location and d is any constant value.

2.7 Compare (CMP)

The CMP instruction acts like the SUB instruction, but the result is discarded. It thus leaves both operands intact but sets the status flags, such as the O (overflow), C (carry), Z (zero) and S (sign flag). It is typically used to determine if two numbers are the same, or if one value is greater, or less than, another value. Examples are:

```
cmp  6,5        ;result is 1, this sets C=0 S=0; Z=0 O=0
cmp  10,10      ;result is 0, this sets Z=1 the rest as above
cmp  5,6        ;result is -1, this sets negative flag S=1
```

2.8 Unary operations (INC, DEC and NEG)

The unary operations operate on a single operand. An INC instruction increments the operand by 1, the DEC instruction decrements the operand by 1 and the NEG instruction makes the operand negative. Examples are:

```
mov al,10
inc al          ; adds 1 onto AL, AL will thus store 11
inc al          ; AL now stores 12
dec al          ; takes 1 away from AL (thus it will be equal to 11)
neg al          ; make AL negative, thus AL stores -11
```

2.9 Boolean bitwise instructions (AND, OR, XOR and NOT)

The Boolean bitwise instructions operate logically on individual bits. The XOR function yields a 1 when the bits in a given bit position differ; the AND function yields a 1 only when the given bit positions are both 1s. The OR operation gives a 1 when any one of the given bit positions are a 1. These operations are summarized in Table 2.2. For example:

```
        00110011              10101111              00011001
AND     11101110      OR      10111111      XOR     11011111
        00100010              10111111              11000110
```

Table 2.2 Bitwise operations.

A	B	AND	OR	XOR
0	0	0	0	0
0	1	0	1	1
1	0	0	1	1
1	1	1	1	0

Examples of Assembly Language instructions which use bitwise operations are:

```
mov al,7dh      ;loads 01111101 into al
and al,03h      ; 01111101 AND 00000011 gives 00000001
                ;   al stores 00000001 or 1
mov ax,03f2h    ; loads 0000 0011 1111 0010 into AX
xor ax,ffffh    ; exclusive OR 1111 1111 1111 1111  with AX,
                ; AX now contain 1111 1100 0000 1101
```

2.10 Shift/rotate instructions

The shift/rotate instructions are:

SHL – shift bits left   SHR–shift bits right
SAL – shift arithmetic left   SAR–shift arithmetic right
RCL – rotate through carry left   RCR –rotate through carry right
ROL – rotate bits left   ROR –rotate bits right

The shift instructions move the bits, with or without the carry flag, and can either be an arithmetic shift or logical shift, whereas the rotate instructions are cyclic and may involve the carry flag. The SHL and SHR shift bits to the left and right, respectively. They shift the bits to the left or right where the bit shifted out is put into the carry flag and the bit shifted in is a 0. The rotate operations (ROL, ROR, RCL, RCR) are cyclic. Rotate with carry instructions (RCL and RCR) rotate the bits using the carry flag. Thus the bit shifted out is put into the carry flag and the bit shift in is taken from the carry flag. The rotate bits (ROL and ROR) rotate the bits without the carry flag. The SAL instruction is identical to SHL, but the SAR instruction differs from SHR in that the most significant bit is shifted to the right for each shift operation. This operation, and the others, are illustrated in Figure 2.2.

The number of shifts on the value is specified either as a unitary value (1) or the number of shift is stored in the counter register (CL). The standard format is:

```
SAR r/m, 1/CL    SAL r/m, 1/CL    SHR r/m, 1/CL    SHL r/m, 1/CL
ROR r/m, 1/CL    ROL r/m, 1/CL    RCR r/m, 1/CL    RCL r/m, 1/CL
```

where r/m is for register or memory and 1 stands for one shift. If any more than one shift is required the CL register is used. These operations take a destination and a counter value stored in CL. For example, with bit pattern:

Initial conditions:

01101011 and carry flag 1

Result after:

```
SHR   00110101  CF 1  → SHL   11010110  CF 0      →
SAR   00110101  CF 1  → SAL   11010110  CF 0      →
ROR   10110101  CF 0  → RCR   10110101  CF 1      →
RCL   11010111  CF 0
```

The following is an example of the SAR instruction:

```
mov cl,03           ; Contents of AX
mov ax,10110111b    ; (10110111b)
sar ax,1            ; shifted one place to the right (0101 1011b)
sar ax,cl           ; shifted three places to the right (0000 0101b)
```

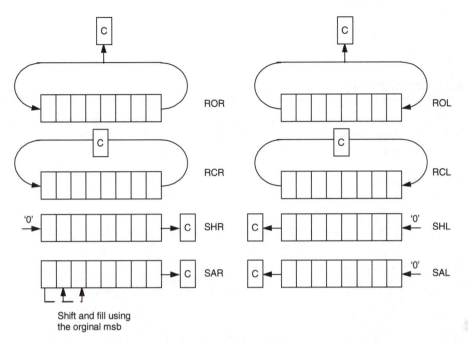

Figure 2.2 Rotate operations.

After `sar ax,1` stores `005Bh` (`0000 0000 0101 1011b`) then the `sar ax,cl` instruction moves the contents of AX by 3 bit positions to the right. The contents of AX after this operation will be `0005h` (`0000 0000 0000 0101b`).

The following shows an example of the `SHR` instruction:

```
mov cl,03          ; Contents of AX
mov ax,10110111b   ; (10110111b)

shr ax,1           ; Shift right one (01011011)
shr ax,cl          ; shift right three (00001011)
```

And an example of the `ROR` instruction:

```
mov cl,03          ; Contents of BX are :
mov bl,10110111b   ; 10110111
ror bl,1           ; rotate one place to the right(1101 1011b)
ror bl,cl          ; rotate three places to the right(0111 1011b)
```

2.11 Unconditional jump (JMP)

The JMP instruction transfers program execution to another part of the program. It uses a label to identify the jump location; this is defined as a name followed by a colon. The JMP instruction is not conditional – the program will always jump. An example is given next:

```
mov al,10101010b
jmp nextst
```

```
                        : :
                        : :
        nextst:  mov bx,10
```

2.12 Conditional jumps

With the JMP the program always goes to the label, but the unconditional jumps will only branch if a certain condition is met, such as if the result is negative, or the result is zero, and so on. Table 2.3 outlines the condition jump instructions.

A few examples are:

```
            mov    al,11
            cmp    al,10
            jle    fred  ; last operation was less than 10
                         ; then branch to label fred

fred2:    mov    ax,300
          sub    ax,1000  ; subtract 1000 from 300
          jg fred5        ; no jump since result was not greater

fred:     sub al,12      ;
          cmp al,0       ;
          jz fred2       ;no jump since not equal to zero
```

Table 2.3 Conditional jump instructions.

Name	Description	Flag tests	Name	Description	Flag tests
JC	jump if carry	C=1	JZ	jump if zero	Z=1
JS	jump if sign	S=1	JNC	jump if not carry	C=0
JNS	jump is not sign	S=0	JL	jump if less	
JNZ	jump if not zero	Z=0	JLE	jump if less or equal	
JGE	jump if greater or equal	S=Ov	JG	jump if greater	Z=0 S=Ov
JA	jump if above	C=0 and Z=0	JNB	jump if not below	
JB	jump if below				

2.13 Subroutine calls (CALL and RET)

Subroutines allow a section of code to be called and for the program to return back to where it was called. The instructions are CALL and RET. An example is given next:

```
            call   fred  ; Goto fred routine
            add    al,bl
                   : :
                   : :

fred:     mov    al,00h
          add    al,bl
          ret            ; return to place that called
```

2.14 PUSH and POP

The PUSH and POP instructions are typically used with subroutines. A PUSH instruction puts the operand onto a temporary storage called a stack (this will be covered in more detail later). The stack is a LIFO (last in, first out) where the last element to be loaded is the first to be taken off, and so on. The POP instruction is used to extract the last value which was put on the stack.

Typically they are used to preserve the contents of various registers so that their contents are recovered after a subroutine is called. For example, if a subroutine modifies the AX, BX and CX registers, then the registers are put on the stack with:

```
PUSH AX
PUSH BX
PUSH CX
```

Next, the subroutine can use these registers for its own use. Finally, within the subroutine, the original registers are restored with:

```
POP CX
POP BX
POP AX
```

The order of the POP instructions must be the reverse of the PUSH instructions so that the contents are properly restored. For example:

```
        call sub1
        add  al,bl
          : :
sub1:   push ax
        push bx
        mov  ax,1111h
        mov  bx,1111h
        add  ax,bx
          : :
        pop bx
        pop ax
        ret          ; return to place that called
```

2.15 Moving around data in memory

Program 2.2 loads the memory locations from DS:0000h to DS:00FFh with values starting at 00h and ending at FFh. After the AL and BX registers have been initialized to 00h then the code runs round a loop until all the memory locations have been loaded. The BX register contains the address the value will be loaded to. This increments each time round the loop. The AL register stores the value to be loaded into the currently specified memory location. Figure 2.3 shows a sample run.

📖 Program 2.2

```
code    segment
assume  cs:code,ds:data
start:
   mov al,00h
```

```
   mov bx,00h
   loop1:
     mov [bx],al
     inc bx
     inc al
     cmp al,0ffh
   jne loop1
   mov  ah,4ch
   int  21h
code     ends
end      start
```

```
+-[_]-CPU 80486---------------------------------Ð-------1-[□] [□]-+
¦ cs:0000 B000             mov   al,00        -  ax 0020  ¦c=1¦
¦ cs:0002 BB0000           mov   bx,0000      _  bx 0020  ¦z=0¦
¦ cs:0005 8807             mov   [bx],al      _  cx 0000  ¦s=0¦
¦ cs:0007 43               inc   bx           _  dx 0000  ¦o=0¦
¦ cs:0008 FEC0             inc   al           _  si 0000  ¦p=0¦
¦ cs:000A>3CFF             cmp   al,FF        _  di 0000  ¦a=1¦
¦ cs:000C 75F7             jne   0005         _  bp 0000  ¦i=1¦
¦ cs:000E B44C             mov   ah,4C        _  sp 0100  ¦d=0¦
¦ cs:0010 CD21             int   21           _  ds 5705  ¦    ¦
¦ cs:0012 50               push  ax           _  es 5705  ¦    ¦
¦ cs:0013 6A01             push  0001         _  ss 5717  ¦    ¦
¦ cs:0015 9AB2467711       call  1177:46B2    _  cs 5715  ¦    ¦
¦ cs:001A FF76FE           push  word ptr [bp -  ip 000A  ¦    ¦
Ã□                                           □¦           ¦    ¦
¦ ds:0000 00 01 02 03 04 05 06 07  □□□□□□□□  ¦           ¦    ¦
¦ ds:0008 08 09 0A 0B 0C 0D 0E 0F □       ¤  +---------------Â
¦ ds:0010 10 11 12 13 14 15 16 17 □□□□¶§§□□  ¦  ss:0102 C033  ¦
¦ ds:0018 18 19 1A 1B 1C 1D 1E 1F □□□□□□-    ¦  ss:0100□000C  ¦
+-------------------------------------------¤---------------+
```

Figure 2.3   Sample debug screen.

2.16 Assembler directives

There are various structure directives that allow the user to structure the program. These are defined in Table 2.4.

Table 2.4   Assembler directives.

Directive	Name	Description
SEGMENT and ENDS	segment definition	The SEGMENT and ENDS directives mark the beginning and the end of a program segment. Its general format is: ``` name segment : : : : main program : : name ends end ```
END	source file end	The END directive marks the end of a module. The assembler will ignore any statements after the end directive.
GROUP	segment group	

ASSUME	segment registers	The ASSUME directive specifies the default segment register name. For example:
		`assume cs:code`
		The general format is
		`assume segmentregister:segmentregistername`
ORG	segment origin	The ORG statement tells the assembler at which location the code should be located.
PROC and ENDP	procedure definition and end	These statements define the start and end of a procedure.

2.17 Data definition

Variables are declared in the data segment. To define a variable the DB (define byte) and DW (define word) macros are used. For example, to define (and initialize) a variable temp, which has the value 15 assigned to it, is declared as follows:

```
temp db 15
```

an uninitialized variable has a value which is a question mark, for example:

```
temp db ?
```

There are other definition types used, these are:

- dd (define doubleword – 2 times 16 bits which is 4 bytes).
- dq (define quadword, which is 8 bytes).
- dt (define 10 bytes).

The data definition is defined within the data segment. In Turbo Assembler (TASM) the data segment is defined after the .DATA directive (as shown in TASM Program 2.4). Microsoft Assembler (MASM) defines the data segment between the data segment and data ends, as shown in MASM Program 2.3.

Program 2.3 declares two variables named val1 and val2. The value val1 is loaded with the value 1234h and val2 is loaded with 5678h. Figure 2.4 shows an example screen after the three mov instructions have been executed. It can be seen val1 has been stored at DS:0000 and val2 at DS:0002.

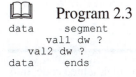 **Program 2.3**

```
data    segment
        val1 dw ?
   val2 dw ?
data    ends

code  segment
assume cs:code,ds:data
```

Program 2.4

```
.MODEL SMALL

.DATA

    val1 dw ?
    val2 dw ?
```

```
                                        .CODE
org 0100h                                   org   0100h
                                            mov   ax,1234h
start:                                      mov   val1,ax
      mov ax,1234h                          mov   val2,5678h
      mov val1,ax
      mov val2,5678h                        mov   ah,4Ch ; DOS exit
                                            int   21h
      mov ah,4Ch ; DOS exit            end
      int 21h
code     ends
end      start
```

```
+-[_]-CPU 80486------------------------------------Ð-------1-[□][□]-+
¦  cs:0000 B83412          mov    ax,1234              -  ax 1234   ¦c=0¦
¦  cs:0003 A30000          mov    [0000],ax            _  bx 0000   ¦z=0¦
¦  cs:0006 C70602007856    mov    word ptr [0002],5678 _  cx 0000   ¦s=0¦
¦  cs:000C>B44C            mov    ah,4C                _  dx 0000   ¦o=0¦
¦  cs:000E CD21            int    21                   _  si 0000   ¦p=0¦
¦  cs:0010 0F              db     0F                   _  di 0000   ¦a=0¦
¦  cs:0011 FE              db     FE                   _  bp 0000   ¦i=1¦
¦  cs:0012 50              push   ax                   _  sp 0100   ¦d=0¦
¦  cs:0013 6A01            push   0001                    ds 5705   ¦   ¦
¦  cs:0015 9AB2467711      call   1177:46B2             _ es 5705   ¦   ¦
¦  cs:001A FF76FE          push   word ptr [bp-02]      _ ss 5717   ¦   ¦
¦  cs:001D 8D8661FE        lea    ax,[bp-019F]          _ cs 5715   ¦   ¦
¦  cs:0021 50              push   ax                    ~ ip 000C   ¦   ¦
Ã□                                                 □¦              ¦   ¦
¦  ds:0000 34 12 78 56 00 9A F0 FE 4□xV Ü-_         ¦              ¦   ¦
¦  ds:0008 1D F0 E0 01 20 24 AA 01 □-Ó□ $¬□         +---------------Â
¦  ds:0010 20 24 89 02 7B 1E ED 0F $ë□{-Ý¤         ¦ ss:0102 C033  ¦
¦  ds:0018 01 01 01 00 02 FF FF FF □□□ □           ¦ ss:0100□000C  ¦
+----------------------------------------------------¤---------------+
```

Figure 2.4   Sample debug screen.

2.18 Equates (EQU)

To define a token to a certain value the EQU (equates) statement can be used. For example:

```
    one       EQU     1
    outA      EQU     1f1h
    PI        EQU     3.14159
    prompt    EQU     'Type Enter'
```

The general format is:

```
        name EQU expression
```

The assembler simply replaces every occurrence of the token with the value given.

2.19 Exercises

In this tutorial the sample code should be inserted, by replacing the highlighted code, into Program 2.5.

📖 Program 2.5

```
code segment
    mov bx,0
    mov [bx],1234h
    mov 2[bx],5678h
    mov 5[bx],1122h
    mov  ah,4ch
    int  21h
code ends
end
```

2.19.1   Enter the following code and run the debugger to determine the values given next.

```
mov al,54h
mov bl,36h
add al,bl
```

AL	Overflow flag
Sign flag	Zero flag
Carry flag	

2.19.2   Enter the following code and run the debugger to determine the values given next.

```
mov al,54h
mov bl,36h
sub al,bl
```

AL	Overflow flag
Sign flag	Zero flag
Carry flag	

2.19.3   Enter the following code and run the debugger to determine the values given next.

```
mov al,47h
mov bl,62h
sub al,bl
```

AL	Overflow flag
Sign flag	Zero flag
Carry flag	

2.19.4   Enter the following code and run the debugger to determine the values given next.

```
mov al,54h
mov bl,36h
and al,bl
```

AL	Overflow flag
Sign flag	Zero flag
Carry flag	

2.19.5   Enter the following code and run the debugger to determine the values given next.

```
mov al,73h
mov bl,36h
xor al,bl
```

AL
Carry flag
Overflow flag
Sign flag
Zero flag

2.19.6   Enter the following code and run the debugger to determine the values given next.

```
mov al,54h
not al
```

AL
Carry flag
Overflow flag
Sign flag
Zero flag

2.19.7   Enter the following code and run the debugger to determine the values given next.

```
mov ax,1f54h
mov bx,5a36h
add al,bl
```

AL
Carry flag
Overflow flag
Sign flag
Zero flag

2.19.8   Enter the following code and run the debugger to determine the values given next.

```
mov ax,3a54h
mov bx,0236h
mov cl,3
shr ax,1
shl bx,cl
```

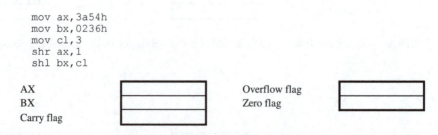

AX
BX
Carry flag

Overflow flag
Zero flag

2.19.9   Enter the following code and run the debugger to determine the values given next.

```
mov ax,3a54h
mov bx,0236h
mov cl,3
sar bx,cl
```

AX
BX
Carry flag

Overflow flag
Zero flag

2.19.10 Enter the following code and run the debugger to determine the values given next.

```
mov ax,3a54h
mov bx,0236h
mov cl,3
ror ax,cl
rcl bx,cl
```

AX
BX
Carry flag

Overflow flag
Zero flag

2.19.11 Enter the following code and run the debugger to determine the values given next.

```
mov al,54h
mov bl,66h
cmp al,bl
```

AL
BL
Carry flag

Overflow flag
Zero flag

2.19.12 Enter the following code and run the debugger to determine the values given next.

```
mov al,32
mov ah,53
mov bx,236
xor ax,bx
```

AX
BX
Carry flag

Overflow flag
Zero flag

2.19.13 Enter the following code and run the debugger to determine the values given next.

```
mov ax,3a54h
mov bx,100h
mov [bx],ax
```

AX
Contents of address 100h
Contents of address 101h

Overflow flag
Zero flag

2.19.14 Enter the following code and run the debugger to determine the values given next.

```
mov ax,3a54h
mov bx,120h
mov 20[bx],ax
```

Contents of address 100h
Contents of address 120h
Contents of address 121h

AX
Zero flag

2.19.15 Enter the following code and run the debugger to determine the values given next.

```
mov al,'a'
mov ah,'b'
```

AL
BL
Carry flag

Overflow flag
Zero flag

2.19.16 Write an Assembly Language program which contains a function which adds the contents of the AX and BX registers and puts the result into the CX register.

2.19.17 Write a program which loads the values 00h, 01h, 02h,...FEh, FFh into the memory locations starting from address DS:0008h. A basic layout is shown below.

```
loop:
    mov al,00h
    mov bx,08h
       :    :
       :    :
    jne loop
```

2.19.18 Write a program which will load the values FFh, FEh, FDh,...01h, 00h into the memory locations starting from address DS:0000h.

2.19.19 Write a program which moves a block of memory from DS:0020h to 0100h to addresses which start at address 0200h.

2.19.20 Write a program which determines the largest byte in the memory locations 0000h to 0050h.

3 80386/80486

3.1 Introduction

The PC had grown from the 8086 processor, which could run 8-bit or 16-bit software. This processor was fine with text-based applications, but struggled with graphical programs, especially with GUIs (Graphical User Interfaces). The original version of Microsoft Windows (Windows Version 1.0 and Version 2.0) ran on these limited processes. The great leap in computing power came with the development of the Intel 80386 processor and with Microsoft Windows 3.0. A key to the success of the 80386 was that it was fully compatible with the previous 8088/8086/80286 processors. This allowed it to run all existing DOS-based programs and new 32-bit applications. The DX version has full 32-bit data and address bus and can thus address up to 4 GB of physical memory. An SX version with a stripped-down 16-bit external data bus and 24-bit address bus version can access only up to 16 MB of physical memory (at its time of release this was a large amount of memory). Most of the time, with Microsoft Windows 3.0, the processor was using only 16 bits, and thus not using the full power of the processor.

The 80486DX basically consists of an improved 80386 with a memory cache and a math co-processor integrated onto the chip. An SX version had the link to the math co-processor broken. At the time, a limiting factor was the speed of the system clock (which was limited to around 25 MHz or 33 MHz). Thus clock doublers, treblers or quadrupers allow the processor to multiply the system clock frequency to a high speed. Thus, internal operations of the processor are carried out at much higher speeds, but accesses outside the processor must slow down the system clock. As most of the operations within the computer involve operations within the processor then the overall speed of the computer is improved (roughly by about 75% for a clock doubler).

3.2 80486 pin out

To allow for easy upgrades and to save space the 80486 and Pentium processors are available in a pin-grid array (PGA) form. A 168-pin PGA 80486 processor is illustrated in Figure 3.1. It can be seen that the 486 processor has a 32-bit address bus (A0–A31) and a 32-bit data bus (D0–D31). The pin definitions are given in Table 3.1.

Table 3.2 defines the how the control signals are interpreted. For the STOP/special bus cycle, the byte enable signals ($\overline{BE0} - \overline{BE3}$) further define the cycle. These are:

- Write back cycle $\overline{BE0}=1$, $\overline{BE1}=1$, $\overline{BE2}=1$, $\overline{BE3}=0$.
- Halt cycle $\overline{BE0}=1$, $\overline{BE1}=1$, $\overline{BE2}=0$, $\overline{BE3}=1$.
- Flush cycle $\overline{BE0}=1$, $\overline{BE1}=0$, $\overline{BE2}=1$, $\overline{BE3}=1$.
- Shutdown cycle $\overline{BE0}=0$, $\overline{BE1}=1$, $\overline{BE2}=1$, $\overline{BE3}=1$.

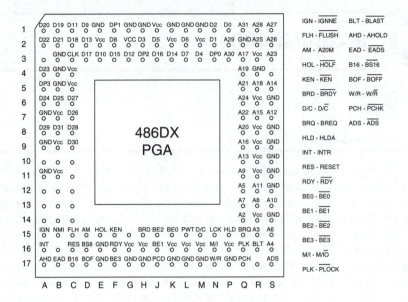

Figure 3.1 i486DX processor.

Table 3.1 80486 signal lines.

Signals	I/O	Description
A2–A31	I/O	The 30 most significant bits of the address bus.
$\overline{\text{A20M}}$	I	When active low, the processor internally masks the address bit A20 before every memory access.
$\overline{\text{ADS}}$	O	Indicates that the processor has valid control signals and valid address signals.
AHOLD	I	When active a different bus controller can have access to the address bus. This is typically used in a multi-processor system.
$\overline{\text{BE0}}$ – $\overline{\text{BE3}}$	O	The byte enable lines indicate which of the bytes of the 32-bit data bus are active.
$\overline{\text{BLAST}}$	O	Indicates that the current burst cycle will end after the next $\overline{\text{BRDY}}$ signal.
$\overline{\text{BOFF}}$	I	The backoff signal informs the processor to deactivate the bus on the next clock cycle.
$\overline{\text{BRDY}}$	I	The burst ready signal is used by an addressed system that has sent data on the data bus or read data from the bus.
BREQ	O	Indicates that the processor has internally requested the bus.
$\overline{\text{BS16}}$, $\overline{\text{BS8}}$	I	The $\overline{\text{BS16}}$ signal indicates that a 16-bit data bus is used, the

		$\overline{\text{BS8}}$ signal indicates that an 8-bit data bus is used. If both are high then a 32-bit data bus is used.
DP0–DP3	I/O	The data parity bits gives a parity check for each byte of the 32-bit data bus. The parity bits are always even parity.
$\overline{\text{EADS}}$	I	Indicates that an external bus controller has put a valid address on the address bus.
$\overline{\text{FERR}}$	O	Indicates that the processor has detected an error in the internal floating-point unit.
$\overline{\text{FLUSH}}$	I	When active the processor writes the complete contents of the cache to memory.
HOLD, HLDA	I/O	The bus hold (HOLD) and acknowledge (HLDA) are used for bus arbitration and allow other bus controllers to take control of the busses.
$\overline{\text{IGNNE}}$	I	When active the processor ignores any numeric errors.
INTR	I	External devices to interrupt the processor use the interrupt request line.
$\overline{\text{KEN}}$	I	This signal stops caching of a specific address.
$\overline{\text{LOCK}}$	O	If active the processor will not pass control to an external bus controller, when it receives a HOLD signal.
$\overline{\text{M/IO}}$, $\overline{\text{D/C}}$, $\overline{\text{W/R}}$	O	See Table 3.2.
NMI	I	The non-maskable interrupt signal causes an interrupt 2.
$\overline{\text{PCHK}}$	O	If it is set active then a data parity error has occurred.
$\overline{\text{PLOCK}}$	O	The active pseudo lock signal identifies that the current data transfer requires more than one bus cycle.
PWT, PCD	O	The page write-through (PWT) and page cache disable (PCD) are used with cache control.
$\overline{\text{RDY}}$	I	When active the addressed system has sent data on the data bus or read data from the bus.
RESET	I	If the reset signal is high for more than 15 clock cycles then the processor will reset itself.

The 486 integrates a processor, cache and a math co-processor onto a single IC. Figure 3.2 shows the main 80386/80486 processor connections. The Pentium processor connections are similar but it has a 64-bit data bus. There are three main interface connections: the memory/IO interface, interrupt interface and DMA interface.

Table 3.2 Control signals.

M/$\overline{\text{IO}}$	D/$\overline{\text{C}}$	W/$\overline{\text{R}}$	*Description*
0	0	0	Interrupt acknowledge sequence
0	0	1	STOP/special bus cycle
0	1	0	Reading from an I/O port
0	1	1	Writing to an I/O port
1	0	0	Reading an instruction from memory
1	0	1	Reserved
1	1	0	Reading data from memory
1	1	1	Writing data to memory

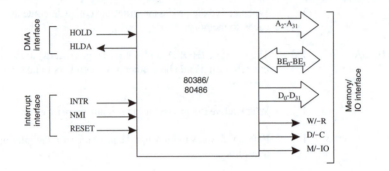

Figure 3.2 Some of the 80386/80486 signal connections.

The write/read (W/$\overline{\text{R}}$) line determines whether data is written to (W) or read from ($\overline{\text{R}}$) memory. PCs can interface directly with memory or can interface to isolated memory. The signal line M/$\overline{\text{IO}}$ differentiates between the two types. If it is high then the processor accesses direct memory; however, if it is low it then accesses isolated memory.

The 80386DX and 80486 have an external 32-bit data bus (D_0–D_{31}) and a 32-bit address bus ranging from A_2 to A_{31}. The two lower address lines, A_0 and A_1, are decoded to produce the byte enable signals $\overline{\text{BE0}}$, $\overline{\text{BE1}}$, $\overline{\text{BE2}}$ and $\overline{\text{BE3}}$. The ⌨ line activates when A_1A_0 is 00, $\overline{\text{BE1}}$ activates when A_1A_0 is 01, $\overline{\text{BE2}}$ activates when A_1A_0 and $\overline{\text{BE3}}$ actives when A_1A_0 is 11. Figure 3.5 illustrates this addressing.

The byte enable lines are also used to access either 8, 16, 24 or 32 bits of data at a time. When addressing a single byte, only the $\overline{\text{BE0}}$ line is active (D_0–D_7), if 16 bits of data are to be accessed then $\overline{\text{BE0}}$ and $\overline{\text{BE1}}$ are active (D_0–D_{15}), if 32 bits are to be accessed then $\overline{\text{BE0}}$, $\overline{\text{BE1}}$, $\overline{\text{BE2}}$ and $\overline{\text{BE3}}$ are active (D_0–D_{31}).

The D/$\overline{\text{C}}$ line differentiates between data and control signals. When it is high then data is read from or written to memory, else if it is low then a control operation is indicated, such as a shutdown command.

The interrupt lines are interrupt request (INTR), non-maskable interrupt request (NMI) and system reset (RESET), all of which are active high signals. The INTR line is activated when an external device, such as a hard disk or a serial port, wishes to communicate with the processor. This interrupt is maskable and the processor can ignore the interrupt if it wants. NMI is a non-maskable interrupt and is always acted on.

When it becomes active the processor calls the non-maskable interrupt service routine. The RESET signal causes a hardware reset and is normally made active when the processor is powered-up.

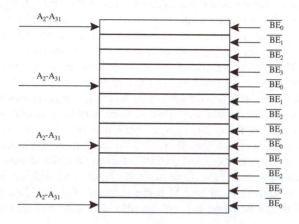

Figure 3.3 Memory addressing.

3.3   80386/80486 registers

The 80386 and 80486 are 32-bit processors and can thus operate on 32-bits at a time. They have expanded 32-bit registers, which can also be used as either 16-bit or 8-bit registers (mainly to keep compatibility with other processors and software). The general purpose registers, such as AX, BX, CX, DX, SI, DI and BP are expanded from the 8086 processor and are named EAX, EBX, ECX, EDX, ESI, EDI and EBP, respectively, as illustrated in Figure 3.4. The CS, SS and DS registers are still 16 bits, but the flag register has been expanded to 32 bits and is named EFLAG.

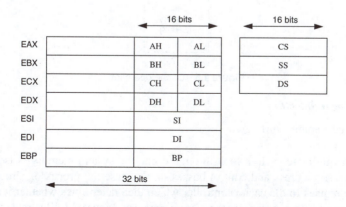

Figure 3.4   80386/80486 registers.

3.4   Memory cache

DRAM is based on the charging and discharge of tiny capacitors. It is thus a relatively slow type of memory compared with SRAM. For example, typical access time for DRAM is 80 ns and a typical motherboard clock speed is 50 MHz. This gives a clock period of 20 ns. Thus, the processor would require five wait states before the data becomes available. A cache memory can be used to overcome this problem. This is a bank of fast memory (SRAM) that uses a cache controller to load data from main memory (typically DRAM) into it. The cache controller guesses the data the processor requires and loads this into the cache memory. Figure 3.5 shows that if the controller guesses correctly then it is a cache hit, however, if it is wrong it is a cache miss. A miss causes the processor to access the memory in the normal way (that is, there may be wait states as the DRAM memory need time to get the data). Typical cache memory sizes are 16 kB, 32 kB and 64 kB for 80486 processors and 256 kB and 512 kB for Pentium processors. This should be compared with the size of the RAM on a PC which is typically at least 32 MB.

The 80486 and Pentium have built-in cache controllers and, at least, 64 kB (or 256 kB for the Pentium) of local SRAM cache memory. This is a first-level cache and the total cache size can be increased with an off-chip (or near-chip) memory (second-level cache).

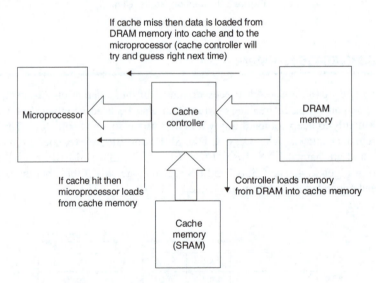

Figure 3.5   Cache operation.

3.4.1 Cache architecture

The main cache architectures are:

- **Look-through cache**. In a look-through cache the system memory is isolated from the processor address and control busses. In this case the processor directly sends a memory request to the cache controller which then determines whether it should forward it to its own memory or the system memory. Figure 3.6 illustrates this type of cache. It can be seen that the cache controls whether the processor address contents are latched through to the DRAM memory and it also controls whether the contents of the DRAM's memory is loaded onto the processor data bus (through the data transceiver). The operation is described as bus cycle forwarding.

- **Look-aside cache**. A look-aside cache is where the cache and system memory connect to a common bus. System memory and the cache controller see the beginning of the processor bus cycle at the same time. If the cache controller detects a cache hit then it must inform the system memory before it tries to find the data. If a cache miss is found then the memory access is allowed to continue.
- **Write-through cache**. With a write-through cache all memory address accesses are seen by the system memory when the processor performs a bus cycle.
- **Write-back cache**. With a write-back cache the cache controller controls all system writes. It thus does not write the system memory unless it has to.

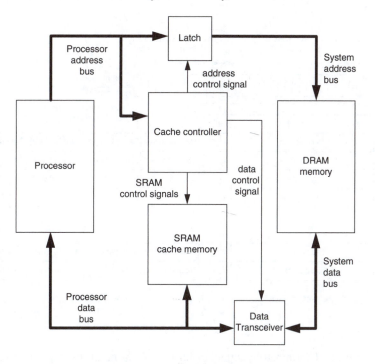

Figure 3.6 Look-through cache.

3.4.2 *Cache organization*

A cache contains a table of data which is likely to be accessed by the processor. The cache controller makes guesses on this data and fills the cache memory. Along with this data the cache must keep a record of the address that the data has been loaded from. The cache controller takes a 32-bit memory address and splits it into three parts:

- A 20-bit tag address (A12–A31).
- An 8-bit set address (A4–A11).
- A 4-bit byte address (A0–A3). A2–A3 identifies the 4-byte word and A0–A1 identifies the byte within the word.

Figure 3.7 illustrates a 4 kB-memory cache. Each entry in the cache has a cache directory entry and a corresponding cache memory entry. The cache directory entry contains information on the actual address of the data in the memory cache. Each address of the entry is defined by the set address and, as this has 8 bits, there are 256 entries in the table. Each entry in the table contains the 20-bit tag address, a write protection bit (W) and a valid bit (V). The W and V bit are used as:

- The V bit identifies that cache memory entry is valid and can thus be used if there is a cache hit for the associated cache directory entry. Initially, at power on, the cache is flushed and all the valid bits are reset. Once data is loaded into the memory cache the valid bits for each entry are then set.
- The W bit identifies that the data in the associated memory entry should not be overwritten.

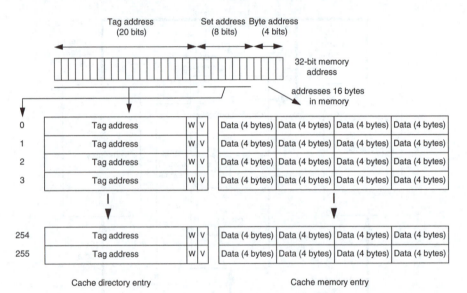

Figure 3.7 Cache directory and memory entries.

A cache hit is determined by simultaneously comparing all the tag addresses in the cache directory with the upper 20 bits of the address on the address bus. If a cache hit is found then the address lines A2 and A3 are used to select the required 32 bits from the 128-bit cache memory entry (known as a cache line).

The cache in Figure 3.7 is a direct memory cache where data from a certain location is only stored at a single place within the cache. Unfortunately, an entry which has the same set address but has a different tag address cannot be simultaneously stored. For example, the 32-bit addresses:

00000000000000000000 00101011 0000
10101010101010101010 00101011 1111

would both be stored at the set address 43 (00101011), as this address is the same they could not be simultaneously stored in the cache.

To overcome this a number of similar cache memories are built up into a number of ways. Typically this is 2-, 4- or 8-way. A 4-way cache with 4 kB in each way gives a total cache size of 16 kB; this is illustrated in Figure 3.8. Multi-way caches have an increased amount of logic, as they must check each of the ways to determine if there is a cache hit. The cache hit rate, though, increases with the number of ways, as it allows an increased number of addresses to be stored at the same time. A multi-way cache is also known as a set associative cache (as opposed to a direct-mapped cache).

The 486 processor has an integrated, on-chip cache which has a 4-way, 16-byte cache line and 128 set addresses. This gives a capacity of 8192 bytes (8 kB). This type of cache is known as an L-1 cache and can significantly improve the performance of the processor, especially when loading code from memory and loading sequentially from memory (as is typical). A linefill sequence occurs when a cache read miss occurs and the 80486 internal cache reads 16 bytes from system memory.

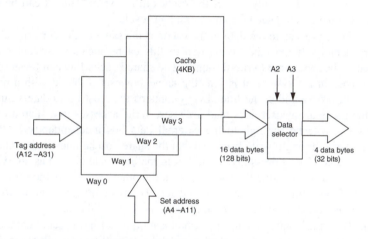

Figure 3.8   Cache with 4 ways.

3.4.3   *Second-level caches*

An L1-cache (first-level cache) provides a relatively small on-chip cache, where an L2-cache (second-level cache) provides an external, on-board, cache, which provides a cache memory of between 128 and 512 kB. The processor looks in its own L1-cache for a cache hit; if none is found then it searches in the on-board L2-cache. A cache hit in the L1-cache will obviously be faster than the off-chip cache.

An L2-cache for the Pentium has a maximum 512 kB-memory size, which has 2 ways. It is typically available as 128 kB, 256 kB or 512 kB. The cache controller internally takes a 32-bit memory address and splits it into three parts:

- A 13-bit tag address (A19–A31).
- A 13-bit set address (A6–A18).
- A 6-bit byte address (A0–A5).

Each cache line contains 64 bytes. A 13-bit set address gives a total of 8192 (2^{13}) addresses.

3.4.4 MESI states

A major problem occurs when there is more than one cache. This can happen when there is an L1-cache and an L2-cache, or when there is more than one processor, each of which has an on-chip cache. The MESI (Modified, Exclusive, Shared, Invalid) protocol is used to synchronize cache operations. The four states defined in the protocol are:

- Modified (M) – In this state the data in the cache is more recent than the corresponding location in memory. The cache line is then marked that it is only available in a single cache of the complete system.
- Exclusive (E) – In this state the data in the cache is the same as the corresponding memory location. If new data is written to a cache location then the system memory is not updated automatically (write-back). On a multi-cache system an exclusive cache line is stored on only one of the caches in a system. Thus it can be read and overwritten without the need for an external bus cycle.
- Shared (S) – In this state the data in the cache is the same as the corresponding location in memory. If new data is written to this cache location, system memory is updated at the same time (write-through). The shared cache line can be stored within other caches in the system; it is – as the name suggests – shared with a number of other caches. A shared cache line always contains the most up-to-date value; in this way, the cache always services read accesses. Write accesses to a shared cache line are always switched through to the external data bus independently of the cache strategy (write-through, write-back), so that the shared cache lines in the other caches are invalidated. The address given out during the bus cycle is used as an external inquiry cycle for invalidating the cache lines in the other caches. As the same time, the contents of the main memory are also updated. The write operation in the local cache itself only updates the contents of the cache; it is not invalidated.
- Invalid (I) – In this state data in the cache location is not most recent data, or a flush has taken place. A cache line marked as invalid is logically not available in the cache, which could be because the cache line itself is empty or contains an invalid entry, that is, not updated. Invalid or empty tag entries also cause cache lines to be marked as invalid. Every access to an invalid cache line leads to a cache miss. In the case of a read access, the cache controller normally initiates a cache line fill (if the line can be cached and its transfer into the cache is not blocked). A write access, however, is switched through to the external bus as a write-through. The MESI protocol will not provide a write-allocate.

3.4.5 Non-cacheable cycles

Some of the cycles which occur within the system are non-cacheable as the required data will not be stored in the cache memory. These include interrupt acknowledgement cycles, memory mapped I/O reads and writes. The cache controller detects these by monitoring the address and control busses. These signals are then passed onto the system via the address latch and data transceiver.

3.4.6 Cache coherency and snooping

An important parameter in the cache is that the data in the cache must be the same as the data in the system memory, that is, cache coherency. For this reason memory writes are forwarded on to system memory immediately in a write-through cache; for a cache write hit both the cache SRAM and system memory are updated.

The cache controller must also be able to monitor writes to system memory by other busmasters. When the cache controller detects a write to system memory by another busmaster, it uses the address on the bus to perform a directory search. If a hit is detected, the directory entry is cleared. If the processor wants information from that same location later, a cache miss occurs, because the directory search results in a miss.

Snooping occurs when the cache controller monitors the address bus when another device is writing to system memory.

3.5   Direct memory access (DMA)

DMA is a method in which an external device takes over the data and address busses for a short time. A DMA controller controls the transfers and makes the request to the processor to take over the transfer.

Two lines control the DMA interface: bus hold acknowledge (HLDA) and bus hold request (HOLD). When the DMA controller wants to take control of the local data and address bus lines it sets the HOLD active, that is, a high level. When the processor has completed its current operation it sets the data and address busses into the high impedance state and then sets the HLDA line active high. The DMA controller can then transfer data directly to memory and when complete it sets the HOLD line inactive. When the processor senses this, it can then take over the control of the busses again.

4 Pentium/Pentium Pro

4.1 Introduction

Intel have gradually developed their range of processors from the original 16-bit 8086 processor to the 32-bit processors, such as the Pentium II. Table 4.1 contrasts the Intel processor range. It can also be seen from the table that the Pentium II processor is nearly more than a thousand times more powerful than an 8086 processor. The original 8086 had just 29 000 transistors and operated at a clock speed of 8 MHz. It had an external 20-bit bus and could thus only access up to 1 MB of physical memory. Compare this with the Pentium II which can operate at over 300 MHz, contains over 6 000 000 transistors and can access up to 64 GB of physical memory.

Table 4.1 Processor comparison.

Processor	Clock (when released)	Register size	External data bus	Max. external memory	Cache	Power (MIPs)
8086	8 MHz	16	16	1 MB		0.8
286	12.5 MHz	16	16	16 MB		2.7
386DX	20 MHz	32	32	4 GB		6.0
486DX	25 MHz	32	32	4 GB	8 kB L-1	20
Pentium	60 MHz	32	64	4 GB	16 kB L-1	100
Pentium Pro	200 MHz	32	64	64 GB	16 kB L-1 256 kB L-2	440
Pentium II	200 MHz	32	64	64 GB	16 kB L-1 512 kB L-2	700

4.2 Intel processor development

The 80386 processor was a great leap in processing power over the 8086 and 80286, but it required an on-board math co-processor to enhance its mathematical operations and it could also only execute one instruction at a time. The 80486 brought many enhancements, such as:

- The addition of parallel execution with the expansion of the Instruction decode and execution units into five pipelined stages. Each of these stages operate in parallel, with the others, on up to five instructions in different stages of execution. This allows up to five instructions to be completed at a time.
- The addition of an 8 kB on-chip cache to greatly reduce the data and code access times.

- The addition of an integrated floating-point unit.
- Support for more complex and powerful systems, such as off-board L-2 cache support and multiprocessor operation.

With the increase in notebook and palmtop computers, the 80486 was also enhanced to support many energy and system management capabilities. These processors were named the 80486SL processors. The new enhancements included:

- System Management Mode. This mode is triggered by the processor's own interrupt pin and allows complex system management features to be added to a system transparently to the operating system and application programs.
- Stop Clock and Auto Halt Powerdown. These allow the processor to either shut itself down (and preserve its current state) or run at a reduced clock rate.

The Intel Pentium processor added many enhancements to the previous processors, including:

- The addition of a second execution pipeline. These two pipelines, named u and v, can execute two instructions per clock cycle. This is known as superscalar operation.
- Increased on-chip L-1 cache, 8 kB for code and another 8 kB for data. It uses the MESI protocol to support write-back mode, as well as the write-through mode (which is used by the 80486 processor).
- Branch prediction with an on-chip branch table that improves looping characteristics.
- Enhancement to the virtual-8086 mode to allow for 4 MB as well as 4 kB pages.
- 128-bit and 256-bit data paths are possible (although the main registers are still 32 bits).
- Burstable 64-bit external data bus.
- Addition of Advanced Programmable Interrupt Controller (APIC) to support multiple Pentium processors.
- New dual processing mode to support dual processor systems.

The Pentium processor has been extremely successful and has helped support enhanced multitasking operating systems such as Windows NT and Windows 95/98. The Intel Pentium Pro enhanced the Pentium processor with the following:

- Addition of a 3-way superscalar architecture, as opposed to a 2-way for the Pentium. This allows three instructions to be executed for every clock cycle.
- Uses enhanced prediction of parallel code (called dynamic execution microarchitecture) for the superscalar operation. This includes methods such as micro-data flow analysis, out-of-order execution, enhanced branch prediction and speculative execution. The three instruction decode units work in parallel to decode object code into smaller operations called micro-ops. These micro-ops then go into an instruction pool, and, when there are no interdependencies they can be executed out-of-order by the five parallel execution units (two integer units, two for floating-point operations and one for memory). A retirement unit retires completed micro-ops in their original program order and takes account of any branches. This recovers the original program flow.

- Addition of register renaming. Multiple instructions not dependent on each other, using the same registers, allow the source and destination registers to be temporarily renamed. The original register names are used when instructions are retired and program flow is maintained.
- Addition of a closely coupled, on-package, 256 kB L-2 cache that has a dedicated 64-bit full clock speed bus. The L-2 cache also supports up to four concurrent accesses through a 64-bit external data bus. Each of these accesses is transaction-oriented where each access is handled as a separate request and response. This allows for numerous requests while awaiting a response.
- Expanded 36-bit address bus to give a physical address size of 64 GB.

The Pentium II processor is a further enhancement to the processor range. Apart from increasing the clock speed it has several enhancements over the Pentium Pro, including:

- Integration of MMX technology. MMX instructions support high-speed multimedia operations and include the addition of eight new registers (MM0 to MM7), four MMX data types and an MMX instruction set.
- Single edge contact (SEC) cartridge packaging. This gives improved handling performance and socketability. It uses surface mount component and has a thermal plate (which accepts a standard heat sink), a cover and a substrate with an edge finger connection.
- Integrated on-chip L-1 cache 16 kB for code and another 16 kB for data.
- Increased size, on-package, 512 kB L-2 cache.
- Enhanced low-power states, such as AutoHALT, Stop-Grant, Sleep and Deep Sleep.

4.3   Terms

Before introducing the Pentium Pro (P-6) various terms have to be defined. These are:

Transaction   Used to define a bus cycle. It consists of a set of phases, which relate to a single bus request.

Bus agent   Devices that reside on the processor bus, that is, the processor, PCI bridge and memory controller.

Priority agent   The device handling reset, configuration, initialization, error detection and handling; generally the processor-to-PCI bridge.

Requesting agent   The device driving the transaction, that is, busmaster.

Addressed agent   The slave device addressed by the transaction, that is, target agent.

Responding agent   The device that provides the transaction response on $\overline{RS2} - \overline{RS0}$ signals.

Snooping agent   A caching device that snoops on the transactions to maintain
                      cache coherency.

Implicit write-back   When a hit to a modified line is detected during the snoop phase,
                      an implicit write-back occurs. This is the mechanism used to
                      write-back the cache line.

4.4   Pentium II and Pentium Pro

A major objective of electronic systems design is the saving of electrical power and the
minimization of electromagnetic interference (EMI). Thus gunning transceiver logic
(GTL) has been used to reduce both power consumption and EMI as it has a low voltage
swing. GTL requires a 1 V reference signal and signals which use GTL logic are terminated to 1.5 V. If a signal is 0.2 V above the reference voltage, that is, 1.2 V, then it is
considered high. If a signal is 0.2 V below the reference voltage, that is, 0.8 V, then it is
considered low.

The Pentium Pro and II support up to four processors on the same bus without extra
supporting logic. Integrated into the bus structure are cache coherency signals, advanced
programmable interrupt control signals and bus arbitration.

A great enhancement of the Pentium Pro bus is data error detection and correction.
The Pentium Pro bus detects and corrects all single-bit data bus errors and also detects
multiple-bit errors on the data bus. Address and control bus signals also have basic parity
protection.

The Pentium Pro bus has a modified line write-back performed without backing off
the current bus owner, where the processor must perform a write-back to memory when
it detects a hit to a modified line. The following mechanism eliminates the need to back-
off the current busmaster. If a memory write is being performed by the current bus owner
then two writes will be seen on the bus, that is, the original one followed by the write-
back. The memory controller latches, and merges the data from the two cycles, and performs one write to DRAM. If the current bus owner is performing a memory read then it
accepts the data when it is being written to memory.

Other enhanced features are:

- Deferred reply transactions stop the processor from having to wait for slow devices;
  transactions that require a long time can be completed later, that is, deferred.
- Deeply pipelined bus transactions where the bus supports up to eight outstanding
  pipelined transactions.

4.5   System overview

Figure 4.1 outlines the main components of a Pentium system and Table 4.2 gives its
main pin connections. A major upgrade is the support for up to four processors. The
memory control and data path control logic provides the memory control signals, that is,
memory address, $\overline{\text{RAS}}$ and $\overline{\text{CAS}}$ signals. The data path logic moves the data between the
processor bus and the memory data bus. The memory interface component interfaces the

memory data bus with the DRAM memory. Both interleaved and non-interleaved methods are generally supported. The memory consists of dual-in-line memory modules, that is, DIMMs. A DIMM module supports 64 data bits, and 8 parity or ECC bits.

The PCI bridge provides the interface between the processor bus and the PCI bus. The standard bridge provides an interface between the PCI bus and the EISA / ISA bus. EISA / ISA Support Component provides the EISA / ISA bus support functions, for example, timers, interrupt control, flash ROM, keyboard interface, LA/SA translation and XD bus control.

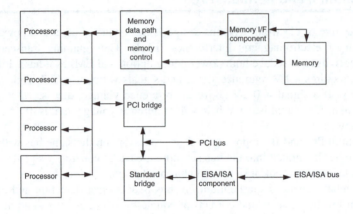

Figure 4.1   P-6 architecture.

4.5.1 Bus transactions

A Pentium bus transaction contains up to six phases; each of these uses a particular set of signals to communicate particular information. The six phases are:

- **Arbitration**. A transaction begins with the arbitration phase when the requesting agent does not already own any of the busses. The bus agent generates the appropriate bus request signals, to get ownership of the busses. This phase is skipped if the bus agent already owns the busses.
- **Request**. The bus agent enters the request phase, once it owns the busses. This phase consists of two clocks. During the first CLK the bus agent drives $\overline{\text{ADS}}$, and an address on the bus; this allows other agents to snoop. During the second CLK other transaction information is driven, for example, Byte enables. All bus agents latch the information provided during the request phase, and store it in their in-order queues.
- **Error**. If a bus agent detects an address or control bus parity error, it must generate the appropriate error signals during the error phase time frame. If an error is indicated during the error phase then the rest of the transaction phases are cancelled.
- **Snoop**. If a transaction is not cancelled during the error phase, then it will have a snoop phase. During this phase all snooping agents indicate if a hit was detected, to a line in the shared or modified state.
- **Response**. If the transaction is not cancelled during the error phase, then it will have a response phase. The response phase indicates the status of the transaction. A hard failure response is provided if a transaction is retired due to an error, and then fails again on a retry. A no data response will be provided if the transaction is complete,

for example, a write transaction. A normal data response will be provided if the transaction has to contain a data phase, for example, a read transaction. A deferred response is provided if the transaction is to be completed later, for example, an I/O read from a slow device. An implicit write-back response will be provided, if modified data has to be written back, for example, a snooping agent detects a hit to a modified line, during a read from or a write to memory. A retry response is provided if a bus agent decides that a transaction must be retired.

- **Data**. If a transaction is not cancelled during the error phase, and did not get a hard failure, deferred or retry response during the response phase, then it will contain a data phase. Data is transferred during the data phase, for example, read data, write data, or implicit write-back data.

4.5.2 *Transaction types*

The P-6 can perform the following types of transaction:

- **I/O write**.
- **I/O read**.
- **Memory write**.
- **Memory read**.
- **Interrupt acknowledge**.
- **Special**. The type of special transaction being requested is determined by the byte enables, $\overline{BE8} - \overline{BE15}$. Special transaction types are:

  ◆ Shutdown.
  ◆ Flush.
  ◆ Halt.
  ◆ SMI acknowledge.
  ◆ Flush acknowledge.
  ◆ Sync.
  ◆ Stop CLK acknowledge.

- **Deferred**. This allows the processor to move onto the next transaction instead of waiting for a response from a slow device. The processor is notified during the response phase of the current transaction, by a bus agent, that the transaction will be deferred and will be completed at a later time. The deferring bus agent then performs a deferred reply transaction and when the original transaction can be completed the deferred reply transaction returns data to complete the earlier I/O transaction. During the request phase of a deferred reply transaction the bus agent identifies who the original requesting agent was, and which transaction the reply is for.

  If the original transaction was a read, then a normal data response would be provided during the deferred reply transaction, that is, a data phase would follow the response phase. If the original transaction was a write, then a no data response would be provided during the deferred reply transaction, that is, the deferred reply transaction will not contain a data phase because the write took place during the data phase of the original transaction.

Table 4.2   Pentium signal lines.

Signals	I/O	Description
$\overline{\text{BSEL}}$	I/O	Bus select is for future use.
DP0–DP63	I/O	64-bit data bus.
$\overline{\text{ADS}}$	O	Indicates that the processor has valid control signals and valid address signals.
AHOLD	I	When active a different bus controller can have access to the address bus. This is typically used in a multi-processor system.
$\overline{\text{BE0}} - \overline{\text{BE3}}$	O	The byte enable lines indicate which of the bytes of the 32-bit data bus are active.
$\overline{\text{BLAST}}$	O	Indicates that the current burst cycle will end after the next $\overline{\text{BRDY}}$ signal.
$\overline{\text{BOFF}}$	I	The backoff signal informs the processor to deactivate the bus on the next clock cycle.
$\overline{\text{BRDY}}$	I	The burst ready signal is used by an addressed system that has sent data on the data bus or read data from the bus.
BREQ	O	Indicates that the processor has internally requested the bus.
$\overline{\text{BS16}}$, $\overline{\text{BS8}}$	I	The $\overline{\text{BS16}}$ signal indicates that a 16-bit data bus is used, the $\overline{\text{BS8}}$ signal indicates that an 8-bit data bus is used. If both are high then a 32-bit data bus is used.
DP0–DP3	I/O	The data parity bits gives a parity check for each byte of the 32-bit data bus. The parity bits are always even parity.
$\overline{\text{EADS}}$	I	Indicates that an external bus controller has put a valid address on the address bus.
$\overline{\text{FERR}}$	O	Indicates that the processor has detected an error in the internal floating-point unit.
$\overline{\text{FLUSH}}$	I	When active the processor writes the complete contents of the cache to memory.
HOLD, HLDA	I/O	The bus hold (HOLD) and acknowledge (HLDA) are used for bus arbitration and allow other bus controllers to take control of the buses.
$\overline{\text{IGNNE}}$	I	When active the processor ignores any numeric errors.
INTR	I	External devices to interrupt the processor use the interrupt request line.
$\overline{\text{KEN}}$	I	This signal stops caching of a specific address.
$\overline{\text{LOCK}}$	O	If active the processor will not pass control to an external bus controller, when it receives a HOLD signal.
$\text{M/}\overline{\text{IO}}$, $\text{D/}\overline{\text{C}}$, $\text{W/}\overline{\text{R}}$	O	See Table 3.2.
NMI	I	The non-maskable interrupt signal causes an interrupt 2.

$\overline{\text{PCHK}}$	O	If it is set active then a data parity error has occurred.
$\overline{\text{PLOCK}}$	O	The active pseudo lock signal identifies that the current data transfer requires more than one bus cycle.
PWT, PCD	O	The page write-through (PWT) and page cache disable (PCD) are used with cache control.
$\overline{\text{RDY}}$	I	When active the addressed system has sent data on the data bus or read data from the bus.
RESET	I	If the reset signal is high for more than 15 clock cycles then the processor resets itself.

4.6   MMX technology

MMX technology has been added to the Pentium processor to enhanced multimedia and communications software. It uses new data types and 57 new instructions to accelerate calculations which are common in audio, 2D and 3D graphics, video, speech synthesis and recognition, and data communications algorithms. The new instructions use a technique known as SIMD (Single Instruction Multiple Data) which allows a single instruction to operate on multiple pieces of data, in parallel. For example, a single MMX instruction can add up to eight integer pairs, in parallel, using 64-bit registers.

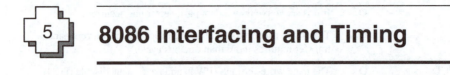

5   **8086 Interfacing and Timing**

5.1   Introduction

There are two main methods of communicating external equipment, either they are mapped into the physical memory and given a real address on the address bus (memory mapped I/O) or they are mapped into a special area of input/output memory (isolated I/O). Figure 5.1 shows the two methods. Devices mapped into memory are accessed by reading or writing to the physical address. Isolated I/O provides ports which are gateways between the interface device and the processor. They are isolated from the system using a buffering system and are accessed by four machine code instructions. The IN instruction inputs a byte, or a word, and the OUT instruction outputs a byte, or a word. C and Pascal compilers interpret the equivalent high-level functions and produce machine code which uses these instructions.

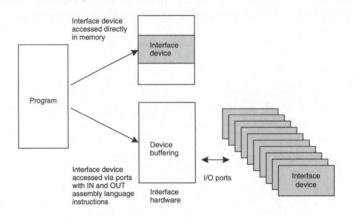

Figure 5.1   Memory mapping or isolated interfacing.

5.2   Interfacing with memory

The 80×86 processor interfaces with memory through a bus controller, as shown in Figure 5.2. This device interprets the microprocessor signals and generates the required memory signals. Two main output lines differentiate between a read or a write operation ($R/\overline{W}$) and between direct and isolated memory access ($M/\overline{IO}$). The $R/\overline{W}$ line is low when data is being written to memory and high when data is being read. When $M/\overline{IO}$ is high, direct memory access is selected and when low, the isolated memory is selected.

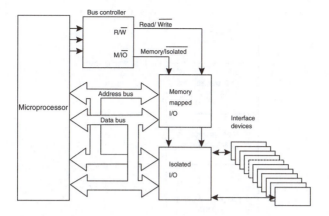

Figure 5.2 Access memory mapped and isolated I/O.

5.3 Memory mapped I/O

Interface devices can map directly onto the system address and data bus. In a PC-compatible system, the address bus is 20 bits wide, from address 00000h to FFFFFh (1 MB). If the PC is being used in an enhanced mode (such as with Microsoft Windows) it can access the area of memory above the 1 MB. If it uses 16-bit software (such as Microsoft Windows 3.1) then it can address up to 16 MB of physical memory, from 000000h to FFFFFFh. If it uses 32-bit software (such as Microsoft Windows 95/98) then the software can address up to 4 GB of physical memory, from 00000000h to FFFFFFFFh. Table 5.1 and Figure 5.3 give a typical memory allocation.

5.4 Isolated I/O

Devices are not normally connected directly onto the address and data bus of the computer because they may use part of the memory that a program uses or they could cause a hardware fault. On modern PCs only the graphics adaptor is mapped directly into memory, the rest communicate through a specially reserved area of memory, known as isolated I/O memory.

Table 5.1 Memory allocation for a PC.

Address	Device
00000h–00FFFh	Interrupt vectors
00400h–0047Fh	ROM BIOS RAM
00600h–9FFFFh	Program memory
A0000h–AFFFFh	EGA/VGA graphics
B0000h–BFFFFh	EGA/VGA graphics
C0000h–C7FFFh	EGA/VGA graphics

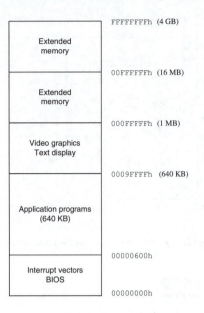

Figure 5.3   Typical PC memory map.

Isolated I/O uses 16-bit addressing from `0000h` to `FFFFh`, thus up to 64 KB of memory can be mapped. Microsoft Windows 95/98 can display the isolated I/O memory map by selecting `Control Panel` → `System` → `Device Manager`, then selecting `Properties`. From the computer properties window the `Input/output (I/O)` option is selected. Figure 5.4 shows an example for a computer in the range from `0000h` to `0064h` and Figure 5.5 shows from `0378h` to `03ffh`.

It can be seen from Figure 5.4 that the keyboard maps into address `0060h` and `0064h`, the speaker maps to address `0061h` and the system timer between `0040h` and `0043h`. Table 5.2 shows the typical uses of the isolated memory area.

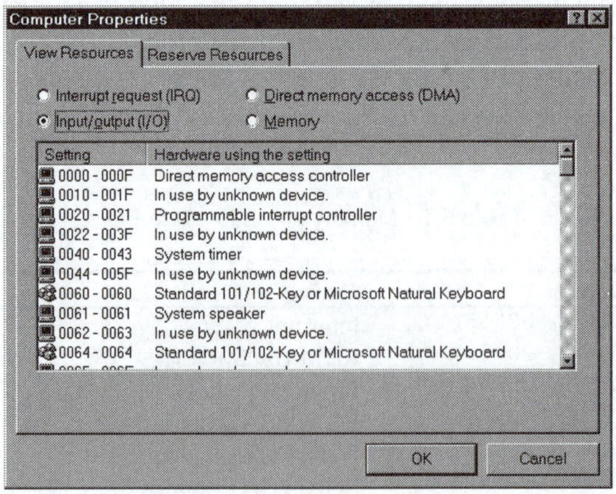

Figure 5.4   Example I/O memory map from `0000h` to `0064h`.

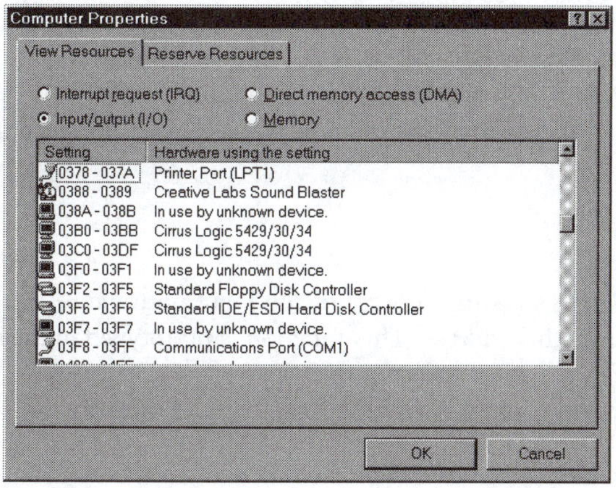

Figure 5.5 Example I/O memory map from `0378h` to `03FFh`.

Table 5.2 Typical isolated I/O memory map.

Address	Device
000h–01Fh	DMA controller
020h–021h	Programmable interrupt controller
040h–05Fh	Counter/Timer
060h–07Fh	Digital I/O
080h–09Fh	DMA controller
0A0h–0BFh	NMI reset
0C0h–0DFh	DMA controller
0E0h–0FFh	Math co-processor
170h–178h	Hard disk (Secondary IDE drive or CD-ROM drive)
1F0h–1F8h	Hard disk (Primary IDE drive)
200h–20Fh	Game I/O adapter
210h–217h	Expansion unit
278h–27Fh	Second parallel port (LPT2:)
2F8h–2FFh	Second serial port (COM2:)
300h–31Fh	Prototype card
378h–37Fh	Primary parallel port (LPT1:)
380h–38Ch	SDLC interface
3A0h–3AFh	Primary binary synchronous port
3B0h–3BFh	Graphics adapter
3C0h–3DFh	Graphics adapter
3F0h–3F7h	Floppy disk controller
3F8h–3FFh	Primary serial port (COM1:)

5.4.1 *Inputting a byte from an I/O port*

The assembly language command to input a byte is:

```
IN AL,DX
```

where DX is the Data Register which contains the address of the input port. The 8-bit value loaded from this address is put into the register AL.

For Turbo/Borland C the equivalent function is inportb(). Its general syntax is as follows:

```
value=inportb(PORTADDRESS);
```

where PORTADDRESS is the address of the input port and value is loaded with the 8-bit value from this address. This function is prototyped in the header file dos.h.

For Turbo Pascal the equivalent is accessed via the port[] array. Its general syntax is as follows:

```
value:=port[PORTADDRESS];
```

where PORTADDRESS is the address of the input port and value the 8-bit value at this address. To gain access to this function the statement uses dos requires to be placed near the top of the program.

Microsoft C++ uses the equivalent _inp() function (which is prototyped in conio.h).

5.4.2   *Inputting a word from a port*

The assembly language command to input a word is:

```
IN AX,DX
```

where DX is the Data Register which contains the address of the input port. The 16-bit value loaded from this address is put into the register AX.

For Turbo/Borland C the equivalent function is inport(). Its general syntax is as follows:

```
value=inport(PORTADDRESS);
```

where PORTADDRESS is the address of the input port and value is loaded with the 16-bit value at this address. This function is prototyped in the header file dos.h.

For Turbo Pascal the equivalent is accessed via the portw[] array. Its general syntax is as follows:

```
value:=portw[PORTADDRESS];
```

where PORTADDRESS is the address of the input port and value is the 16-bit value at this address. To gain access to this function the statement uses dos requires to be placed near the top of the program.

Microsoft C++ uses the equivalent _inpw() function (which is prototyped in conio.h).

5.4.3 *Outputting a byte to an I/O port*

The assembly language command to output a byte is:

```
OUT DX,AL
```

> where DX is the Data Register which contains the address of the output port. The 8-bit value sent to this address is stored in register AL.

For Turbo/Borland C the equivalent function is outportb(). Its general syntax is as follows:

```
outportb(PORTADDRESS,value);
```

> where PORTADDRESS is the address of the output port and value is the 8-bit value to be sent to this address. This function is prototyped in the header file dos.h.

For Turbo Pascal the equivalent is accessed via the port[] array. Its general syntax is as follows:

```
port[PORTADDRESS]:=value;
```

> where PORTADDRESS is the address of the output port and value is the 8-bit value to be sent to that address. To gain access to this function the statement uses dos requires to be placed near the top of the program.

Microsoft C++ uses the equivalent _outp() function (which is prototyped in conio.h).

5.4.4 *Outputting a word*

The assembly language command to input a byte is:

```
OUT DX,AX
```

> where DX is the Data Register which contains the address of the output port. The 16-bit value sent to this address is stored in register AX.

For Turbo/Borland C the equivalent function is outport(). Its general syntax is as follows:

```
outport(PORTADDRESS,value);
```

> where PORTADDRESS is the address of the output port and value is the 16-bit value to be sent to that address. This function is prototyped in the header file dos.h.

For Turbo Pascal the equivalent is accessed via the port[] array. Its general syntax is as follows:

```
portw[PORTADDRESS]:=value;
```

where PORTADDRESS is the address of the output port and value is the 16-bit value to be sent to that address. To gain access to this function the statement uses dos requires to be placed near the top of the program.

Microsoft C++ uses the equivalent _outp() function (which is prototyped in conio.h).

5.5   Timing

Each instruction takes a finite time to complete. The speed of operation is determined by the processor clock speed. To determine how long a certain instruction will take determine the number of clock cycles to execute it and multiply this by the clock period. For example, if the clock rate is 8 MHz then the clock period is 0.125 μs. Table 5.3 gives the number of clock cycles for various instructions. Note that different processors take differing number of clock cycles to execute each command. Notice also that the 80386 processor is around twice as fast as the 8086 for many of the commands. This is due to improved architecture.

Table 5.3   Instruction timings for different processors.

Command	Example	8086	80286	80386
mov	mov ax,1234	4	2	2
mov	mov dx,ax	2	2	2
out	out dx,al	8	3	11
inc	inc ax	3	2	2
dec	dec bx	3	2	2
and	and ax,0b6h	4	3	2
jne (nj)	jne fred	16(4)	7(3)	7(3)
div	div cx	80 (b)	14 (b)	14 (b)
		144 (w)	22 (w)	22 (w)
nop	nop	2	2	2

where (b) – byte divide, (w) – word divide, (nj) – no jump.

For example, the mov ax,1234 statement takes 0.5 μs assuming an 8 MHz clock. Note the great improvement in the 80286/386 over the 8086 in dealing with mathematics operations. In the 8086 it takes 144 clock cycles to perform a word divide while the 80386 only takes 22 clock cycles (nearly seven times faster). The following program outputs an incremented value every two seconds.

```
loop:      mov    dx,1f3h    ; control register address
           mov    al,90h     ; set port A input, port B output
           out    dx,al

           mov    dx,1f0h
           in     al,dx      ;read byte from port A

           mov    dx,1f1h
           out    dx,al      ; send byte to port B

           call   delay
           jmp    loop

; two second delay loop for 8MHz clock
```

```
delay:    mov    ax,13
outer:    mov    bx,64777                      ;;; ) outer
inner:    dec    bx          ;;;;; ) inner
          jnz inner          ;;;;; ) loop
          dec ax
          jnz outer                      ;;; ) loop
          ret
```

The second (inner) loop:

```
inner: dec bx
       jnz inner
```

will be executed 64 777 times. The number of cycles to do a `dec` and a `jnz` is 3+16 cycles. Thus it takes 19 cycles to complete this loop. The total time to complete this inner loop is thus:

number of cycles $\times$ clock period $= 19 \times 0.125\,\mu s\ = 2.375\,\mu s$

Total time to complete this loop is $64\,777 \times 2.375\,\mu s\ = 0.1538\,s$

This inner loop is executed 13 times, thus the total delay time is $13 \times 0.1538 = 2\,s$.

In general, for a general-purpose loop with A and B as the variables in AX and BX, then:

```
delay:    mov    ax,A          ; 4 clock cycles
outer:    mov    bx,B          ; 4
inner:    dec    bx            ; 3
          jnz inner            ; 16
          dec ax               ; 3
          jnz outer            ; 16
          ret
```

First the inner loop:

```
inner:         dec    bx       ; 3
               jnz inner       ; 16
```

then the number of cycles for inner loop will be B×19

```
inner:         dec    bx       ; 3
               jnz inner       ; 16
               dec ax          ; 3
               jnz outer       ; 16
```

Number of cycles is thus approximately: A×((B×19)+16+3).

If $19 \times B$ is much greater than 19 then the following approximation can be made:

Number of cycles = 19×A×B

Thus:

$$\text{Time taken} = \frac{\text{Number of clock cycles}}{\text{Clock frequency}}$$

$$= \frac{19 \times A \times B}{\text{Clock frequency}}$$

For example, in the last example (assuming a 4 MHz clock) the value of A is 13 and B is 64 777, thus:

$$\text{Time taken} = \frac{19 \times 13 \times 64\,777}{8 \times 10^6} = 2\,\text{s}$$

Typical processor clocks are:

8086	4.77 MHz, 8 MHz.
80386	16 MHz, 25 MHz, 33 MHz.
80486	33 MHz, 50 MHz, 66 MHz, 100 MHz.
Pentium	60 MHz, 90 MHz, 120 MHz, 233MHz, 400 MHz.

6 UART and PIC

6.1 Introduction

This chapter discusses two important devices: the UART and PIC. Their functionality is now integrated into a multi-function device, but they still operate as if they were discrete devices. The UART transmits and receives characters using RS-232. This will be discussed in more detail in Chapters 15 and 16. The PIC is used to interrupt the processor.

6.2 Universal Asynchronous Receiver Transmitter (8250)

The 8250 IC is a 40-pin IC and is used to transmit and receive asynchronous serial communications. Figure 6.1 shows the logic arrangement of the signals and their pin numbers. The connection to the system microprocessor is made through the data bus (D_0–D_7) and the handshaking and address lines ($\overline{\text{DOSTR}}$, $\overline{\text{DISTR}}$, A_2, A_1, A_0, RESET, and so on).

When the processor wishes to write data to the 8250 it sets the DOSTR and $\overline{\text{DOSTR}}$ (Data Output STRobe) lines active, that is, high and low, respectively. When it wants to read data from the 8250 it sets the DISTR and $\overline{\text{DISTR}}$ (Data Input STRobe) lines active, that is, high and low, respectively.

There are seven registers with the device, these are TD/RD Buffer, Interrupt Enable, Interrupt Identify, and so on (refer to Figure 6.5). They are selected using the three addressed lines: A_2, A_1 and A_0. If the address $A_2A_1A_0$ is a 000 then the TD/RD register is address, an address of 001 selects the Interrupt Identify register, and so on. The timings of the transfers are controlled by the write (DOSTR) and read (DISTR) control signals.

The main input RS-232 handshaking lines are: $\overline{\text{RI}}$ (ring indicate), $\overline{\text{DSR}}$ (Data Set Ready) and $\overline{\text{CTS}}$ (Clear to Send), and the main output handshaking lines are: $\overline{\text{RTS}}$ (Ready to Send) and $\overline{\text{DTR}}$ (Data Terminal Ready). Serial data is output from SOUT and inputted from SIN. Refer to Chapter 15 for more information on RS-232 handshaking.

The clock input lines XTAL1 and XTAL2 connect to a crystal to control the internal clock oscillator. Normally on a PC this clock frequency is set at 1.8432 MHz; see Section 6.2.2. The BAUDOT line is the clock frequency divided by 16 and is equal to the Baud rate. As the 1.843 MHz clock is divided by 16 then the maximum Baud rate will thus be 1 843 000 divided by 16, which gives 115 200 Baud.

The 8255 generates hardware interrupts on the INT line. A low input on the RESET input initializes the device and causes the internal registers of the 8250 to be reset. It is normally connected so that at power-up the RESET line is low for a short time.

The 16450 is the 16-bit equivalent of the 8250.

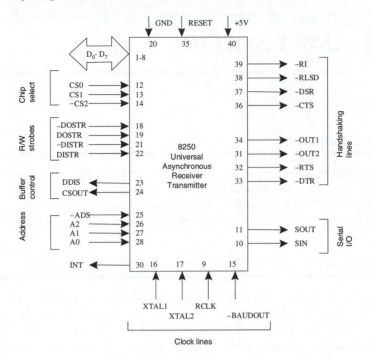

Figure 6.1   8250 pin connections.

6.2.1   Frame format

RS-232 uses asynchronous communications which has a start–stop data format, as shown in Figure 6.2. Each character is transmitted one at a time with a delay between them. This delay is called the inactive time and is set at a logic level high (–12 V) as shown in Figure 6.2. The transmitter sends a start bit to inform the receiver that a character is to be sent in the following bit transmission. This start bit is always a '0'. Next, 5, 6 or 7 data bits are sent as a 7-bit ASCII character, followed by a parity bit and finally either 1, 1.5 or 2 stop bits. Figure 6.3 shows a frame format and an example transmission of the character 'A', using odd parity. The timing of a single bit sets the rate of transmission. Both the transmitter and receiver need to be set to the same bit-time interval. An internal clock on both sets this interval. These only have to be roughly synchronized and approximately at the same rate as data is transmitted in relatively short bursts.

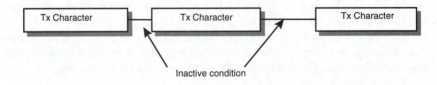

Figure 6.2   Asynchronous communications.

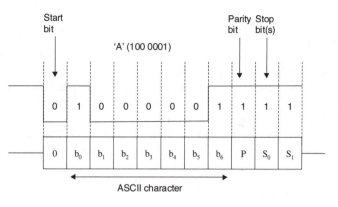

Figure 6.3   RS-232 frame format.

Example

An RS-232 serial data link uses 1 start bit, 7 data bits, 1 parity bit, 2 stop bits, ASCII coding and even parity. Determine the message sent from the following bit stream.

First bit sent
⇓
111110100000101100000111111111111111110000011111111100011001111101010
    0111111111111

ANSWER

The format of the data string sent is given next:

{idle} 11111 {start bit} 0 {'A'} 1000001 {parity bit} 0 {stop bits } 11 {start bit} 0
{'p'} 0000111 {parity bit} 1 {stop bits} 11   {idle} 11111111   {start bit} 0 {'p'}
0000111 {parity bit} 1 {stop bits} 11 {idle} 11 {start bit} 0 {'L'} 0011001 {parity bit}
1 {stop bits} 11

The message sent was thus 'AppL'.

Parity

Error control is data added to transmitted data in order to detect or correct an error in transmission. RS-232 uses a simple technique known as parity to provide a degree of error detection.

A parity bit is added to transmitted data to make the number of 1s sent either even (even parity) or odd (odd parity). It is a simple method of error coding and only requires exclusive-OR (XOR) gates to generate the parity bit. The parity bit is added to the transmitted data by inserting it into the shift register at the correct bit position.

A single parity bit can only detect an odd number of errors, that is, 1, 3, 5, and so on. If there is an even number of bits in error then the parity bit will be correct and no error will be detected. This type of error coding is not normally used on its own where there is the possibility of several bits being in error.

Baud rate

One of the main parameters which specify RS-232 communications is the rate of transmission at which data is transmitted and received. It is important that the transmitter and receiver operate at, roughly, the same speed.

For asynchronous transmission the start and stop bits are added in addition to the 7 ASCII character bits and the parity. Thus a total of 10 bits are required to transmit a single character. With 2 stop bits, a total of 11 bits are required. If 10 characters are sent every second and if 11 bits are used for each character, then the transmission rate is 110 bits per second (bps).

	Bits
ASCII character	7
Start bit	1
Stop bit	2
Total	10

Table 6.1 lists how the bit rate relates to the characters sent per second (assuming 10 transmitted bits per character). The bit rate is measured in bits per second (bps).

In addition to the bit rate, another term used to describe the transmission speed is the Baud rate. The bit rate refers to the actual rate at which bits are transmitted, whereas the Baud rate relates to the rate at which signalling elements, used to represent bits, are transmitted. Since one signalling element encodes one bit, the two rates are then identical. Only in modems does the bit rate differ from the Baud rate.

Table 6.1 Bits per second related to characters sent per second.

Speed (bps)	Characters / second
300	30
1200	120
2400	240

Bit stream timings

Asynchronous communications is a stop–start mode of communication and both the transmitter and receiver must be set up with the same bit timings. A start bit identifies the start of transmission and is always a low logic level. Next, the least significant bit is sent followed by the rest of the 7-bit ASCII character bits. After this, the parity bit is sent followed by the stop bit(s). The actual timing of each bit relates to the Baud rate and can be determined using the following formula:

$$\text{Time period of each bit} = \frac{1}{\text{Baud rate}} \text{ s}$$

For example, if the Baud rate is 9600 Baud (or bps) then the time period for each bit sent is 1/9600 s, or 104 µs. Table 6.2 shows some bit timings as related to the Baud rate. An example of the voltage levels and timings for the ASCII character 'V' is given in Figure 6.4.

Table 6.2 Bit timings related to Baud rate.

Baud rate	Time for each bit (µs)
1200	833
2400	417
9600	104˙
19200	52

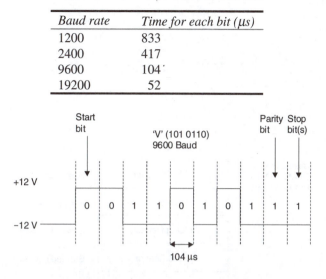

Figure 6.4 ASCII 'V' at RS-232 voltage levels.

6.2.2 Programming RS-232

Normally, serial transmission is achieved via the RS-232 standard. Although 25 lines are defined usually only a few are used. Data is sent along the TD line and received by the RD line with a common ground return. The other lines, used for handshaking, are RTS (Ready to Send) which is an output signal to indicate that data is ready to be transmitted and CTS (Clear to Send), which is an input indicating that the remote equipment is ready to receive data.

The 8250 IC is commonly used in serial communications. It can either be mounted onto the motherboard of the PC or fitted to an I/O card. This section discusses how it is programmed.

Programming the serial device

The main registers used in RS-232 communications are the Line Control Register (LCR), the Line Status Register (LSR) and the Transmit and Receive buffers (see Figure 6.5). The Transmit and Receive buffers share the same addresses.

The base address of the primary port (COM1:) is normally set at 3F8h and the secondary port (COM2:) at 2F8h. A standard PC can support up to four COM ports. These addresses are set in the BIOS memory and the address of each of the ports is stored at address locations 0040:0000 (COM1:), 0040:0002 (COM2:), 0040:0004 (COM3:) and 0040:0008 (COM4:). Program 6.1 can be used to identify these addresses. The statement:

```
ptr=(int far *)0x0400000;
```

initializes a far pointer to the start of the BIOS communications port addresses. Each address is 16 bits, thus the pointer points to an integer value. A far pointer is used as this can access the full 1 MB of memory, a non-far pointer can only access a maximum of 64 KB.

📖   Program 6.1

```
#include <stdio.h>
#include <conio.h>
int    main(void)
{
int    far *ptr; /* 20-bit pointer */
       ptr=(int far *)0x0400000; /* 0040:0000   */ clrscr();
       printf("COM1: %04x\n",*ptr);
       printf("COM2: %04x\n",*(ptr+1));
       printf("COM3: %04x\n",*(ptr+2));
       printf("COM4: %04x\n",*(ptr+3));
       return(0);
}
```

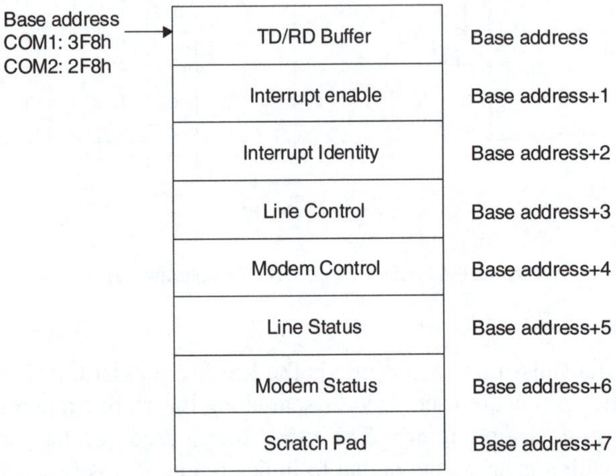

Base address		
COM1: 3F8h →	TD/RD Buffer	Base address
COM2: 2F8h	Interrupt enable	Base address+1
	Interrupt Identity	Base address+2
	Line Control	Base address+3
	Modem Control	Base address+4
	Line Status	Base address+5
	Modem Status	Base address+6
	Scratch Pad	Base address+7

Figure 6.5 Serial communication registers.

Test run 6.1 shows a sample run. In this case there are four COM ports installed on the PC. If any of the addresses is zero then that COM port is not installed on the system.

💻   Sample run 6.1

```
COM1: 03f8
COM2: 02f8
COM3: 03e8
COM4: 02e8
```

Line Status Register (LSR)

The LSR determines the status of the transmitter and receiver buffers. It can only be read from, and all the bits are automatically set by hardware. The bit definitions are given in Figure 6.6. When an error occurs in the transmission of a character one (or several) of the error bits is (are) set to a '1'.

One danger when transmitting data is that a new character can be written to the transmitter buffer before the previous character has been sent. This overwrites the contents of the character being transmitted. To avoid this the status bit S_6 is tested to determine if there is still a character still in the buffer. If there is then it is set to a '1', else the transmitter buffer is empty.

To send a character:

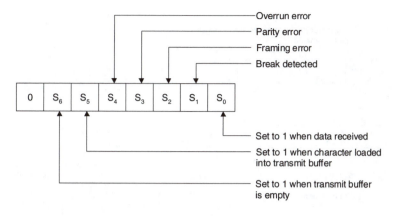

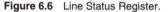

Figure 6.6 Line Status Register.

> *Test Bit 6 until set;*
> *Send character;*

A typical Pascal routine is:

```
repeat
    status := port[LSR] and $40;
until (status=$40);
```

When receiving data the S_0 bit is tested to determine if there is a bit in the receiver buffer. To receive a character:

> *Test Bit 0 until set;*
> *Read character;*

A typical Pascal routine is:

```
repeat
        status := port[LSR] and $01;
until (status=$01);
```

Figure 6.7 shows how the LSR is tested for the transmission and reception of characters.

Line Control Register (LCR)

The LCR sets up the communications parameters. These include the number of bits per character, the parity and the number of stop bits. It can be written to or read from and has a similar function to that of the control registers used in the PPI and PTC. The bit definitions are given in Figure 6.8.

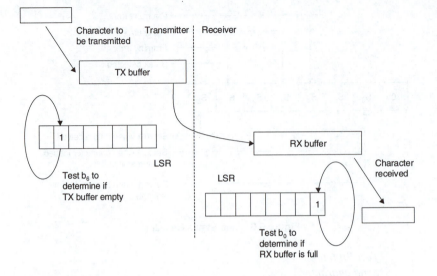

Figure 6.7   Testing of the LSR for the transmission and reception of characters.

The msb, C_7, must to be set to a '0' in order to access the transmit and receive buffers, (TX/RX buffer) else if it is set to a '1', the Baud rate divider is accessed. The Baud rate is set by loading an appropriate 16-bit divisor, with the lower 8 bits of the divisor put into the TX/RX buffer address and the upper 8 bits put into the next address after the TX/RX buffer. The value loaded depends on the crystal frequency connected to the IC. Table 6.3 shows divisors for a crystal frequency is 1.8432 MHz. In general the divisor, N, is related to the Baud rate by:

$$Baud\ rate = \frac{Clock\ frequency}{16 \times N}$$

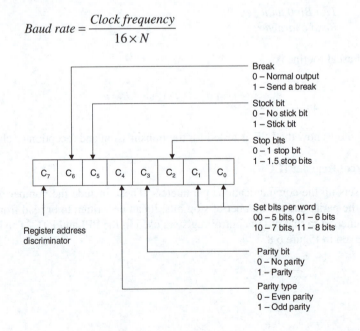

Figure 6.8   Line Control Register.

For example, for 1.8432 MHz and 9600 Baud $N = 1.8432 \times 10^6/(9600 \times 16) = 12$ (000Ch).

Table 6.3   Baud rate divisors.

Baud rate	Divisor (value loaded into Tx/Rx buffer)
110	0417h
300	0180h
600	00C0h
1200	0060h
1800	0040h
2400	0030h
4800	0018h
9600	000Ch
19200	0006h

Register addresses

The addresses of the main registers are given in Table 6.4. To load the Baud rate divisor, first the LCR bit 7 is set to a '1', then the LSB is loaded into divisor LSB and the MSB into the divisor MSB register. Finally, bit 7 is set back to a '0'. For example, for 9600 Baud, COM1 and 1.8432 MHz clock then 0Ch is loaded in 3F8h and 00h into 3F9h.

When bit 7 is set at a '0' then a read from base address reads from the RD buffer and a write operation writes to the TD buffer. An example of this is shown in Figure 6.9.

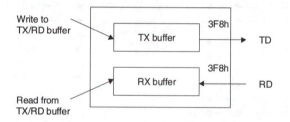

Figure 6.9   Read and write from TD/RD buffer.

Table 6.4   Serial communications addresses.

Primary	Secondary	Register	Bit 7 of LCR
3F8h	2F8h	TD buffer	'0'
3F8h	2F8h	RD buffer	'0'
3F8h	2F8h	Divisor LSB	'1'
3F9h	2F9h	Divisor MSB	'1'
3FBh	2FBh	Line Control Register	
3FDh	2FDh	Line Status Register	

6.3   Programmable Interrupt Controller (8259)

The 8259 IC is a 28-pin IC and is used to generate processor interrupts. Figure 6.10 shows the logic arrangement of the signals and their pin numbers. The connection to the microprocessor is made through the data bus (D_0–D_7) and the handshaking and address lines ($\overline{\text{RD}}$, $\overline{\text{WR}}$, A_0, INT and $\overline{\text{INTA}}$).

It has two registers, these are Interrupt Control Port (ICP) and the Interrupt Mask Register (IMR), refer to Section 8.5.2. The IMR enables and disables interrupt from interrupting the processor. As there are only two registers there is only one address line, A_0. If A_0 is a 0 then the ICP is addressed, if A_0 is 1 then the IMR is selected. The timing of the transfers is controlled by the read ($\overline{RD}$) and write ($\overline{WR}$) control signals.

When one of the interrupt lines becomes active and if that interrupt has been enabled then the 8259 line generates an interrupt on the processor by setting the interrupt line (INT) high. If the processor accepts the interrupt then it returns an acknowledgement with the $\overline{INTA}$ line. When the PIC receives this acknowledgement then it outputs the type number of the highest-priority active interrupt on the data bus lines D0–D7. The processor then reads this.

The chip select signal ($\overline{CS}$) must be a low for the device to be activated.

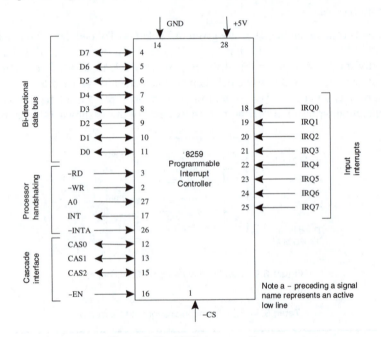

Figure 6.10   8259 pin connections.

7 PPI and PTC

7.1 Introduction

Two important devices which are used inside the PC and can also be used by external devices are the PPI (Programmable Peripheral Interface) and PTC (Programmable Timer/Counter). These devices are normally mapped into the isolated I/O memory map.

7.2 Programmable Peripheral Interface (8255)

The 8255 IC is a 40-pin IC which is used to input and/or output digital signals. Figure 7.1 shows the logic arrangement of the signals and their pin numbers. The connection to the system microprocessor is through the data bus (D0–D7), and the handshaking and address lines ($\overline{RD}$, $\overline{WR}$, A1, A0 and RESET).

There are four registers in the device; these are Port A, Port B, Port C and the Control Register. Port A, Port B and Port C link to the input/output lines PA0–PA7, PB0–PB7 and PC0–PC7, respectively. The register is selected using the two address lines, A0 and A1, these are selected by setting A1A0 to:

00 selects Port A.	01 selects Port B.
10 selects Port C.	11 selects Control Register.

The other signal lines are:

- $\overline{RD}$, $\overline{WR}$. These control transfers for read ($\overline{RD}$) and write ($\overline{WR}$) operations.
- RESET. A low input on the RESET input initializes the device and causes a reset of the internal registers of the 8255. This is normally connected so that at power-up the RESET line is low for a short time.
- $\overline{CS}$. This is the chip select signal and must be a low to activate the device.

7.2.1 Programming the PPI

Each 8255 has 24 input/output lines. These are grouped into three groups of 8 bits and are named Port A, Port B and Port C. A single 8-bit register, known as the Control Register, programs the functionality of these ports. Port C can be split into two halves to give Port C (upper) and Port C (lower). The ports and the Control Register map into the input/output memory with an assigned base address. The arrangement of the port addresses with respect to the base address is given in Table 7.1.

Figure 7.2 shows the functional layout of the 8255. The Control Register programs each of the ports to be an input or an output and also their mode of operation. There are four main parts which are programmed: Port A, Port B, Port C (upper) and Port C (lower).

Table 7.1   PPI addresses.

Port address	Function
BASE_ADDRESS	Port A
BASE_ADDRESS+1	Port B
BASE_ADDRESS+2	Port C
BASE_ADDRESS+3	Control Register

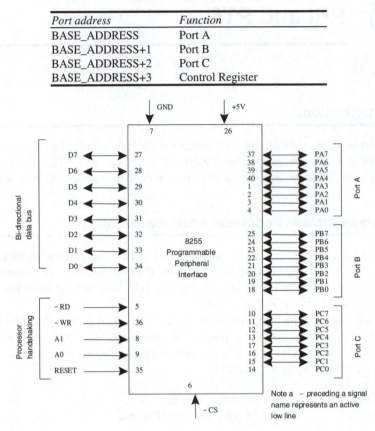

Figure 7.1   8255 pin connections.

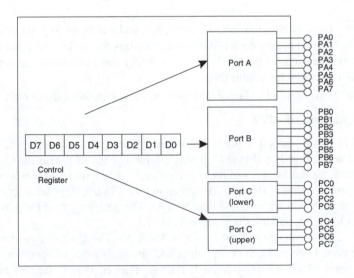

Figure 7.2   Layout of PPI.

Figure 7.3 shows the definition of the Control Register bits. The msb (most significant bit) D7 either makes the device active or inactive. If it is set to a 0 it is inactive, else it will be active. The input/output status of Port A is set by D4. If it is a 0 then Port A is an output, else it is an input. The status of Port B is set by D1, Port C (lower) by D0 and Port C (upper) by D3.

Port A can operated in one of three modes – 0, 1 and 2. These are set by bits D5 and D6. If they are set to 00 then Mode 0 is selected, 01 to Mode 1 and 10 to Mode 2. Port B can be used in two modes (Mode 0 and 1) and which set by bit D2. Examples of bit definitions and the mode of operation are given in Table 7.2.

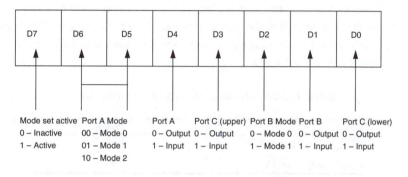

Figure 7.3   PPI Control Register bit definitions.

Mode 0

Mode 0 is the simplest mode and has no handshaking. In this mode the bits on Port C can be programmed as inputs or outputs.

Mode 1

Mode 1 allows handshaking for data synchronization. Handshaking is normally required when one device is faster than another. In a typical handshaking operation the originator of the data asks the recipient if it is ready to receive data. If it is not then the recipient sends back a 'not ready for data' signal. When it is ready it sends a 'ready for data' signal. The originator then sends the data and the recipient sets the 'not ready for data' signal until it has read the data.

If Ports A and B are inputs then the bits on Port C have the definitions given in Table 7.3.

Table 7.2   Example bit patterns for Control Register.

Bit pattern	Mode of operation
01101000	Device is inactive as D7 set to 0
10011000	Mode 0 Port A input, Port C (upper) input Mode 0 Port B output, Port C (lower) output
10101000	Mode 1 Port A output, Port C (upper) input Mode 0 Port B output, Port C (lower) output

Table 7.3 Mode 1 handshaking lines for inputting data.

Signal	Port A	Port B
Strobe ($\overline{\text{STB}}$)	PC4	PC2
Input Buffer full (IBF)	PC5	PC1

When inputting data, the $\overline{\text{STB}}$ going low (active) writes data into the port. After this data is written into the port, the IBF line automatically goes high. This remains high until the data is read from the port.

If any of the ports are outputs, then the bit definitions of Port C are as given in Table 7.4. In this mode, writing data to the port causes the $\overline{\text{OBF}}$ line to go low. This indicates that data is ready to be read from the port. The $\overline{\text{OBF}}$ line stays low until $\overline{\text{ACK}}$ is pulled low (the recipient has read the data).

Table 7.4 Mode 1 handshaking lines for outputting data.

Signal	Port C	Port B
Output Buffer Full ($\overline{\text{OBF}}$)	PC7	PC1
Acknowledge ($\overline{\text{ACK}}$)	PC6	PC2

Mode 2

This mode allows bi-directional I/O. The signal lines are given in Table 7.5.

Table 7.5 Mode 2 operation for bi-directional I/O.

Signal	Port A
$\overline{\text{OBF}}$	PC7
$\overline{\text{ACK}}$	PC6
$\overline{\text{STB}}$	PC4
IBF	PC5

7.2.2 Digital I/O programs

Program 7.1 outputs the binary code from 0 to 255 to Port B with a one-second delay between changes. The program exits when the output reaches 255. A delay routine has been added which uses the system timer. Figure 7.4 shows a typical set-up to test the program where Port B has been connected to eight light-emitting diodes (LEDs).

In 8086 Assembly Language a macro is defined using the equ statement. Program 7.1 uses these to define the port addresses. This helps to make the program more readable and makes it easier to make global changes. For example, a different base address is relatively easy to set up, as a single change to BASE_ADDRESS automatically updates all port defines in the program. In this case the base address is 3B0h. This address should be changed to the required base address of the DIO card.

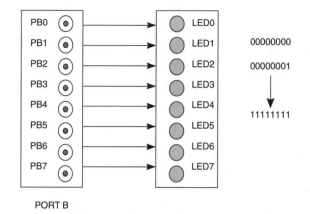

PORT B

Figure 7.4   Possible system set-up.

The statements:

```
        mov dx,CNTRLREG      ; set up PPI with
        mov al,90h           ; Port B as Output
        out dx,al
```

outputs the value 90h (1001 0000b) to the Control Register (CNTRLREG). The statements:

```
        mov ax,00h
loop1:
        mov dx,PORTB
        out dx,al            ; output to Port B

        call delay
        inc ax
        cmp ax,100h
        jnz loop1            ; repeat until all 1s
```

initially sets the AL register to 00h. The next two statements (mov dx, PORTB and out dx,al) output the value of AL to Port B. Next the delay routine is called (with call delay). This routine delays for a period of 1 second. Next the AL register is incremented (inc al). After this the AL register value is compared with 100h (0001 0000 0000b). The results of the compare statement is not equal to zero then the program loops back to the loop1: label.

📖 Program 7.1

```
code        SEGMENT
            ASSUME cs:code
BASEADDRESS EQU     03B0h ; change this as required
PORTA       EQU     BASEADDRESS
PORTB       EQU     BASEADDRESS+1
CNTRLREG    EQU     BASEADDRESS+3
;     program to output to Port B counts in binary until from 00000000
;     to 11111111 with approximately 1 second delay between changes
start:
        mov dx,CNTRLREG      ; set up PPI with
        mov al,90h           ; Port B as Output
        out dx,al
```

```
                mov ax,00h
loop1:
                mov dx,PORTB
                out dx,al                ; output to Port B

                call delay
                inc ax
                cmp ax,100h
                jnz loop1                ; repeat until all 1s

                mov ah,4cH               ; program exit
                int 21h                  ;

                ; ROUTINE TO GIVE 1 SECOND DELAY USING THE PC TIMER
DELAY:    push ax
                push bx
                mov ax,18                ; 18.2 clock ticks per second;
                ; Address of system timer on the PC is 0000:046C (low word)
                ; and 0000:046E (high word)
                mov bx,0
                mov es,bx
                ; Add the number of required ticks of the clock (ie 18)
                add ax,es:[46CH]
                mov bx,es:[46EH]

loop2:    ; Compare current timer count with AX and BX
                ;  if they are equal 1 second has passed
                cmp bx,es:[46EH]
                ja loop2
                jb over
                cmp ax,es:[46CH]
                jg loop2

over:     pop bx
                pop ax
                ret

code      ENDS
                END    start
```

Program 7.2 reads the binary input from Port A and sends it to Port B. It will stop only when all the input bits on port A are 1s. It shows how a byte can be read from a port and then outputted to another port. Port A is used, in this example, as the input and Port B as the output. Figure 7.5 shows how Port A could be connected to input switches and Port B to the light-emitting diodes (LEDs). Loading the bit pattern 90h into the Control Register initializes the correct set-up for Ports A and B.

Programs 7.3 and 7.4 show an example of how a C/C++ program interfaces with the isolated I/O. They use the functions _outp() to output a byte to a port and _inp() to input a byte from a port.

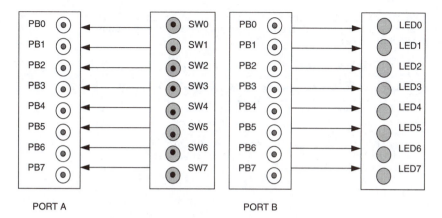

PORT A   PORT B

Figure 7.5 Typical system set-up.

📖 Program 7.2

```
code        SEGMENT
            ASSUME cs:code
; program to read from Port A and send to
; Port B. Program stops with all 1's
start:
            mov dx,3B3h
            mov al,90h
            out dx,al
loop:
            mov dx,3B0h
            in al,dx          ; read from Port A

            mov dx,3B1h
            out dx,al         ; output to Port B

            cmp al,ffh
            jnz loop:         ; repeat until all 1s
            mov ah,4cH        ; program exit
            int 21h           ;
code        ENDS
            END     start
```

📖 Program 7.3

```
/*    ppi_1.c                                                      */
/*    Program that will count from 0 to 255                        */
/*    and display it to PORT B. Onesecond between counts           */

#define    BASE_ADDRESS   0x3B0 /* change this as required         */
#define    PORTA          BASE_ADDRESS
#define    PORTB          (BASE_ADDRESS+1)
#define    PORTC          (BASE_ADDRESS+2)
#define    CNTRL_REG      (BASE_ADDRESS+3)

// #include    <dos.h>     /* required for outportb() */
#include    <conio.h>   /* required for _outp() */
#include    <time.h>    /* required for time() */
#include    <stdio.h>   /* required for printf() */

void my_delay(int secs);

int    main(void)
{
```

```
/*     NOTE: It may be better to define i is an integer (int)      */
/*     as it is easier to display the value in the debugger        */
unsigned char i=0;

     _outp(CNTRL_REG,0x90);

     // for Turbo C use outportb(CNTRL_REG,0x90);
          /*set A input, B output*/
     for (i=0;i<=255;i++)
     {
          _outp(PORTB,i);
          // for Turbo C use outportb(PORTB,i);
          my_delay(1);                    /* wait 1 second */
          printf("%d ",i);
     }
     return(0);
}

void my_delay(int secs)
{
time_t oldtime,newtime;

     time(&oldtime);
     do
     {
          time(&newtime);
     } while ((newtime-oldtime)<secs);
}
```

📖 Program 7.4

```
/*     ppi_2.c                                                      */

#define     BASE_ADDRESS   0x3B0 /* change this as required          */
#define     PORTA          BASE_ADDRESS
#define     PORTB          (BASE_ADDRESS+1)
#define     PORTC          (BASE_ADDRESS+2)
#define     CNTRL_REG      (BASE_ADDRESS+3)

// #include   <dos.h>      /* required for outportb() */
#include    <conio.h>     /* required for _outp() */
#include    <time.h>      /* required for time() */
#include    <stdio.h>     /* required for printf() */

void  my_delay(int secs);

int   main(void)
{
unsigned char i=0;

     _outp(CNTRL_REG,0x90);

     /*     for Turbo C use outportb(CNTRL_REG,0x90);    */
     /*     set A input, B output                        */
     do
     {
          i=_inp(PORTA);    /* read from Port A     */
          _outp(PORTB,i);   /* output to Port B     */
          /* for Turbo C use i=inportb(PORTA) and */
          /* outportb(PORTB,i);                      */
          my_delay(1);                 /* wait 1 second */
          printf("Input value is %d\n",i);
     } while (i!=0xff);
     return(0);
}
```

```
void my_delay(int secs)
{
time_t oldtime,newtime;
      time(&oldtime);
      do
      {

         time(&newtime);
      } while ((newtime-oldtime)<secs);
}
```

7.3 Programmable Timer Controller (8254)

The 8254 IC is a 24-pin IC and is used to count pulses or in timing applications. Figure 7.6 shows the logic arrangement of the signals and their pin numbers. The connection to the system microprocessor is made through the data bus (D0–D7) and the handshaking and address lines ($\overline{RD}$, $\overline{WR}$, A1 and A0).

There are four registers in the device; these are Counter 0, Counter 1, Counter 2 and the Control Register. The register is selected using the two address lines, A0 and A1, these are selected by setting A1A0 to:

00 selects Counter 0.   01 selects Counter 1.
10 selects Counter 2.   11 selects Control Register.

The other signal lines are:

- $\overline{RD}$, $\overline{WR}$. These control transfers for read ($\overline{RD}$) and write ($\overline{WR}$) operations.
- RESET. A low input on the RESET input initializes the device and causes a reset of the internal registers of the 8254. This is normally connected so that at power-up the RESET line is low for a short time.
- $\overline{CS}$. This is the chip select signal and must be a low to activate the device.

PC systems can be fitted with an 8254 PTC (programmable timer/counter) integrated circuit (IC) to give timing and counting capabilities. Each IC has 24 pins and contains three timer/counters, each of which can be programmed with differing functions. Typically, they are fitted onto a multi-function DIO interface card, as illustrated in Figure 7.7, or are fitted to a counter/timer I/O board. In-line switches or wire jumpers normally set the base address at which these ICs map into the isolated memory. Connection to external equipment is typically achieved via a D-type connector or two 50-way IDC connectors.

The connections to each timer/counter are:

- CLOCK INPUT
- GATE
- OUTPUT

The input line is CLOCK INPUT, the output is OUTPUT and the timer is disabled/enabled by the GATE line. A high level on the GATE enables the timer, else it is disabled. If the GATE is not connected then the input level floats. This is sensed as a high input and the counter will be active.

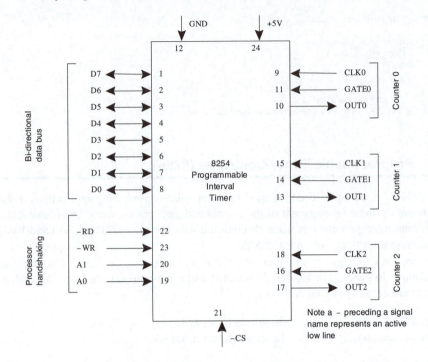

Figure 7.6   8254 pin connections.

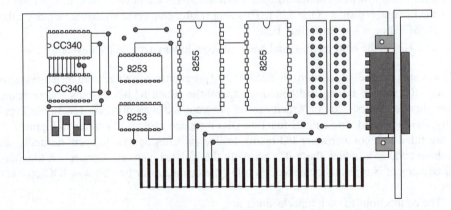

Figure 7.7   DIO with PTC ICs.

Each counter has a 16-bit counter register which gives a count range of 0000000000000000b (0 or 0000h) to 1111111111111111b (65 535 or FFFFh) and it always counts down. A diagram of a counter is given in Figure 7.8. The Control Register programs each of the three timer/counters on each IC. Its address is set with respect to the base address, as given in Table 7.6.

Table 7.6 PTC addresses.

Function	Address	Used as
Counter 0 Read/Write Buffer	BASE_ADDRESS	16-bit register
Counter 1 Read/Write Buffer	BASE_ADDRESS+1	16-bit register
Counter 2 Read/Write Buffer	BASE_ADDRESS+2	16-bit register
Counter Control Register	BASE_ADDRESS+3	To program the counters

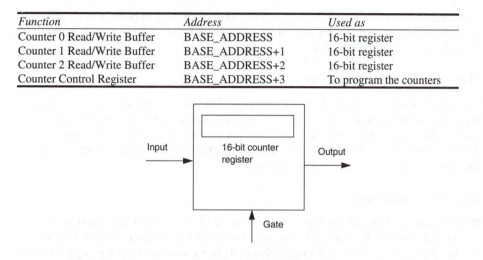

Figure 7.8 Diagram of counter/timer circuit.

7.3.1 Control Register

The Control Register programs the functionality of each of the three counters/timers. Figure 7.9 shows the format of this register. The counter to be programmed is set up by setting bits SC1 and SC0. If a PC card is used then only 8 bits can be loaded to or read from the PTC at a time. Thus to access the 16-bit counter register there must be two read or write operations. Bits RL1 and RL0 control the method of access. If these are set to 11 then the first byte written/read to/from the counter register is the LSB (least significant byte). The next write/read accesses the MSB (the most significant byte). Mode bits M2, M1 and M0 control the mode of the counter; these are discussed in the next section.

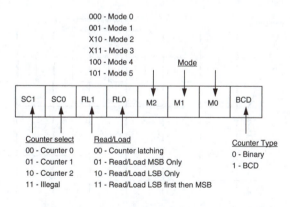

Figure 7.9 Timer Control Register bit definition.

7.3.2 Modes

The bits M2, M1 and M0 in the counter Control Register program the PTC mode.

Mode 0 (interrupt on terminal count)

In this mode the output is initially low and stays low until the number of clock cycles has been counted. If the gate is low the output is disabled. Figure 7.10 shows an example of Mode 0 with a counter value of 4.

Mode 1 (programmable one-shot)

The programmable one-shot mode is similar to Mode 0, but the output starts initially high. The output goes low at the start of the count and remains low until the count finishes. It then goes high. A low to high transition on the GATE input initiates the count. A low or high level on the GATE after this has no effect on the count. Figure 7.11 shows an example of Mode 1 with a counter value of 4.

Mode 2 (rate generator)

In this mode the inputted clock pulses are divided by the value in the counter register. The output goes low for one cycle and high for the rest of the cycle. Figure 7.12 shows an example of Mode 2 with a counter value of 4. In this case the output is high for three cycles and low for one. As with Mode 1 the count is initiated by a low to high transition on the GATE.

Mode 3 (square wave generator)

The square wave generator is similar to Mode 2 but the output is a square wave when the value in the counter is even or is high for an extra cycle more when the value of the count is odd. Figure 7.13 shows an example of Mode 3 with a counter value of 4. In this case the output is low for 2 cycles and high for 2 cycles.

If the counter is loaded with 5 the output is high for 3 cycles and low for 2. As with Mode 1 the count is initiated by a low to high transition on the GATE.

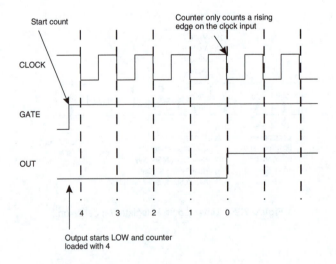

Figure 7.10   Mode 0 operation.

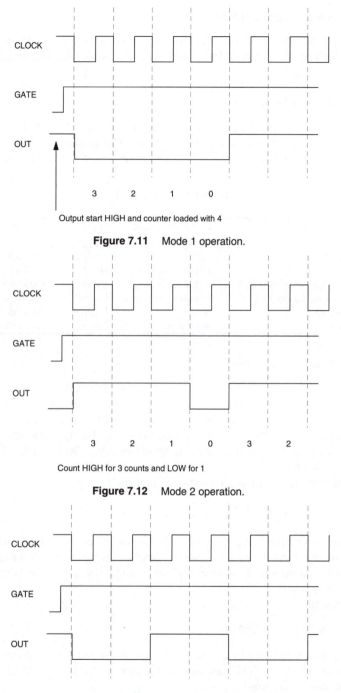

CLOCK
GATE
OUT
3
2
1
0
Output start HIGH and counter loaded with 4

Figure 7.11 Mode 1 operation.

CLOCK
GATE
OUT
3
2
1
0
3
2
Count HIGH for 3 counts and LOW for 1

Figure 7.12 Mode 2 operation.

CLOCK
GATE
OUT
Count HIGH for 2 counts and LOW for 2

Figure 7.13 Mode 3 operation.

Mode 4 (software triggered strobe)

This mode is similar to Mode 2 except that the GATE does not initiate the count. The output goes high for the count and goes low for one clock cycle. The output then goes back to high.

Mode 5 (hardware triggered strobe)

This mode is similar to Mode 2 except that the GATE input has no effect on the count. It starts counting after the rising edge of the input and then goes low for one clock period when the count is reached. Table 7.7 summarizes the control that the gate has on the mode.

Table 7.7   Gate control.

Mode	GATE low	GATE low–high transition	GATE high	Output signal
0	Disable	None	Enable	see Figure 7.10
1	None	Initiate counting	None	see Figure 7.11
2	Disable. Set output high	Initiate counting	Enable	see Figure 7.12
3	Disable. Set output high	Initiate counting	Enable	see Figure 7.13
4	Disable	None	Enable	As mode 2
5	None	Start count	None	As mode 2

7.3.3   Producing timer programs

Program 7.4 uses Mode 3 to produce a square wave of a frequency that is the input clock divided by an entered value. This clock input can be taken from an electronic clock output (for example, 25 kHz) or could be taken from a switched input. An oscilloscope (or LED if the input is relatively slow) can be used to display the input and output. Note that the GATE must be high in order for the counter to be active, a low disables the count and sets the output to a high.

The mode of counter 0 is set up using the statement:

```
_outp(CNTRL_REG, 0x36);
```

which loads the bit pattern `0011 0110b` into the Control Register. Taking each of the bits in turn, starting from the most significant bit, then `00` sets up counter 0, `11` specifies that the LSB will be loaded into the counter register then the MSB, `011` selects mode 3 and `0` specifies a binary count.

The statement:

```
_outp(COUNTER0, d & 0x00FF);
```

masks off the least significant byte (LSB) of the variable `d` and puts it into the LSB of the counter register. The most significant byte of `d` is then loaded into the MSB of the counter by the following statement:

```
_outp(COUNTER0, d >> 8);
```

This uses the shift right operator (`>>`) to move the MSB bits eight positions to the right (that is, into the LSB positions).

📖 Program 7.5

```
/*    This program divides the input clock on counter 0    */
/*    by an entered value. The GATE is set to a high and    */
/*    the output is OUT0.                                    */
#include <stdio.h>

#define  BASE_ADDRESS    0x3B8 /* change for system used on */
#define  COUNTER0        BASE_ADDRESS
#define  COUNTER1        (BASE_ADDRESS+1)
#define  COUNTER2        (BASE_ADDRESS+2)
#define  CNTRL_REG       (BASE_ADDRESS+3)

void  set_up_PTC(int); /* ANSI C prototype definitions */
int   main(void)
{
int    Divide;

      puts("Enter the value the clock to be divided by>");
      scanf("%d",&Divide);
      set_up_PTC(Divide);
      puts("The Programmable counter is programmed");
      return(0);
}

void set_up_PTC(int d)
{
      outportb(CNTRL_REG, 0x36);
      /*0011 0110 - Binary Select (0)                              */
      /*Mode Select 3 (011) Square wave generator                  */
      /*Read/Load Low Byte then High Byte (11)                     */
      /*Counter 0 selected (0)                                     */
      _outp(COUNTER0, d & 0x00FF);/*Load low byte into counter     */
      _outp(COUNTER0, d >> 8);   /*Load high byte into counter     */
}
```

Program 7.6 uses Mode 2 to produce a rate generator.

📖 Program 7.6

```
/*    This program divides the input clock on counter 0             */
/*    by an entered value to produce a rate generator.              */
/*    The GATE is set to a high and the output is OUT0.             */
/*    The output goes low for one cycle then high for the rest      */
#define  BASE_ADDRESS    0x3B8 /* change for system used on         */
#define  COUNTER0        BASE_ADDRESS
#define  COUNTER1        (BASE_ADDRESS+1)
#define  COUNTER2        (BASE_ADDRESS+2)
#define  CNTRL_REG       (BASE_ADDRESS+3)

#include <stdio.h>
#include <dos.h>

void  set_up_PTC(int); /* ANSI C prototype definition  */
int   main(void)
{
int    Divide;
      puts("Enter value clock to be divided by>>");
      scanf("%d",&Divide);
      set_up_PTC(Divide);
      puts("The Programmable counter is programmed");
      return(0);
}

void  set_up_PTC(int d)
```

```
{
        outportb(CNTRL_REG, 0x34);
        /*0011 0100 - Binary Select (0)                             */
        /*Mode Select 2 (010) Rate generator                        */
        /*Read/Load Low Byte then High Byte (11)                    */
        /*Counter 0 selected (0)                                    */

        _outp(COUNTER0, d & 0x00FF);/*Load low byte into counter    */
        _outp(COUNTER0, d >> 8);  /*Load high byte into counter     */
}
```

Program 7.7 is an assembly language program, divide by 10 counter.

Program 7.7

```
code            SEGMENT
                ASSUME cs:code
BASEADDRESS     EQU     03B8H     ; change this as required
COUNTER0        EQU     BASEADDRESS
COUNTER1        EQU     BASEADDRESS+1
CNTRLREG        EQU     BASEADDRESS+3
; 8088 program to set up divide by 10 counter.
start:
        mov dx,CNTRLREG     ; Control Reg.
        mov al,36h          ;
        out dx,al           ; Square wave, etc.
        mov dx,COUNTER0
        mov dx,10           ; Low byte
        out al,dx
        mov al,00           ; High byte
        out al,dx
        mov ah,4cH          ; program exit
        int 21h             ;
code    ENDS
        END     start
```

7.3.4 Pulse counting programs

In Program 7.8 the PTC counts a number of clock pulses on Counter 0. These pulses could be generated by many means, such as from switches, clock pulses, and so on. The counter always counts down and is initialized with 1111 1111 1111 1111b with the lines:

```
_outp(CNTRL_REG,0x30);
_outp(COUNTER0,0xff);      /* load LSB    */
_outp(COUNTER0,0xff);      /* load MSB    */
```

and this is latched into the counter register using the statement:

```
_outp(CNTRL_REG, 0x00);
```

The getcount() function contains the statements given next. It reads the LSB and MSB of the counter register. Then scales them so that the MSB is placed above the LSB. This is achieved by shifting the bits in the MSB by eight positions to the left. The scaled value is then subtracted from the initialized value to produce the final count.

```
lsb=inportb(portid);
msb=inportb(portid);
return(0xffff-(lsb+(msb<<8)));
```

📖 Program 7.8

```
/* Program which will determine the number of             */
/* clock pulses on Counter 0                              */
#include <stdio.h>
#include <conio.h>   /* required for clrscr() and kbhit() */

#define  BASE_ADDRESS   0x3B8 /* change for system used on */
#define  COUNTER0       BASE_ADDRESS
#define  COUNTER1       (BASE_ADDRESS+1)
#define  COUNTER2       (BASE_ADDRESS+2)
#define  CNTRL_REG      (BASE_ADDRESS+3)

int      getcount(int portid);
void     set_up_PTC(void);

int      main(void)
{
int      count;
      set_up_PTC();
      do
      {
         clrscr();
         count=getcount(COUNTER0);
         printf("count is %d\n",count);
         delay(1000);
      } while (!kbhit());
      return(0);
}

void  set_up_PTC(void)
{
      _outp(CNTRL_REG, 0x30);
      _outp(COUNTER0,0xff);       /* reset counter */
      _outp(COUNTER0,0xff);       /* reset counter */
      _outp(CNTRL_REG, 0x00);     /* latch counter */
}
int      getcount(int portid)
{
int      lsb,msb;
      /* Count starts from 0xffff and then counts down    */
      lsb=inportb(portid);
      msb=inportb(portid);
      return(0xffff-(lsb+(msb<<8)));
}
```

7.4 Exercises

Using C, Pascal or Assembly Language complete the following.

7.4.1   Write a program to input a byte from Port A.

7.4.2   Write a program which will send to Port B all 1s.

7.4.3   Write a program which will read a byte from Port A. This byte is then sent to Port B.

7.4.4   Write a program that sends a 'walking-ones' code to Port B. The delay between changes should be one second. A 'walking-ones' code is as follows:

```
00000001
00000010
00000100
00001000
   :  :
10000000
00000001
00000010
```
and so on.

7.4.5   Write separate programs which output the patterns in (a) and (b). The sequences are as follows:

(a)
```
00000001
00000010
00000100
00001000
00010000
00100000
01000000
10000000
01000000
   ::
00000001
00000010
```
and so on.

(b)
```
10000001
01000010
00100100
00011000
00100100
01000010
10000001
01000010
00100100
```
and so on.

7.4.6   Write separate programs which output the following sequences:

(a)
```
1010 1010
0101 0101
1010 1010
0101 0101
```
and so on.

(b)
```
1111 1111
0000 0000
1111 1111
0000 0000
```
and so on.

(c)
```
0000 0001
0000 0011
0000 1111
0001 1111
0011 1111
0111 1111
1111 1111
0000 0001
0000 0011
0000 0111
0000 1111
0001 1111
```
and so on.

(d)
```
0000 0001
0000 0011
0000 0111
0000 1111
0001 1111
0011 1111
0111 1111
1111 1111
0111 1111
0011 1111
0001 1111
0000 1111
```
and so on.

(e)   The inverse of (d) above.

7.4.7   Write a program that reads a byte from Port A and send the 1s complement representation to Port B. Note that 1s complement is all bits inverted.

7.4.8   Change the program in Exercise 7.4.7 so that it gives the 2s complement value on Port B. *Hint*: Either complement all the bits of the value and add 1 or send the negated value.

7.4.9   Write a program which will count from 00h to ffh will 1s delay between each count. The output should go to Port B.

7.4.10   Write a program which will sample Port A every 1s then send it to Port B.

7.4.11   Write a program which will simulate the following logic functions.

        NOT   PB0 = not (PA0)
        AND   PB0 = PA0 and PA1
        OR   PB0 = PA0 or PA1

where PA0 is bit 0 of Port A, PA1 is bit 1 of Port A and PB0 is bit 0 of Port B.

7.4.12   Write a program which will simulate a traffic light sequence. The delay between changes should be approximately 1 second.

        PB0 is RED   PB1 is AMBER   PB2 is GREEN

and the sequence is:

        RED → AMBER → GREEN → AMBER →
        RED → AMBER → GREEN
        and so on.

7.4.13   Modify the program in 7.4.12 so that the sequence is:

        RED   → RED and AMBER   →   GREEN   →
        AMBER → RED   →   RED and AMBER→
        GREEN   *and so on.*

7.4.14   Write a program which will input a value from Port A. This value is sent to Port B and the bits are rotated with a delay of 1 second.

7.4.15   Write a program which will sample Port A when bit 0 of Port C is changed from a 0 to a 1. Values are then entered via Port A by switching PC0 from a 0 to a 1. These values are put into memory starting from address 100h. The end of the input session is given by PC1 being set (that is, PC1 is equal to a 1). When this is set all the input values are sent to Port B with a 2 s interval.

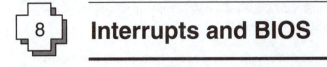

Interrupts and BIOS

8.1 Introduction

Computer systems either use polling or interrupt-driven software to service external equipment. With polling the computer continually monitors a status line and waits for it to become active, while an interrupt-driven device sends an interrupt request to the computer, which is then serviced by an interrupt service routine (ISR). Interrupt-driven devices are normally better in that the computer is thus free to do other things, while polling slows the system down as it must continually monitor the external device. Polling can also cause problems because a device may be ready to send data and the computer is not watching the status line at that point. Figure 8.1 illustrates polling and interrupt-driven devices.

The generation of an interrupt can occur by hardware or software, as illustrated in Figure 8.2. If a device wishes to interrupt the processor it informs the programmable interrupt controller (PIC). The PIC then decides whether it should interrupt the processor. If there is a processor interrupt then the processor reads the PIC to determine which device caused the interrupt. Then, depending on the device that caused the interrupt, a call to an ISR is made. The ISR then communicates with the device and processes any data. When it has finished the program execution returns to the original program.

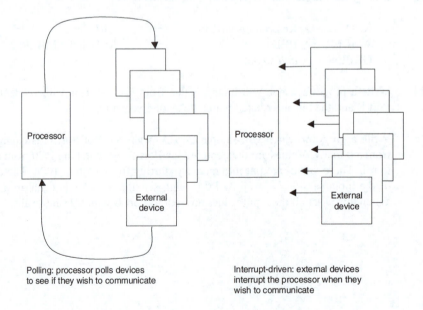

Figure 8.1 Polling and interrupt-driven communications.

A software interrupt causes the program to interrupt its execution and go to an interrupt service routine. Typical software interrupts include reading a key from the keyboard, outputting text to the screen and reading the current date and time.

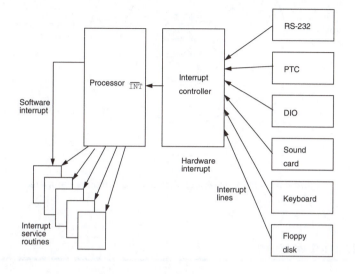

Figure 8.2   Interrupt handling.

8.2   BIOS and the operating system

The Basic Input/Output System (BIOS) communicates directly with the hardware of the computer. It consists of a set of programs which interface with devices such as keyboards, displays, printers, serial ports and disk drives. These programs allow the user to write application programs that contain calls to these functions, without having to worry about controlling them or which type of equipment is being used. Without BIOS the computer system would simply consist of a bundle of wires and electronic devices.

There are two main parts to BIOS. The first part is permanently stored in a ROM (the ROM BIOS). It is this part that starts the computer (or boots it) and contains programs which communicate with resident devices. The second stage is loaded when the operating system is started. This part is non-permanent.

An operating system allows the user to access the hardware in an easy-to-use manner. It accepts commands from the keyboard and displays them to the monitor. The Disk Operating System, or DOS, gained its name from its original purpose of providing a controller for the computer to access its disk drives. The language of DOS consists of a set of commands which are entered directly by the user and are interpreted to perform file management tasks, program execution and system configuration. It makes calls to BIOS to execute these. The main functions of DOS are to run programs, copy and remove files, create directories, move within a directory structure and to list files. The relationship between the computer's hardware, BIOS, DOS and application programs is illustrated in Figure 8.3. Microsoft Windows 95/98/NT calls BIOS programs directly.

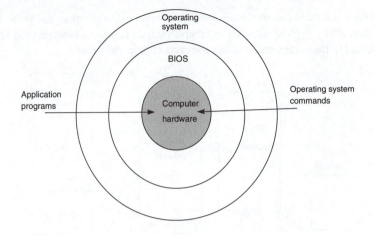

Figure 8.3   Interface between the user and computer hardware.

8.3   Interrupt vectors

Interrupt vectors are addresses which inform the interrupt handler as to where to find the ISR. All interrupts are assigned a number from 0 to 255. The interrupt vectors associated with each interrupt number are stored in the lower 1024 bytes of PC memory. For example, interrupt 0 is stored from `0000:0000` to `0000:0003`, interrupt 1 from `0000:0004` to `0000:0007`, and so on. The first two bytes store the offset and the next two store the segment address. Program 8.1 can be used to determine the addresses of the ISRs. Sample run 8.1 shows an example run. In this case, the address of the ISR for interrupt 0 is `0EE5:0158`, for interrupt 1 it is `0070:06F4`.

📖 Program 8.1

```
#include <stdio.h>

int    main(void)
{
int    far    *ptr;
int    seg,off,intr;

    ptr=(int far *)0x00;

    puts("INT ADDRESS");

    for (intr=0;intr<16;intr++)
    {
        off=*ptr;
        ptr++;

        seg=*ptr;
        ptr++;

        printf("%02d %04x:%04x\n",intr,seg,off);
    }
    return(0);
}
```

Each interrupt number is assigned a predetermined task, as outlined in Table 8.1. An interrupt can be generated either by external hardware, software, or by the processor. Interrupts 0, 1, 3, 4, 6 and 7 are generated by the processor. Interrupts from 8 to 15 and interrupt 2 are generated by external hardware. These get the attention of the processor by activating an interrupt request (IRQ) line. For example, the `IRQ0` line connects to the system timer, the keyboard to `IRQ1`, and so on. Most other interrupts are generated by software.

⌨ Sample run 8.1

```
INT ADDRESS
00 0ee5:0158
01 0070:06f4
02 0707:0016
03 0070:06f4
04 0070:06f4
05 f000:ff54
06 f000:50b2
07 f000:3509
08 0955:0000
09 ca51:1923
10 f000:3509
11 d101:02cd
12 f000:3509
13 f000:3509
14 0705:00b7
15 0070:06f4
```

Table 8.1 Interrupt handling.

Interrupt	Name	Generated by
00 (00h)	Divide error	processor
01 (00h)	Single step	processor
02 (02h)	Non-maskable interrupt	external equipment
03 (03h)	Breakpoint	processor
04 (04h)	Overflow	processor
05 (05h)	Print screen	Shift-Print screen key stroke
06 (06h)	Reserved	processor
07 (07h)	Reserved	processor
08 (08h)	System timer	hardware via IRQ0
09 (09h)	Keyboard	hardware via IRQ1
10 (0Ah)	Reserved	hardware via IRQ2
11 (0Bh)	Serial communications (COM2)	hardware via IRQ3
12 (0Ch)	Serial communications (COM1)	hardware via IRQ4
13 (0Dh)	Reserved	hardware via IRQ5
14 (0Eh)	Floppy disk controller	hardware via IRQ6
15 (0Fh)	Parallel printer	hardware via IRQ7
16 (10h)	BIOS – Video access	software
17 (11h)	BIOS – Equipment check	software
18 (12h)	BIOS – Memory size	software
19 (13h)	BIOS – Disk operations	software
20 (14h)	BIOS – Serial communications	software
22 (16h)	BIOS – Keyboard	software
23 (17h)	BIOS – Printer	software
25 (19h)	BIOS – Reboot	software
26 (1Ah)	BIOS – Time of day	software

28 (1Ch)	BIOS – Ticker timer	software
33 (21h)	DOS – DOS services	software
39 (27h)	DOS – Terminate and stay resident	software

8.4   Processor interrupts

The processor-generated interrupts normally occur either when a program causes a certain type of error or if it is being used in a debug mode. In the debug mode the program can be made to break from its execution when a break-point occurs. This allows the user to test the current status of the computer. It can also be forced to step through a program one operation at a time (single step mode).

8.4.1   Interrupt 00h: Divide error

If the divisor of a divide operation is zero, or if the quotient overflows, then the processor generates an interrupt 00h. Many compilers use their own ISR for this interrupt as this allows the program to handle the error without crashing it.

8.4.2   Interrupt 02h: Non-maskable interrupt

This interrupt is used by external equipment to flag that a serious fault has occurred. Typical non-maskable interrupts (NMIs) are:

- For power-failure procedures;
- Memory parity error;
- Breakout switch on hardware debuggers;
- Co-processor interrupt;
- I/O channel check;
- Disk-controller power-on request.

8.5   Hardware interrupts

Hardware interrupts allow external devices to gain the attention of the processor. Depending on the type of interrupt the processor leaves the current program and goes to a special program called an interrupt service routine (ISR). This program communicates with the device and processes any data. After it has completed its task, the program execution returns to the program that was running before the interrupt occurred. Examples of interrupts include the processing of keys from a keyboard and data from a sound card.

If a device wishes to interrupt the processor, it must inform the programmable interrupt controller (PIC). The PIC then decides if it should interrupt the processor. If it does then the processor reads the PIC to determine which device caused the interrupt. Then, depending on the device that caused the interrupt, a call to an ISR is made. Each PIC allow access to eight interrupt request lines and most modern PCs use two PICs to give access to 16 interrupt lines.

8.5.1   Interrupt vectors

Each device that requires to be 'interrupt-driven' is assigned an IRQ (interrupt request) line. Each IRQ is active high. The first eight (IRQ0–IRQ7) map into interrupts 8 to 15

(08h–0Fh) and the next eight (IRQ8–IRQ15) into interrupts 112 to 119 (70h–77h). Table 8.2 outlines the usage of each of these interrupts. When IRQ0 is made active the ISR corresponds to interrupt vector 8. IRQ0 normally connects to the system timer, the keyboard to IRQ1, and so on. The standard set-up of these interrupts is illustrated in Figure 8.4. The system timer interrupts the processor 18.2 times per second and is used to update the system time. When the keyboard has data it interrupts the processor with the IRQ1 line.

Data received from serial ports interrupts the processor with IRQ3 and IRQ4 and the parallel ports use IRQ5 and IRQ7. If one of the parallel, or serial ports does not exist then the IRQ line normally assigned to it can be used by another device. It is typical for interrupt-driven I/O cards, such as a sound card, to have a programmable IRQ line which is mapped to an IRQ line that is not being used.

Table 8.2 Interrupt handling.

Interrupt	Name	Generated by
08 (08h)	System timer	IRQ0
09 (09h)	Keyboard	IRQ1
10 (0Ah)	Reserved	IRQ2
11 (0Bh)	Serial communications (COM2:)	IRQ3
12 (0Ch)	Serial communications (COM1:)	IRQ4
13 (0Dh)	Parallel port (LPT2:)	IRQ5
14 (0Eh)	Floppy disk controller	IRQ6
15 (0Fh)	Parallel printer (LPT1:)	IRQ7
112 (70h)	Real-time clock	IRQ8
113 (71h)	Redirection of IRQ2	IRQ9
114 (72h)	Reserved	IRQ10
115 (73h)	Reserved	IRQ11
116 (74h)	Reserved	IRQ12
117 (75h)	Math co-processor	IRQ13
118 (76h)	Hard disk controller	IRQ14
119 (77h)	Reserved	IRQ15

Note that several devices can use the same interrupt line. A typical example is COM1: and COM3: sharing IRQ4 and COM2: and COM4: sharing IRQ3. If they do share then the ISR must be able to poll the shared devices to determine which of them caused the interrupt. If two different types of device (such as a sound card and a serial port) use the same IRQ line then there may be a contention problem as the ISR may not be able to communicate with different types of interfaces.

The Microsoft program MSD.EXE and similar utilities can be used to display the current usage of the IRQ lines. A sample run of MSD is given in Sample run 8.2.

Microsoft Windows 95/98 contains a useful program which determines the usage of the system interrupts. It is selected from Control Panel by selecting System→ Device Manager→ Properties. Figure 8.5 shows a sample window. In this case, it can be seen that the system timer uses IRQ0, the keyboard uses IRQ1, the PIC uses IRQ2, and so on. Notice that a Sound Blaster is using IRQ5. This interrupt is normally reserved for the secondary printer port. If there is no printer connected then IRQ5 can be used by another device. Some devices can have their I/O address and interrupt line changed. An example is given in Figure 8.6. In this case the IRQ line is set to IRQ7 and the base address is 378h.

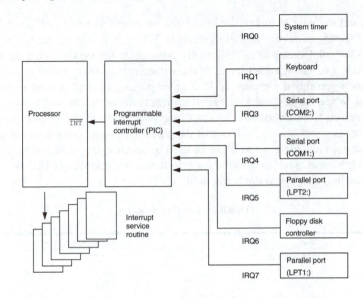

Figure 8.4   Standard usage of IRQ lines.

🖥 Sample run 8.2

```
IRQ  Address   Description     Detected     Handled By
---  -------   -----------     --------     ----------
0    0955:0000 Timer Click     Yes          win386.exe
1    CA51:1923 Keyboard        Yes          Block Device
2    F000:3509 Second 8259A    Yes          BIOS
3    D101:02CD COM2: COM4:     COM2:        MOUSE
4    F000:3509 COM1: COM3:     COM1:        BIOS
5    F000:3509 LPT2:           Yes          BIOS
6    0705:00B7 Floppy Disk     Yes          Default Handlers
7    0070:06F4 LPT1:           Yes          System Area
8    0705:0052 Real-Time Clock Yes          Default Handlers
9    F000:34F1 Redirected IRQ2 Yes          BIOS
10   F000:3509 (Reserved)                   BIOS
11   F000:3509 (Reserved)                   BIOS
12   0705:00FF (Reserved)                   Default Handlers
13   F000:34FA Math Coprocessor Yes         BIOS
14   0705:0117 Fixed Disk      Yes          Default Handlers
15   0705:012F (Reserved)                   Default Handlers
```

IRQ0: System timer

The system timer uses `IRQ0` to interrupt the processor 18.2 times per second and is used to keep the time-of-day clock updated.

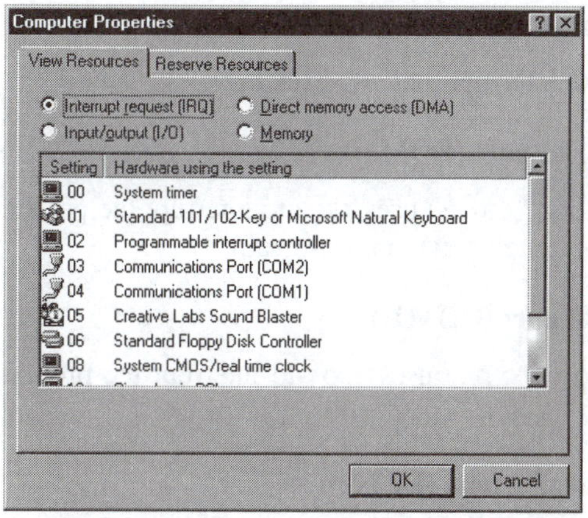

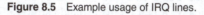

Figure 8.5 Example usage of IRQ lines.

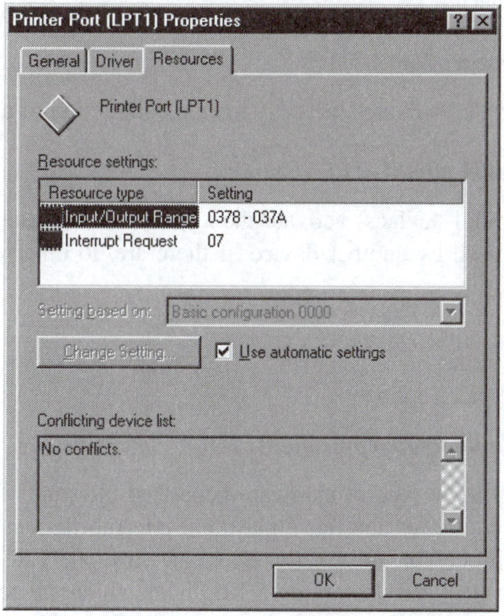

Figure 8.6 Example usage of IRQ lines.

IRQ1: Keyboard data ready

The keyboard uses `IRQ1` to signal to the processor that data is ready to be received from the keyboard. This data is normally a scan code, but the interrupt handler performs differently for the following special keystrokes:

- *Ctrl-Break* invokes interrupt 1Bh;
- *SysRq* invokes interrupt 15h/AH=85h;
- *Ctrl-Alt-Del* performs hard or soft reboot;
- *Shift-PrtSc* invokes interrupt 05h.

IRQ2: Redirection of IRQ9

The BIOS redirects the interrupt for IRQ9 back here.

IRQ3: Secondary serial port (COM2:)

The secondary serial port (COM2:) uses IRQ3 to interrupt the processor. Typically, COM3: to COM8: also use it, although COM3: may use IRQ4.

IRQ4: Primary serial port (COM1:)

The primary serial port (COM1:) uses IRQ4 to interrupt the processor. Typically, COM3: also uses it.

IRQ5: Secondary parallel port (LPT2:)

On older PCs the IRQ5 line was used by the fixed disk. On new systems the secondary parallel port uses it. Typically, it is used by a sound card on PCs which have no secondary parallel port connected.

IRQ6: Floppy disk controller

The floppy disk controller activates the IRQ6 line on completion of a disk operation.

IRQ7: Primary parallel port (LPT1:)

Printers (or other parallel devices) activate the IRQ7 line when they become active. As with IRQ5 it may be used by another device, if there are no other devices connected to this line.

IRQ9

Redirected to IRQ2 service routine.

8.5.2 *Programmable interrupt controller (PIC)*

The PC uses the 8259 IC to control hardware-generated interrupts. It is known as a programmable interrupt controller and has eight input interrupt request lines and an output line to interrupt the processor. Originally, PCs had only one PIC and eight IRQ lines (IRQ0–IRQ7). Modern PCs can use up to 15 IRQ lines which are set up by connecting a secondary PIC interrupt request output line to the IRQ2 line of the primary PIC. The interrupt lines on the secondary PIC are then assigned IRQ lines of IRQ8 to IRQ15. This set-up is shown in Figure 8.7. When an interrupt occurs on any of these lines it is sensed by the processor on the IRQ2 line. The processor then interrogates the primary and secondary PIC for the interrupt line which caused the interrupt.

The primary and secondary PICs are programmed via port addresses 20h and 21h, as given in Table 8.3.

The operation of the PIC is programmed using registers. The IRQ input lines are either configured as level-sensitive or edge-triggered interrupt. With edge-triggered interrupts a change from a low to a high on the IRQ line causes the interrupt. A level-sensitive interrupt occurs when the IRQ line is high. Most devices generate edge-triggered interrupts.

Table 8.3   Interrupt port addresses.

Port address	Name	Description
20h	Interrupt control port (ICR)	Controls interrupts and signifies the end of an interrupt
21h	Interrupt mask register (IMR)	Used to enable and disable interrupt lines

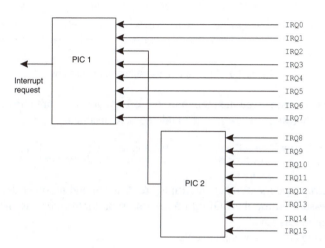

Figure 8.7   PC PIC connections.

The PIC controllers can be set up in many different modes using ICW (initialization command words); refer to an Intel data book for more information on these modes. The following code initializes the PICs with edge-triggered interrupts and interrupt lines IRQ8–IRQ15 enabled.

```
#define   ICR   0x20  /* Interrupt control port             */
#define   IMR   0x21  /* Interrupt mask register port       */

outportb(ICR,0x13);  /* edge triggered, one 8259, ICW4 required  */
outportb(IMR,8);     /* use interrupt vectors 08h-0Fh for IRQ0-IRQ7 */
outportb(IMR,9);     /* ICW4: buffered mode, normal EOI, 8088     */
```

Note that this initialization is normally carried out when the system is rebooted and there is thus no need to reinitialize it in a user program (unless any of the initialization parameters require to be changed). After initialization these ports are used either to enable or disable interrupt lines using the IMR or to control the interrupts with the ICR.

In the IMR an interrupt line is enabled by setting the assigned bit to a 0 (zero). This allows the interrupt line to interrupt the processor. Figure 8.8 shows the bit definitions of the IMR. For example, if bit 0 is set to a 0 then the system timer on IRQ0 is enabled.

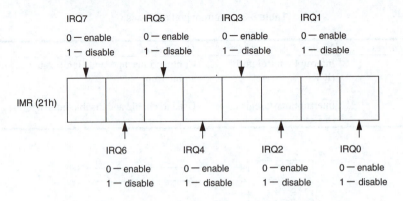

Figure 8.8   Interrupt mask register bit definitions.

In the example code given next the lines `IRQ0`, `IRQ1` and `IRQ6` are allowed to interrupt the processor, whereas `IRQ2`, `IRQ3`, `IRQ4` and `IRQ7` are disabled.

```
outportb(IMR,0xBC); /* 1011 1100 enable disk (bit 6),
                keyboard (1) and timer (0) interrupts */
```

When an interrupt occurs all other interrupts are disabled and no other device can interrupt the processor. Setting the EOI bit on the interrupt control port, as shown in Figure 8.9, enables interrupts again.

The following code enables interrupts:

```
#define    EOI   0x20
           outportb(ICR,EOI);   /* EOI command */
```

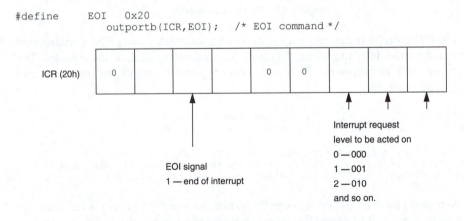

Figure 8.9   Interrupt control register bit definitions.

8.6   Generating software interrupts

In Turbo/Borland C there are four main functions to interrupt the processor: `int86x()`, `intdos()`, `intr()` and `int86()`. These functions are prototyped in the header file `dos.h`. This header file also contains a structure definition that allows a C program to gain access to the processor's registers. Parameters are passed into and out of the interrupt service routines via these registers. The format of the structure is:

```
struct    WORDREGS
{
      unsigned int ax;
      unsigned int bx;
      unsigned int cx;
      unsigned int dx;
      unsigned int si;
      unsigned int di;
      unsigned int cflag;
}
struct    BYTEREGS
{
      unsigned char al,ah;
      unsigned char bl,bh;
      unsigned char cl,ch;
      unsigned char dl,dh;
}

union REGS
{
      struct    WORDREGS x;
      struct    BYTEREGS h;
}
```

Registers are accessed either as 8-bit registers (such as AL, AH) or 16-bit registers (such as AX, BX). If a structure name regs is declared, then:

regs.h.al   accesses the 8-bit AL register

regs.x.ax   accesses the 16-bit AX register.

The syntax of the function int86() is:

```
int86(int intno, union REGS *inregs, union *outregs);
```

where the interrupt number is the first argument of the parameter list, the input registers are passed as the second argument and the output registers the third. Parameters are passed to the interrupt routine by setting certain input registers and parameters are passed back from the interrupt in the output registers.

BIOS interrupt 14h can be used to transmit and receive characters and also to determine the status of the serial port. Table 8.4 lists the main interrupt calls. Program 8.2 initializes COM2: with 4800 Baud, even parity, 1 stop bit and 7 data bits.

Program 8.2
```c
#include <stdio.h>
#include <dos.h>
int    main(void)
{
union REGS inregs,outregs;

      inregs.h.ah=0x00;
      inregs.h.al=0xD2;      /*    1101 0010                            */
                             /*    110 - 4800 bps, 10 - even parity,    */
                             /*    0 - 1 stop bit, 10 - 7 data bits     */
      inregs.x.dx=0x01;      /* COM2:                                   */
      int86(0x14,&inregs,&outregs);
      return(0);
}
```

Table 8.4   BIOS serial communications interrupts.

Description	Input registers	Output registers
Initialize serial port	AH = 00h AL = port parameters (see Figure 12.3) DX = port number (00h–03h)	AH = line status (see get status) AL = modem status (see get status)
Write character to port	AH = 01h AL = character to write DX = port number (00h–03h)	AH bit 7 clear if successful AH bit 7 set on error AH bits 6–0 = port status (see get status)
Read character from port	AH = 02h DX = port number (00h–03h)	Return: AH = line status (see get status) AL = received character if AH bit 7 clear
Get port status	AH = 03h DX = port number (00h–03h)	AH = line status bit 7: timeout 6: transmit shift register empty 5: transmit holding register empty 4: break detected 3: framing error 2: parity error 1: overrun error 0: receive data ready

In Visual C++ the inline assembler allows assembly language code to be embedded with C++ code. This code can use any C variable or function name that is in scope. The __asm keyword invokes the inline assembler and can appear wherever a C statement is legal. The following code is a simple __asm block enclosed in braces.

```
__asm
{
/* Initialize serial port */
      mov dx,0x01;   /* COM2:                     */
      mov al,0xD2;   /* serial port parameters */
      mov ah,0x0;    /* initialize serial port */
      int 14h;
      line_status=ah;
      modem_status=al;
}
```

Note these statements can also be inserted after the __asm keyword, such as:

```
__asm mov dx,0x01;   /* COM2:                     */
__asm mov al,0xD2;   /* serial port parameters */
__asm mov ah,0x0;    /* initialize serial port */
__asm int 14h;
__asm line_status=ah;
__asm modem_status=al;
```

8.6.1   Interrupt 1Ch: BIOS system timer tick

The PC system clock is updated 18.2 times every second. This clock update is automatically generated by the system timer tick interrupt. It is possible to use it to create a multitasking system. To achieve this the timer ISR is redirected from the system time update to a user-defined routine. This is achieved using the function setvect(intr,handler), where intr is the interrupt number and handler is the name of the new ISR for this interrupt.

In Program 8.3, the function `my_interrupt()` is called 18.2 times every second. Each time it is called a variable named `count` is incremented by one (notice in the main program there are no calls to this function). The main program tests the variable `count` and if it is divisible by 18 then the program displays a new count value.

In order to leave the system in the way in which it was started then the old ISR address must be restored. To achieve this the `getvect()` function is used to get the address of the interrupt routine at the start of the program. This is then restored with `setvect()` at the end. A test run is shown in Sample run 8.3.

📖 Program 8.3

```
#include <stdio.h>
#include <dos.h>
#include <conio.h>
void interrupt (*oldvect)(void);
void interrupt my_interrupt();

long count=0;

int main(void)
{
long   oldcount=0,newcount=0;
       puts("Press any key to exit");
       oldvect= getvect(0x1C); /* save the old interrupt vector      */
       setvect(0x1C,my_interrupt);/* install the new interrupt handler */
       do
       {
           if (!(count % 18))
           {
               newcount=count;
               if (oldcount!=newcount) printf("%ld\n",count);
               oldcount=count;
           }
       } while (!kbhit());
       /* set the old interrupt handler back */
       setvect(0x1c, oldvect);
       return 0;
}

void interrupt my_interrupt(void)
{
       count++;
       oldvect(); /* call the old routine */
}
```

💻 Sample run 8.3

```
Press any key to exit
18
36
54
72
90
108
126
144
162
180
198
216
```

8.7   Exercises

8.7.1   Using BIOS interrupt 10h, write a program that contains the following functions.

Function	Description
ch=read_character(x,y)	read character from screen position (x,y) and put the result into ch
moveto(x,y)	move the screen cursor to position (x,y)
get_cursor(&x,&y)	get the current cursor position and return it in x and y

8.7.2   Using DOS interrupt (21h) write a program that determines the DOS version. Note that DOS uses a major and minor number for version control. The general format is VER MAJOR.MINOR. For example,

🖥 **Sample run 8.4**
```
DOS Ver 3.01 is major 3 and minor 1.
```

Check the version number using the DOS command *VER*.

8.7.3   Using DOS interrupt (21h) write a program that determines the amount of free and total disk space on the default disk drive.

8.7.4   Using DOS interrupts, write a program that determines the system time.

8.7.5   Modify the DOS interrupt program that displays the date so that it will display the actual day (e.g. SUNDAY, etc.) and not the day of the week. For example

🖥 **Sample run 8.5**
```
Current Date is WEDNESDAY 9/9/1993
```

8.7.6   Using DOS interrupts write a program that displays if a key has been pressed.

8.7.7   Program 8.4 uses a DOS interrupt. When it is run it prints the text PROGRAM START but does not print the text PROGRAM END. Explain why.

📖 **Program 8.4**
```c
#include <stdio.h>
#include <dos.h>

int   main(void)
{
union REGS inregs,outregs;
  puts("PROGRAM STARTED");

  inregs.h.ah=0x4c;
```

```
int86(0x21,&inregs,&outregs);
puts("PROGRAM END");

return(0);
}
```

8.7.8   Using BIOS video interrupt 10h write programs which perform the following:

(a)   fill a complete screen with the character 'A' of a text colour of red with a background of blue;

(b)   repeat (a), but the character displayed should cycle from 'A' to 'Z' with a one-second delay between outputs;

(c)   repeat (a), but the foreground colour should cycle through all available colours with a one-second delay between outputs;

(d)   repeat (a) so that the background colour cycles through all available colours with a one-second delay between outputs.

8.7.9   Using BIOS keyboard interrupt 16h write a program that displays the status of the Shift, Caps lock, Cntrl, Scroll and Num keys.

8.7.10   If there is a line printer connected to the parallel port then write a program which sends text entered from a keyboard to the printer. The message should be entered followed by a CNTRL-D (4 ASCII). Use BIOS printer interrupt 17h.

   The program should also contain error checking of each character sent. Errors should include printer out-of-paper, printer time out and printer I/O error. If possible, test the program by switching the printer off while it is printing.

8.7.11   Distinguish between polling and interrupt-driven devices. What is the main advantage of using interrupt-driven devices.

8.7.12   Figure 8.5 shows an example usage of interrupt. Determine the device which is using the shown interrupts.

8.7.13   Find a PC and using Control Panel or MSD determine the usage of the interrupts.

8.7.14   Explain how hardware interrupts (IRQ0-IRQ15) are mapped into interrupt vectors.

8.7.15   How does the PC use IRQ3 and IRQ4 to communicate with the serial ports? What happens when there are four serial ports connected?

8.7.16   Explain how the interrupt mask register is used to enable and disable interrupts.

9 Interfacing Standards

9.1   Introduction

The type of interface card used greatly affects the performance of a PC system. Early models of PCs relied on expansion options to improve their specification. These expansion options were cards that plugged into an expansion bus. Eight slots were usually available and these added memory, video, fixed and floppy disk controllers, printer output, modem ports, serial communications and so on.

There are eight main types of interface busses available for the PC. The number of data bits they handle at a time determines their classification. They are:

- PC (8-bit)   ISA (16-bit)
- EISA (32-bit)   MCA (32-bit)
- VL-Local Bus (32-bit) PCI bus (32/64-bit)
- SCSI (16/32-bit)   PCMCIA (16-bit)

9.2   PC bus

The PC bus uses the architecture of the Intel 8088 processor which has an external 8-bit data bus and 20-bit address bus. A PC bus connector has a 62-pin printed circuit card edge connector and a long narrow or half-length plug-in card. Since it uses a 20-bit address bus it can address a maximum of 1 MB of memory. The transfer rate is fixed at 4.772 727 MHz, thus a maximum 4 772 727 bytes can be transferred every second. Dividing a crystal oscillator frequency of 14.31818 MHz by three derives this clock speed. Figure 9.1 shows a PC card. Table 9.1 defines the bus signals for the PC bus and Figure 9.2 defines the signal connections. The direction of the signal is taken as input if a signal comes from the ISA bus controller and an output if it comes from the slave device. An input/output identifies that the signal can originate from either the ISA controller or the slave device.

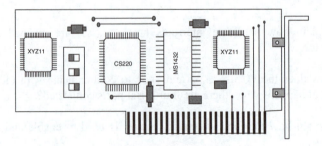

Figure 9.1   PC card.

Table 9.1   8-bit PC bus connections.

Signal	Name	Description
SA0–SA19	Address bus (input/output)	The lower 20 bits of the system address bus.
AEN	Address enable (output)	The address enable allows for an expansion bus board to disable its local I/O address decode logic. It is active high. When active, address enable indicates that either DMA or refresh are in control of the busses.
D0–D7	Data bus (input/output)	The 8 data bits that allow a transfer between the busmaster and the slave.
CLK	Clock (output)	The bus CLK is set to 4.772 727 MHz (for PC bus and 8.33 MHz for ISA bus) and provides synchronization of the data transmission (it is derived from the OSC clock).
ALE	Address latch (output)	The bus address latch indicates to the expansion bus that the address bus and bus cycle control signals are valid. It thus indicates the beginning of a bus cycle on the expansion bus.
$\overline{\text{IOR}}$	I/O read (input/output)	I/O read command signal indicates that an I/O read cycle is in progress.
$\overline{\text{IOW}}$	I/O write (input/output)	I/O write command signal indicates that an I/O write bus cycle is in progress.
$\overline{\text{SMEMR}}$	System memory read (output)	System memory read signal indicates a memory read bus cycle for the 20-bit address bus range (0h to FFFFFh).
$\overline{\text{SMEMW}}$	System memory write (output)	System memory write signal indicates a memory read bus cycle from the 20-bit address bus range (0h to FFFFFh).
IO CH RDY	Bus ready (input)	The bus ready signal allows a slave to lengthen the amount of time required for a bus cycle.
$\overline{\text{0WS}}$	Zero wait states (input)	The zero wait states (or no wait state) allows a slave to shorten the amount of time required for a bus cycle.
DRQ1–DRQ3	DMA request (input)	The DMA request indicates that a slave device is requesting a DMA transfer.
$\overline{\text{DACK1}}$ – $\overline{\text{DACK3}}$	DMA acknowledge (output)	The DMA acknowledge indicates to the requesting slave that the DMA is handling its request.
$\overline{\text{REF}}$	Refresh (output)	The refresh signal is used to inform a memory board that it should perform a refresh cycle.

T/C	Terminal count (input)	The Terminal count indicates that the DMA transfer has been successful and all the bytes have been transferred.
IRQ2-IRQ7	Interrupt request	The interrupt request signals indicate that the slave device is requesting service by the processor.
OSC	Crystal oscillator (output)	The crystal oscillator signal is a 14.31818 MHz signal provided for use by expansion boards. This clock speed is three times the CLK speed.
RESET DRV	Reset drive (output)	Resets plug-in boards connected to the ISA bus.
IO CH CHK	I/O check (input)	The I/O check signal indicates that a memory slave has detected a parity error.
±5V, ±12V and GND	Power (output)	

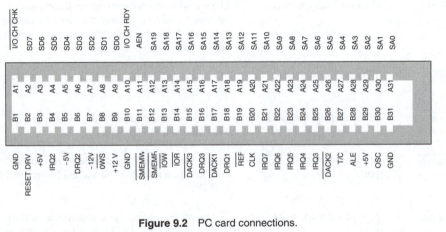

Figure 9.2 PC card connections.

9.3 ISA bus

IBM developed the ISA (Industry Standard Architecture) for their 80286-based AT (Advanced Technology) computer. It had the advantage of being able to deal with 16 bits of data at a time. An extra edge connector gives compatibility with the PC bus. This gives an extra 8 data bits and 4 address lines. Thus, the ISA bus has a 16-bit data and a 24-bit address bus, which gives a maximum of 16 MB of addressable memory and like the PC bus it uses a fixed clock rate of 8 MHz. The maximum data rate is thus 2 bytes (16 bits) per clock cycle, giving a maximum throughput of 16 MB/sec. In machines that run faster than 8MHz the ISA bus runs slower than the rest of the computer.

A great advantage of PC bus cards is that they can be plugged into an ISA bus connector. ISA cards are very popular as they give good performance for most interface applications. The components used are extremely cheap and it is a well-proven and reliable technology. Typical applications include serial and parallel communications, networking cards and sound cards. Figure 9.3 illustrates an ISA card and Table 9.2 gives the pin connections for the bus. It can be seen that there are four main sets of connections, the A, B, C and D sections. The standard PC bus connection contains the A and B sections. The A section includes the address lines A0–A19 and 8 data lines, D0–D7. The B section contains interrupt lines, IRQ0–IRQ7, power supplies and various other control signals. The extra ISA lines are added with the C and D section; these include the address lines, A17–A23, data lines D8–D15 and interrupt lines IRQ10–IRQ14.

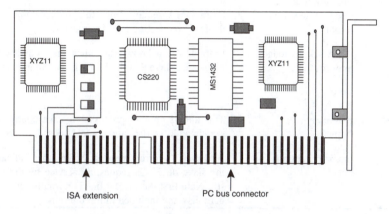

Figure 9.3 ISA card.

The Industry Standard Architecture (ISA) bus uses a 16-bit data bus (D0–D15) a 24-bit address bus (A0–A24) and the CLK signal is set to 8.33 MHz. Figure 9.4 illustrates the ISA bus pin connections and Table 9.2 lists the extra pin connections.

The $\overline{\text{SMEMR}}$ and $\overline{\text{SMEMW}}$ lines are used to transfer data for the lowest 1 MB (0h to FFFFFh) of memory (where the S prefix can be interpreted as small memory model) and the signals $\overline{\text{MEMR}}$ and $\overline{\text{MEMW}}$ are used to transfer data between 1 MB (FFFFFh) and 16 MB (FFFFFFh). For example, if reading from address 001000h then the $\overline{\text{SMEMR}}$ line is made active low, while if the address is 1F0000h then the $\overline{\text{MEMR}}$ line is made active. For a 16-bit transfer the $\overline{\text{M16}}$ and $\overline{\text{IO16}}$ lines are made active.

Table 9.2 Extra 16-bit ISA bus connections.

Signal	Name	Description
A17–A23	Address bus (input/output)	The upper 7 bits of the address of the system address bus.
$\overline{\text{SBHE}}$	System byte high enable (output)	The system byte high enable indicates that data is expected on the upper 8 bits of the data bus (D8–D15).
D8–D15	Data bus (input/output)	The upper 8 bits of the data bus provide for the second half of the 16-bit data bus.
$\overline{\text{MEMR}}$	Memory read (input/output)	The memory read command indicates a memory read when the memory address is in the range 100000h–FFFFFFh (16 MB of memory).

$\overline{\text{MEMW}}$	Memory write (input/output)	The memory write command indicates a memory write when the memory address is in the range 100000h – FFFFFFh (16 MB of memory).
$\overline{\text{M16}}$	16-bit memory slave	Indicates that the addressed slave is a 16-bit memory slave.
$\overline{\text{IO16}}$	16-bit I/O slave (input/output)	Indicates that the addressed slave is a 16-bit I/O slave.
DRQ0, DRQ5–DRQ7	DMA request lines (input)	Extra DMA request lines that indicate that a slave device is requesting a DMA transfer.
$\overline{\text{DACK0}}$, $\overline{\text{DACK5}}$ – $\overline{\text{DACK7}}$	DMA acknowledge lines (output)	Extra DMA acknowledge lines that indicate to the requesting slave that the DMA is handling its request.
$\overline{\text{MASTER}}$	Bus ready (input)	This allows another processor to take control of the system address, data and control lines.
IRQ9– IRQ12, IRQ14, IRQ15	Interrupt requests (input)	Additional interrupt request signals that indicate that the slave device is requesting service by the processor. Note that the IRQ13 line is normally used by the hard disk and included in the IDE bus.

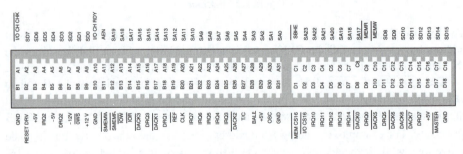

Figure 9.4   ISA bus connections.

9.3.1 Handshaking lines

Figure 9.5 shows typical connections to the ISA bus. The ALE (sometimes known as BALE) controls the address latch and, when active low, it latches the address lines A2–A19 to the ISA bus. The address is thus latched when ALE goes from a high to a low.

The Pentium's data bus is 64 bits wide, whereas the ISA expansion bus is 16 bits wide. It is the bus controller's function to steer data between the processor and the slave device for either 8-bit or 16-bit communications. For this purpose the bus controller monitors $\overline{\text{BE0}}$ - $\overline{\text{BE3}}$, W/$\overline{\text{R}}$, $\overline{\text{M16}}$, and $\overline{\text{IO16}}$ to determine the movement of data.

When the processor outputs a valid address it sets address lines (AD2–AD31), the byte enables ($\overline{\text{BE0}}$ - $\overline{\text{BE3}}$) and sets ADS active. The bus controller then picks up this address and uses it to generate the system address lines, SA0–SA19 (which are just a copy of the lines A2–A19). The bus controller then uses the byte enable lines to generate the address bits SA0 and SA1.

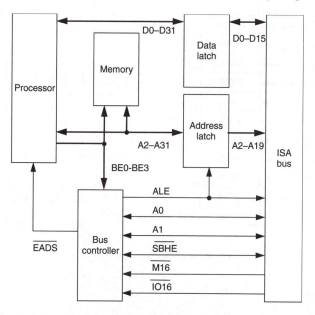

Figure 9.5   ISA bus connections.

The $\overline{\text{EADS}}$ signal returns an active low signal to the processor if the external bus controller has sent a valid address on address pins A2–A21.

It can be seen from Figure 9.6 that the $\overline{\text{BE0}}$ line accesses the addresses ending with 0h, 4h, 8h and Ch, the $\overline{\text{BE1}}$ line accesses addresses ending with 1h, 5h, 9h and Dh, the $\overline{\text{BE2}}$ line accesses addresses ending with 2h, 6h, Ah and Eh, and so on.

Thus if the $\overline{\text{BE0}}$ line is low and $\overline{\text{SBHE}}$ is high then a single byte is accessed through D0–D7. If $\overline{\text{SBHE}}$ is low then a word is accessed and D0–D15 contains the data.

Table 9.3 shows three examples of handshaking lines. The first is an example of a byte transfer with an 8-bit slave at an even address. The second example gives a byte transfer for an 8-bit slave at an odd address. Finally, the table shows a 2-byte transfer with a 16-bit slave at an even address.

If a 32-bit data is to be accessed then $\overline{\text{BE0}}-\overline{\text{BE3}}$ will be 0000 which makes 4 bytes active. The bus controller will then through cycle from SA0, SA1 = 00 to SA0, SA1 = 11. Each time 8 data bits are placed into a copy buffer, which are then passed to the processor as 32 bits.

Table 9.3   Example handshaking lines.

$\overline{\text{BE0}}$	$\overline{\text{BE1}}$	$\overline{\text{BE2}}$	$\overline{\text{BE3}}$	$\overline{\text{IO16}}$	$\overline{\text{M16}}$	$\overline{\text{SBHE}}$	SA0	SA1	*Data*
0	1	1	1	1	1	1	0	0	SD0–SD7
1	0	1	1	1	1	0	1	0	SD8–SD15
0	0	1	1	0	1	0	0	0	SD0–SD15

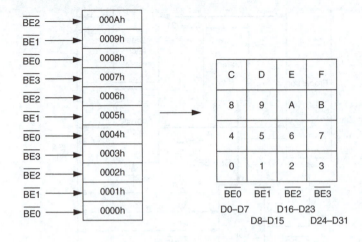

Figure 9.6   Address decoding.

9.3.2   82344 IC

Much of the electronics in a PC have been integrated onto multifunction ICs. The 82344 IC is one that interfaces directly to the ISA bus. Figure 9.7 shows its pin connections.

9.4   MCA bus

IBM developed the Microchannel Interface Architecture (MCA) bus for their PS/2 computers. This bus is completely incompatible with the ISA bus and can operate as a 16-bit or a 32-bit data bus. The main technical difference between the MCA and PC/ISA (and EISA) is that MCA has a synchronous bus whereas PC/ISA/EISA use an asynchronous bus. An asynchronous bus works at a fixed clock rate whereas a synchronous bus data transfer is not dependent on a fixed clock. Synchronous busses take their timings from the devices involved in the data transfer (that is, the processor or system clock). The original MCA specification resulted in a maximum transfer rate of 160 MB/sec. Very few manufacturers adopted MCA technology and it is mainly found in IBM PS/2 computers.

9.5   EISA bus

Several manufacturers developed the EISA (Extended Industry Standard Architecture) bus in direct competition to the MCA bus. It provides compatibility with PC/ISA but not with MCA. The EISA connector looks like an ISA connector. It is possible to plug an ISA card into an EISA connector, but a special key allows the EISA card to insert deeper into the EISA bus connector. It then makes connections with a 32-bit data and address bus. An EISA card has twice the number of connections over an ISA card and there are extra slots that allow it to be inserted deeper into the connector. The ISA card only connects with the upper connectors because it has only a single key slot.

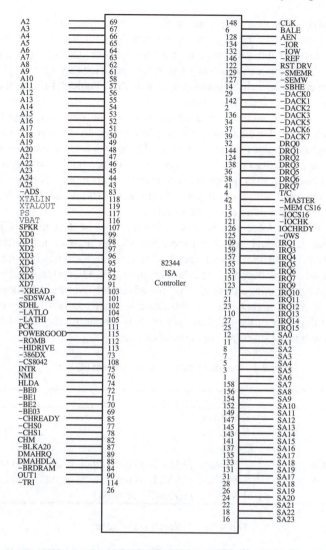

Figure 9.7 82344 IC connections.

EISA uses an asynchronous transfer at a clock speed of 8 MHz. It has a full 32-bit data and address bus and can address up to 4 GB of memory. In theory, the maximum transfer rate is 4 bytes for every clock cycle. Since the clock runs at 8 MHz, the maximum data rate is 32 MB/sec.

9.6 Comparison of different types

Data throughput depends on the number of bytes being communicated for each transfer and the speed of the transfer. With the PC, ISA and EISA busses this transfer rate is fixed at 8 MHz, whereas the PCI and VL local busses use the system clock (typically,

33 MHz or 50 MHz). For many applications the ISA bus offers the best technology as it has been around for a long time, it gives a good data throughput and it is relatively cheap and reliable. It has a 16-bit data bus and can thus transfer data at a maximum rate of 16 MB/sec. The EISA bus can transfer 4 bytes for each clock cycle, thus if 4 bytes are transferred for each clock cycle, it is twice as fast as ISA. Table 9.4 shows the maximum data rates for the different interface cards.

The type of interface technology used depends on the data throughput. Table 9.5 shows some typical transfer data rates. The heaviest usage on the system are microprocessor to memory and graphics adapter transfers. These data rates depend on the application and the operating system used. Graphical user interface (GUI) programs have much greater data throughput than programs running in text mode. Notice that a high-specification sound card with recording standard quality (16-bit samples at 44.1 kHz sampling rate) only requires a transfer rate of 88 kB/sec.

A standard Ethernet local area network card transfers at data rates of up 10 Mbps (approx. 1 MB/sec), although new fast Ethernet cards can transfer at data rates of up to 100 Mbps (approx. 10 MB/sec). These transfers thus require local bus type interfaces.

The PCI local bus has become a standard on most new PC systems and has replaced the VL-local bus for graphics adapters. It has the advantage over the VL-local bus in that it can transfer at much higher rates. Unfortunately, most available software packages cannot use the full power of the PCI bus because they do not use the full 64-bit data bus. PCI and VL-local bus are discussed in the next chapter.

Table 9.4   Maximum data rates for different I/O cards.

I/O card	Maximum data rate
PC	8 MB/sec
ISA	16 MB/sec
EISA	32 MB/sec
VL-Local bus	132 MB/sec (33 MHz system clock using 32-bit transfers)
PCI	264 MB/sec (33 MHz system clock using 64-bit transfers)
MCA	20 MB/sec (160 MB/sec burst)

Table 9.5   Typical transfer rates.

Device	Transfer rate	Application
Hard disk	4 MB/sec	Typical transfer
Sound card	88 kB/sec	16-bit, 44.1 kHz sampling
LAN	1 MB/sec	10 Mbit/sec Ethernet
RAM	66 MB/sec	Microprocessor to RAM
Serial Communications	1 kB/sec	9600 bps
Super VGA	15 MB/sec	1024×768 pixels with 256 colours

9.7   Exercises

9.7.1   Prove, apart from the MCA bus, the transfer rates given in Table 9.4.

9.7.2   If an audio card is using 16-bit sampling at a rate of 44.1 kHz, prove that the transfer rate for stereo sound will be 176.4 kB/sec. Show also that this is equivalent to 1.411 Mbps (note that this approximates the standard rate for CD-ROMs). Can this rate be transferred using the ISA bus?

9.7.3   Using the transfer rate derived in Exercise 9.7.2 determine the maximum transfer speed of a ×32 CD-ROM drive.

9.7.4   Explain the difference between the method of transfer for the asynchronous busses (such as PC, ISA, EISA and PCI) and an synchronous bus (such as MCA).

9.7.5   Determine amount of data for a single screen that is required to be transferred for the following screen resolutions:

(a) 800×600, 65 536 colours [960 000 B/sec].
(b) 800×600, 16 777 216 colours [1 440 000 B/sec].
(c) 1024×768, 65 536 colours [1 572 864 B/sec].

Determine the maximum number of screen updates with a 32-bit PCI bus for each of the above.

9.7.6   Identify the main ISA signal lines and how they are used to transfer data. Answer clearly the following:

(a) What are the main differences between a PC card and an ISA card?
(b) How are the byte enable lines used?
(c) How is a read or write transfer identified?
(d) How is a memory read/write or isolated memory read/write transfer identified?
(e) Describe the interrupt lines which are available on a PC card and an ISA card.
(f) Typically, what devices could be supported by a PC card (that is, what devices use the interrupts that a PC card can support)? How does this relate to the original specification of the PC?

10 Local Bus

10.1 Introduction

The main problem with the PC, ISA and EISA busses is that the transfer rate is normally much slower than the system clock. This is wasteful in processor time and generally reduces system performance. For example, if the system clock is running at 50 MHz and the EISA interface operates at 8 MHz then for 84% of the data transfer time the processor is doing nothing. This chapter discusses the main local busses and the next discusses motherboard design.

10.2 VESA VL-local bus

An improvement to the ISA interface is to transfer data at the speed of the system clock. For this reason the Video Electronics Standards Association (VESA) created the VL-local bus to create fast processor-to-video card transfers. It uses a standard ISA connector with an extra connection to tap into the system bus (Figure 10.1).

Memory, graphics and disk transfers are the heaviest for data transfer rates, whereas applications such as modems, Ethernet and sound cards do not require fast transfer rates. The VL-local bus addresses this by allowing the processor, memory, graphics and disk controller access to a 33 MHz/32-bit local bus. Other applications still use the normal ISA bus, as shown in Figure 10.2. The graphics adapter and disk controller connect to the local bus whereas other slower peripherals connect to the slower 8 MHz/16-bit ISA bus. A maximum of three devices can connect to the local bus (normally graphics and disk controllers). Note that the speed of the data transfer is dependent on the clock rate of the system and that the maximum clock speed for the VL-local bus is 33 MHz.

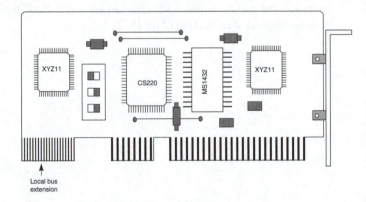

Figure 10.1 VL-local bus interface card.

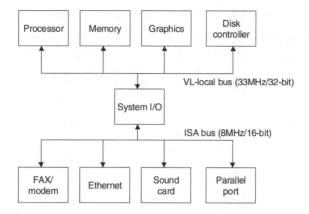

Figure 10.2   VESA VL-local bus architecture.

Table 10.1 lists the pin connections for the 32-bit VL-local bus and it shows that, in addition to the standard ISA connector, there are two sides of connections, the A and the B side. Each side has 58 connections giving 116 connections. It has a full 32-bit data and address bus. The 32 data lines are labelled DAT00–DAT31 and 32 address lines are labelled from ADR00 to ADR31. Note that while the data and address lines are contained within the extra VL-local bus extension, some of the standard ISA lines are used, such as the IRQ lines.

10.3 PCI bus

Intel have developed a new standard interface, named the PCI (Peripheral Component Interconnection) local bus, for the Pentium processor. This technology allows fast memory, disk and video access. A standard set of interface ICs known as the 82430 PCI chip-set is available to interface to the bus.

As with the VL-local bus, the PCI bus transfers data using the system clock, but has the advantage over the VL-local Bus in that it can operate over a 32-bit or 64-bit data path. The high transfer rates used in PCI architecture machines limit the number of PCI bus interfaces to two or three (normally the graphics adapter and hard disk controller). If data is transferred at 64 bits (8 bytes) at a rate of 33 MHz then the maximum transfer rate is 264 MB/sec. Figure 10.3 shows PCI architecture. Notice that an I/O bridge gives access to ISA, EISA or MCA cards. Unfortunately, to accommodate for the high data rates and for a reduction in the size of the interface card, the PCI connector is not compatible with PC, ISA or EISA.

The maximum data rate of the PCI bus is 264 MB/sec, which can only be achievable using 64-bit software on a Pentium-based system. On a system based on the 80486 processor this maximum data will only be 132 MB/sec (that is, using a 32-bit data bus).

The PCI local bus is a radical re-design of the PC bus technology and is logically different from the ISA and VL-local bus. Table 10.2 lists the pin connections for the 32-bit PCI local bus and it shows that there are two lines of connections, the A and the B side. Each side has 64 connections giving 128 connections. A 64-bit, 2×94-pin connector version is also available. The PCI bus runs at the speed of the motherboard which for the Pentium processor is typically 33 MHz or 50 MHz (as compared to the VL-local bus which gives a maximum transfer rate of 33 MHz).

Table 10.1   32-bit VESA VL-local bus connections.

Pin	Side A	Side B	Pin	Side A	Side B
1	D0	D1	30	A17	A16
2	D2	D3	31	A15	A14
3	D4	GND	32	VCC	A12
4	D6	D5	33	A13	A10
5	D8	D7	34	A11	A8
6	GND	D9	35	A9	GND
7	D10	D11	36	A7	A6
8	D12	D13	37	A5	A4
9	VCC	D15	38	GND	$\overline{\text{WBACK}}$
10	D14	GND	39	A3	$\overline{\text{BE0}}$
11	D16	D17	40	A2	VCC
12	D18	VCC	41	NC	$\overline{\text{BE1}}$
13	D20	D19	42	$\overline{\text{RESET}}$	$\overline{\text{BE2}}$
14	GND	D21	43	$D / \overline{C}$	GND
15	D22	D23	44	$M / \overline{IO}$	$\overline{\text{BE3}}$
16	D24	D25	45	$W / \overline{R}$	$\overline{\text{ADS}}$
17	D26	GND	46	KEY	KEY
18	D28	D27	47	KEY	KEY
19	D30	D29	48	$\overline{\text{RDYRTN}}$	$\overline{\text{LRDY}}$
20	VCC	D31	49	GND	$\overline{\text{LDEV}}$
21	A31	A30	50	IRQ9	$\overline{\text{LREQ}}$
22	GND	A28	51	$\overline{\text{BRDY}}$	GND
23	A29	A26	52	$\overline{\text{BLAST}}$	$\overline{\text{LGNT}}$
24	A27	GND	53	ID0	VCC
25	A25	A24	54	ID1	ID2
26	A23	A22	55	GND	ID3
27	A21	VCC	56	LCLK	ID4
28	A19	A20	57	VCC	NC
29	GND	A18	58	$\overline{\text{LBS16}}$	$\overline{\text{LEADS}}$

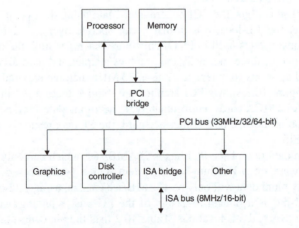

Figure 10.3   PCI bus architecture.

Table 10.2 32-bit PCI local bus connections.

Pin	Side A	Side B	Pin	Side A	Side B
1	−12V	$\overline{TRST}$	32	AD17	AD16
2	TCK	+12V	33	$\overline{C/BE2}$	+3.3V
3	GND	TMS	34	GND	$\overline{FRAME}$
4	TDO	TDI	35	$\overline{IRDY}$	GND
5	+5V	+5V	36	+3.3V	$\overline{TRDY}$
6	+5V	$\overline{INTA}$	37	$\overline{DEVSEL}$	GND
7	$\overline{INTB}$	$\overline{INTC}$	38	GND	$\overline{STOP}$
8	$\overline{INTD}$	+5V	39	$\overline{LOCK}$	+3.3V
9	$\overline{PRSNT1}$	Reserved	40	$\overline{PERR}$	SDONE
10	Reserved	+5V(I/O)	41	+3.3V	$\overline{SBO}$
11	$\overline{PRSNT2}$	Reserved	42	$\overline{SERR}$	GND
12	GND	GND	43	+3.3V	PAR
13	GND	GND	44	$\overline{C/BE1}$	AD15
14	Reserved	Reserved	45	AD14	+3.3V
15	GND	$\overline{RST}$	46	GND	AD13
16	CLK	+5V(I/O)	47	AD12	AD11
17	GND	$\overline{GNT}$	48	AD10	GND
18	$\overline{REQ}$	GND	49	GND	AD09
19	+5V(I/O)	Reserved	50	KEY	KEY
20	AD31	AD30	51	KEY	KEY
21	AD29	+3.3V	52	AD08	$\overline{C/BE0}$
22	GND	AD28	53	AD07	+3.3V
23	AD27	AD26	54	+3.3V	AD06
24	AD25	GND	55	AD05	AD04
25	+3.3V	AD24	56	AD03	GND
26	$\overline{C/BE3}$	IDSEL	57	GND	AD02
27	AD23	+3.3V	58	AD01	AD00
28	GND	$\overline{FRAME}$	59	+5V(I/O)	+5V(I/O)
29	AD21	AD20	60	$\overline{ACK64}$	$\overline{REQ64}$
30	AD19	GND	61	+5V	+5V
31	+3.3V	$\overline{TRDY}$	62	+5V	+5V

10.3.1 PCI operation

The PCI bus cleverly saves lines by multiplexing the address and data lines. It has two modes (Figure 10.4):

- Multiplexed mode. The address and data lines are used alternately. First the address is sent, followed by a data read or write. Unfortunately, this requires two or three clock cycles for a single transfer (either an address followed by a read or write cycle, or an address followed by read and write cycle). This causes a maximum data write transfer rate of 66 MB/s (address then write) and a read transfer rate of 44 MB/s (address, write then read), for a 32-bit data bus width.
- Burst mode. The multiplexed mode obviously slows down the maximum transfer rate. Additionally, it can be operated in burst mode, where a single address can be initially sent, followed by implicitly addressed data. Thus, if a large amount of sequentially addressed memory is transferred then the data rate approach the maximum transfer of 133 MB/s for a 32-bit data bus and 266 MB/s for a 64-bit data bus.

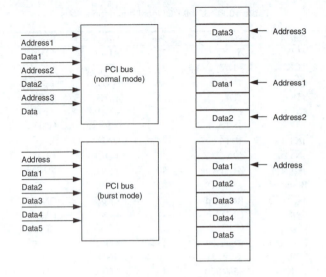

Figure 10.4   PCI bus transfer modes.

If the data from the processor is sequentially address data then PCI bridge buffers the incoming data and then releases it to the PCI bus in burst mode. The PCI bridge may also use burst mode when there are gaps in the addressed data and use a handshaking line to identify that no data is transferred for the implied address. For example in Figure 10.4 the burst mode could involve Address+1, Address+2 and Address+3 and Address+5, then the byte enable signal can be made inactive for the fourth data transfer cycle.

To accommodate the burst mode, the PCI bridge has a prefetch and posting buffer on both the host bus and the PCI bus sides. This allows the bridge to build the data access up into burst accesses. For example, the processor typically transfers data to the graphics card with sequential accessing. The bridge can detect this and buffer the transfer. It will then transfer the data in burst mode when it has enough data. Figure 10.5 shows an example where the PCI bridge buffers the incoming data and transfers it using burst mode. The transfers between the processor and the PCI bridge, and between the PCI bridge and the PCI bus can be independent where the processor can be transferring to its local memory while the PCI bus is transferring data. This helps to decouple the PCI bus from the processor.

The primary bus in the PCI bridge connects to the processor bus and the secondary bus connects to the PCI bus. The prefetch buffer stores incoming data from the connected bus and the posting buffer holds the data ready to be sent to the connected bus.

The PCI bus also provides for a configuration memory address (along with direct memory access and isolated I/O memory access). This memory is used to access the configuration register and 256-byte configuration memory of each PCI unit.

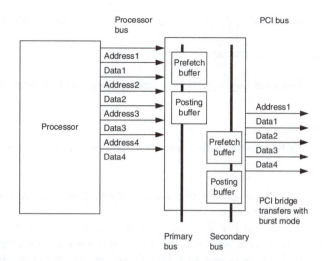

Figure 10.5   PCI bridge using buffering for burst transfer.

10.3.2 PCI bus cycles

The PCI has built-in intelligence where the command/byte enable signals ($\overline{\text{C/BE3}} - \overline{\text{C/BE0}}$) are used to identify the command. They are given by:

$\overline{\text{C/BE3}}$	$\overline{\text{C/BE2}}$	$\overline{\text{C/BE1}}$	$\overline{\text{C/BE0}}$	*Description*
0	0	0	0	INTA sequence
0	0	0	1	Special cycle
0	0	1	0	I/O read access
0	0	1	1	I/O write access
0	1	1	0	Memory read access
0	1	1	1	Memory write access
1	0	1	0	Configuration read access
1	0	1	1	Configuration write access
1	1	0	0	Memory multiple read access
1	1	0	1	Dual addressing cycle
1	1	1	0	Line memory read access
1	1	1	1	Memory write access with invalidations

The PCI bus allows any device to talk to any other device, thus one device can talk to another without the processor being involved. The device that starts the conversion is known as the initiator and the addressed PCI device is known as the target. The sequence of operation for write cycles, in burst mode, is:

- Address phase. The transfer data is started by the initiator activating the $\overline{\text{FRAME}}$ signal. The command is set on the command lines ($\overline{\text{C/BE3}} - \overline{\text{C/BE0}}$) and the address/data pins (AD31–AD0) are used to transfer the address. The bus then uses the byte enable lines ($\overline{\text{C/BE3}} - \overline{\text{C/BE0}}$) to transfer a number of bytes.
- The target sets the $\overline{\text{TRDY}}$ signal (target ready) active to indicate that the data has on the AD31–AD0 (or AD62–AD0 for a 64-bit transfer) lines is valid. In addition, the initiator indicates its readiness to the PCI bridge by setting the $\overline{\text{IRDY}}$ signal (indicator ready) active. Figure 10.6 illustrates this.

- The transfer continues using the byte enable lines. The initiator can block transfers if it sets $\overline{\text{IRDY}}$ and the target with $\overline{\text{TRDY}}$.
- Transfer is ended by deactivating the $\overline{\text{FRAME}}$ signal.

The read cycle is similar but the $\overline{\text{TRDY}}$ line is used by the target to indicate that the data on the bus is valid.

10.3.3 PCI commands

The first phase of the bus access is the command/addressing phase. Its main commands are:

- INTA sequence. Addresses an interrupt controller where interrupt vectors are transferred after the command phase.
- Special cycle. Used to transfer information to the PCI device about the processor's status. The lower 16 bits contain the information codes, such as 0000h for a processor shutdown, 0001h for a processor halt, 0002h for *x*86 specific code and 0003h to FFFFh for reserved codes. The upper 16 bits (AD31–AD16) indicate *x*86 specific codes when the information code is set to 0002h.
- I/O read access. Indicates a read operation for I/O address memory, where the AD lines indicate the I/O address. The address lines AD0 and AD1 are decoded to define whether an 8-bit or 16-bit access is being conducted.
- I/O write access. Indicates a write operation to an I/O address memory, where the AD lines indicate the I/O address.
- Memory read access. Indicates a direct memory read operation. The byte-enable lines ($\overline{\text{C/BE3}}-\overline{\text{C/BE0}}$) identify the size of the data access.
- Memory write access. Indicates a direct memory write operation. The byte-enable lines ($\overline{\text{C/BE3}}-\overline{\text{C/BE0}}$) identify the size of the data access.

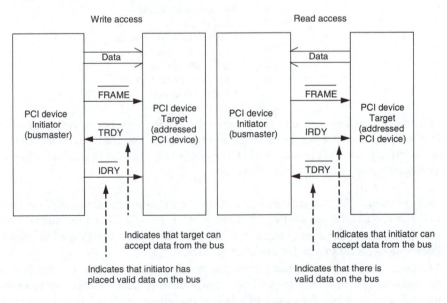

Figure 10.6   PCI handshaking.

- Configuration read access. Used when accessing the configuration address area of a PCI unit. The initiator sets the IDSEL line activated to select it. It then uses address bits AD7–AD2 to indicate the addresses of the double words to be read (AD1 and AD0 are set to 0). The address lines AD10–AD18 can be used for selecting the addressed unit in a multi-function unit.
- Configuration write access. As the configuration read access, but data is written from the initiator to the target.
- Memory multiple read access. Used to perform multiple data read transfers (after the initial addressing phase). Data is transferred until the initiator sets the $\overline{\text{FRAME}}$ signal inactive.
- Dual addressing cycle. Used to transfer a 64-bit address to the PCI device (normally only 32-bit addresses are used) in either a single or a double clock cycle. In a single clock cycle the address lines AD63–AD0 contain the 64-bit address (note that the Pentium processor only has a 32-bit address bus, but this mode has been included to support other systems). With a 32-bit address transfer the lower 32 bits are placed on the AD31–AD0 lines, followed by the upper 32 bits on the AD31–AD0 lines.
- Line memory read access. Used to perform multiple data read transfers (after the initial addressing phase). Data is transferred until the initiator sets the $\overline{\text{FRAME}}$ signal inactive.
- Memory write access with invalidations. Used to perform multiple data write transfers (after the initial addressing phase).

10.3.4 PCI interrupts

The PCI bus support four interrupts ($\overline{\text{INTA}}$ – $\overline{\text{INTD}}$). The $\overline{\text{INTA}}$ signal can be used by any of the PCI units, but only a multi-function unit can use the other three interrupt lines ($\overline{\text{INTB}}$ – $\overline{\text{INTD}}$). These interrupts can be steered, using system BIOS, to one of the IRQx interrupts by the PCI bridge. For example, a 100 Mbps Ethernet PCI card can be set to interrupt with $\overline{\text{INTA}}$ and this could be steered to IRQ10.

10.3.5 Bus arbitration

Busmasters are devices on a bus which are allowed to take control of the bus. For this purpose, PCI uses the $\overline{\text{REQ}}$ (request) and $\overline{\text{GNT}}$ (grant) signals. There is no real standard for this arbitration, but normally the PCI busmaster activates the $\overline{\text{REQ}}$ signal to indicate a request to the PCI bus, and the arbitration logic must then activate the $\overline{\text{GNT}}$ signal so that the requesting master gains control of the bus. To prevent a bus lock-up, the busmaster is given 16 CLK cycles before a time-overrun error occurs.

10.3.6 Other PCI pins

The other PCI pins are:

- $\overline{\text{RST}}$ (Pin A15). Resets all PCI devices.
- $\overline{\text{PRSNT1}}$ and $\overline{\text{PRSNT2}}$ (Pins B9 and B11). These, individually, or jointly, show that there is an installed device and what the power consumption is. A setting of 11 (that is, $\overline{\text{PRSNT1}}$ is a 1 and $\overline{\text{PRSNT2}}$ is a 1) indicates no adapter installed, 01 indicates maximum power dissipation of 25 W, 10 indicates a maximum dissipation of 15 W and 00 indicate a maximum power dissipation of 7.5 W.
- $\overline{\text{DEVSEL}}$ (Pin B37). Indicates that addressed device is the target for a bus operation.

- TMS (test mode select), TDI (test data input), TDO (test data output), $\overline{\text{TRST}}$ (test reset), TCK (test clock). Used to interface to the JTAG boundary scan test.
- IDSEL (Pin A26). Used for device initialization select signal during the accessing of the configuration area.
- $\overline{\text{LOCK}}$ (Pin A15). Indicates that an addressed device is to be locked-out of bus transfers. All other unlocked device can still communicate.
- PAR, $\overline{\text{PERR}}$ (Pins A43 and B40). The parity pin (PAR) is used for even parity for AD31–AD0 and C/BE3–C/BE0, and $\overline{\text{PERR}}$ indicates that a parity error has occurred.
- SDONE, $\overline{\text{SBO}}$ (Pins A40 and A41). Used in snoop cycles. SDONE (snoop done) and $\overline{\text{SBO}}$ (snoop back off signal).
- $\overline{\text{SERR}}$ (Pin B42). Used to indicate a system error.
- $\overline{\text{STOP}}$ (Pin A38). Used by a device to stop the current operation.
- $\overline{\text{ACK64}}$, $\overline{\text{REQ64}}$ (Pins B60 and A60). The $\overline{\text{REQ64}}$ signal is an active request for a 64-bit transfer and $\overline{\text{ACK64}}$ is the acknowledge for a 64-bit transfer.

10.3.7 Configuration address space

Each PCI device has 256 bytes of configuration data, which is arranged as 64 registers of 32 bits. It contains a 64-byte predefined header followed by an extra 192 bytes which contain extra configuration data. Figure 10.7 shows the arrangement of the header. The definitions of the fields are:

- Unit ID and Man. ID. A Unit ID of FFFFh defines that there is no unit installed, while any other address defines its ID. The PCI SIG, which is the governing body for the PCI specification, allocates a Man. ID. This ID is normally shown at BIOS start-up. Section 10.5 gives some example Man. IDs (and Plug-and-Play IDs).
- Status and Command.
- Class code and Revision. The class code defines PCI device type. It splits into two 8-bit values with a further 8-bit value that defines the programming interface for the unit. The first defines the unit classification (00h for no class code, 01h for mass storage, 02h for network controllers, 03h for video controllers, 04h for multimedia units, 05h for memory controller and 06h for a bridge), followed by a subcode which defines the actual type. Typical codes are:

- 0100h. SCSI controller.
- 0101h. IDE controller.
- 0102h. Floppy controller.
- 0200h. Ethernet network adapter.
- 0201h. Token ring network adapter.
- 0202h. FDDI network adapter.
- 0280h. Other network adapter.
- 0300h. VGA video adapter.
- 0301h. XGA video adapter.
- 0380h. Other video adapter.
- 0400h. Video multimedia device.
- 0401h. Audio multimedia device.

- 0480h. Other multimedia device.
- 0500h. RAM memory controller.
- 0501h. Flash memory controller.
- 0580h. Other memory controller.
- 0600h. Host.
- 0601h. ISA Bridge.
- 0602h. EISA Bridge.
- 0603h. MAC Bridge.
- 0604h. PCI–PCI Bridge.
- 0680h. Other Bridge.

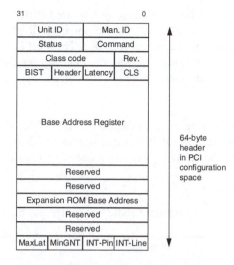

31   0

Unit ID	Man. ID
Status	Command
Class code	Rev.
BIST | Header | Latency	CLS

Base Address Register

Reserved

Reserved

Expansion ROM Base Address

Reserved

Reserved

| MaxLat \| MinGNT \| INT-Pin \| INT-Line |

64-byte header in PCI configuration space

Figure 10.7 PCI configuration space.

- BIST, Header, Latency, CLS. The BIST (Built-in Self Test) is an 8-bit field, where the most significant bit defines if the device can carry out a BIST, the next bit defines if a BIST is to be performed (a 1 in this position indicates that it should be performed) and bits 3–0 define the status code after the BIST has been performed (a value of zero indicates no error). The Header field defines the layout of the 48 bytes after the standard 16-byte header. The most significant bit of the Header field defines whether the device is a multi-function device or not. A 1 defines a multi-function unit. The CLS (Cache Line Size) field defines the size of the cache in units of 32 bytes. Latency indicates the length of time for a PCI bus operation, where the amount of time is the latency+8 PCI clock cycles.
- Base Address Register. This area of memory allows the device to be programmed with an I/O or memory address area. It can contain a number of 32- or 64-bit addresses. The format of a memory address is:

Bit 64–4 Base address.
Bit 3 PRF. Prefetching, 0 identifies not possible, 1 identifies possible.
Bit 2, 1 Type. 00 – any 32-bit address, 01 – less than 1MB, 10 – any 64-bit address and 11 – reserved.
Bit 0 0. Always set to a 0 for a memory address.

For an I/O address space it is defined as:

Bit 31–2 Base address.
Bit 1, 0 01. Always set to a 01 for an I/O address.

- Expansion ROM Base Address. Allows a ROM expansion to be placed at any position in the 32-bit memory address area.
- MaxLat, MinGNT, INT-Pin, INT-Line. The MinGNT and MaxLat registers are read-only registers that define the minimum and maximum latency values. The INT-Line

field is a 4-bit field that defines the interrupt line used (IRQ0–IRQ15). A value of 0 corresponds to IRQ0 and a value of 15 corresponds to IRQ15. The PCI bridge can then redirect this interrupt to the correct IRQ line. The 4-bit INT-pin defines the interrupt line that the device is using. A value of 0 defines no interrupt line, 1 defines $\overline{\text{INTA}}$, 2 defines $\overline{\text{INTB}}$, and so on.

10.3.8 I/O addressing

The standard PC I/O addressing ranges from 0000h to FFFFh, which gives an addressable space of 64 kB, whereas the PCI bus can support a 32-bit or 64-bit addressable memory. The PCI device can be configured using one of two mechanisms.

Configuration mechanism 1

Passing two 32-bit values to two standard addresses configures the PCI bus:

Address	Name	Description
0CF8h	Configuration Address	Used to access the configuration address area.
0CFCh	Configuration Data	Used to read or write a 32-bit (double word) value to the configuration memory of the PCI device.

The format of the Configuration Address register is:

Bit 31   ECD (Enable CONFIG_DATA) bit. A 1 activates the CONFIG_DATA register, while a 0 disables it.

Bit 30–24 Reserved.

Bit 23–16 PCI bus number. Defines the number of the number of the PCI bus (to a maximum of 256).

Bit 15–11 PCI unit. Selects a PCI device (to a maximum of 32). PCI thus supports a maximum of 256 attached buses with a maximum of 32 devices on each bus.

Bit 10–8   PCI function. Selects a function within a PCI multi-function device (one of eight functions).

Bit 7–2   Register. Selects a Dword entry in a specified configuration address area (one of 64 Dwords).

Bit 1, 0   Type. 00 – decode unit, 01 – CONFIG_ADDRESS value copy to AD*x*.

Configuration mechanism 2

In this mode, each PCI device is mapped to a 4 kB I/O address range between C000h and CFFFh. This is achieved by used in the activation register CSE (Configuration Space Enable) for the configuration area at the port address 0CF8h. The format of the CSE register is located at 0CF8h and is defined as:

Bit 7–4   Key. 0000 – normal mode, 0001…1111 – configuration area activated. A value other than zero for the key activates the configuration area mapping, that is, all I/O addresses to the 4 kB range between C000h and CFFFh would be performed as normal I/O cycles.

Bit 3–1   Function. Defines the function number within the PCI device (if it represents a multi-function device).

Bit 0   SCE. 0 defines a configuration cycle, 1 defines a special cycle.

The forward register is stored at address 0CFAh and contains:

Bit 7–0   PCI bus.

The I/O address is defined by:

Bit 31–12   Contains the bit value of 0000Ch.
Bit 11–8   PCI unit.
Bit 7–2   Register index.
Bit 1, 0   Contains the bit value of 00b.

10.4 Exercises

10.4.1   Explain how PCI architecture uses bridges.

10.4.2   Explain how the 32-bit PCI bus transfers data. Prove that the maximum data rate for a 32-bit PCI in its normal mode is only 66 MB/s. Explain the mechanism that the PCI bus uses to increase the maximum data rate to 132 MB/s.

10.4.3   How does buffering in the PCI bridge aid the transfer of data to and from the processor?

10.4.4   Explain how the PCI bus uses the command phase to set up a peripheral.

10.4.5   How are interrupt lines used in the PCI bus? Explain how these interrupts can be steered to the ISA bus interrupt lines.

10.4.6   Outline the concept of bus mastering and how it occurs on the PCI bus. What signal lines are used?

10.4.7   Explain how the PCI bus uses configuration addresses.

10.5 Example manufacturer and Plug-and-Play IDs

Manufacturer	Man. ID	PNP ID	Manufacturer	Man. ID	PnP ID
NCR	1000	4096	Toshiba	102f	4143
Motorola	1057	4183	Compaq	1032	4146
Mitsubishi	1067	4199	HP	103c	4156
EPSON	1008	4104	Intel	8086	32902
Yamaha	1073	4211	Adaptec	9004	36868
Cyrix	1078	4216	Matsushita	10f7	4343
Tseng Labs	100c	4108	Creative	10f6	4342

Motherboard Design

11.1 Introduction

This chapter analyzes a Pentium-based motherboard. An example board is the Intel 430HX motherboard that supports most Pentium processors and has the following component parts:

- PCIset components. 82438 System Controller (TXC) and 82371SB PCI ISA Xcelerator (PIIX3).
- 82091AA (AIP) for serial and parallel ports, and floppy disk controller.
- DRAM main memory. These are arranged either as SIMMs or DIMMs.
- L-2 cache SRAM. Support for up to 256 kB level-2 cache.
- Universal Serial Bus (USB).
- Interface slots (typically 4 PCI and 3 ISA).
- 1 Mbit flash RAM.

Figure 11.1 illustrates the main connections of the PCIset (which are the TXC and PIIX3 devices). The TXC allows for a host-to-PCI bridge, whereas the PIIX3 device supports:

- PCI-to-ISA bridge.
- Fast IDE.
- APIC (Advanced Programmable Interrupt Controller) support.
- USB host/hub controller. Connection to the Universal Serial Bus.
- Power management.

The 430HX board has 3 V and 5 V busses. PCI bus connections are 5 V and the Pentium bus is 3 V. An upgraded TX board includes the upgraded 82439 System Controller (MTXC) and the 82371AB PCI ISA Xcelerator (PIIX4).

11.2 Pentium processor

Figure 11.2 illustrates the main connections to the Pentium II processor (note that a # symbol after the signal name identifies an active low signal). It can be seen that it has:

- 64-bit data bus ($D0-D63$) which connects to the TXC ($HD0-HD63$).
- 32-bit address bus ($A0-A31$) which connects to the TXC ($HA0-HA31$).
- 8-byte address lines ($\overline{BE0}-\overline{BE7}$) to allow the processor to access from 1 to 8 bytes (64 bits) at a time, which connects to TXC ($\overline{HBE0}-\overline{HBE7}$).
- Read/write line ($W/\overline{R}$) which connects to TXC ($HW/\overline{R}$).
- Memory/IO ($HM/\overline{IO}$) which connects to TXC ($HM/\overline{IO}$).
- Data/control ($HD/\overline{C}$) which connects to TXC ($HD/\overline{C}$).

The host bus (the connections between the processor and the TXC) typically runs at 60/66 MHz and the PCI bus typically run at 30/33 MHz.

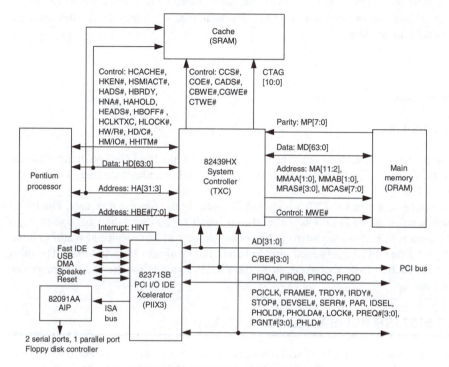

Figure 11.1   PCIset system architecture.

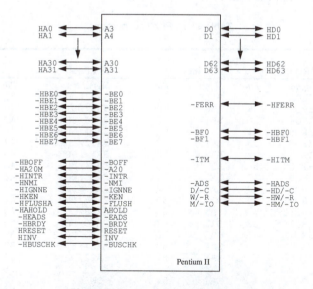

Figure 11.2   Pentium II connections.

It can be seen that the interface between the processor and the TXC device has an address bus from A3 to A31. These provide access to addresses in banks of 8 bytes. The byte enable lines ($\overline{HBE0} - \overline{HBE7}$) provide the lower address lines. Thus, 8 bits, 16 bits, 32 bits or 64 bits can be accessed at a time. For example, to address the 8 bytes from the following binary address:

0110 1110 0000 0110 0110 0110 0110 *XXXX*b

then the address:

6E00666*x*h

would be put on the address bus. Then to access the 16 bits from 6E06661h to 6E06662h then the $\overline{HBE1}$ and $\overline{HBE2}$ lines would be made active, all the other byte lines will be inactive.

It can be seen that the TXC device handles most of the processor signals. The PIIX3 device handles all the interrupts within the computer (IRQ0–IRQ15 and PCIRQA–PCIRQD) and connects directly to the interrupt line of the processor. This device also allows interrupts to be steered to unassigned interrupt and allow supports Plug-and-Play. The other direct connection from the processor to the PIIX3 device is for the math co-processor error interrupt.

11.3 82371SB PCI ISA Xcelerator (PIIX3)

The PIIX3 is a 208-pin QFP (Quad flat pack) IC which integrates much of the functionality of the ISA bus interface onto a single device. Table 11.1 outlines the main connections to the PIIX3 IC. The PIIX4 is a 324-pin device.

Table 11.1   PIIX3 connections.

PCI Address/ Data lines		IRQ lines		ISA lines		ISA lines	
Signal	*Pin*	*Signal*	*Pin*	*Signal*	*Pin*	*Signal*	*Pin*
AD0	206	IRQ1	4	BALE	64	SA8/DD0	55
AD1	205	IRQ3	58	AEN	20	SA9/DD1	50
AD2	204	IRQ4	56	LA17	86	SA10/DD2	49
AD3	203	IRQ5	34	LA18	84	SA11/DD3	48
AD4	202	IRQ6	33	LA19	82	SA12/DD4	47
AD5	201	IRQ7	32	LA20	80	SA13/DD5	46
AD6	200	-IRQ8	5	LA21	76	SA14/DD6	45
AD7	199	IRQ9	10	LA22	74	SA15/DD7	44
AD8	197	IRQ10	73	LA23	72	SA16/DD8	43
AD9	194	IRQ11	75	SA0	69	SA17/DD9	41
AD10	193	IRQ12/M	77	SA1	68	SA18/DD10	40
AD11	192	IRQ14	83	SA2	67	SA19/DD11	39
AD12	191	IRQ15	81	SA3	66	SA20/DD12	38
AD13	190			SA4	63	SA21/DD13	37
AD14	189			SA5	61	SA22/DD14	36
AD15	188			SA6	59	SA23/DD15	35
AD16	177			SA7	57	-OWS	15
AD17	176			DRQ0	87	-SMEMW	22
AD18	175			DRQ1	30	-SMEMR	19
AD19	174			DRQ2	12	-IOW	24
AD20	173			DRQ3	25	-IOR	23

AD21	172	DRQ5	91	-REFRESH	31
AD22	171	DRQ6	95	T/C	62
AD23	168	DRQ7	99	OSC	
AD24	166	-DACK0	85	-MEMCS16	70
AD25	165	-DACK1	29	-IOCS16	71
AD26	164	-DACK2	60	-MASTER	
AD27	163	-DACK3	21	IOCHK	6
AD28	162	-DACK5	89	IOCHRDY	18
AD29	161	-DACK6	93	-SBHE (DD12)	
AD30	160	-DACK7	97	-MEMR	88
AD31	159	RSTISA		-MEMW	90

USB

Signal	Pin	Signal	Pin	Signal	Pin
USBP1-	143	USBP1+	142	USBCLK	146
USBP0-	145	USBP0+	144		

PCI control lines

C/BE0#	198	FRAME#	179	PIRQA	149
C/BE1#	187	DEVSEL#	184	PIRQB	150
C/BE2#	178	IRDY#	180	PIRQC	151
C/BE3#	167	STOP#	185	PIRQD	152
		PHLDA#	110		
		SERR#	3		
		TRDY#	181		

PIIX3's functionality includes:

- Enhanced 7-channel DMA with two 8237 controllers. This is supported with the handshaking lines DRQ0–DRQ7 and $\overline{DRQ0}-\overline{DRQ7}$.
- ISA–PCI bridge.
- Fast IDE support for up to four disk drives (two masters and two slaves). It supports mode 4 timings which gives transfer rates of up to 22 MB/s.
- I/O APIC (Advanced Programmable Interrupt Controller) support.
- Implementation of PCI 2.1 which allows for PCI auto-configuration.
- Incorporates 82C54 timer for system timer, refresh request and speaker output tone.
- Non-maskable interrupts (NMI).
- PCI clock speed of 25/33 MHz. Motherboard configurable clock speed (normally 33 MHz).
- Plug-and-Play support with one steerable interrupt line and one programmable chip select. The motherboard interrupt MIRQ0 can be steered to any one of 11 interrupts (IRQ3–IRQ7, IRQ9–IRQ12, IRQ14 and IRQ15).
- Steerable PCI interrupts for PCI device Plug-and-Play. The PCI interrupt lines (PIRQA–PIRQD) can be steered to one of 11 interrupts (IRQ3–IRQ7, IRQ9–IRQ12, IRQ14 and IRQ15).
- Support for PS/2-type mouse and serial port mouse. IRQ12/M can be enabled for the PS/2-type mouse or disabled for a serial port mouse.
- Support for 5 ISA slots. Typical applications for ISA include 10 Mbps Ethernet adapter cards, serial/parallel port cards, sound cards, and so on.
- System Power Management. Allows the system to operate in a low-power state without being powered-down. This can be triggered either by a software, hardware or external event. It uses the programmable $\overline{SMI}$ (system management interrupt) line.
- Math Co-processor error function. The $\overline{FERR}$ line goes active (LOW) when a math co-processor error occurs. The PIIX3 device automatically generates an IRQ13 interrupt and sets the INTR line (HINT) to the processor. The PXII3 device then sets the

$\overline{\text{IGNNE}}$ active and INTR inactive when there is a write to address F0h.

- Two 82C59 controllers with 14 interrupts. The interrupt lines IRQ1, IRQ3–IRQ15 are available (IRQ0 is used by the system time and IRQ2 by the cascaded interrupt line). When an interrupt occurs the PIIX3 uses the HINT line to interrupt the processor.
- Universal Serial Bus with root hub and two USB ports. With the USB the host controller transfers data between the system memory and USB devices. This is achieved by processing data structures set up to by the Host Controller Driver (HCD) software and generating the transaction on USB.

The PCI bus address lines (AD0–AD22) connect to the TXC IC and the available interrupt lines at IRQ1, IRQ2–IRQ12, IRQ14 and IRQ15 (IRQ0 is generated by the system timer and IRQ2 is the cascaded interrupt line). The PS/2-type mouse uses the IRQ12/M line.

11.4 82438 System Controller (TXC)

The 324-pin TXC BGA (ball grid array) provides an interface between the processor, DRAM and the external busses (such as the PCI, ISA, and so on). Table 11.2 outlines its main pin connections. The TXC's functionality includes:

- Supports 50 MHz, 60 MHz and 66 MHz host system bus.
- Integrated DRAM controller. Supports four CAS lines and eight RAS lines. The memory supports symmetrical and asymmetrical addressing for 1 MB, 2 MB and 4 MB-deep SIMMs and symmetrical addressing for 16 MB-deep SIMMs.
- Integrated second-level cache controller. Supports up to 512 KB of second-level cache with synchronous pipelined burst SRAM.
- Dual processor support.
- Optional parity with 1 parity bit for every 8 bits stored in the DRAM.
- Optional error checking and correction on DRAM. The ECC mode is software configurable and allows for single-bit error correction and multi-bit error detection on single nibbles in DRAM.
- Swappable memory bank support. This allows memory banks to be swapped-out.
- PCI 2.1 compliant bus.
- Supports USB.

The TXC controls the processor cycles for:

- Second-level cache transfer. The processor directly sends data to the second-level cache and the TXC controls its operation.
- All other processor cycles. The TXC directs all other processor cycles to their destination (DRAM, PCI or internal TXC configuration space).

11.5 Error detection and correction

Parity or error correction can be configured by software (parity is the default). The ECC mode provides single-error correction, double-error detection and detection of all errors in a single nibble for the DRAM memory.

Table 11.2 TXC connections.

PCI Address/ Data bus		Processor Addresses bus		Processor Data bus			
Signal	*Pin*	*Signal*	*Pin*	*Signal*	*Pin*	*Signal*	*Pin*
AD0	15			HD0	305	HD32	179
AD1	14			HD1	307	HD33	178
AD2	33			HD2	306	HD34	149
AD3	13	HA3	275	HD3	308	HD35	180
AD4	52	HA4	315	HD4	285	HD36	136
AD5	32	HA5	252	HD5	286	HD37	135
AD6	12	HA6	316	HD6	265	HD38	138
AD7	51	HA7	312	HD7	212	HD39	125
AD8	11	HA8	272	HD8	245	HD40	126
AD9	50	HA9	271	HD9	287	HD41	115
AD10	30	HA10	311	HD10	267	HD42	137
AD11	10	HA11	291	HD11	288	HD43	117
AD12	49	HA12	251	HD12	225	HD44	128
AD13	29	HA13	310	HD13	268	HD45	114
AD14	9	HA14	270	HD14	247	HD46	127
AD15	48	HA15	290	HD15	266	HD47	102
AD16	47	HA16	250	HD16	248	HD48	101
AD17	27	HA17	309	HD17	247	HD49	116
AD18	7	HA18	289	HD18	246	HD50	104
AD19	46	HA19	269	HD19	214	HD51	103
AD20	26	HA20	249	HD20	228	HD52	81
AD21	6	HA21	273	HD21	213	HD53	84
AD22	45	HA22	254	HD22	226	HD54	82
AD23	25	HA23	253	HD23	201	HD55	61
AD24	66	HA24	294	HD24	215	HD56	83
AD25	44	HA25	293	HD25	203	HD57	63
AD26	24	HA26	274	HD26	202	HD58	62
AD27	4	HA27	313	HD27	191	HD59	41
AD28	23	HA28	314	HD28	204	HD60	42
AD29	3	HA29	255	HD29	193	HD61	43
AD30	22	HA30	295	HD30	192	HD62	21
AD31	2	HA31	292	HD31	194	HD63	1
PCI control lines							
C/BE0#	21	FRAME#	86	PREQ0#	67	PGNT0#	68
C/BE1#	31	DEVSEL#	89	PREQ1#	69	PGNT1#	70
C/BE2#	8	IRDY#	88	PREQ2#	71	PGNT2#	72
C/BE3#	5	STOP#	91	PREQ3#	73	PGNT3#	74
		LOCK#	85				
		PHOLD#	64				
		PHLDA#	65				
		PAR	92				
		SERR#	93				

Cache Memory Tag		DRAM Parity		DRAM Address lines		DRAM Data lines			
Signal	*Pin*	*Signal*	*Pin*	*Signal*	*Pin*	*Signal*	*Pin*	*Signal*	*Pin*
CTAG0	207	MP0	133			MD0	304	MD32	283
CTAG1	260	MP1	123			MD1	241	MD33	263
CTAG2	261	MP2	146	MA2	317	MD2	243	MD34	244
CTAG3	281	MP3	113	MA3	297	MD3	224	MD35	221
CTAG4	238	MP4	132	MA4	277	MD4	210	MD36	209
CTAG5	282	MP5	124	MA5	257	MD5	198	MD37	190
CTAG6	302	MP6	134	MA6	237	MD6	176	MD38	175
CTAG7	322	MP7	122	MA7	298	MD7	161	MD39	160
CTAG8	303			MA8	258	MD8	111	MD40	112
CTAG9	323			MA9	319	MD9	90	MD41	98
CTAG10	324			MA10	318	MD10	59	MD42	60
				MA11	278	MD11	58	MD43	20
				MAA0	276	MD12	38	MD44	77
				MAA1	236	MD13	36	MD45	56
				MAB0	296	MD14	35	MD46	75

MAB1	256	MD15	53	MD47	54
MWE#	235	MD16	262	MD48	284
		MD17	264	MD49	242
		MD18	222	MD50	223
		MD19	208	MD51	211
		MD20	200	MD52	199
		MD21	189	MD53	188
		MD22	174	MD54	162
		MD23	148	MD55	147
		MD24	99	MD56	100
		MD25	97	MD57	79
		MD26	78	MD58	40
		MD27	19	MD59	39
		MD28	57	MD60	18
		MD29	17	MD61	37
		MD30	76	MD62	16
		MD31	34	MD63	55

Cache address lines

MRASR0#	121	MCASR0#	145	MCASR4#	130
MRASR1#	110	MCASR1#	159	MCASR5#	144
MRASR2#	109	MCASR2#	131	MCASR6#	120
MRASR3#	96	MCASR3#	173	MCASR7#	172

Cache control lines

CBWE#	321	COE#	259	CCS#	300	CADS#	299
CGWE#	320	CADV#	279	TWE#	280	GWE#	320
BWE	321					

11.6 PCI interface

The TXC supports up to four PCI busmasters and provides the interface between PCI and main memory. It can operate the PCI interface at 25 MHz, 30 MHz or 33 MHz. When used as a PCI master the PIIX3 runs cycles on behalf of DMA, ISA masters or a busmaster IDE.

11.7 82091AA (AIP)

The AIP device integrates the serial ports, parallel ports and floppy disk interfaces. Figure 11.3 shows its connections and Figure 11.4 shows the interconnection between the AIP and the PIIX3 device. The osc frequency is set to 14.21818 MHz. It can be seen that the range of interrupts for the serial, parallel and floppy disk drive is IRQ3, IRQ4, IRQ5, IRQ6 and IRQ7. Normally the settings are:

- IRQ3.   Secondary serial port (COM2/COM4).
- IRQ4.   Primary serial port (COM1/COM3).
- IRQ6.   Floppy disk controller.
- IRQ7.   Parallel port (LPT1).

Figure 11.4 shows the main connections between the TXC, PIIX3 and the AIP. It can be seen that the AIP uses many of the ISA connections (such as $\overline{\text{ows}}$, IOCHRDY, and so on). The interface between the TXC and the PIIX3 defines the PCI bus and the interface between the PIIX3 and AIP defines some of the ISA signals. It can be seen that the AIP can support up to 8 DMA transfers (DRQ0–DRQ7).

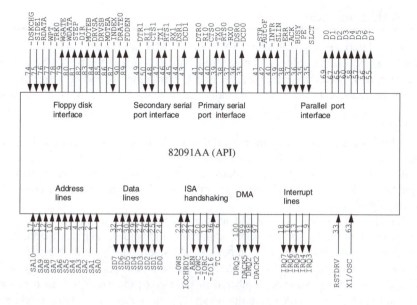

Figure 11.3   API IC.

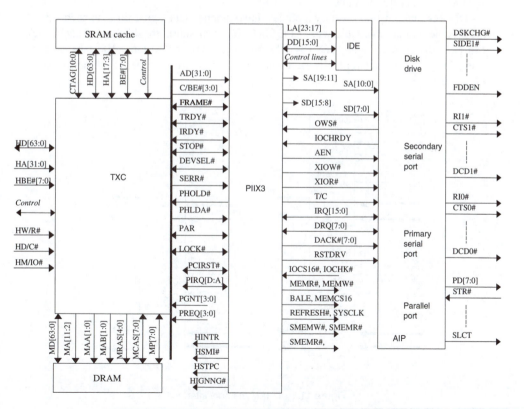

Figure 11.4   Connections between TXC, PIIX3 and AIP.

11.8 DRAM interface

The DRAM interface supports from 4 MB to 512 MB with eight row address lines ($\overline{\text{MRAS0}}$ – $\overline{\text{MRAS7}}$), eight column address lines ($\overline{\text{MCAS0}}$ – $\overline{\text{MCAS7}}$) and a 64-bit data path with 8 parity bits. It can use either a 3.3 V or 5 V power supply and both standard page mode and extended data out (EDO) memory are supported with a mixture of memory sizes for 1 MB, 2 MB and 4 MB-deep SIMMs and symmetrical addressing for 16 MB-deep SIMMs.

Each SIMM (single in-line memory module) has 12 input address lines and has a 32-bit data output. They are normally available with 72 pins (named tabs) on each side. These pins can read the same signal because they are shorted together on the board. For example tab 1 (pin 1) on side A is shorted to tab 1 on side B. Thus the 144 tabs only give 72 useable signal connections.

Figure 11.5 shows how the DRAM memory is organized. It shows banks 1 and 2 (and does not show banks 3 and 4). Each bank has two modules, such that modules 0 and 1 are in bank 1, modules 2 and 3 are in bank 2, and so on. The bank is selected with the $\overline{\text{MRAS}}$ lines; for example, bank 1 is selected with $\overline{\text{MRAS0}}$ and $\overline{\text{MRAS1}}$, bank 1 by $\overline{\text{MRAS2}}$ and $\overline{\text{MRAS3}}$, and so on. An even-numbered module gives the lower 32 bits (MD0–MD31) and the odd-numbered modules give the upper 32 bits (MD32–MD63). Each module also provides 4 parity bits (MP0–MP3 and MP4–MP7). Note that the MAA0 and MAA1, and MAB0 and MAB1 signals are the same.

DIMMs (dual in-line memory modules) have independent signal lines on each side of the module and are available with 72 (36 tabs on each side), 88 (44 tabs on each side), 144 (72 tabs on each side), 168 (84 tabs on each side) or 200 tabs (100 tabs on each side). They give greater reliability and density and are used in modern high performance PC servers.

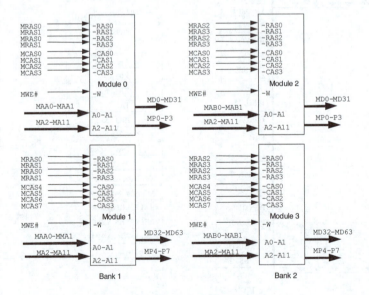

Figure 11.5   DRAM memory interface.

11.9 Clock rates

The system board runs at several clock frequencies. These are:

- Processor speed, such as 66 MHz.
- PCI bus speed.
- 24 or 48 MHz. USB.
- 12 MHz. Keyboard.

- 24 MHz. Floppy clock.
- 14 MHz. ISA bus OSC.
- 8 MHz. ISA bus clock.

The ICS9159-02S IC provides for each of these clock speeds. The input to the device is a 14.31818 MHz crystal clock, as illustrated in Figure 11.6. Two jumpers (Jumper 1 and Jumper 2) set the system speed. These set the system clock speed to either 50 MHz, 60 MHz or 66 MHz.

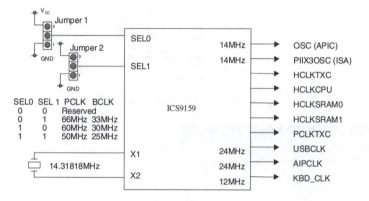

Figure 11.6   Clock generator device.

11.10 ISA/IDE interface

The IDE and ISA busses share several data, address and control lines. Figure 11.7 shows the connections to the busses. A multiplexor (MUX) is used to select either the ISA or IDE interface lines. The IDE interface uses the DD[12:0] and LA[23:17] lines, and the ISA uses these lines as $\overline{SBHE}$, SA[19:8], CS1S, CS3S, CS1P, CS3P and DA[2:0].

The IDE adapter is a 40-pin header connector. It is thus very easy to insert in the wrong way or to the wrong pins. For this reason all the input and output pins are short-circuit protected. The data lines connect to the IDE through 22 Ω resistors and are pulled-up with 4.7 kΩ resistors, and the address lines connect to the IDE through 33 Ω resistors.

11.11 DMA interface

The PIIX3 device incorporates the functionality of two 8237 DMA controllers to give seven independently programmable channels (Channels 0–3 and Channels 5–7). DMA channel 4 is used to cascade the two controllers and defaults to cascade mode in the DMA channel mode (DCM) register. Figure 11.8 shows the interface connections and that DMA channel 4 is used for the cascaded controller.

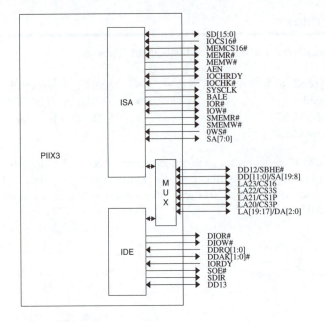

Figure 11.7 IDE/ISA interface with PIIX3.

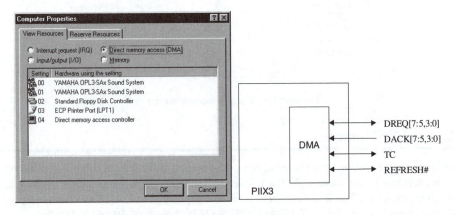

Figure 11.8 DMA interface.

11.12 Interval timer

The PIIX3 contains three 8251-compatible counters which are contained in one PIIX3 timer unit, referred to as Timer-1. The 14.21818 MHz counters normally use OSC as a clock source. Each counter provides an essential system function, such as:

- Counter 0, which connects to the IRQ0 line and provides a system timer interrupt for a time-of-day, diskette time-out, and so on.
- Counter 1, which generates a refresh request signal.
- Counter 2, which generates the speaker tone.

11.13 Interrupt controller

The PXII3 incorporates two 8259-compatible interrupt controllers and provides an ISA-compatible interrupt controller. These are cascaded to give 13 external and 3 internal interrupts. The primary interrupt controller connects to IRQ0–IRQ7 and the secondary connects to IRQ8–IRQ15. The three internal interrupts are:

- IRQ0. Used by the system timer and is connected to Timer 1, Counter 0.
- IRQ2. Used by the primary and secondary controller (see Figure 8.7 in Section 8.5.2).
- IRQ13. Used by the math co-processor, which is connected to the $\overline{FERR}$ pin on the processor.

The interrupt unit also supports interrupt steering. PIIX3 also supports interrupt steering where the four PCI active low interrupts ($\overline{PIRQA}$ – $\overline{PIRQD}$) can be internally routed to one of 11 interrupts (IRQ15, IRQ14, IRQ12–IRQ9, IRQ7–IRQ3).

11.14 Mouse function

The mouse normally either connects to one of the serial ports (COM1: or COM2:) or a PS/2-type connector. If they connect to the PS/2-type connector then IRQ12 is used (see Figure 11.9), else a serial port connected mouse uses the serial interrupts (such as IRQ4 for COM1 and IRQ3 for COM2). Thus, a system with a serial connected mouse must have the IRQ12/M interrupt disabled. This is typically done with a motherboard jumper (to enable or disable the mouse interrupt) or by BIOS steering.

11.15 Power management

PIIX3 has extensive power management capabilities and permits the system to operate in a low-power state without being powered-down. In a typical desktop PC, there are two states – Power On and Power Off. Leaving a system powered on, when not in use, wastes power. PIIX3 provides a fast on/off feature that creates a third state called Fast Off. When in the Fast Off state, the system consumes less power than the Power-On state.
The PIIX3's power management function is based on two modes:

- System Management Mode (SMM). Software (called SMM code) controls the transitions between the Power On state and the Fast Off state. PIIX3 invokes this software by generating an SMI to the CPU (asserting the $\overline{SMI}$ signal).
- Advanced Power Management (APM).

11.16 Universal serial bus

PIIX3 contains a USB. The host controller includes the root hub and two USB ports. This allows up to two USB peripheral devices to be directly connected to the PIIX3 without an external hub. If more devices are required, an external bus can be connected to either of the built-in ports. The USB's PCI configuration registers are located in function 2, PCI configuration space.

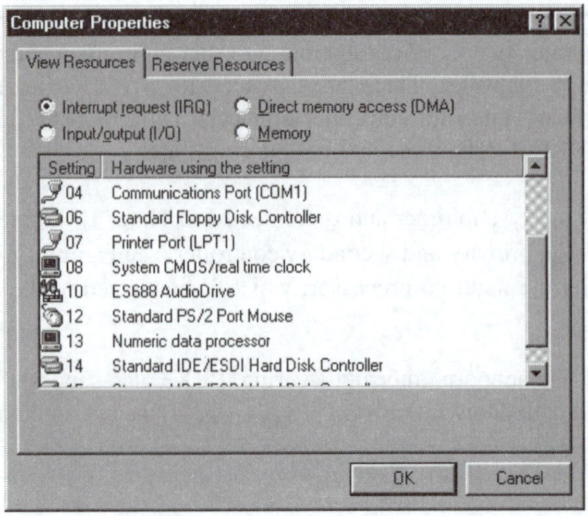

Figure 11.9   Interrupts usage showing PS/2 port mouse.

The PIIX3 host controller completely supports the standard Universal Host Controller Interface (UHCI) and thus, takes advantage of the standard software drivers written to be compatible with UHCI. Its advantages are:

- Automatic mapping of function to driver and configuration.
- Supports synchronous and asynchronous transfer types.
- Self-identifying peripherals that can be hot-plugged.
- Supports up to 127 devices.
- Supports error-handling and fault-recovery.
- Guaranteed bit rate with low delay times.

11.17 Mouse and keyboard interface

The mouse and keyboard interface uses the 8242 device, as illustrated in Figure 11.10. It can be seen that the two interrupts which are available are IRQ1 (the keyboard interrupt) and IRQ12 (PS/2 style mouse). If the mouse connects to the serial port then the IRQ12 line does not cause an interrupt. All clock frequencies are derived from the keyboard clock frequency (see Figure 11.6).

11.18 Example ATX motherboard

Figure 11.11 shows an example ATX motherboard. It supports the Pentium II though a Slot 1 SEC socket and is based on Intel 440LX chipset. It is similar to the HX motherboard (which has a Socket 7 processor connector) but has the following:

- DIMM connection for up to 384 MB for memory. Support for synchronous 100 MHz DRAM (SDRAM) for a 64/72-bit data path with autodetection for any combination of 4/16/64 MB DRAM modules.

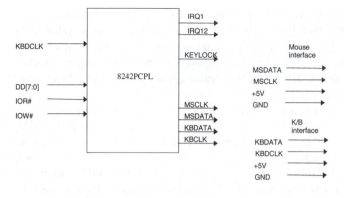

Figure 11.10 Mouse and keyboard interface.

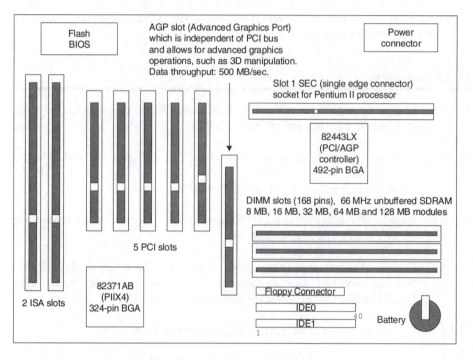

Figure 11.11 Typical LX motherboard.

- Support for Slot 1 SEC to inserting the processor into the motherboard. This allows for easy upgrade of the processor. Normally the processor is inserted into the motherboard so that the fan is near to its location. This overcomes the problem of mounting a fan on top of the Socket 7 based processor. The Pentium II also has an integrated heat sink and integrated Level-2 cache which is on the substrate for the SEC cartridge.
- Intel 82443LX PCI/AGP controller (PAC). This supports the PCI bus and the Advanced Graphics Port (AGP). The AGP transfers at 133 MHz and can achieve a maximum data rate of 500 MB/s. It is enhanced for graphics transfers and gives pipe-

lined-memory read and write operations that hides any memory access delays.

- 82371AB PCI/ISA IDE Xcellerator (PIIX4). Support for PCI bridge, USB controller, IDE controller, DMA controller, Interrupt controller, Power management and real-time clocks. The IDE interface supports Mode 3 and Mode 4 transfers at up to 16 MB/s and also Ultra DMA/33 which gives synchronous DMA transfers at up to 33 MB/s. It also supports ATAPI devices (such as CD-ROMs).

- National Semiconductor PC97307 Super I/O Controller. Supports two serial ports, a multimode parallel port (standard mode, EPP and ECP), floppy disk controller (DP8473 and N82077 compatible), keyboard controller, mouse controller and Infra-red communications controller. The serial ports contain two 16450/166550A-compatible UARTs which have an integrated 16-byte FIFO buffer for storing in-coming and outgoing characters. The floppy disk controller also has a 16-byte FIFO buffer.

- Support for LS-120 MB floppy disk drives and Desktop Management Interface (DMI). DMI is a management system for networked PC, where a system manager can control the settings remotely.

11.19 Exercises

11.19.1   Outline the importance of the TXC (system controller) device in the PC. Outline also the main ICs that are used in a PC.

11.19.2   Describe, in detail, the architecture of the HX PCI chip-set, and how the Pentium processor communicates with: DRAM memory, Level-2 SRAM cache, the PCI bus, the ISA bus and the IDE bus.

11.19.3   Explain, with reference to the PIIX3 and Pentium processor, how interrupts on the PCI and ISA busses are dealt with.

11.19.4   Explain, with reference to the Level-1 cache, the Level-2 cache and DRAM, how the processor accesses memory. What advantage does Level-1 over Level-2 cache, and the advantage that these have over DRAM.

11.19.5   Discuss the power management modes supported by the PXII3.

11.19.6   Which interrupts are supported with the AIP and where are they typically used?

11.19.7   Explain how the ISA and IDE busses share the same control and data lines.

11.19.8   Contrast the HX motherboard with the LX motherboard.

11.19.9   What are the advantages of using a SEC connected processor rather than a Socket 7 connected processor?

11.19.10 If possible, open up a PC and identify the ICs on the motherboard.

12 IDE and Mass Storage

12.1 Introduction

This chapter and the next chapter discuss IDE and SCSI interfaces which are used to interface to disk drives and mass storage devices. Disks are used to store data reliably in the long term. Typical disk drives either store binary information as magnetic fields on a fixed disk (as in a hard disk drive), a plastic disk (as in a floppy disk or tape drive), or as optical representation (on optical disks).

The main sources of permanent read/writeable storage are:

- Magnetic tape – where the digital bits are stored with varying magnetic fields. Typical devices are tape cartridges, DAT and 8 mm video tape.
- Magnetic disk – as with the magnetic tape the bits are stored as varying magnetic fields on a magnetic disk. This disk can be either permanent (such as a Winchester hard disk) or flexible (such as a floppy disk). Large capacity hard disks allow storage of several GBs of data. Normally fixed disks are designed to a much higher specification than floppy disks and can thus store much more information.
- Optical disk – where the digital bits are stored as pits on an optical disk. A laser then reads these bits. This information can either be read-only (CD-ROM), write-once read many (WORM) or can be reprogrammable. A standard CD-ROM stores up to 650 MB of data. Their main disadvantage in the past has been their relative slowness as compared with Winchester hard disks; this is now much less of a problem as speeds have steadily increased over the years.

12.2 Tracks and sectors

A disk must be formatted before it is used, which allows data to be stored in a logical manner. The format of the disk is defined by a series of tracks and sectors on either one or two sides. A track is a concentric circle around the disk where the outermost track is track 0. The next track is track 1 and so on, as shown in Figure 12.1. Each of these tracks is divided into a number of sectors. The first sector is named sector 1, the second is sector 2, and so on. Most disks also have two sides: the first side of the disk is called side 0 and the other is side 1.

Figure 12.1 also shows how each track is split into a number of sectors, in this case there are eight sectors per track. Typically, each sector stores 512 bytes. The total disk space, in bytes, will thus be given by:

$$\text{Disk space} = \text{No. of sides} \times \text{tracks} \times \text{sectors per track} \times \text{bytes per sector}$$

For example, a typical floppy disk has two sides, 80 tracks per side, 18 sectors per track and 512 bytes per sector, so:

$$
\begin{aligned}
\text{Disk capacity} \quad &= 2 \times 80 \times 18 \times 512 &&= 1\,474\,560\,\text{B} \\
&= 1\,474\,560 / 1\,024\,\text{kB} = 1\,440\,\text{kB} \\
&= 1440 / 1024\,\text{MB} &&= 1.4\,\text{MB}
\end{aligned}
$$

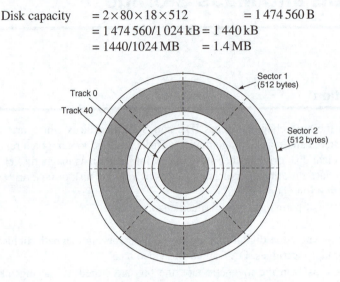

Figure 12.1   Tracks and sectors on a disk.

12.3 Floppy disks

A 3½-inch DD (double density) disk can be formatted with 2 sides, 9 sectors per track and 40 tracks per side. This gives a total capacity of 720 kB. A 3½-inch HD (high density) disk has a maximum capacity when formatted with 80 tracks per side.

A 5¼-inch DD disk can be formatted with two sides, nine sectors per disk with either 40 or 80 tracks per side. The maximum capacity of these formats is 360 kB (40 tracks) or 720 kB (80 tracks). A 5¼-inch HD disk can be formatted with 15 sectors per track which gives a total capacity of 1.2 MB. When reading data the disks rotate at 300 rpm. Table 12.1 outlines the differing formats.

Table 12.1   Capacity of different disk types.

Size	Tracks per side	Sectors per track	Capacity
5¼ "	40	9	360 kB
5¼ "	80	15	1.2 MB
3½ "	40	9	720 kB
3½ "	80	18	1.44 MB

12.4 Fixed disks

Fixed disks store large amounts of data and vary in their capacity, from several MB to several GB. A fixed disk (or hard disk) consists of one or more platters which spin at around 3 000 rpm (10 times faster than a floppy disk). A hard disk with four platters is shown in Figure 12.2. Data is read from the disk by a flying head, which sits just above the surface of the platter. This head does not actually touch the surface as the disk is spinning so fast. The distance between the platter and the head is only about 10 μin (which is no larger than the thickness of a human hair or a smoke particle). It must thus be protected from any outer particles by sealing it in an airtight container. A floppy disk is prone to wear as the head touches the disk as it reads but a fixed disk has no wear as its heads never touch the disk.

One problem with a fixed disk is head crashes, typically caused when the power is abruptly interrupted or if the disk drive is jolted. This can cause the head to crash into the disk surface. In most modern disk drives the head is automatically parked when the power is taken away. Older disk drives that do not have automatic head parking require a program to park the heads before the drive is powered down.

There are two sides to each platter and, like floppy disks, each side divides into a number of tracks which are subdivided into sectors. A number of tracks on fixed disks are usually named cylinders. For example, a 40 MB hard disk has two platters with 306 cylinders, four tracks per cylinder, 17 sectors per track and 512 bytes per sector, thus each side of a platter stores:

$$
\begin{aligned}
306 \times 4 \times 17 \times 512\,\text{B} &= 10\,653\,696\,\text{B} \\
&= 10\,653\,696/\,1\,048\,576\,\text{MB} \\
&= 10.2\,\text{MB}
\end{aligned}
$$

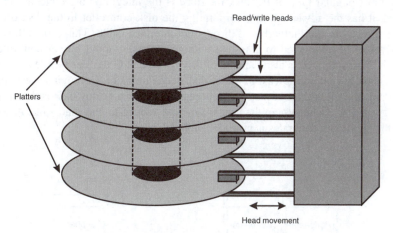

Figure 12.2   Hard disk with four platters.

12.5 Drive specifications

Access time is the time taken for a disk to locate data. Typical access times for modern disk drives range from 10 to 30 ms. The average access time is the time for the head to travel half way across the platters. Once the head has located the correct sector then there may be another wait until it locates the start of the data within the sector. If it is positioned at a point after the start of the data, it requires another rotation of the disk to locate the data. This average wait, or latency time, is usually taken as half of a revolution of the disk. If the disk spins at 3600 rpm then the latency is 8.33 ms.

The main parameters that affect the drive specification are the data transfer rate and the average access time. The transfer rate is dependent upon the interface for the controller/disk drive and system/controller and the access time is dependent upon the disk design.

12.6 Hard disk/CD-ROM interfaces

There are two main interfaces involved with hard disks (and CD-ROMs). One connects the disk controller to the system (system/controller interface) and the other connects the disk controller to the disk drive (disk/controller interface).

The controller can be interfaced by standards such as ISA, EISA, MCA, VL-local bus or PCI bus. For the interface between the disk drive and the controller then standards such as ST-506, ESDI, SCSI or IDE can be used. Seagate Technologies developed ST-506 and is used in many older machines with hard disks of a capacity less than 40 MB. The enhanced small disk interface (ESDI) is capable of transferring data between itself and the processor at rates approaching 10 MB/s.

The small computer system interface (SCSI) allows up to seven different disk drives or other interfaces to be connected to the system through the same interface controller. SCSI is a common interface for large capacity disk drives and is illustrated in Figure 12.3.

The most popular type of PC disk interface is the integrated drive electronics (IDE) standard. It has the advantage of incorporating the disk controller in the disk drive, and attaches directly to the motherboard through an interface cable. This cable allows many disk drives to be connected to a system without worrying about bus or controller conflicts. The IDE interface is also capable of driving other I/O devices besides a hard disk. It also normally contains at least 32 kB of disk cache memory. Common access times for an IDE are often less than 16 ms, where access times for a floppy disk is about 200 ms. With a good disk cache system the access time can reduce to less than 1 ms. A comparison of the maximum data rates is given in Table 12.2.

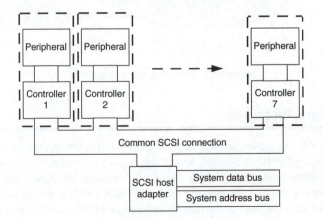

Figure 12.3   SCSI interface.

Table 12.2 Capacity of different disk types.

Interface	Maximum data rate
ST-506	0.6 MB/s
ESDI	1.25 MB/s
DIE	8.3 MB/s
E-DIE	16.6 MB/s
SCSI	4 MB/s
SCSI-II	10 MB/s

A typical modern PC contains two IDE connections on the motherboard, named IDE0 and IDE1. The IDE0 connection connects to the master drive (C:) and IDE1 to the slave drive (D:). These could connect either to two hard disks or, possibly, to one hard disk and a CD-ROM drive (or even a tape backup system). Unfortunately, the IDE standard only allows disk access up to 528 MB. A new standard called Enhanced-IDE (E-IDE) allows for disk capacities of over this limit. The connector used is the same as IDE but the computers' BIOS must be able to recognize the new standard. Most computers manufactured since 1993 are able to fully access E-IDE disk drives.

The specification for the IDE and E-IDE are:

- IDE.
  - Maximum of two devices (hard disks).
  - Maximum capacity for each disk of 528 MB.
  - Maximum cable length of 18 inches.
  - Data transfer rates of 3.3, 5.2 and 8.3 MB/s.
- E-IDE.
  - Maximum of four devices (hard disks, CD-ROM and tape).
  - Uses two ports (for master and slave).
  - Maximum capacity for each disk is 8.4 GB.
  - Maximum cable length of 18 inches.
  - Data transfer rates of 3.3, 5.2, 8.3, 11.1 and 16.6 MB/s.

12.7 IDE interface

The most popular interface for hard disk drives is the Integrated Drive Electronics (IDE) interface. Its main advantage is that the hard disk controller is built into the disk drive and the interface to the motherboard simply consists of a stripped-down version of the ISA bus. The most common standard is the ANSI-defined ATA-IDE standard. It uses a 40-way ribbon cable to connect to 40-pin header connectors. Table 12.3 lists the pin connections. It has a 16-bit data bus (D0–D15) and the only available interrupt line used is IRQ14 (the hard disk uses IRQ14).

The standard allows for the connection of two disk drives in a daisy chain configuration. This can cause problems because both drives have controllers within their drives. The primary drive (Drive 0) is assigned as the master and the secondary driver (Drive 1) as the slave. Setting jumpers on the disk drive sets a drive as a master or a slave. They can also be set by software using the Cable Select (CSEL) pin on the interface.

E-IDE has various modes (ANSI modes) of operation, these are:

- Mode 0. 600 ns read/write cycle time. 3.3 MB/s burst data transfer rate.
- Mode 1. 383 ns read/write cycle time. 5.2 MB/s burst data transfer rate.
- Mode 2. 240 ns read/write cycle time. 8.3 MB/s burst data transfer rate.
- Mode 3. 180 ns read/write cycle time. 11.1 MB/s burst data transfer rate.
- Mode 4. 120 ns read/write cycle time. 16.6 MB/s burst data transfer rate.

Table 12.3   IDE connections.

Pin	IDE signal	AT signal	Pin	IDE signal	AT signal
1	RESET	RESET DRV	2	GND	–
3	D7	SD7	4	D8	SD8
5	D6	SD6	6	D9	SD9
7	D5	SD5	8	D10	SD10
9	D4	SD4	10	D11	SD11
11	D3	SD3	12	D12	SD12
13	D2	SD2	14	D13	SD13
15	D1	SD1	16	D14	SD14
17	D0	SD0	18	D15	SD15
19	GND	–	20	KEY	–
21	DRQ3	DRQ3	22	GND	–
23	$\overline{\text{IOW}}$	$\overline{\text{IOW}}$	24	GND	–
25	$\overline{\text{IOR}}$	$\overline{\text{IOR}}$	26	GND	–
27	IOCHRDY	IOCHRDY	28	CSEL	–
29	$\overline{\text{DACK3}}$	$\overline{\text{DACK3}}$	30	GND	–
31	IRQ14	IRQ14	32	$\overline{\text{IOCS16}}$	$\overline{\text{IOCS16}}$
33	Address bit 1	SA1	34	$\overline{\text{PDIAG}}$	–
35	Address bit 0	SA0	36	Address bit 2	SA2
37	$\overline{\text{CS1FX}}$	–	38	$\overline{\text{CS3FX}}$	–
39	SP / $\overline{\text{DA}}$	–	40	GND	–

12.8 IDE communication

The IDE (or AT bus) is the *de facto* standard for most hard disks in PCs. It has the advantage over older type interfaces that the controller is integrated into the disk drive. Thus the computer only has to pass high-level commands to the unit and the actual control can be achieved with the integrated controller. Several companies developed a standard command set for an ATA (AT attachment). Commands included:

- Read sector buffer. Reads contents of the controller's sector buffer.
- Write sector buffer. Writes data to the controller's sector buffer.
- Check for active.
- Read multiple sectors.
- Write multiple sectors.
- Lock drive door.

The control of the disk is achieved by passing a number of high-level commands through a number of I/O port registers. Table 12.3 outlines the pin connections for the IDE connector. Typically pin 20 is missing on the connector cable so that it cannot be inserted in the wrong way, although most systems buffer the signals so that the bus will not be damaged if the cable is inserted in the wrong way. The five control signals, which are unique to the IDE interface (and not the AT bus), are:

- $\overline{CS3FX}$, $\overline{CS1FX}$. These are used to identify either the master or the slave.
- $\overline{PDIAG}$ (Passed diagnostic). Used by the slave drive to indicate that it has passed its diagnostic test.
- SP/$\overline{DA}$ (Slave present/drive active). Used by the slave drive to indicate that it is present and active.

The other signals are:

- IOCHRDY. This signal is optional and is used by the drive to tell the processor that it requires extra clock cycles for the current I/O transfer. A high level informs the processor that it is ready, while a low informs it that it need more time.
- DRQ3, $\overline{DACK3}$. These are used for DMA transfers.

12.8.1 AT task file

The processor communicates with the IDE controller through data and control registers (typically known as the AT task file). The base registers used are between 1F0h and 1F7h for the primary disk (170h and 177h for secondary), and 3F6h (376h for secondary), as shown in Figure 12.4. Their function is:

Port	Function	Bits	Direction
1F0h	Data register	16	R/W
1F1h	Error register	8	R
	Precompensation	8	W
1F2h	Sector count	8	R/W
1F3h	Sector number	8	R/W
1F4h	Cylinder LSB	8	R/W
1F5h	Cylinder MSB	8	R/W
1F6h	Drive/head	8	R/W
1F7h	Status register	8	R
	Command register	8	W
3F6h	Alternative status reg.	8	R
	Digital output reg.	8	W
3F7h	Drive address	8	R

Data register (1F0h)

The data register is a 16-bit register that is used to read/write data from/to the disk.

Error register (1F1h)

The error register is read-only and contains error information relating to the last command. Its definitions are:

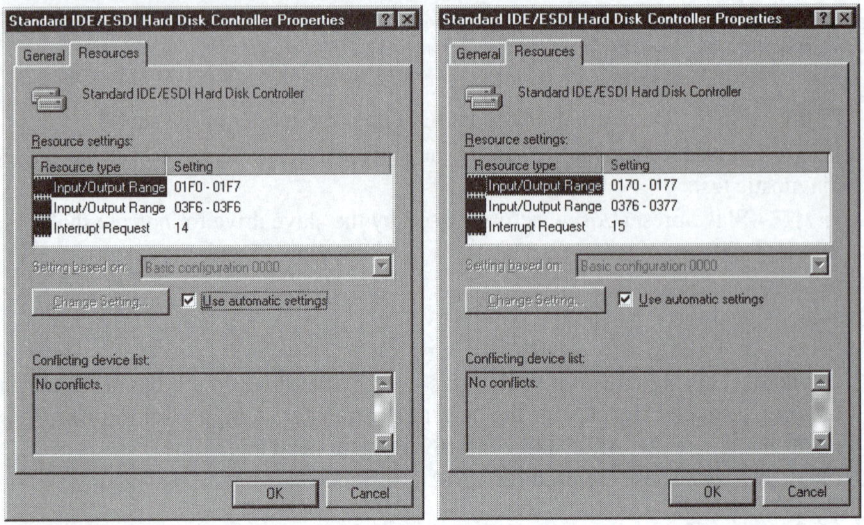

Figure 12.4   Typical hard-disk controller settings for the primary and secondary drive.

b_7	b_6	b_5	b_4	b_3	b_2	b_1	b_0
BBK	UNC	MCNID	MCR	ABT	NT0		NDM

where:

- BBK.   Set to 1 if the sector is bad.
- UNC.   Set to 1 if there is an unrecoverable error.
- NID.   Set to 1 if mark not found.
- ABT.   Set to 1 if command aborted.
- NT0.   Set to 1 if track 0 not found.
- MC.   Set to 1 identifies that the medium has changed (E-IDE only). The E-IDE standard support disks which can be changed while the system is running (such as CD-ROMs, tape drives, and so on).
- MCR.   Set to 1 identifies that the medium requires to be changed (E-IDE only).

Sector count register (1F2h)

This is a read/write 8-bit register that defines the number of sectors to be read, written or verified. Each transfer to/from the disk causes the register value to be decremented by one.

Sector number register (1F3h)

This is a read/write 8-bit register that defines the start sector to be read, written or verified. After each transfer to/from the disk, the register contains the last processed sector.

Cylinder register (1F4h/1F5h)

These are read/write 8-bit registers which define the LSB (1F4h) and MSB (1F5h) of the cylinder number. The two registers are capable of containing a 16-bit value. In standard IDE the cylinder number is 10-bit and can only vary from 0 to 1023 (0 to $2^{10}-1$). For E-IDE the value can be a 16-bit value and can thus vary from 0 to 65 535 (0 to $2^{16}-1$). This is one of the main reasons that E-IDE can address much more data than IDE. For example:

Drive/head register (1F6h)

This is a read/write 8-bit register that defines the currently used head. Its definitions are:

b_7	b_6	b_5	b_4	b_3	b_2	b_1	b_0
1	L	1	DRV	HD_3	HD_2	HD_1	HD_0

where:

- L. Set to a 1 if LBA (logical block addressing) mode else set to a 0 if CHS (E-IDE only).
- DRV. Set to 1 for the slave, else it is master.
- HD_3–HD_0. Identifies head number, where 0000 identifies head 0, 0001 identifies head 1, and so on.

Status register (1F7h)

The 1F7h register has two modes. If it is written-to then it is a command register (see next section), else if it is read-from then it is a status register. The status register is a read-only 8-bit register that contains status information from the previously issued command. Its definitions are:

b_7	b_6	b_5	b_4	b_3	b_2	b_1	b_0
BUSY	RDY	WFT	SKT	DRQ	COR	IDX	ERR

where:

- BUSY. Set to 1 if the drive is busy.
- RDY. Set to 1 if the drive is ready.
- WFT. Set to 1 if there is a write fault.
- SKT. Set to 1 if head seek positioning is complete.
- DRQ. Set to 1 if data can be transferred.
- COR. Set to 1 if there is a correctable data error.
- IDX. Set to 1 identifies that the disk index has just passed.
- ERR. Set to 1 identifies that the error register contains error information.

Command register (1F7h)

If the 1F7h register is written-to then it is a command register. The command register is an 8-bit register that can contain commands, such as:

Command	b_7	b_6	b_5	b_4	b_3	b_2	b_1	b_0	Related registers
Calibrate drive	0	0	0	1	–	–	–	–	1F6h
Read sector	0	0	1	0	–	–	L	R	1F2h–1F6h
Write sector	0	0	1	1	–	–	L	R	1F2h–1F6h
Verify sector	0	1	0	0	–	–	–	R	1F2h–1F6h
Format track	0	1	0	1	–	–	–	–	1F3h–1F6h
Seek	0	1	1	1	–	–	–	–	1F4h–1F6h
Diagnostics	1	0	0	1	–	–	–	–	1F2h,1F6h
Read sector buffer	1	1	1	0	0	1	0	0	1F6h
Write sector buffer	1	1	1	0	1	0	0	0	1F6h
Identify drive	1	1	1	0	1	1	–	–	1F6h

where R is the set to a 0 if the command is automatically retried and L identifies the long-bit.

Digital output register (3F6h)

This is a write-only 8-bit register that allows drives to be reset and also IRQ14 to be masked. Its definitions are:

b_7	b_6	b_5	b_4	b_3	b_2	b_1	b_0
–	–	–	–	–	SRST	$\overline{\text{IEN}}$	–

where:

- SRST. Set to a 1 to reset all connected drives, else accept the command.
- $\overline{\text{IEN}}$. Controls the interrupt enable. If set to 1 then IRQ14 is always masked, else interrupt after each command.

Drive address register (3F7h)

The drive address register is a read-only register that contains information on the active drive and drive head. Its definitions are:

b_7	b_6	b_5	b_4	b_3	b_2	b_1	b_0
–	$\overline{\text{WTGT}}$	$\overline{\text{HS3}}$	$\overline{\text{HS2}}$	$\overline{\text{HS1}}$	$\overline{\text{HS0}}$	$\overline{\text{DS1}}$	$\overline{\text{DS0}}$

where:

- $\overline{\text{WTGT}}$. Set to a 1 if the write gate is closed, else the write gate is open.
- $\overline{\text{HS3}} - \overline{\text{HS0}}$. 1s complement value of currently active head.
- $\overline{\text{DS1}} - \overline{\text{DS0}}$. Identifies the selected drive.

12.8.2 Command phase

The IRQ14 line is used by the disk when it wants to interrupt the processor, either when it wants to read or write data to/from memory. For example, using Microsoft C++ (for Borland replace _outp() and _inp() with outport() and inportb()) to write to a disk at cylinder 150, head 0 and sector 7:

```c
#include <conio.h>

int main(void)
{
int         sectors=4, sector_no=7, cylinder=150, drive=0, command=0x33, i;
unsigned    int buff[1024], *buff_pointer;

    do
    {
        /* wait until BSY signal is set to a 1 */

    } while (( _inp(0x1f7) & 0x80) != 0x80);

    _outp(0x1f2,sectors);       /* set number of sectors        */
    _outp(0x1f3,sector_no);     /* set sector number            */
    _outp(0x1f4,cylinder & 0x0ff);  /* set cylinder number LSB  */
    _outp(0x1f5,cylinder & 0xf00);  /* set cylinder number MSB  */
    _outp(0x1f6,drive);         /* set DRV=0 and head=0         */
    _outp(0x1f7,command);           /* 0011 0011 (write sector)     */

    do
    {
        /* wait until BSY signal is set to a 1 and DRQ is set to a 1 */

    } while ( ((_inp(0x1f7) & 0x80) != 0x80) && ((_inp(0x1f7) & 0x08)
            !=0x08) );
    buff_pointer= buff;

    for (i=0;i<512;i++,buff_pointer++)
    {
        _outp(0x1f0,*buff_pointer); /* output 16-bits at a time */
    }
    return(0);
}
```

Note that if the L bit is set then an extra 4 ECC (error correcting code) bytes must be written to the sector (thus a total of 516 bytes are written to each sector). The code used is cyclic redundancy check which, while it cannot correct errors, is very powerful at detecting them.

12.8.3 E-IDE

The main differences between IDE and E-IDE are:

- E-IDE supports removable media.
- E-IDE supports a 16-bit cylinder value, which gives a maximum of 65 636 cylinders.
- Higher transfer rates. In mode 4, E-IDE has a 120 ns read/write cycle time, which gives a 16.6 MB/s burst data transfer rate.
- E-IDE supports LBA (logical block addressing) which differs from CHS (cylinder head sector) in that the disk drive appears to be a continuous stream of sequential blocks. The addressing of these blocks is achieved from within the controller and the system does not have to bother about which cylinder, header and sector is being used.

IDE is limited to 1024 cylinders, 16 heads (the drive/head register has only 4 bits for the number of heads) and 63 sectors, which gives:

$$\text{Disk capacity} = 1024 \times 16 \times 63 \times 512 \quad = 504 \text{ MB}$$

With enhanced BIOS this is increased to 1024 cylinders, 256 heads (8-bit definition for the number of heads) and 63 sectors, to give:

$$\text{Disk capacity} = 1024 \times 256 \times 63 \times 512 = 7.88\,\text{GB}$$

With E-IDE the maximum possible is 65 536 cylinders, 256 heads and 63 sectors, to give:

$$\text{Disk capacity} = 65536 \times 256 \times 63 \times 512 = 128\,\text{GB}$$

Normally a 3½ inch hard disk would be limited around two platters, with four heads. Thus, the capacity is around 8.1 GB.

12.9 File systems

Windows NT supports three different types of file system:

- FAT (file allocation table) – as used by MS-DOS, OS/2 and Windows NT. A single volume can be up to 2 GB (now increased to 4GB). The maximum file size is 4GB. It has no built-in security but can be access through Windows 95/98, MS-DOS and Windows NT.
- HPFS (high performance file system) – a UNIX-style file system which is used by OS/2 and Windows NT. A single volume can be up to 8 GB. MS-DOS applications cannot access files.
- NTFS (NT file system) – as used by Windows NT. A single volume can be up to 64 TB (based on current hardware, but, theoretically, 16 exabytes). It has built-in security and also supports file compression/decompression. MS-DOS applications, themselves, cannot access the file system but they can when run with Windows NT, nor can Windows 95/98.

The FAT file system is widely used and supported by a variety of operating systems, such as MS-DOS, Windows NT and OS/2. If a system is to use MS-DOS it must be installed with a FAT file system.

12.9.1 FAT

The standard MS-DOS FAT file and directory-naming structure allows an 8-character file name and a 3-character file extension with a dot separator (.) between them (the 8.3 file name). It is not case sensitive and the file name and extension cannot contain spaces and other reserved characters, such as:

```
" / \ : ; | = , ^ * ? .
```

With Windows NT and Windows 95/98 the FAT file system supports long file names which can be up to 255 characters. The name can also contain multiple spaces and dot separators. File names are not case sensitive, but the case of file names is preserved (a file named `FredDocument.XYz` will be displayed as `FredDocument.XYz` but can be accessed with any of the characters in upper or lower case.

Each file in the FAT table has four attributes (or properties): read-only, archive, system and hidden (as shown in Figure 12.5). The FAT uses a linked list where the file's directory entry contains its beginning FAT entry number. This FAT entry in turn contains the location of the next cluster if the file is larger than one cluster, or a marker that designates this is included in the last cluster. A file which occupies 12 clusters will have 11 FAT entries and 10 FAT links.

The main disadvantage with FAT is that the disk is segmented into allocated units (or clusters). On large-capacity disks these sectors can be relatively large (typically 512 bytes/sector). Disks with a capacity of between 256 MB and 512 MB use 16 sectors per cluster (8 kB) and disks from 512 MB to 1 GB use 32 sectors per cluster (16 kB). Drives up to 2 GB use 64 sectors per cluster (32 kB). Thus if the disk has a capacity of 512 MB then each cluster will be 8 kB. A file which is only 1 kB will thus take up 8 kB of disk space (a wastage of 7 kB), and a 9 kB file will take up 16 kB (a wastage of 7 kB). Thus a file system which has many small files will be inefficient on a cluster-based system. A floppy disk normally uses one cluster per sector (512 bytes).

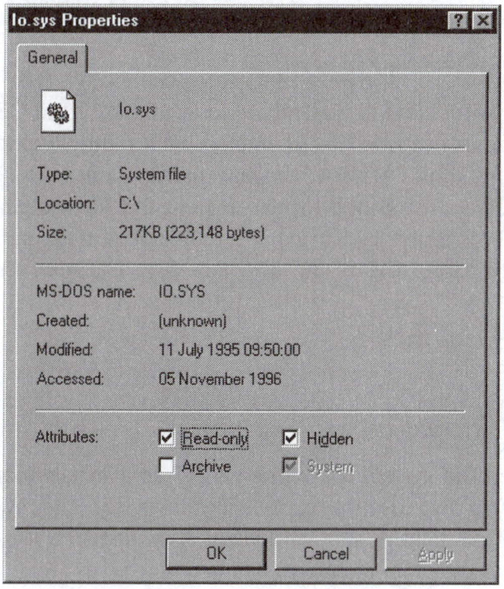

Figure 12.5 File attributes.

Windows 95/98 and Windows NT support up to 255 characters in file names; unfortunately, MS-DOS and Windows 3.*x* applications cannot read them. To accommodate this, every long file name has an autogenerated short file name (in the form xxxxxxxx.yyy). Table 12.4 shows three examples. The conversion takes the first six characters of the long name then adds a *~number* to the name to give it a unique name. File names with the same initial six characters are identified with different *numbers*. For example, Program Files and Program Directory would be stored as PROGRA~1 and PROGRA~2, respectively. Sample run 12.1 shows a listing from Windows NT. The left-hand column shows the short file name and the far right-hand column shows the long file name.

Table 12.4   File name conversions.

Long file name	Short file name
Program Files	PROGRA~1
Triangular.bmp	TRIANG~1.BMP
Fredte~1.1	FRED.TEXT.1

Sample run 12.1

```
EXAMPL~1 DOC   4,608   05/11/96   23:36 Example Document 1.doc
EXAMPL~2 DOC   4,608   05/11/96   23:36 Example Document 2.doc
EXAMPL~3 DOC   4,608   05/11/96   23:36 Example Document 3.doc
EXAMPL~4 DOC   4,608   05/11/96   23:36 Example Document 4.doc
EXAMPL~5 DOC   4,608   05/11/96   23:36 Example Document 5.doc
EXAMPL~6 DOC   4,608   05/11/96   23:36 Example Document 6.doc
EXAMPL~7 DOC   4,608   05/11/96   23:36 Example Document 7.doc
EXAMPL~8 DOC   4,608   05/11/96   23:39 Example assignment A.doc
EXAMPL~9 DOC   4,608   05/11/96   23:40 Example assignment B.doc
EXAMP~10 DOC   4,608   05/11/96   23:40 Example assignment C.doc
```

12.9.2 HPFS (high-performance file system)

HPFS is supported by OS/2 and is typically used to migrate from OS/2 to Windows NT. It allows long file names of up to 254 characters with multiple extensions. As with the Windows 95/98 and Windows NT FAT system the file names are not case sensitive but preserve the case. HPFS uses B-tree format to store the file system directory structure. The B-tree format stores directory entries in an alphabetic tree, and binary searches are used to search for the target file in the directory list. The reserved characters for file names are:

```
"  /  \  :  <  >  |  *  ?
```

12.9.3 NTFS (NT file system)

NTFS is the preferred file system for Windows NT as it makes more efficient usage of the disk and it offers increased security. It allows for file systems up to 16 EB (16 exabytes, or 1 billion gigabytes, or 2^{64} bytes). As with HPFS it uses B-tree format for storing the file systems directory structure. Its main objectives are:

- To increase reliability. NTFS automatically logs all directory and file updates which can be used to redo or undo failed operations resulting from system failures such as power losses, hardware faults, and so on.
- To provide sector sparing (or hot fixing). When NTFS finds errors in a bad sector, it causes the data in that sector to be moved to a different section and the bad sector to be marked as bad. No other data is then written to that sector. Thus, the disk fixes itself as it is working and there is no need for disk repair programs (FAT only marks bad areas when formatting the disk).
- Increases file system size (up to 16 EB).
- To enhance security permissions.
- To support POSIX requirements, such as case-sensitive naming, addition of a time stamp to show the time the file was last accessed and hard links from one file (or directory) to another.

The reserved characters for file names are:

`` / \ : < > | * ?

12.10 Coping with disk errors

Most network operating systems (such as Windows NT, NetWare and OS/2) provide for reliable storage that can cope with disk errors. The main techniques used are disk mirroring, disk duplexing and disk striping.

12.10.1 Disk mirroring

Network servers normally support disk mirroring which protects against hard disk failure. It uses two partitions on different disk drives which are connected to the same controller. Data written to the first (primary) partition is mirrored automatically to the secondary partition. If the primary disk fails then the system uses the partition on the secondary disk. Mirroring also allows unallocated space on the primary drive to be allocated to the secondary drive. On a disk mirroring system the primary and secondary partitions have the same drive letter (such as C: or D:) and users are unaware that disks are being mirrored.

12.10.2 Disk duplexing

Disk duplexing means that mirrored pairs are controlled by different controllers. This provides for fault tolerance on both disk and controller. Unfortunately, it does not support multiple controllers connected to a single disk drive.

12.10.3 Striping with parity

Network servers normally support disk striping with parity. This technique is based on RAID 5 (Redundant Array of Inexpensive Disks), where a number of partitions on different disks are combined to make one large logical drive. Data is written in stripes across all of the disk drives and additional parity bits. For example, if a system has four disk drives then data is written to the first three disks and the parity is written to the fourth drive. Typically the stripe is 64 kB, thus 64 kB will be written to Drive 1, the same to Drive 2 and Drive 3, then the parity of the other three to the fourth. The following example illustrates the concept of RAID where a system writes the data 110, 000, 111, 100 to the first three drives, this gives parity bits of 1, 1, 0 and 0.

   If one of the disk drives fails then the addition of the parity bit allows the bits on the failed disk to be recovered. For example, if disk 3 fails then the bits from the other disk are simply XOR-ed together to generate the bits from the failed drive. If the data on the other disk drives is 111 then the recovered data gives 0, 001 gives 0, and so on.

Disk 1	Disk 2	Disk 3	Disk 4 (Odd parity)
1	1	0	1
0	0	0	1
1	1	1	0
1	0	0	0

The 64 kB stripes of data are also interleaved across the disks. The parity block is written to the first disk drive, then in the next block to the second, and so on. A system with four disk drives would store the following data:

Disk 1	Disk 2	Disk 3	Disk 4
Parity block 1	Data block A	Data block B	Data block C
Data block D	Parity block 2	Data block E	Data block F
Data block G	Data block H	Parity block 3	Data block I

Each of the data blocks will be 64 kB, which is also equal to the parity block. The interlacing of the data ensures that the parity stripes are not all on the same disk. Thus there is no single point of failure for the set.

Striping of data improves reading performance when each of the disk drives has a separate controller, because the data is simultaneously read by each of the controllers and simultaneously passed to the systems. It thus provides fast reading of data but only moderate writing performance (because the system must calculate the parity block).

The main advantages of RAID 5 can be summarized as:

- It recovers data when a single disk drive or controller fails (RAID level 0 does not use a parity block thus it cannot regenerate lost data).
- It allows a number of small partitions to be built into a large partition.
- Several disks can be mounted as a single drive.
- Performance can be improved with multiple disk controllers.

The main disadvantages of RAID 5 are:

- It requires increased memory because of the parity block.
- Performance is reduced when one of the disks fails because of the need to regenerate the failed data.
- It increases the amount of disk space as it has an overhead due to the parity block (although the overhead is normally less than disk mirroring, which has a 50% overhead).
- It requires at least three disk drives.

12.11 Optical storage

Optical storage devices can store extremely large amounts of digital data. They use a laser beam which reflects from an optical disk. If a pit exists in the disk then the laser beam does not reflect back. Figure 12.6 shows the basic mechanism for reading from optical disks. A focusing lens directs the laser light to an objective lens that focuses the light onto a small area on the disk. If a pit exists then the light does not reflect back from the disk. If the pit does not exist then it is reflected and directed through the objective lens and a quarter-wave plate to the polarized prism. The quarter-wave polarizes the light by 45° and thus the reflected light will have a polarization by 90°, with respect to the original incident light in the prism. The polarized prism then directs this polarized light to the sensor.

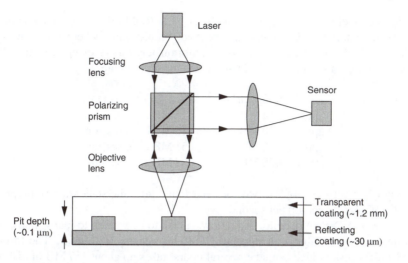

Figure 12.6 Reading from an optical disk.

12.11.1 CD-ROM

In a permanent disk (also known as compact disk, or CD) the pits are set up by pressing then onto the disk at production. The data on this type of disk is permanent and cannot be reprogrammed to store different data, and is known as CD-ROM (compact disk read-only memory). This type of disk is normally only cost effective in large quantities.

Standard CD-ROM disks have a diameter of 120 mm (4.7 inch) and a thickness of 1.2 mm. They can store up to 650 MB of data which gives around 72 minutes of compressed video (MPEG format with near VCR quality) or uncompressed hi-fi audio. The reflective coating (normally aluminium) on the disk is approximately 30 μm and the pits are approximately 0.1 μm long and deep. A protective transparent coating is applied on top of the reflective coating with a depth of 1.2 mm (the approximate thickness of the disk). The protective coating also help to focus the light beam from about 0.7 mm on the surface of the coating to the 0.1 μm pit.

Data is stored on the disk as a spiral starting from the outside and ending at the inside. The thickness of the track is 1.6 μm, which gives a total spiral length of 5.7 km.

12.11.2 WORM drives

WORM (write-once read many) disks allow data to be written to the optical disk once. The data is then permanent and thus cannot be altered. They are typically used in data logging applications and in making small volumes of CD-ROMs. A 350 mm (14 inch) WORM disk can store up to 10 GB of data (5 GB per side). This gives around 15 hours of compressed video (MPEG format with near VCR quality).

WORM disks consist of two pieces of transparent material (normally glass) with a layer of metal (typically tellurium) sandwiched in-between. Initially the metal recording surface is clear. A high-intensity laser beam then writes information to the disk by burning small pits into the surface.

12.11.3 CD-R/ CD-RW disks

CD-R (CD-Recordable) disks are write-once disks that can store up to 650 MB of data or

74 minutes of audio. For a disk to be read by any CD-ROM drive they must comply with ISO 9660 format. A CD-R disk can also be made multi-session where a new file system is written each time the disk is written–to. Unfortunately this takes up around 14 MB of header data for each session. Typical parameters for sessions are:

No. of sessions	Header information	Data for each session
1	approx. 14 MB	636 MB one session
5	approx. 70 MB	116 MB each session
10	approx. 140 MB	51 MB each session
30	approx. 420 MB	7.7 MB each session

Typically CD recorders write at two (or even four) times the standard writing/playback speed of 150 kB (75 sectors) per second.

A CD-RW (CD-ReWriteable) disk allows a disk to be written-to many times, but the file format is incompatible with standard CD-ROM systems (IS0 9660). The formatting of the CD-RW disk (which can take several hours) takes up about 157 MB of disk space, which only leaves about 493 MB for data.

New CD-R/CD-RW writing systems incorporate a smart laser system that eradicates the problem of dirt on the disk. It does this by adjusting the write power of the laser using Automatic Power Control. This allows the unit to continue to write when it encounters minor media errors such as dirt, smudges, small scratches, and so on.

12.11.4 CD-ROM disk format

The two main standard for writing a CD-ROM are ISO 9660 and UDF (Universal Disk Format). The ISO 9660 disk unfortunately uses 14 MB for each session write.

In 1980, Philips NV and Sony Corporation announced the CD-DA (digital audio) format and in 1983 they released the standard for CD-ROM. Then, in 1988, they released the Red Book standard for recordable CD audio disks (CD-DA)

This served as a blueprint for the Yellow Book specification for CD-ROMs (CD-ROM and CD-ROM-XA Data Format) and the Orange Book Parts 1 and 2 specifications for CD-Recordable (CD-R/CD-E (CD-Recordable/CD-Erasable)). In the Red Book standard a disk is organized into a number of segments:

- Lead In. Contains the disk's table of contents that specifies the physical location of each track.
- Program Area. Contains the actual disk data or audio data and is divided up into 99 tracks, with a two-second gap between each track.
- Lead Out. Contains a string of zeros which is a legacy of the old Red Book standard. These zeros enabled old CD players to identify the end of a CD.

The CD is laid out in a number of sectors. Each of these sectors contains 2352 bytes, made up of 2048 bytes of data and other information such as headers, sub-headers, error detection code, and so on. The data is organized into logical blocks. After each session a logical block has a logical address, which is used by the drive to find a particular logical block number (LBN).

Within the tracks the CD can contain either audio or computer data. The most common formats for computer data are ISO 9660, hierarchical file system (HFS) and the Joliet file system.

The ISO 9660 standard was developed at a time when disks required to be mass-replicated. It thus wrote the complete file system at the time of creation, as there was no need for incremental creation. Now, with CD-R technology, it is possible to incrementally write to a disk. This is described as multi-session. Unfortunately, after each session a new Lead In and Lead Out must be written (requiring a minimum of 13 MB of disk space). This consists of:

- 13.2 MB for the Lead Out for the first session and 4.4 MB for each subsequent session.
- 8.8 MB for Lead In for each session.

Thus multi-session is useful for writing large amounts of data for each session, but is not efficient when writing many small updates. Most new CD-R systems now use a track-at-once technique which stores the data one track at a time and only writes the Lead In and Lead Out data when the session is actually finished. In this technique, the CD can be build up with data over a long time period. Unfortunately, the disk cannot be read by standard CD-ROM drives until the session is closed (and written with the ISO 9660 format). Another disadvantage is that the Red Book only specifies up to 99 tracks for each CD.

Unfortunately, ISO 9660 is not well-suited for packet writing and is likely to be phased out over the coming years.

12.11.5 Magneto-optical (MO) disks

As with CD-R disks, magneto-optical (MO) disks allow data to be rewritten many times. These disks use magnetic and optical fields to store the data. Unfortunately, the disk must first be totally erased before writing data (although new developments are overcoming this limitation).

12.11.6 Transfer rates

Optical disks spin at variable speeds, they spin at a lower rate on the outside of the disk than on the inside. Thus, the disk increases its speed progressively as the data is read from the disk. The actual rate at which the drive reads the data is constant for the disk. The basic transfer rate for a typical CD-ROM is 150 kB/s. This has recently been increased to 300 kB/s ($\times$2 CD drives), 600 kB/s ($\times$4), 900 kB/s ($\times$6), 1.5 MB/s ($\times$10) and even 3.6 MB/s ($\times$24).

12.11.7 Standards

Data disks are described in the following standards books, each of them specific to an area or application type. They can be obtained by becoming a licensed CD developer with Philips and they apply to media, hardware, operating systems, file systems and software.

Red Book	World standard for all audio Compact Disks (CD-DA).
Yellow Book	CD-ROM and CD-ROM-XA data formats.
Green Book	CD-I data formats and operating systems (photo).
White Book	CD-I (video).
Orange Book	CD-R/CD-E (CD-Recordable/CD-Eraseable).
Blue Book	CD-Enhanced (CD Extra, CD Plus).

12.11.8 Silver, green, blue or gold

CD-ROMs are available in a number of colours, these are:

- Silver. These are read-only disks which are a stamped as an original disk.
- Gold. These are recordable disks which use a basic phthalocyanine formulation which was patented by Mitsui Toatsu Chemicals (MTC) of Japan, and is licensed to other phthalocyanine media manufacturers. They generally work better with 2× writing speeds as some models of disk cannot be written to at 1× writing speed.
- Green. These are recordable disks which are based on cyanine-based formulations. They are not covered by a governing patent, and are more or less unique to the individual manufacturers. An early problem was encountered with cyanine-based disks as the dye became chemically unstable in the presence of sunlight. Other problems included a wide variation in electrical performance depending on write speed and location (inner or outer portion of the disk). Eventually, in 1995, some stabilizing compounds were added. The best attempt produced a metal-stabilized cyanine dye formulation that gave excellent overall performance. Gradually the performance of these disks is approaching gold disk performance.
- Blue. These are recordable disks which are based on an Azo media. This was designed and manufactured by Mitsubishi Chemical Corporation (MCC) and marketed through its US subsidiary, Verbatim Corporation.

12.12 Magnetic tape

Magnetic tapes use a thin plastic tape with a magnetic coating (normally of ferric oxide). Most modern tapes are either reel-to-reel or cartridge type. A reel-to-reel tape normally has two interconnected reels of tape with tension arms (similar to standard compact audio cassettes). The cartridge type has a drive belt to spin the reels; this mechanism reduces the strain on the tape and allows faster access speeds.

Magnetic tapes have an extremely high capacity and are relatively cheap. Data is saved in a serial manner with one bit (or one record) at a time. This has the disadvantage that they are relatively slow when moving back and forward within the tape to find the required data. Typically it may take many seconds (or even minutes) to search from the start to the end of a tape. In most applications, magnetic tapes are used to backup a system. This type of application requires a large amount of data to be stored reliably over time but the recall speed is not important.

The most common types of tape are:

- Reel-to-reel tapes – the tapes have two interconnected reels with an interconnecting tape which is tensioned by tension arms. They were used extensively in the past to store computer-type data but have been replaced by the following three types (8 mm, QIC and DAT tapes).
- 8 mm video cartridge tapes – this type of tape was developed to be used in video cameras and is extremely compact. As with video tapes the tape wraps round the read/write head in a helix.
- Quarter inch cartridge (QIC) tapes – a QIC is available in two main sizes: 5¼-inch and 3½-inch. They give capacities of 40 MB to tens of GB.

- Digital audio tapes (DAT) – this type of tape was developed to be used in hi-fi applications and is extremely compact. As with the 8 mm tape, the tape wraps round the read/write head in a helix. The tape itself is 4 mm wide and can store several GBs of data with a transfer rate of several hundred kbps.

12.12.1 QIC tapes

QIC tapes are available in two sizes: 5¼ inch and 3½ inch. The tape length ranges from 200 to 1000 feet, with a tape width of ¼ inch. Typical capacities range from 40 MB to tens of GB. A single capstan drive is driven by the tape drive. Figure 12.7 illustrates a QIC tape.

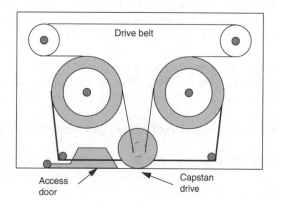

Figure 12.7   QIC tape.

12.12.2 8 mm video tape

The 8 mm video tape is a high specification tape and was originally used in video cameras. These types are also known as Exabyte after the company that originally developed a backup system using 8 mm video tapes. They can be used to store several GB of data with a transfer rate of 500 kbps. In order to achieve this high transfer rate the read/write head spins at 2000 rpm and the tape passes it at a relatively slow speed.

12.12.3 Digital audio tape (DAT)

The DAT tape is a high specification tape and was originally used in the music industry.

12.13 Exercises

12.13.1   What is the main advantage, apart from increased transfer rate, that IDE has over older interface standards, such as ST-506 and ESDI?

12.13.2   Explain how IDE differs from E-IDE and how E-IDE supports larger disk capacities.

12.13.3   How does E-IDE use modes to define the maximum transfer rate. Which mode is the fastest?

12.13.4 Show that the maximum capacity of IDE is 528 MB and that the maximum capacity (per disk) is 8.4 GB for E-IDE.

12.13.5 Which IRQ does an IDE connected disk drive normally use and what is the size of its data bus?

12.13.6 A floppy disk ribbon cable has a cable twist to differentiate between the A: drive and the B: drive. How does the ribbon cable that connects two IDE connected drives differ? In addition, how many wires does the ribbon cable have?

12.13.7 Outline how three hard disks and a CD-ROM can be connected to the IDE bus? What settings are required for the disks to connect properly? Which signal line differentiates between a master and a slave?

12.13.8 How are I/O addresses used to communicate with hard disks? How is data transferred to and from the disk? What are the standard address ranges for the primary and the secondary? If possible, check these on an available PC.

12.13.9 Which register is used to identify a hard disk error? Explain its operation.

12.13.10 Which is the IDE signal line that identifies if a slave device exists?

12.13.11 Outline the main disadvantages of FAT.

12.13.12 Describe the main file systems supported in Windows NT and their advantages.

12.13.13 Explain the main methods that Windows NT and NetWare use to deal with disk errors.

12.13.14 Prove that, 16-bit, 44.1 kHz sampled, stereo audio gives approximately 65 minutes for a 650 MB optical disk.

13 SCSI

13.1 Introduction

SCSI is often the best choice of bus for high-specification systems. It has many advantages over IDE, these include:

- A single bus system for up to seven connected devices.
- It supports many different peripherals, such as hard disks, tape drives, CD-ROMs, and so on.
- It supports device priority where a higher SCSI-ID has priority over a lower SCSI-ID.
- It supports both high-quality connectors and cables, and low-quality connectors and ribbon cable.
- It supports differential signals, which gives longer cable lengths.
- Extended support for commands and messaging.
- Devices do not need individual IRQ lines (as they do in IDE) as the controller communicates with the devices. Thus it requires only a single IRQ line.
- It has great potential for faster transfer and enhanced peripheral support.

13.2 SCSI types

SCSI has an intelligent bus subsystem and can support multiple devices cooperating currently, where each device is assigned a priority. The main types of SCSI are:

- SCSI-I. Transfer rate of 5 MB/sec with an 8-bit data bus and seven devices per controller.
- SCSI-II. Support for SCSI-I and with one or more of the following:
  - Fast SCSI which uses a synchronous transfer to give 10 MB/s transfer rate. The initiator and target initially negotiate to see if they can both support synchronous transfer. If they can they then go into a synchronous transfer mode.
  - Fast/Wide-SCSI-II which doubles the data bus width to 16 bits and gives a 20 MB/s transfer rate.
  - 15 devices per master device.
  - Tagged command queuing (TCQ) which greatly improves performance and is supported by Windows NT, NetWare and OS/2.
  - Multiple commands sent to each device.
  - Commands executed in whatever sequence will maximize device performance.
- Ultra-SCSI (SCSI-III) which operates either as 8-bit or 16-bit giving a 20 MB/sec or 40 MB/s transfer rate.

13.2.1 SCSI-II

SCSI-II supports Fast SCSI, which is basically SCSI-I operating at a rate of 10 MB/s (using Synchronous vs. Asynchronous), and Wide-SCSI which uses a 64-pin connector and has a 16-bit data bus. The SCSI-II controller is also more efficient and processes commands up to seven times faster than SCSI-I.

The SCSI-II drive latency is much less than SCSI-I because it uses tagged command queuing (TCQ) which allows multiple commands to be sent to each device. These then hold their own commands and execute them in sequence that maximizes system performance (such as by minimizing disk rotation latency). Table 13.1 shows examples of Fast SCSI-II and Fast/Wide-SCSI-II. It can be seen that both disks have predictive failure analysis (PFA) and automatic defect reallocation (ADR).

The normal 50-core cable is typical known as A-cable, while the 68-core cable is known as B-cable.

Table 13.1   Comparison of SCSI-II disks.

	Seek time (ms)	Latency (ms)	Rotational speed (rpm)	Sustained data read (MB/s)	PFA	ADR
1GB SCSI-II Fast	10.5	5.56	5400	4	✓	✓
4.5GB SCSI-II Fast/Wide	8.2	4.17	7200	12	✓	✓

13.2.2 Ultra-SCSI

Ultra-SCSI (or SCSI-III) allows for 20 MB/s burst transfers on an 8-bit data path and 40 MB/s burst transfer on a 16-bit data path. It uses the same cables as SCSI-II and the maximum cable length is 1.5 m. Ultra-SCSI disks are compatible with SCSI-II controllers; however, the transfer will be at the slower speed of the SCSI controller. SCSI disks are compatible with Ultra-SCSI controllers; however, the transfer will be at the slower speed of the SCSI disk.

SCSI-I and Fast SCSI-II use a 50-pin 8-bit connector, while Fast/Wide-SCSI-II and Ultra-SCSI use a 68-pin 16-bit connector. The 16-bit connector is physically smaller than the 8-bit connector and the 16-bit connector cannot connect directly to the 8-bit connector. The cable used is called P-cable and replaces the A/B-cable.

Note that SCSI-II and Ultra-SCSI require an active terminator on the last external device. Table 13.2 compares the main types of SCSI.

Table 13.2   SCSI types.

	Data bus (bits)	Transfer rate (MB/s)	Tagged command queuing	Parity checking	Maximum devices	Pins on cable and connector
SCSI-I	8	5	×	×/✓ (opt.)	7	50
SCSI-II Fast	8	10	✓	✓	7	50
SCSI-II Fast/Wide	16	20	✓	✓	15	68
Ultra-SCSI	32	40	✓	✓	15	68

13.3 SCSI Interface

In its standard form the Small Computer Systems Interface (SCSI) standard uses a 50-pin header connector and a ribbon cable to connect to up to eight devices. It overcomes the problems of the IDE, where devices are assigned to be either a master or a slave. SCSI and Fast SCSI transfer data one byte at a time with a parity check on each byte. SCSI-II, Wide-SCSI and Ultra-SCSI use a 16-bit data transfer and a 68-pin connector. Table 13.3 lists the pin connections for SCSI-I (single-ended cable) and Fast SCSI (differential cable) and Table 13.4 lists the pin connections for SCSI-II, Wide-SCSI and Ultra-SCSI. With Wide-SCSI and Ultra-SCSI there are 24 data bits ($\overline{D8} - \overline{D31}$) and three associated parity bits ($\overline{D(PARITY1)} - \overline{D(PARITY3)}$).

Table 13.3   SCSI-I and Fast SCSI connections.

Single-ended cable				Differential cable			
Pin	*Signal*	*Pin*	*Signal*	*Pin*	*Signal*	*Pin*	*Signal*
1	GND	2	$\overline{D0}$	1	GND	2	GND
3	GND	4	$\overline{D1}$	3	$+\overline{D0}$	4	$-\overline{D0}$
5	GND	6	$\overline{D2}$	5	$+\overline{D1}$	6	$-\overline{D1}$
7	GND	8	$\overline{D3}$	6	$+\overline{D2}$	8	$-\overline{D2}$
9	GND	10	$\overline{D4}$	8	$+\overline{D3}$	10	$-\overline{D3}$
11	GND	12	$\overline{D5}$	11	$+\overline{D4}$	12	$-\overline{D4}$
13	GND	14	$\overline{D6}$	13	$+\overline{D5}$	14	$-\overline{D5}$
15	GND	16	$\overline{D7}$	15	$+\overline{D6}$	16	$-\overline{D6}$
17	GND	18	$\overline{D(PARITY)}$	17	$+\overline{D7}$	18	$-\overline{D7}$
19	GND	20	GND	19	D(PARITY)	20	$-\overline{D(PARITY)}$
21	GND	22	GND	21	DIFFSEN	22	GND
23	RESERVED	24	RESERVED	23	RESERVED	24	RESERVED
25	Open	26	TERMPWR	25	TERMPWR	26	TEMPWR
27	RESERVED	28	RESERVED	27	RESERVED	28	RESERVED
29	GND	30	GND	29	$+\overline{ATN}$	30	$-\overline{ATN}$
31	GND	32	$\overline{ATN}$	31	GND	32	GND
33	GND	34	GND	33	$+\overline{RST}$	34	$-\overline{RST}$
35	GND	36	$\overline{BSY}$	35	$+\overline{ACK}$	36	$-\overline{ACK}$
37	GND	38	$\overline{ACK}$	37	$+\overline{RST}$	38	$-\overline{RST}$
39	GND	40	$\overline{RST}$	39	$+\overline{MSG}$	40	$-\overline{MSG}$
41	GND	42	$\overline{MSG}$	41	$+\overline{SEL}$	42	$-\overline{SEL}$
43	GND	44	$\overline{SEL}$	43	$+\overline{C}/D$	44	$-\overline{C}/D$
45	GND	46	$\overline{C}/D$	45	$+\overline{REQ}$	46	$-\overline{REQ}$
47	GND	48	$\overline{REQ}$	47	$+\overline{I}/O$	48	$-\overline{I}/O$
49	GND	50	$\overline{I}/O$	49	GND	50	GND

13.3.1 Signals

A SCSI bus is made up of a SCSI host adapter connected to a number of SCSI units via a SCSI bus. As all units connect to a common bus, only two units can transfer data at a time, either from one SCSI unit to another or from one SCSI unit to the SCSI host. The great advantage of this transfer is that is does not involve the processor.

Table 13.4   SCSI-II, Wide-SCSI and Ultra-SCSI.

Pin	Signal	Pin	Signal	Pin	Signal	Pin	Signal
1	GND	18	TERMPWR	35	GND	52	$\overline{D19}$
2	GND	19	GND	36	$\overline{D8}$	53	$\overline{D20}$
3	GND	20	GND	37	$\overline{D9}$	54	$\overline{D21}$
4	GND	21	GND	38	$\overline{D10}$	55	$\overline{D22}$
5	GND	22	GND	39	$\overline{D11}$	56	$\overline{D23}$
6	GND	23	GND	40	$\overline{D12}$	57	$\overline{D(PARITY2)}$
7	GND	24	GND	41	$\overline{D13}$	58	$\overline{D24}$
8	GND	25	GND	42	$\overline{D14}$	59	$\overline{D25}$
9	GND	26	GND	43	$\overline{D15}$	60	$\overline{D26}$
10	GND	27	GND	44	$\overline{D(PARITY1)}$	61	$\overline{D27}$
11	GND	28	GND	45	$\overline{ACKB}$	62	$\overline{D28}$
12	GND	29	GND	46	GND	63	$\overline{D29}$
13	GND	30	GND	47	$\overline{REQB}$	64	$\overline{D30}$
14	GND	31	GND	48	$\overline{D16}$	65	$\overline{D31}$
15	GND	32	GND	49	$\overline{D17}$	66	$\overline{ATN}$
16	GND	33	GND	50	TERMPWR	67	$\overline{D(PARITY3)}$
17	TERMPWR	34	GND	51	TERMPWR	68	GND

Each unit on a SCSI is assigned a SCSI-ID address. As SCSI-I has an 8-bit data bus this address can range from 0 to 7 (where 7 is normally reserved for a tape drive). The host adapter takes one of the addresses and thus a maximum of seven units can connect to the bus. Most systems allow the units to take on any SCSI-ID address, but older system required boot drives to be connected to a specific SCSI address. On boot the host adapter sends out a 'Start Unit' command to each SCSI unit. This allows each unit to start in an orderly manner (and not overload the local power supply). The host starts with the highest priority address (ID=7) and finishes with the lowest address (ID=0). Typically, the ID is set with a rotating switch selector or by three jumpers.

SCSI defines an initiator control and a target control. The initiator requests functions from a target, which then executes the function, as illustrated in Figure 13.1. The initiator effectively takes over the bus for the time to send a command, the target then executes the command and contacts the initiator to transfer data. The bus will then be free for other transfers.

The main signals are:

- $\overline{BSY}$. Indicates that the bus is busy, or not (an OR-tied signal).
- $\overline{ACK}$. Activated by the initiator to indicate an acknowledgement for a $\overline{REQ}$ information transfer handshake.
- $\overline{RST}$. When active (low) resets all the SCSI devices (an OR-tied signal).
- $\overline{ATN}$. Activated by the initiator to indicate the attention state.
- $\overline{MSG}$. Activated by the target to indicate the message phase.
- $\overline{SEL}$. Activated by the initiator and is used to select a particular target device (an OR-tied signal).
- $\overline{C}/D$ (control/data). Activated by the target to identify if there is data or control on the SCSI bus.

- $\overline{\text{REQ}}$. Activated by the target to acknowledge a request for an $\overline{\text{ACK}}$ information transfer handshake.
- $\overline{\text{I}} / \text{O}$ (input/output). Activated by the target to show the direction of the data on the data bus. Input defines that data is an input to the initiator, else, it is an output.

Each of the control signals can be true or false. They can be:

- OR-tied driven, where the driver does not drive the signal to the false state. In this case any SCSI device can pull the signal false whenever it is released by another device. If any driver is asserted, then the signal is true. The $\overline{\text{BSY}}$, $\overline{\text{SEL}}$, and $\overline{\text{RST}}$ signals are OR-tied. In the ordinary operation of the bus, the $\overline{\text{BSY}}$ and $\overline{\text{RST}}$ signals may be simultaneously driven true by several drivers.
- Non-OR-tied driven where the signal may be actively driven false. No signals other than $\overline{\text{BSY}}$, $\overline{\text{RST}}$, and $\overline{\text{D(PARITY)}}$ are simultaneously driven by two or more drivers.

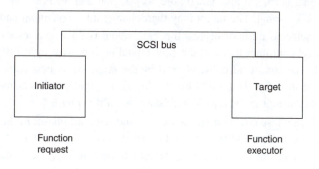

Figure 13.1 Initiator and target in SCSI.

13.4 SCSI operation

The SCSI bus allows any unit to talk to any other unit, or the host to talk to any unit. Thus there must be some way of arbitration where units capture the bus. The main phases that the bus goes through are:

- **Free-bus**. In this state no units are either transfering data or have control of the bus. It is identified by disactive $\overline{\text{SEL}}$ and $\overline{\text{BSY}}$ lines (both will be high). In this state any unit can capture the bus.
- **Arbitration**. In this state a unit can take control of the bus and become an initiator. To do this it activates the $\overline{\text{BSY}}$ signal and puts its own ID address on the data bus. Next, after a delay, it tests the data bus to determine if a higher-priority unit has put its own address on the bus. If it has then it allows the other unit(s) access to the bus. If its address is still on the bus then it asserts the $\overline{\text{SEL}}$ line. After a delay, it then has control of the bus.
- **Selection**. In this state the initiator selects a target unit and gets the target to carry out a given function, such as reading or writing data. The initiator outputs the OR-value of its SCSI-ID and the target's SCSI-ID onto the data bus (for example, if the initiator is 2 (0000 0100) and the target is 5 (0010 0000) then the OR-ed ID on the bus will be

0010 0100.). The target then determines that its ID is on the data bus and sets the $\overline{\text{BSY}}$ line active. If this does not happen within a given time then the initiator deactivates the $\overline{\text{SEL}}$ signal, and the bus becomes free. The target determines that it is selected when the $\overline{\text{SEL}}$ signal and its SCSI-ID bit are active and the $\overline{\text{BSY}}$ and $\overline{\text{I}}/\text{O}$ signals are false. It then asserts the $\overline{\text{BSY}}$ signal within a selection abort time.

- **Reselection**. When the arbitration phase is complete, the winning SCSI device asserts the $\overline{\text{BSY}}$ and $\overline{\text{SEL}}$ signals and has delayed at least a bus clear delay plus a bus settle delay. The winning SCSI device sets the data bus to a value that is the logical OR of its SCSI-ID bit and the initiator's SCSI-ID bit. Sometimes the target takes a while reply to the initiator's request. The initiator determines that it is reselected when the $\overline{\text{SEL}}$ and $\overline{\text{I}}/\text{O}$ signals and its SCSI-ID bit are true and the $\overline{\text{BSY}}$ signal is false. The reselected initiator then asserts the $\overline{\text{BSY}}$ signal within a selection abort time of its most recent detection of being reselected. An initiator does not respond to a reselection phase if other than two SCSI-ID bits are on the data bus. After the target detects that the $\overline{\text{BSY}}$ signal is true, it also asserts the $\overline{\text{BSY}}$ signal and waits a given time delay to release the $\overline{\text{SEL}}$ signal. The target may then change the $\overline{\text{I}}/\text{O}$ signal and the data bus. After the reselected initiator detects the $\overline{\text{SEL}}$ signal is false, it releases the $\overline{\text{BSY}}$ signal. The target continues to assert the $\overline{\text{BSY}}$ signal until it gives up the SCSI bus.

- **Command**. The command phase is used by the target to request command information from the initiator. The target asserts the $\overline{\text{C}}/\text{D}$ signal and negates the $\overline{\text{I}}/\text{O}$ and $\overline{\text{MSG}}$ signals during the $\overline{\text{REQ}}/\overline{\text{ACK}}$ handshake(s) of this phase.

- **Data**. The data phase covers both the data in and data out phase. In the data in phase the target requests that data is to be sent to the initiator. It (the target) asserts the $\overline{\text{I}}/\text{O}$ signal and negates the $\overline{\text{C}}/\text{D}$ and $\overline{\text{MSG}}$ signals during the $\overline{\text{REQ}}/\overline{\text{ACK}}$ handshake(s) of this phase. In the data out phase the target requests that data be sent from the initiator to the target. For this the target negates the $\overline{\text{C}}/\text{D}$, $\overline{\text{I}}/\text{O}$, and $\overline{\text{MSG}}$ signals during the $\overline{\text{REQ}}/\overline{\text{ACK}}$ handshake(s) of this phase.

- **Message**. The message phase covers both the message out and message in phase. The first byte transferred can be either a single-byte message or the first byte of a multiple-byte message. Multiple-byte messages are completely contained within a single message phase.

- **Status**. The status phase allows the target to request status information from the initiator. For this the target asserts the $\overline{\text{C}}/\text{D}$ and $\overline{\text{I}}/\text{O}$ signals and negate the $\overline{\text{MSG}}$ signal during the $\overline{\text{REQ}}/\overline{\text{ACK}}$ handshake of this phase.

Typical times are:

- Arbitration delay, 2–4 µs. This is the minimum time that the SCSI device waits from asserting $\overline{\text{BSY}}$ for arbitration until the data bus can be examined to see if arbitration has been won.
- Power-on to selection time, 10 s. This is the maximum time from power start-up until a SCSI target is able to respond with appropriate status and sense data.
- Selection abort time, 200 µs. This is the maximum time that a target (or initiator) takes from its most recent detection of being selected (or reselected) until asserting a $\overline{\text{BSY}}$ response. This is required to ensure that a target (or initiator) does not assert $\overline{\text{BSY}}$ after an aborted select (or reselection) phase.

- Selection time out delay, 250 ms. The minimum time that a SCSI device waits for a $\overline{\text{BSY}}$ response during the selection or reselection phase before starting the time out procedure.
- Disconnection delay, 200 µs. The minimum time that a target waits after releasing $\overline{\text{BSY}}$ before entering an arbitration phase when implementing a disconnect message from the initiator.
- Reset hold time, 23 µs. The minimum time for which $\overline{\text{RST}}$ is asserted.

The signals $\overline{\text{C}}/\text{D}$, $\overline{\text{I}}/\text{O}$, and $\overline{\text{MSG}}$ differentiate the different information transfer phases, as summarized in Table 13.5. The target drives these signals and thus controls the operation of the bus. The initiator requests a message out phase with the $\overline{\text{ATN}}$ signal, while the target initiates a bus free phase by releasing the $\overline{\text{MSG}}$, $\overline{\text{C}}/\text{D}$, $\overline{\text{I}}/\text{O}$, and $\overline{\text{BSY}}$ signals.

Information transfer phases use one or more $\overline{\text{REQ}}/\overline{\text{ACK}}$ handshakes to control the transfer. Each $\overline{\text{REQ}}/\overline{\text{ACK}}$ handshake allows the transfer of one byte of information. During this phase the $\overline{\text{BSY}}$ signal remain active (low) and the $\overline{\text{SEL}}$ signal false (high). Additionally, during this phase, the target continuously uses the $\overline{\text{REQ}}/\overline{\text{ACK}}$ handshake(s) with the $\overline{\text{C}}/\text{D}$, $\overline{\text{I}}/\text{O}$, and $\overline{\text{MSG}}$ signals so that these control signals are valid for a bus settle delay before assertioning the $\overline{\text{REQ}}$ signal of the first handshake and remain valid until after the negation of the $\overline{\text{ACK}}$ signal at the end of the handshake of the last transfer of the phase.

Table 13.5 Information transfer phases.

$\overline{\text{MSG}}$	$\overline{\text{C}}/\text{D}$	$\overline{\text{I}}/\text{O}$	Phase	Direction
0	1	1	–	–
0	1	0	–	–
0	0	1	Message out	Initiator→target
0	0	0	Message in	Initiator←target
1	1	1	Data out	Initiator→target
1	1	0	Data in	Initiator←target
1	0	1	Command	Initiator→target
1	0	0	Status	Initiator←target

The $\overline{\text{I}}/\text{O}$ signal controls the information direction. When low, information is transferred from the target to the initiator and when high, the transfer is from the initiator to the target.

The handshaking operation for a transfer to the initiator is as follows:

- $\overline{\text{I}}/\text{O}$ signal is set low.
- Target sets the data bus lines and asserts the $\overline{\text{REQ}}$ signal.
- Initiator reads the data bus and then indicates its acceptance of the data by asserting the $\overline{\text{ACK}}$ signal.
- Target may change or release the data bus.
- Target negates the $\overline{\text{REQ}}$ signal.
- Initiator negates the $\overline{\text{ACK}}$ signal.
- Target then transfers data using the data bus and the $\overline{\text{REQ}}$ signal, and so on.

The handshaking operation for a transfer from the initiator is as follows:

- $\bar{I}/O$ signal is set high.
- Target asserts the $\overline{REQ}$ signal (requesting information).
- Initiator puts data on bus and asserts the $\overline{ACK}$ signal.
- Target reads the data bus and negates the $\overline{REQ}$ signal (acknowledging transfer).
- Initiator continues to transfer data, and so on.

13.5 SCSI pointers

SCSI provides for three pointers for each I/O process (called saved pointers), for command, data, and status. When an I/O process becomes active, its three saved pointers are copied into the initiator's set of three current pointers. These current pointers point to the next command, data, or status byte to be transferred between the initiator's memory and the target.

13.6 Message system description

The message system allows the initiator and the target to communicate over the interface connection. Each message can be one or more bytes in length. In a single message phase, one or more messages can be transmitted (but a message cannot be split between multiple message phases). Table 13.6 lists the message format, where the first byte of the message determines the format. The initiator ends the message out phase (by negating $\overline{ATN}$) when it sends certain messages identified in Table 13.7. Single-byte messages consist of a single byte transferred during a message phase.

Table 13.6   Message format.

Value	Message format
00h	One-byte message (command complete)
01h	Extended messages
02h–1Fh	One-byte messages
20h–2Fh	Two-byte messages
30h–7Fh	Reserved
80h–FFh	One-byte message (identify)

Table 13.7   Message codes.

Code	Message	Direction	Description
00h	Command complete	In	Sent from a target to an initiator to indicate a successful completion of a process. After sending this message, the target by releasing the $\overline{BSY}$ signal and the bus becomes free. The target detects a success when it detects the negation of $\overline{ACK}$ for the command complete message with

the $\overline{\text{ATN}}$ signal false.

03h	Restore pointers	In	
04h	Disconnect	In/Out	Sent from target to inform an initiator that the present connection is going to be broken. After sending this message, the target releases the $\overline{\text{BSY}}$ signal goes into the bus free phase. It then considers the message transmission to be successful when it detects the negation of the $\overline{\text{ACK}}$ signal.
05h	Initiator detected error	Out	
06h	Abort	Out	Sent from initiator to reset the connection. The target then goes to the bus free phase following its receipt.
07h	Message reject	Out	Sent to indicate that the last message or message byte was invalid (or not implemented).
08h	No operation	Out	Sent when the initiator does not currently have any other valid message to send.
09h	Message parity error	Out	
0Ah	Linked command complete	In	
0Bh	Linked command complete (with flag)	In	
0Ch	Bus device reset	Out	Forces a hard reset on the selected SCSI device.
0Dh	Abort tag	Out	
0Eh	Clear queue	Out	
0Fh	Initiate recovery	In/Out	
10h	Release recovery	Out	
11h	Terminate I/O process	Out	
12h–1Fh	Reserved		
23h	Ignore wide residue (2 bytes)		
24h–2Fh	Reserved for 2-byte messages		
30h–7Fh	Reserved		
80h–FFh	Identify	In/Out	

13.7 SCSI commands

Commands are sent from the initiator to the target. The first byte of all SCSI commands contains an operation code, followed by a command descriptor block and finally the control byte.

The formats of the command descriptor block for 6-byte commands are:

Byte 0. Operation code.
Byte 1. Logical unit number (MSB, if required).
Byte 2. Logical block address.
Byte 3. Logical block address (LSB, if required).
Byte 4. Transfer length (if required) / Parameter list length (if required) / Allocation length (if required).
Byte 5. Control.

13.7.1 Operation code

Figure 13.2 shows the operation code of the command descriptor block. It has a group code field and a command code field. The 3-bit group code field provides for eight groups of command codes and the 5-bit command code field provides for 32 command codes in each group.

The group code specifies one of the following groups:

- Group 0 – 6-byte commands.
- Group 1/2 – 10-byte commands.
- Group 3/4 – reserved.

- Group 5 – 12-byte commands.
- Group 6/7 – vendor-specific.

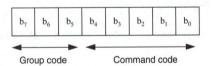

Figure 13.2   Operation code.

13.7.2 Logical unit number

The logical unit number (LUN) is defined in the identify message. The target ignores the LUN specified within the command descriptor block if an identify message was received (normally the logical unit number in the command descriptor block is set to zero).

13.7.3 Logical block address

The logical block address (LBA) on a disk drive starts a zero after a drive partition and is contiguous up to the last logical block on that device.

A 10-byte and a 12-byte command descriptor block contains a 32-bit logical block addresses, whereas a 6-byte command descriptor block contains a 21-bit logical block address.

13.7.4 Transfer length

The transfer length field specifies the amount of data to be transferred (normally the number of blocks). For several commands, the transfer length indicates the requested number of bytes to be sent as defined in the command description. Commands that uses 1 byte for the transfer length thus allow up to 256 blocks of data for one command (a value of 0 identifies a transfer bock of 256 blocks).

13.7.5 Parameter list length

The parameter list length specifies the number of bytes to be sent during the data out phase. It is typically used in command descriptor blocks for parameters that are sent to a target (such as, mode parameters, diagnostic parameters, log parameters, and so on).

13.7.6 Allocation length

The allocation length field specifies the maximum number of bytes that an initiator has allocated for returned data. The target ends the data in phase when allocation length bytes have been transferred or when all available data have been transferred to the initiator, whichever is less. The allocation length is used to limit the maximum amount of data returned to an initiator.

13.7.7 Control field

The control field is the last byte of every command descriptor block. Its format is shown in Figure 13.3. The flag bit specifies which message the target should return to the initiator. If the link bit is a 1 and the command completes without error. If the link bit is 0 and the flag bit is 1 the target returns check condition status.

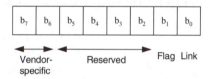

Figure 13.3 Control field.

13.7.8 Command code

Commands for all device types include (bold type identifies the mandatory commands and the operation code is given in parentheses):

- Change definition (40h). Modifies the operating definition of the selected logical unit or target.
- Compare (39h). Compares data on one logical unit with another.
- Copy (18h). Copies data from one logical unit to another or the same logical unit. The logical unit that receives and performs the copy command is the copy manager and is responsible for copying data from the source device to the destination device.
- Copy and compare (3Ah). Performs a copy and compare command.
- **Inquiry** (12h). Requests that information regarding parameters of the target and its attached peripheral device(s) be sent to the initiator.
- Log select (4Ch). Allows an initiator to manage statistical information maintained by the device about the device or its logical units (used with Log sense).
- Log sense (4Dh). Allows the initiator to retrieve statistical information from the device about the device or its logical units (used with Log select).

- Mode select (15h). Allows the initiator to specify medium, logical unit, or peripheral device parameters to the target (used with Mode sense).
- Mode sense (1Ah). Allows the target to report parameters to the initiator (used with Mode select).
- Read buffer (3Ch). Used with the write buffer command as a diagnostic function for testing target memory and the SCSI bus integrity.
- Receive diagnostic results (1Ch). Requests analysis data be sent to the initiator after a send diagnostic.
- **Request sense** (03h). Requests that the target transfer sense data to the initiator.
- **Send diagnostic** (1Dh). Requests the target to perform diagnostic operations on it-self, on the logical unit, or on both.
- **Test unit ready** (00h). Provides a means to check if the logical unit is ready.
- Write buffer (3Bh). Used with the read buffer command as a diagnostic for testing target memory and the SCSI bus integrity.

13.8 Status

The status phase normally occurs at the end of a command (although in some cases it may occur before transferring the command descriptor block). Figure 13.4 shows the format of the status byte and Table 13.8 defines some status byte codes. The status byte is sent from the target to the initiator during the status phase at the completion of each command unless the command is terminated by one of the following events:

- Abort message.
- Abort tag message.
- Bus device reset message.

- Clear queue message.
- Hard reset condition.
- Unexpected disconnect.

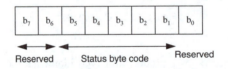

Figure 13.4   Status field.

13.9 Exercises

13.9.1   Explain the main differences between SCSI-I, SCSI-II and Ultra-SCSI. Out-line their maximum data throughput, the connectors used and the size of their data busses. Also, Outline some of the advantages of SCSI over busses such as the ISA bus.

13.9.2   State the SCSI lines that are used for simple error detection. Why is it not pos-sible to detect which bits are in error?

13.9.3   Discuss the main system lines that are used in the SCSI bus and the operation of OR-tied driven signals.

Table 13.8 Status byte codes.

Bit value of status bit								Status	Description
7	6	5	4	3	2	1	0		
R	R	0	0	0	0	0	R	Good	Target has successfully completed the command.
R	R	0	0	0	0	1	R	Check condition	Contingent allegiance condition has occurred.
R	R	0	0	0	1	0	R	Condition met	This status returned whenever the requested operation is satisfied.
R	R	0	0	1	0	0	R	Busy	Target is busy and is unable to accept a command.
R	R	0	1	0	0	0	R	Immediate	Successfully completed command in a series of linked commands (except the last command).
R	R	0	1	0	1	0	R	Immediate-condition met	Used in combination of the CONDITION MET and INTERMEDIATE statuses.
R	R	0	1	1	0	0	R	Reservation conflict	Initiator attempts to access a logical unit or an extent within a logical unit that is reserved with a conflicting reservation type for another SCSI device.
R	R	1	0	0	0	1	R	Command conflict	Target ends the current I/O process after receiving a TERMINATE I/O PROCESS message.
R	R	1	0	1	0	0	R	Queue full	Used with tagged queuing.
R	R	R	R	R	R	R	R	Reserved	

13.9.4 Outline the main phases that the initiator and target go through in setting up a connection. Also, outline the important of device time-outs for the different SCSI phases.

13.9.5 Discuss how the $\overline{\text{MSG}}$, $\overline{\text{C}}/\text{D}$ and $\overline{\text{I}}/\text{O}$ signal signals are used to set up different transfer phases.

13.9.6 Explain how SCSI uses the SCSI-ID address to set up a device priority system.

13.9.7 Discuss the usage of the message phase in SCSI and give typical examples of its usage.

13.9.8 Discuss the usage of the command phase in SCSI and give typical examples of its usage.

13.9.9 Discuss the usage of the status phase in SCSI and give typical examples of its usage.

14 PCMCIA

14.1 Introduction

The Personal Computer Memory Card International Association (PCMCIA) interface allows small thin cards to be plugged into laptop, notebook or palmtop computers. It was originally designed for memory cards (Version 1.0) but has since been adopted for many other types of adapters (Version 2.0), such as fax/modems, sound-cards, local area network cards, CD-ROM controllers, digital I/O cards, and so on. Most PCMCIA cards comply with either PCMCIA Type II or Type III. Type I cards are 3.3 mm thick, Type II cards take cards up to 5 mm thick, Type III allows cards up to 10.5 mm thick. A new standard, Type IV, takes cards which are greater than 10.5 mm. Type II interfaces can accept Type I cards, Type III accept Types I and II and Type IV interfaces accepts Types I, II and III.

The PCMCIA standard uses a 16-bit data bus (D0–D15) and a 26-bit address bus (A0–A25), which gives an addressable memory of 2^{26} bytes (64 MB). The memory is arranged as:

- Common memory and attribute memory, which gives a total addressable memory of 128 MB.
- I/O addressable space of 64 k 8-pin ports.

The PCMCIA interface allows the PCMCIA device to map into the main memory or into the I/O address space. For example, a modem PCMCIA device would map its registers into the standard COM port addresses (such as 3F8h–3FFh for COM1 or 2F8h–2FF for COM2). Any accesses to the mapped memory area will be redirected to the PCMCIA rather that the main memory or I/O address space. These mapped areas are called windows. A window is defined with a START address and a LAST address. The PCMCIA control register contains these addresses.

14.2 PCMCIA connections

Table 14.1 shows the pin connections.

14.3 PCMCIA signals

The main PCMCIA signals are:

- A25–A0, D15–D0. Data bus (D15–D0) and a 26-bit memory address (A25–A0) or 16-bit I/O memory address (A15–A0).

Table 14.1 PCMCIA connections.

Pin	Signal	Pin	Signal	Pin	Signal	Pin	Signal
1	GND	18	Vpp1	35	GND	52	Vpp2
2	D3	19	A16	36	*See below*	53	A22
3	D4	20	A15	37	D11	54	A23
4	D5	21	A12	38	D12	55	A24
5	D6	22	A7	39	D13	56	A25
6	D7	23	A6	40	D14	57	RFU
7	$\overline{\text{CARD ENABLE 1}}$	24	A5	41	D15	58	RESET
8	A10	25	A4	42	*See below*	59	$\overline{\text{WAIT}}$
9	$\overline{\text{OUTPUT ENABLE}}$	26	A3	43	REFRESH	60	$\overline{\text{INPACK}}$
10	A11	27	A2	44	$\overline{\text{IOR}}$	61	$\overline{\text{REGISTER SELECT}}$
11	A9	28	A1	45	$\overline{\text{IOW}}$	62	$\overline{\text{SPKR}}$
12	A8	29	A0	46	A17	63	$\overline{\text{STSCHG}}$
13	A13	30	D0	47	A18	64	D8
14	A14	31	D1	48	A19	65	D9
15	*See below*	32	D2	49	A20	66	D10
16	$\overline{\text{READY}}$ / $\overline{\text{BUSY}}$	33	$\overline{\text{IOIS16}}$	50	A21	67	$\overline{\text{CARD DETECT 2}}$
17	+5V	34	GND	51	+5V	68	GND

Pin 15 $\overline{\text{WRITE ENABLE / PROGRAM}}$ Pin 33 $\overline{\text{IOIS16}}$ (Write Protect)

Pin 36 $\overline{\text{CARD DETECT 1}}$ Pin 42 $\overline{\text{CARD ENABLE 2}}$

- $\overline{\text{CARD DETECT 1}}$, $\overline{\text{CARD DETECT 2}}$. Used to detect if a card is present in a socket. When a card is inserted one of these lines is pulled to a low level.
- $\overline{\text{CARD ENABLE 1}}$, $\overline{\text{CARD ENABLE 2}}$. Used to enable the upper 8-bits of the data bus ($\overline{\text{CARD ENABLE 1}}$) and/or the lower 8 bits of the data bus ($\overline{\text{CARD ENABLE 2}}$).
- $\overline{\text{OUTPUT ENABLE}}$. Set low by the computer when reading data from the PCMCIA unit.
- $\overline{\text{REGISTER SELECT}}$. Set high when accessing common memory or a low when accessing attribute memory.
- RESET. Used to reset the PCMCIA card.
- REFRESH. Used to refresh PCMCIA memory.
- $\overline{\text{WAIT}}$. Used by the PCMCIA device when it cannot transfer data fast enough and requests a wait cycle.
- $\overline{\text{WRITE ENABLE / PROGRAM}}$. Used to program the PCMCIA device.
- Vpp1, Vpp2. Programming voltages for flash memories.
- $\overline{\text{READY}}$ / $\overline{\text{BUSY}}$. Used by the PCMCIA card when it is ready to process more data (when a high) or is still occupied by a previous access (when it is a low).
- $\overline{\text{IOIS16}}$. Used to indicate the state of the write-protect switch on the PCMCIA card. A high level indicates that the write-protect switch has been set.
- $\overline{\text{INPACK}}$. Used by the PCMCIA card to acknowledge the transfer of a signal.
- $\overline{\text{IOR}}$. Used to issue an I/O read access from the PCMCIA card (must be used with an active $\overline{\text{REGISTER SELECT}}$ signal).
- $\overline{\text{IOW}}$. Used to issue an I/O write access to the PCMCIA card (must be used with an active $\overline{\text{REGISTER SELECT}}$ signal).
- $\overline{\text{SPKR}}$. Used by PCMCIA card to send audio data to the system speaker.
- $\overline{\text{STSCHG}}$. Used to identify that the card has changed its status.

14.4 PCMCIA registers

A typical PCMCIA Interface Controller (PCIC) is the 82365SL. Figure 14.1 shows the main registers for the first socket. The second socket index values are simply offset by 40h. Figure 14.2 shows that the base address of the PCIC is, in Windows, set to 3E0h, by default. Figure 14.3 shows an example of a FIRST and LAST memory address. The PCIC is accessed using two addresses: 3E0h and 3E1h. The I/O windows 0/1 are accessed through:

- 08h/0Ch for the low byte of the FIRST I/O address.
- 09h/0Dh for the high byte of the FIRST I/O address.
- 0Ah/0Eh for the high byte of the LAST I/O address.
- 0Bh/0Fh for the high byte of the LAST I/O address.

Register index

Index	Register
00h →	PCIC indentification
01h →	Interface status
02h →	Power supply (RESETDRV)
03h →	Interrupt control
04h →	Card status change
05h →	Configuration
06h →	Memory window enable
07h →	I/O window control
08h →	FIRST setup for I/O window 0 (lo)
09h →	FIRST setup for I/O window 0 (hi)
0Ah →	LAST setup for I/O window 0 (lo)
0Bh →	LAST setup for I/O window 0 (hi)
0Ch →	FIRST setup for I/O window 1 (lo)
0Dh →	FIRST setup for I/O window 1 (hi)
0Eh →	LAST setup for I/O window 1 (lo)
0Fh →	LAST setup for I/O window 1 (hi)
10h →	FIRST setup for memory window 0 (lo)
11h →	FIRST setup for memory window 0 (hi)
12h →	LAST setup for memory window 1 (lo)
13h →	LAST setup for memory window 1(hi)

Figure 14.1 PCMCIA controller status and control registers.

The registers are accessed by loading the register index into 3E0h and then the indexed register is accessed through the 3E1h. The memory windows 0/1/2/3/4 are accessed through:

- 10h/18h/20h/28h/30h for the low byte of the FIRST memory address.
- 11h/19h/21h/29h/31h for the high byte of the FIRST memory address.
- 12h/1Ah/22h/2Ah/32h for the low byte of the LAST memory address.
- 13h/1Bh/23h/2Bh/33h for the high byte of the LAST memory address.
- 14h/1Ch/24h/2Ch/34h for the low byte of the card offset.

- 15h/1Dh/25h/2Dh/35h for the high byte of the card offset.

For example, to load a value of 22h into the Card status change register, the following would be used:

```
_outp(0x3E0,5h);  /* point to Card status change register       */
_outp(0x3E1,22h);   /* load 22h into Card status change register  */
```

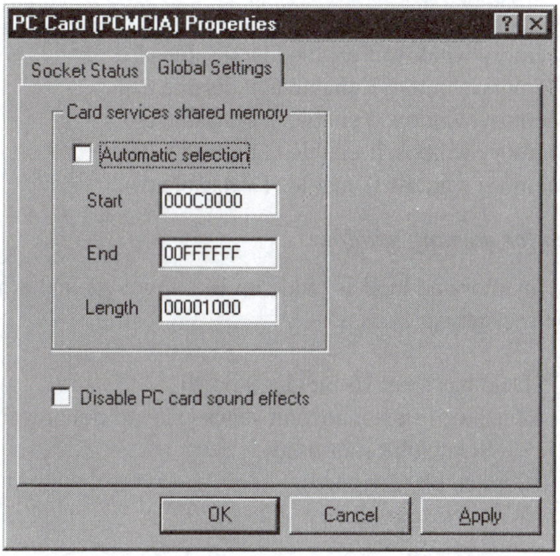

Figure 14.2   Start and end of shared memory.

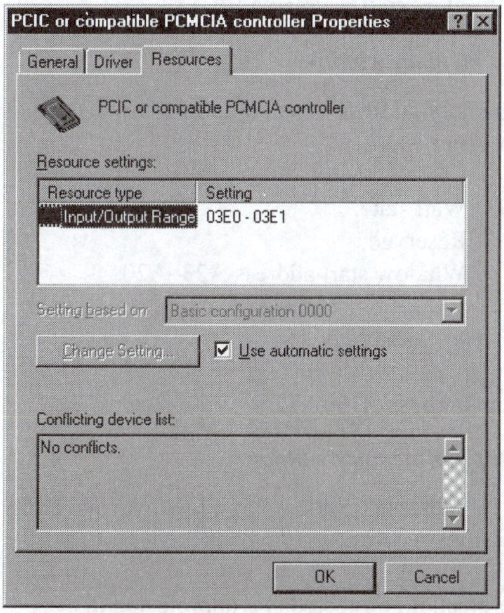

Figure 14.3   Base address of the PCIC.

14.4.1 Window enable register

The Window enable register has a register index of 06h (and 46h for the second socket). The definition of the register is:

Bit 7   IOW1.   I/O window 1 enable (1)/ disable (0).
Bit 6   IOW0.   I/O window 0 enable (1)/ disable (0).
Bit 5   DEC.   If active (1) $\overline{\text{MEMCS16}}$ generated from A23–A12, else from A23–A17.
Bit 4   MW4.   Memory window 4 enable (1)/ disable (0).
Bit 3   MW3.   Memory window 3 enable (1)/ disable (0).
Bit 2   MW2.   Memory window 2 enable (1)/ disable (0).
Bit 1   MW1.   Memory window 1 enable (1)/ disable (0).
Bit 0   MW0.   Memory window 0 enable (1)/ disable (0).

14.4.2 FIRST setup for memory window

The FIRST window memory address is made up of a low byte and a high byte. The format of the high-byte register is:

Bit 7   DS.   Data bus size: 16-bit (1)/ 8-bit (0).
Bit 6   0WS.   Zero wait states: no wait states (1)/ additional wait states (0).
Bit 5   SCR1.   Scratch bit (not used).
Bit 4   SCR0.   Scratch bit (not used).
Bit 3–0   Window start address A23–A20.

The format of the low-byte register is:

Bit 7–0   A19–A12. Window start address A19–A12.

14.4.3 LAST setup for memory window

The LAST window memory address is made up of a low byte and a high byte. The format of the high-byte register is:

Bit 7, 6   WS1, WS0.   Wait state.
Bit 5, 4   Reserved.
Bit 3–0   A23–A20.   Window start address A23–A20.

The format of the low-byte register is:

Bit 7–0   Window start address A19–A12.

14.4.4 Card offset setup for memory window

The card offset memory address is made up of a low byte and a high byte. The format of the high-byte register is:

Bit 7   WP   Write protection: protected (1)/ unprotected (0).
Bit 6   REG $\overline{\text{REGISTER SELECT}}$ enabled. If set to a 1 then access to attribute memory, else common memory.

Bit 5–0   Window start address A25–A20.

The format of the low-byte register is:

Bit 7–0   Window start address A19–A12.

14.4.5 FIRST setup for I/O window

The FIRST window I/O address is made up of a low byte and a high byte. The format of the high-byte register is:

Bit 7–0   A15–A8.

The format of the low-byte register is:

Bit 7–0   A7–A8.

14.4.6 LAST setup for I/O window

The LAST window I/O address is made up of a low byte and a high byte. The format of the high-byte register is:

Bit 7–0   A15–A8.

The format of the low-byte register is:

Bit 7–0   A7–A8.

14.4.7 Control register for I/O address window

The Control register for the I/O address window is made up from a single byte. Its format is:

Bit 7, 3   WS1, WS0.   Wait states for Window 1 and 0.
Bit 6, 2   0WS1, 0WS0. Zero wait states for Window 1 and 0.
Bit 5, 1   CS1, CS0. $\overline{IOIS16}$ source. Select $\overline{IOIS16}$ from PC (1) or select data size from DS1 and DS0 (0).
Bit 4, 0   DS1, DS0.   Data size: 16-bit (1)/ 8-bit (0).

14.4.8 Examples

A typical application of the PCMCIA socket is to use it for a modem. This is an example of a setting to set up a modem on the COM2 port. For this purpose, the socket must be set up to map into the I/O registers from 02F8h to 02FFh. The following code will achieve this:

```
/* load 02f8 into FIRST and 02FFh into LAST registers
*/
_outp(0x3E0,08h);    /* point to FIRST low byte                 */
_outp(0x3E1,f8h);    /* load f8h into FIRST low byte            */

_outp(0x3E0,09h);    /* point to FIRST high byte                */
_outp(0x3E1,02h);    /* load 02h into FIRST high byte            */

_outp(0x3E0,0Ah);    /* point to LAST low byte                  */
```

```
_outp(0x3E1,ffh);     /* load ffh into LAST low byte                  */

_outp(0x3E0,0Bh);     /* point to LAST high byte                      */
_outp(0x3E1,02h);     /* load 02h into LAST high byte                 */

/*setup control register: no wait states, 8-bit data access
       */
_outp(0x3E0,07h);     /* point to I/O Control register                */
_outp(0x3E1,00h);     /* load 00h into register                       */

/* enable window 0 */
_outp(0x3E0,06h);     /* point to memory enable window                */
_outp(0x3E1,04h);     /* load 0100 0000b to enable I/O window 0        */
```

14.5 Exercises

14.5.1   Prove that the maximum address memory with PCMCIA is 64 MB.

14.5.2   Explain how I/O registers are used to program the PCMCIA device.

14.5.3   Show the lines of C code that would be required to mount a primary serial port (3F8h–3FFh) and an ECP printer port (378h–37Ah).

14.5.4   Show the lines of C code that would be required to mount a primary (1F0h–1F7h) and a secondary hard disk (170h–177h).

14.5.5   How would the programming for extra memory differ from an isolated I/O device?

15 RS-232

15.1 Introduction

RS-232 is one of the most widely used techniques used to interface external equipment to computers. It uses serial communications where one bit is sent along a line, at a time. This differs from parallel communications which send one or more bytes, at a time. The main advantage of serial communications over parallel communications is that a single wire is needed to transmit and another to receive. RS-232 is a *de facto* standard that most computer and instrumentation companies comply with. The Electronics Industries Association (EIA) standardized it in 1962. Unfortunately, this standard only allows short cable runs with low bit rates, such as a bit rate of 19 600 bps for a maximum distance of 20 metres. New serial communications standards, such as RS-422 and RS-449, allow very long cable runs and high bit rates. For example, RS-422 allows a bit rate of up to 10 Mbps over distances of up to one mile, using twisted-pair, coaxial cable or optical fibres. The new standards can also be used to create computer networks. This chapter introduces the RS-232 standard and gives simple programs which can be used to transmit and receive using RS-232. Chapter 16 uses an interrupt-driven technique to further enhance the transmission and reception.

15.2 Electrical characteristics

15.2.1 Line voltages

The electrical characteristics of RS-232 define the minimum and maximum voltages of a logic '1' and '0'. A logic '1' ranges from -3 V to -25 V, but will typically be around -12 V. A logical '0' ranges from 3 V to 25 V, but will typically be around $+12$ V. Any voltage between -3 V and $+3$ V has an indeterminate logical state. If no pulses are present on the line then the voltage level is equivalent to a high level, that is -12 V. A voltage level of 0 V at the receiver is interpreted as a line break or a short circuit. Figure 15.1 shows an example transmission.

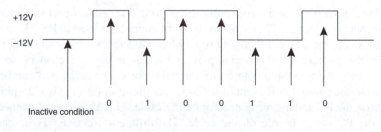

Figure 15.1 RS-232 voltage levels.

15.2.2 DB25S connector

The DB25S connector is a 25-pin D-type connector and gives full RS-232 functionality. Figure 15.2 shows the pin number assignment. A DCE (the terminating cable) connector has a male outer casing with female connection pins. The DTE (the computer) has a female outer casing with male connecting pins. There are three main signal types: control, data and ground. Table 15.1 lists the main connections. Control lines are active high, that is they are high when the signal is active and low when inactive.

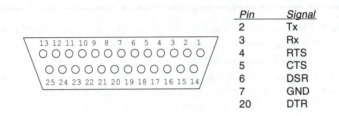

Pin	Signal
2	Tx
3	Rx
4	RTS
5	CTS
6	DSR
7	GND
20	DTR

Figure 15.2   RS-232 DB25S connector.

15.2.3 DB9S connector

The 25-pin connector is the standard for RS-232 connections but as electronic equipment becomes smaller, there is a need for smaller connectors. For this purpose most PCs now use a reduced function 9-pin D-type connector rather than the full function 25-way D-type. As with the 25-pin connector the DCE (the terminating cable) connector has a male outer casing with female connection pins. The DTE (the computer) has a female outer casing with male connecting pins. Figure 15.3 shows the main connections.

Pin	Signal
2	Rx
3	Tx
4	DTR
5	GND
6	DSR
7	RTS
8	CTS

Figure 15.3   RS-232 DB9S Interface.

15.2.4 PC connectors

All PCs have at least one serial communications port. The primary port is named COM1: and the secondary is COM2:. There are two types of connectors used in RS-232 communications; these are the 25- and 9-way D-type. Most modern PCs use either a 9-pin connector for the primary (COM1:) serial port and a 25-pin for a secondary serial port (COM2:), or they use two 9-pin connectors for serial ports. The serial port can be differentiated from the parallel port in that the 25-pin parallel port (LPT1:) is a 25-pin female connector on the PC and a male connector on the cable. The 25-pin serial connector is a male on the PC and a female on the cable. The different connector types can cause problems in connecting devices. Thus, a 25-to-9 pin adapter is a useful attachment, especially to connect a serial mouse to a 25-pin connector.

Table 15.1   Main pin connections used in 25-pin connector.

Pin	Name	Abbreviation	Functionality
1	Frame Ground	FG	This ground normally connects the outer sheath of the cable to earth ground.
2	Transmit Data	TD	Data is sent from the DTE (computer or terminal) to a DCE via TD.
3	Receive Data	RD	Data is sent from the DCE to a DTE (computer or terminal) via RD.
4	Request to Send	RTS	DTE sets this active when it is ready to transmit data.
5	Clear to Send	CTS	DCE sets this active to inform the DTE that it is ready to receive data.
6	Data Set Ready	DSR	Similar functionality to CTS but activated by the DTE when it is ready to receive data.
7	Signal Ground	SG	All signals are referenced to the signal ground (GND).
20	Data Terminal Ready	DTR	Similar functionality to RTS but activated by the DCE when it wishes to transmit data.

15.3 Frame format

See Section 6.2.

15.4 Communications between two nodes

RS-232 is intended to be a standard but not all manufacturers abide by it. Some implement the full specification while others implement just a partial specification. This is mainly because not every device requires the full functionality of RS-232; for example, a modem requires many more control lines than a serial mouse.

The rate at which data is transmitted and the speed at which the transmitter and receiver can transmit/receive the data dictates whether data handshaking is required.

15.4.1 Handshaking

In the transmission of data there can be either no handshaking, hardware handshaking or software handshaking. If no handshaking is used then the receiver must be able to read the received characters before the transmitter sends another. The receiver may buffer the received character and store it in a special memory location before it is read. This memory location is named the receiver buffer. Typically, it may only hold a single character. If it is not emptied before another character is received then any character previously in the buffer will be overwritten. An example of this is illustrated in Figure 15.4. In this case the receiver has read the first two characters successfully from the receiver buffer, but it did not read the third character as the fourth transmitted character has overwritten it in the receiver buffer. If this condition occurs then some form of handshaking must be used to stop the transmitter sending characters before the receiver has had time to service the received characters.

Hardware handshaking involves the transmitter asking the receiver if it is ready to receive data. If the receiver buffer is empty it will inform the transmitter that it is ready to receive data. Once the data is transmitted and loaded into the receiver buffer, the transmitter is informed not to transmit any more characters until the character in the receiver buffer has been read. The main hardware handshaking lines used for this purpose are:

- CTS   –   Clear to Send.
- RTS   –   Ready to Send.
- DTR   –   Data Terminal Ready.
- DSR   –   Data Set Ready.

Software handshaking involves sending special control characters. These include the DC1–DC4 control characters.

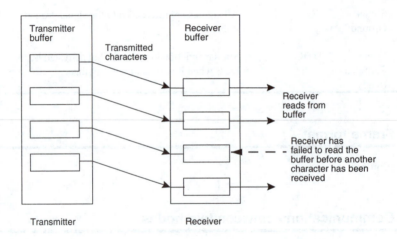

Figure 15.4   Transmission and reception of characters.

15.4.2 RS-232 set-up

Windows 95/98 allow the serial port setting to be set by selecting Control Panel → System → Device Manager → Ports (COM and LPT) → Port Settings. The settings of the communications port (the IRQ and the port address) can be changed by selecting Control Panel → System → Device Manager → Ports (COM and LPT) → Resources for IRQ and Addresses. Figure 15.5 shows example parameters and settings. The selectable baud rates are typically 110, 300, 600, 1200, 2400, 4800, 9600 and 19 200 Baud for an 8250-based device. A 16650 compatible UART speed also gives enhanced speeds of 38400, 57 600, 115 200, 230 400, 460 800 and 921 600 Baud. Notice that the flow control can either be set to software handshaking (X-ON/X-OFF), hardware handshaking or none.

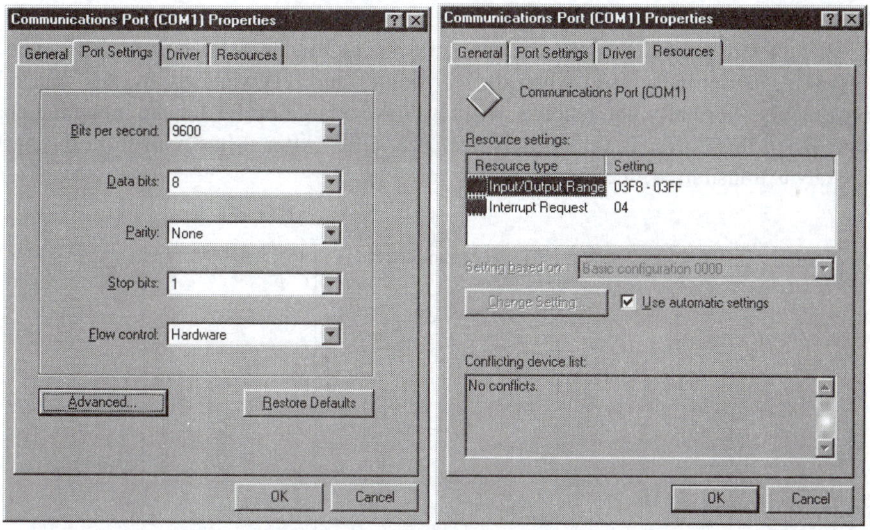

Figure 15.5   Changing port setting and parameters.

The parity bit can either be set to none, odd, even, mark or space. A mark in the parity option sets the parity bit to a '1' and a space sets it to a '0'.

In this case COM1: is set at 9600 Baud, 8 data bits, no parity, 1 stop bit and no parity checking.

15.4.3 Simple no-handshaking communications

In this form of communication it is assumed that the receiver can read the received data from the receive buffer before another character is received. Data is sent from a TD pin connection of the transmitter and is received in the RD pin connection at the receiver. When a DTE (such as a computer) connects to another DTE, then the transmit line (TD) on one is connected to the receive (RD) of the other and vice versa. Figure 15.6 shows the connections between the nodes.

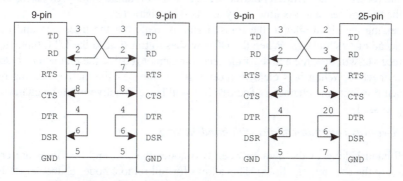

Figure 15.6   RS-232 connections with no hardware handshaking.

15.4.4 Software handshaking

Two ASCII characters start and stop communications. These are X-ON (^S , Cntrl-S or

ASCII 11) and X-OFF (^Q, Cntrl-Q or ASCII 13). When the transmitter receives an X-OFF character it ceases communications until an X-ON character is sent. This type of handshaking is normally used when the transmitter and receiver can process data relatively quickly. Normally, the receiver will also have a large buffer for the incoming characters. When this buffer is full it transmits an X-OFF. After it has read from the buffer the X-ON is transmitted; see Figure 15.7.

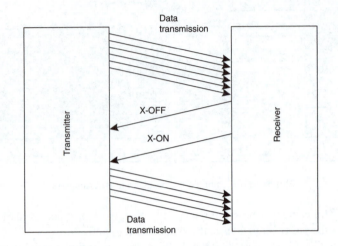

Figure 15.7   Software handshaking using X-ON and X-OFF.

15.4.5 Hardware handshaking

Hardware handshaking stops characters in the receiver buffer from being overwritten. The control lines used are all active high. Figure 15.8 shows how the nodes communicate. When a node wishes to transmit data it asserts the RTS line active (that is, high). It then monitors the CTS line until it goes active (that is, high). If the CTS line at the transmitter stays inactive then the receiver is busy and cannot receive data, at the present. When the receiver reads from its buffer the RTS line will automatically go active indicating to the transmitter that it is now ready to receive a character.

Receiving data is similar to the transmission of data, but the lines DSR and DTR are used instead of RTS and CTS. When the DCE wishes to transmit to the DTE the DSR input to the receiver will become active. If the receiver cannot receive the character, it sets the DTR line inactive. When it is clear to receive it sets the DTR line active and the remote node then transmits the character. The DTR line will be set inactive until the character has been processed.

15.4.6 Two-way communications with handshaking

For full handshaking of the data between two nodes the RTS and CTS lines are crossed over (as are the DTR and DSR lines). This allows for full remote node feedback (see Figure 15.9).

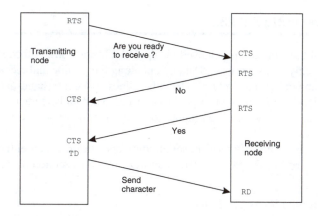

Figure 15.8 Handshaking lines used in transmitting data.

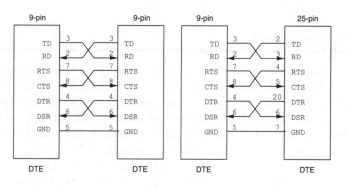

Figure 15.9 RS-232 communications with handshaking.

15.4.7 DTE–DCE connections (PC to modem)

A further problem occurs in connecting two nodes. A DTE–DTE connection requires crossovers on their signal lines, whereas DTE–DCE connections require straight-through lines. Figure 15.10 shows an example connection for a computer to modem connection.

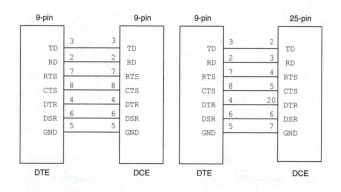

Figure 15.10 DTE to DCE connections.

15.5 Programming RS-232

Normally, serial transmission is achieved via the RS-232 standard. Although 25 lines are defined usually only a few are used. Data is sent along the TD line and received by the RD line with a common ground return. The other lines, used for handshaking, are RTS (Ready to Send) which is an output signal to indicate that data is ready to be transmitted and CTS (Clear to Send), which is an input indicating that the remote equipment is ready to receive data.

The 8250 IC is commonly used in serial communications. It can either be mounted onto the motherboard of the PC or fitted to an I/O card. This section discusses how it is programmed.

15.5.1 Programming the serial device

See Section 6.2.2.

15.6 RS-232 programs

Figure 15.11 shows the main RS-232 connection for 9- and 25-pin connections without hardware handshaking. The loopback connections are used to test the RS-232 hardware and the software, while the null modem connections are used to transmit characters between two computers. Program 15.1 uses a loopback on the TD/RD lines so that a character sent by the computer will automatically be received into the receiver buffer. This set-up is useful in testing the transmit and receive routines. The character to be sent is entered via the keyboard. A Cntrl-D (^D) keystroke exits the program.

Program 15.2 can be used as a sender program (send.c) and Program 15.3 can be used as a receiver program (receive.c). With these programs the null modem connections shown in Figure 15.11 are used.

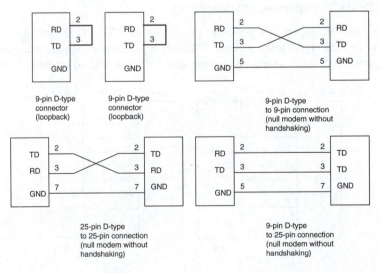

Figure 15.11   System connections.

Note that Programs 15.1 to 15.3 are written for Microsoft Visual C. For a Borland
C/C++ program change _inp for inportb and _outp for outportb.

Program 15.1

```
/*    This program transmits a character from COM1: and receives  */
/*    it via this port. The TD is connected to RD.                */

#define  COM1BASE      0x3F8
#define  COM2BASE      0x2F8
#define  TXDATA        COM1BASE
#define  LCR           (COM1BASE+3) /*  0x3FB line control     */
#define  LSR           (COM1BASE+5) /*  0x3FD line status      */

#include <conio.h>  /* required for getch()                    */
#include <stdio.h>

/* Some ANSI C prototype definitions  */
void  setup_serial(void);
void  send_character(int ch);
int   get_character(void);

int      main(void)
{
int      inchar,outchar;

     setup_serial();
     do
     {
        puts("Enter char to be transmitted (Cntrl-D to end)");
        outchar=getch();
        send_character(outchar);
        inchar=get_character();
        printf("Character received was %c\n",inchar);
     } while (outchar!=4);
     return(0);
}

void     setup_serial(void)
{
     _outp( LCR, 0x80);
     /* set up bit 7 to a 1 to set Register address bit  */

     _outp(TXDATA,0x0C);
     _outp(TXDATA+1,0x00);
     /* load TxRegister with 12, crystal frequency is 1.8432MHz */

     _outp(LCR, 0x0A);
     /* Bit pattern loaded is 00001010b, from msb to lsb these are:  */
     /* 0 - access TD/RD buffer,  0 - normal output               */
     /* 0 - no stick bit , 0 - even parity                        */
     /* 1 - parity on, 0 - 1 stop bit                             */
     /* 10 - 7 data bits                                          */
}

void  send_character(int ch)
{
char  status;
     do
     {
        status = _inp(LSR) & 0x40;
     } while (status!=0x40);
     /*repeat until Tx buffer empty ie bit 6 set*/

     _outp(TXDATA,(char) ch);
```

```
}

int    get_character(void)
{
int    status;
       do
       {
           status = _inp(LSR) & 0x01;
       } while (status!=0x01);
       /* Repeat until bit 1 in LSR is set */
       return( (int)_inp(TXDATA));
}
```

📖 Program 15.2

```
/*       send.c                                           */
#define  TXDATA    0x3F8
#define  LSR       0x3FD
#define  LCR       0x3FB

#include <stdio.h>
#include   <conio.h>   /* included for getch           */
#include   <dos.h>

void     setup_serial(void);
void     send_character(int ch);

int      main(void)
{
int      ch;
       puts("Transmitter program. Please enter text (Cntl-D to end)");
       setup_serial();
       do
       {
          ch=getche();
          send_character(ch);
       } while (ch!=4);
       return(0);
}

void  setup_serial(void)
{
       _outp( LCR, 0x80);
       /* set up bit 7 to a 1 to set Register address bit        */
       _outp(TXDATA,0x0C);
       _outp(TXDATA+1,0x00);
       /* load TxRegister with 12, crystal frequency is 1.8432MHz   */
       _outp(LCR, 0x0A);
       /* Bit pattern loaded is 00001010b, from msb to lsb these are:   */
       /* Access TD/RD buffer, normal output, no stick bit        */
       /* even parity, parity on, 1 stop bit, 7 data bits         */
}
void  send_character(int ch)
{
char  status;
       do
       {
           status = _inp(LSR) & 0x40;
       } while (status!=0x40);
       /*repeat until Tx buffer empty ie bit 6 set*/
       _outp(TXDATA,(char) ch);
}
```

📖 Program 15.3

```
/*       receive.c                                        */
```

```
#define    TXDATA    0x3F8
#define    LSR       0x3FD
#define    LCR       0x3FB
#include   <stdio.h>
#include   <conio.h>    /* included for getch            */
#include   <dos.h>

void       setup_serial(void);
int        get_character(void);
int        main(void)
{
int        inchar;

      setup_serial();
      do
      {
         inchar=get_character();
         putchar(inchar);
      }  while (inchar!=4);
      return(0);
}
void setup_serial(void)
{
      _outp( LCR, 0x80);
      /* set up bit 7 to a 1 to set Register address bit       */
      _outp(TXDATA,0x0C);
      _outp(TXDATA+1,0x00);
      /* load TxRegister with 12, crystal frequency is 1.8432MHz   */
      _outp(LCR, 0x0A);
      /* Bit pattern loaded is 00001010b, from msb to lsb these are:   */
      /* Access TD/RD buffer, normal output, no stick bit           */
      /* even parity, parity on, 1 stop bit, 7 data bits            */
}
int    get_character(void)
{
int    status;
      do
      {
         status = _inp(LSR) & 0x01;
      } while (status!=0x01);
      /* Repeat until bit 1 in LSR is set */
      return( (int)_inp(TXDATA));
}
```

15.7 Standard Windows serial communications programs

Often an RS-232 communication program requires to be tested for the transmitted characters. In electrical circuits a digital meter is used to test points. The equivalent in RS-232 communications is the Terminal (in Windows 3.*x*) and HyperTerminal (in Windows 95/98). In Windows 95/98 it must be installed on the computer; this is either done automatically or can be added with Control Panel → Add/Remove Program → Windows Set Up → Communications (as shown in Figure 15.12). It can be seen that, in this case, the HyperTerminal program has been installed (as well as Direct Cable Connection and Dial-up Networking). The Direct Cable Connection allows two computers to be connected together using RS-232. Once connected the connection allows the computers to share resources such as their disk drives (hard disk and floppy disk), files, CD-ROMs, and so on. The Dial-up Networking program allows a computer to connect to a remote network using a modem.

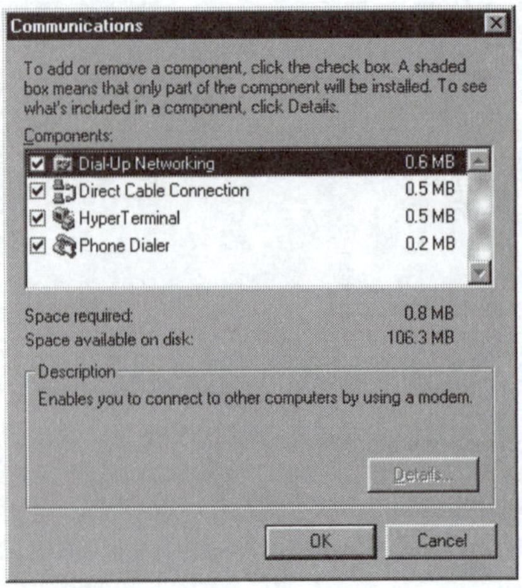

Figure 15.12   Install communications programs.

15.7.1 HyperTerminal and Terminal

The HyperTerminal (and Terminal, in Windows 3.*x*) allow the transmission and reception of RS-232 characters. In Windows 95/98 it is selected from Start → Program → Accessories → HyperTerminal, in Windows 3.*x* it is selected from the Accessories group. The left-hand side of Figure 15.13 shows an example HyperTerminal folder. This contains previously set-up connections (such as CompuServe and MCI Mail). Activating Hypertrm accesses the HyperTerminal program. After this, the user is prompted for the connection name and the associated icon (as shown in the right-hand side of Figure 15.13).

   After this the user enters the telephone number (if it connects via a modem) or the communication port. Figure 15.14 shows that, in this case, the connection is set for a direct connect to COM1. After this the program prompts the user for the communications port settings (this will be the same as the system settings). A sample window is shown on the right-hand side of Figure 15.14. Finally, the main screen is shown (as shown in Figure 15.15). The program can then be used to either send or receive characters (typically it is used to test other programs and/or communications hardware).

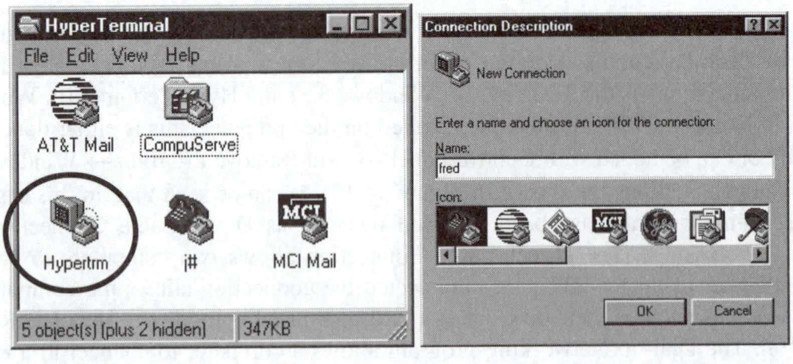

Figure 15.13   HyperTerminal folder and connection name window.

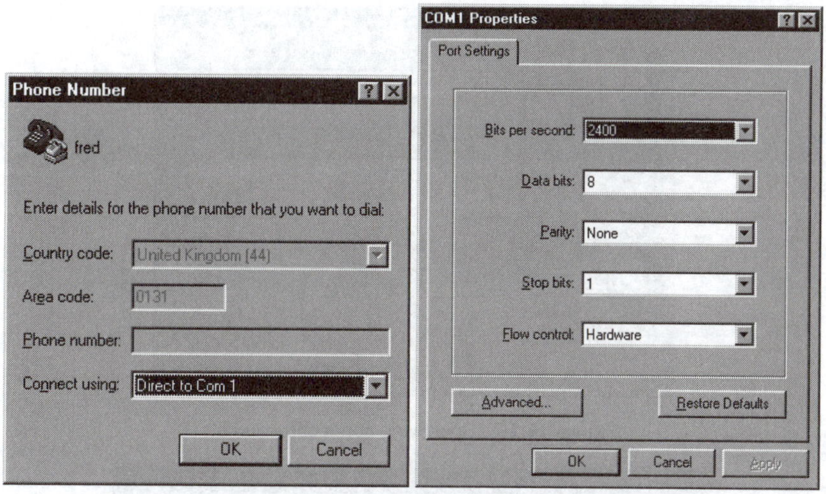

Figure 15.14   HyperTerminal set-up windows.

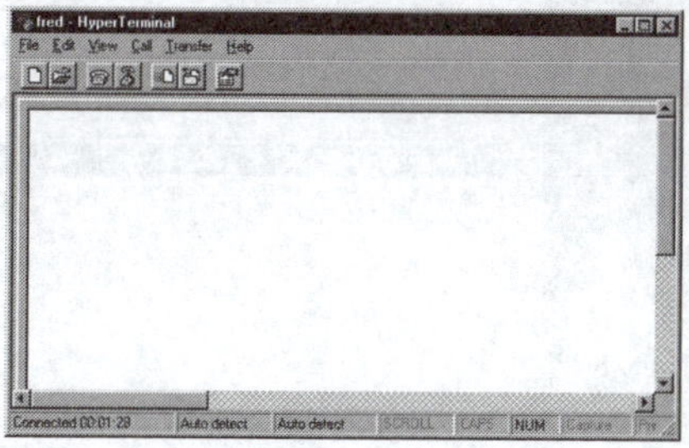

Figure 15.15   HyperTerminal.

15.7.2 Dial-up networking

The point-to-point protocol (PPP) is a set of industry standard protocols which allow a remote computer to connect to a remote network using a dial-up connection. Windows 95/98 can connect to a remote network using this protocol and the Dial-up Networking facility. It is typically used to connect to an Internet provider or to an organizational network.

To set it up in Windows 95/98 the user first selects the `Dial-Up Network` program from within `My Computer`. Next, the user selects the name of the connection, as shown in Figure 15.16.

After this the user enters the telephone number of the remote modem with the local code and country code. Figure 15.17 shows an example set-up (note that the telephone number has been set at 0131-xxx xxxx).

After the Next option is selected a connection icon is made, as shown in Figure 15.18.

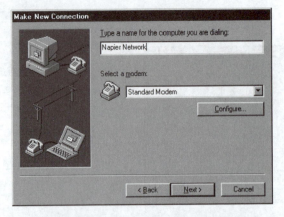

Figure 15.16   Specifying connection name.

Figure 15.17   Specifying telephone number.

Figure 15.18   Connection icon.

Next the server type is set by selecting the File → Properties option to give the window shown in Figure 15.19 (right-hand side). From this window the Server Type option is selected. This will then show the window shown in Figure 15.20. The type of server should be set to:

```
PPP; Windows 95; Windows NT
```

and the protocol to:

```
TCP/IP
```

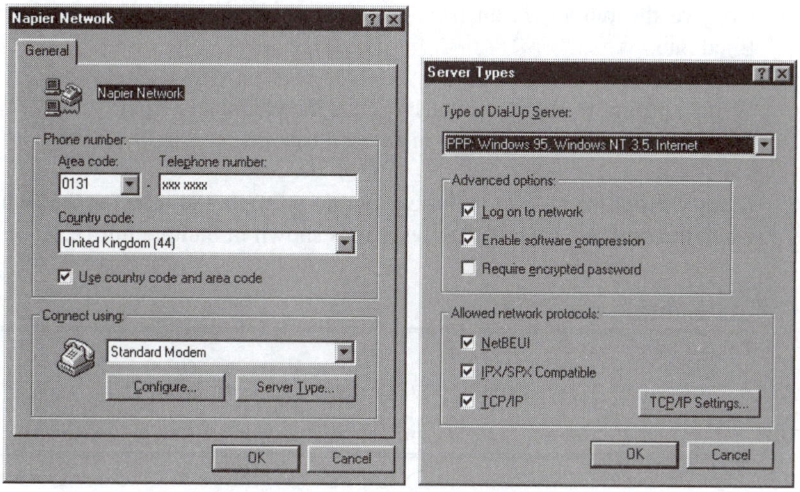

Figure 15.19 Connection settings and server types.

After these have been set the user can log into the remote network, as shown in Figures 15.20 and 15.21.

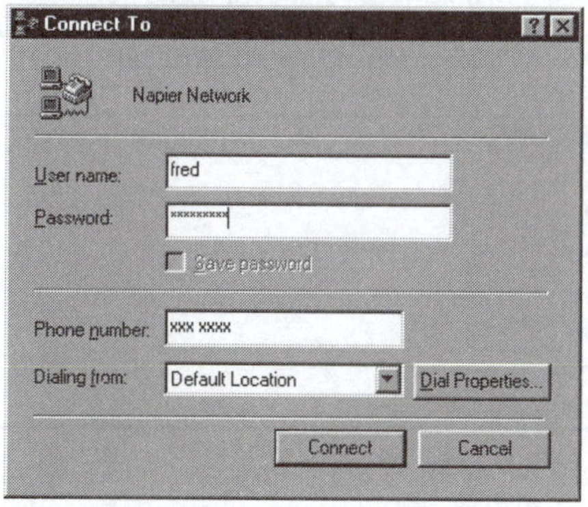

Figure 15.20 Connection setting.

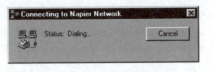

Figure 15.21   Dialing message.

15.8 Exercises

15.8.1   Write a program that continuously sends the character 'A' to the serial line. Observe the output on an oscilloscope and identify the bit pattern and the Baud rate.

15.8.2   Write a program that continuously sends the characters from 'A' to 'Z' to the serial line. Observe the output on an oscilloscope.

15.8.3   Modify Program 15.1 so that the program prompts the user for the Baud rate when the program is started. A test run is shown in Sample run 15.1.

🖥 Sample run 15.1

```
Enter baud rate required:
1   110          2   150        3   300         4   600
5   1200         6   2400       7   4800        8   9600
>> 8
RS232 transmission set to 9600 baud
```

15.8.4   Complete Table 15.2 to give the actual time to send 1000 characters for the given Baud rates. Compare these values with estimated values.

Note that approximately 10 bits are used for each character thus 960 characters/sec will be transmitted at 9600 Baud.

Table 15.2   Baud rate divisors.

Baud rate	Time to send 1000 characters (sec)
110	
300	
600	
1200	
2400	
4800	
9600	
19200	

15.8.5   Modify the setup_serial() routine so that the RS232 parameters can be passed to it. These parameters should include the comport (either COM1: or COM2:), the Baud rate, the number of data bits and the type of parity. An outline of the modified function is given in Program 15.4.

📖 Program 15.4

```
#define    COM1BASE 0x3F8
#define    COM2BASE 0x2F8
#define    COM1       0
#define    COM2       1
enum       baud_rates  {BAUD110,BAUD300,BAUD600,BAUD1200,
                          BAUD2400,BAUD4800,BAUD9600};
enum       parity      {NO_PARITY,EVEN_PARITY,ODD_PARITY};
enum       databits    {DATABITS7,DATABITS8};
#include <conio.h>
#include <dos.h>
#include <stdio.h>
void  setup_serial(int comport, int baudrate, int parity,
                    int databits);
void  send_character(int ch);
int   get_character(void);
int   main(void)
{
int   inchar,outchar;

    setup_serial(COM1,BAUD2400,EVEN_PARITY,DATABITS7);
    ::::::::::::etc.
}

void  setup_serial(int comport, int baudrate,
                    int parity, int databits)
{
int   tdreg,lcr;
    if (comport==COM1)
    {
        tdreg=COM1BASE;   lcr=COM1BASE+3;
    }
    else
    {
        tdreg=COM2BASE;   lcr=COM2BASE+3;
    }
    _outp( lcr, 0x80);
    /* set up bit 7 to a 1 to set Register address bit     */
    switch(baudrate)
    {
    case BAUD110:  _outp(tdreg,0x17);_outp(tdreg+1,0x04); break;
    case BAUD300:  _outp(tdreg,0x80);_outp(tdreg+1,0x01); break;
    case BAUD600:  _outp(tdreg,0x00);_outp(tdreg+1,0xC0); break;
    case BAUD1200: _outp(tdreg,0x00);_outp(tdreg+1,0x40);break;
    case BAUD2400: _outp(tdreg,0x00);_outp(tdreg+1,0x30);break;
    case BAUD4800: _outp(tdreg,0x00);_outp(tdreg+1,0x18);break;
    case BAUD9600: _outp(tdreg,0x00);_outp(tdreg+1,0x0C);break;
    }
        :::::::::: etc.
}
```

15.8.6 One problem with Programs 15.2 and 15.3 is that when the return key is pressed only one character is sent. The received character will be a carriage return which returns the cursor back to the start of a line and not to the next line. Modify the receiver program so that a line feed will be generated automatically when a carriage return is received. Note a carriage return is an ASCII 13 and line feed is a 10.

15.8.7 Modify the get_character() routine so that it returns an error flag if it detects an error or if there is a time out. Table 15.3 lists the error flags and the returned error value. An outline of the C code is given in Program 15.5. If a character is not received within 10 s an error message should be displayed.

📖 Program 15.5

```c
#include <stdio.h>
#include <dos.h>
#define  TXDATA    0x3F8
#define  LSR        0x3FD
#define  LCR        0x3FB
void      show_error(int ch);
int       get_character(void);
enum      RS232_errors   {PARITY_ERROR=-1, OVERRUN_ERROR=-2,
          FRAMING_ERROR=-3, BREAK_DETECTED=-4, TIME_OUT=-5};
int       main(void)
{
int       inchar;
   do
   {
      inchar=get_character();
      if (inchar<0) show_error(inchar);
      else printf("%c",inchar);
   } while (inchar!=4);
   return(0);
}
void      show_error(int ch)
{
   switch(ch)
   {
   case PARITY_ERROR: printf("Error: Parity error/n"); break;
   case OVERRUN_ERROR: printf("Error: Overrun error/n"); break;
   case FRAMING_ERROR: printf("Error: Framing error/n"); break;
   case BREAK_DETECTED: printf("Error: Break detected/n");break;
   case TIME_OUT: printf("Error: Time out/n"); break;
   }
}
int    get_character(void)
{
int    instatus;
   do
   {
      instatus = _inp(LSR) & 0x01;
      if (instatus & 0x02) return(BREAK_DETECTED);
                     :::: etc
   } while (instatus!=0x01 );
   return( (int) _inp(TXDATA) );
}
```

Table 15.3   Error returns from get_character().

Error condition	Error flag return	Notes
Parity error	−1	
Overrun error	−2	
Framing error	−3	
Break detected	−4	
Time out	−5	get_character() should time out if no characters are received with 10 seconds.

Test the routine by connecting two PCs together and set the transmitter with differing RS-232 parameters.

16 **Interrupt-driven RS-232**

16.1 Interrupt-driven RS-232

Interrupt-driven devices are efficient on processor time as they allow the processor to run a program without having to poll the devices. This allows fast devices almost instant access to the processor and stops slow devices from 'hogging' the processor. For example, a line printer tends to be slow in printing characters. If the printer only interrupted the processor when it was ready for data then the processor can do other things while the printer is printing the character. Another example can be found in serial communications. Characters sent over an RS-232 link are transmitted and received relatively slowly. In a non-interrupt-driven system the computer must poll the status register to determine if a character has been received, which is inefficient in processor time. But, if the amount of time spent polling the status register is reduced, there is a possibility of the computer missing the received character as another could be sent before the first is read from the receiver buffer. If the serial communications port was set up to interrupt the processor when a new character arrived then it is guaranteed that the processor will always process the receiver buffer.

A major disadvantage with non-interrupt-driven software is when the processor is involved in a 'heavy processing' task such as graphics or mathematical calculations. This can have the effect of reducing the amount of time that can be spent in polling and/or reading data.

16.2 Win32 programs

The problem with many C/C++ programs is that some of the application functions, such as graphics and communications, are not standardized. Thus, the graphics function to draw a circle in one development system might be different from another. Win32 overcomes this by providing a set of standard functions and is common across all development systems. These will be discussed in more detail in Chapter 29. In RS-232, the functions used include: OpenFile, ReadFile, SetCommState, SetCommMask, WaitCommEvent, WriteFile, and CloseFile. The program writen in this chapter illustrates the operation of interrupt-driven RS-232; it is likely in non-DOS-based operating systems (such as Windows NT and Windows 95/98) that the Win32 function will be used. These functions isolate the operation of the hardware from the program. They also automatically buffer the transmitted and received characters. The program in this chapter helps to illustrate the operation of the hardware.

16.3 DOS-based RS-232 program

Program 16.1 is a simple interrupt-driven DOS-based RS-232 program which is written for Turbo/Borland C/C++. If possible, connect two PCs together with a cable which swaps the TX and RX lines, as shown in Figure 15.11. Each of the computers should be able to transmit and receive concurrently. A description of this program is given in the next section. The header file associated with this program is `serial.h`.

📖 Program 16.1

```c
#include <dos.h>
#include <conio.h>
#include <stdio.h>
#include <bios.h>
#include "serial.h"
void  interrupt rs_interrupt(void);

void  setup_serial(void);
void  send_character(int ch);
int   get_character(void);
int   get_buffer(void);
void  set_vectors(void);
void  reset_vectors(void);
void  enable_interrupts(void);
void  disable_interrupts(void);

void  interrupt(*oldvect)();

char  buffer[RSBUFSIZE];

unsigned int    startbuf=0,endbuf = 0;

int   main(void)
{
int   ch, done  = FALSE;
      setup_serial();
      set_vectors(); /* set new interrupt vectors and store old ones    */
      enable_interrupts();
      printf("Terminal emulator, press [ESC] to quit\n");
      do
      {
          if (kbhit())
          {
              ch=getche();
              if (ch==ESC) break;
              send_character(ch);
          }
          /* empty RS232 buffer   */
          do
          {
              if ((ch=get_buffer()) != -1) putch(ch);
          } while (ch!=-1);
      } while (!done);
      disable_interrupts();
      reset_vectors();
      return(0);
}

void  interrupt rs_interrupt(void)
{
      disable();
      if ((inportb(IIR) & RX_MASK) == RX_ID)
      {
          buffer[endbuf] = inportb(RXR);
          endbuf++;
          if (endbuf == RSBUFSIZE) endbuf=0;
      }
      /* Set end of interrupt flag */
```

```
            outportb(ICR, EOI);
            enable();
}

void      setup_serial(void)
{
int       RS232_setting;
          RS232_setting=BAUD1200 | STOPBIT1 | NOPARITY | DATABITS7;
          bioscom(0,RS232_setting,COM1);
}

void   send_character(int ch)
{
char   status;
          do
          {
             status = inportb(LSR) & 0x40;
          } while (status!=0x40);
          /*repeat until Tx buffer empty ie bit 6 set*/
          outportb(TXDATA,(char) ch);
}

int    get_character(void)
{
int    status;
          do
          {
             status = inportb(LSR) & 0x01;
          } while (status!=0x01);
          /* Repeat until bit 1 in LSR is set */
          return( (int)inportb(TXDATA));
}

int    get_buffer(void)
{
int    ch;
          if (startbuf == endbuf) return (-1);
          ch = (int) buffer[startbuf];
          startbuf++;
          if (startbuf == RSBUFSIZE) startbuf = 0;
          return (ch);
}

void   set_vectors(void)
{
     oldvect = getvect(0x0C);
     setvect(0x0C, rs_interrupt);
}

/* Uninstall interrupt vectors before exiting the program */
void   reset_vectors(void)
{
     setvect(0x0C, oldvect);
}

void      disable_interrupts(void)
{
int       ch;
       disable();
       ch = inportb(IMR) | ~IRQ4; /* disable IRQ4 interrupt */
       outportb(IMR, ch);
       outportb(IER, 0);
       enable();
}

void      enable_interrupts(void)
{
```

```
int   ch;
      disable();
      /* initialize rs232 port   */
      ch = inportb(MCR) | MC_INT;
      outportb(MCR, ch);
      /* enable interrupts for IRQ4*/
      outportb(IER, 0x01);
      ch = inportb(IMR) & IRQ4;
      outportb(IMR, ch);
      enable();
}
```

📖 Header file 16.1: serial.h

```
#define  FALSE         0
/* RS232 set up parameters*/
#define COM1           0
#define COM2           1

#define DATABITS7      0x02
#define DATABITS8      0x03

#define STOPBIT1       0x00
#define STOPBIT2       0x04

#define NOPARITY       0x00
#define ODDPARITY      0x08
#define EVENPARITY     0x18

#define BAUD110        0x00
#define BAUD150        0x20
#define BAUD300        0x40
#define BAUD600        0x60
#define BAUD1200       0x80
#define BAUD2400       0xA0
#define BAUD4800       0xC0
#define BAUD9600       0xE0

#define ESC            0x1B       /* ASCII Escape character         */
#define RSBUFSIZE      10000      /* RS232 buffer size              */

#define COM1BASE       0x3F8      /* Base port address for COM1     */

#define TXDATA         COM1BASE        /* Transmit register         */
#define RXR            COM1BASE        /* Receive register          */
#define IER            (COM1BASE+1)    /* Interrupt Enable          */
#define IIR            (COM1BASE+2)    /* Interrupt ID              */
#define LCR            (COM1BASE+3)    /* Line control              */
#define MCR            (COM1BASE+4)    /* Line control              */
#define LSR            (COM1BASE+5)    /* Line Status               */

#define RX_ID          0x04
#define RX_MASK        0x07
#define MC_INT         0x08

/*    Addresses of the 8259 Programmable Interrupt Controller (PIC).*/

#define IMR            0x21 /* Interrupt Mask Register port         */
#define ICR            0x20 /* Interrupt Control Port               */

/*    An end of interrupt needs to be sent to the Control Port of   */
/*    the 8259 when a hardware interrupt ends.                      */
#define EOI            0x20 /* End Of Interrupt                     */

#define IRQ4           0xEF /* COM1                                 */
```

16.3.1 Description of program

The initial part of the program sets up the required RS-232 parameters. It uses `bi-oscom()` to set `COM1:` with the parameters of 1200 bps, 1 stop bit, no parity and 7 data bits.

```
void    setup_serial(void)
{
int     RS232_setting;
     RS232_setting=BAUD1200 | STOPBIT1 | NOPARITY | DATABITS7;
     bioscom(0,RS232_setting,COM1);
}
```

After the serial port has been initialized the interrupt service routine for the `IRQ4` line is set to point to a new 'user-defined' service routine. The primary serial port `COM1:` sets the `IRQ4` line active when it receives a character. The interrupt associated with `IRQ4` is 0Ch (12). The `getvect()` function gets the ISR address for this interrupt, which is then stored in the variable `oldvect` so that at the end of the program it can be restored. Finally, in the `set_vectors()` function, the interrupt assigns a new 'user-defined' ISR (in this case it is the function `rs_interrupt()`).

```
void    set_vectors(void)
{
     oldvect = getvect(0x0C);       /* store IRQ4 interrupt vector    */
     setvect(0x0C, rs_interrupt); /* set ISR to rs_interrupt()        */
}
```

At the end of the program the ISR is restored with the following code.

```
void    reset_vectors(void)
{
     setvect(0x0C, oldvect);        /* reset IRQ4 interrupt vector */
}
```

The `COM1:` port is initialized for interrupts with the code given next. The statement

```
     ch = inportb ( MCR ) | 0x08;
```

resets the RS-232 port by setting bit 3 for the modem control register (MCR) to a 1. Some RS-232 ports require this bit to be set. The interrupt enable register (IER) enables interrupts on a port. Its address is offset by 1 from the base address of the port (that is, 0x3F9 for `COM1:`). If the least significant bit of this register is set to a 1 then interrupts are enabled, else they are disabled.

To enable the `IRQ4` line on the PIC, bit 5 of the IMR (interrupt mask register) is to be set to a 0 (zero). The statement:

```
     ch = inportb(IMR) & 0xEF;
```

achieves this as it bitwise ANDs all the bits, except for bit 4, with a 1. This is because any bit which is ANDed with a 0 results in a 0. The bit mask `0xEF` has been defined with the macro `IRQ4`.

```
void    enable_interrupts(void)
{
int    ch;
     disable();
```

```
      ch = inportb(MCR) | MC_INT; /* initialize rs232 port */
      outportb(MCR, ch);
      outportb(IER, 0x01);
      ch = inportb(IMR) & IRQ4;
      outportb(IMR, ch);  /* enable interrupts for IRQ4*/

      enable();
}
```

At the end of the program the function `disable_interrupts()` sets the IER register to all 0s. This disables interrupts on the `COM1:` port. Bit 4 of the IMR is also set to a 1 which disables `IRQ4` interrupts.

```
void    disable_interrupts(void)
{
int     ch;

      disable();
      ch = inportb(IMR) | ~IRQ4; /* disable IRQ4 interrupt */
      outportb(IMR, ch);
      outportb(IER, 0);
      enable();
}
```

The ISR for the `IRQ4` function is set to `rs_interrupt()`. When it is called, the Interrupt Status Register (this is named IIR to avoid confusion with the interrupt service routine) is tested to determine if a character has been received. Its address is offset by 2 from the base address of the port (that is, 0x3FA for `COM1:`). The first 3 bits give the status of the interrupt. A `000b` indicates that there are no interrupts pending, a `100b` that data has been received, or a `111b` that an error or break has occurred. The statement `if ((in-portb(IIR) & 0x7) == 0x4)` tests if data has been received. If this statement is true then data has been received and the character is then read from the receiver buffer array with the statement `buffer[endbuf] = inportb(RXR);`. The end of the buffer variable (`endbuf`) is then incremented by 1.

   At the end of this ISR the end of interrupt flag is set in the interrupt control register with the statement `outportb(ICR, 0x20);`. The `startbuf` and `endbuf` variables are global, thus all parts of the program have access to them.

   Turbo/Borland functions `enable()` and `disable()` in `rs_interrupt()` are used to enable and disable interrupts, respectively.

```
void  interrupt rs_interrupt(void)
{
      disable();
      if ((inportb(IIR) & RX_MASK) == RX_ID)
      {
         buffer[endbuf] = inportb(RXR);
         endbuf++;
         if (endbuf == RSBUFSIZE) endbuf=0;
      }
      /* Set end of interrupt flag */
      outportb(ICR, EOI);
      enable();
}
```

The `get_buffer()` function is given next. It is called from the main program and it tests the variables `startbuf` and `endbuf`. If they are equal then it returns –1 to the `main()`. This indicates that there are no characters in the buffer. If there are characters in the buffer then the function returns, the character pointed to by the `startbuf` variable. This variable is then incremented. The difference between `startbuf` and `endbuf` gives the number of characters in the buffer. Note that when `startbuf` or `endbuf` reach the end of the buffer (`RSBUFSIZE`) they are set back to the first character, that is, element 0.

```
int    get_buffer(void)
{
int    ch;

       if (startbuf == endbuf) return (-1);
       ch = (int) buffer[startbuf];
       startbuf++;
       if (startbuf == RSBUFSIZE) startbuf = 0;
       return (ch);
}
```

The `get_character()` and `send_character()` functions are similar to those developed in Chapter 7. For completeness, these are listed next.

```
void   send_character(int ch)
{
char   status;
       do
       {
           status = inportb(LSR) & 0x40;
       } while (status!=0x40);

       /*repeat until Tx buffer empty ie bit 6 set*/
       outportb(TXDATA,(char) ch);
}

int        get_character(void)
{
int        status;

       do
       {
           status = inportb(LSR) & 0x01;
       } while (status!=0x01);
       /* Repeat until bit 1 in LSR is set */
       return( (int)inportb(TXDATA));
}
```

The `main()` function calls the initialization and the de-initialization functions. It also contains a loop, which continues until the Esc key is pressed. Within this loop, the keyboard is tested to determine if a key has been pressed. If it has then the `getche()` function is called. This function returns a key from the keyboard and displays it to the screen. Once read into the variable `ch` it is tested to determine if it is the Esc key. If it is then the program exits the loop, else it transmits the entered character using the `send_character()` function. Next the `get_buffer()` function is called. If there are no characters in the buffer then a –1 value is returned, else the character at the start of the buffer is returned and displayed to the screen using `putch()`.

```
int        main(void)
{
int        ch, done  = FALSE;

       setup_serial();
       /* set new interrupt vectors and store old ones   */
```

```
set_vectors();
enable_interrupts();
printf("Terminal emulator, press [ESC] to quit\n");
do
{
   if (kbhit())
   {
      ch=getche();
      if (ch==ESC) break;
      send_character(ch);
   }
   /* empty RS232 buffer  */
   do
   {
      if ((ch=get_buffer()) != -1) putch(ch);
   } while (ch!=-1);
} while (!done);
disable_interrupts();
reset_vectors();
return(0);
}
```

16.4 Exercises

16.4.1   Modify Program 16.1 so that a new-line character is displayed properly.

16.4.2   Prove that Program 16.1 is a true multitasking system by inserting a delay in the main loop, as shown next. The program should be able to buffer all received characters and display them to the screen when the sleep delay is over.

```
do
{
   sleep(10);
      /* go to sleep for 10 seconds, real-time system    */
      /* will  buffer all received characters            */
   if (kbhit())
   {
      ch=getche();
      if (ch==ESC) break;
      send_character(ch);
   }
   /* empty RS232 buffer  */
   do
   {
      if ((ch=get_buffer()) != -1) putch(ch);
   } while (ch!=-1);
} while (!done);
```

16.4.3   Modify Program 16.1 so that the transmitted characters are displayed in the top half of the screen and then received in the bottom half of the screen.

16.4.4   Modify Program 16.1 so that it communicates via COM2: (if the PC has one).

16.4.5   Using a loopback connection on a serial port, write a program, which sends out the complete ASCII table and checks it against the received characters.

16.4.6 Outline how a program could communicate with a serial port card with eight serial lines on it. Normally the IRQ lines for COM3 to COM8 can set to either IRQ3 to IRQ4 with jumpers on the board. Investigate typical base addresses for COM3 to COM8. Explain how multiple devices can be connected to a single interrupt line.

16.4.7 Implement a program which has a write buffer system. This should fill a buffer with characters and only send them once every 30 seconds. Modify the program so that the user can enter the delay time.

16.4.8 Write a program which sends the complete contents of a text file from one computer to another. The receiving program should wait for the sending program to send the file and the sending program should prompt the user on the name of the file. The sending program must thus identify the name of the file to the receiver. A typical protocol could be:

1. Send name of the file followed by an invalid file name character, such as:

   ```
   myfile.txt*
   ```

   which would identify that the name of the file to be sent is `myfile.txt`.

2. Send each of the characters in the file one by one. The end of the file is then identified by the end-of-file (EOF) character.

16.4.9 Modify the program in Exercise 16.4.8 so that a binary file can be sent. Note that in a binary file the EOF character can occur at a point in the file. There are two possible methods which can be used to implement this. These are:

- Implement a time-out on the characters received. When no characters have been received after, say, 1 second then it is assumed that the EOF has occurred. The receiver will then close the file.

- The sender sends some initial information on the filename, number of bytes in the file, date and time, and so on. This could be a fixed format header.

- Send a second EOF character whenever there is an EOF character which is not the EOF marker. Thus when the receiver receives two consecutive EOF characters, it simply deletes one of them. When it receives a single EOF character (within a given time) then it knows it is at the end of the file.

16.4.10 Modify the program in Exercise 16.4.10 so that a user on the receiving computer can specify the filename which is to be sent from the sending program.

Parallel Port

17

17.1 Introduction

This chapter discusses parallel communications. The Centronics printer interface transmits 8 bits of data at a time to an external device, normally a printer. Normally it uses a 25-pin D-type connector to connect to a 36-pin Centronics printer interface. In the past, it has been one of the most under used parts of a PC and was not normally used to interface to other equipment. This was because, as a standard, it could only transmit data in one direction (from the PC to the external device). Some interface devices overcame this by using four of the input handshaking lines to input data and then multiplexing using an output handshaking line to multiplex them to produce 8 output bits.

As technology has improved there has been a great need for an inexpensive, external bi-directional port to connect to devices such as tape backup drives, CD-ROMs, and so on. The Centronics interface unfortunately lacks speed (150 kB/s), has limited length of lines (2 m) and very few computer manufacturers have complied with an electrical standard.

Thus, in 1991, several manufacturers (including IBM and Texas Instruments) formed a group called NPA (National Printing Alliance). Their original objective was to develop a standard for control printers over a network. To achieve this a bi-directional standard was developed which was compatible with existing software. This standard was submitted to the IEEE and was published as the IEEE 1284-1994 Standard (as it was released in 1994 and was developed by the IEEE 1284 committee).

With this standard all parallel ports use a bi-directional link in either a compatible, nibble or byte mode. These modes are relatively slow, as the software must monitor the handshaking lines (and gives rates up to 100 kB/s). To allow high speed the EPP (Enhanced Parallel Port) and ECP (Extended Capabilities Port Protocol) modes have been developed to allow high-speed data transfer using automatic hardware handshaking. In addition to the previous three modes, EPP and ECP are being implemented on the latest I/O controllers by most of the Super I/O chip manufacturers. These modes use hardware to assist in the data transfer. For example, in EPP mode, a byte of data can be transferred to the peripheral by a simple OUT instruction and the I/O controller handles all the handshaking and data transfer to the peripheral.

17.2 Data handshaking

Figure 17.1 shows the pin connections on the PC connector. The data lines (D0–D7) output data from the PC and each of the data lines has an associated ground line (GND).

The main handshaking lines are $\overline{\text{ACK}}$, BUSY and $\overline{\text{STROBE}}$. Initially the computer places the data on the data bus, then it sets the $\overline{\text{STROBE}}$ line low to inform the external device that the data on the data bus is valid. When the external device has read the data it sets the $\overline{ACK}$ lines low to acknowledge that it has read the data. The PC then waits for the printer to set the BUSY line inactive, that is, low. Figure 17.2 shows a typical hand-shaking operation and Table 17.1 outlines the definitions of the pins.

The parallel interface can be accessed either by direct reads to and writes from the I/O memory addresses or from a program which uses the BIOS printer interrupt. This interrupt allows a program either to get the status of the printer or to write a character to it. Table 17.2 outlines the interrupt calls.

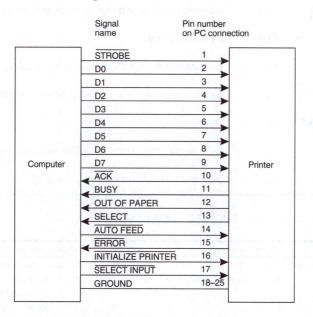

Figure 17.1 Centronics parallel interface showing pin numbers on PC connector.

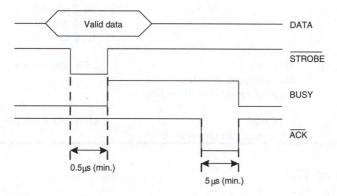

Figure 17.2 Data handshaking with the Centronics parallel printer interface.

17.2.1 BIOS printer

Program 17.1 uses the BIOS printer interrupt to test the status of the printer and outputs characters to the printer.

Table 17.1   Signal definitions.

Signal	In/out	Description
STROBE	Out	Indicates that valid data is on the data lines (active low)
AUTOFEED	Out	Instructs the printer to insert a line feed for every carriage return (active low)
SELECT INPUT	Out	Indicates to the printer that it is selected (active low)
INIT	Out	Resets the printer
ACK	In	Indicate that the last character was received (active low)
BUSY	In	Indicates that the printer is busy and thus cannot accept data
OUT OF PAPER	In	Out of paper
SELECT	In	Indicates that the printer is on-line and connected
ERROR	In	Indicates that an error exists (active low)

Table 17.2   BIOS printer interrupt.

Description	Input registers	Output registers

Initialize printer port	AH = 01h
	DX = printer number (00h–02h)
		AH = printer status
		    bit 7: not busy
		    bit 6: acknowledge
		    bit 5: out of paper
		    bit 4: selected
		    bit 3: I/O error
		    bit 2: unused
		    bit 1: unused
		    bit 0: timeout

Write character to printer	AH = 00h AL = character to write DX = printer number (00h–02h)	AH = printer status
Get printer status	AH = 02h DX = printer number (00h–02h)	AH = printer status

📖 Program 17.1

```
#include <dos.h>
#include <stdio.h>
#include <conio.h>

#define  PRINTERR -1

void   print_character(int ch);
int    init_printer(void);

int    main(void)
```

```
{
int    status,ch;

       status=init_printer();
       if (status==PRINTERR) return(1);

       do
       {
          printf("Enter character to output to printer");
          ch=getch();
          print_character(ch);
       } while (ch!=4);
       return(0);
}

int    init_printer(void)
{
union REGS inregs,outregs;

       inregs.h.ah=0x01; /* initialize printer */
       inregs.x.dx=0; /* LPT1: */
       int86(0x17,&inregs,&outregs);
       if (inregs.h.ah & 0x20)
       { puts("Out of paper"); return(PRINTERR); }
       else if (inregs.h.ah & 0x08)
       { puts("I/O error"); return(PRINTERR); }
       else if (inregs.h.ah & 0x01)
       { puts("Printer timeout"); return(PRINTERR); }

       return(0);
}

void  print_character(int ch)
{
union REGS inregs,outregs;

       inregs.h.ah=0x00; /* print character */
       inregs.x.dx=0; /* LPT1: */
       inregs.h.al=ch;

       int86(0x17,&inregs,&outregs);
}
```

17.3 I/O addressing

17.3.1 Addresses

The printer port has three I/O addresses assigned for the data, status and control ports. These addresses are normally assigned to:

Printer	Data register	Status register	Control register
LPT1	378h	379h	37ah
LPT2	278h	279h	27ah

The DOS debug program is used to display the base addresses for the serial and parallel ports by displaying the 32 memory location starting at 0040:0008. For example:

```
-d 40:00
0040:0000   F8 03 F8 02 00 00 00 00-78 03 00 00 00 00 29 02
```

The first four 16-bit addresses give the serial communications ports. In this case there are two COM ports at address 03F8h (COM1) and 02F8h (for COM2). The next four 16-bit addresses give the parallel port addressees. In this case, there are two parallel ports; one at 0378h (LPT1) and one at 0229h (LPT4).

17.3.2 Output lines

Figure 17.3 shows the bit definitions of the registers. The Data port register links to the output lines. Writing a 1 to the bit position in the port sets the output high, while a 0 sets the corresponding output line to a low. Thus to output the binary value 1010 1010b (AAh) to the parallel port data then using Borland C:

```
outportb(0x378,0xAA);   /* in Visual C this is _outp(0x378,0xAA); */
```

The output data lines are each capable of sourcing 2.6 mA and sinking 24 mA; it is thus essential that the external device does not try to pull these lines to ground.

The Control port also contains five output lines, of which the lower four bits are $\overline{\text{STROBE}}$, $\overline{\text{AUTO FEED}}$, INIT and $\overline{\text{SELECT INPUT}}$, as illustrated in Figure 17.3. These lines can be used as either control lines or as data outputs. With the data line, a 1 in the register gives an output high, while the lines in the Control port have inverted logic. Thus, a 1 to a bit in the register causes an output low.

Program 17.2 outputs the binary pattern 0101 0101b (55h) to the data lines and sets $\overline{\text{SELECT INPUT}}$ =0, INIT=1, $\overline{\text{AUTO FEED}}$ =1, and $\overline{\text{STROBE}}$ =0, the value of the Data port will be 55h and the value written to the Control port will be XXXX 1101 (where X represents don't care). The value for the control output lines must be inverted, so that the $\overline{\text{STROBE}}$ line will be set to a 1 so that it will be output as a LOW.

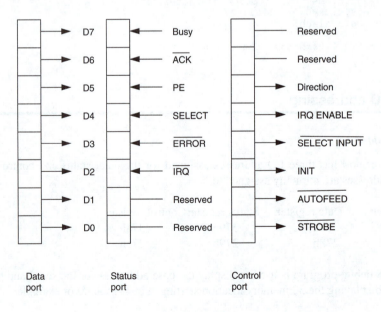

Figure 17.3   Port assignments.

📖 **Program 17.2**

```
#define DATA       0x378
#define STATUS     DATA+1
#define CONTROL    DATA+2
int   main(void)
{
int out1,out2;
      out1 = 0x55;            /* 0101 0101 */
      outportb(DATA, out1);
      out2 = 0x0D;            /* 0000 1101 */
      outportb(CONTROL, out2); /* STROBE=LOW, AUTOFEED=HIGH, etc */
      return(0);
}
```

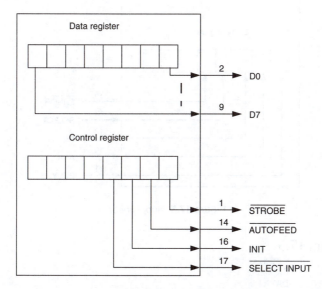

Figure 17.4 Output lines.

The setting of the output value (in this case, `out2`) looks slightly confusing, as the output is the inverse of the logical setting (that is, a 1 sets the output low). An alternative method is to exclusive-OR (EX-OR) the output value with $B which inverts the 1st, 2nd and 4th least significant bits ($\overline{\text{SELECT INPUT}}=0$, $\overline{\text{AUTOFEED}}=1$, and $\overline{\text{STROBE}}=0$), while leaving the 3rd least significant bit (INIT) untouched. Thus, the following will achieve the same as the previous program:

```
out2 = 0x06;                 /* 0000 0110 */
outportb(CONTROL, out2 ^ 0xb); /* STROBE=LOW, AUTOFEED=HIGH, etc */
```

If the 5th bit on the control register (IRQ Enable) is written as 1 then the output on this line will go from a high to a low which will cause the processor to be interrupted.

The control lines are driven by open collector drivers pulled to +5 Vdc through 4.7 kΩ resistors. Each can sink approximately 7 mA and maintain 0.8 V down-level.

17.3.3 Inputs

There are five inputs from the parallel port (BUSY, $\overline{\text{ACK}}$, PE, SELECT and $\overline{\text{ERROR}}$).

The status of these lines can be found by simply reading the upper 5 bits of the Status register, as illustrated in Figure 17.5.

Unfortunately, the BUSY line has an inverted status. Thus when a LOW is present on BUSY, the bit will actually be read as a 1. For example, Program 17.3 reads the bits from the Status register, inverts the BUSY bit and then shifts the bits three places to the right so that the 5 inputs bits are in the 5 least significant bits.

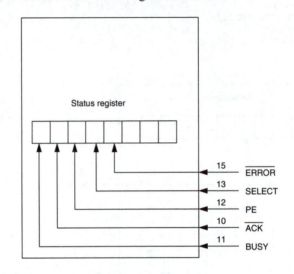

Figure 17.5 Input lines.

📖 Program 17.3

```
#include          <stdio.h>
#define DATA       0x378
#define STATUS     DATA+1
int   main(void)
{
unsigned int in1;

        in1 = inportb(STATUS); /* read from status register */

        in1 = in1 ^ 0x80        /* invert  BUSY bit */
        in1 = in1 >> 3;         /* move bits so that the inputs are the least
                                   significant bits */
        printf("Status bits are %d\n",in1);
        return(0);
}
```

17.3.4 Electrical interfacing

The output lines can be used to drive LEDs. Figure 17.6 shows an example circuit where a LOW output will cause the LED to be ON while a HIGH causes the output to be OFF. For an input an open push button causes a HIGH input on the input.

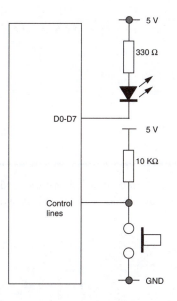

Figure 17.6   Interfacing to inputs and outputs.

17.3.5 Simple example

Program 17.4 uses a push button connected to pin 11 (BUSY). When the button is open then the input to BUSY will be a HIGH and the most significant bit in the status register will thus be a 0 (as the BUSY signal is inverted). When the button is closed then this bit will be a 1. This is tested with:

```
if (in1&0x80)==1)
```

When this condition is TRUE (that is, when the button is closed) then the output data lines (D0–D7) will flash on and off with a delay of 1 second between flashes. An output of all 1s to the data lines causes the LEDs to be off and all 0s cause the LEDs to be on.

📖 Program 17.4

```
/*    Flash LEDs on and off when the push button connected to BUSY */
/*    is closed                                                    */
#include <stdio.h>
#include <dos.h>

#define DATA      0x378
#define STATUS    DATA+1
#define CONTROL   DATA+2

int main(void)
{
int in1;
    do
    {
        in1 = inportb(STATUS);

        if (in1&0x80)==1)   /* if switch closed this is TRUE */
        {
            outportb(DATA,0x00);    /* LEDs on */
```

```
            delay(1000);
            outportb(DATA, 0xff);    /* LEDs off   */
            delay(1000);
        }
    else
        outportb(DATA,0x01); /* switch open */
    } while (!kbhit());
    return(0);
}
```

17.4   Exercises

17.4.1   Write a program that sends a 'walking-ones' code to the parallel port. The delay between changes should be 1 second. A 'walking-ones' code is as follows:

```
                    00000001
                    00000010
                    00000100
                    00001000
                      : :
                    10000000
                    00000001
                    00000010
```
and so on.

Hint: Use a do...while loop with either the shift left operators (<<) or output the values 0x01, 0x02, 0x04, 0x08, 0x10, 0x20, 0x40, 0x80, 0x01, 0x02, and so on.

17.4.2   Write separate programs which output the patterns in (a) and (b). The sequences are as follows:

(a)	(b)
00000001	10000001
00000010	01000010
00000100	00100100
00001000	00011000
00010000	00100100
00100000	01000010
01000000	10000001
10000000	01000010
01000000	00100100
00100000	00011000
00010000	00100100
::	*and so on.*
00000001	
00000010	
and so on.	

17.4.3   Write separate programs which output the following sequences:

(a)	(b)
1010 1010	1111 1111
0101 0101	0000 0000
1010 1010	1111 1111
0101 0101	0000 0000
and so on.	and so on.

(c)
```
0000 0001
0000 0011
0000 1111
0001 1111
0011 1111
0111 1111
1111 1111
0000 0001
0000 0011
0000 0111
0000 1111
0001 1111
```
and so on.

(d)
```
0000 0001
0000 0011
0000 0111
0000 1111
0001 1111
0011 1111
0111 1111
1111 1111
0111 1111
0011 1111
0001 1111
0000 1111
```
and so on.

(e)   The inverse of (d) above.

17.4.4   Binary coded decimal (BCD) is used mainly in decimal displays and is equivalent to the decimal system where a 4-bit code represents each decimal number. The first 4 bits represent the units, the next 4 the tens, and so on. Write a program that outputs to the parallel port a BCD sequence with a 1-second delay between changes. A sample BCD table is given in Table 17.3. The output should count from 0 to 99.

Hint: One possible implementation is to use two variables to represent the units and tens. These would then be used in a nested loop. The resultant output value will then be (tens << 4)+units. An outline of the loop code is given next.

```
for (tens=0;tens<10;tens++)
    for (units=0;units<10;units++)
    {

    }
```

17.4.5   Write a program which interfaces to a 7-segment display and displays an incremented value every second. Each of the segments should be driven from one of the data lines on the parallel port. For example:

Value	Segment							Hex
	A	B	C	D	E	F	G	Value
0	1	1	1	0	1	1	1	77h
1	0	0	1	0	0	1	0	12h
2	1	1	0	1	0	1	1	6Bh
:				:	:			
9	0	0	1	1	1	1	1	1Fh

Two ways of implementing this are either to determine the logic for each segment or to have a basic lookup table, such as:

```
int seg_val[8]={0x77, 0x12, 0x6B, ... 0x1F};

    val=seq_val(count % 10);
            /* mask-off the least-significant digit */
        outportb(0x378,seg_val[val]);
```

Table 17.3   BCD conversion.

Digit	BCD
00	00000000
01	00000001
02	00000010
03	00000011
04	00000100
05	00000101
06	00000110
07	00000111
08	00001000
09	00001001
10	00010000
11	00010001
.	.
.	.
.	.
97	10010111
98	10011000
99	10011001

18 Interrupt-driven Parallel Port

18.1 Introduction

The previous chapter discussed how the parallel port is used to output data. This chapter discusses how an external device can interrupt the processor. It does this by hooking onto the interrupt server routine for the interrupt that the port is attached to. Normally this interrupt routine serves as a printer interrupt (such as lack of paper, paper jam, and so on). Thus, an external device can use the interrupt service routine to transmit data to or from the PC.

18.2 Interrupts

Each parallel port is hooked to an interrupt. Normally the primary parallel port is connected to IRQ7. It is assumed in this chapter that this is the case. As with the serial port this interrupt line must be enabled by setting the appropriate bit in the interrupt mask register (IMR), which is based at address 21h. The bit for IRQ7 is the most significant bit, and it must be set to a 0 to enable the interrupt. As with the serial port, the end of interrupt signal must be acknowledged by setting the EOI signal bit of the interrupt control register (ICR) to a 1. See Section 8.5.2 for more information on these operations.

The interrupt on the parallel port is caused by the $\overline{\text{ACK}}$ line (pin 10) going from a high to a low (just as a printer would acknowledge the reception of a character). For this interrupt to be passed to the PIC then bit 4 of the control port (IRQ Enable) must be set to a 1.

18.3 Example program

Program 18.1 is a simple interrupt-driven parallel port Borland C program. The program interrupts the program each time the $\overline{\text{ACK}}$ line is pulled LOW. When this happens the output value should change corresponding to a binary count (0000 0000 to 1111 1111, and then back again). The user can stop the program by pressing any key on the keyboard. Figure 18.1 shows a sample setup with a push button connected to the $\overline{\text{ACK}}$ line and LEDs connected to the output data lines.

📖 Program 18.1

```
/* Program to sample data from the parallel port */
/* when the ACK line goes low                     */
#include <stdio.h>
#include <bios.h>
#include <conio.h>
#include <dos.h>
#define  TRUE    1
```

```
#define  FALSE     0
#define  DATA      0x378
#define  STATUS    DATA+1
#define  CONTROL   DATA+2
#define  IRQ7      0x7F  /* LPT1 interrupt */
#define  EOI       0x20  /* End of Interrupt */
#define  ICR       0x20  /* Interrupt Control Register*/
#define  IMR       0x21  /* Interrupt Mask Register*/

void  interrupt far pl_interrupt(void);
void  setup_parallel (void);
void  set_vectors(void);
void  enable_interrupts(void);
void  disable_interrupts(void);
void  reset_vectors(void);
void  interrupt far (*oldvect)();
int   int_flag = TRUE;
int   outval=0;

int main(void)
{
      set_vectors();
      setup_parallel();
      do
      {
        if (int_flag)
          {
            printf("New value sent\n");
            int_flag=FALSE;
          }
      } while (!kbhit());
      reset_vectors();
      return(0);
}

void  setup_parallel(void)
{

   outportb(CONTROL, inportb(CONTROL) | 0x10);
                 /* Set Bit 4 on control port to a 1 */
}

void interrupt far pl_interrupt(void)
{
      disable();
      outportb(DATA,outval);
      if (outval!=255) outval++; else outval=0;
      int_flag=TRUE;
      outportb(ICR,EOI);
      enable();
}

void set_vectors(void)
{
int int_mask;
      disable();                      /* disable all ints       */
      oldvect=getvect(0x0f);          /* save any old vector     */
      setvect (0x0f,pl_interrupt);  /* set up for new int serv   */
}

void  enable_interrupts(void)
{
int ch;
      disable();
      ch=inportb(IMR);
      outportb(IMR, ch & IRQ7);
      enable();
```

```
}

void  disable_interrupts(void)
{
int ch;
      disable();
      outportb(IMR, ch & ~IRQ7);
      enable();
}

void  reset_vectors(void)
{
      setvect(0x0f,oldvect);
}
```

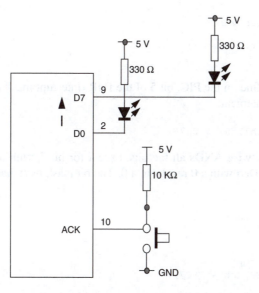

Figure 18.1   Example setup for interrupt-driven parallel port.

18.4 Program explanation

The initial part of the program enables the interrupt on the parallel port by setting bit 4 of the control register to 1.

```
void  setup_parallel(void)
{
   outportb(CONTROL, inportb(CONTROL) | 0x10); /* Set Bit 4 on control
port*/
}
```

After the serial port has been initialized the interrupt service routine for the IRQ7 line is set to point to a new 'user-defined' service routine. The primary parallel port LPT1: normally sets the IRQ7 line active when the $\overline{\text{ACK}}$ line goes from a high to a low. The interrupt associated with IRQ7 is 0Fh (15). The getvect() function gets the ISR address for this interrupt, which is then stored in the variable oldvect so that at the end of the program it can be restored. Finally, in the `set_vectors()` function, the interrupt assigns a new 'user-defined' ISR (in this case it is the function `pl_interrupt()`).

```
void set_vectors(void)
{
int int_mask;
        disable();   /* disable all ints */
        oldvect=getvect(0x0f);   /* save any old vector */
        setvect (0x0f,pl_interrupt);   /* set up for new int serv */
}
```

At the end of the program the ISR is restored with the following code.

```
void  reset_vectors(void)
{
        setvect(0x0f,oldvect);
}
```

To enable the `IRQ7` line on the PIC, bit 5 of the IMR (interrupt mask register) is to be set to a 0 (zero). The statement:

```
        ch = inportb(IMR) & 0x7F;
```

achieves this as it bitwise ANDs all the bits, except for bit 7, with a 1. This is because any bit which is ANDed with a 0 results in a 0. The bit mask `0x7F` has been defined with the macro `IRQ7`.

```
void  enable_interrupts(void)
{
int ch;
        disable();
        ch=inportb(IMR);
        outportb(IMR, ch & IRQ7);
        enable();
}
```

At the end of the program the interrupt on the parallel port is disabled by setting bit 7 of the IMR to a 1; this disables `IRQ7` interrupts.

```
void  disable_interrupts(void)
{
int ch;
        disable();
        outportb(IMR, ch & ~IRQ7);
        enable();
}
```

The ISR for the `IRQ7` function is set to `pl_interrupt()`. It outputs the value of `outval`, which is incremented each time the interrupt is called (note that there is a roll-over statement which resets the value of `outval` back to zero when its value is 255). At the end of the ISR the end of interrupt flag is set in the interrupt control register with the statement `outportb(ICR, EOI);`.

```
void interrupt far pl_interrupt(void)
{
        disable();
        outportb(DATA,outval);
        if (outval!=255) outval++; else outval=0;
```

```
        int_flag=TRUE;
        outportb(ICR,EOI);
        enable();
}
```

The `main()` function calls the initialization and the de-initialization functions. It also contains a loop which continues until any key is pressed. Within this loop the keyboard is tested to determine if a key has been pressed. The interrupt service routine sets `int_flag`. If the main routine detects that it is set it displays the message 'New value sent' and resets the flag.

```
int main(void)
{
    set_vectors();
    outportb(CONTROL, inportb(CONTROL) | 0x10);
                /* set bit 4 on control port to logic one */
    do
    {
        if (int_flag)
        {
            printf("New value sent\n");
            int_flag=FALSE;
        }
    } while (!kbhit());
    reset_vectors();
    return(0);
}
```

18.5 Exercises

18.5.1   Write a program that counts the number of pushes of a button. The display should show the value.

18.5.2   Modify the program developed in Exercise 18.5.1 so that it outputs the count value to the parallel port.

18.5.3   Modify the program developed in Exercise 17.4.5 so that the display is incremented when the user presses a button.

18.5.4   Write a program in which the user presses a button which causes the program to read from the parallel port.

18.5.5   Write a printer driver in which a string buffer is passed to it and this is then outputted to the printer. The driver should include all the correct error checking (such as out-of-paper, and so on).

19 Enhanced Parallel Port

19.1 Introduction

The Centronics parallel port only allows data to be sent from the host to a peripheral. To overcome this the IEEE have published the 1284 standard which is entitled 'Standard Signaling Method for a Bi-directional Parallel Peripheral Interface for Personal Computers'. It allows for bi-directional communication and high communication speeds, while it is backwardly compatible with existing parallel ports.

The IEEE 1284 standard defines the following modes:

- Compatibility mode (forward direction only). This mode defines the transfer of data between the PC and the printer (Centronics mode, as covered in the two previous two chapters).
- Nibble mode (reverse direction). This mode defines how 4 bits are transferred, at a time, using status lines for the input data (sometimes known as Hewlett Packard Bitronics). The Nibble mode can thus be used for bi-directional communication, with the data lines being used as outputs. To input a byte thus requires two nibble cycles.
- Byte mode (reverse direction). This mode defines how 8 bits are transferred at a time.
- Enhanced Parallel Port (EPP). This mode defines standard bi-directional communications and is used by many peripherals, such as CD-ROMs, tape drives, external hard disks, and so on.

19.2 IEEE 1284 Data Transfer Modes

In the IEEE 1284 standard, the control and status signals for nibble, byte and EPP modes have been renamed. It also classifies the modes as forward (data goes from the PC), reverse (data is sent to the PC) and bi-directional. Both the compatibility and nibble modes can be implemented with all parallel ports (as the nibble mode uses the status lines and the compatibility mode only outputs data). Some parallel ports support input and output on the data lines and thus support the byte mode. This is usually implemented by the addition of a direction bit on the control register.

19.3 Compatibility mode

The compatibility mode was discussed in Chapters 17 and 18. In this mode the program sends data to the data lines and then sets the $\overline{\text{STROBE}}$ low and then high (see Figure 19.1). This then latches the data to the printer. The operations that the program does are:

1. Data is written to the data register.
2. The program reads from the status register to test to see if the BUSY signal is low (that is, the printer is not busy).
3. If the printer is not busy then the program sets the $\overline{\text{STROBE}}$ line active low.
4. The program then makes the $\overline{\text{STROBE}}$ line high by de-asserting it.

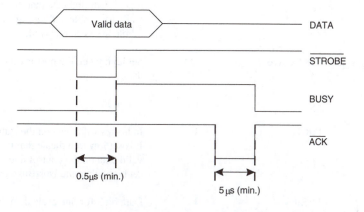

DATA

STROBE

BUSY

$\overline{\text{ACK}}$

0.5µs (min.)

5 µs (min.)

Figure 19.1   Compatibility mode transfer.

19.4 Nibble mode

This mode defines how 4 bits are transferred, at a time, using status lines for the input data (sometimes known as Hewlett Packard Bi-tronics). The Nibble mode can thus be used for bi-directional communication, with the data lines being used as outputs. To input a byte thus requires two nibble cycles.

As seen in Chapter 3 there are five inputs from the parallel port (BUSY, $\overline{\text{ACK}}$, PE, SELECT and $\overline{\text{ERROR}}$). The status of these lines can be found by simply reading the upper 5 bits of the status register. The BUSY, PE, SELECT and $\overline{\text{ERROR}}$ are normally used with $\overline{\text{ACK}}$ to interrupt the processor.

Table 19.1 defines the names of the signal in the nibble mode and Figure 19.2 shows the handshaking for this mode.

The nibble mode has the following sequence:

1. Host (PC) indicates that it is ready to receive data by setting HostBusy low.
2. The peripheral then places the first nibble on the status lines.
3. The peripheral indicates that the data is valid on the status line by setting PtrClk low.
4. The host then reads from the status lines and sets HostBusy high to indicate that it has received the nibble, but it is not yet ready for another nibble.
5. The peripheral sets PtrClk high as an acknowledgement to the host.
6. Repeat steps 1–5 for second nibble.

Table 19.1   Nibble mode signals.

Compatibility signal name	Nibble mode name	In/out	Description
$\overline{\text{STROBE}}$	$\overline{\text{STROBE}}$	O	Not used.
$\overline{\text{AUTO FEED}}$	HostBusy	O	Host nibble mode handshake signal. It is set low to indicate that the host is ready for nibble and set high when the nibble has been received.
$\overline{\text{SELECT INPUT}}$	1284Active	O	Set high when the host is transferring data.
$\overline{\text{INIT}}$	$\overline{\text{INIT}}$	O	Not used.
$\overline{\text{ACK}}$	PtrClk	I	Indicates valid data on the status lines. It is set low to indicate that there is valid data on the control lines and then set high when the HostBusy going high.
BUSY	PtrBusy	I	Data bit 3 for one cycle then data bit 7.
PE	AckDataReq	I	Data bit 2 for one cycle then data bit 6.
SELECT	Xflag	I	Data bit 1 for one cycle then data bit 5.
$\overline{\text{ERROR}}$	$\overline{\text{DataAvail}}$	I	Data bit 0 for one cycle then data bit 4.
D0–D7	D0–D7		Not used.

These operations are software intensive as the driver requires to set and read the handshaking lines. This limits transfer to about 50 KBytes/s. Its main advantage is that it works with all printer ports because it uses the standard Centronics setup and is normally used in low-speed bi-directional operations, such as ADC adapters, reading data from switches, and so on.

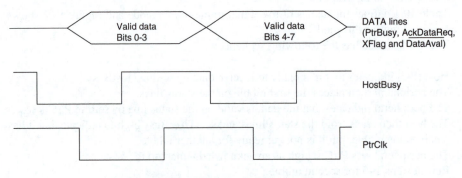

Figure 19.2   Nibble mode data transfer cycle.

19.5 Byte mode

The byte mode is often known as a bi-directional port and it uses bi-directional data lines. It has the advantage over nibble mode in that it only takes a single cycle to transfer a byte. Unfortunately, it is only compatible with newer ports. Table 19.2 defines the names of the signal in the nibble mode and Figure 19.3 shows the handshaking for this mode.

The byte mode has the following sequence:

1. The host (PC) indicates that it is ready to receive data by setting HostBusy low.
2. The peripheral then places the byte on the status lines.
3. The peripheral indicates that the data is valid on the status line by setting PtrClk low.
4. The host then reads from the data lines and sets HostBusy high to indicate that it has received the nibble, but it is not yet ready for another nibble.
5. The peripheral sets PtrClk high as an acknowledge to the host.
6. The host then acknowledges the transfer by pulsing HostClk.

Table 19.2 Byte mode signals.

Compatibility signal name	Byte mode name	In/out	Description
STROBE	HostClk	O	Used as an acknowledgement signal. It is pulsed low after each transferred byte.
AUTO FEED	HostBusy	O	It is set low to indicate that the host is ready for nibble and set high when the nibble has been received.
SELECT INPUT	1284Active	O	Set high when the host is transferring data.
INIT	INIT	O	Not used.
ACK	PtrClk	I	Indicates valid data byte. It is set low to indicate that there is valid data on the data lines and then set high when the HostBusy going high.
BUSY	PtrBusy	I	Busy status (for forward direction).
PE	AckDataReq	I	Same as DataAvail.
SELECT	Xflag	I	Not used.
ERROR	DataAvail	I	Indicates that there is reverse data available.
D0–D7	D0–D7	I/O	Input/output data lines.

19.6 EPP

The Enhanced Parallel Port (EPP) mode defines standard bi-directional communications and is used by many peripherals, such as CD-ROMs, tape drives, external hard disks, and so on.

The EPP protocol provides four types of data transfer cycles:

1. Data read and write cycles. These involve transfers between the host and the peripheral.
2. Address read and write cycle. These pass address, channel, or command and control information.

Table 19.3 defines the names of the signals in the nibble mode and Figure 19.4 shows the handshaking for this mode. The $\overline{\text{WRITE}}$ signal occurs automatically when the host writes data to the output lines.

The data write cycle has the following sequence:

1. Program executes an I/O write cycle to the base address port + 4 (EPP Data Port); see Table 19.4. Then the following occurs with hardware:
2. The $\overline{\text{WRITE}}$ line is set low which puts the data on the data bus.
3. The $\overline{\text{DATASTB}}$ is then set low.
4. The host waits for peripheral to set the $\overline{\text{WAIT}}$ line high.
5. The $\overline{\text{DATASTB}}$ and $\overline{\text{WRITE}}$ are then set high and the cycle ends.

The important parameter is that it takes just one memory mapped I/O operation to transfer data. This gives transfer rates of up to 2 million bytes per second. While it is not as fast as a peripheral transferring over the ISA, it has the advantage that the peripheral can transfer data at a rate that is determined by the peripheral (ISA has a fixed transfer rate).

19.6.1 EPP registers

Several extra ports are defined; these are the EPP address register and the EPP data register. The EPP address register has an offset of 3 bytes from the base address and the EPP data register is offset by 4 bytes. Table 19.4 defines the registers.

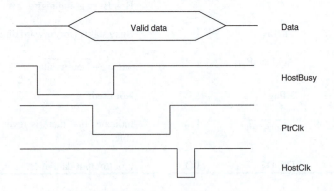

Figure 19.3 Byte mode data transfer cycle.

Table 19.3 EPP mode signals.

Compatibility signal name	EPP mode name	In/out	Description
STROBE	WRITE	O	A low for a write operation while a high indicates a read operation.
AUTO FEED	DATASTB	O	Indicates a data read or write operation.
SELECT INPUT	ADDRSTROBE	O	Indicates an address read or write operation.
INIT	RESET	O	Peripheral reset when low.
ACK	INTR	I	Peripheral sets this line low when it wishes to interrupt to the host.
BUSY	WAIT	I	When it is set low it indicates that it is valid to start a cycle, else if it is high then it is valid to end the cycle.
PE	User defined	I	Can be set by each peripheral.
SELECT	User defined	I	Can be set by each peripheral.
ERROR	User defined	I	Can be set by each peripheral.
D0–D7	AD0–AD7	I/O	Bi-directional address and data lines.

Table 19.4 EPP register definitions.

Port Name	I/O address	Read/write	Description
Data register	BASE_AD	W	
Status register	BASE_AD +1	R	
Control register	BASE_AD +2	W	
EPP address port	BASE_AD+3	R/W	Generates EPP address read or write cycle.
EPP data port	BASE_AD+4	R/W	Generates EPP data read or write cycle.

19.7 ECP

The extended capability port (ECP) protocol was proposed by Hewlett Packard and Microsoft as an advanced mode for communication with printer and scanner type peripherals. It provides a high performance bi-directional data transfer between a host and a peripheral.

ECP provides the following cycle types in both the forward and reverse directions:

- Data cycles.
- Command cycles. The command cycles are divided into 2 types: Run Length Count and Channel address.

It supports several enhancements, such as:

- Run Length Encoding (RLE). This allows for real-time compression with compression ratios of up to 64:1. RLE allows multiple occurrences of a sequence to be sent as a short code. Typically graphics images and video information have long sequences of the same data.
- Forward and reverse channel FIFOs.
- DMA.
- Programmed I/O with a standard addressing structure.
- Channel addressing. This supports many logical devices connected to a single parallel port connection. Each of the devices can have its own connection. Typically a FAX, modem, printer and CD-ROM drive could be connected to a single parallel port connection.

In the ECP protocol the signal lines have been renamed to be consistent with an ECP handshake. Table 19.5 describes these signals.

Table 19.5 ECP mode signals.

Compatibility signal name	ECP mode name	In/out	Description
STROBE	HostClk	O	Along with PeriphAck it is used to transfer data or address information in the forward direction.
AUTO FEED	HostAck	O	Gives Command/Data status in the forward direction.
SELECT INPUT	1284Active	O	Set to a high when host is a transfer mode.
INIT	ReverseRequest	O	Active low puts the channel into the reverse direction.
ACK	PeriphClk	I	Along with HostAck it is used to transfer data in the reverse direction.
BUSY	PeriphAck	I	Along with HostClk it is used to transfer data or address information in the forward direction.
PE	nAckReverse	I	Active low to acknowledge nReverseRequest.
SELECT	Xflag	I	Extensibility flag.
ERROR	nPeriphRequest	I	Active low to indicate the availability of reverse data.
D0–D7	Data[8:1]	I/O	Data lines.

Figure 19.4 shows two forward transfer cycles, a data cycle followed by a command cycle. An active HostAck signal indicates that it is a data cycle, else it is a command cycle. In the command cycle the data byte represents either:

- RLE count. If the most significant bit of the data byte is a 0 then the rest of the bytes represent the Run Length Count (0–127).
- Channel address. If the most significant bit of the data byte is a 1 then the rest of the bytes represent a channel address.

Forward Transfer phase is as follows:

1. Host sets the HostAck signal to identify if the transfer is a data or a command cycle Host puts its data on the data bus. (A).
2. Host sets HostClk low to indicate valid data. (B).
3. The peripheral sets PeriphAck high to acknowledge the transfer. (C).
4. Host sets HostClk high which clocks data into the peripheral. (D).
5. Peripheral sets PeriphAck low to indicate that it is ready for more data. (E).

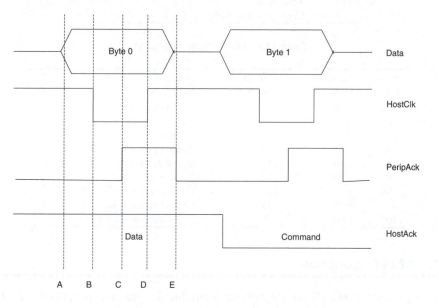

Figure 19.4 ECP forward data and Command cycle.

The reverse transfer is as follows:

1. Host identifies a reverse channel transfer by setting nReverseRequest low.
2. Peripheral acknowledges this by setting nAckReverse low.
3. Peripheral puts its data on the data bus and sets PeriphAck high.
4. Peripheral sets PeriphClk low to indicate valid data.
5. Host acknowledges this by setting HostAck high.
6. Peripheral sets PeriphClk high which clocks data into the host.
7. Host sets HostAck low to indicate that it is ready for the next transfer.

ECP registers

ECP mode has a standard set of I/O registers using a number of modes (as defined in Table 19.6). The additional registers have been added at an offset of 400h from the base port, as given in Table 19.7. Note that only extra three I/O addresses have been added. It can be seen from Figure 19.5 that the ECP driver uses the address 378h to 37Ah and 778h to 77Ah (offset from the base register by 400h). The configuration of the ECP is setup using the ECR register.

Table 19.6   ECR Register Modes.

Mode	Description
000	SPP mode
001	Bi-directional mode (Byte mode)
010	Fast Centronics
011	ECP Parallel Port mode
100	EPP Parallel Port mode (note 1)
101	(reserved)
110	Test mode
111	Configuration mode

Table 19.7   ECP register description.

Offset	Read/Write	ECP Mode	Function
000	R/W	000–001	Data register
000	R/W	011	ECP address FIFO
001	R/W	All	Status register
002	R/W	All	Control register
400	R/W	010	Parallel port data FIFO
400	R/W	011	ECP data FIFO
400	R/W	110	Test FIFO
400	R	111	Configuration register A
401	R/W	111	Configuration register B
402	R/W	All	Extended control register

19.8 1284 Negotiation

The negotiation mode allows the host to determine the attached peripherals and the method used to control them. It has been designed so that is does not affect older devices, which do not respond to the negotiation phase.

In the negotiation phase, the host places a request on the data lines, such as:

- Setup a mode.
- Request a device ID.

It then goes into a negotiation sequence and uses an extensibility byte, as defined in Table 19.8.

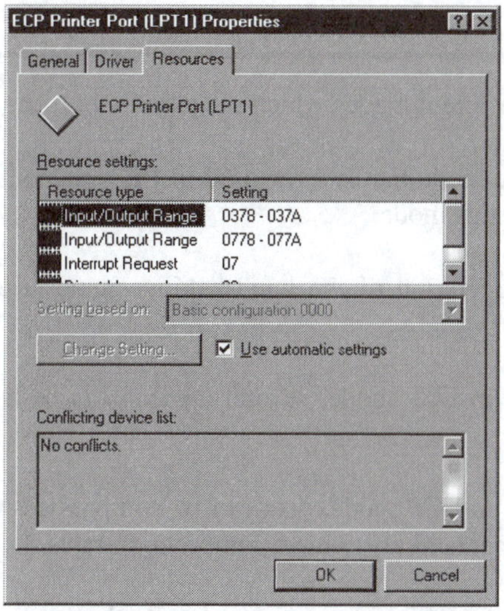

Figure 19.5   ECP register settings.

The negotiation is as follows:

1. Host puts the required extensibility byte on the data bus.
2. Host indicates the negotiation phase by setting nSelectIn high and nAutoFeed.
3. Compliant peripherals respond by setting nAck low, nError, PE high and Select high.
4. Host sets nStrobe low which clocks the extensibility byte into the peripheral.
5. Host sets nStrobe high and nAutoFeed high to acknowledge the transfer.
6. Peripheral then sets PE low, nError low and Select high.
7. Peripheral sets nAck high to signal that the negotiation sequence is over.

Table 19.8   Extensibility byte bit values.

Bit	Description	Valid bit values
8	Request Extensibility Link	1000 0000
7	Request EPP Mode	0100 0000
6	Request ECP Mode with RLE	0011 0000
5	Request ECP Mode without RLE	0001 0000
4	Reserved	0000 1000
3	Request Device ID	Return data using mode:
		Nibble Mode 0000 0100
		Byte Mode 0000 0101
		ECP Mode without RLE 0001 0100
		ECP Mode with RLE0011 0100
2	Reserved	0000 0010
1	Byte Mode	0000 0001
none	Nibble Mode	0000 0000

19.9 Exercises

19.9.1 Discuss the different modes which the parallel port can be put into.

19.9.2 Why is nibble mode hardly ever used in PC systems? Show the handshaking that occurs in this mode.

19.9.3 Discuss the operation of the handshaking signals used in the compatibility mode.

19.9.4 Explain how, in ECP mode, several devices can be connected onto the same bus.

19.9.5 Explain how, in ECP mode, data can be compressed. Give an example of the type of data that is likely to have compression rates.

19.9.6 Explain how the ECP mode uses the standard printer port addresses and extra registers.

19.9.7 Explain how the ECR register is used to setup the mode in which the ECP mode is used.

20 Modems

20.1 Introduction

Modems (MOdulator/DEModulator) connect digital equipment to a telephone line. It connects digital equipment to a speech bandwidth-limited communications channel. Typically, modems are used on telephone lines, which have a bandwidth of between 400 Hz and 3.4 kHz. If digital pulses were applied directly to these lines, they would end up severely distorted.

Modem speeds range from 300 bps to 56 kbps. A modem normally transmits about 10 bits per character (each character has 8 bits). Thus the maximum rate of characters for a high-speed modem is 2880 characters per second. This chapter contains approximately 15 000 characters and thus to transmit the text in this chapter would take approximately 5 seconds. Text, itself, is relatively fast transfer, unfortunately even compressed graphics can take some time to be transmitted. A compressed image of 20 KB (equivalent to 20 000 characters) will take nearly 6 seconds to load on the fastest modem.

The document that was used to store this chapter occupies, in an uncompressed form, 360 KB. Thus to download this document over a modem, on the fastest modem, would take:

$$\text{Time taken} = \frac{\text{Total file size}}{\text{Characters per second}} = \frac{360\,000}{2\,800} = 125\,\text{s}$$

A 14.4 kbps modem would take 250 seconds. Typically home users connect to the Internet and WWW through a modem (although increasingly ISDN is being used). The example above shows the need to compress files when transferring them over a modem. On the WWW, documents and large files are normally compressed into a ZIP file and images and video compressed in GIF and JPG.

Most modems are able to do the following:

- Automatically dial (known as Auto-dial) another modem using either touch-tone or pulse dialing.
- Automatically answer (known as Auto-answer) calls and make a connection with another modem.
- Disconnect a telephone connection when data transfer has completed or if an error occurs.
- Automatic speed negotiation between the two modems.
- Convert bits into a form suitable for the line (modulator).
- Convert received signals back into bits (demodulator).
- Transfer data reliably with the correct type of handshaking.

Figure 20.1 shows how two computers connect to each other using RS-232 converters and modems. The RS-232 converter is normally an integral part of the computer, while the modem can either be external or internal to the computer. If it is externally connected then it is normally connected by a cable with a 25-pin male D-type connector on either end.

Modems are either synchronous or asynchronous. A synchronous modem recovers the clock at the receiver. There is no need for start and stop bits in a synchronous modem. Asynchronous modems are, by far, the most popular types. Synchronous modems have a typical speed of 56 kbps whereas for asynchronous modems it is 33 kbps. A measure of the speed of the modem is the Baud rate or bps (bits per second).

There are two types of circuit available from the public telephone network: either direct dial or a permanent connection. The direct dial type is a dial-up network where the link is established in the same manner as normal voice calls with a standard telephone or some kind of an automatic dial/answer machine. They can use either touch-tones or pulses to make the connection. With private line circuits, the subscriber has a permanent dedicated communication link.

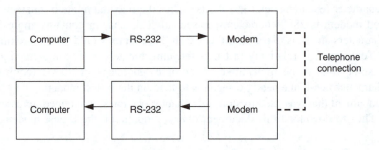

Figure 20.1   Data transfer using modems.

20.2 RS-232 communications

The communication between the modem and the computer is via RS-232. RS-232 uses asynchronous communication which has a start–stop data format. Each character is transmitted one at a time with a delay between characters. This delay is called the inactive time and is set at a logic level high as shown in Figure 20.2. The transmitter sends a start bit to inform the receiver that a character is to be sent in the following bit transmission. This start bit is always a '0'. Next 5, 6 or 7 data bits are sent as a 7-bit ASCII character, followed by a parity bit and finally either 1, 1.5 or 2 stop bits. The rate of transmission is set by the timing of a single bit. Both the transmitter and receiver need to be set to the same bit-time interval. An internal clock on both of them sets this interval. They only have to be roughly synchronized and approximately at the same rate as data is transmitted in relatively short bursts.

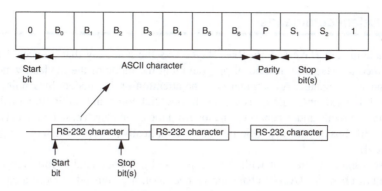

Figure 20.2 RS-232 frame format.

20.2.1 Bit rate and the Baud rate

One of the main parameters for specifying RS-232 communications is the rate at which data is transmitted and received. It is important that the transmitter and receiver operate at roughly the same speed.

For asynchronous transmission the start and stop bits are added in addition to the seven ASCII character bits and the parity. Thus a total of 10 bits are required to transmit a single character. With 2 stop bits, a total of 11 bits are required. If 10 characters are sent every second and if 11 bits are used for each character, then the transmission rate is 110 bits per second (bps). The fastest modem thus has a character transmission rate of 2880 characters per second.

In addition to the bit rate, another term used to describe the transmission speed is the Baud rate. The bit rate refers to the actual rate at which bits are transmitted, whereas the Baud rate is to the rate at which signalling elements, used to represent bits, are transmitted. Since one signalling element encodes 1 bit, the two rates are then identical. Only in modems does the bit rate differ from the Baud rate.

20.3 Modem standards

The CCITT (now known as the ITU) has defined standards which relate to RS-232 and modem communications. Each uses a V. number to define their type. Modems tend to state all the standards they comply with. An example FAX/modem has the following compatibility:

- V.32bis (14.4 Kbps).   V.32   (9.6 Kbps).
- V.22bis (2.4 Kbps).   V.22   (1.2 Kbps).
- Bell 212A (1.2 Kbps).   Bell 103 (300 bps).
- V.17   (14.4 bps FAX).   V.29   (9.6 Kbps FAX).
- V.27ter (4.8 Kbps FAX).   V.21   (300 bps FAX - secondary channel).
- V.42bis (data compression).   V.42   (error correction).
- MNP5   (data compression).   MNP2–4 (error correction).

A 28.8 Kbps modem also supports the V.34 standard.

20.4 Modem commands

Most modems are Hayes compatible. Hayes was the company that pioneered modems and defined the standard method of programming the mode of the modem, which is the AT command language. A computer gets the attention of the modem by sending an 'AT' command. For example, 'ATDT' is the touch-tone dial command. Initially, a modem is in the command mode and accepts commands from the computer. These commands are sent at either 300 bps or 1200 bps (the modem automatically detects which of the speeds is being used).

Most commands are sent with the AT prefix. Each command is followed by a carriage return character (ASCII character 13 decimal); a command without a carriage return character is ignored (after a given time delay). More than one command can be placed on a single line and, if necessary, spaces can be entered to improve readability. Commands can be sent in either upper or lower case. Table 20.1 lists some AT commands. The complete set is defined in Appendix D.

Table 20.1   Example AT modem commands.

Command	Description
ATDT54321	Automatically phone number 54321 using touch-tone dialling. Within the number definition, a comma (,) represents a pause and a W waits for a second dial tone and an @ waits for a 5 second silence.
ATPT12345	Automatically phone number 12345 using pulse dialling.
AT S0=2	Automatically answer a call. The S0 register contains the number of rings the modem uses before it answers the call. In this case there will be two rings before it is answered. If S0 is zero then the modem will not answer a call.
ATH	Hang up telephone line connection.
+++	Disconnect line and return to on-line command mode.
AT A	Manually answer call.
AT E0	Commands are not echoed (AT E1 causes commands to be echoed). See Table 20.2.
AT L0	Low speaker volume (AT L1 gives medium volume and AT L2 gives high speaker volume).
AT M0	Internal speaker off (AT M1 gives internal speaker on until carrier detected, AT M2 gives the speaker always on, AT M3 gives speaker on until carrier detect and while dialling).
AT Q0	Modem sends responses (AT Q1 does not send responses). See Table 20.2.
AT V0	Modem sends numeric responses (AT V1 sends word responses). See Table 20.2.

The modem can enter one of two states: the normal state and the command state. In the normal state the modem transmits and/or receives characters from the computer. In the command state, characters sent to the modem are interpreted as commands. Once a command is interpreted, the modem goes into the normal mode. Any characters sent to the modem are then sent along the line. To interrupt the modem so that it goes back into command mode, three consecutive '+' characters are sent, i.e. '+++'.

After the modem has received an AT command it responds with a return code. Some return codes are given in Table 20.2 (a complete set is defined in Appendix D). For example, if a modem calls another which is busy then the return code is 7. A modem dialling another modem returns the codes for OK (when the ATDT command is received), CONNECT (when it connects to the remote modem) and CONNECT 1200 (when it detects the speed of the remote modem). Note that the return code from the modem can be suppressed by sending the AT command 'ATQ1'. The AT code for it to return the code is 'ATQ0'; normally this is the default condition.

Table 20.2   Example return codes.

Message	Digit	Description
OK	0	Command executed without errors
CONNECT	1	A connection has been made
RING	2	An incoming call has been detected
NO CARRIER	3	No carrier detected
ERROR	4	Invalid command
CONNECT 1200	5	Connected to a 1200 bps modem
NO DIALTONE	6	Dial-tone not detected
BUSY	7	Remote line is busy
NO ANSWER	8	No answer from remote line
CONNECT 600	9	Connected to a 600 bps modem
CONNECT 2400	10	Connected to a 2400 bps modem
CONNECT 4800	11	Connected to a 4800 bps modem
CONNECT 9600	13	Connected to a 9600 bps modem
CONNECT 14400	15	Connected to a 14 400 bps modem
CONNECT 19200	61	Connected to a 19 200 bps modem
CONNECT 28800	65	Connected to a 28 800 bps modem
CONNECT 1200/75	48	Connected to a 1200/75 bps modem

Figure 20.3 shows an example session when connecting one modem to another. Initially the modem is set up to receive commands from the computer. When the computer is ready to make a connection it sends the command 'ATDH 54321' which makes a connection with telephone number 54321 using tone dialling. The modem then replies with an OK response (a 0 value) and the modem tries to make a connection with the remote modem. If it cannot make the connection it sends back a response of NO CARRIER (3), BUSY (7), NO DIALTONE (6) or NO ANSWER (8). If it does connect to the remote modem then it returns a connect response, such as CONNECT 9600 (13). The data can then be transmitted between the modem at the assigned rate (in this case 9600 bps). When the modem wants to end the connection it gets the modem's attention by sending it three '+' characters ('+++'). The modem will then wait for a command from the host computer. In this case the command is hang-up the connection (ATH). The modem will then return an OK response when it has successfully cleared the connection.

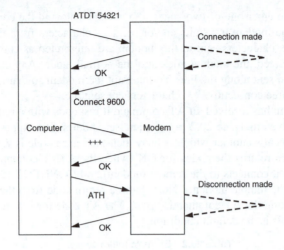

Figure 20.3   Commands and responses when making a connection.

The modem contains various status registers called the S-registers which store modem settings. Table 20.3 lists some of these registers (Appendix D gives a complete listing). The S0 register sets the number of rings that must occur before the modem answers an incoming call. If it is set to zero (0) then the modem will not answer incoming calls. The S1 register stores the number of incoming rings when the modem is rung. S2 stores the escape character, normally this is set to the '+' character and the S3 register stores the character which defines the end of a command, normally the CR character (13 decimal).

Table 20.3   Modem registers.

Register	Function	Range [typical default]
S0	Rings to auto-answer	0–255 rings [0 rings]
S1	Ring counter	0–255 rings [0 rings]
S2	Escape character	[43]
S3	Carriage return character	[13]
S6	Wait time for dial-tone	2–255 s [2 s]
S7	Wait time for carrier	1–255 s [50 s]
S8	Pause time for automatic dialling	0–255 [2 s]

20.5 Modem setups

Figure 20.4 shows a sample window from the Microsoft Windows Terminal program (in both Microsoft Windows 3.*x* and Windows 95/98). It shows the Modem commands window. In this case, it can be seen that when the modem dials a number the prefix to the number dialled is 'ATDT'. The hang-up command sequence is '+++ ATH'. A sample dialling window is shown in Figure 20.5. In this case the number dialled is 9,123456789. A ',' character represents a delay. The actual delay is determined by the value in the S8 register (see Table 20.3). Typically, this value is about 2 seconds.

On many private switched telephone exchanges a 9 must prefix the number if an out-

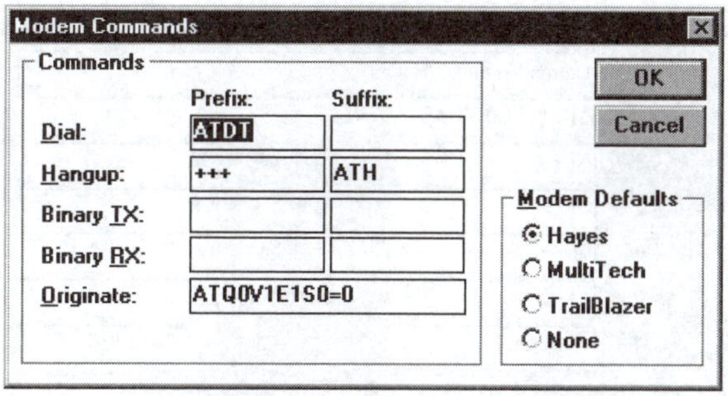

Figure 20.4 Modem commands.

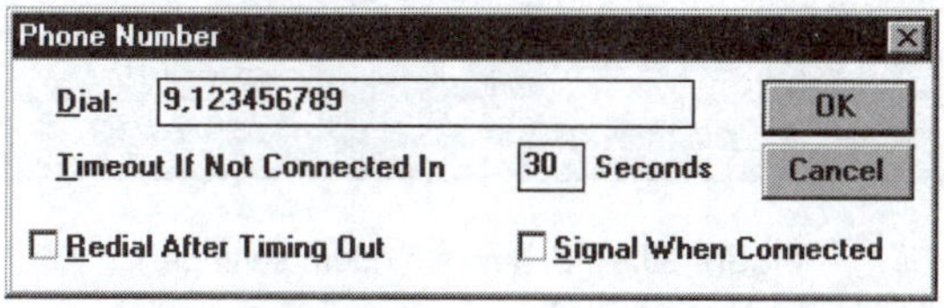

Figure 20.5 Dialling a remote modem.

side line is required. A delay is normally required after the 9 prefix before dialling the actual number. To modify the delay to 5 seconds, dial the number 9 0112432 and wait 30 seconds for the carrier, then the following command line can be used:

```
ATDT 9,0112432 S8=5 S7=30
```

It can be seen in Figure 20.4 that a prefix and a suffix are sent to the modem. This is to ensure there is a time delay between the transmission prefix and the suffix string. For example, when the modem is to hang-up the connection, the '+++' is sent followed by a delay then the 'ATH'.

In Figure 20.4 there is an option called <u>O</u>riginate. This string is sent initially to the modem to set it up. In this case the string is 'ATQ0V1E1S0=0'. The Q0 part informs the modem to return a send status code. The V1 part informs the modem that the return code message is to be displayed rather than just the value of the return code; for example, it displays CONNECT 1200 rather than the code 5 (V0 displays the status code). The E1 part enables the command message echo (E0 disables it).

Figure 20.6 shows the modem setup windows for CompuServe access. The string in this case is:

```
ATS0=0 Q0 V1 &C1&D2^M
```

as previously seen, S0 stops the modem from auto-answering. V1 causes the modem to respond with word responses. &C1 and &D2 set up the hardware signals for the modem. Finally ^M represent Cntrl-M which defines the carriage return character.

The modem reset command in this case is AT &F. This resets the modem and restores the factor default settings.

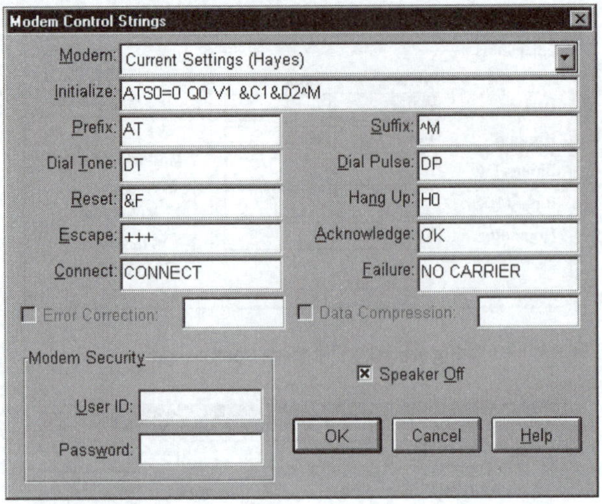

Modem Control Strings   ☒

    <u>M</u>odem: Current Settings (Hayes)   ▼

    <u>I</u>nitialize: ATS0=0 Q0 V1 &C1&D2^M

    <u>P</u>refix: AT   S<u>u</u>ffix: ^M

    Dial <u>T</u>one: DT   <u>D</u>ial Pulse: DP

    <u>R</u>eset: &F   Ha<u>n</u>g Up: H0

    <u>E</u>scape: +++   Acknowledge: OK

    <u>C</u>onnect: CONNECT   <u>F</u>ailure: NO CARRIER

    ☐ Error Correction: [   ]   ☐ Data Compression: [   ]

    Modem Security   ☒ Speaker O<u>f</u>f

    <u>U</u>ser ID: [   ]

    Pass<u>w</u>ord: [   ]   [OK] [Cancel] [Help]

Figure 20.6   Example modem settings.

20.6 Modem indicators

Most external modems have status indicators to inform the user of the current status of a connection. Typically, the indicator lights are:

- AA – is ON when the modem is ready to receive calls automatically. It flashes when a call is incoming. If it is OFF then it will not receive incoming calls. Note that if the S0 register is loaded with any other value than 0 then the modem goes into auto-answer mode. The value stored in the S0 register determines the number of rings before the modem answers.
- CD – is ON when the modem detects the remote modem's carrier, else it is OFF.
- OH – is ON when the modem is on-hook, else it is OFF.
- RD – flashes when the modem is receiving data or is getting a command from the computer.
- SD – flashes when the modem is sending data.
- TR – shows that the DTR line is active (i.e. the computer is ready to transmit or receive data).
- MR – shows that the modem is powered-up.

20.7 Profile viewing

The settings of the modem can be determined by using the AT command with &V. An example is shown next (which uses the program in Chapter 15). In this it can be seen that the settings include: B0 (CCITT 300 or 1200 bps for call establishment), E1 (enable command echo), L2 (medium volume), M1 (speaker is off when receiving), Q1 (prohibits modem from sending result codes to the DTE) T (set tone dial) and V1 (display result codes in a verbose form). It can be seen that the S0 register is set to 3 which means that the modem waits for three rings before it will automatically answer the call.

```
+++
AT &V
ACTIVE PROFILE:
B0 E1 L2 M1 Q1 T V1 X4 Y0 &C1 &D0 &E0 &G2 &L0 &M0 &O0 &P1 &R0 &S0 &X0 &Y1
%A000 %C1 %D1 %E1 %P0 %S0 \A3 \C0 \E0 \G0 \J0 \K5 \N6 \Q0 \T000 \V1 \X0
S00:003 S01:000 S06:004 S07:045 S08:002 S09:006 S10:014 S11:085 S12:050
S16:1FH S18:000 S21:20H S22:F6H S23:B2H S25:005 S26:001 S27:60H S28:00H
STORED PROFILE 0:
B0 E1 L2 M1 Q0 T V1 X4 Y0 &C1 &D2 &E0 &G2 &L0 &M0 &O0 &P1 &R0 &S0 &X0
%A000 %C1 %D1 %E1 %P0 %S0 \A3 \C0 \E0 \G0 \J0 \K5 \N6 \Q3 \T000 \V1 \X0
S00:000 S16:1FH S21:30H S22:F6H S23:89H S25:005 S26:001 S27:000 S28:000
STORED PROFILE 1:
B0 E0 L2 M1 Q1 T V1 X4 Y0 &C1 &D0 &E0 &G2 &L0 &M0 &O0 &P1 &R0 &S0 &X0
%A000 %C1 %D1 %E1 %P0 %S0 \A3 \C0 \E0 \G0 \J0 \K5 \N6 \Q0 \T000 \V1 \X0
S00:003 S16:1FH S21:20H S22:F6H S23:95H S25:005 S26:001 S27:096 S28:000
TELEPHONE NUMBERS:
&Z0=
&Z1=
&Z2=
&Z3=
```

20.8 Test modes

There are several modes associated with the modems.

20.8.1 Local analogue loopback (&T1)

In the analogue loopback test the modem connects the transmit and receive lines on its output, as illustrated in Figure 20.7. This causes all transmitted characters to be received. It is initiated with the &T1 mode. For example:

```
AT &Q0          <Enter>
AT S18=0 &T1 <Enter>
CONNECT 9600
Help the bridge is on fire <Enter>
+++
OK
AT &T0
OK
```

The initial command AT &Q0 sets the modem into an asynchronous mode (stop–start). Next the AT S18=0 &T1 command sets the timer test time to zero (which disables any limit to the time of the test) and &T1 sets an analogue test. The modem responds with the message CONNECT 9600. Then the user enters the text Help .... on fire followed by an <Enter>. Next the user enters three + characters which puts the modem back into command mode. Finally the user enters AT &T0 which disables the current test.

If a time-limited test is required then the S18 register is loaded with the number of seconds that the test should last. For example, a test that last 2 minutes will be set-up with:

```
AT S18=120 &T1
```

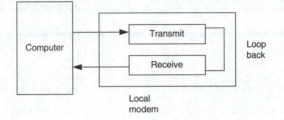

Figure 20.7 Analogue loopback with self-test.

20.8.2 Local analog loopback with self-test (&T8)

In the analog loopback test with self-test the modem connects the transmit and receive lines on its output and then automatically sends a test message which is then automatically received, as illustrated in Figure 20.8. The local error checker then counts the number of errors and displays a value when the test is complete. For example, the following test has found two errors:

```
AT  &Q0       <Enter>
AT  S18=0 &T8 <Enter>
+++
AT  &T0
002
OK
```

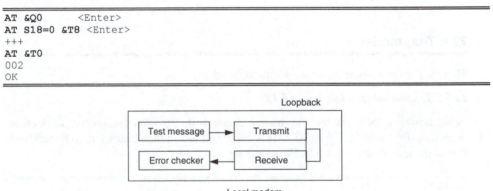

Figure 20.8 Analog loopback with self-test.

20.8.3 Remote digital loopback (&T6)

The remote digital loopback checks the local computer to modem connection, the local modem, the telephone line and the remote modem. The remote modem performs a loopback at the connection from the remote modem to its attached computer. Figure 20.9 illustrates the test setup. An example session is:

```
AT  &Q0          <Enter>
AT  S18=0 &T6 <Enter>
CONNECT 9600
Help the bridge is on fire <Enter>
+++
OK
AT  &T0
OK
```

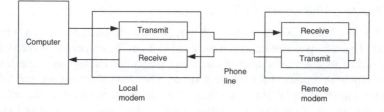

Figure 20.9   Remote digital loopback test.

20.8.4 Remote digital loopback with self-test (&T7)

The remote digital loopback with self-test checks the local computer to modem connection, the local modem, the telephone line and the remote modem. The remote modem performs a loopback at the connection from the remote modem to its attached computer. The local modem sends a test message and checks the received messages for errors. On completion of the test, the local modem transmits the number of errors. Figure 20.10 illustrates the test setup. An example session is:

```
AT &Q0        <Enter>
AT S18=0 &T7 <Enter>
+++
AT &T0
004
OK
```

or with a test of 60 seconds then the user does not have to send the break sequence:

```
AT &Q0         <Enter>
AT S18=60 &T7 <Enter>
004
OK
```

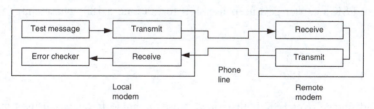
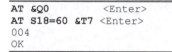

Figure 20.10   Remote digital loopback test with self-test.

20.9 Digital modulation

Digital modulation changes the characteristic of a carrier according to binary information. With a sine wave carrier the amplitude, frequency or phase can be varied. Figure 20.11 illustrates the three basic types: amplitude-shift keying (ASK), frequency-shift keying (FSK) and phase-shift keying (PSK).

20.9.1 Frequency-shift keying (FSK)

FSK, in the most basic case, represents a 1 (a mark) by one frequency and a 0 (a space) by another. These frequencies lie within the bandwidth of the transmission channel.

On a V.21, 300 bps, full-duplex modem the originator modem uses the frequency 980 Hz to represent a mark and 1180 Hz a space. The answering modem transmits with 1650 Hz for a mark and 1850 Hz for a space. The four frequencies allow the caller originator and the answering modem to communicate at the same time; that is full-duplex communication.

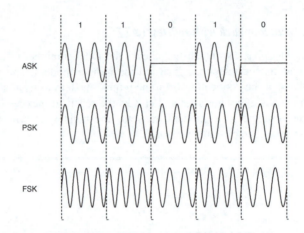

Figure 20.11   Waveforms for ASK, PSK and FSK.

FSK modems are inefficient in their use of bandwidth, with the result that the maximum data rate over normal telephone lines is 1800 bps. Typically, for rates over 1200 bps, other modulation schemes are used.

20.9.2 Phase-shift keying (PSK)

In coherent PSK a carrier gets no phase shift for a 0 and a 180° phase shift for a 1, as given next:

$$0 \quad \Rightarrow \quad 0°$$
$$1 \quad \Rightarrow \quad 180°$$

Its main advantage over FSK is that since it uses a single frequency it uses much less bandwidth. It is thus less affected by noise. It has an advantage over ASK because its information is not contained in the amplitude of the carrier, thus again it is less affected by noise.

20.9.3 M-ary modulation

With *M*-ary modulation a change in amplitude, phase or frequency represents one of *M* possible signals. It is possible to have *M*-ary FSK, *M*-ary PSK and *M*-ary ASK modulation schemes. This is where the Baud rate differs from the bit rate. The bit rate is the true measure of the rate of the line, whereas the Baud rate only indicates the signalling element rate, which might be a half or a quarter of the bit rate.

For four-phase differential phase-shift keying (DPSK) the bits are grouped into two and each group is assigned a certain phase shift. For 2 bits there are four combinations: a 00 is coded as 0°, 01 coded as 90°, and so on:

$$00 \Rightarrow \quad 0° \qquad 01 \Rightarrow \quad 90°$$
$$11 \Rightarrow \quad 180° \qquad 10 \Rightarrow \quad 270°$$

It is also possible to change a mixture of amplitude, phase or frequency. *M*-ary amplitude-phase keying (APK) varies both the amplitude and phase of a carrier to represent *M* possible bit patterns.

M-ary quadrature amplitude modulation (QAM) changes the amplitude and phase of the carrier. 16-QAM uses four amplitudes and four phase shifts, allowing it to code 4 bits at a time. In this case, the baud rate will be a quarter of the bit rate.

Typical technologies for modems are:

FSK	– used up to 1200 bps
Four-phase DPSK	– used at 2400 bps
Eight-phase DPSK	– used at 4800 bps
16-QAM	– used at 9600 bps

20.10 Typical modems

Most modern modems operate with V.22bis (2400 bps), V.32 (9600 bps), V.32bis (14 400 bps); some standards are outlined in Table 20.4. The V.32 and V.32bis modems can be enhanced with echo cancellation. They also typically have built-in compression using either the V.42bis standard or MNP level 5.

Table 20.4 Example AT modem commands.

ITU recommendation	Bit rate (bps)	Modulation
V.21	300	FSK
V.22	1 200	PSK
V.22bis	2 400	ASK/PSK
V.27ter	4 800	PSK
V.29	9 600	PSK
V.32	9 600	ASK/PSK
V.32bis	14 400	ASK/PSK
V.34	28 800	ASK/PSK

20.10.1   *V.42bis and MNP compression*

There are two main standards used in modems for compression. The V.42bis standard is defined by the ITU and the MNP (Microcom Networking Protocol) has been developed by a company named Microcom. Most modems will try to compress using V.42bis but if this fails they try MNP level 5. V.42bis uses the Lempel-Ziv algorithm which builds dictionaries of code words for recurring characters in the data stream. These code words normally take up fewer bits than the uncoded bits. V.42bis is associated with the V.42 standard which covers error correction.

20.10.2   V.22bis modems

V.22bis modems allow transmission at up to 2400 bps. It uses four amplitudes and four phases. Figure 20.12 shows the 16 combinations of phase and amplitude for a V.22bis modem. It can be seen that there are 12 different phase shifts and four different amplitudes. Each transmission is known as a symbol, thus each transmitted symbol contains 4 bits. The transmission rate for a symbol is 600 symbols per second (or 600 Baud), thus the bit rate will be 2 400 bps.

Trellis coding tries to ensure that consecutive symbols differ as much as possible.

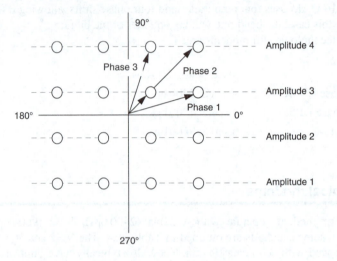

Figure 20.12   Phase and amplitude coding for V.32.

20.10.3   V.32 modems

V.32 modems include echo cancellation which allows signals to be transmitted in both directions at the same time. Previous modems used different frequencies to transmit on different channels. Echo cancellation uses DSP (digital signal processing) to subtract the sending signal from the received signal.

V.32 modems use trellis encoding to enhance error detection and correction. They encode 32 signaling combinations of amplitude and phase. Each of the symbols contains 4 data bits and a single trellis bit. The basic symbol rate is 2400 bps, thus the actual data rate will be 9600 bps. A V.32bis modem uses 7 bits per symbol, thus the data rate will be 14 400 bps (2400×6).

20.11 Fax transmission

Facsimile (fax) transmission involves the transmission of images over a telephone line using a modem. A standalone fax consists of:

- An image scanner.
- A graphics printer (normally a thermal printer).
- A transmission/reception modem.

The fax scans an A4 image with 1142 scan lines (3.85 lines per millimetre) and 1728 pixels per line. The EIA and ITU originally produced the RS-328 standard for the transmission of analogue voltage levels to represent different brightness. The ITU recommendations are known as Group I and Group II standards. The Group III standard defines the transmission of faxes using digital transmission with 1142×1728 pixels of black or white. Group IV is an extension to Group III but allows different grey scales and also colour (unfortunately it requires a high bit rate).

An A4 scan would consist of 1 976 832 (1142×1728) scanned elements. If each element is scanned for black and white, then, at 9600 bps, it would take over 205 s to transmit. Using RLE coding can drastically reduce this transmission time.

20.11.1   Modified Huffman coding

Group III compression uses modified Huffman code to compress the transmitted bit stream. It uses a table of codes in which the most frequent run lengths are coded with a short code. Typically, documents contain long runs of white or black. A compression ratio of over 10:1 is easily achievable (thus a single-page document can be sent in under 20 s, for a 9600 bps transmission rate). Table 20.5 shows some code runs of white and Table 20.6 shows some codes for runs of black. The transmitted code always starts on white code. The codes range from 0 to 63. Values from 64 to 2560 use two codes. The first gives the multiple of 64 followed by the normally coded remainder.

For example, if the data to be encoded is:

16 white, 4 black, 16 white, 2 black, 63 white, 10 black, 63 white

it would be coded as:

```
101010  011 101010  11 00110100  0000100  00110100
```

This would take 40 bits to transmit the coding, whereas it would take 304 bits (i.e. 16 + 4 + 16 + 2 + 128 + 10 + 128). This results in a compression ratio of 7.6:1.

Table 20.5   White run length coding.

Run length	Coding	Run length	Coding	Run length	Coding
0	00110101	1	000111	2	0111
3	1000	4	1011	5	1100
6	1110	7	1111	8	10011
9	10100	10	00111	11	01000
12	001000	13	000011	14	110100
15	110101	16	101010	17	101011
18	0100111	19	0001100	61	00110010
62	00110011	63	00110100	EOL	00000000001

Table 20.6 Black run length coding.

Run length	Coding	Run length	Coding	Run length	Coding
0	0000110111	1	010	2	11
3	10	4	011	5	0011
6	0010	7	00011	8	000101
9	000100	10	0000100	11	0000101
12	0000111	13	00000100	14	00000111
15	000011000	16	0000010111	17	0000011000
18	0000001000	19	00001100111	61	000001011010
62	0000001100110	63	000001100111	EOL	00000000001

20.12 Exercises

20.12.1 Which modem indicators would be ON when a modem has made a connection and is receiving data? Which indicators would be flashing?

20.12.2 Which modem indicators would be ON when a modem has made a connection and is sending data? Which indicators will be flashing?

20.12.3 Investigate the complete set of AT commands by referring to a modem manual or reference book.

20.12.4 Investigate the complete set of S-registers by referring to a modem manual or reference book.

20.12.5 Determine the location of modems on a network or in a works building. If possible, determine the type of data being transferred and its speed.

20.12.6 Connect a modem to a computer and dial a remote modem.

20.12.7 If possible connect two modems together and, using a program such as `Terminal`, transfer text from one computer to the another.

21 VB (Introduction)

21.1 Introduction

Microsoft Windows has become the *de facto* PC operating system. All versions up to, and including, Windows 3.*x* used DOS as the core operating system. New versions of Windows, such as Windows NT and Windows 95/98 do not use DOS and can thus use the full capabilities of memory and of the processor. The most popular programming languages for Windows programming are:

- Microsoft Visual Basic.
- Microsoft Visual C++ and Borland C++.
- Delphi (which is available from Borland).

Visual Basic has the advantage over the other languages in that it is relatively easy to use and to program with, although the development packages which are used with C++ and Delphi make constructing the user interface relatively easy. Visual Basic Version 4 is shown in Figure 21.1 and Version 5 is shown in Figure 21.2.

21.2 Event-driven programming

Traditional methods of programming involve writing a program which flows from one part to the next in a linear manner. Most programs are designed using a top-down structured design, where the task is split into a number of submodules and these are then called when they are required. This means that it is relatively difficult to interrupt the operation of a certain part of a program to do another activity, such as updating the graphics display.

Visual Basic in general is:

- **Object-oriented**. Where the program is designed around a number of ready-made objects.
- **Event-driven**. Where the execution of a program is not predefined and its execution is triggered by events, such as a mouse click, a keyboard press, and so on.
- **Designed from the user interface outwards**. The program is typically designed by first developing the user interface and then coded to respond to events within the interface.

21.3 Visual Basic files

A listing of a sample directory which contains Visual Basic files is:

```
DDE        BAS          143  12/01/96   0:00  DDE.BAS
DDE        VBP          338  12/01/96   0:00  DDE.VBP
EXECUTE    FRM        2,431  12/01/96   0:00  EXECUTE.FRM
MAIN       FRM       18,468  12/01/96   0:00  MAIN.FRM
```

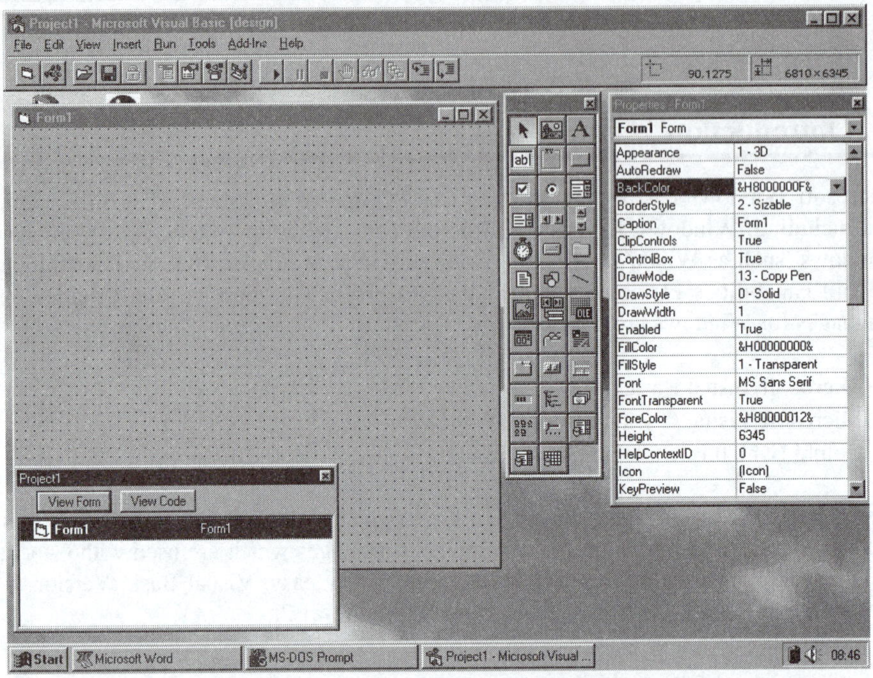

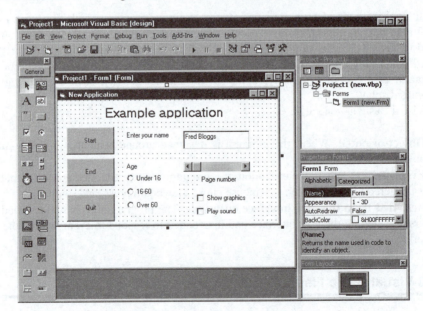

Figure 21.1   Visual Basic 4 user interface.

Figure 21.2   Visual Basic 5 user interface.

The files are:

- **Project files**. Projects bind together the individual elements of a Visual Basic program. Initially the user creates a project file for the program and this is loaded whenever the program is being developed. The default extension for a project is either .MAK or .VBP. Projects make it easier to control the various elements of a program.
- **Modules**. Code that is attached to a form is accessible from anywhere on that form, but a program may have more than one form. It will sometimes be necessary to have program code that can be reached from any form, and in this case the code would be written on a module. Modules disappear from view when the program runs – only forms have an on-screen existence. There may be several modules in one program, and each is saved as a separate file. These are marked by a .BAS extension.
- **Forms**. A form forms the anchor for all parts of a Visual Basic program. Initially it is a blank window and the user pastes controls onto it to create the required user interface. Code is then associated with events on the form, such as responding to a button press or a slider control, although some control elements do not have associated code. A program can have one or more forms, each of which displays and handles data in different ways. To make forms shareable with other programs then each is saved separately with a .FRM extension.
- **Icons**. These are, normally, small graphics images and have a .ICO extension.
- **Graphics images**. These are normally either BMP (bitmapped) files or WMF (windows metafile) files with the .BMP and .WMF extensions, respectively.
- **Others**. Other files also exist, such as VBX which is Visual Basic eXtension.

21.4 Other terms

Visual Basic uses a number of other terms to describe design procedure, these are:

- **Controls**. The VB interface contains a window with control objects which are pasted onto a form. These controls can be simple text, menus, spreadsheet grids, radio buttons, and so on. Each control has a set of properties that defines their operation, such as their colour, the font size, whether it can be resized, and so on. Some controls, such as command buttons and menus, and normally have code attached to them, but simple controls, such as text and a graphics image can exist on a form with no associated code.
- **Procedures**. As with C and Pascal, Visual Basic uses procedures, or subroutines, to structure code. Most of these are associated with an event that occurs from a control and some will be stand-alone with no associated event.

21.5 Main screen

Figure 21.3 shows the Visual Basic 5 desktop (Visual Basic 4 is similar, but the windows float on the display). It contains a menu form, controls, main form, project windows and properties window.

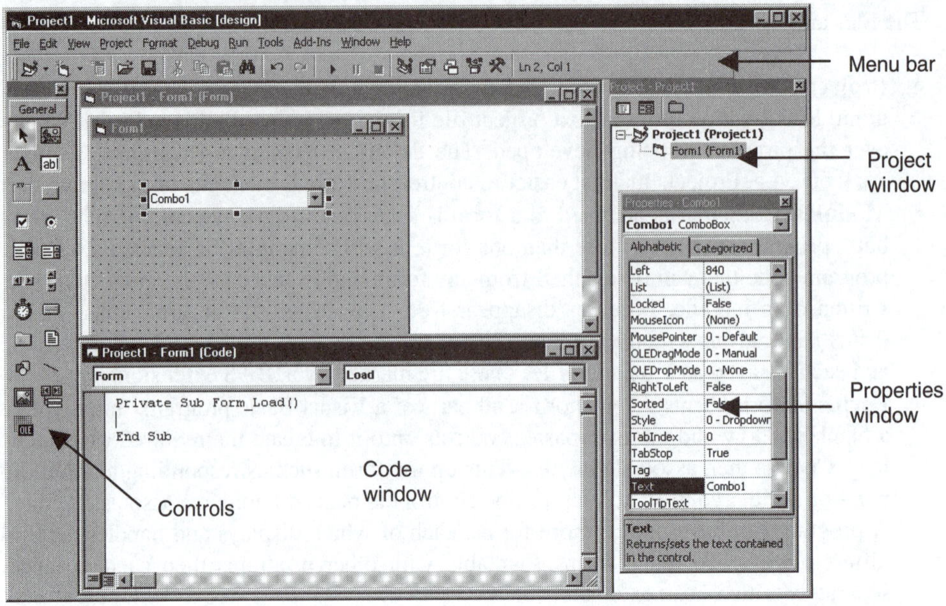

Figure 21.3   Visual Basic 5 desktop.

21.5.1 Menu bar and toolbar

The menu bar and tool bar appear in a single, floating window, as shown in Figure 21.4. The menu bar contains options for file manipulation (File), editing (Edit), viewing (View), running (Run), testing the program (Debug), manipulating windows (Window) and getting help (Help). These can either be selected with the mouse, using the function key F10 and then selecting the option with the arrow keys and pressing return or use the hot key. The hot key is Alt and the underlined character, thus Alt-F selects the File menu, Alt-E selects the Edit menu, and so on.

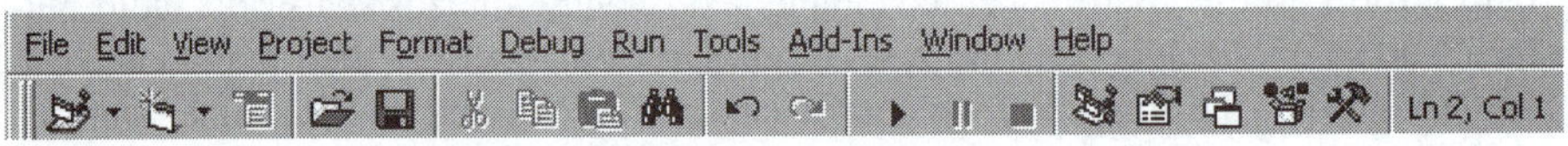

Figure 21.4   Visual Basic 5 menu bar and toolbar.

The toolbar contains shortcut buttons for commonly used menu items. To the right of the toolbar there are two indicators; these display the position and size of a selected form or control. This area of the window is also used in the compilation phase to display the status of the compilation.

The toolbar buttons are:

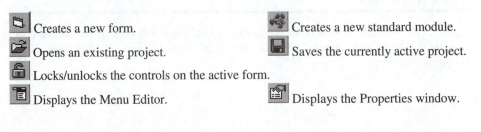

Creates a new form.

Opens an existing project.

Locks/unlocks the controls on the active form.

Displays the Menu Editor.

Creates a new standard module.

Saves the currently active project.

Displays the Properties window.

Displays the Object Browser.   Displays the Project window.

Runs the application.   Pauses program execution.

Stops execution.   Toggles a breakpoint (breakpoint on or off).

Displays the value of the current selection in the Code window.

Displays the structure of active calls.

Traces through each line of code and steps into procedures.

Executes code one procedure or statement at a time in the Code window.

21.5.2 Project window

The Project window displays all the forms and modules used in the currently active project; an example is shown in Figure 21.5. A new project is opened by selecting New Project from the File menu, whereas to open an existing project the Open Project option is selected from the File menu, else the open existing project option is selected from the toolbar.

Only one project can be opened at a time, but that project can have any number of forms. In the Project window the user can do the following:

• Open a Form window for an existing form by selecting the form name and clicking the View Form button.
• Open the Code window for an existing form by selecting the module name and clicking the View Code button.
• Remove a file from a project by selecting the file in the Project window, and then from the File menu choose Remove File.

Figure 21.5   Visual Basic Project window.

21.5.3 Form window

The Form window, as shown in Figure 21.6, creates application windows and dialog boxes. A new form is created by selecting the Form from the Insert menu (or use the toolbar shortcut) and an existing form is opened by selecting the form name and then clicking the View Form button. An existing form is added to a project by selecting the Add File command from the File menu. Any associated code on a form can be viewed by clicking on the View Code button.

Each form has a Control-menu box, Minimize and Maximize buttons, and a title bar, and can be moved and resized. Table 21.1 shows the key combinations in the Form window.

21.5.4 Toolbox

The Toolbox contains the icons for controls. These are standard Visual Basic controls and any custom controls and insertable objects, as shown in Figure 21.7. The Toolbox is displayed, if it is not already in view, with Toolbox from the View menu and it is closed by double-clicking the Control-menu box.

Figure 21.6 shows some typical controls, these include:

- 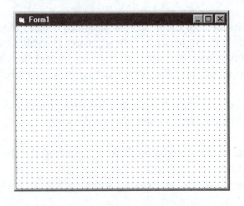 **Pointer**. The pointer does not draw any control objects and is used to resize or move a control once it has been drawn on a form. When a control is added to a form then the pointer is automatically selected.

Figure 21.6   Visual Basic Form window.

Table 21.1   Key combinations in Form window.

Key combination	Operation
alpha	Enter a value in the Properties window for the selected property.
CLICK–Drag	Select multiple controls.
CTRL+CLICK+ DRAG	Add or remove controls from the current selection.
CTRL–C	Copy the selected controls to the Clipboard.
CTRL–CLICK	Add or remove a control from the selection.
CTRL–E	Display the Menu Editor.
CTRL–J	Bring control to front (if controls are overlapping).
CTRL–K	Send control to back (if controls are overlapping).
CTRL–V	Paste from Clipboard onto the form.
CTRL–X	Cut the selected controls to the Clipboard.

CTRL–Z	Undo a deleted control.
DEL	Delete the selected controls.
F4	Display the Properties window.
F7	Open the Code window for the selected object.
SHIFT–CTRL– *alpha*	Select a property in the Property list of the Properties window.
SHIFT–TAB	Cycle backward through controls in tab order.
TAB	Cycle forward through controls in tab order.

- **PictureBox**. Displays graphical images (BMP, WMF, ICO or DIB).

- **Label**. Used to display text that cannot be changed by the user.

- **TextBox**. Allows the user to either enter or change text.

- **Frame**. Used to create a graphical or functional grouping for controls. These are grouped by first drawing a Frame around them and then drawing controls inside the frame.

- **CommandButton**. Used to carry out a command.

- **CheckBox**. Used to create a check box, where the user can indicate if something is on or off (true or false), or, when there is more than one option, a multiple of choices.

- **OptionButton**. Used to display a number of options but only one can be chosen (this differs from the check box which only allows one option to be chosen).

- **ComboBox**. Used to give a combination of a list box and test box, where the user can either enter a value in a text box or choose an item from the list.

- **ListBox**. Used to display a list of items and the user is allowed to choose one of them. This list has a scroll button to allow the list to be scrolled.

- **HScrollBar** (horizontal scroll bar). Used to scroll up and down through a list of text or graphical information. It can also be used to indicate the current position on a scale or by the user to indicate a given strength of value.

- **VScrollBar** (vertical scroll bar). Used to scroll across a list of text or graphical information. It can also be used to indicate the current position on a scale or by the user to indicate a given strength of value.

- **Timer**. Used to generate timed events at given intervals.

- 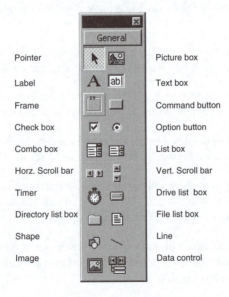 **DriveListBox**. Used to display currently connected disk drives.

- **DirListBox** (directory list box). Used to display directories and paths.

- **FileListBox**. Used to display a list of files.

- **Shape**. Used to draw shapes, such as rectangles, rounded rectangles, squares, rounded squares, ovals or circles.

- **Line**. Used to draw a variety of line styles on your form at design time (transparent, solid, dash, dot, dash-dot and dash-dot-dot).

- **Image**. Used to display a graphical image, such as a bitmap (BMP), icon (ICO), or metafile (WMF). These images can only be used to display an image and do not have the same control functions as PictureBox.

- **Data**. Used to provide access to data in databases.

- **OLE Controller**. Used to link and embed objects from other applications (such as Word Documents, Excell Spreadsheets, and so on). OLE stands for Object Linking and Embedding.

- **CommonDialog**. Used to create customized dialog boxes for operations such as printing files, opening and saving files, setting fonts and help functions.

- **DBList** (data-bound list box). Used as an enhanced ListBox which can be customized to display a list of items from which the user can choose one. The list can be scrolled if it has more items than can be displayed at one time.

Figure 21.7   Toolbox controls.

- **DBCombo** (data-bound combo box). Used as an enhanced Combo which can be customized to display a list of items from which the user can choose one. Used to draw a combination list box and text box. The user can either choose an item from the list or enter a value in the text box.

- **DBGrid** (data-bound grid). Use to display a series of rows and columns and to manipulate the data in its cells. DBGrid is a custom control and has increased data access capabilities that the standard Grid does not have.

21.6 Properties window

The Properties window displays the properties of the currently selected form, control or menu. They allow selection of properties such as the colour, font type and size of text, background colour of a form, type of graphic image, and so on.

First, the item to be changed is selected and then the Properties option is chosen from the View menu, else the function key F4. The Property window is closed with a double-click on the Control-menu box.

The Properties window contains two main parts, these are:

- **The Object box**. This is found below the title bar and identifies the currently selected form or control on the form. In Figure 21.8 the command button has an associated Properties window. The Object box in this case is:

```
Command1 CommandButton
```

Where CommandButton is the control item and is named Command1, other control items are PictureBox, Label, TextBox, Frame, CheckBox, OptionButton, ComboBox, ListBox, HScrollBar, VScrollBar, Timer, DriveListBox, FileListBox, Shape, Line, Image, Data, and so on. Click the arrow at the right side of the Object box (▼) to get a list of the controls on the current form. From the list, choose the current form or a control on the form whose properties you want to change. An example is given in Figure 21.9. In this case there are three command buttons (named Command1, Command2 and Command3) on the form, a drive list box (named Drive1), and so on. The list also contains the currently active form (in this case it is named Form1). Names of controls are assigned consecutively, so that the first command button is Command1, the second is Command2, and so on.

- **The Properties list**. This is a two-column list that shows all properties associated with a form or control and their current settings. To change a properties setting then the properties name is selected and the new setting is either typed or selected from a menu. Properties that have predefined settings (such as a range of colours or true/false) display the list of settings by clicking the down arrow at the right of the settings box (▼), or they can be cycled through by double-clicking the property name in the left column. In Figure 21.8 the Default property has either a True or False setting. A ▪▪▪ in the second column indicates either the selection of colours from a palette or the selection of picture files through a dialog box.

Figure 21.10 shows an example of colour settings. Note that the colour appears as a 24-bit hexadecimal equivalent (with 8 other attribute bits), but when the user selects the colour it appears as a colour in the palette. This 24-bit colour is made up from red, green and blue (RGB). The standard format is:

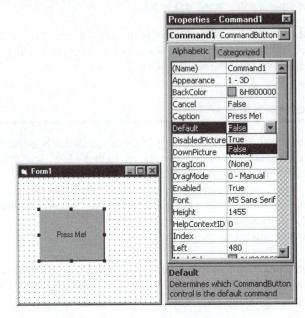

Figure 21.8 Properties window.

&H*aa*BBGGRR&

The RR hexadecimal digits give the strength of the red from 00h to FFh (0 to 255), the GG hexadecimal digits give the strength of green and BB gives the strength of blue. Thus for the colour strength parts: white is &H*aa*FFFFFF&, black is &H*aa*000000&, red is &H*aa*0000FF&, yellow is &H*aa*00FFFF& and cyan is &H*aa*FFFF00&.

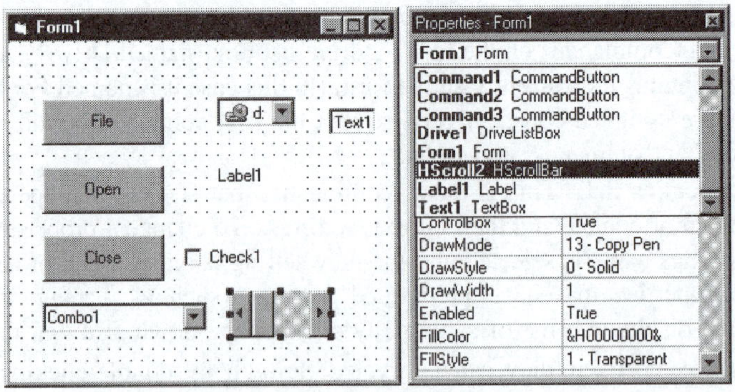

Figure 21.9 Example list of controls.

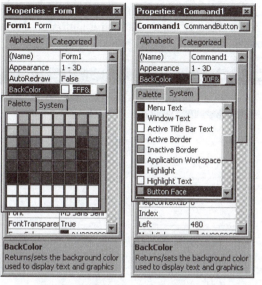

Figure 21.10 Setting colour.

21.7 Controls and Event

Controls have associated properties and a number of events. These events can be viewed by double-clicking on a control or by selecting View Code from Project window. Figure 21.11 shows an example of the Code windows. It can be seen that the object can be selected by pulling down the menu of the left-hand side and the associated events in the right-hand menu. The associated code with that object and event is shown in the window below these menu options.

```
Project1 - Form1 (Code)

Command1                          Click

(General)
Command1
Command2
Form
Label1                    Then
Label2                 :1.Text) + 32
Text1
Text2

              Text2.Text = "INVALID"
        End If

    End Sub

    Private Sub Command2_Click()
```

Figure 21.11 Selecting objects.

Figure 21.12 shows an example of the events that occur when the control is a command button (in this case the object is Command1). It can be seen that the associated events are: Click, DragDrop, DragOver, GotFocus, KeyDown, KeyPress and KeyUp.

Each of these can have associated sections of code to react to the event. For example, the Click event occurs when the user clicks the mouse button on the command button and KeyDown is initiated when a key has been pressed down.

```
Project1 - Form1 (Code)                              _ □ ×
Command1                    ▼   Click                          ▼
(General)
Command1
Command2
Form
Label1                          Then
Label2                          1.Text) + 32
Text1
Text2
            Text2.Text = "INVALID"
        End If

    End Sub

    Private Sub Command2_Click()
```

Figure 21.12   Events when the control is a command button.

21.8 Programming language

Visual Basic has an excellent on-line manual in which the user can either search for the occurrence of keywords (with <u>H</u>elp → <u>S</u>earch For Help On) or view the contents of the manual (<u>H</u>elp → <u>C</u>ontents). The left-hand side of Figure 21.13 shows an example manual page after the user has selected <u>H</u>elp → <u>C</u>ontents → Visual Basic Help, and then leads to other parts of the manual, such as the Programming Language and Contents Topic. The left-hand side of Figure 21.13 shows an example of the Contents list.

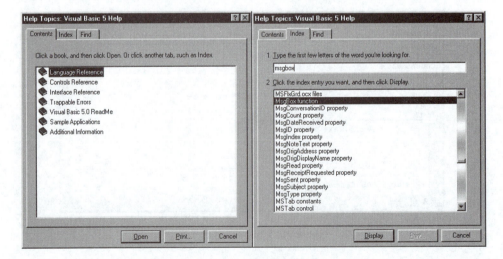

Figure 21.13   Visual Basic 5 on-line help manual.

21.9 Entering a program

To start the development of a program with no controls on a form then the user selects the View Code from the Project window. Figure 21.14 shows the basic steps (a right mouse click on the form allows the user to select from a quick menu). After the View Code is selected then the user selects the Form object from within the form code window. Next the code is entered between the `Private Sub Load_From()` and `End Sub`. This code is automatically run when the form is run, as the procedure is Load. The code in Figure 21.14 simply displays the text 'Hello to you' to a window.

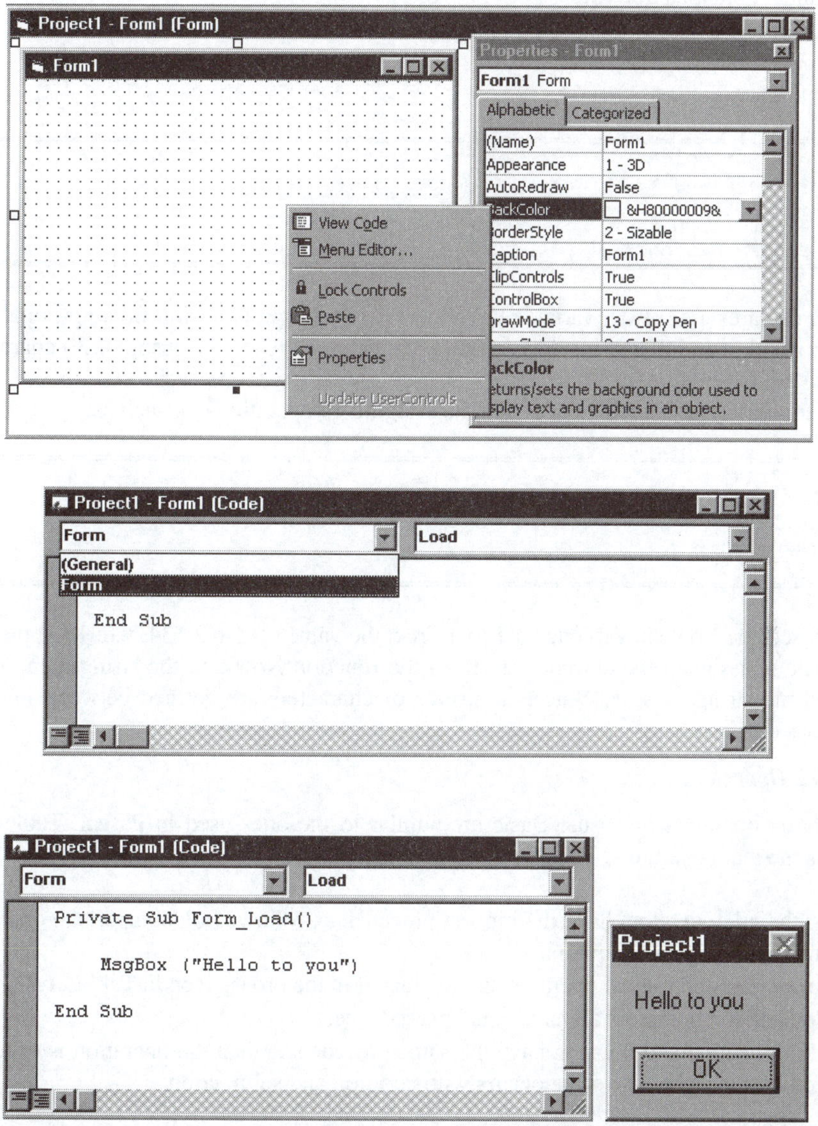

Figure 21.14 Steps taken to enter code.

21.10 Language reference

This section contains a condensed reference to Visual Basic.

21.10.1 Data types and declaring variables

A variable is declared with the Dim keyword. These variables must conform to the following:

- Begin with an alphabet character.
- Cannot contain a dot, '$', '!', '@', '#' or '%'.
- Must be less than 256 characters long.

Examples are:

```
Dim val1 As Boolean
Dim x, y As Single
Dim i As Integer
Dim newdate As Date
Dim name As String * 30
```

which declares a Boolean variable called val1, two single precision floating-point variables: x and y, an integer named i, a date named newdate and a string of 30 characters named name.

Variables are assigned values with the assignment operation (=), such as:

```
val1 = True
x = 2.134
y = 10.1
newdate = Now
name = "Fred"
```

which sets the Boolean variable val1 to a True, the value of x to 2.134, y to 10.1, the date newdate is assigned the current date from the function Now and the string name is assigned the string "Fred". Note that strings of characters are defined between inverted commas ("").

21.10.2 Operators

The basic operators in Visual Basic are similar to the ones used in Pascal. Table 21.2 shows the main operators. The operator precedence is:

- Arithmetic operators have the highest precedence, followed by comparison operators and finally logical operators.
- Arithmetic and logical operators are evaluated in the order given in Table 21.2.
- Comparison operators all have equal precedence.
- Multiplication and division have the same precedence, then the operation is executed from left to right. The same occurs with addition and subtraction.

Table 21.2   Operator precedence.

Arithmetic	Comparison	Logical
Exponentiation (^)	Equality (=)	Not
Negation (–)	Inequality (<>)	And
Multiplication and division (*,/)	Less than (<)	Or
Integer division (\)	Greater than (>)	Xor
Modulo arithmetic (Mod)	Less than or Equal to (<=)	
Addition and subtraction (+,–)	Greater than or Equal to (>=)	
String concatenation (&)		

21.10.3 Data types

As with C and Pascal, Visual Basic has a whole range of data types. Their range depends on their format (such as characters, integers and floating-point values) and the number of bytes used to store them. Table 21.3 outlines the main predefined (intrinsic) data types. A user-defined type can also be defined using the Type statement.

The main data types are:

Boolean   Boolean variables can either be True or False and are stored as 16-bit (2-byte) values. Boolean variables are displayed as either True or False. Like C, when other numeric data types are converted to Boolean values then a 0 becomes False and any other values become True. When Boolean values are converted to other data types, False becomes 0 while True becomes –1.

Byte   Byte variables are stored as unsigned, 8-bit (1-byte) ranging from 0 to 255.

Table 21.3   Data types.

Data type	Storage size	Range
Boolean	2 bytes	True or False
Byte	1 byte	0 to 255
Integer	2 bytes	–32 768 to 32 767
Long (long integer)	4 bytes	–2 147 483 648 to 2 147 483 647
Single (single-precision floating-point)	4 bytes	$\pm3.402823\times10^{38}$ to $\pm1.401298\times10^{-45}$
Double (double-precision floating-point)	8 bytes	$\pm4.94065645841247\times10^{-324}$ to $\pm1.79769313486232\times10^{308}$
Currency (scaled integer)	8 bytes	$\pm922\ 337\ 203\ 685\ 477.5808$
Date	8 bytes	January 1, 100 to December 31, 9999.
String (variable length)	10 bytes + string length	0 to approximately 2 billion
String (fixed length)	Length of string	1 to approximately 65 400

Currency   Currency data types are normally used in money calculations which have high accuracy. They are stored in 64-bit (8-byte) integer format which are scaled by 10 000 to give a fixed-point number with 19 significant digits and 4 decimal places. This gives a range of presentation providing a range of ±922 337 203 685 477.5808.

Date   Date variables are stored as IEEE 64-bit (8-byte) floating-point numbers that represent dates ranging from 1 January 100 to 31 December 9999 and times from 0:00:00 to 23:59:59. Literal dates must be enclosed within number sign characters (#), for example, #January 1, 1993# or #1 Jan 93#. Any recognizable literal date values can be assigned to Date variables.

Double   Double (double-precision floating-point) variables are stored as IEEE 64-bit (8-byte) floating-point numbers ranging in value from ±4.94065645841247×10^{-324} to ±1.79769313486232×10^{308}.

Integer   Integer variables are stored as 16-bit (2-byte) numbers ranging in value from −32 768 to 32 767.

Long   Long (long integer) variables are stored as signed 32-bit (4-byte) numbers ranging in value from −2 147 483 648 to 2 147 483 647.

Single   Single (single-precision floating-point) variables are stored as IEEE 32-bit (4-byte) floating-point numbers, ranging in value from ±3.402823×10^{38} to ±1.401298×10^{-45}.

String   There are two kinds of strings:
Variable-length strings: which can contain up to 2 147 483 648 (2^{31}) characters (or 65 536 for Microsoft Windows version 3.1 and earlier).
Fixed-length strings: which can contain up to 65 536 (2^{16}) characters.

21.10.4 Convert between data types

Visual Basic has strong data type checking where the compiler generates an error when one data type is assigned directly to a variable with another data type. Thus different data types may need to be converted into another type so that they can be used. The basic conversion functions are:

Cbool(*expr*)   Which converts an expression into Boolean. The expression argument is any valid numeric or string expression. If the expression is zero then a False is returned, else a True is returned.

Cbyte(*expr*)   Which converts an expression into Byte. The expression argument is any valid numeric or string expression. If the expression lies outside the acceptable range for the Byte data type then an error occurs.

Ccur(*expr*)   Which converts an expression into Currency. The expression argument is any valid numeric or string expression. If the expression lies outside the acceptable range for the Currency data type then an error occurs.

Cdate(*expr*)   Which converts an expression into Date. The date argument is any valid date expression.

Cdbl(*expr*)   Which converts an expression into Double. The expression argument is any valid numeric or string expression.

Cint(*expr*)   Converts an expression to an Integer. The expression argument is any valid numeric or string expression. Cint differs from the Fix and Int functions, which truncate, rather than round, the fractional part of a number. When the fractional part is exactly 0.5, the Cint function always rounds it to the nearest even number. For example, 0.5 rounds to 0, and 1.5 rounds to 2.

Clng(*expr*)   Which converts an expression into Long. The expression argument is any valid numeric or string expression. As with Cint the value is rounded to the nearest whole number.

Csng(*expr*)   Which converts an expression into Single. The expression argument is any valid numeric or string expression. If the expression lies outside the acceptable range for the Single data type, an error occurs.

Cstr(*expr*)   Which converts an expression into String. The expression argument is any valid numeric or string expression. If the expression is Boolean then a string is returned with either True or False, else a numeric value returns a string containing the number.

Int(*expr*)
Fix(*expr*)   Returns the integer portion of a number. Int differs from Fix in that Int when the number is negative returns the first negative integer which is less than or equal to the number, whereas Fix returns the first negative integer greater than or equal to the number. For example, if the value is –12.3 then Int converts this to –13 while Fix converts it to –12.

A typical conversion is from a numeric or date variable into a string format. Program 21.1 shows an example of a Visual Basic program which contains the CStr function which is used to convert from two floating-point values (x and y), an integer (i) and date (newdate) into a string format. This is then used to display the values to a window using the MsgBox function. The program also uses the Fix function to round-up the value of x. Figure 21.3 shows a sample run.

Program 21.1

```
Private Sub Form_Load()
Dim x, y As Double
Dim i As Integer
Dim newdate As Date

  x = 43.2
  y = 3.221
  i = 100
  newdate = #1/1/99#
  MsgBox ("Values of x and y are: " + CStr(x) + "," + CStr(y))
  MsgBox ("The whole part of x is : " + CStr(Fix(x)))
  MsgBox ("Date is : " + CStr(newdate))
  MsgBox ("Value of i is " + CStr(i))
End Sub
```

21.10.5 Input/output

The functions that can be used to input and output information are InputBox and MsgBox, respectively. Both these functions input and output information in the form of a string of characters. Thus when outputting non-string variables, such as integers and floating-point values, they must first be converted to a string using one of the string conversion functions. The same must be done for input, where the input string must be converted into the required data type, again using the data type conversion functions.

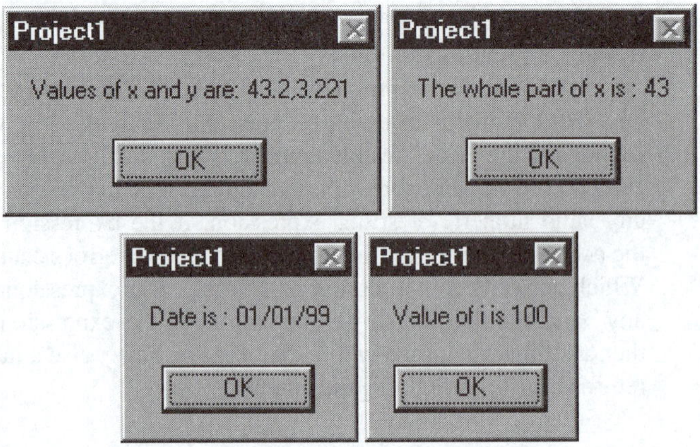

Figure 21.15 Sample run for Program 21.1.

Output

The MsgBox function displays a message in a dialog box with specified buttons and then waits for the user to select a button. The value returned indicates the chosen button. The basic format is:

MsgBox(*prompt*[, *buttons*][, *title*][, *helpfile, context*])

where the parameters in brackets are optional. The parameters are:

prompt   String to be displayed in the dialog box.

buttons   Numeric value that is the sum of values that specifies the number, the types of buttons to display, the icon style and the default button. Table 21.4 outlines these values and if it is omitted then the default value for buttons is 0.

title   String which contains the title bar of the dialog box. If it is omitted then the application name is placed in the title bar.

helpfile   String that identifies the Help file to use to provide context-sensitive Help for the dialog box. If helpfile is provided then context must also be provided.

context   Numeric value that is the Help context number the Help author assigned to the appropriate Help topic. If context is provided, helpfile must also be provided. When both helpfile and context are provided, the user can press F1 to view the Help topic corresponding to the context.

Table 21.4 defines the button settings. The values from 0 to 5 define the type of the button to be displayed. For example, a value of 5 will have two buttons, which are Retry and Cancel. The values 16, 32, 48 and 64 identify the icon to be displayed. For example, a value of 32 will display a question bubble. The 0, 256 and 512 define which button is the default. Each of these values can be added together to create the required set of buttons, icon and default button. For example, to create a dialog box with the OK and Cancel buttons, a Critical icon and the Cancel button to be the default, then the setting would be:

```
setting = 1 + 16 + 256
```

which is 273. Note that to aid documentation in the program then the predefined constant values can be used, so for the previous example:

```
setting = vbOKCancel + vbCritical + vbDefaultButton2
```

Table 21.4 Button settings.

Constant	Value	Description
vbOKOnly	0	Display OK button only.
vbOKCancel	1	Display OK and Cancel buttons. See example 1 in Figure 21.16.
vbAbortRetryIgnore	2	Display Abort, Retry, and Ignore buttons. See example 2 in Figure 21.16.
vbYesNoCancel	3	Display Yes, No, and Cancel buttons. See example 3 in Figure 21.16.
vbYesNo	4	Display Yes and No buttons. See example 4 in Figure 21.16.
vbRetryCancel	5	Display Retry and Cancel buttons. See example 5 in Figure 21.16.
vbCritical	16	Display Critical Message icon. See example 1 in Figure 21.17.
vbQuestion	32	Display Warning Query icon. See example 2 in Figure 21.17.
vbExclamation	48	Display Warning Message icon. See example 3 in Figure 21.17.
vbInformation	64	Display Information Message icon. See example 4 in Figure 21.17.
vbDefaultButton1	0	First button is default.
vbDefaultButton2	256	Second button is default.
vbDefaultButton3	512	Third button is default.

The MsgBox function returns a value depending on the button pressed; these return values are outlined in Table 21.5. For example, if the user presses the OK button then the return value will be 1. If the dialog box has a Cancel button then the user pressing ESC has the same effect as choosing Cancel. If the dialog box contains a Help button, context-sensitive Help is provided for the dialog box. However, no value is returned until one of the other buttons is chosen.

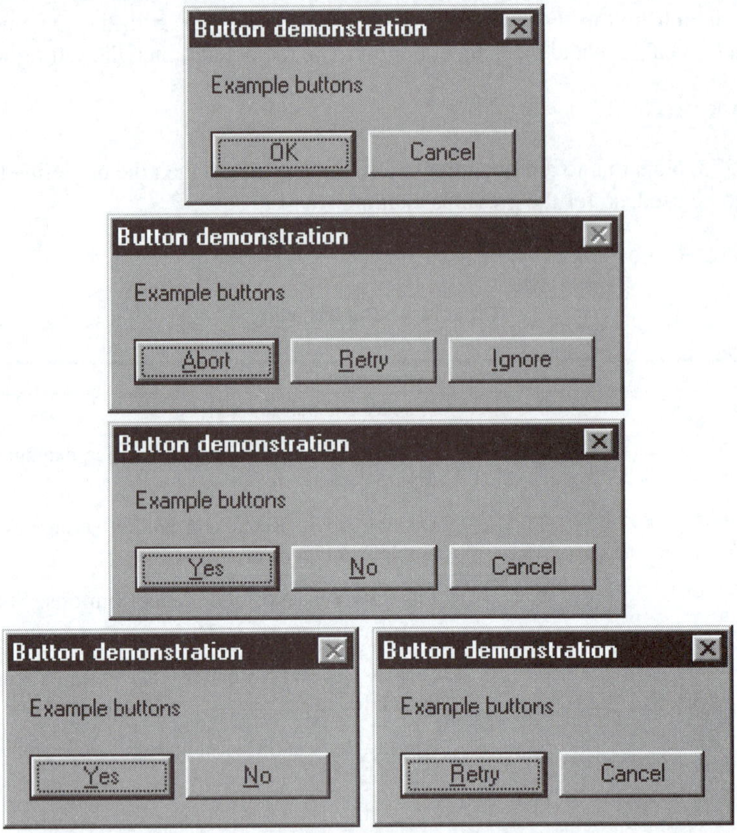

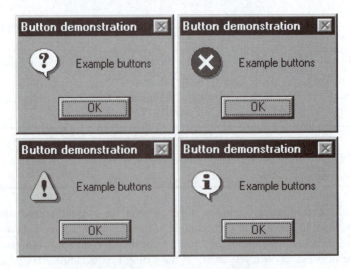

Figure 21.16 Buttons for MsgBox.

Figure 21.17 Icons for MsgBox.

Table 21.5   MsgBox return values.

Constant	Value	Button chosen
vbOK	1	OK
vbCancel	2	Cancel
vbAbort	3	Abort
vbRetry	4	Retry
vbIgnore	5	Ignore
vbYes	6	Yes
vbNo	7	No

Program 21.2 gives an example of a program which displays a dialog box with Yes and No buttons, and a question mark icon. The response will thus either be a 6 (if the Yes button is selected) or a 7 (if the No button is selected). Figure 21.18 shows a sample run.

📖 Program 21.2

```
Private Sub Form_Load()
Dim msg, title As String
Dim style, response As Integer
   msg = "Example buttons"
   style = vbYesNo + vbQuestion
   title = "Button demonstration"
   response = MsgBox(msg, style, title)
   MsgBox ("Response was " + CStr(response))
End Sub
```

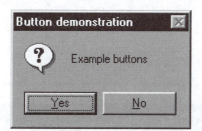

Figure 21.18   Example run.

Input

The InputBox function prompts the user to input text, or choose a button. It then returns the contents of the text box. The basic format is:

  InputBox(*prompt*[, *title*][, *default*][, *xpos*][, *ypos*][, *helpfile, context*])

where the parameters in brackets are optional. The parameters are:

prompt   String of be displayed in the dialog box.
title   String which contains the title bar of the dialog box. If it is omitted then the application name is placed in the title bar.

default   String displayed in the text box and is the default response if no other input is provided. Omitting this field makes the text box initially empty.

xpos   Numeric value that specifies (in twips) the horizontal distance of the left edge of the dialog box from the left edge of the screen. Omitting this field makes the dialog box horizontally centreed.

ypos   Numeric value that specifies (in twips) the vertical distance of the upper edge of the dialog box from the top of the screen. Omitting this field makes the dialog box is vertically positioned approximately one-third of the way down the screen.

helpfile   String that identifies the Help file to use to provide context-sensitive Help for the dialog box. If helpfile is provided then context must also be provided.

context   Numeric value that is the Help context number the Help author assigned to the appropriate Help topic. If context is provided, helpfile must also be provided. When both helpfile and context are provided, the user can press F1 to view the Help topic corresponding to the context.

Program 21.3 shows an example usage of the InputBox function. In this case the message for the title is 'Input demonstration', the default value is '10' and the value is return into the `inval` variable.

📖 Program 21.3

```
Private Sub Form_Load()
Dim msg, title, default As String
Dim inval As Integer
   msg = "Enter a value"
   title = "Input demonstration"
   default = "10"
   inval = InputBox(msg, title, default)
   MsgBox ("Value is " + CStr(inval))
End Sub
```

Figure 21.19   Example run.

21.10.6 Decisions and loops

The decisions and loops in Visual Basic are similar to the ones used in C and Pascal.

If statement

The basic if statement format is:

```
if (expression) then
    statement block
end if
```

or, in general:

```
if (condition1) then
    statement block
elseif (condition2)
      statement block
 ::::
else
      statement block
end if
```

where the condition can be a numeric or string expression that evaluates to True or False. The statement block contains one or more statements separated by colons.

As with C and Pascal, if the first condition is True then the first statement block is executed, else if the second condition is True then the second statement block is executed, and so on. If none of the conditions are True then the final else statement block is executed (if it exists).

Note that Else and ElseIf are both optional and there can be any number of ElseIf clauses but none of them can occur after the Else clause

Program 21.4 gives an example of a program in which the user enters a value from 0 to 2 and the program displays the equivalent resistor colour code.

📖 Program 21.4

```
Private Sub Form_Load()
Dim msg, title, default As String
Dim inval As Integer

msg = "Enter color code value (0-2)"
title = "Color code"
default = "0"

inval = InputBox(msg, title, default)

If (inval = 0) Then
    MsgBox ("BLACK")
ElseIf (inval = 1) Then
    MsgBox ("BROWN")
ElseIf (inval = 2) Then
    MsgBox ("RED")
ElseIf (inval > 2 And inval < 10) Then
    MsgBox ("Colors not added")
Else
    MsgBox ("No color value")
End If
End Sub
```

Case

The Case statement is similar to the case and switch statements used in Pascal and C. Its general form is:

```
Select Case expression
Case expressionval1
```

```
      statement block1
Case expressionval2
      statement block2
Case Else
      else statement block1
End Select
```

The expression can be any numeric or string expression. A match of the expression to the expression value causes the corresponding statement block to be executed. If none of the blocks match then the Case Else statement block is executed. If testexpression matches any expressionlist expression associated with a Case clause, the statements following that Case clause are executed up to the next Case clause, or, for the last clause, up to the End Select. Control then passes to the statement following End Select. If testexpression matches an expressionlist expression in more than one Case clause, only the statements following the first match are executed.

Multiple expressions or ranges can be added to the Case cause, such as:

```
Case -1 To 3, 10 To 20, 51, 53
```

It is also possible to specify ranges and multiple expressions for strings. For example, the following matches the string to 'apple' and everything, alphabetically between 'banana' and 'carrot':

```
Case "apple", "banana" To "carrot"
```

Program 21.5 shows an example of a program which is similar to Program 21.4 but uses a Case statement to select the resistor colour code.

📖 Program 21.5

```
Private Sub Form_Load()
Dim msg, title, default As String
Dim inval As Integer
    msg = "Enter color code value (0-9)"
    title = "Color code"
    default = "0"

    inval = InputBox(msg, title, default)

    Select Case inval
    Case 0
         MsgBox ("BLACK")
    Case 1
         MsgBox ("BROWN")
    Case 2
         MsgBox ("RED")
    Case 3, 4, 5, 6, 7, 8, 9
         MsgBox ("Colors not added")
    Case Else
         MsgBox ("No Color")
    End Select
End Sub
```

For loop

The For loop is similar to the for loop in Pascal. It repeats a group of statements a number of times. Its general form is:

```
For counter = start To end [Step step]
       statements
Next [counter]
```

or

```
For counter = start To end Step stepsize
       statements
Next [counter]
```

where counter is a numeric variable which has used a loop counter, start is the Initial value of the counter, end is the final value of the counter and step is the amount by which the count is changed for each loop. This value can either be positive or negative. The default step size, if not specified, is 1.

Program 21.6 uses a For loop to calculate the factorial value of an entered value (Figure 21.20 shows a sample run).

📖 Program 21.6

```
Private Sub Form_Load()
Dim fact As Long
Dim i, inval As Integer

    inval = InputBox("Enter a value")
    fact = 1
    For i = 2 To inval
           fact = fact * i
    Next i
    MsgBox ("Factorial of " + CStr(inval-1) + " is " + CStr(fact))
End Sub
```

Figure 21.20 Example run.

Do ... while loop

The Do...while loop is similar to the while() statements used in Pascal and C. Its general forms are:

```
Do While condition              Do Until condition
     statement block                 statement block
Loop                            Loop

Do                              Do
     statement block                statement block
Loop While condition            Loop Until condition
```

Program 21.7 uses a do...while loop to test to see if the user input is within a valid range. In this case the valid input is between 0 and 10 for the voltage input and greater than 0 and up to 10 for the current input. If the user enters a value which is outside this range then a MsgBox is displayed with an error message (INVALID: re-enter).

📖 Program 21.7

```
Private Sub Form_Load()
Dim voltage, current, resistance As Double
    Do
        voltage = InputBox("Enter a voltage (0-10)")
        If (voltage < 0 Or voltage > 10) Then
            MsgBox ("INVALID: re-enter")
        End If
    Loop While (voltage < 0 Or voltage > 10)
    Do
        current = InputBox("Enter a current (0-10)")
        If (current <= 0 Or current > 10) Then
            MsgBox ("INVALID: re-enter")
        End If
    Loop While (current <= 0 Or current > 10)
    resistance = voltage / current
    MsgBox ("Resistance is " + Cstr(resistance))
End Sub
```

21.11 Exercises

21.11.1   Complete Program 21.5 so that it implements the complete resistor colour code.

21.11.2   Change the program in Exercise 21.11.1 so that it loops until the user enters a valid value (between 0 and 9).

21.11.3   Change the program in Exercise 21.11.2 so that after the result has been displayed the user is prompted as to whether to repeat the program (OK) or exit the program (Cancel).

21.11.4   Write a program which will continually display the current date and time. The sample code given next displays a single date and time.

```
Private Sub Form_Load()
Dim CurrDate, CurrTime As Date

  CurrTime = Time ' System time
  CurrDate = Date    ' System date
  MsgBox (CurrTime + CurrDate)

End Sub
```

21.11.5   Modify the program in Exercise 21.11.4 so that the OK and Cancel buttons are shown. If the user selects the Cancel button then the program should exit, else the program should display the new date. The sample code given below displays a single date and time with the OK and Cancel buttons.

```
Private Sub Form_Load()
Dim CurrDate, CurrTime As Date
Dim response As Integer

CurrTime = Time ' System time
CurrDate = Date  ' System date
response = MsgBox(CurrDate +
    CurrTime,vbOKCancel, "Date")

End Sub
```

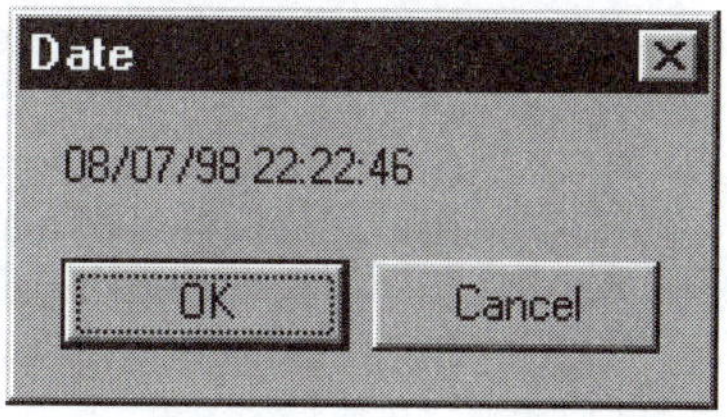

21.11.6 Place a `CommandButton` on a form and display its properties. Note all of the properties and, with the help of the help manual, identify the function of each of the properties. Note that help on a property can be found by highlighting the property and pressing F1.

21.11.7 With a `CommandButton` identify the events that are associated with it.

21.11.8 Determine the actual colours of the following RGB Colour values:

(i)   &H0080FF80&   (ii)   &H00FF8080&
(iii) &H00C000C0&   (iv) &H00E0E0E0&

21.11.9 Conduct the following:

(i)   Add a command button to a form.
(ii)   Change the text on the `CommandButton` to 'EXIT'.
(iii) Change the font on the `CommandButton` to 'Times Roman' and the font size to 16.
(iv)   Resize the `CommandButton` so that the text fits comfortably into the button.
(iv)   Change the background colour of the form to yellow.
(v)   Change the Caption name of the form to 'My Application'.

21.11.10 Develop the form given in Figure 21.21.

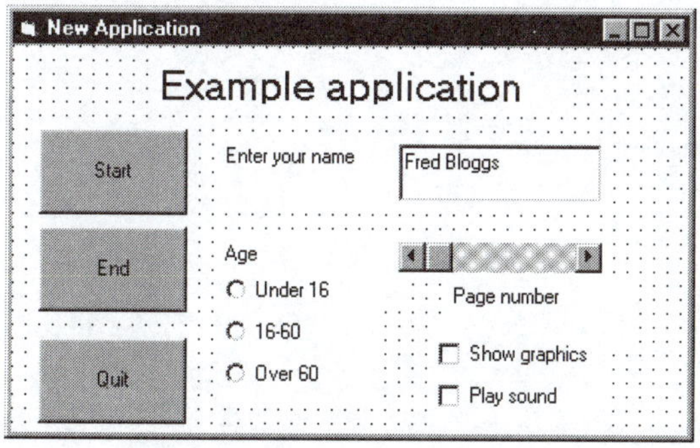

Figure 21.21 Exercise.

21.11.11 Explain why, in the previous exercise, a radio button is used for the age option and a check box is used to select the choices of Show Graphics and Play

Sounds. Which of the following would be radio buttons or check boxes?

    (i)   Items on a shopping list.
    (ii)   Selection of a horse to win a race.
    (iii)   Selection of paint colour on a new car.
    (iv)   Selection of several modules on a course.

22 VB (Forms)

22.1 Introduction

This chapter discusses how forms are constructed and how code is associated with the form.

22.2 Setting properties

Each control object has a set of properties associated with it. For example, the TextBox control in Figure 22.1 has an object name of Text1. This object has a number of associated properties, such as Alignment, Appearance, BackColour, and so on. These properties can be changed within the program by using the dot notation. For example, to change the font to 'Courier New', the text displayed in the object to 'Hello' and the height of the window to 1000 the following can be used:

```
Text1.Font = "Courier New"
Text1.Text = "FALSE"
Text1.Height = 1000
```

Properties - Text1

Text1 TextBox

Alphabetic | Categorized

(Name)	Text1
Alignment	0 - Left Justify
Appearance	1 - 3D
BackColor	&H80000005&
BorderStyle	1 - Fixed Single
DataField	
DataSource	
DragIcon	(None)
DragMode	0 - Manual
Enabled	True
Font	MS Sans Serif
ForeColor	&H80000008&
Height	1455

(Name)
Returns the name used in code to identify an object.

Figure 22.1   Object properties.

22.3 Forms and code

Visual Basic programs are normally designed by first defining the user interface (the form) and writing the code which is associated with events and controls. The best way to illustrate the process is with an example.

22.3.1 Multiple choice example

In this example the user is to design a form with a simple question and three optional examples. It should display if the answer is correct (TRUE) or wrong (FALSE). The program should continue after each selection until the user selects an exit button.

Step 1: The label control is selected [A]. Then the text 'What is the capital of France' is entered in the caption field, as shown in Figure 22.2.

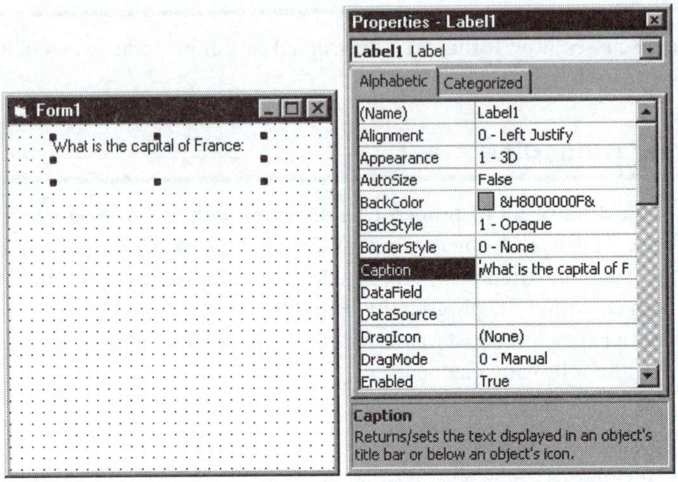

Figure 22.2   Step 1.

Step 2: Next, the user adds a command button by selecting the command control [□]. The button is then added to the form and the Caption property is set to 'Edinburgh', as shown in Figure 22.3.

Step 3: Next, the user adds another command button by selecting the command control. The button is then added to the form and the Caption property is set to 'Paris', as shown in Figure 22.4.

Step 4: Next, the user adds another command button by selecting the command control. The button is then added to the form and the Caption property is set to 'Munich', as shown in Figure 22.5.

Step 5: Next, the user adds a TextBox [ab]. This is then added to the right-hand side of the form, as shown in Figure 22.6. The Text property is then changed to have an empty field. The TextBox will be used to display text from the program.

Step 6: Next, the user adds another command button by selecting the command control. The button is then added to the form and the Caption property is set to 'Exit', as shown in Figure 22.7. A character in the name can be underlined by putting an & before it. Thus '&Exit' will be displayed as 'Exit'.

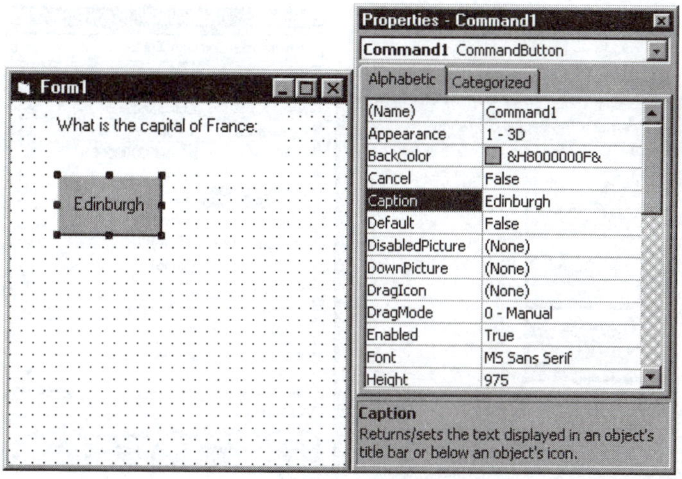

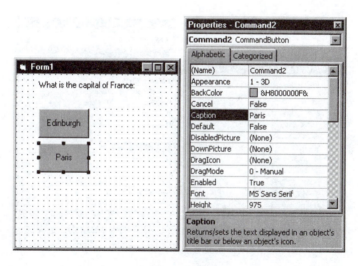

Figure 22.3   Step 2.

Figure 22.4   Step 3.

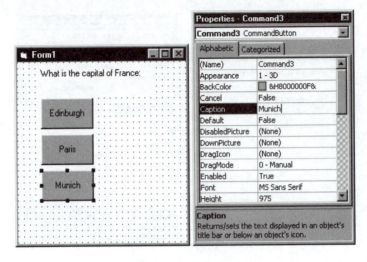

Figure 22.5 Step 4.

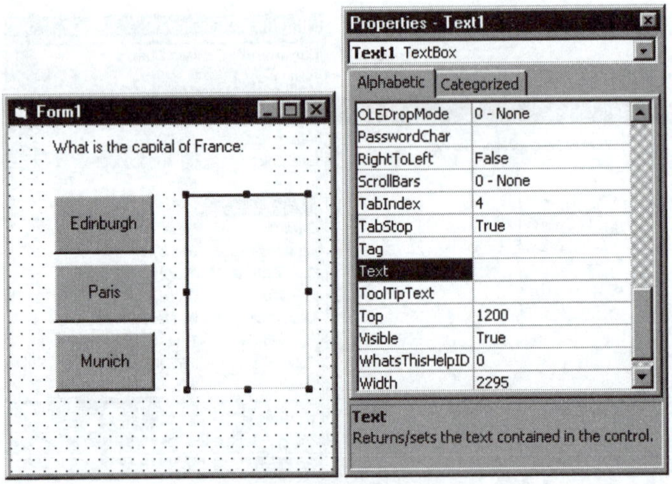

Figure 22.6 Step 5.

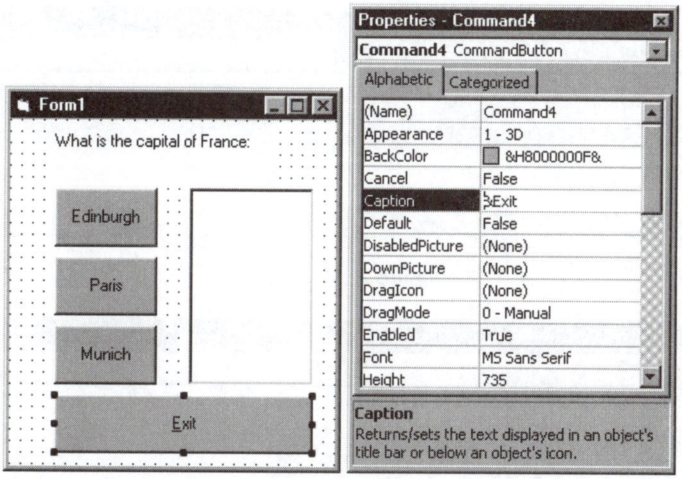

Figure 22.7   Step 6.

Step 7: Next, the code can be attached to each of the command buttons. This is done by either double-clicking on the command button or by selecting the button and pressing the F7 key. To display to the TextBox (the object named Text1) then the text property is set with:

```
Text1.Text = "FALSE"
```

which displays the string "FALSE" to the text window. The associated code is shown in Figure 22.8.

Step 8: Next, the code associated with the second command button is set, with:

```
Text1.Text = "TRUE"
```

as shown in Figure 22.9.

Step 9: Next, the code associated with the third command button is set (Figure 22.10), with:

```
Text1.Text = "FALSE"
```

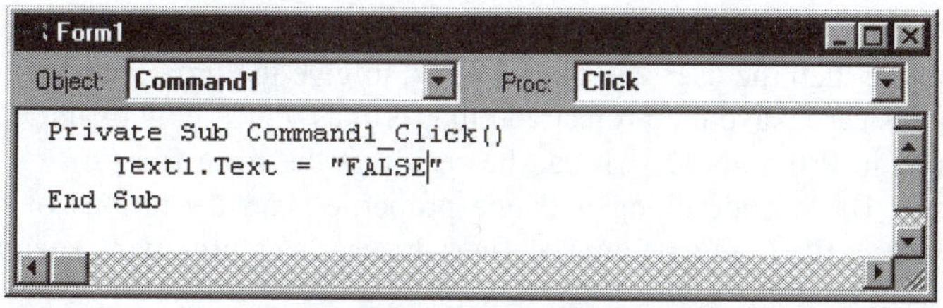

Figure 22.8   Step 7.

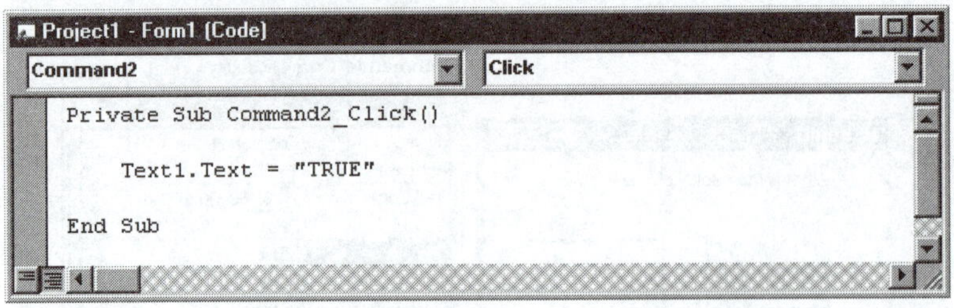

```
Project1 - Form1 (Code)                                    _ □ ×
Command2                        ▼    Click                    ▼
    Private Sub Command2_Click()

        Text1.Text = "TRUE"

    End Sub
```

Figure 22.9   Step 8.

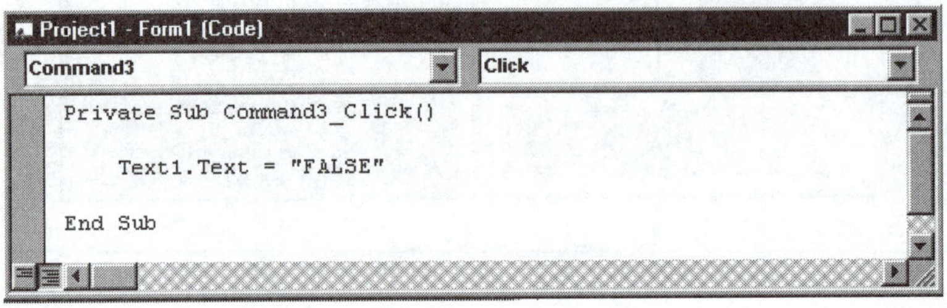

```
Project1 - Form1 (Code)                                    _ □ ×
Command3                        ▼    Click                    ▼
    Private Sub Command3_Click()

        Text1.Text = "FALSE"

    End Sub
```

Figure 22.10   Step 9.

Step 10: Finally, the code associated with the exit command button is set by adding the
code:

```
End
```

which causes the program to end; the code is shown in Figure 22.11.

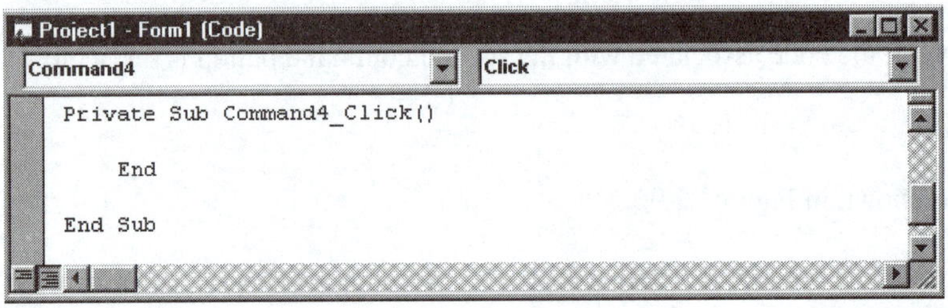

```
Project1 - Form1 (Code)                                    _ □ ×
Command4                        ▼    Click                    ▼
    Private Sub Command4_Click()

        End

    End Sub
```

Figure 22.11   Step 10.

The program can then be executed with Run → Start. Figure 22.12 shows a sample run.
Next the form and the project are saved using the File → Save option. If the file has not
been saved before then the user will be prompted to give the project and the form a new
file name. In this case, save the project and the form as VB22_01.VBP and VB22_01.FRM.
These are listed in Program 22.1. It can be seen that the form file (VB22_01.FRM) contains the Visual Basic code along with the properties and definitions of the controls,
whereas the project file (VB22_01.VBP) defines the user's environment, such as:

- The names of any forms.
- The control types.

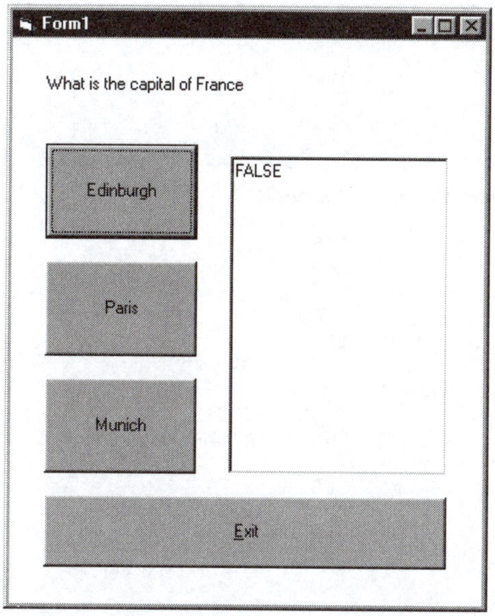

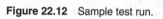

Figure 22.12   Sample test run.

📖   **Program 22.1** (vb22_01.FRM)

```
VERSION 5.00
Begin VB.Form Form1
   BackColor       =    &H8000000E&
   Caption         =    "Form1"
   ClientHeight    =    5790
   ClientLeft      =    4275
   ClientTop       =    3900
   ClientWidth     =    4950
   LinkTopic       =    "Form1"
   ScaleHeight     =    5790
   ScaleWidth      =    4950
   Begin VB.CommandButton Command4
      Caption      =    "&Exit"
      Height       =    735
      Left         =    360
      TabIndex     =    5
      Top          =    4680
      Width        =    4215
   End
   Begin VB.TextBox Text1
      Height       =    3255
      Left         =    2280
      TabIndex     =    4
      Top          =    1200
      Width        =    2295
   End
   Begin VB.CommandButton Command3
      Caption      =    "Munich"
      Height       =    975
      Left         =    360
      TabIndex     =    3
      Top          =    3480
      Width        =    1575
   End
   Begin VB.CommandButton Command2
```

```
        Caption         =       "Paris"
        Height          =       975
        Left            =       360
        TabIndex        =       2
        Top             =       2280
        Width           =       1575
    End
    Begin VB.CommandButton Command1
        Caption         =       "Edinburgh"
        Height          =       975
        Left            =       360
        TabIndex        =       1
        Top             =       1080
        Width           =       1575
    End
    Begin VB.Label Label1
        BackColor       =       &H8000000E&
        Caption         =       "What is the capital of France"
        Height          =       495
        Left            =       360
        TabIndex        =       0
        Top             =       360
        Width           =       3495
    End
End
Attribute VB_Name = "Form1"
Attribute VB_GlobalNameSpace = False
Attribute VB_Creatable = False
Attribute VB_PredeclaredId = True
Attribute VB_Exposed = False
Private Sub Command1_Click()
    Text1.Text = "FALSE"
End Sub

Private Sub Command2_Click()
    Text1.Text = "TRUE"
End Sub

Private Sub Command3_Click()
    Text1.Text = "FALSE"
End Sub

Private Sub Command4_Click()
    End
End Sub
```

📖 Program 22.1 (vb22_01.VBP)

```
Type=Exe
Form=new.frm
Reference=*\G{00020430-0000-0000-C000-
000000000046}#2.0#0#..\WINDOWS\SYSTEM\StdOle2.tlb#OLE Automation
Startup="Form1"
Command32=""
Name="Project1"
HelpContextID="0"
CompatibleMode="0"
MajorVer=1
MinorVer=0
RevisionVer=0
AutoIncrementVer=0
ServerSupportFiles=0
VersionCompanyName="Napier University"
CompilationType=0
OptimizationType=0
```

```
FavorPentiumPro(tm)=0
CodeViewDebugInfo=0
NoAliasing=0
BoundsCheck=0
OverflowCheck=0
FlPointCheck=0
FDIVCheck=0
UnroundedFP=0
StartMode=0
Unattended=0
ThreadPerObject=0
MaxNumberOfThreads=1
```

22.4 Temperature conversion program

In this example the user will enter either a temperature in Centigrade or Fahrenheit and the program will convert to an equivalent Fahrenheit or Centigrade temperature. The steps taken, with reference to Figure 22.13, are:

1. Add a Label control and change its Caption property to 'Centigrade'.
2. Add a Label control and change its Caption property to 'Fahrenheit'.
3. Add a TextBox control and put it beside the Centigrade Label. Next, change its Text property to '0'.
4. Add a TextBox control and put it beside the Fahrenheit Label. Next, change its Text property to '32'.
5. Add a CommandButton control and put it below the text boxes. Next, change its Caption property to 'C to F'. This command button will convert the value in Centigrade to Fahrenheit and put the result in the Fahrenheit text box.
6. Add a CommandButton control and put it beside the other command button. Next, change its Caption property to 'F to C'. This command button will convert the value in Fahrenheit to Centigrade and put the result in the Centigrade text box.

Select the form and change the Caption property to "Temperature Conversion". Next, the code associated with each control can be added, as follows:

1. First add code to the first command button (C to F) which will be used to convert the text from the Centigrade text box (Text1) and display it to the Fahrenheit text box (Text2). This is achieved with:

```
Private Sub Command1_Click()
Dim val As Double

    val = 9 / 5 * CDbl(Text1.Text) + 32
    Text2.Text = CStr(val)

End Sub
```

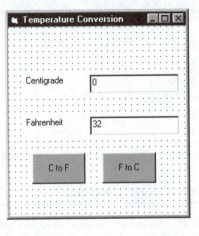

Figure 22.13 Temperature conversion form.

2. Next, add code to the second command button (F to C) which will be used to convert the text from the Fahrenheit text box (Text2) and display it to the Centigrade text box (Text1). This is achieved with:

```
Private Sub Command2_Click()
Dim val As Double
    val = 5 / 9 * (CDbl(Text2.Text) - 32)
    Text1.Text = CStr(val)
End Sub
```

A test run of the program is given in Figure 22.14.

The temperature conversion program up to this point has several weaknesses. One of these is that it does not have an exit option (this will be left as an exercise) and the other is that the user can enter a value which is not a valid temperature value and the program accepts it. For example, if the user enters a string of characters then the program stops and displays the message shown in Figure 22.15.

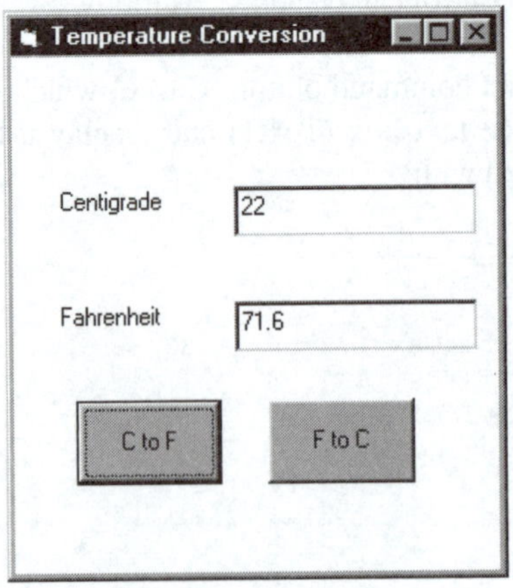

Figure 22.14 Sample run.

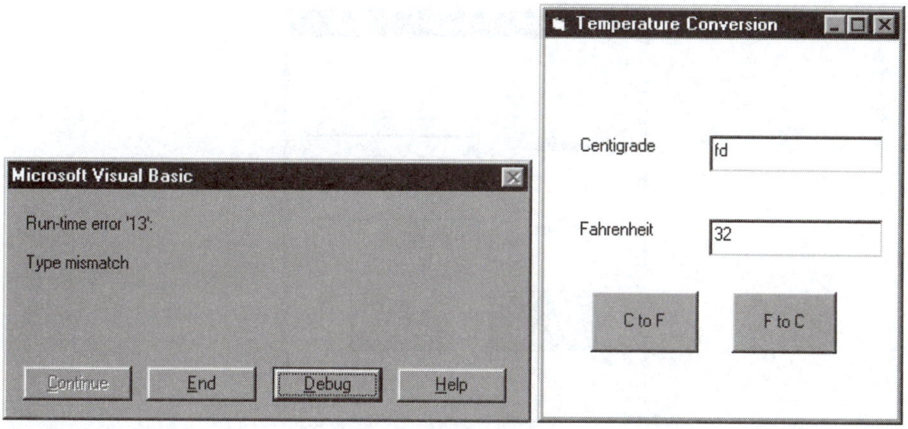

Figure 22.15 Sample run with invalid input.

To overcome this problem the value that is entered is tested to see if it is a valid numeric value, using the `IsNumeric()` function. This returns a TRUE if the value can be converted to a numeric value, else a FALSE. The modified code for the two command buttons is given next and a sample run is shown in Figure 22.16.

```
Private Sub Command1_Click()
Dim val As Double

    If (IsNumeric(Text1.Text)) Then
        val = 9 / 5 * CDbl(Text1.Text) + 32
        Text2.Text = CStr(val)
    Else
        Text2.Text = "INVALID"
    End If

End Sub
```

```
Private Sub Command2_Click()
Dim val As Double

    If (IsNumeric(Text1.Text)) Then
        val = 5 / 9 * (CDbl(Text2.Text) - 32)
        Text2.Text = CStr(val)
    Else
        Text2.Text = "INVALID"
    End If

End Sub
```

22.5 Quadratic roots program

In this example the program calculates the roots of a quadratic equation with user-entered values of a, b and c. The general form of a quadratic equation is:

$$ax^2 + bx + c = 0$$

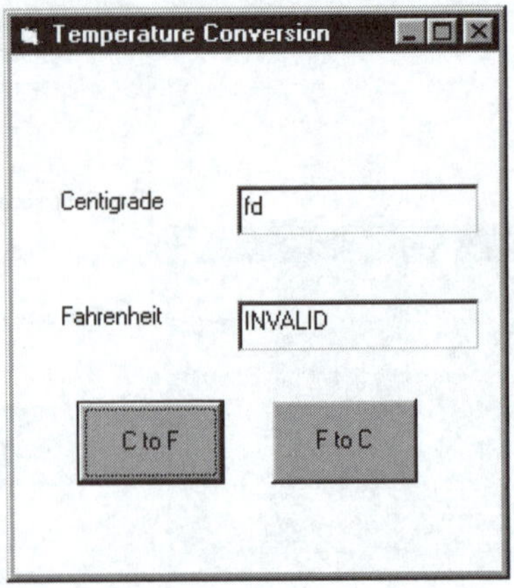

Figure 22.16 Sample run with invalid input.

the general solution is:

$$x_{1,2} = \frac{-b \pm \sqrt{b^2 - 4ac}}{2a}$$

This leads to three types of roots, these are:

if ($b^2 > 4ac$) then there are two real roots;
else if ($b^2 = 4ac$) then there is a single root of $-b/4a$;
else if ($b^2 < 4ac$) then these are two complex roots which are:

$$x_{1,2} = -\frac{b}{2a} \pm j\frac{\sqrt{4ac - b^2}}{2a}$$

The steps taken, with reference to Figure 22.17, are:

1. Add a Label control and change its Caption property to 'a'.
2. Add a Label control and change its Caption property to 'b'.
3. Add a Label control and change its Caption property to 'c'.
4. Add a Label control and change its Caption property to 'x1'.
5. Add a Label control and change its Caption property to 'x2'.
6. Add a TextBox control and put it beside the 'a' Label. Next change its Text property to '0' (this is the Text1 object).
7. Add a TextBox control and put it beside the 'b' Label. Next change its Text property to '0' (this is the Text2 object).
8. Add a TextBox control and put it beside the 'c' Label. Next change its Text property to '0' (this is the Text3 object).
9. Add a TextBox control and put it beside the 'x1' Label. Next change its Text property to '0' (this is the Text4 object).
10. Add a TextBox control and put it beside the 'x2' Label. Next change its Text prop-

erty to '0' (this is the Text5 object).

11. Add a CommandButton control and put it below the text boxes. Next, change its Caption property to 'Calculate'. This command button will be used to determine the roots of the equation.

12. Add a CommandButton control and put it beside the other command button. Next, change its Caption property to 'Exit'. This command button will be used to exit the program.

13. Select the form and change the Caption property to 'Quadratic Equation'.

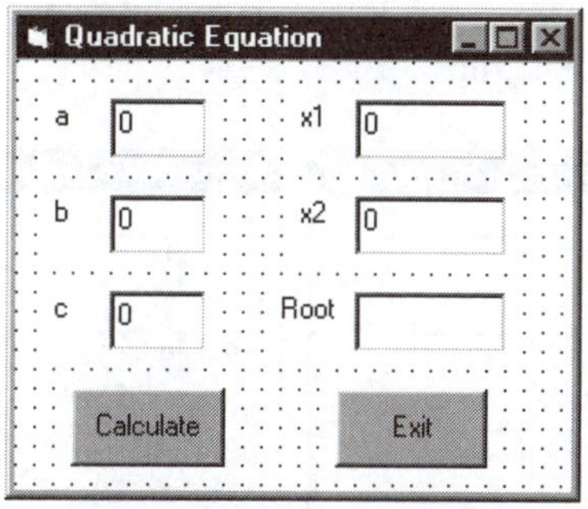

Figure 22.17   Quadratic equation form.

Next, the code associated with each control can be added, as follows:

1. First add code to the first command button (Calculate) which will be used to calculate the roots and display to the roots text box (Text4 and Text5). This is achieved with:

```
Private Sub Command1_Click()
Dim a, b, c As Double
Dim aval, bval, cval As String

    aval = Text1.Text
    bval = Text2.Text
    cval = Text3.Text
    a = CDbl(aval)
    b = CDbl(bval)
    c = CDbl(cval)

    If (Not (IsNumeric(aval)) Or _
        Not (IsNumeric(bval)) Or Not (IsNumeric(cval))) Then
        Text4.Text = ""
        Text5.Text = ""
        Text6.Text = "INVALID"
    ElseIf ((b * b) > (4 * a * c)) Then
        Text4.Text = CStr((-b + Sqr(b * b - 4 * a * c)) / (2 * a))
        Text5.Text = CStr((-b - Sqr(b * b - 4 * a * c)) / (2 * a))
        Text6.Text = "Real"
    ElseIf (b * b < 4 * a * c) Then
        Text4.Text = CStr(-b / (2 * a))
        Text5.Text = "j" + CStr(Sqr(4 * a * c - b * b) / (2 * a))
        Text6.Text = "Complex"
    Else
        Text4.Text = CStr(-b / (2 * a))
        Text5.Text = ""
        Text6.Text = "Singlar"
```

```
        End If
    End Sub
```

Notice that the code includes the _ character which allows the programmer to continue a statement onto another line.

2. Next, add code to the second command button (Exit):

```
    Private Sub Command2_Click()
        End
    End Sub
```

Figure 22.18 shows two sample runs.

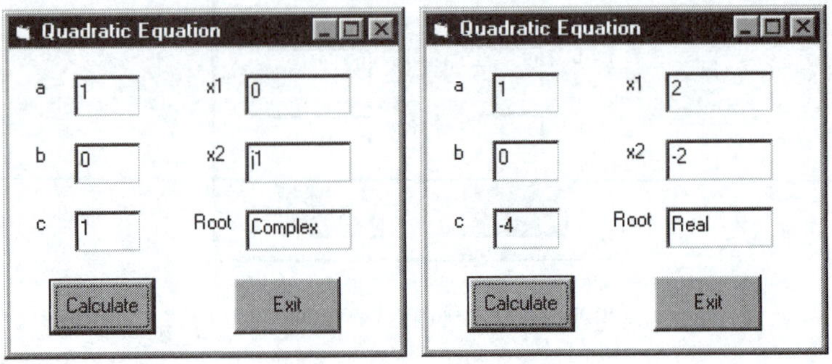

Figure 22.18   Sample runs.

22.6 Resistance calculation with slider controls program

An excellent method of allowing the user to input a value within a fixed range is to use a slider control. These slider controls can either be vertical (VScroll) or horizontal (HScroll). The main properties, as shown in left-hand side of Figure 22.19, of a scroll bar are:

- Max. Which defines the maximum value of the scroll bar.
- Min. Which defines the minimum value of the scroll bar.
- Value. Which gives the current slider value.

As an example, a horizontal slider will be setup with a voltage range of 0 to 100. The value of the slider will be shown. The steps taken, with reference to the right-hand side of Figure 22.19, are:

1. Add a Label control and change its Caption property to 'Voltage'.
2. Add a Label control and change its Caption property to '0'.
3. Add an HScrollBar control below the labels. Next, change its Max property to '100' and its Min property to '0'.

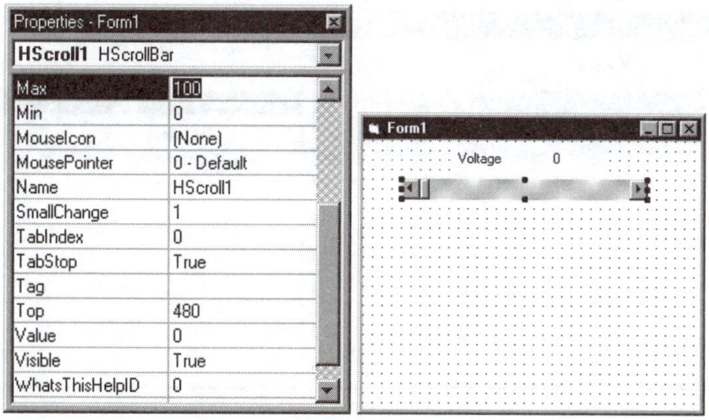

Figure 22.19 Scroll bar properties and voltage form.

Next the code associated with each control can be added, as follows:

1. Add code to the horizontal scroll bar which will be used to display its value to the voltage value label (Label2). This is achieved with:

```
Private Sub HScroll1_Change()
    Label2.Caption = HScroll1.Value
End Sub
```

This will take the value from the scroll bar (HScroll1.Value) and display to the second label box (Label2). When the program is run then the user can move the scroll bar back and forward which causes a change in the displayed voltage value (from 0 to 100). A sample run is shown in the left-hand side of Figure 22.20.

This project can now be enhanced by adding another slider for current and displaying the equivalent resistance (which is voltage divided by current). The steps taken, with reference to the right-hand side of Figure 22.20, are:

1. Add a Label control and change its Caption property to 'Voltage'.
2. Add a Label control and change its Caption property to '0'.
3. Add an HScrollBar control below the labels (HScroll1). Next, change its Max property to '100' and its Min property to '0'.
4. Add a Label control and change its Caption property to 'Current'.
5. Add a Label control and change its Caption property to '0'.
6. Add an HScrollBar control below the labels (HScroll2). Next change its Max property to '100' and its Min property to '0'.
7. Add a Label control and change its Caption property to 'Resistance'.
8. Add a Label control and change its Caption property to '0'.

Next, the code associated with each control can be added, as follows:

1. Add code to the first horizontal scroll bar (HScroll1) which will be used to display its value to the voltage value label (Label2). The resistance label (Label6) is also updated with the result of the voltage divided by the current. This is achieved with:

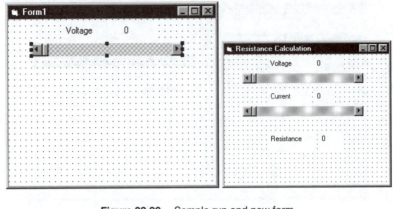

Figure 22.20   Sample run and new form.

```
Private Sub HScroll1_Change()
    Label2.Caption = HScroll1.Value
    If (HScroll2.Value <> 0) Then
        Label6.Caption = 100 * HScroll1.Value / HScroll2.Value
    End If
End Sub
```

2. Add code to the second horizontal scroll bar (HScroll2) which will be used to display its value to the current value label (Label4) with the value of the scroll bar divided by 100. The resistance label (Label6) is also updated with the result of the voltage divided by the current. This is achieved with:

```
Private Sub HScroll2_Change()
    Label4.Caption = HScroll2.Value / 100
    If (HScroll2.Value <> 0) Then
        Label6.Caption = 100 * HScroll1.Value / HScroll2.Value
    End If
End Sub
```

The left-hand side of Figure 22.21 shows a sample run.

One of the problems of the design is that the controls and form have names which do not document their function. Visual Basic uses a naming convention which uses the type of control and consecutively adds a number, as shown in the design in the right-hand side of Figure 22.21. In this case an improved naming convention might be:

```
Label1      Voltage_Label       Label2      Voltage_Show
Label3      Current_Label       Label4      Current_Show
Label5      Resistance_Label    Label6      Resistance_Show
HScroll1    Voltage_Value       HScroll2    Current_Value
Form1       Resistance_Calc
```

These are set by selecting the properties of each of the objects and then changing the Name property to the required name. An example of changing the name of the form to `Resistance_Calc` is given in the left-hand side of Figure 22.22.

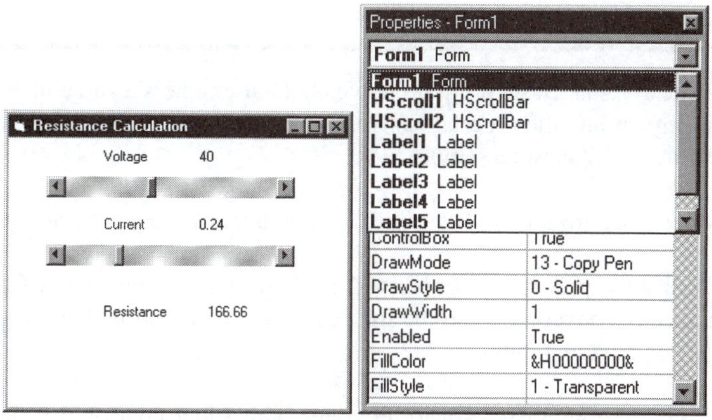

Figure 22.21 Sample run and object names.

The right-hand side of Figure 22.22 shows the list of objects after each of their names has been changed. Notice that it is now easier to locate the required object.

Next the code must be modified so that the references are to the newly named objects. The code for the voltage scroll bar (Voltage_Value) is now:

```
Private Sub Voltage_Value_Change()
    Voltage_Display.Caption = Voltage_Value.Value
    If (Current_Value.Value <> 0) Then
      Resistance_Value.Caption = 100 * Voltage_Value.Value / Current_Value.Value
    End If
End Sub
```

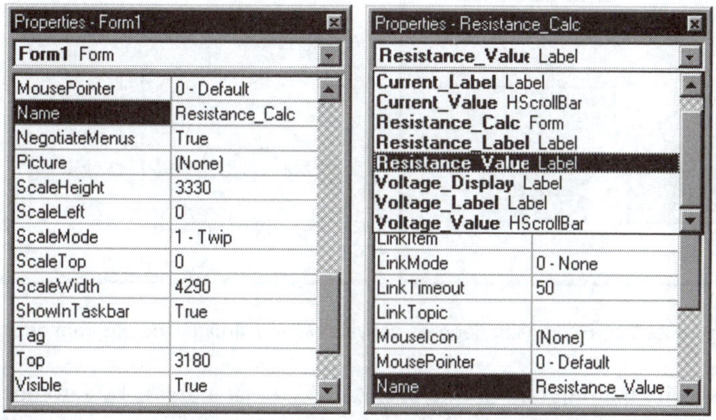

Figure 22.22 Changing the name of the form.

and the code for the current scroll bar (Current_Value) is now:

```
Private Sub Current_Value_Change()
    Current_Display.Caption = Current_Value.Value / 100
    If (Current_Value.Value <> 0) Then
        Resistance_Value.Caption = 100 * Voltage_Value.Value /
                                   Current_Value.Value
    End If
End Sub
```

22.7 Exercises

22.7.1   Write a Visual Basic program in which the user enters a value in either radians or degrees and the program converts to either degrees or radians, respectively. Figure 22.24 shows a sample run.

22.7.2   Modify the program in Exercise 22.7.1 so that invalid entries are not accepted.

22.7.3   Modify the program in Exercise 22.7.2 so that the conversion value is automatically converted when the user enters a value (that is, there is no need for the command buttons).

22.7.4   Write separate Visual Basic programs with slider controls for the following formula:

(i) $F = ma$ range: $m = 0.01$ to 1000 g, $a = 0.01$ to 100 m.s^{-2}
(ii) $V = IR$ range: $I = 0.1$ to 100 A, $V = 0.1$ to 100 V

22.7.5   Write a Visual Basic program that calculates the values of m and c for a straight line. The values of (x_1, y_1) and (x_2, y_2) should be generated with slider controls (with a range of -100 to $+100$ for each of the values). Figure 22.23 shows a sample design.

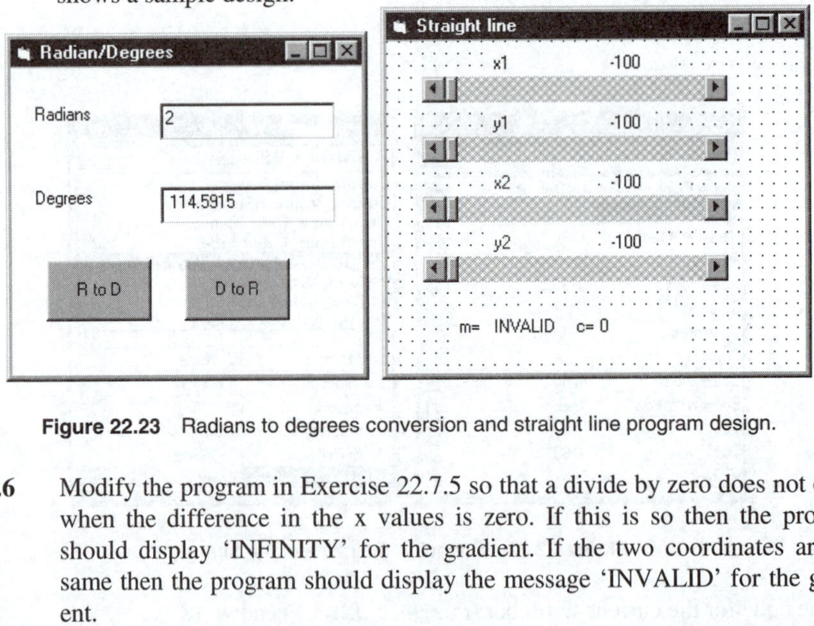

Figure 22.23   Radians to degrees conversion and straight line program design.

22.7.6   Modify the program in Exercise 22.7.5 so that a divide by zero does not occur when the difference in the x values is zero. If this is so then the program should display 'INFINITY' for the gradient. If the two coordinates are the same then the program should display the message 'INVALID' for the gradient.

22.7.7   Write a Visual Basic program which has a multiple choice option question which is repeated. The program should keep a running tally of the number of correct answers and the number of incorrect answers.

23 VB (Menus)

23.1 Introduction

This chapter discusses how menus and dialog boxes are used.

23.2 Menu editor

Most Windows programs have menus in which the user selects from a range of defined pull-down menus with defined options. Visual Basic has an easy-to-use function called the Menu editor which is used to create custom menus. The Menu editor is started from the Tools menu or from the toolbar shortcut ▤.

Figure 23.1 shows an example screen from the Menu editor. It includes:

- **Caption**. Which is a text box in which the name of the menu bar or menu option is entered. A hyphen (-) is entered as a caption if a menu separator bar is required.

  This bar helps to separate menu options. Often in menus the user can select a menu option by pressing the Alt key and an assigned key (hot key). To specify the Alt-hot key then an & is inserted before the letter of the menu option. When the program is run then this letter is underlined. For example, `Fi&le` would be displayed as `File` and the assigned keys would be Alt-L. A double ampersand specifies the ampersand character.
- **Name**. Which is a text box in which the control name for the menu option is specified. This is used by the program code and is not displayed to the user when the program is run.
- **Index**. Which is a numeric value that can be used to specify the menu option. Typically it is used when calling a single function which services several menu items. For example, a File menu may have the options: New, Open and Save, then a single function could be created to service these requests and the index value would be used to indicate which option has been selected.
- **Shortcut**. Which is a pull-down menu that can be used to specify a shortcut key (Cntrl-A to Cntrl-Z, F1 to F12, Cntrl-F1 to Cntrl-F12, Shift-F1 to Shift-F12, Shift-Cntrl-F1 to Shift-Cntrl-F12, Cntrl-Ins, Shift-Ins, Del, Shift-Del, Alt-Bkspace).
- **HelpContextID**. Which is a text box in which a unique numeric value is specified for the context ID. This value can be used to find the appropriate Help topic in the Help file identified by the HelpFile property.
- **NegotiatePosition**. Which is a pull-down list box which allows the user to specify the menu's NegotiatePosition property and determine how the menu appears in a form. Value options are 0 (None), 1 (Left) and 2 (Middle) and 3 (Right).
- **Checked**. Which is a checkbox which specifies if a check mark is to appear initially at the left of a menu item. It is generally used to specify if a toggled menu option is initially on or off.

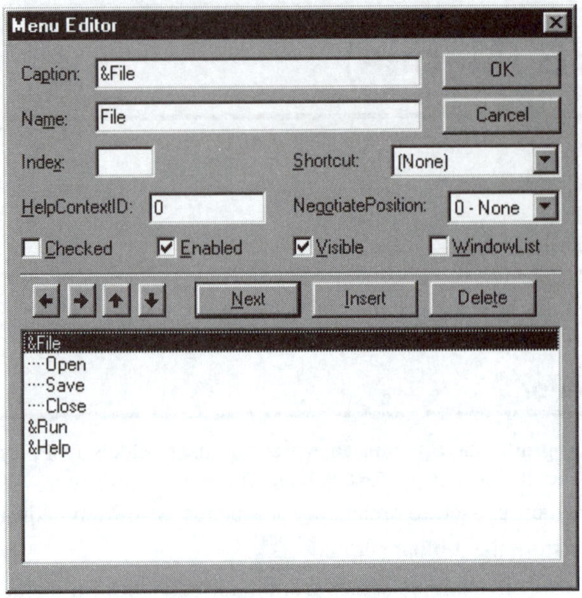

Figure 23.1   Menu editor.

- **Enabled**. Which is a checkbox which specifies if the menu item is to respond to events. If it is not enabled then the menu item appears dimmed.
- **Visible**. Which is a checkbox which specifies if the menu item is to appear in the menu.

23.2.1 Creating a menu system

The user enters the caption and name and then uses the outlining buttons to either promote or demote the item to a higher or lower level (with the left and right arrow buttons) or up and down (with the up and down arrow buttons). With this up to four levels of submenus can be created.

The list box displays a hierarchical list of menu items with indented submenu items which indicate their hierarchical position. A menu option is inserted using the Insert button and deleted with the Delete button. The OK button closes the Menu Editor and saves the most recent changes.

The code associated with a menu item is defined by the menu item name. For example, if a menu item has the caption of `File` and a name of `FileOption` then the associated code function will be `FileOption_Click`.

For example for create a menu with:

```
File            Exit
    Open
    Save
    Close
```

1. Create a caption `&File` and add the name of `MenuFile`. Next, press the Next button.
2. Create a caption `&Open` and add the name of `MenuFileItem`. Add an index value of 0. Then select the right arrow button to move the option to the next level, as shown in Figure 23.2. Next, press the Next button.

3. Create a caption &Save and add the name of MenuFileItem. Add an index value of 1, as shown in Figure 23.3. Next, press the Next button.
4. Create a caption &Close and add the name of MenuFileItem. Add an index value of 2, as shown in Figure 23.4. Next, press the Next button.
5. Create a caption &Exit and add the name of Exit. Then select the left arrow button to move the option to the next level, as shown in Figure 23.5. Next press the OK button and the form shown in the left-hand side of Figure 23.6 should be displayed.

The associated code modules which are related to these menus items are MenuFile_Click(), MenuFileItem_Click()and Exit_Click(). The MenuFileItem_ Click() module has the Index parameter passed to it. This has a value of 0 when Open is selected, a 1 when Save is selected and a 2 when Close is selected. The MenuFileItem is specified with:

```
Private Sub MenuFileItem_Click(Index As Integer)

End Sub
```

thus the value of Index will either be 0, 1 or 2.

Next, a text box is added to the form (Text1), as shown in the right-hand side of Figure 23.6. The resulting objects are shown in Figure 23.7.

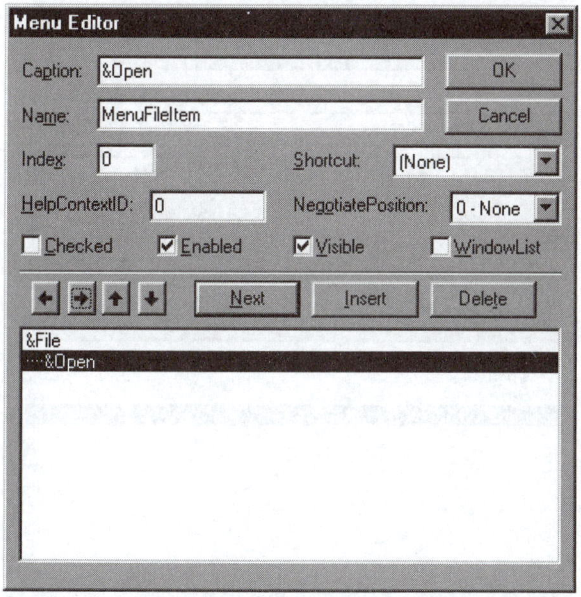

Figure 23.2   Adding a menu item.

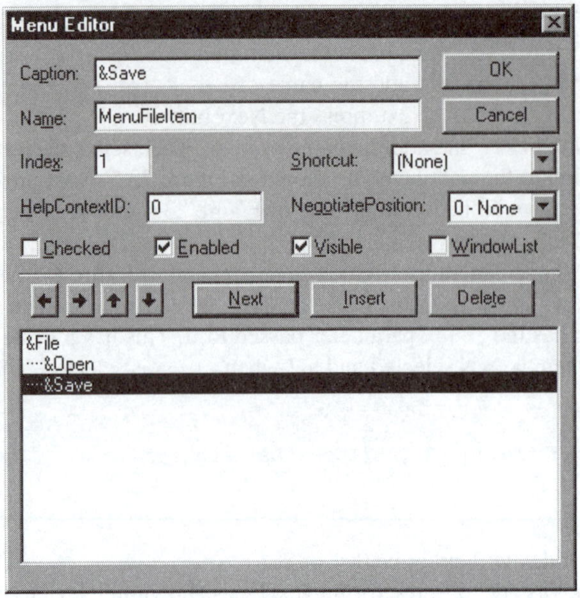

Figure 23.3   Adding a menu option.

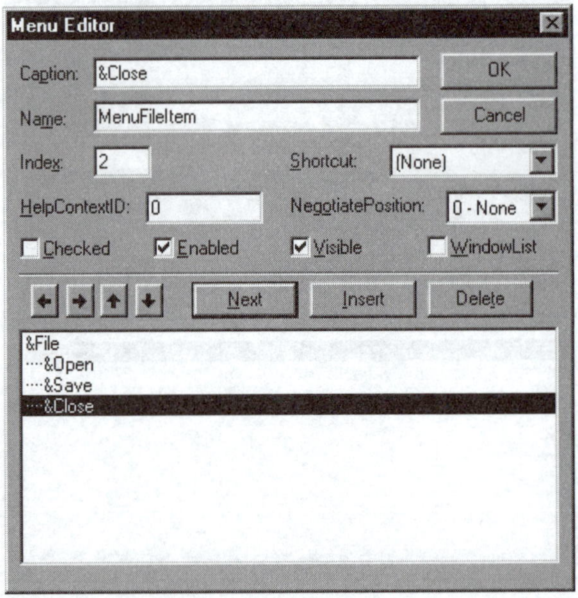

Figure 23.4   Adding a menu option.

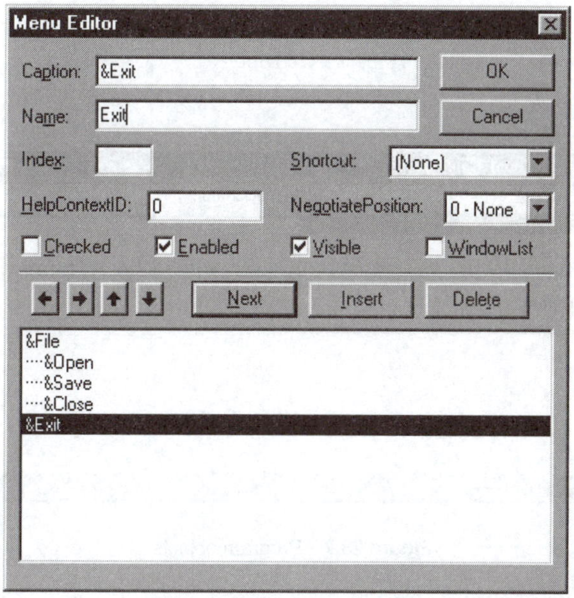

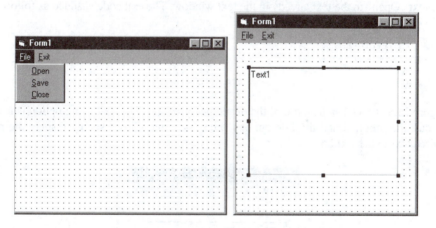

Figure 23.5 Adding a menu option.

Figure 23.6 Created menu and adding a text box.

Next, the code can be added. The `MenuFileItem` object services the Open, Save and Close options and the Index parameter passed into it. In the code below the Case statement is used to test the Index parameter and, in this case, display some text to the text box.

📖 Program 23.1

```
Private Sub MenuFileItem_Click(Index As Integer)
    Select Case Index
    ' Check index value of selected menu item.
    Case 0
        Text1.Text = Text1.Text & " Open "
    Case 1
```

```
            Text1.Text = Text1.Text & " Save "
    Case 2
            Text1.Text = Text1.Text & " Close "
    End Select
End Sub
```

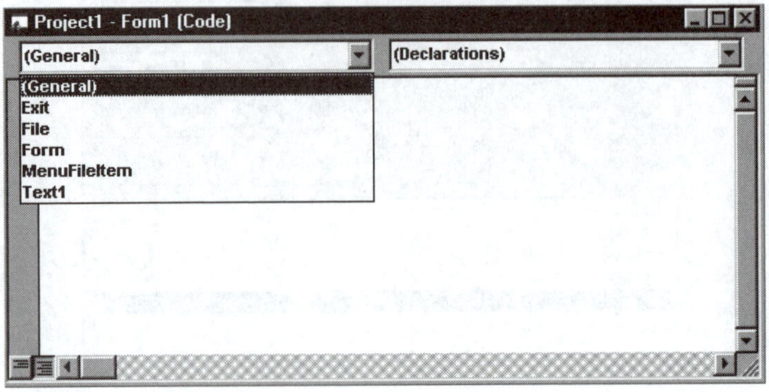

Figure 23.7 Program objects.

This code appends either "Open", "Save" or "Close" to the text box (Text1). The & character concatenates two strings together, thus the code `Text1.Text & "Open"` simply adds the text "Open" to the text already in the text window. The exit code is added as follows:

📖 Program 23.2

```
Private Sub Exit_Click()
     End
End Sub
```

Figure 23.8 shows a sample run of the developed program. The Exit menu option is used to quit the program and the File options (File, Save and Close) simply display the required text to the text box.

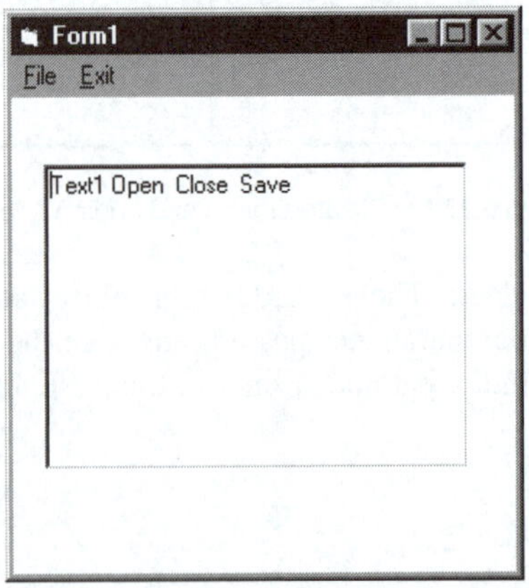

Figure 23.8 Sample run.

23.3 Common dialog control

The CommonDialog control allows for file operations such as opening, saving or printing files. It is basically a control between Visual Basic and the Microsoft Windows dynamic-link library COMMDLG.DLL. Thus this file must be in the Microsoft Windows SYSTEM directory for the common dialog control to work. In Visual Basic 5 the CommonDialog control is added by selecting Project → Components and then activating Microsoft Common Dialog Control.

A dialog box is added to an application by first adding the CommonDialog control to a form and setting its properties. When developing the program the common dialog box is displayed as an icon on the form. A program calls the dialog with one of the following (assuming that the dialog box is named CommonDialog1):

CommonDialog1.Filter
A string which displays the filename filter. The | character is used to differentiate different For example the following filter enables the user to select text files or graphic files that include bitmaps and icons:

```
Text (*.txt)|*.txt|Pictures(*.bmp;*.ico)|*.bmp;*.ico
```

CommonDialog1.Filename
Which returns or sets the path and filename of a selected file.

CommonDialog1.FilterIndex
Defines the default filter (with reference to the Filter).

CommonDialog1.ShowSave
Returns or sets the path and filename of a selected file. Displays the CommonDialog control's Save As dialog box. The object placeholder represents an object expression that evaluates to an object in the Applies To list.

CommonDialog1.ShowOpen
Displays the CommonDialog control's Open dialog box.

CommonDialog1.ShowPrinter
Displays the CommonDialog control's Printer dialog box.

CommonDialog1.ShowFont
Displays the CommonDialog control's Font dialog box.

CommonDialog1.ShowHelp
Runs WINHELP.EXE and displays the specified help file.

A dialog box is added to a form in any position, as shown in Figure 23.9. This box can be placed anywhere as it will not be seen on the form when the program is run.

Figure 23.9 Sample run.

The common dialog box can be used to determine the filename of a file to be opened or saved. It is used in Program 23.3 (which is a modification of Program 23.1) in the Open and Save file menu options. The filter is set to:

```
"All Files (*.*)|*.*|Text Files (*.txt)|*.txt|Temp Files (*.tmp)|*.tmp"
```

This displays, in the Type of File field, the three options `"All Files (*.*), *.*, Text Files (*.txt), *.txt` and `Temp Files (*.tmp)|*.tmp"`. The default file type is set to the second option with the filter index setting of:

```
        CommonDialog1.FilterIndex = 2
```

Figure 23.10 shows a sample run and the dialog box. It can be seen that the default Type of File is set to `"Text Files (*.txt)"` and Figure 23.10 also shows an example message box.

📖 Program 23.3
```
Private Sub MenuFileItem_Click(Index As Integer)
Dim filename As String

    Select Case Index
    Case 0
    CommonDialog1.Filter = _
    "All Files (*.*)|*.*|Text Files (*.txt)|*.txt|Temp Files (*.tmp)|*.tmp"
    CommonDialog1.FilterIndex = 2
    CommonDialog1.ShowOpen
    filename = CommonDialog1.filename
    MsgBox ("Open Filename: " & filename)
    Case 1
        CommonDialog1.Filter = _
        "All Files (*.*)|*.*|Text Files (*.txt)|*.txt|Temp Files (*.tmp)|*.tmp"
    CommonDialog1.FilterIndex = 2
    CommonDialog1.ShowSave
    filename = CommonDialog1.filename
    MsgBox ("Save Filename: " & filename)
    Case 2
    Text1.Text = Text1.Text & " Close "
    End Select
End Sub
```

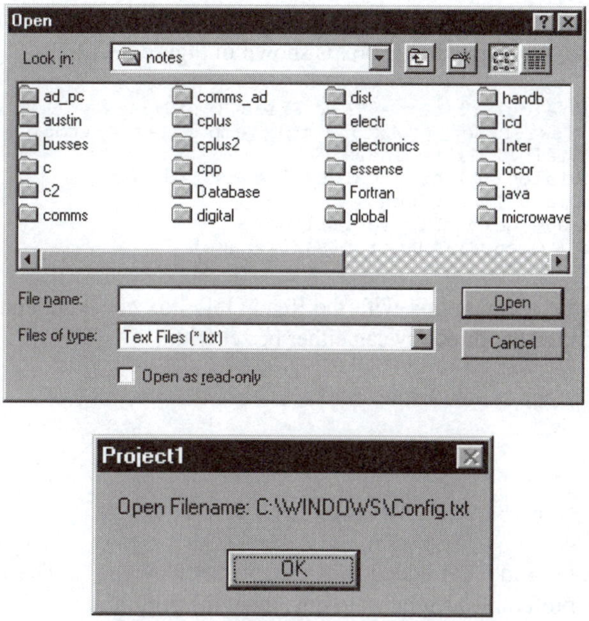

Figure 23.10 Sample run.

23.3.1 File Open/Save dialog box flags

Various flags can be set before the File Open/Save dialog box. These are defined in Table 23.1 and are set with:

```
CommonDialog1.Flags= flag1 + flag2 + ...
```

The flags can either be defined with their constant name (such as `cdlOFNReadOnly`) or by the value (0x01). These values or names can be added together to achieve the required functionality. For example, modifying the previous example to check the read-only check box for Open dialog box. A sample dialog box is shown in Figure 23.11.

```
CommonDialog1.Filter = "All Files (*.*)|*.*|
    Text Files (*.txt)|*.txt|Temp Files (*.tmp)|*.tmp"
CommonDialog1.FilterIndex = 2
CommonDialog1.Flags = cdlOFNHideReadOnly
CommonDialog1.ShowOpen
filename = CommonDialog1.filename
MsgBox ("Open Filename: " & filename)
```

For example, modifying the previous example to hide the Read-Only check box. A sample dialog box is shown in Figure 23.12.

```
CommonDialog1.Filter = "All Files (*.*)|*.*|
    Text Files (*.txt)|*.txt|Temp Files (*.tmp)|*.tmp"
CommonDialog1.FilterIndex = 2
CommonDialog1.Flags = cdlOFNHideReadOnly
CommonDialog1.ShowOpen
filename = CommonDialog1.filename
MsgBox ("Open Filename: " & filename)
```

For example, modifying the previous example to Allow the File Name list box to have multiple selections. A sample dialog box is shown in Figure 23.13.

```
CommonDialog1.Filter = "All Files (*.*)|*.*|
    Text Files (*.txt)|*.txt|Temp Files (*.tmp)|*.tmp"
CommonDialog1.FilterIndex = 2
CommonDialog1.Flags = cdlOFNAllowMultiselect
CommonDialog1.ShowOpen
filename = CommonDialog1.filename
MsgBox ("Open Filename: " & filename)
```

The flag settings for a dialog box with the Read-Only box checking and that the user is not allowed to change the directory can either be set with:

```
CommonDialog1.Flags = cdlOFNReadOnly + cdlOFNNoChangeDir
```

or

```
CommonDialog1.Flags = 9
```

which is 1 (`cdlOFNReadOnly`) added to 8 (`cdlOFNNoChangeDir`). The method of using lable constants is preferable as it helps to document the program.

Table 23.1   CommonDialog control constants.

Constant	Value	Description
cdlOFNReadOnly	&H1 (1)	Checks Read-Only check box for Open and Save As dialog boxes; see Figure 23.13.
cdlOFNOverwritePrompt	&H2 (2)	Causes the Save As dialog box to generate a message box if the selected file already exists.
cdlOFNHideReadOnly	&H4 (4)	Hides the Read-Only check box; see Figure 23.14.
cdlOFNNoChangeDir	&H8 (8)	Sets the current directory to what it was when the dialog box was invoked.
cdlOFNHelpButton	&H10 (16)	Causes the dialog box to display the Help button.
cdlOFNNoValidate	&H100 (256)	Allows invalid characters in the returned filename.
cdlOFNAllowMultiselect	&H200 (512)	Allows the File Name list box to have multiple selections; see Figure 23.15.
cdlOFNExtensionDifferent	&H400 (1024)	The extension of the returned filename is different from the extension set by the DefaultExt property.
cdlOFNPathMustExist	&H800 (2096)	User can enter only valid path names.
cdlOFNFileMustExist	&H1000 (4096)	User can enter only names of existing files.

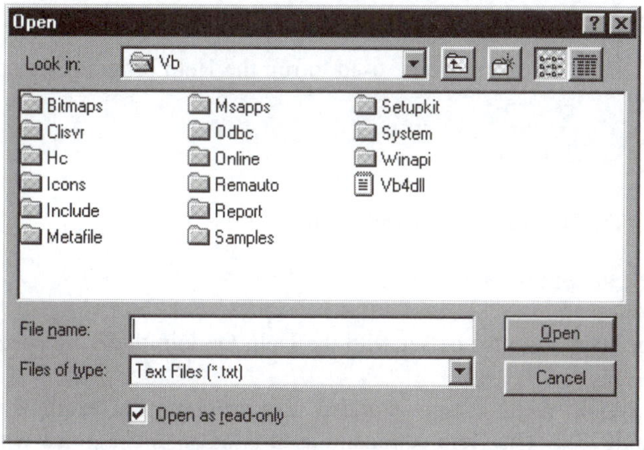

Figure 23.11 Sample run.

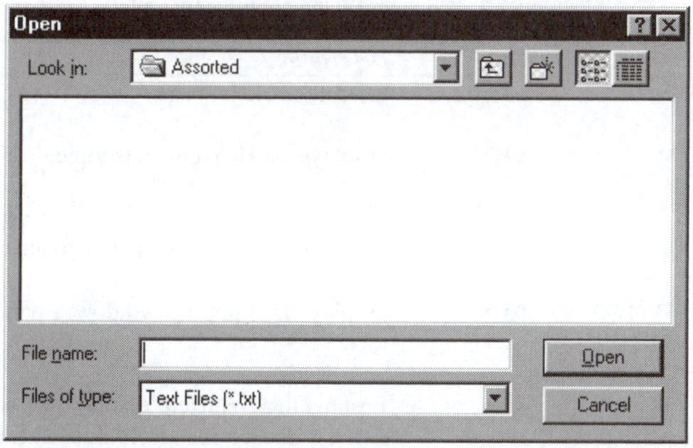

Figure 23.12 Sample run.

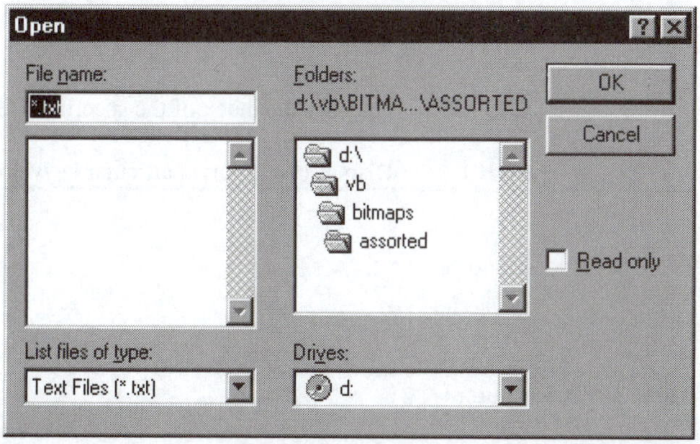

Figure 23.13 Sample run.

23.3.2 Showing help manuals

The Common Dialog box can also be used to run the Help program `WINHELP.EXE`. This is achieved by:

```
CommonDialog1.ShowHelp
```

and the name of the help manual is specified by:

```
CommonDialog1.HelpFile = filename
```

Various options flags can also be set with the Help Option; these are specified in Table 23.2.

Typically, a Help menu option is added to a program. An example Help event is given in Program 23.4. The Help command used is `cdlHelpContents` which shows the index page of the Help manual. Figure 23.14 shows an example of a run.

Table 23.2   CommonDialog control constants.

Constant	Value	Description
cdlHelpCommand	&H102	Executes a Help macro.
cdlHelpContents	&H3	Displays the Help contents topic.
cdlHelpContext	&H1	Displays Help for a particular context.
cdlHelpContextPopup	&H8	Displays in a pop-up window a particular Help topic.
cdlHelpForceFile	&H9	Ensures that WinHelp displays the correct Help file. If the correct Help file is currently displayed, no action occurs. If the incorrect Help file is displayed, WinHelp opens the correct file.
CdlHelpHelpOnHelp	&H4	Displays Help for using the Help application itself.
CdlHelpIndex	&H3	Displays the index of the specified Help file.
CdlHelpKey	&H101	Displays Help for a particular keyword.

📖 Program 23.4

```
Private Sub Help_Click()
Dim filename As String

    CommonDialog1.Filter = "All Files (*.*)|*.*|Help Files (*.hlp)|*.hlp"
    CommonDialog1.FilterIndex = 2
    CommonDialog1.ShowOpen
    filename = CommonDialog1.filename
    CommonDialog1.HelpFile = filename
    CommonDialog1.HelpCommand = cdlHelpContents
    CommonDialog1.ShowHelp
End Sub
```

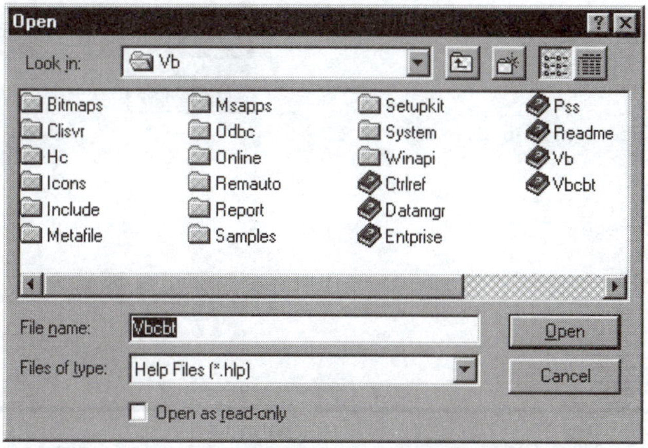

Figure 23.14 Selecting Help file.

23.4 Running an application program

Visual Basic allows for the execution of applications with the Shell command. Its format is:

Shell(*pathname[, windowstyle]*)

where the *windowstyle* is as defined in Table 23.3. If this argument is missing then the *windowstyle* is that the program is started with a minimized focus.

Table 23.3 Windowstyle named argument.

Constant	Val	Description
vbHide	0	Window is hidden and focus is passed to the hidden window.
vbNormalFocus	1	Window has focus and is restored to its original size and position.
vbMinimizedFocus	2	Window is displayed as an icon with focus.
vbMaximizedFocus	3	Window is maximized with focus.
vbNormalNoFocus	4	Window is restored to its most recent size and position. The currently active window remains active.
vbMinimizedNoFocus	6	Window is displayed as an icon. The currently active window remains active.

The following shows an example of executing the Calc.exe and Notepad.exe programs:

📖 Program 23.5

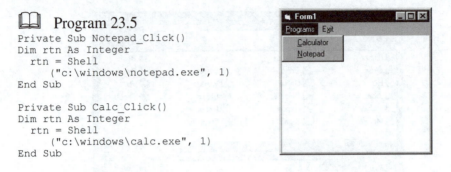

```
Private Sub Notepad_Click()
Dim rtn As Integer
  rtn = Shell
     ("c:\windows\notepad.exe", 1)
End Sub

Private Sub Calc_Click()
Dim rtn As Integer
  rtn = Shell
     ("c:\windows\calc.exe", 1)
End Sub
```

23.5 Exercises

23.5.1   Write a Visual Basic program with the following menu system:

```
File            Edit            View            Help
   Open            Copy            Normal
   Save            Paste           Full Screen
   Close           Select All
```

23.5.2   Modify the menu system in Exercise 23.5.1 so that the program displays the function of the menu option.

23.5.3   Expand Program 23.5 and its menu system so that it runs other Windows programs. An example could be:

```
Utils           WordProcessing      Spreadsheets   Exit
   Calculator      Word                Lotus123
   Notepad         AmiPro              Excel
   Paint
```

23.5.4   Integrate some of the programs from previous chapters into a single program with menu options. For example, the menu system could be:

```
Programs
   Temperature Conversion
   Quadratic Equation
   Straight Line
Exit
```

One possible method of implementing this program is to compile the temperature conversion, quadratic equation and straight-line programs to an EXE (File → Make EXE file...). Then run the Shell function from the object call.

```
rtn = Shell("tempcon.exe", 1)
```

24 VB (Events)

24.1 Introduction

Visual Basic differs from many other programming languages in that it is event-driven where the execution of a program is defined by the events that happen. This is a different approach to many programming languages which follow a defined sequence of execution and the programmer must develop routines which react to events. This chapter discusses the events that happen in Visual Basic.

24.2 Program events

Each object in Visual Basic has various events associated with it. For example, the single click on an object may cause one event but a double-click causes another. The events are displayed at the right-hand side of the code window. An example is shown in Figure 24.1 which in this case shows the events: KeyPress, KeyUp, LinkClose, LinkError, LinkExecute, LinkOpen and Load. The name of the routine which contains the code for the event and object is in the form:

```
Private Sub ObjectName_Event()
End
```

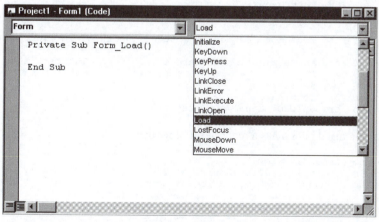

Figure 24.1 Form events.

The main events that occur in Visual Basic include:

- **MouseDown**. Which occurs when the user presses the mouse button down.
- **MouseMove**. Which occurs when the user moves the mouse.

- **MouseUp**. Which occurs when the user releases the mouse button.
- **Click**. Which occurs when a user performs a single click of the mouse button on the object.
- **DblClick**. Which occurs when a user performs a double-click of the mouse button on the object.
- **KeyUp**. Which occurs when the user releases a key.
- **KeyDown**. Which occurs when the user presses a key.
- **KeyPress**. Which occurs when the user presses and releases a key (the KeyDown and KeyUp events).
- **Load**. Which occurs when a form is loaded.
- **DragDrop**. Which occurs at the begin and end of a drag operation of any control.
- **LostFocus**. Which occurs when an object loses the focus, either by user action, such as tabbing to or clicking another object.
- **Resize**. Which occurs when a form is first displayed or if the object size is changed.
- **Unload**. Which occurs when a form is about to be removed from the screen.

Not all controls and forms (objects) have all the events associated with them. For example a form may have the following:

```
Private Sub Form_Activate()
Private Sub Form_Click()
Private Sub Form_Deactivate()
Private Sub Form_DblClick()
Private Sub Form_DragDrop(Source As Control, X As Single, Y As Single)
Private Sub Form_DragOver(Source As Control, X As Single, Y As Single, State
As Integer)
Private Sub Form_KeyDown(KeyCode As Integer, Shift As Integer)
Private Sub Form_KeyPress(KeyAscii As Integer)
Private Sub Form_KeyUp(KeyCode As Integer, Shift As Integer)
Private Sub Form_Load()
Private Sub Form_LostFocus()
Private Sub Form_MouseDown(Button As Integer, Shift As Integer, X As Single,
Y As Single)
Private Sub Form_MouseMove(Button As Integer, Shift As Integer, X As Single,
Y As Single)
Private Sub Form_MouseUp(Button As Integer, Shift As Integer, X As Single,
                                Y As Single)
Private Sub Form_Resize()
Private Sub Form_Terminate()
Private Sub Form_Unload(Cancel As Integer)
```

whereas a command button has a reduced set of routines:

```
Private Sub Command1_Click()
Private Sub Command1_DragDrop(Source As Control, X As Single, Y As Single)
Private Sub Command1_DragOver(Source As Control, X As Single, Y As Single,
                                State As Integer)
Private Sub Command1_GotFocus()
Private Sub Command1_KeyDown(KeyCode As Integer, Shift As Integer)
Private Sub Command1_KeyPress(KeyAscii As Integer)
Private Sub Command1_KeyUp(KeyCode As Integer, Shift As Integer)
Private Sub Command1_LostFocus()
Private Sub Command1_MouseDown(Button As Integer, Shift As Integer, X As
Single, Y As Single)
Private Sub Command1_MouseMove(Button As Integer, Shift As Integer, X As
Single, Y As Single)
```

```
Private Sub Command1_MouseUp(Button As Integer, Shift As Integer, X As
Single, Y As Single)
```

The parameters passed into the routine depend on the actions associated with the events. For example, the KeyPress event on a command button causes the routine:

```
Private Sub Command1_KeyPress(KeyAscii As Integer)

End
```

to be called. The value of KeyAscii will contain the ASCII value of the character press.

The MouseDown event for a command button has the following routine associated with it:

```
Private Sub Command1_MouseDown(Button As Integer, Shift As Integer, X As
Single, Y As Single)
```

where the value of Button is the value of the button press (0 for none, 1 for the left button and 2 for the right button). Shift specifies if the Shift key has been pressed, and X, Y specify the x, y coordinates of the mouse point. The following sections discuss some events which occur.

24.2.1 Click

The Click event occurs when the user presses and then releases a mouse button over an object. When the object is a form, the event occurs when the user clicks on a blank area or a disabled control. If the object is a control, the event occurs when the user:

- Clicks on a control with any of the mouse buttons. When the control is a CheckBox, CommandButton, or OptionButton control then the Click event occurs only when the user clicks the left mouse button.
- Presses the Alt-*hotkey* for a control, such as pressing Alt-X for the E&xit control property name.
- Presses the Enter key when the form has a command button.
- Presses the Space key when a command button, option button or check box control has the focus.

24.2.2 DblClick

The DblClick event occurs when the user presses and releases the mouse button twice over an object. In a form, it occurs when the user double-clicks either on a disabled control or a blank area of a form. On a control, the event happens when the user:

- Double-clicks on a control with the left mouse button.
- Double-clicks an item within a ComboBox control whose Style property is set to 1 (Simple).

An example form is shown in Figure 24.2. In this case, a text box is added to the form. Then the following code is added to the form:

```
Private Sub Form_DblClick()
    Text1.Text = "MISS"
```

```
End Sub
```

which will display the text 'MISS' when the user clicks on any blank area on the form. The following code is added to the text box:

```
Private Sub Text1_DblClick()
    Text1.Text = "HIT"
End Sub
```

which displays the text 'HIT' when the user double-clicks on the text box.

Figure 24.2 Sample run.

24.2.3 MouseUp, MouseDown

The MouseUp event occurs when the user releases the mouse button and the Mouse-Down event when the user presses a mouse button. The standard formats, on a form, for the associated routines are:

```
Private Sub Form_MouseDown(button As Integer, shift As Integer,
                           x As Single, y As Single)

Private Sub Form_MouseUp(button As Integer, shift As Integer,
                         x As Single, y As Single)
```

where
- button identifies which button was pressed (MouseDown) or released (MouseUp). The first bit of the value identifies the left button, the second identifies the right button and the third bit identifies the middle button. Thus a value of one identifies the left button, a value of two identifies the right and a value of four identifies the middle button (if the mouse has one). A combination of these values can be used to identify button press combinations, such as a value of six identifies that the middle and right buttons have been pressed. Table 24.1 shows the constant names for the buttons.
- shift identifies the state of the Shift, Cntrl, and Alt keys when the button was pressed (or released). The first bit of the value identifies the Shift key, the second bit identifies the Cntrl key and the third bit identifies the Alt key. Thus a value of one identifies the Shift key, a value of two identifies the Cntrl key and a value of four

identifies the Alt key. A combination of these values can be used to identify key combinations, such as a value of 6 identifies that the Cntrl and Alt keys are pressed. Table 24.2 shows the constant names for the keys.

- x, y identifies the current location of the mouse pointer. The x and y values are relatively to the ScaleHeight, ScaleWidth, ScaleLeft, and ScaleTop properties of the object.

An example of code for the MouseDown event is given next and a sample run is shown in Figure 24.3.

```
Private Sub Text1_MouseDown(Button As Integer, Shift As Integer, X As
Single, Y As Single)
    If (Button = vbLeftButton) Then
        Text1.Text = "LEFT BUTTON " & X & " " & Y
    ElseIf (Button = vbRightButton) Then:
        Text1.Text = "RIGHT BUTTON " & X & " " & Y
    ElseIf (Button = vbMiddleButton) Then:
        Text1.Text = "MIDDLE BUTTONS " & X & " " & Y
    End If
End Sub
```

Table 24.1 Button constants.

Constant (Button)	Value	Description
vbLeftButton	1	Left button is pressed
vbRightButton	2	Right button is pressed
vbMiddleButton	4	Middle button is pressed

Table 24.2 Button constants.

Constant	Value	Description
vbShiftMask	1	Shift key is pressed
vbCtrlMask	2	Ctrl key is pressed
vbAltMask	4	Alt key is pressed

24.2.4 MouseMove

The MouseMove event occurs when the user moves the mouse. Thus, it is continually called as the mouse cursor moves across an object. The standard forms, on a form, for the associated routines are:

```
Private Sub Form_MouseMove(button As Integer, shift As Integer,
          x As Single , y As Single)

Private Sub object_MouseMove(button As Integer, shift As Integer,
          x As Single, y As Single)
```

where button, shift, x and y have the same settings as the ones defined in the previous section.

Figure 24.3 Sample run.

An example of code for the MouseMove event is given next and a sample code is shown in Figure 24.4. Figure 24.5 shows a sample run. In this case, the x and y coordinate is the mouse pointer and the buttons pressed are displayed to the text box.

```
Private Sub Form_MouseMove(Button As Integer, Shift As Integer,
              X As Single, Y As Single)
    Text1.Text = "X,Y:" & X & " " & Y & " Button:" & Button
End Sub
```

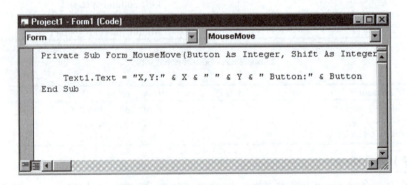
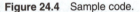

Figure 24.4 Sample code.

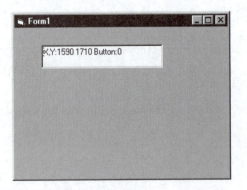

Figure 24.5 Sample run.

24.2.5 Drag and drop

The DragDrop event occurs at the end of a drag and drop operation of any control. The standard formats, on a form, for the associated routines are:

```
Private Sub Form_DragDrop(source As Control, x As Single, y As Single)

Private Sub object_DragDrop([index As Integer,]source As Control,
                  x As Single, y As Single)
```

where:
- source is the control being dragged.
- x, y specifies the current x and y coordinate of the mouse pointer within the target form or control. The x and y values are relative to the ScaleHeight, ScaleWidth, ScaleLeft, and ScaleTop properties of the object.

24.2.6 KeyPress

The KeyPress event occurs when the user presses and releases a key (the KeyDown and KeyUp events). The standard formats of the associated routines are:

```
Private Sub Form_KeyPress(Keyascii As Integer)
Private Sub object_KeyPress(Keyascii As Integer)
```

where Keyascii specifies a standard ANSI keycode; this can be converted into an ASCII character with the conversion function:

```
Chr(KeyAscii)
```

An example of code for the KeyPress event is given next and a sample run is shown in Figure 24.6. For this program, the user can type in the blank area on the form (the grey area) and the text will be displayed in the text box.

```
Private Sub Form_KeyPress(KeyAscii As Integer)
    Text1.Text = Chr(KeyAscii)
End Sub
```

Figure 24.6 Sample run.

24.2.7 LostFocus

The LostFocus event occurs when an object loses the focus, either by user action, such as tabbing to or clicking another object. The standard formats, on a form and an object, for the associated routines are:

```
Private Sub Form_LostFocus()
Private Sub object_LostFocus()
```

24.2.8 Resize

The Resize event occurs when a form is first displayed or if the object size is changed. The standard formats, on a form and an object, for the associated routines are:

```
Private Sub Form_Resize()
Private Sub object_Resize(height As Single, width As Single)
```

where:

- height is a value specifying the new height of the control.
- width is a value specifying the new width of the control.

24.2.9 Unload

The Unload event occurs when a form is about to be removed from the screen. Then if the form is reloaded the contents of all its controls are reinitialized. The standard formats, on an object, for the associated routines are:

```
Private Sub object_Unload(cancel As Integer)
```

where cancel determines whether the form is removed from the screen. If it is 0 then the form is removed else it will not be removed.

24.3 Exercises

24.3.1   Write a Visual Basic program which has a single form and a text box. The text box should show all of the events that occur with the form, that is:

Activate, Click, DblClick, Deactivate, DragDrop, DragOver, and so on.

Investigate when these events occur. Notice that when an event has code attached then the procedure name in the View Code pull-down menu becomes highlighted.

24.3.2   Write a Visual Basic program which has a single command button and a text box. The text box should show all of the events that occur with the command button, that is:

Click, KeyDown, KeyPress, KeyUp, MouseDown, MouseUp, and so on.

Investigate when these events occur.

24.3.3   Write a Visual Basic program in which the program displays the message 'IN TEXT AREA' when the mouse is within the textbox area and 'OUT OF

TEXT AREA' when it is out of the textbox area.

24.3.4   Write a Visual Basic program which has a command button. If the user presses any lower case letter then the program ends, else it should continue. A sample event which quits when the letter 'x' is pressed is given next:

```
Private Sub Command1_KeyPress(KeyAscii As Integer)
    If (Chr(KeyAscii) = "x") Then
        End
    End If
End Sub
```

24.3.5   Modify the program in Exercise 24.3.4 so that if the user clicks on the form (and not on the command button) the program automatically prompts the user for his/her name. This name should then appear in the command button caption property (Command1.caption). An outline of the event is given next:

```
Private Sub Form_Click()
Dim username As String

    username = InputBox("Enter your name")
     ::::::

End Sub
```

24.3.6   Write a Visual Basic program which displays the message 'So long and thanks for the fish' when the main form is Unloaded. The form should be removed from the screen.

24.3.7   Write a Visual Basic program with a textbox which displays the current keypress, including Alt-, Ctrl- and Shift- keystrokes.

24.3.8   Modify the program in Exercise 24.3.7 so that it also displays the mouse button press and the coordinates of the mouse.

25 VB (Graphics and Timer)

25.1 Introduction

This chapter discusses how graphics files are loaded into the program and how graphic objects can be drawn.

25.2 Loading graphics files

Visual Basic allows a graphic file to be loaded into a form, a picturebox or an image control. The standard function is:

```
LoadPicture(graphfile)
```

where *graphfile* specifies the name of the graphics file; if no name is given then the graphic in the form, picture box or image control is cleared. The standard graphics files supported by Visual Basic are:

- **BMP**. Windows bitmap file.
- **ICO**. Icon file.
- **RLE**. Run-length encoded files.
- **WMF**. Windows metafile files.

Normally graphics files are displayed in a PictureBox ⬚. Thus to display the graphic file "CLOUD.BMP" to Picture1 then:

```
Picture1.Picture = LoadPicture("CLOUD.BMP")
```

A picture can be loaded put into the clipboard using:

```
Clipboard.SetData LoadPicture(filename)
```

The following example loads a graphics file into a PictureBox. Figure 25.1 shows a sample form which contains a PictureBox, a CommandButton and a DialogBox.
The code added to the command button is as follows:

```
Private Sub Command1_Click()
Dim filename As String

    CommonDialog1.Filter = _
     "All Files (*.*)|*.*|Text Files (*.bmp)|*.bmp|Icon Files
(*.ico)|*.ico"

        CommonDialog1.FilterIndex = 2
        CommonDialog1.ShowOpen
        filename = CommonDialog1.filename
        Picture1.Picture = LoadPicture(filename)
End Sub
```

Figure 25.1 Form.

This will display a dialog box with the default file setting of *.BMP. After the user has selected a graphic then the LoadPicture function is used to display the graphic file to the PictureBox (Picture1). Figure 25.2 shows a sample dialog box and Figure 25.3 shows a sample graphic.

Figure 25.2 Dialog box.

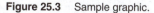

Figure 25.3 Sample graphic.

One problem with the previous example code is that a non-graphic file could be loaded and the program would not give an error message. The following code overcomes this by testing for an error. This is achieved by testing the `Err` parameter after the picture has been loaded. If it is set to TRUE then an error message is displayed and, after the user has accepted the error, then the picture will be cleared from the picture box.

```
Private Sub Command1_Click()
Dim filename,Msg As String
    CommonDialog1.Filter = _
    "All Files (*.*)|*.*|Text Files (*.bmp)|*.bmp|Icon Files
(*.ico)|*.ico"
    CommonDialog1.FilterIndex = 2
    CommonDialog1.ShowOpen
    filename = CommonDialog1.filename
    Picture1.Picture = LoadPicture(filename)
    If Err Then
        Msg = "Error loading graphics file."
        MsgBox Msg
        Picture = LoadPicture()
    End If
End Sub
```

25.3 Colours

The background and foreground colour of an object can be modified with the Back-Colour or ForeColour property, respectively. The standard form is:

object.BackColor= *colour*
object.ForeColor= *colour*

A colour is defined as its RGB (red/green/blue) strength, with a hexadecimal strength from &H00 to &H77 for each colour. The valid ranges of colour are thus from 0 to &HFFFFFF.

25.3.1 RGB function

The RGBColour function returns the hexadecimal colour value given the three strengths of red, green and blue. Its standard form is:

colour=RGB (*red, green, blue*)

where red, green and blue are a value from 0 to 255. Table 25.1 gives some example colours with their RGB colour. For example:

```
Form.BkColor=QBColor(0,0,255)      ' set background color to Blue
Form.ForeColor=QBColor(255,255,0)  ' set foreground color to Yellow
```

25.3.2 QBColour function

The QBColour function has a limited range of 15, typically colours as specified in Table 25.2. For example, the following sets the

```
Form.BkColor=QBColor(1)    ' set background color to Blue
Form.ForeColor=QBColor(6)  ' set foreground color to Yellow
```

Table 25.1 Colour strengths.

Colour	Red value	Green value	Blue value
Black	0	0	0
Blue	0	0	255
Green	0	255	0
Cyan	0	255	255
Red	255	0	0
Magenta	255	0	255
Yellow	255	255	0
White	255	255	255

Table 25.2 Colour values.

Number	Colour	Number	Colour
0	Black	8	Grey
1	Blue	9	Light blue
2	Green	10	Light green
3	Cyan	11	Light cyan
4	Red	12	Light red
5	Magenta	13	Light magenta
6	Yellow	14	Light yellow
7	White	15	Bright white

25.4 Drawing

Visual Basic has a wide range of drawing functions (graphics methods); these include:

- **Line**. Draws lines and rectangles on an object.
- **Circle**. Draws a circle, ellipse, or arc on an object.
- **Cls**. Clears graphics and text from a Form or PictureBox.
- **FillColour**. Returns or sets the colour used to fill in shapes (drawn by Line and Circle graphics methods).
- **FillStyle**. Returns or sets the pattern used to fill Shapes (as created by Line or Circle graphics methods).

25.4.1 Line

The Line graphic method draws lines and rectangles on an object. Its standard form is:

object.Line Step (*x1, y1*) - Step (*x2, y2*), *colour*, BF

where († identifies optional parameter, ‡ identifies required parameter):

- Step. Keyword specifying the starting point coordinates. †
- (*x1, y1*). Define the starting point coordinates of a line or rectangle. If they are omitted then the line starts at the current x,y position (CurrentX and CurrentY). †
- Step. Keyword specifying the end point coordinates. †
- (*x2, y2*) Define the end point coordinates of a line or rectangle. ‡

- *colour*. Defines the RGB colour used to draw the line. If it is omitted then the ForeColour property setting is used. †
- B. If the B option is added then a box is drawn using the coordinates for opposite corners. †
- F. If the F option is added then the box is filled with the same colour as the line colour. †

The CurrentX and CurrentY values are set to the end of the line after a line has been drawn. The DrawWidth property sets the width of the line and DrawMode and Draw-Style properties define the way that the line or box is drawn.

The following code is added to a form and with the Click event. It displays 15 solid rectangles of a random size and random colour. The QBColour function is used to display one of the 16 predefined colours. Note that the Rnd function returns a random number from 0 to 1.

```
Private Sub Form_Click()
Dim x1, x2, y1, y2, i As Integer

    For i = 1 To 15
        ForeColor = QBColor(i)
        x1 = ScaleWidth * Rnd
        y1 = ScaleHeight * Rnd
        x2 = ScaleWidth * Rnd
        y2 = ScaleHeight * Rnd
        Line (x1, y1)-(x2, y2), , BF
    Next i
End Sub
```

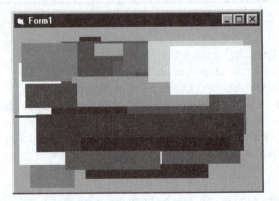

Figure 25.4   Sample graphic.

25.4.2 Circle

The Circle graphic method draws a circle, ellipse or an arc on an object. Its standard form is:

object.Circle Step (*x*, *y*), *radius*, *colour*, *start*, *end*, *aspect*

where († identifies optional parameter, ‡ identifies required parameter):

- Step. Keyword specifying that the centre of the circle, ellipse, or arc is relative to the current coordinates given by the CurrentX and CurrentY properties of the object. †
- (*x, y*). Value which gives the coordinates of the centre of the circle, ellipse or arc. ‡
- *radius*. Value which specifies the radius of the circle, ellipse or arc. ‡
- *colour*. Value which specifies the colour of the circle's outline. If omitted, the value of the ForeColour property is used. †
- *start, end*. Values specifying the start and end angle (in radians) for a drawn arc, partial circle or ellipse, start and end specify (in radians) the beginning and end positions of the arc. †
- *aspect*. Value specifying the aspect ratio of the circle. The default value is 1.0, which yields a perfect circle. †

The QBColour or RGB function are typically used to set the colour. A circle is filled with a defined colour with the FillColour property and the fill style is set by the FillStyle properties. The DrawWidth property defines the width of the line used to draw the circle, ellipse, or arc.

The following example code draws 10 circles of increasing size of a random colour. Figure 25.5 shows a sample run.

```
Private Sub Form_Click()
Dim x, y, Radius, RadiusInc As Double
Dim i As Integer

    x = ScaleWidth / 2 ' Set X position.
    y = ScaleHeight / 2    ' Set Y position.
    If (ScaleWidth > ScaleHeight) Then
        RadiusInc = ScaleHeight / 20
    Else
        RadiusInc = ScaleWidth / 20
    End If

    For i = 1 To 10 ' Set radius.
        Radius = Radius + RadiusInc
        Circle (x, y), Radius, RGB(Rnd * 255, Rnd * 255, Rnd * 255)
    Next i
End Sub
```

Figure 25.5 Sample graphic.

25.4.3 DrawWidth

The DrawWidth property returns or sets the line width of a graphic method. To set the width of line the following is used:

object.DrawWidth = *size*

where the *size* is a value from 1 (the default) to 32 767 and is measured in pixels.

25.4.4 DrawStyle

The DrawWidth property returns or sets the line style of a graphic method. To set the line style the following is used:

object.DrawWidth = *value*

where *value* is a number from 0 (the default) to 6 which corresponds to the following line styles:

0 Solid.	1 Dash.	2 Dot.
3 Dash-Dot.	4 Dash-Dot-Dot.	5 Transparent.
6 Inside Solid.		

For example, to set a line style on a Form to dashed:

```
DrawWidth=1
```

25.4.5 FillColour

The FillColour property returns or sets the colour used to fill in shapes, circles and boxes. To set the fill colour the following is used:

object.FillColor = *value*

where the *size* is a hexadecimal colour and by default it is Black.

25.4.6 FillStyle

The FillStyle property returns or sets the fill style of a graphic method. To set the line style the following is used:

object.FillStyle = *value*

where *value* is a number from 0 (the default) to 6 which corresponds to the following line styles:

0 Solid.	1 (Default) Transparent.	2 Horizontal Line.
3 Vertical Line.	4 Upward Diagonal.	5 Downward Diagonal.
6 Cross.	7 Diagonal Cross.	

The following example displays 15 randomly filled circles with a radius of 200 pixels. It is initiated with the user clicks on the form. Figure 25.6 shows a sample run.

```
Private Sub Form_Click()
Dim x1, x2, y1, y2, i As Integer
    For i = 1 To 15
        ForeColor = QBColor(i)
        FillStyle = Int(7 * Rnd)
        x1 = ScaleWidth * Rnd
        y1 = ScaleHeight * Rnd
        x2 = ScaleWidth * Rnd
        y2 = ScaleHeight * Rnd
        Circle (x1, y1), 200
    Next i
End Sub
```

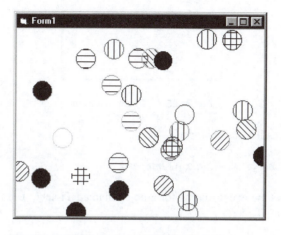

Figure 25.6   Sample graphic.

25.4.7 CurrentX, CurrentY

The CurrentX and CurrentY properties return or set the horizontal and vertical (CurrentY) coordinates, respectively. The standard format is:

object.CurrentX = *x*
object.CurrentY = *y*

The (0,0) co-ordinate is at the upper left-hand corner of an object.

25.4.8 Cls

The Cls method clears graphics and text generated at run time from a Form or Picture-Box. Its standard form is:

object.Cls

25.5 Timer

A Timer control ![timer icon] can be used to create accurate timings. Figure 25.7 shows a timer control added to a form. This control will be invisible to the user when the program is executed. The properties of the timer object are:

- **Enable**. When set to a True the timer object is enabled, else it is disabled.
- **Interval**. This sets the timer interval in milliseconds. For example, Timer1.interval=1000 will set the Timer1 object to an interval of 1 second.

Figure 25.7　Timer on a form.

The event that is called has the form:

```
Private Sub object_Timer([index As Integer])
```

Figure 25.8 shows the event routine for a object named Timer1. The name of this routine is thus Timer1_Timer.

```
Project1 - Form1 (Code)
Timer1                              Timer
    Private Sub Timer1_Timer()
        i = i + 1
        Cls
        If (i = 1) Then
            FillStyle = 0
        ElseIf (i = 2) Then
            FillStyle = 2
        ElseIf (i = 3) Then
            FillStyle = 3
            i = 0
        End If
        Circle (500, 500), 400
    End Sub
```

Figure 25.8　Timer event.

The following program uses the timer to update the fill pattern of a circle. There are three different fill patterns and these are called with a one second interval. The timer event is defined as

```
Private Sub Timer1_Timer()
    i = i + 1
    Cls
    If (i = 1) Then
        FillStyle = 0
    ElseIf (i = 2) Then
        FillStyle = 2
    ElseIf (i = 3) Then
```

```
        FillStyle = 3
        i = 0
    End If
    Circle (500, 500), 400
End Sub
```

The initial value of I and the interval are defined with the loading of the form with:

```
Private Sub Form_Load()
    Timer1.Interval = 1000
    i = 0
End Sub
```

Finally to set the value of i to be global then the following is added to the (general), (declarations):

```
Dim i As Integer
```

25.6 Exercises

25.6.1   Write a program which displays a coloured rectangle in the middle of a form. Each time the user clicks on the form the rectangle should change colour.

25.6.2   Write a Visual Basic program which automatically moves a rectangle from the top left-hand side of the screen to the bottom right-hand side. The program should quit once it reaches the bottom corner.

25.6.3   Write a Visual Basic program which randomly moves a small rectangle around the screen. If the rectangle touches any of the edges it should rebound off the edge.

25.6.4   Write a Visual Basic program in which the user controls the movement of a small rectangle by the arrow keys.

25.6.5   Write a Visual Basic program which displays a circle on the form which follows the user's mouse cursor (note: use the `cls` function to get rid of the existing circle).

25.6.6   Write separate Visual Basic programs which draw the following objects:

(i)   A car.   (ii)   A ship.   (iii)   A house.

25.6.7   Write a Visual Basic program which displays the following images. Use the timer and `cls` functions to create a timing delay of 1 second between each image display (the animation should look as if it is winking).

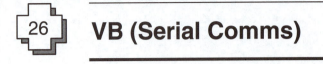

VB (Serial Comms)

26.1 Introduction

This chapter discusses how Visual Basic can be used to access serial communication functions. Windows hides much of the complexity of serial communications and automatically puts any received characters in a receive buffer and characters sent into a transmission buffer. The receive buffer can be read by the program whenever it has time and the transmit buffer is emptied when it is free to send characters.

26.2 Communications control

Visual Basic allows many additional components to be added to the toolbox. The Microsoft Comm component is used to add a serial communication facility.

This is added to the toolbox with: `Project → Components` (Ctrl-T)

or in Visual Basic 4 with: `Tools → Custom Controls` (Ctrl-T)

Notice that both are selected by using the Ctrl-T keystroke. Figure 26.1 shows how a component is added in Visual Basic 4 and shows how it is added in Visual Basic 5. This then adds a Comms Component 🦉 into the toolbox, as shown in Figure 26.2.

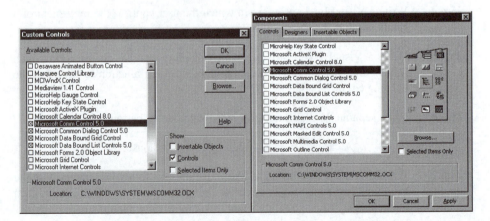

Figure 26.1 Adding Microsoft Comm component with Visual Basic 4/5.

Figure 26.2 Toolbox showing Comms components.

In order to use the Comms component the files MSCOMM16.OCX (for a 16-bit module) or MSCOMM32.OCX (for a 32-bit module) must be present in the \WINDOWS\SYSTEM directory. The class name is MSComm.

The communications control provides the following two ways for handling communications:

- **Event-driven**. Event-driven communications is the best method of handling serial communication as it frees the computer to do other things. The event can be defined as the reception of a character, a change in CD (carrier detect) or a change in RTS (request to send). The OnComm event can be used to capture these events. and also to detect communications errors.

- **Polling**. CommEvent properties can be tested to determine if an event or an error has occurred. For example, the program can loop waiting for a character to be received. Once it is, the character is read from the receive buffer. This method is normally used when the program has time to poll the communications receiver or that a known response is imminent.

Visual Basic uses the standard Windows drivers for the serial communication ports (such as serialui.dll and serial.vxd). The communication control is added to the application for each port. The parameters (such as the bit rate, parity, and so on) can be changed by selecting Control Panel → System → Device Manager → Ports (COM and LPT) → Port Settings. The settings of the communications port (the IRQ and the port address) can be changed by selecting Control Panel → System → Device Manager → Ports (COM and LPT) → Resources for IRQ and Addresses. Figure 26.3 shows example parameters and settings.

26.3 Properties

The Comm component is added to a form whenever serial communications are required (as shown in left-hand side of Figure 26.4). The right-hand side of Figure 26.5 shows its properties. By default, the first created object is named MSComm1 (the second is named MSComm2, and so on). It can be seen that the main properties of the object are: CommPort, DTREnable, EOFEnable, Handshaking, InBufferSize, Index, InputLen, InputMode, Left, Name, NullDiscard, OutBufferSize, ParityReplace, RThreshold, RTSEnable, Settings, SThreshold, Tag and Top. The main properties are defined in Table 26.1.

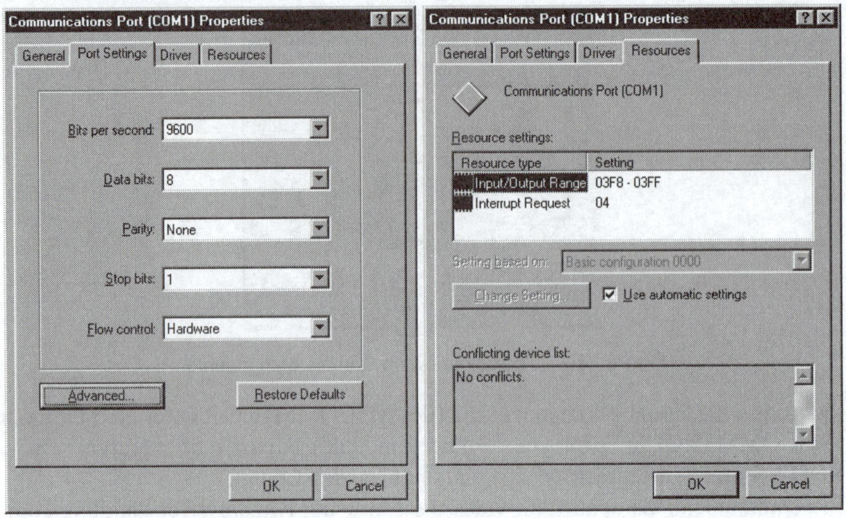

Figure 26.3 Changing port setting and parameters.

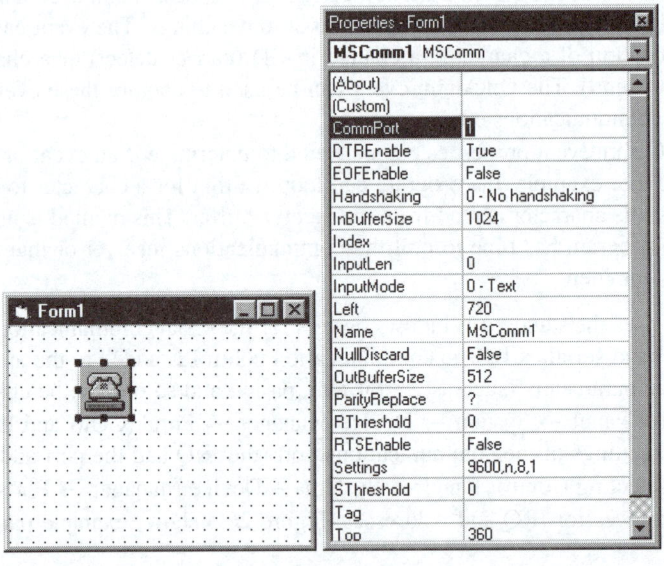

Figure 26.4 Communications control and MS Comm Properties.

Table 26.1 The main communications control properties.

Properties	Description
CommPort	Sets and returns the communications port number.
Input	Returns and removes characters from the receive buffer.
Output	Writes a string of characters to the transmit buffer.
PortOpen	Opens and closes a port, and gets port settings
Settings	Sets and returns port parameters, such as bit rate, parity, number of data bits and so on.

26.3.1 Settings

The Settings property sets and returns the RS-232 parameters, such as Baud rate, parity, the number of data bit, and the number of stop bits. Its syntax is:

[form.]MSComm.Settings*[= setStr$]*

where the strStr is a string which contains the RS-232 settings. This string takes the form:

```
"BBBB,P,D,S"
```

where BBBB defines the Baud rate, P the parity, D the number of data bits, and S the number of stop bits.

The following lists the valid Baud rates (default is 9600 Baud):

110, 300, 600, 1200, 2400, 9600, 14 400, 19 200, 38 400, 56 000, 128 000, 256 000.

The valid parity values are (default is N): E (Even), M (Mark), N (None), O (Odd), S (Space).

The valid data bit values are (default is 8): 4, 5, 6, 7 or 8.

The valid stop bit values are (default is 1). 1, 1.5 or 2.

An example of setting a control port to 4800 Baud, even parity, 7 data bits and 1 stop bit is:

```
Com1.Settings = "4800,E,7,1"
```

26.3.2 CommPort

The CommPort property sets and returns the communication port number. Its syntax is:

[form.]MSComm.CommPort*[= portNumber%]*

which defines the portNumber from a value between 1 and 99. A value of 68 is returned if the port does not exist.

26.3.3 PortOpen

The PortOpen property sets and returns the state of the communications port. Its syntax is:

[form.]MSComm.PortOpen*[= {True | False}]*

A True setting opens the port, while a False closes the port and clears the receive and transmit buffers (this automatically happens when an application is closed).

The following example opens communications port number 1 (COM1:) at 4800 Baud with even parity, 7 data bits and 1 stop bit:

```
Com1.Settings = "4800,E,7,1"
Com1.CommPort = 1
Com1.PortOpen = True
```

26.3.4 Inputting data

The three main properties used to read data from the receive buffer are Input, InBuffer-Count and InBufferSize.

Input

The Input property returns and removes a string of characters from the receive buffer. Its syntax is:

[*form.*]*MSComm.*Input

To determine the number of characters in the buffer the InBufferCount property is tested (to be covered in the next section). Setting InputLen to 0 causes the Input property to read the entire contents of the receive buffer.

Program 26.1 shows an example of how to read data from the receiver buffer.

Program 26.1

```
' Check for characters in the buffer
If Com1.InBufferCount Then
     ' Read data in the buffer
     InStr$ = Com1.Input
End If
```

InBufferSize

The InBufferSize property sets and returns the maximum number of characters that can be received in the receive buffer (by default it is 1024 bytes). Its syntax is:

[*form.*]*MSComm.*InBufferSize[= *numBytes%*]

The size of the buffer should be set so that it can store the maximum number of characters that will be received before the application program can read them from the buffer.

InBufferCount

The InBufferCount property returns the number of characters in the receive buffer. It can also be used to clear the buffer by setting the number of characters to 0. Its syntax is:

[*form.*]*MSComm.*InBufferCount[= *count%*]

26.3.5 Outputting data

The three main properties used to write data to the transmit buffer are Output, OutBufferCount and OutBufferSize.

Output

The Output property writes a string of characters to the transmit buffer. Its syntax is:

*[form.]MSComm.*Output*[= outString$]*

Program 26.2 uses the KeyPress event on a form to send the character to the serial port.

📖 Program 26.2

```
Private Sub Form_KeyPress (KeyAscii As Integer)
     if (Com1.OutBufferCount < Com1.OutBufferSize)
         Com1.Output = Chr$(KeyAscii)
End Sub
```

OutBufferSize

The OutBufferSize property sets and returns the number of characters in the transmit buffer (default size is 512 characters). Its syntax is:

*[form.]MSComm.*OutBufferSize*[= NumBytes%]*

OutBufferCount

The OutBufferCount property returns the number of characters in the transmit buffer. The transmit buffer can also be cleared by setting it to 0. Its syntax is:

*[form.]MSComm.*OutBufferCount*[= 0]*

26.3.6 Other properties

Other properties are:

- **Break**. Sets or clears the break signal. A True sets the break signal, while a False clears the break signal. When True character transmission is suspended and a break level is set on the line. This continues until Break is set to False. Its syntax is:

  *[form.]MSComm.*Break*[= {True | False}]*

- **CDTimeout**. Sets and returns the maximum amount of time that the control waits for a carried detect (CD) signal, in milliseconds, before a timeout. Its syntax is:

  *[form.]MSComm.*CDTimeout*[= milliseconds&]*

- **CTSHolding**. Determines whether the CTS line should be detected. CTS is typically used for hardware handshaking. Its syntax is:

  *[form.]MSComm.*CTSHolding*[= {True | False}]*

- **DSRHolding**. Determines the DSR line state. DSR is typically used to indicate the presence of a modem. If the setting is a True then the DSR line is high, else it is low. Its syntax is:

  *[form.]MSComm.*DSRHolding*[= setting]*

- **DSRTimeout**. Sets and returns the number of milliseconds to wait for the DSR signal before an OnComm event occurs. Its syntax is:

[*form.*]*MSComm*.DSRTimeout[= *milliseconds&*]

- **DTEEnable**. Determines whether the DTR signal is enabled. It is typically sent from the computer to the modem to indicate that it is ready to receive data. A True setting enables the DTR line (output level high). Its syntax is:

  [*form.*]*MSComm*.DTREnable[= {*True* | *False*}]

- **RTSEnable**. Determines whether the RTS signal is enabled. Normally used to handshake incoming data and is controlled by the computer. Its syntax is:

  [*form.*]*MSComm*.RTSEnable[= {*True* | *False*}]

- **NullDiscard**. Determines whether null characters are read into the receive buffer. A True setting does not transfer the characters. Its syntax is:

  [*form.*]*MSComm*.NullDiscard[= {*True* | *False*}]

- **SThreshold**. Sets and returns the minimum number of characters allowable in the transmit buffer before the OnComm event. A 0 value disables generating the On-Comm event for all transmission events, while a value of 1 causes the OnComm event to be called when the transmit buffer is empty. Its syntax is:

  [*form.*]*MSComm*.SThreshold[= *numChars%*]

- **Handshaking**. Sets and returns the handshaking protocol. It can be set to no hand-shaking, hardware handshaking (using RTS/CTS) or software handshaking (XON/XOFF). Valid settings are given in Table 26.2. Its syntax is:

  [*form.*]*MSComm*.Handshaking[= *protocol%*]

- **CommEvent**. Returns the most recent error message. Its syntax is:

  [*form.*]*MSComm*.CommEvent

Table 26.2   Settings for handshaking.

Setting	Value	Description
ComNone	0	No handshaking (Default).
ComXOnXOff	1	XON/XOFF handshaking.
ComRTS	2	RTS/CTS handshaking.
ComRTSXOnXOff	3	RTS/CTS and XON/XOFF handshaking.

When a serial communication event (OnComm) occurs then the event (error or change) can be determined by testing the CommEvent property. Table 26.3 lists the error values and Table 26.4 lists the communications events.

Table 26.3 CommEvent property.

Setting	Value	Description
comBreak	1001	Break signal received.
comCTSTO	1002	CTSTimeout. Occurs when transmitting a character and CTS was low for CTSTimeout milliseconds.
comDSRTO	1003	DSRTimeout. Occurs when transmitting a character and DTR was low for DTRTimeout milliseconds.
comFrame	1004	Framing Error.
comOverrun	1006	Port Overrun. The receive buffer is full and another character was written into the buffer, overwriting the previously received character.
comCDTO	1007	CDTimeout. Occurs CD was low for CDTimeout milliseconds, when transmitting a character.
comRxOver	1008	Receive buffer overflow.
comRxParity	1009	Parity error.
comTxFull	1010	Transmit buffer full.

Table 26.4 Communications events.

Setting	Value	Description
comEvSend	1	Character has been sent.
comEvReceive	2	Character has been received.
comEvCTS	3	Change in CTS line.
comEvDSR	4	Change in DSR line from a high to a low.
comEvCD	5	Change in CD line.
comEvRing	6	Ring detected.
comEvEOF	7	EOF character received.

26.4 Events

The Communication control generates an event (OnComm) when the value CommEvent property changes its value. Figure 26.5 shows the event subroutine and Program 26.3 shows an example event routine which tests the CommEvent property. It also shows the property window which is shown with a right click on the comms component.

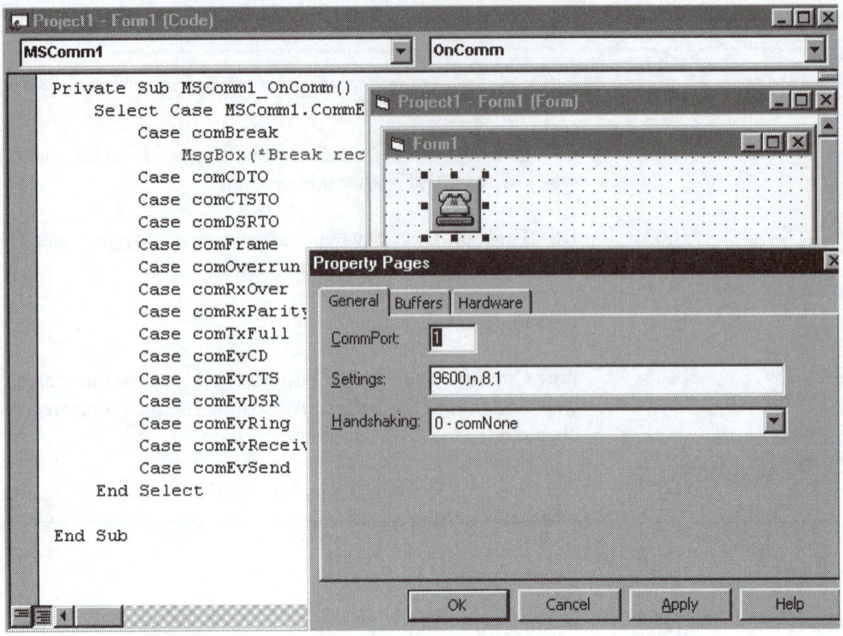

Figure 26.5   OnComm event.

Program 26.3

```
Private Sub MSComm_OnComm ()
     Select Case MSComm1.CommEvent
         Case comBreak        ' A Break was received.
         MsgBox("Break received")
         Case comCDTO          ' CD (RLSD) Timeout.
         Case comCTSTO         ' CTS Timeout.
         Case comDSRTO         ' DSR Timeout.
         Case comFrame         ' Framing Error
         Case comOverrun       ' Data Lost.
         Case comRxOver        ' Receive buffer overflow.
         Case comRxParity      ' Parity Error.
         Case comTxFull        ' Transmit buffer full.
         Case comEvCD          ' Change in the CD.
         Case comEvCTS         ' Change in the CTS.
         Case comEvDSR         ' Change in the DSR.
         Case comEvRing        ' Change in the RI.
         Case comEvReceive
         Case comEvSend
     End Select
End Sub
```

26.5 Example program

Program 26.4 shows a simple transmit/receive program which uses COM1: to transmit and receive. A loopback connection which connects the transmit line to the receive line can be used to test the communications port. All the characters that are transmitted should be automatically received. A sample form is given in Figure 26.6.

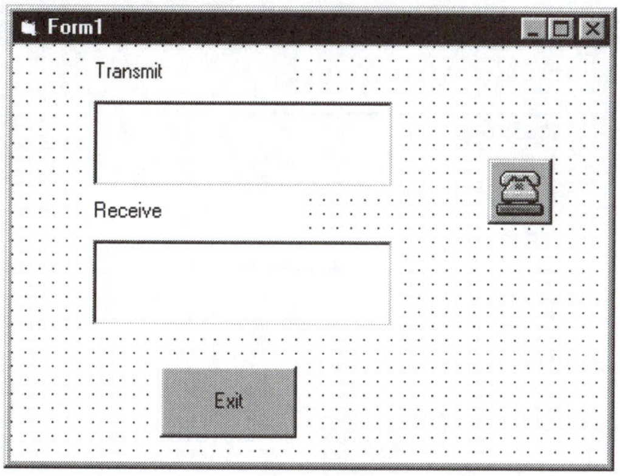

Figure 26.6   Simple serial communications transmit/receive form.

The loading of the form (Form_Load) is called when the program is initially run. This is used to set-up the communication parameters (in this case to 9600 Baud, no parity, 8 data bits and 1 stop bit). When the user presses a key on the form the Form_Keypress event is called. This is then used to transmit the entered character and display it to the Transmit text window (Text1). When a character is received the OnComm event is called and the MSComm1.CommEvent is set to 2 (comEvReceive) which identifies that a character has been received. This character is then displayed to the Receive text window (Text2). Figure 26.7 shows a sample run.

📖 Program 26.4

```
Private Sub Form_Load()

   MSComm1.CommPort = 1             ' Use COM1.
   MSComm1.Settings = "9600,N,8,1"  ' 9600 baud, no parity, 8 data,
                                    '  and 1 stop bit.
   MSComm1.InputLen = 0             ' Read entire buffer when Input
                                    ' is used
   MSComm1.PortOpen = True          ' Open port
End Sub

Private Sub Form_KeyPress(KeyAscii As Integer)
    MSComm1.Output = KeyAscii
    Text1.Text = KeyAscii
End Sub

Private Sub MSComm1_OnComm()
    If (MSComm1.CommEvent = comEvReceive) Then
        Text2.Text = MSComm1.Input
    End If
End Sub


Private Sub Command1_Click()
    End
End Sub
```

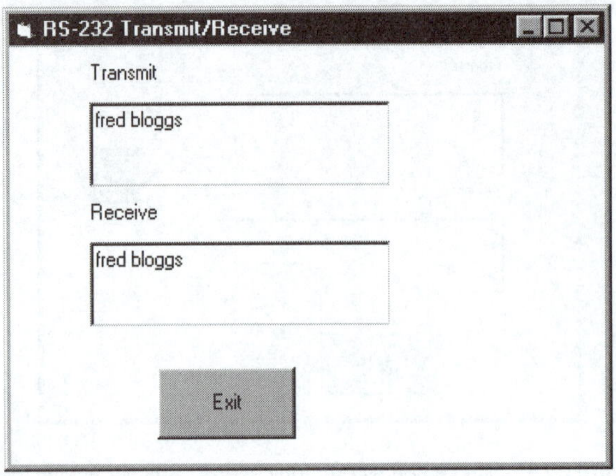

Figure 26.7   Sample run.

26.6 Error messages

Table 26.5 identifies the run-time errors that can occur with the Communications control.

Table 26.5   Error messages.

Error number	Message explanation	Error number	Message explanation
8000	Invalid operation on an opened port	8010	Hardware is not available
8001	Timeout value must be greater than zero	8011	Cannot allocate the queues
8002	Invalid port number	8012	Device is not open
8003	Property available only at run-time	8013	Device is already open
8004	Property is read-only at run-time	8014	Could not enable Comm notification
8005	Port already open	8015	Could not set Comm state
8006	Device identifier is invalid	8016	Could not set Comm event mask
8006	Device identifier is invalid	8018	Operation valid only when the port is open
8007	Unsupported Baud rate	8019	Device busy
8008	Invalid Byte size is invalid	8020	Error reading Comm device
8009	Error in default parameters		

26.7 RS-232 polling

The previous program used interrupt-driven RS-232. It is also possible to use polling to communicate over RS-232. Program 26.5 uses COM2 to send the message 'Hello' and then waits for a received string. It determines that there has been a response by continually testing the number of received characters in the receive buffer (InBufferCount). When there is more than one character in the input buffer it is read.

📖 Program 26.5

```
Private Sub Form_Load()
  Dim Str As String                  ' String to hold input

  MSComm1.CommPort = 2               ' Use COM2
  MSComm1.Settings = "9600,N,8,1"    ' 9600 baud, no parity, 8 data,
                                     ' and 1 stop bit
  MSComm1.InputLen = 0               ' Read entire buffer when Input
                                     ' is used
  MSComm1.PortOpen = True            ' Open port

  Text1.Text = "Sending: Hello"
  MSComm1.Output = "Hello"        ' Send message

  Do  ' Wait for response from port
      DoEvents
  Loop Until MSComm1.InBufferCount >= 2
  Str = MSComm1.Input                ' Read input buffer
  Text1.Text = "Received: " + Str
  MSComm1.PortOpen = False  ' Close serial port.
End Sub
```

26.8 Exercises

26.8.1   List the properties of the MSComm control and outline their uses.

26.8.2   Write a Visual Basic program that continuously sends the character 'A' to the serial line. If possible, observe the output on an oscilloscope and identify the bit pattern and the baud rate.

26.8.3   Write a program that continuously sends the characters from 'A' to 'Z' to the serial line. If possible, observe the output on an oscilloscope.

26.8.4   Write a Visual Basic program that prompts the user for the main RS-232 parameters, such as bit rate, parity, and so on. The user should then be able to transmit and receive with those parameters.

26.8.5   If possible, connect two computers together with a serial link and write a program which uses full-duplex communications.

26.8.6   If possible, connect two computers together with a serial link and write a program which uses full-duplex communications.

26.8.7   Write a program which tests some of the run-time errors given in Table 26.5.

26.8.8   Investigate the Handshaking property of the MSComm control. Its settings are:

0 –	comNone	1 –	comXOnXoff
2 –	comRTS	3 –	comRTSXOnXoff

Windows 95/98/NT (Introduction)

27.1 Introduction

DOS has long been the Achilles heel of the PC and has limited its development. It has also been its strength in that it provides a common platform for all packages. DOS and Windows 3.x operated in a 16-bit mode and had limited memory accessing. Windows 3.0 provided a great leap in PC systems as it provided an excellent graphical user interface to DOS. It suffered from the fact that it still used DOS as the core operating system. Windows 95/98 and Windows NT have finally moved away from DOS and operate as full 32-bit protected-mode operating systems. Their main features are:

- Run both 16-bit and 32-bit application programs.
- Allow access to a large virtual memory (up to 4 GB).
- Support for pre-emptive multitasking and multithreading of Windows-based and MS-DOS-based applications.
- Support for multiple file systems, including 32-bit installable file systems such as VFAT, CDFS (CD-ROM) and network redirectors. These allow better performance, use of long file names, and are an open architecture to support future growth.
- Support for 32-bit device drivers which give improved performance and intelligent memory usage.
- A 32-bit kernel which includes memory management, process scheduling and process management.
- Enhanced robustness and cleanup when an application ends or crashes.
- Enhanced dynamic environment configuration.

The three most widely used operating systems are MS-DOS, Microsoft Windows and UNIX. Microsoft Windows comes in many flavours; the main versions are outlined below and Table 27.1 lists some of their attributes.

- Microsoft Windows 3.x – 16-bit PC-based operating system with limited multitasking. It runs from MS-DOS and thus still uses MS-DOS functionality and file system structure.
- Microsoft Windows 95/98 – robust 32-bit multitasking operating system (although there are some 16-bit parts in it) which can run MS-DOS applications, Microsoft Windows 3.x applications and 32-bit applications.
- Microsoft Windows NT – robust 32-bit multitasking operating system with integrated networking. Networks are around NT servers and clients. As with Microsoft Windows 95/98 it can run MS-DOS, Microsoft Windows 3.x applications and 32-bit applications.

Windows NT and 95/98 provide excellent network support as they can communicate directly with many different types of network, protocols and computer architectures.

They can network to make peer-to-peer connections and also connections to servers for access to file systems and print servers.

Windows NT has more security in running programs than Windows 95/98 as programs and data are insulated from the operation of other programs. The operating system parts of Windows NT and Windows 95/98 run at the most trusted level of privilege of the Intel processor, which is ring zero. Application programs run at least trusted level of privilege, which is ring three. These programs can use either a 32-bit flat mode or any of the memory models, such as large, medium, compact or small.

Table 27.1   Windows comparisons.

	Windows 3.1	*Windows 95/98*	*Windows NT*
Pre-emptive multitasking		✓	✓
32-bit operating system		✓	✓
Long file names		✓	✓
TCP/IP	✓	✓	✓
32-bit applications		✓	✓
Flat memory model		✓	✓
32-bit disk access	✓	✓	✓
32-bit file access	✓	✓	✓
Centralized configuration storage		✓	✓
OpenGL 3D graphics			✓

27.2 Architecture

There was a great leap in performance between the 16-bit Windows 3.*x* operating system (which was built on DOS) to Windows 95/98 and Window NT. Apart from running in a dual 16-bit and 32-bit mode they also allow for application robustness. Figure 27.1 outlines the internal architecture of Windows 95/98.

27.3 Windows registry

On DOS-based systems, the main configuration files were AUTOEXEC.BAT, CONFIG.SYS and INI files. INI files were a major problem in that each application program and device driver configuration required one or more of these file to store default settings (such as IRQ, I/O addresses, default directories, and so on). Several important INI files are:

- WIN.INI. Information about the appearance of the Windows environment.
- SYSTEM.INI. System-specific information on the hardware and device driver configuration of the system.

In Windows 95/98/NT use a central database called the Registry which stores user-specific and configuration-specific information at a single location. This location could be on the local computer or stored on a networked computer. It thus allows network managers to standardize the configuration of networked PCs.

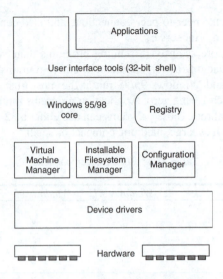

Figure 27.1   Windows 95/98 architecture.

When a computer initially is upgraded from Windows 3.*x* to Windows 95/98 the upgrade program reads the SYSTEM.INI file and system-specific information which it then puts into the Registry. Many INI files are still retained on the system as many Win16-based applications use them. For example, Microsoft Word Version 6 uses the WINWORD6.INI to store package information, such as: location of filters, location of spell checker, location of grammar checker, and so on. An example is:

```
[Microsoft Word]
WPHelp=0
Hyphenate 1033,0=C:\MSOFFICE\WINWORD\HYPH.DLL,C:\MSOFFICE\WINWORD\HY_EN.
NoLongNetNames=Yes
USER-DOT-PATH=C:\MSOFFICE\WINWORD\TEMPLATE
PICTURE-PATH=C:\MSOFFICE\WINWORD
PROGRAMDIR=C:\MSOFFICE\WINWORD
TOOLS-PATH=C:\MSOFFICE\WINWORD
STARTUP-PATH=C:\DOCS\NOTES\
INI-PATH=C:\MSOFFICE\WINWORD
DOC-PATH=C:\DOCS\NOTES\
Hyphenate 2057,0=C:\MSOFFICE\WINWORD\HYPH.DLL,C:\MSOFFICE\WINWORD\HY_EN.
```

An important role for the Registry is to store hardware-specific information which can be used by hardware detection and Plug-and-Play programs. The Configuration Manager determines the configuration of installed hardware (such as, IRQs, I/O addresses, and so on) and it uses this information to update the Registry. This allows new devices to be installed and checked to see if they conflict with existing devices. If they are Plug-and-Play devices then the system assigns hardware parameters which do not conflict with existing devices.

The advantages of the Registry over INI files include:

- **No limit to size and data type**. The Registry has no size restriction and can include binary and text values (INI files are text based and are limited to 64 kB in size).
- **Hierarchical information**. The Registry is hierarchically arranged, whereas INI files

are non-hierarchical and support only two levels of information.

- **Standardized setup**. The Registry provides a standardized method of setting up programs, whereas many INI files contain a whole host of switches and entries, and are complicated to configure.

- **Support for user-specific information**. The Registry allows the storage of user-specific information, using the `Hkey_Users` key. This allows each user of a specific computer (or a networked computer) to have their own user-specific information. INI files do not support this.

- **Remote administration and system policies**. The Registry can be used to remotely administer and set system policies (which are stored as Registry values). These can be downloaded from a central server each time a new user logs on.

The Registry will be discussed in more detail in the next chapter. Figure 27.2 shows an example of the Registry in Windows 95/98.

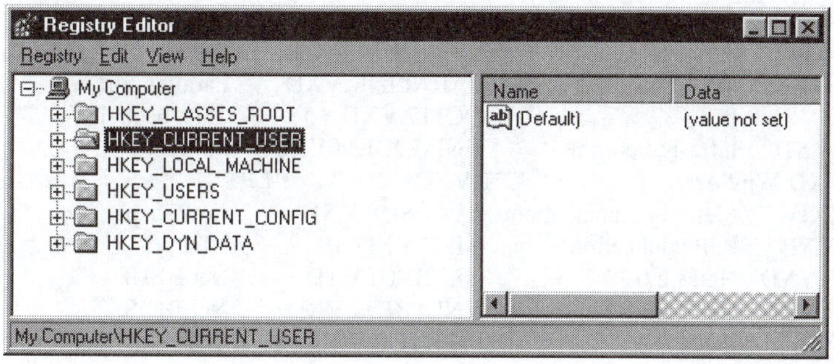

Figure 27.2 Example registry.

27.4 Device drivers

In Windows 3.*x*, device drivers were complex entities and were, in part, static and unchanging. Windows 95/98/NT now provide enhanced support for hardware devices and peripherals including disk devices. Windows NT will be discussed in Section 27.11. Windows 95/98 uses a universal driver/mini-driver architecture that makes writing device-specific code much easier.

The universal driver provides for most of the code for a specific class of device (such as for printers or mice) and the mini-driver is a relatively small and simple driver that provides for the additional information for the hardware.

The actual system interface to the hardware (or some software parts) is through a virtual device driver (VxD), which is a 32-bit, protected-mode driver. These keep track of the state of the device for each application and ensure that the device is in the correct state whenever an application continues. This allows for multitasking programming and also for multi-access for a single device. VxD files also support hardware emulation, such as in the case of the MS-DOS device driver, where any calls to the PC hardware can be handled by the device driver and not by the physical hardware. Typical VxD drivers are:

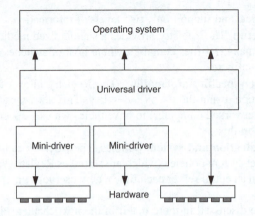

Figure 27.3   Device drivers.

EISA.VXD	EISA bus driver	ISAPNP.VXD	ISA Plug-and-Play
SERIAL.VXD	Serial port	LPTENUM.VXD	Parallel port
MSMOUSE.VXD	MS Mouse	PARALINK.VXD	Parallel port
PCI.VXD	PCI	QC117.VXD	Tape backup
IRCOMM.VXD	Infra-red comms.	UNIMODEM.VXD	Modem
WSOCK.VXD	WinSock	LPT.VXD	LPT
VMM32.VXD	Memory management	JAVASUP.VXD	JavaScript
PPPMAC.VXD	PPP connection	NDIS.VXD	NDIS
NDIS2SUP.VXD	NDIS 2.0	NETBEUI.VXD	Net BEUI
NWREDIR.VXD	NetWare Redirect	VNETBIOS.VXD	Net BIOS
WSIPX.VXD	IPX	WSHTCP.VXD	TCP

In Windows 95/98, VxD files are loaded dynamically and are thus only loaded when they are required, whereas in Windows 3.*x* they were loaded statically (and thus took up a lot of memory). In Window 3.*x* these virtual device drivers have a 386 file extension.

27.5 Configuration Manager

A major drawback with Windows 3.*x* and DOS is that they did not automate PC configuration. For this purpose, Windows 95/98 has a Configuration Manager. The left-hand side of Figure 27.4 shows how it integrates into the system and the right side of Figure 27.4 shows an example device connection of a PC. Its aim is to:

- Determine, with the aid of several subcomponents, each bus and each device on the system, and their configuration settings. This is used to ensure that each device has unique IRQs and I/O port addresses and that there are no conflicts with other devices. With Plug-and-Play, devices can be configured so that they do not conflict with other devices.
- Monitor the PC for any changes to the number of devices connected and also the device types. If it detects any changes then it manages the reconfiguration of the devices.

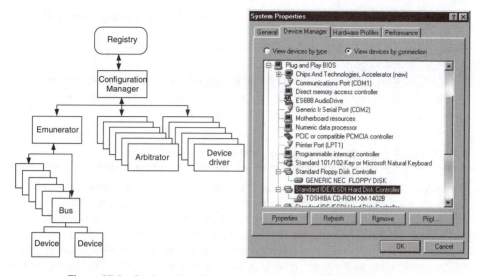

Figure 27.4 Configuration Manager and example connection of devices.

The operation is as follows:

1. The Configuration Manager communicates with each of the bus enumerators and asks them to identify all the devices on the buses and their respective resource requirements. A bus enumerator is a driver that is responsible for creating a hardware tree, which is a hierarchical representation of all the buses and devices on a computer. Figure 27.5 shows an example tree.
2. The bus enumerator locates and gathers information from either the device drivers or the BIOS services for that particular device type. For example, the CD-ROM bus enumerator calls the CD-ROM drivers to gather information.
3. Each of the drivers is then loaded and wait for the Configuration Manager to assign their specific resources (such as IRQs, I/O addresses, and so on).

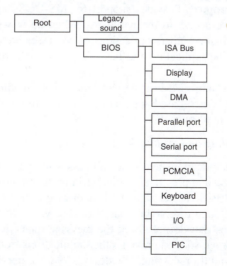

Figure 27.5 Hierarchical representation of the system.

4. Configuration Manager calls on resource arbitrators to allocate resources for each device.
5. Resource arbitrators identify any devices which are conflicting and tries to resolve them.
6. The Configuration Manager informs all device drivers of their device configuration. This process is repeated when the BIOS or one of the other bus enumerators informs Configuration Manager about a system configuration change.

27.6 Virtual Machine Manager (VMM)

The perfect environment for a program is to run on a stand-alone, dedicated computer, which does not have any interference from any other programs and can have access to any device when it wants. This is the concept of the Virtual Machine. In Windows 95/98 the Virtual Machine Manager (VMM) provides each application with the system resources when it needs them. It creates and maintains the virtual machine environments in which applications and system processes run (in Windows 3.*x* the VMM was called WIN386.EXE).

The VMM is responsible for three areas:

- **Process scheduling**. This is responsible for scheduling processes. It allows for multiple applications to run concurrently and also for providing system resources to the applications and other processes that run. This allows multiple applications and other processes to run concurrently, using either cooperative multitasking or pre-emptive multitasking.
- **Memory paging**. Windows 95/98/NT uses a demand-paged virtual memory system, which is based on a flat, linear address space accessed using 32-bit addresses. The system allocates each process a unique virtual address space of 4 GB. The upper 2 GB is shared, while the lower 2 GB is private to the application. This virtual address space is divided into equal blocks (or pages).
- **MS-DOS Mode support**. Provides support for MS-DOS-based applications which must have exclusive access to the hardware. When an MS-DOS-based application runs in this mode then no other applications or processes are allowed to compete for system resources. The application thus has sole access to the resources.

Windows 95/98 has a single VMM (named System VMM) in which all system processes run. Win32-based and Win16-based applications run within this VMM. Each MS-DOS-based application runs in its own VM.

27.6.1 Process scheduling and multitasking

This allows multiple applications and other processes to run concurrently, using either cooperative multitasking and pre-emptive multitasking. In Windows 3.*x*, applications ran using cooperative multitasking. This method requires that applications check the message queue periodically and to give-up control of the system to other applications. Unfortunately, applications that do not check the message queue at frequent intervals can effectively 'hog' the processor and prevent other applications from running. As this does not provide effective multi-processing, Windows 95/98/NT uses pre-emptive multitasking for Win32-based applications (but also supports cooperative multitasking for computability reasons). Thus, the operating system takes direct control away from the application tasks.

Win16 programs need to yield to other tasks in order to multitask properly, whereas Win32-based programs do not need to yield to share resources. This is because Win32-based applications (called processes) use multithreading, which provides for multiprocessing. A thread in a program is a unit of code that can get a time slice from the operating system to run concurrently with other code units. Each process consists of one or more execution threads that identify the code path flow as it is run on the operating system. A Win32-based application can have multiple threads for a given process. This enhances the running of an application by improving throughput and responsiveness. It allows processes for smooth background processing.

27.6.2 Memory paging

Windows 95/98/NT use a demand-paged virtual memory system, which is based on a flat, linear address space using 32-bit addresses. The system allocates each process a unique virtual address space of 4 GB (which should be enough for most applications). The upper 2 GB is shared, while the lower 2 GB is private to the application. This virtual address space divides into equal blocks (or pages), as illustrated in Figure 27.6.

Demand paging is a method by which code and data are moved in pages from physical memory to a temporary paging file on disk. When required, information is then paged back into physical memory.

The functions of the Memory Pager are:

- To map virtual addresses from the process's address space to physical pages in memory. This then hides the physical organization of memory from the process's threads and ensures that the thread can access the required memory when required. It also stops other processes from writing to another memory location.

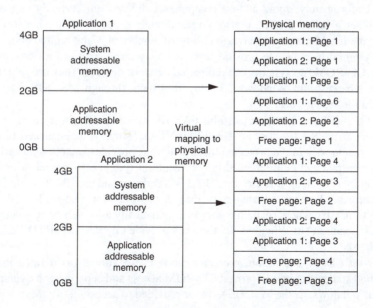

Figure 27.6 Memory paging.

- To support a 16-bit segmented memory model for Windows 3.*x* and MS-DOS applications. In this addressing scheme the addresses are made from a 16-bit segment address and a 16-bit offset address (see Section 1.3).

Windows 95/98/NT use the full addressing capabilities of the 80x86/Pentium processors by supporting a flat, linear memory model for 32-bit operating system functionality and Win32-based applications. This linear addressing model simplifies the development process for application vendors, and removes the performance penalties of a segmented memory architecture.

27.7 Multiple file systems

Windows 95/98/NT supports a layered file system architecture that directly supports multiple file systems (such as, FAT and CDFS). Windows 95/98/NT have great performance improvements over Windows 3.*x*, for example:

- Support for 32-bit protected-mode code when reading and writing information to and from a file system.
- Support for 32-bit dynamically allocated cache size.
- Support for an open file system architecture to enhance future system support.

Figure 27.7 shows the file system architecture used by Windows 95/98. It has the following components:

- IFS (Installable File System) Manager. This is the arbiter for the access to different file system components. On MS-DOS and Windows 3.*x* it was provided by interrupt 21h. Unfortunately, some add-on components did not run correctly and interfered with other installed drivers. It also did not directly support multiple network redirections (the IFS Manager can have an unlimited number of 32-bit redirectors).
- File system drivers. These provide support file systems, such as FAT-based disk devices, CD-ROM file systems and redirected network devices. They are ring 0 components, whereas with Windows 3.*x* supported them through MS-DOS. The two enhanced file systems are:
  - 32-bit VFAT. The 'legacy' 16-bit FAT file system suffers from many problems, such as the 8.3 file format. The 32-bit VFAT format is an enhanced form which works directly in the protected mode, and thus provides smooth multitasking as it is reentrant and multithreaded (a non reentrant system does not allow an interrupt within an interrupt). It uses the VFAT.VXD driver and uses 32-bit code for all file accesses. Another advantage is that it provides for real-mode disk caching (VCACHE), where cache memory is automatically allocated or deallocated when it is required (In Windows 3.*x* this was provided by the SMARTDRV.EXE program).
  - 32-bit CDFS. The 32-bit, protected-mode CDFS format (as defined in the ISO 9660 standard) gives improved CD-ROM access and support for a dynamic cache (in Windows 3.*x* the MSCDEX driver provided to access CD-ROMs).

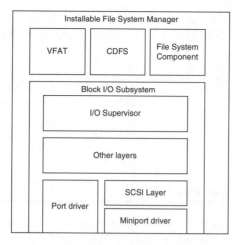

Figure 27.7 File system architecture.

- Block I/O subsystem. This is responsible for the actual physical access to the disk drive. Its components are:

  - **Input/Output Supervisor** (IOS). This component provides for an interface between the file systems and drivers. It is responsible for the queuing of file service requests and for routing the requests to the appropriate file system driver.
  - **Port driver**. This component is a 32-bit, protected-mode driver that communicates with a specific IDE disk device. It implements the functionality of the SCSI manager and miniport driver.
  - **SCSI layer**. This component is a 32-bit, protected-mode, universal driver model architecture for communicating with SCSI devices. It provides all the high-level SCSI functionality, and then uses a miniport driver to handle device-specific I/O calls.
  - **Miniport driver**. In Windows 95/98 these miniport driver models are used to write device-specific code. The Windows 95/98 miniport driver is a 32-bit protected-mode code, and is binary-compatible with Windows NT miniport drivers.

In Windows 95/98, the I/O Supervisor (IOS) is a VxD that controls and manages all protected-mode file system and block device drivers. It loads and initializes protected-mode device drivers and provides services needed for I/O operations. In Windows 3.*x* the I/O Supervisor was *BLOCKDEV. Other responsibilities of the IOS include:

- Registering drivers.
- Routing and queuing I/O requests, and sending asynchronous notifications to drivers as needed.
- Providing services that drivers can use to allocate memory and complete I/O requests.

On Windows 95/98, the IOS stores port drivers, miniport and VxD drivers in the SYSTEM\IOSUBSYS directory. The PDR file extension identifies the port drivers, MPD identifies miniport drivers and VxD (or 386) identifies the VxD drivers. Other clients or virtual device drivers should be stored in other directories and explicitly loaded using device= entries in SYSTEM.INI. A sample listing of the IOSUBSYS directory is given next:

```
Directory of C:\WINDOWS\SYSTEM\IOSUBSYS
AIC78XX.MPD    AMSINT.MPD    APIX.VXD      ATAPCHNG.VXD
BIGMEM.DRV     CDFS.VXD      CDTSD.VXD      CDVSD.VXD
DISKTSD.VXD    DISKVSD.VXD   DRVSPACX.VXD  ESDI_506.PDR
HSFLOP.PDR     NCRC710.MPD   NCRC810.MPD   NECATAPI.VXD
RMM.PDR        SCSI1HLP.VXD  SCSIPORT.PDR  TORISAN3.VXD
VOLTRACK.VXD
```

27.8 Core system components

The core of Windows 95/98 has three components: User, Kernel, and GDI (graphical device interface), each of which has a pair of DLLs (one for 32-bit accesses the other for 16-bit accesses). The 16-bit DLLs allow for Win16 and MS-DOS computability.

Figure 27.8 shows that the lowest-level services provided by the Windows 95/98 Kernel are implemented as 32-bit code. In Windows 95/98 the names of the files are GDI32.DLL, KERNAL32.DLL and USER32.DLL; these are contained in the \WINDOWS\SYSTEM directory.

27.8.1 User

The User component provides input and output to and from the user interface. Input is from the keyboard, mouse, and any other input device and the output is to the user interface. It also manages interaction with the sound driver, timer, and communications ports.

Win32 applications and Windows 95/98 use an asynchronous input model for system input. With this devices have an associated interrupt handler (for example, the keyboard interrupts with IRQ1) which converts the interrupt into a message. This message is then sent to a raw input thread area, which then passes the message to the appropriate message queue. Each Win32 application can have its own message queue, whereas all Win16 applications share a common message queue. Win32 messages will be discussed in Chapter 31.

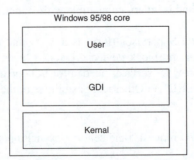

Figure 27.8   Core components.

27.8.2 Kernel

The Kernel provides for core operating system components including file I/O services, virtual memory management, task scheduling and exception handling, such as:

- File I/O services.
- Exceptions. These are events that occur as a program runs and call additional software which is outside the normal flow of control. For example, if an application generates an exception, the Kernel is able to communicate that exception to the application to perform the necessary functions to resolve the problem. A typical exception is caused by a divide-by-zero error in a mathematical calculation, an exception routine can be designed so that it handles the error and does not crash the program.
- Virtual memory management. This resolves import references and supports demand paging for the application.
- Task scheduling. The Kernel schedules and runs threads of each process associated with an application.
- Providing services to both 16-bit and 32-bit applications by using a thinking process which is the translation process between 16-bit and 32-bit formats. It is typically used by a Win16 program to communicate with the 32-bit operating system core.

Virtual memory allows processes to allocate more memory than can be physically allocated. The operating system allocates each process a unique virtual address space, which is a set of addresses available for the process's threads. This virtual address space appears to be 4 GB in size, where 2 GB are reserved for program storage and 2 GB for system storage.

Figure 27.9 illustrates where the system components and applications reside in virtual memory. Its contents are:

- 3 GB–4 GB. All Ring 0 components.
- 2 GB–3 GB. Operating system core components and shared DLLs. These are available to all applications.
- 4 MB–2 GB. Win32-based applications, where each has its own address space. This memory is protected so that other programs cannot corrupt or otherwise hinder the application.
- 0–640 kB. Real-mode device drivers and TSRs.

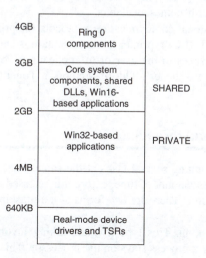

Figure 27.9 System memory usage.

27.8.3 GDI

The Graphical Device Interface (GDI) is the graphical system that:

- Manages information that appears on the screen.
- Draws graphic primitives and manipulates bitmaps.
- Interacts with device-independent graphics drivers, such as display and printer drivers.

The graphics subsystem provides input and output graphics support. Windows uses a 32-bit graphics engine (known as DIB, Device-independent Bitmaps) which:

- Directly controls the graphics output on the screen.
- Provides a set of optimized generic drawing functions for monochrome, 16-colour, 16-bit high colour, 256-colour, and 24-bit true colour graphic devices. It also supports Bézier curves and paths.
- Support for Image Colour Matching for better colour matching between display and colour output devices.

The Windows graphics subsystem is included as a universal driver with a 32-bit mini-driver. The mini-driver provides only for the hardware-specific instructions.

The 32-bit Windows 95/98 printing subsystem has several enhancements over Windows 3.*x*; these include:

- They use a background thread processing to allow for smooth background printing.
- Smooth printing where the operating system only passes data to the printer when it is ready to receive more information.
- They send enhanced metafile (EMF) format files, rather than raw printer data. This EMF information is interpreted in the background and the results are then sent to the printer.
- Support for deferred printing, where a print job can be sent to a printer and then stored until the printer becomes available.
- Support for bi-directional communication protocols for printers using the Extended Communication Port (ECP) printer communication standard. ECP mode allows printers to send messages to the user or to application programs. Typical messages are: 'Paper Jam', 'Out-of-paper', 'Out-of-Memory', 'Toner Low', and so on.
- Plug-and-Play.

27.9 Multitasking and threading

Multitasking involves running several tasks at the same time. It normally involves running a process for a given amount of time, before it is released and allowing another process a given amount of time. There are two forms of multitasking; these are:

- Pre-emptive multitasking. This type of multitasking involves the operating system controlling how long a process stays on the processor. This allows for smooth multitasking and is used in Windows NT/95/98 32-bit programs.

- Cooperative multitasking. This type of multitasking relies on a process giving up the processor. It is used with Windows 3.*x* programs and suffers from processor hogging, where a process can stay on a processor and the operating system cannot kick it off.

The logical extension to multitasking programs is to split a program into a number of parts (threads) and run each of these on the multitasking system (multithreading). A program which is running more than one thread at a time is known as a multithreaded program. Multithreaded programs have many advantages over non-multithreaded programs, including:

- They make better use of the processor, where different threads can be run when one or more threads are waiting for data. For example, a thread could be waiting for keyboard input, while another thread could be reading data from the disk.
- They are easier to test, where each thread can be tested independently of other threads.
- They can use standard threads, which are optimized for a given hardware.

They also have disadvantages, including:

- The program has to be planned properly so that threads must know on which threads they depend.
- A thread may wait indefinitely for another thread which has crashed or terminated.

The main difference between multiple processes and multiple threads is that each process has independent variables and data, while multiple threads share data from the main program.

27.9.1 Scheduling

Scheduling involves determining which thread should be run on the process at a given time. This element in time is named a time slice, and its actual value depends on the system configuration.

Each thread currently running has a base priority. The programmer who created the program sets this base priority level of the thread. This value defines how the thread is executed in relation to other system threads. The thread with the highest priority gets use of the processor.

NT and 95/98 have 32 priority levels. The lowest priority is 0 and the highest is 31. A scheduler can change a thread's base priority by increasing or decreasing it by two levels. This changes the thread's priority.

The scheduler is made up from two main parts:

- **Primary scheduler**. This scheduler determines the priority numbers of the threads which are currently running. It then compares their priority and assigns resources to them depending on their priority. Threads with the highest priority are executed for the current time slice. When two or more threads have the same priority then the threads are put on a stack. One thread is run and then put to the bottom of the stack, then the next is run and it is put to the bottom, and so on. This continues until all threads with the same priority have been run for a given time slice.

- **Secondary scheduler**. The primary scheduler runs threads with the highest priority, whereas the secondary scheduler is responsible for increasing the priority of non-executing threads (which are all other threads apart from the currently executed thread). It is thus important for giving low priority threads a chance to run on the operating system. Threads which are given a higher or lower priority are:

    - A thread which is waiting for user input has its priority increased.
    - A thread that has completed a voluntary wait also has its priority increased.
    - Threads with a computation-bound thread get their priorities reduced. This prevents the blocking of I/O operations.

    Apart from these, all threads get a periodic increase. This prevents lower-priority threads hogging shared resources that are required by higher-priority threads.

27.9.2 Priority inheritance boosting

One problem that can occur is when a low priority thread accesses resources which are required by a higher priority thread. For example, an RS-232 program could be loading data into memory while another program requires to access the memory. One method which can be used to overcome this is Priority Inheritance Boosting. In this case, low priority threads gets a boost so that they can quickly release resources. For example, if a system has three threads: Thread A, Thread B and Thread C. If Thread A has the highest priority and it requires a resource from Thread C then Thread C gets a boost in its priority. Thread A remains blocked until Thread C releases the required resource. When it does release it then Thread C goes back to its normal priority and Thread A then gets access to the resource.

27.10 Plug-and-Play process

Plug-and-Play allows the operating system to configure hardware as required. On system startup, the configuration manager scans the system hardware. When it finds a new Plug-and-Play device it does the following:

- **Sets the device into configuration mode**. This is achieved by using 3 I/O ports. Some data (the initiation key) is written to one of the ports and enables the Plug-and-Play logic.
- **Isolates and identifies each device**. Each device is isolated, one at a time. The method used is to assign each device a unique number, which is a unique handle for the device. This number is made from a device ID and a serial number.
- **Determines device specifications**. Each device sends its functionality to the operating system, such as how many joysticks it supports, its audio functions, its networking modes, and so on.
- **Allocates resources**. The operating system then allocates resources to the device depending on its functionality and the Plug-and-Play device is informed of the allocated resources (such as IRQs, I/O addresses, DMA channels, and so on). It also checks for conflicts on these resources.
- **Activates device**. When the above have been completed the device is enabled. Only the initiation key can re-initialize the device.

27.11 Windows NT architecture

Windows NT uses two modes:

- User mode. This is a lower privileged mode than kernal mode. It has no direct access to the hardware or to memory. It interfaces to the operating system through well-defined API (Application Program Interface) calls.
- Kernal mode. This is a privileged mode of operation and allows all code direct access to the hardware and memory, including memory allocated to user mode processes. Kernal mode processes also have a higher priority over user mode processes.

Figure 27.10 shows an outline of the architecture of NT. It can be seen that only the kernal mode has access to the hardware. This kernal includes executive services which include managers (for I/O, interprocess communications, and so on) and device drivers (which control the hardware). Its parts include:

- Microkernel. Controls basic operating system services, such as interrupt handling and scheduling.
- HAL. This is a library of hardware-specific programs which give a standard interface between the hardware and software. This can either be Microsoft written or manufacturer provided. They have the advantage of allowing for transportability of programs across different hardware platforms.
- Win32 Window Manager. Supports Win32, MS-DOS and Windows 3.*x* applications.

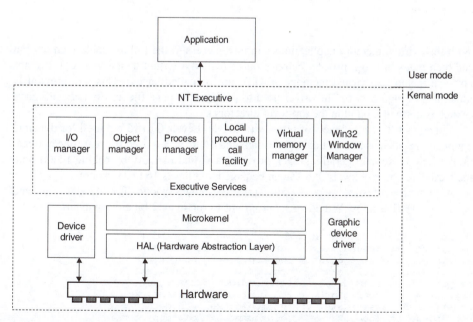

Figure 27.10   NT architecture.

27.11.1 MS-DOS support

Windows NT supports MS-DOS-based applications with an NT Virtual DOS Machine (NTVDM), where each MS-DOS application has its own NTVDM. The NTVDM is started by the application Ntvdm.exe and when this has started the application communicates with two system files Ntio.sys (equivalent to IO.SYS) and Ntdos.sys (equivalent to MSDOS.SYS). Note that the AUTOEXEC.BAT and CONFIG.SYS files have also been replace by Autoexec.nt and Config.nt (which are normally located in \WINNT\System32).

Multiple NTVDMs have the advantage of being reliable because if one NTVDM fails then it does not affect any others. It also allows MS-DOS-based applications to be multitasked. Unfortunately, each NTVDM needs at least 1 MB of physical memory.

Some MS-DOS applications require direct access to the hardware. NT supports this by providing virtual device drivers (VDDs). These detect a call to hardware and communicate with the NT 32-bit device driver.

Windows NT communicates with hardware through device drivers. These drivers have a .sys file extension. An example listing of these is given next:

```
Directory of C:\WINNT\system32\drivers

afd.sys         atapi.sys        atdisk.sys       beep.sys
cdaudio.sys     cdfs.sys         cdrom.sys        changer.sys
cirrus.sys      disk.sys         diskdump.sys     diskperf.sys
fastfat.sys     floppy.sys       ftdisk.sys       hpscan16.sys
i8042prt.sys    kbdclass.sys     ksecdd.sys       modem.sys
mouclass.sys    msfs.sys         mup.sys          ndis.sys
netdtect.sys    npfs.sys         ntfs.sys         null.sys
parallel.sys    parport.sys      parvdm.sys       pcmcia.sys
scsiport.sys    scsiprnt.sys     scsiscan.sys     serial.sys
sfloppy.sys     streams.sys      tape.sys         tdi.sys
vga.sys         videoprt.sys
```

With this, virtual memory applications can have access to the full available memory but NT then maps this to a private memory range (called a virtual memory space). It maps physical memory to virtual memory in 4 kB blocks (called pages). This was previously illustrated in Figure 27.6. The driver used to perform the page file access is Pagefile.sys (which is normally found in the top-level directory).

Windows NT has 32 levels of priority (0 to 31). Levels 0 to 15 are used for dynamic applications (such as non-critical operations) and 16 to 31 are used for real-time applications (such as Kernal operations). NT provides a virtual memory by paging file(s) onto the hard disk. Priority levels 0 to 15 can be paged, but levels 16 to 31 cannot.

A summary of the system32 directory is shown below. The wowdeb.exe and wowexec.exe files allow Windows 3.*x* programs to run in a 32-bit environment.

```
Directory of C:\winnt\system32
ansi.sys        append.exe       at.exe           atsvc.exe
attrib.exe      autoexec.nt      backup.exe       bootok.exe
bootvrfy.exe    cacls.exe        chcp.com         chkdsk.exe
clipsrv.exe     comm.drv         command.com      comp.exe
compact.exe     config.nt        control.exe      convert.exe
country.sys     csrss.exe        dcomcnfg.exe     ddeshare.exe
ddhelp.exe      ebug.exe         diskcomp.com     diskcopy.com
diskperf.exe    doskey.exe       dosx.exe         DRIVERS
```

```
edit.com        exe2bin.exe     expand.exe      fastopen.exe
fc.exe          find.exe        findstr.exe     finger.exe
fontview.exe    forcedos.exe    format.com      ftp.exe
gdi.exe         graftabl.com    graphics.com    grpconv.exe
help.exe        himem.sys       inetins.exe     internat.exe
kb16.com        keyb.com        keyboard.drv    keyboard.sys
krnl386.exe     label.exe       lights.exe      lodctr.exe
mem.exe         mode.com        more.com        mpnotify.exe
mscdexnt.exe    nddeagnt.exe    nddeapir.exe    net.exe
nlsfunc.exe     notepad.exe     ntdos.sys       ntio.sys
ntvdm.exe       os2ss.exe       pax.exe         pentnt.exe
ping.exe        portuas.exe     posix.exe       print.exe
psxss.exe       rdisk.exe       recover.exe     redir.exe
replace.exe     restore.exe     rpcss.exe       rundll32.exe
runonce.exe     savedump.exe    setup.exe       setver.exe
share.exe       shmgrate.exe    skeys.exe       smss.exe
sort.exe        SPOOL           sprestrt.exe    subst.exe
syncapp.exe     sysedit.exe     systray.exe     taskman.exe
taskmgr.exe     telnet.exe      tree.com        unlodctr.exe
ups.exe         user.exe        userinit.exe    VIEWERS
win.com         winhlp32.exe    winspool.exe    winver.exe
wowdeb.exe      wowexec.exe
```

27.12 Exercises

27.12.1   Discuss the architecture of the 32-bit Windows system.

27.12.2   Discuss how Windows 95/98 use VxD device drivers to interface to the hardware. How do equipment manufacturers develop drivers which use the VxD drivers. How do device drivers in NT differ from Windows 95/98?

27.12.3   Explain how the Configuration Manager is used to determine the devices which are connected to the system.

27.12.4   Explain how the operation of the Virtual Machine Manager.

27.12.5   Explain the main differences between pre-emptive and co-operative multitasking. Discuss also how multitasking and threading is implemented.

27.12.6   Discuss how 95/98 use a priority systems to schedule processes.

Windows Registry

28.1 Introduction

The Registry is logically stored as a single entity, but it physically consists of two different files. These are:

- USER.DAT. Contains user-specific information for different user profiles.
- SYSTEM.DAT. Contains hardware-specific and computer-specific settings.

By default, USER.DAT and SYSTEM.DAT are stored in the Windows home directory or the SYSTEM subdirectory, but both these files can be located in physically different locations. For example, a typical setup might be to store USER.DAT on a user's network login directory and the SYSTEM.DAT located on the local hard disk. This will allow the user to see the same user interface no matter which machine the user is logged into.

The following shows the different DAT files (note that they are hidden by default):

```
C:\WINDOWS>dir *.dat /a

SYSTEM    DAT    2,145,516  23/11/97  21:16  SYSTEM.DAT
USER      DAT      279,352  23/11/97  21:00  USER.DAT
VIEWS     DAT        3,584  22/06/97  15:48  VIEWS.DAT
EXTEND    DAT        6,892  27/07/97  17:03  extend.dat
PIPEDLG   DAT           79  10/08/97  14:10  PIPEDLG.DAT
```

28.1.1 Recovering Registry data

Each time Windows 95/98 successfully starts then the operating system backs up the Registry by copying the current SYSTEM.DAT and USER.DAT files to SYSTEM.DA0 and USER.DA0, respectively. If Windows 95/98 fails to start then the user can copy the backed-up Registry from the last successful startup to the current Registry. The following shows the backed-up files:

```
C:\WINDOWS>DIR *.DA0 /S /A
Directory of C:\WINDOWS

USER      DA0      279,352  23/11/97  13:18  USER.DA0
SYSTEM    DA0    2,145,516  23/11/97  13:18  SYSTEM.DA0
```

28.2 Windows 95/98 and the Registry

The program REGEDIT.EXE allows a user to view and edit the contents of the local Registry or on a networked computer.

When Windows 95/98 starts, the operating system stores and checks the configuration information in the Registry for most configuration settings. Windows 95/98 and applications use the Register when:

- Running Windows 95/98 Setup. This including adding new hardware or setting up an application program.
- Installing/re-installing Windows 95/98. Information from INI files is added to the Registry.
- Adding/removing a Plug-and-Play-compliant device. Each time you add or remove a Plug-and-Play-compliant device on a computer running Windows 95/98, configuration data is added to the Registry.
- Using device driver communications. Device drivers send and receive load parameters and configuration data from the Registry.
- Making changes to system policies, user profiles and administrative tools.

28.2.1 Registry structure

The Registry Editor displays the contents of the Registry database in six subtrees. These six subtrees are HKEY_CLASSES_ROOT, HKEY_CURRENT_USER, HKEY_ LOCAL_MACHINE, HKEY_USERS, HKEY_CURRENT_CONFIG and HKEY_ DYN_DATA, as shown in Figure 28.1.

In the Registry, each individual key can contain data items called value entries and can also contain additional subkeys. Keys are roughly equivalent to directories and value entries equivalent to files. Each of the root key names begins with 'HKEY_'. This indicates that the key is a unique identifier, called a handle, that can be used by a program to access resources.

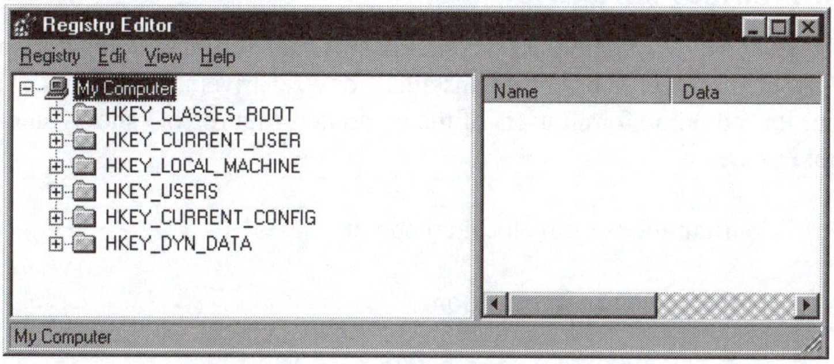

Figure 28.1   Registry Editor example screen.

28.2.2 Value entries

The Registry Editor has two window panes. On the right the value entries are associated and the left pane is used to select the key. Each value entry has three parts: a data type (which appears as an icon), a name and the value. The different data types are:

Binary data
Most hardware information is stored as binary data. This can either be in hexadecimal or a binary format. Figure 28.2 shows an example.

String   A readable text form, which allows values to be searched for. For example, HardWareKey: 'INFRARED/0000/COM'.

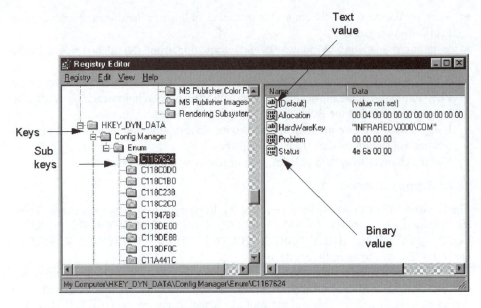

Figure 28.2   Registry Editor.

28.2.3 HKEY_LOCAL_MACHINE

The HKEY_LOCAL_MACHINE key contains software settings, computer-specific information about the type of hardware installed, device drivers, applications, and other information. It is common for all users of the computer. Figure 28.3 shows an example.
    The subkeys are:

Config   Configurations of the local computer.

Enum   Hardware device information.

Hardware   Serial port and modem information.

Network   Network information which contains user login information, such as the
            user name, primary network provider, and the system policies.

Security   Information about the network security provider and remote administration
            capabilities.

Software   Information on installed software and configuration data.

System   System startup information, such as device driver loading, Windows 95/98
            services and operating system behaviour.

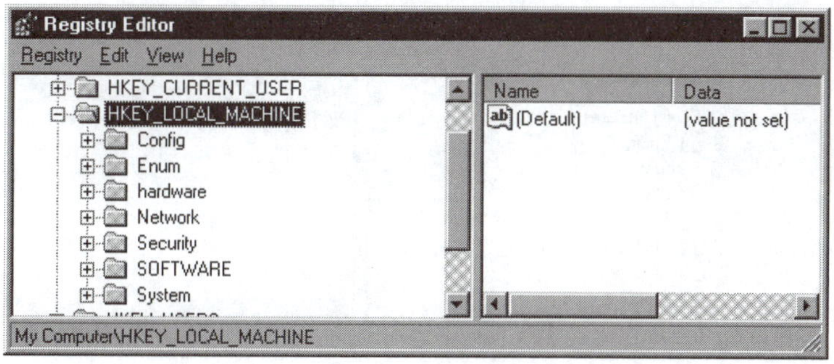

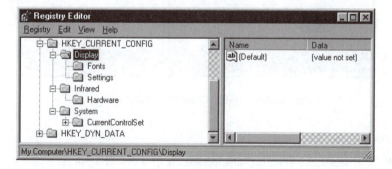

Figure 28.3   HKEY_LOCAL_MACHINE settings.

28.2.4 HKEY_CURRENT_CONFIG

The HKEY_CURRENT_CONFIG key points to a branch of the HKEY_LOCAL_ MACHINE\Config subtree that contains information about the current configuration of hardware attached to the computer and any alternative hardware configurations for the computer. For example, it is typical for a portable computer to have multiple configurations with docking stations and PCMCIA cards. Each alternative configuration has a unique identifier, and this configuration ID has a subkey under the Config key. Each configuration appears in the list of hardware profiles in the System option in Control Panel. Figure 28.4 shows an example.

When the computer is started for the first time, Windows 95 creates a new configuration for the new configuration ID, and a new Config subkey is added to the Registry. After this the computer is started and Windows 95/98 checks the hardware configurations and automatically selects the appropriate configuration, and the settings for the related Config subkey.

Figure 28.4   HKEY_CURRENT_CONFIG settings.

28.2.5 HKEY_DYN_DATA

The HKEY_DYN_DATA key points to a branch of HKEY_LOCAL_MACHINE that contains the dynamic status information for various devices as part of the Plug-and-Play information. The information for each device includes the related hardware key and the device's status, including problems. Figure 28.5 shows an example.

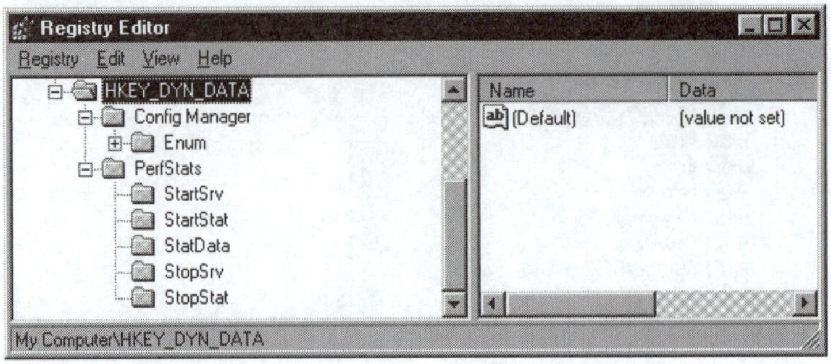

Figure 28.5   HKEY_DYN_DATA settings.

28.2.6 HKEY_CLASSES_ROOT

The HKEY_CLASSES_ROOT key points to a branch of HKEY_LOCAL_MACHINE that describes various software settings. It contains information on OLEs, file associations (for example the ZIP file extension might be associated with the PKZIP package), Windows shortcuts and core aspects of the user interface. Figure 28.6 shows an example.

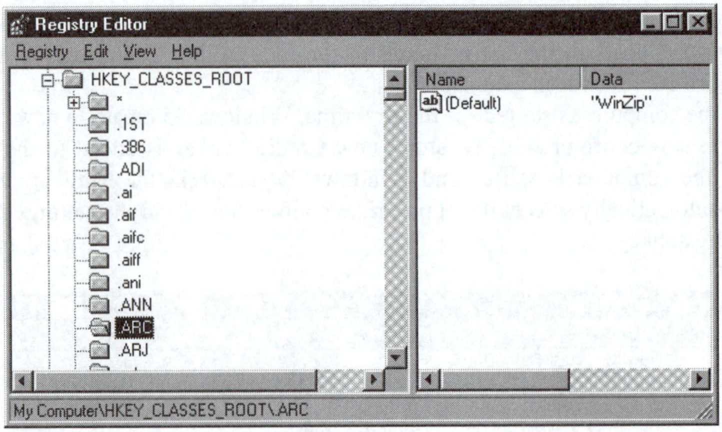

Figure 28.6   HKEY_CLASSES_ROOT settings.

28.2.7 HKEY_USERS

The HKEY_USERS key contains information about users who log on to the computer. This includes both general user information (all users who log onto the computer) and user-specific information. This includes information on the defaults settings for applications, desktop configurations, and so on. Figure 28.7 shows an example.

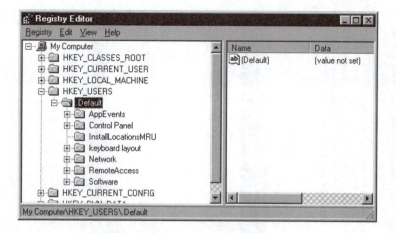

Figure 28.7   HKEY_USERS settings.

28.2.8 HKEY_CURRENT_USER

The HKEY_CURRENT_USER key points to a branch of HKEY_USERS for the user who is currently logged on. Figure 28.8 shows an example.

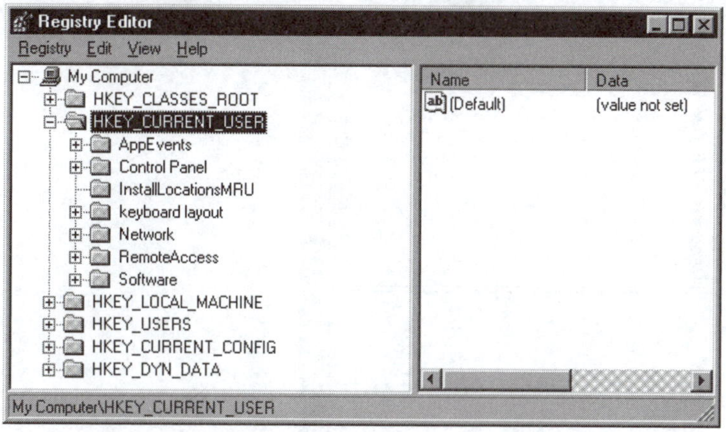

Figure 28.8   HKEY_CURRENT_USER settings.

28.3 Windows NT and the Registry

The program REGEDT32.EXE allows a user to view and edit the contents of the local Registry or on a networked computer. An example is shown in Figure 28.9.

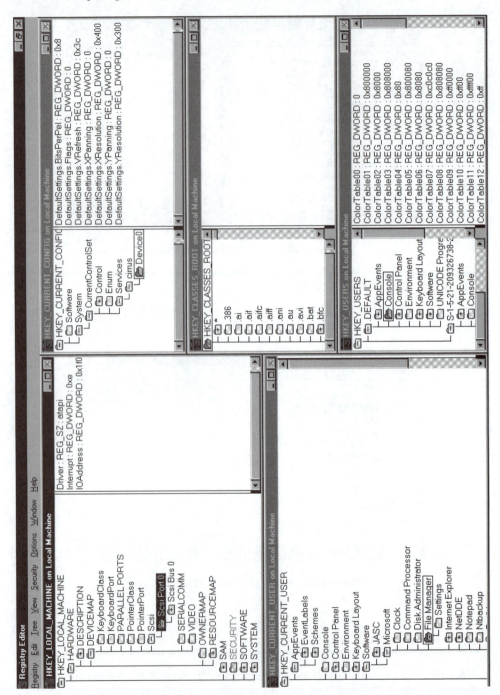

Figure 28.9   Example Windows NT Registry.

28.4 INF files

Device information (INF) files are used to provide information used by Windows 95 to install software for a given hardware device. These files are provided by hardware manufacturers and they define the resources and files required for each class of device.

The format of the INF files is:

- Section names are enclosed in brackets ([ ]) and must be unique within an INF file.
- Keys within a section do not have to be unique, but the order of keys within a section is significant.
- Private sections in an INF file are not evaluated by Windows 95/98.

The operating system detects the unique ID of each device installed. For the device identified, a specific section of the INF file provides information on that class of device; the following describes the information contained in a typical INF file section. The following section defines some of the INF section names. Figure 28.10 shows a listing of some INF files (Keyboard.inf, Locale.inf, Msbatch.inf, and so on).

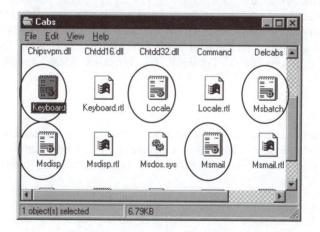

Figure 28.10 Listing of some INF files.

28.4.1 INF file format

INF files organize information into sections which define the information that Setup and the hardware detection process use to determine the resource needs of the hardware device and to install software for that device. Typical INF sections are:

[Version]   A simple header that identifies the INF and the type of hardware device (such as a network card, CD-ROM drive, and so on).

[Manufacturer] and [Manufacturer Name]
Lists the manufacturers of the device.

[Install]   Describes the device driver and any physical attributes of the hardware device.

[ClassInstall] Defines a new class for this device (such as a new type of device).
[Strings]   Defines all localizable strings used in the INF file.

Each of these section can contain one or more entries. Typically an entry consists of a key and a value separated by an equals sign. A comment within an INF file is given after a semi-colon. For example:

```
Class=Keyboard   ; the device is a keyboard (of course).
```

[Version]

A typical format is:

```
[Version]
Signature="$Chicago$"
Class=class-name
Provider =INF_creator
LayoutFile=filename.inf
```

where class-name defines the class in the Registry for any device installed from this INF. Typical class-names are: Adapter, Cdrom, Display, EISADevices Fdc, Hdc, Keyboard, Modem, Monitor, Mouse, NetNetService, Nodriver, PCMCIA, Ports, Printer, SCSIAdapter and System. filename.inf is the INF file that contains the layout information (source disks and files). Typically, for Windows 95/98 components, this is LAYOUT.INF.

[Install]

The [Install] section defines additional sections in the INF file that have device descriptions and instructions for installing files. A Reboot or Restart entry can be added to force a system restart or reboot when it performs the commands in the [Install] section. Its format is:

```
[install-section-name]
LogConfig = log-config-section-name[,log-config-section-name]...
Copyfiles=file-list-section[,file-list-section]...
Renfiles=file-list-section[,file-list-section]...
Delfiles=file-list-section[,file-list-section]...
UpdateInis=update-ini-section[,update-ini-section]...
UpdateIniFields=update-inifields-section[,update-inifields-section]...
AddReg=add-registry-section[,add-registry-section]...
DelReg=del-registry-section[,del-registry-section]...
Ini2Reg=ini-to-registry-section[,ini-to-registry-section]...
UpdateCfgSys=update-config-section
UpdateAutoBat=update-autoexec-section
Reboot | Restart
```

The CopyFiles entry allows a single file to be copied directly from the copy line. An individual file is copied by prefixing the file name with an @ symbol. The destination for the file copied using this notation will be the DefaultDestDir as defined in the [DestinationDirs] section.

[Manfacturer]

The [Manufacturer] section identifies the device manufacturer and also specifies the name of the [Manufacturer-name] section that contains additional information about the device driver.

The [Manufacturer] format is:

```
[Manufacturer]
manufacturer-name | %strings-key%=manufacturer-name-section
```

where manufacturer-name is the name of the manufacturer. This name can be any combination of printable characters, but must uniquely identify the manufacturer and must be enclosed in double quotation marks. strings-key is the name of a string as defined in a [Strings] section. manufacturer-name-section is the name of the [Manufacturer Name] section. This name can be any combination of printable characters, but must uniquely identify the manufacturer's name.

[Manufacturer-name]

The [Manufacturer-name] section provides a device description and identifies the [Install] section for the installed device. There must also be a manufacturer-name-section name in the [Manufacturer] section. The [Manufacturer-name] format is:

```
[manufacturer-name]
device-description=install-section-name,    device-id[,compatible-device-
id]...
```

where device-description is the device to install, install-section-name is the name of the [Install] section for this device, device-id Identifier for this device and compatible-device-id is an identifier of a compatible device (more than one name can be given, separated by a comma).

[Log-config-section-name]

The [Log-config-section-name] section defines specific configuration details. These may include IRQ allocation, memory ranges, I/O ports and DMA channels. Its format is:

```
[log-config-section-name]
ConfigPriority = priority-value
MemConfig = mem-range-list
I/OConfig = io-range-list
IRQConfig = irq-list
DMAConfig = dma-list
```

[Update-autoexec-section]

The [Update-autoexec-section] section defines the commands to modify the AUTOEXEC.BAT file. If it is used then the update-autoexec-section name must appear in an UpdateAutoBat entry in the [Install] section. Its format is:

```
[update-autoexec-section]
CmdDelete=command-name
CmdAdd=command-name[,command-parameters]
UnSet=env-var-name
PreFixPath=ldid[,ldid]
RemOldPath=ldid[,ldid]
TmpDir=ldid[,subdir]
```

[Update-config-section]

The [Update-config-section] section defines the commands to add, delete, or rename commands in CONFIG.SYS. The update-config-section name must appear in an Up-dateCfgSys entry in the [Install] section. Its format is:

```
[update-config-section]
DevRename=current-dev-name,new-dev-name
DevDelete=device-driver-name
DevAddDev=driver-name,configkeyword[,flag][,param-string]
Stacks=dos-stacks-values
Buffers=legal-dos-buffer-value
Files=legal-dos-files-value
LastDrive=legal-dos-lastdrive-value
```

[Update-ini-section]

The [Update-ini-section] section replaces, deletes or adds entries in the specified INI file. If it is used then the update-ini-section name must appear in an UpdateIni entry in the [Install] section. Its format is:

```
[update-ini-section]
ini-file, ini-section, [old-ini-entry], [new-ini-entry], [flags]
```

[Update-inifields-section]

The [Update IniFields] section replaces, adds, and deletes fields in the value of a given INI entry. It if is used then the update-inifields-section name must appear in an Up-dateIniFields entry in the [Install] section. Its format is:

```
[update-inifields-section]
ini-file, ini-section, profile-name, [old-field], [new-field]
```

[Add-registry-section]

The [Update IniFields] section adds subkeys or value names to the Registry, optionally setting the value. The add-registry-section name must appear in an AddReg entry in the [Install] section. Its format is:

```
[add-registry-section]
reg-root-string, [subkey], [value-name], [Flag], [value]
```

[Del-registry-section]

The [Delete Registry] deletes a subkey or value name from the Registry. The del-registry-section name must appear in an DelReg entry in the [Install] section. The [Delete Registry] format is:

```
[del-registry-section]
reg-root-string, subkey, [value-name]
```

[Ini-to-registry-section]

The [ini-to-registry-section] section moves lines or sections from an INI file to the Registry, creating or replacing an entry under the given key in the Registry. The ini-to-registry-section name must appear in an Ini2Reg entry in the [Install] section. Its format is:

```
[ini-to-registry-section]
ini-file, ini-section, [ini-key], reg-root-string, subkey, flags
```

28.5 Exercises

28.5.1   Identify the main registry files. What happens when Windows 95/98 boots and fails to start. How might a user protect against incorrect settings in the registry?

28.5.2   Outline the advantages of the registry over INI files (see this and the previous chapter for information).

28.5.3   If possible, find a PC and locate some INF files. What is their contents?

28.5.4   If possible, find a PC and examine the registry with REGEDIT. Identify some of its contents.

28.6 Sample INF file

```
; Copyright (c) 1993-1995, Microsoft Corporation
[version]
LayoutFile=layout.inf
signature="$CHICAGO$"
Class=Keyboard
Provider=%MS%
SetupClass=BASE

[DestinationDirs]
MS_KBD_ENH_CopyFiles = 11      ; LDID_SYS
KBD_VxDs             = 22      ; LDID_VMM32
KBD_VxDs_Del         = 11      ; LDID_SYS

[ClassInstall]
Addreg=KeyboardReg

[KeyboardReg]
HKR,,,,%KeyboardClassName%
HKR,,Icon,,"-3"

[ControlFlags]
ExcludeFromSelect=*PNP030b                          ; Special default ID

[Manufacturer]
%Std-Keyboards%=MS_KBD

[MS_KBD]
%*PNP0300.DeviceDesc%     = PC_XT_83_Inst,*PNP0300  ;PC/XT (83-Key)
%*PNP0301.DeviceDesc%     = PC_AT_84_Inst,*PNP0301  ;PC/AT (84-Key)
%*PNP0302.DeviceDesc%     = PC_XT_84_Inst,*PNP0302  ;PC/XT (84-Key)
%*PNP0303.DeviceDesc%     = PC_AT_Enh_Inst,*PNP0303 ;PC/AT Enh(101/102-Key)
%*PNP030b.DeviceDesc%     = PC_AT_Enh_Inst,*PNP030b ;Default keyboard

[SysCfgClasses]
Keyboard, %*PNP0303.DeviceDesc%,ROOT,,%KeyboardClassName%

[*PNP0300.det]
LogConfig      = kbdlc
[*PNP0301.det]
LogConfig      = kbdlc
```

```
[*PNP0302.det]
LogConfig           = kbdlc
[*PNP0303.det]
LogConfig           = kbdlc
 [*PNP030b.det]
LogConfig           = kbdlc


[PC_XT_83_Inst]    ;*PNP0300
LogConfig           = kbdlc
CopyFiles           = MS_KBD_ENH_CopyFiles, KBD_VxDs
DelFiles            = KBD_VxDs_Del
UpdateInis          = PC_XT_83_Inis, Keyb.Common.Inis
AddReg=Keyb.Common.Reg
AddReg              = MS_KBD_AddReg


[PC_AT_84_Inst]    ;*PNP0301
LogConfig           = kbdlc
CopyFiles           = MS_KBD_ENH_CopyFiles, KBD_VxDs
DelFiles            = KBD_VxDs_Del
UpdateInis          = PC_AT_84_Inis, Keyb.Common.Inis
AddReg=Keyb.Common.Reg
AddReg              = MS_KBD_AddReg


[PC_AT_84_Inst.PosDup]
*PNP0303


[PC_XT_84_Inst]    ;*PNP0302
LogConfig           = kbdlc
CopyFiles           = MS_KBD_ENH_CopyFiles, KBD_VxDs
DelFiles            = KBD_VxDs_Del
UpdateInis          = PC_XT_84_Inis, Keyb.Common.Inis
AddReg=Keyb.Common.Reg
AddReg              = MS_KBD_AddReg


[PC_AT_Enh_Inst]   ;*PNP0303
LogConfig           = kbdlc
CopyFiles           = MS_KBD_ENH_CopyFiles, KBD_VxDs
DelFiles            = KBD_VxDs_Del
UpdateInis          = PC_AT_Enh_Inis, Keyb.Common.Inis
AddReg=Keyb.Common.Reg
AddReg              = MS_KBD_AddReg


[kbdlc]
ConfigPriority=HARDWIRED
IOConfig=60-60(ffff::)
IOConfig=64-64(ffff::)
IRQConfig=1


[MS_KBD_ENH_CopyFiles]
keyboard.drv


[MS_KBD_AddReg]
HKR,,DriverDesc,,"Keyboard Driver"
HKR,,DevLoader,,*CONFIGMG


[PC_XT_83_Inis]
system.ini,boot.description,,"keyboard.typ=%*PNP0300.DeviceDesc%"
system.ini,keyboard,,"subtype=42"
system.ini,keyboard,,"type=1"


[PC_AT_84_Inis]
system.ini,boot.description,,"keyboard.typ=%*PNP0301.DeviceDesc%"
system.ini,keyboard,,"subtype=0"
system.ini,keyboard,,"type=3"


[PC_XT_84_Inis]
system.ini,boot.description,,"keyboard.typ=%*PNP0302.DeviceDesc%"
system.ini,keyboard,,"subtype="
system.ini,keyboard,,"type=1"


[PC_AT_Enh_Inis]
system.ini,boot.description,,"keyboard.typ=%*PNP0303.DeviceDesc%"
system.ini,keyboard,,"subtype="
system.ini,keyboard,,"type=4"


[Keyb.Common.Inis]
```

```
system.ini,keyboard,,"keyboard.dll="
system.ini,boot,,"keyboard.drv=keyboard.drv"

; Install *vkd unless "device=alrvkd.386", "keyboard=alrvkd.386", "device=vkd.386",
or "keyboard=vkd.386" is already present
system.ini, 386enh, "keyboard=alrvkd.386", "~SetupTemp~=*",3
system.ini, 386enh, "device=alrvkd.386", "~SetupTemp~=*",3
system.ini, 386enh, "keyboard=vkd.386", "~SetupTemp~=*",3
system.ini, 386enh, "device=vkd.386", "~SetupTemp~=*",3
system.ini, 386enh,, "keyboard=*vkd"
system.ini, 386enh, "~SetupTemp~=*", "keyboard=*vkd",3

; always combine *vkd into VMM32.VxD:
wininit.ini, CombineVxDs,,"%22%\vkd.vxd=%11%\vmm32.vxd"

[Keyb.Common.Reg]
HKLM,System\CurrentControlSet\Control\VMM32Files,vkd.vxd,1,

[KBD_VxDs]
vkd.vxd

[KBD_VxDs_Del]
vkd.386

[Strings]
KeyboardClassName      = "Keyboard"
MS                     = "Microsoft"
Std-Keyboards = "(Standard keyboards)"
*PNP0300.DeviceDesc    = "PC/XT Keyboard (83-Key)"
*PNP0301.DeviceDesc    = "PC/AT Keyboard (84-Key)"
*PNP0302.DeviceDesc    = "PC/XT Keyboard (84-Key)"
*PNP0303.DeviceDesc    = "Standard 101/102-Key or Microsoft Natural Keyboard"
*PNP030a.DeviceDesc    = "AT&T 302 Keyboard"
*PNP030b.DeviceDesc    = "PC/AT Enhanced Keyboard (101/102-Key)" ; default
```

29 Win32 Introduction

29.1 Introduction

Win32 is a standard programming model which allows a Windows program to run as a full 32-bit program. It also gives access to a great deal of advanced Windows functions. Its main advantages are:

- A 32-bit programming model for Windows 3.x that shares binary compatibility with Windows NT and Windows 95/98.
- The ability to produce an application program which can be used with Windows NT, Windows 95/98, and Windows 3.x.
- Full OLE (object linking and embedding) support, including 16-bit/32-bit interoperability. OLE allows the application program to share data where an OLE server provides information for an OLE client.
- Improved performance with 32-bit operations.
- Access to a large number of Win32 APIs (application programming interfaces) for Windows NT and Windows 95/98 (such as Windows, Menus, Resources, Memory Management, Graphics, File Compression, and so on).
- Win32 semantics for the application programming interface (API).

Win32s is an operating system extension that allows Win32 applications for Windows NT and Windows 95/98 to run on Windows version 3.x. At the heart of Win32s is a virtual device driver (VxD) and a number of dynamic-link libraries (DLLs). These extend Windows 3.x to support Win32-based applications. On Windows NT and Windows 95/98 there is no need to distribute extra files, while Windows 3.x requires the installation of the Win32 files.

29.1.1 Win32 APIs

There are a great deal of extra APIs that can be used with Win32; these can be classified as:

- Creating windows.
- Windows support functions.
- Message processing.
- Menus.
- Resources.
- Dialog boxes.
- User input functions.
- Memory management.
- GDI (graphical device interface).
- Bitmaps, icons and metafiles.
- Printing and text output.
- Painting and drawing.
- File I/O.
- Clipboard. Support for public and private clipboards.
- Registry. Support for functions which access the Registry.
- Initialization files. Support for functions which access INI files.
- System information.

- String manipulation.
- Timers.
- Processes and threads.
- Error and exception processing.
- MDI (multiple document interface).
- Help files.
- File compression/decompression.

- DLLs.
- Network support (NetBios and Windows sockets 1.1 APIs).
- Multimedia support (sound APIs).
- OLE and DDE (dynamic data exchange).
- TrueType fonts.

29.2 Win32s and Windows 3.x

Figure 29.1 shows how Windows 3.*x* uses Win32 and the general flow of control. The gray boxes represent Win32s components and the hatched box represents Windows 3.*x* components. Most calls are passed to Windows 3.*x*, which actually implements the call.

When a 32-bit application is run on a Windows 3.*x* operating system it dynamically connects to W32SCOMB.DLL, which is the combined Win32s version of the Win32 system DLLs, such as KERNEL32.DLL, GDI32.DLL, and USER32.DLL. The W32SCOMB DLL also contains the Windows 3.*x* window manager, graphics interface and kernel services DLLs.

The translation between 16-bit and 32-bit operations is conducted by WIN32S16 .DLL. A ring 0 kernel provides the low-level system services (VxD level), such as exception handling, floating-point trap emulation and low-level memory management. Few applications are allowed to directly communicate with this level and it is left to VxD files to communicate with this level.

A Win32 loader is used to execute the Win32 program. When the 32-bit executable is run then the Windows 3.*x* loader tries to load the executable. If it fails to load it then the Win32s loader is called to determine whether it is a Win32 executable. These services are provided in W32SKRNL.DLL.'

Win32s also hooks to the Windows 3.*x* resource loader. This allows application icons and other resource-viewing utilities to appear correctly in the Program Manager. Thus when Windows 3.*x* reads tries to read from a resource then Win32s fabricates the resource as a 16-bit resource. Thus 32-bit resources can be added to Windows 3.*x* so that they are transparent to both the programmer and the user.

Windows 3.x has a shared memory approach where all Windows processes operate within a global memory heap. Windows NT is a more robust operating system where processes have their own private address space. Thus, Win32-based applications running on Windows 3.x coexist in the same shared global memory heap as other Windows applications.

29.3 Exceptions

Many errors can occur in a program. In most programming language they can cause a program to crash or act unpredictably. For example, some languages can cause a run-time error when the program accesses an array element which is outside the number of elements which have been declared. In C++ an error causes an exception, which can be tested and handled in the required mode. The format is:

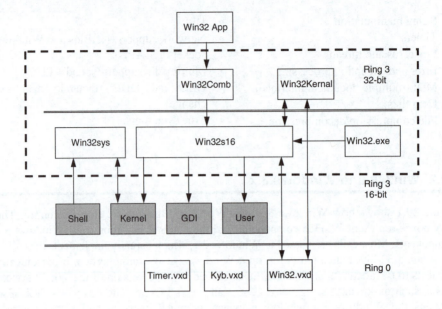

Figure 29.1   Win32s control.

```
try
{
      // statements to catch if an exception occurs
}
except (EXCEPTION_FLAG)
{
     // the catch is called when an exception occurs
}
```

When an exception occurs within the `try`, the rest of the statements within the `try` statement are not executed and the program goes to the `catch` statements. After completing the exception the program does not return to the `try` statement.

   Typical exceptions are:

- Breakpoints. Hardware-defined breakpoint.
- Divide-by-zero. Integer or floating-point divide-by-zero.
- Numerical overflow. Integer or floating-point overflow where an exponent overflows positively.
- Numerical underflow. Integer or floating-point underflow where an exponent overflows negatively.
- Memory access violation. Program has tried to access an area of memory which it is not allows to access.
- Illegal instruction.
- Single step operation. Single step debug mode.
- Privileged instruction.

Win32 Basics

30.1 Introduction

This section discusses some of the main Win32 API function calls and how to make a basic Windows program.

30.2 Main program

A Win32 program differs from a normal C program in that the main function is named `WinMain`, which has the return type of `int WINAPI`. The header file `windows.h` normally requires to be included as this contains definitions, macros, and structures that allow portability between different versions of Microsoft Windows. Program 30.1 shows a skeleton program.

Program 30.1

```
#include <windows.h>

int WINAPI WinMain(HINSTANCE hInstance, HINSTANCE hPrev,
            LPSTR lpCmd,    int nShow)
{

    return(0);
}
```

The parameters to the `WinMain` function are:

hInstance   This identifies the current instance of an application.

hPrev   This identifies the previous instance of the application and is always a NULL for a Win32-based application.

lpCmd   Identifies the command line string.

nShow   This is set to a flag which identifies how the window is to be shown. Typical settings are:

`SW_HIDE`
This hides the current window and activates another window.

`SW_MINIMIZE`
This activates a window which is minimized.

`SW_RESTORE`
This activates and displays a window.

`SW_SHOW`
This activates a window and displays it in its current size and position.

`SW_SHOWMAXIMIZED`

This activates a window which is maximized.

`SW_SHOWMINIMIZED`

This activates a window and displays it as an icon.

`SW_SHOWMINNOACTIVE`

This displays a window as an icon (the current window stays active).

`SW_SHOWNA`

Displays a window in its current state. The active window remains active.

`SW_SHOWNOACTIVATE`

Displays a window in its most recent size and position. The active window remains active.

`SW_SHOWNORMAL`

This activates and restores the window to its normal settings.

The definitions are as follows:

```
#define SW_HIDE             0
#define SW_SHOWNORMAL       1
#define SW_NORMAL           1
#define SW_SHOWMINIMIZED    2
#define SW_SHOWMAXIMIZED    3
#define SW_MAXIMIZE         3
#define SW_SHOWNOACTIVATE   4
#define SW_SHOW             5
#define SW_MINIMIZE         6
#define SW_SHOWMINNOACTIVE  7
#define SW_SHOWNA           8
#define SW_RESTORE          9
#define SW_SHOWDEFAULT      10
#define SW_MAX              10
```

Figure 30.1 shows a sample parameter from the command line parameters. It can be seen that in this case the `nCmdShow` parameter has been set at 1 (which is `SW_NORMAL`. The `lpCmdLine` parameter, in this case, is a NULL string (at the address `0x8156cfd`). Notice that the pointers in Win32 are full 32-bit pointers (they have 8 hexadecimal digits) and not segmented pointers (such as `8156:4321`).

Figure 30.1   Sample run.

30.2.1 Windows.h

Several new standard data types are defined in `windows.h`, these include:

`WINAPI`   This is equivalent to using `far pascal` in API declarations.

LPCSTR	This is defined as (const char FAR *) and is the same LPSTR, except it is used for read-only string pointers.
UINT	This is the unsigned int type and is used to create a portable unsigned integer type whose size is determined by the host environment (such as 32-bit integers for Windows NT/95/98).
LRESULT	This is used as a return value of windows procedures.
LPARAM	This is used in the declaration of *lParam* which is the fourth parameter of a Windows procedure.
WPARAM	This is used in the declaration of *wParam* which is the third parameter of a Windows procedure.
LPVOID	This is declared as (void *) and is a generic pointer type.

30.3 Creating windows

30.3.1 MessageBox

The MessageBox function creates and displays a window that has a specified message and caption. It also contains a combination of the predefined icons and push buttons described in the MessageBox styles list. Its standard format is:

```
int MessageBox( LPCTSTR lpszText, LPCTSTR lpszCaption, UINT nType);
```

Table 30.1 defines the parameters. The return value specifies the result of the function. A zero return identifies that there is not enough memory to create the message box.

Then *nTypes* can be used to set the icon to be displayed. Typical types, with their bitmask, are:

MB_ICONHAND and MB_ICONSTOP   MB_ICONQUESTION

MB_ICONASTERISK and MB_ICONINFORMATION

MB_ICONEXCLAMATION

Table 30.1 MessageBox parameters.

Parameter	Description
lpszText	String containing the message to be displayed.
lpszCaption	String to be used for the message-box caption.
nType	Specifies the contents and behaviour of the message box.

Program 30.2 shows a simple example of a message box and Figure 30.2 shows a sample run. In this the information icon is used. The button types can either be MB_OK (single OK button), MB_OKCANCEL (OK button and a Cancel button), MB_ABORT RETRYIGNORE (Abort, Retry and Ignore buttons), MB_YESNOCANCEL (Yes, No and Cancel buttons), MB_YESNO (Yes and No button) or MB_RETRYCANCEL (Retry and Cancel buttons). Refer to Figures 21.16 and 21.17 in the Visual Basic section for the layout of these buttons.

The definition of the buttons is:

```
#define MB_OK                  0x00000000L
#define MB_OKCANCEL            0x00000001L
#define MB_ABORTRETRYIGNORE    0x00000002L
#define MB_YESNOCANCEL         0x00000003L
#define MB_YESNO               0x00000004L
#define MB_RETRYCANCEL         0x00000005L

#define MB_ICONHAND            0x00000010L
#define MB_ICONQUESTION        0x00000020L
#define MB_ICONEXCLAMATION     0x00000030L
```

Program 30.2

```
#include <windows.h>

int WINAPI WinMain(HINSTANCE hInstance, HINSTANCE hPrev,
        LPSTR lpCmd,   int nShow)
{
char msg[128];
    wsprintf(msg, "My name is Fred");
    MessageBox(GetFocus(), msg, "My first Window",
                    MB_OK | MB_ICONINFORMATION);
    return(0);
}
```

Figure 30.2   Sample run.

The return value for the MessageBox() function is one of the following:

IDABORT	Abort button pressed	IDNO	No button pressed
IDCANCEL	Cancel button pressed	IDOK	OK button pressed
IDIGNORE	Ignore button pressed	IDRETRY	Retry button was selected
IDYES	Yes button pressed.		

Program 30.3 uses the return value for the MessageBox() function to determine the button that has been pressed. The program loops until the user presses the OK button. Figure 30.3 shows a sample run.

📖 **Program 30.3**

```
#include <windows.h>

int WINAPI WinMain(HINSTANCE hInstance, HINSTANCE hPrev,
          LPSTR lpCmd,   int nShow)
{
int rtn;

    do
    {
       rtn=MessageBox(GetFocus(), "Exit?", "Program Exit",
                          MB_OKCANCEL | MB_ICONEXCLAMATION);

    } while (rtn==IDCANCEL);
    return(0);
}
```

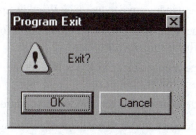

Figure 30.3   Sample run.

30.3.2 WNDCLASS

The main steps taken upon creating a window are:

- Define Windows class (WNDCLASS).
- Register Windows class with RegisterClass.
- Create window with CreateWindow.
- Display window with ShowWindow.
- Update window with UpdateWindow.

The standard format for the Windows class attributes is:

```
typedef struct _WNDCLASS {
    UINT     style;
    WNDPROC  lpfnWndProc;
    int      cbClsExtra;
    int      cbWndExtra;
    HANDLE   hInstance;
    HICON    hIcon;
    HCURSOR  hCursor;
    HBRUSH   hbrBackground;
    LPCTSTR  lpszMenuName;
    LPCTSTR  lpszClassName;
} WNDCLASS;
```

where

style   Specifies the class style(s) as defined in Appendix C.2.1. Typical defines
are:

CS_HREDRAW
Draws entire window when there is any movement or size adjustment in
the width of the client area.
CS_VREDRAW
Redraws entire window when there is any movement or size adjustment in
the height of the client area.

lpfnWndProc Points to the windows procedure (see Windows procedure section).

cbClsExtra Specifies the number of extra bytes to allocate following the window-class
structure. This is initially set to zero.

cbWndExtra Specifies the number of extra bytes to allocate following the window instance. This is initially set to zero.

hInstance   Identifies the instance that the window procedure of this class is within.

hIcon   Identifies the class icon which is a handle of an icon resource.

hCursor   Identifies the class icon which is a handle of a cursor resource.

hbrBackground
Identifies the class background brush which is a handle to the physical
brush to be used for painting the background, or it can be a colour value. If
it is a colour value then 1 must be added to it. Appendix C.2.2 defines the
valid colour values.

lpszMenuName
Points to a null-terminated character string that specifies the resource name
of the class menu, as the name appears in the resource file.

lpszClassName
Points to a null-terminated string which specifies the window class name.
This name is used when creating the window.

An example window class definition is given next. In this case the Windows procedure is
defined as WndProc. The LoadIcon function has been used to define the GENERIC.ICO
icon.

```
WNDCLASS    wc;

    wc.style         = CS_HREDRAW | CS_VREDRAW;
    wc.lpfnWndProc   = (WNDPROC)WndProc;
    wc.cbClsExtra    = 0;
    wc.cbWndExtra    = 0;
    wc.hInstance     = hInstance;
    wc.hIcon         = LoadIcon (hInstance, "Generic");
    wc.hCursor       = LoadCursor(NULL, IDC_ARROW);
    wc.hbrBackground = (HBRUSH)(COLOR_WINDOW+1);
    wc.lpszMenuName  = "Generic";
    wc.lpszClassName = "Generic";
```

30.3.3 RegisterClass

The `RegisterClass` function registers a window class for subsequent use in calls to the `CreateWindow`. If the function succeeds then the return value is an atom (a TRUE or FALSE value) that uniquely identifies the class being registered, else a zero is returned. Its standard format is:

```
ATOM RegisterClass(CONST WNDCLASS * lpWndClass );
```

where

lpWndClass   Points to a `WNDCLASS` structure.

30.3.4 LoadIcon

The `LoadIcon` function loads the specified icon resource for the program. If the function succeeds then the return value is the handle to the icon, else a NULL is returned. Its standard form is:

```
HICON LoadIcon(HINSTANCE   hInstance, LPCTSTR   lpIconName );
```

where

hInstance   Identifies an instance of the module whose executable file contains the icon to be loaded. This parameter must be NULL when a standard icon is being loaded.

lpIconName   Points to a null-terminated string that contains the name of the icon resource to be loaded.

For a predefined Windows icon the *hInstance* parameter is set to a NULL and the *lpIconName* parameter has one of the following:

IDI_APPLICATION	Default application icon.
IDI_ASTERISK	Asterisk.
IDI_EXCLAMATION	Exclamation point.
IDI_HAND	Hand-shaped icon.
IDI_QUESTION	Question mark.

30.3.5 LoadCursor

The `LoadCursor` function loads the specified cursor resource for the program. If the function succeeds then the return value is the handle to the cursor, else a NULL is returned. Its standard form is:

```
HCURSOR LoadCursor(HINSTANCE hInstance,LPCTSTR lpCursorName);
```

where

hInstance   Identifies an instance of the module whose executable file contains the cursor to be loaded.

lpCursorName

> Points to a null-terminated string that contains the name of the cursor resource to be loaded.

For a predefined Windows cursor the *hInstance* parameter is set to a NULL and the *lpCursorName* parameter has one of the following:

IDC_APPSTARTING	Standard arrow and small hourglass.
IDC_ARROW	Standard arrow.
IDC_CROSS	Crosshair.
IDC_IBEAM	Text I-beam.
IDC_NO	Slashed circle.
IDC_SIZEALL	Same as IDC_SIZE.
IDC_SIZENESW	Double-pointed arrow pointing northeast and southwest.
IDC_SIZENS	Double-pointed arrow pointing north and south.
IDC_SIZENWSE	Double-pointed arrow pointing northwest and southeast.
IDC_SIZEWE	Double-pointed arrow pointing west and east.
IDC_UPARROW	Vertical arrow.
IDC_WAIT	Hourglass.

30.3.6 CreateWindow

The CreateWindow function creates either an overlapped, pop-up or child window. It specifies all the parameters that define the window, such as its class, its title, its style, and the initial position and size of the window. Its standard format is:

```
HWND CreateWindow( LPCTSTR lpClassName, LPCTSTR lpWindowName,
    DWORD dwStyle, int x, int y, int nWidth,int nHeight, HWND hWndParent,
    HMENU hMenu, HANDLE   hInstance, LPVOID lpParam );
```

The parameters are:

lpClassName Points to a null-terminated string that specifies the window class name. This class name must first be registered with the RegisterClass function (or any of the predefined control-class names).

lpWindowName

> A null-terminated string which defines the window's name.

dwStyle   This specifies the style of the windows which can be a combination of the window styles and control styles (see Section 30.3.4, Section 30.3.5 and Section 30.3.6).

x   Specifies the initial horizontal position of the window. If this parameter is set to CW_USEDEFAULT then the default position is for the window's upper-left corner and it ignores the *y* parameter.

y   Specifies the initial vertical position of the window.

nWidth   Specifies the width, in device units, of the window. If *nWidth* is CW_USEDEFAULT then the default width and height for the window are selected.

nHeight   Specifies the height, in device units, of the window. If *nWidth* is set to CW_USEDEFAULT then *nHeight* is ignored.

hWndParent This identifies the parent or owner window of the window being created. A valid window handle must be supplied when a child window or an owned window is created.

hMenu Identifies a menu, or specifies a child-window identifier depending on the window style. For an overlapped or pop-up window, *hMenu* identifies the menu to be used with the window; it can be NULL if the class menu is to be used.

hInstance Identifies the instance of the module to be associated with the window.

lpParam Points to a value passed to the window through the CREATESTRUCT structure.

If the function succeeds then the return value will be the handle of the new window, else it will return a NULL. On an error, the GetLastError function can be called to determine the error.

Program 30.4 shows a simple program which creates a window at position (0,0) with a width of 100 and a height of 50. Initially the windows class is registered (with RegisterClass). If this function fails then it returns a zero value and the GetLastError() function is called to determine the error. Next, if the windows class is successfully registered, the window is created. If there is a failure in creating the window then the CreateWindow function returns a NULL, otherwise it returns a window handle. Figure 30.4 shows a sample run.

Program 30.4

```
#include <windows.h>
LRESULT CALLBACK WinProc(HWND, UINT, WPARAM, LPARAM);

int WINAPI WinMain(HINSTANCE hInst, HINSTANCE hPrev, LPSTR lpCmd, int nShow)
{
    HWND hWnd;
    WNDCLASS wc;
    BOOL rtn;
    int err;
    MSG message;

    wc.style=CS_HREDRAW | CS_VREDRAW;
    wc.lpfnWndProc=(WNDPROC)WinProc;
    wc.cbClsExtra=0;    wc.cbWndExtra=0;
    wc.hInstance=hInst; wc.hIcon=LoadIcon(hInst,"test");
    wc.hCursor=LoadCursor(NULL,IDC_ARROW);
    wc.hbrBackground=(HBRUSH)(COLOR_WINDOW+1);
    wc.lpszMenuName=NULL;
    wc.lpszClassName="test";

    rtn=RegisterClass(&wc);
    if (rtn==0) err=GetLastError();

    hWnd= CreateWindow("test", "Main", WS_OVERLAPPEDWINDOW,
        0, 0 , 50, 100 , NULL, NULL, hInst, NULL);

    if (hWnd==NULL) err=GetLastError();

    if (!hWnd)
    {
        MessageBox(GetFocus(), "Cannot create window","Error",
            MB_OK | MB_ICONINFORMATION);
```

```
            return(0);
        }

    ShowWindow(hWnd,nShow);
    UpdateWindow(hWnd);

    while (GetMessage(&message,NULL,0,0))
    {
        TranslateMessage(&message);
        DispatchMessage(&message);
    }
    return(0);
}

LRESULT CALLBACK WinProc(HWND hWnd, UINT message,
                    WPARAM wParam, LPARAM lParam)
{
    switch (message)
    {
    case WM_COMMAND: break;
    case WM_DESTROY: PostQuitMessage(0); break;
    default: return(DefWindowProc(hWnd, message,wParam,lParam));
    }
    return(0);
}
```

Figure 30.4 Sample run.

Control class

See Appendix C.1.1.

Window styles

See Appendix C.1.2.

Button styles

See Appendix C.1.3.

Combo box

See Appendix C.1.4.

Edit control styles

See Appendix C.1.5.

List box

See Appendix C.1.6.

Scroll bars

See Appendix C.1.7.

Static control

See Appendix C.1.8.

Dialog box

See Appendix C.1.9.

30.3.7 ShowWindow

After the `CreateWindow` is used to define a window the `ShowWindow` function can then be used to specify the window's displaying state. It returns a TRUE if the window was previously visible, else it return a FALSE. Its syntax is:

```
BOOL ShowWindow(HWND hWnd, int nCmdShow);
```

The parameters are:

HWnd   Identifies the handle of the window (which is created with the `CreateWindow` function).

nCmdShow   Defines how the window is displayed. The parameters include:

`SW_HIDE`	Hides the window and activates another one.
`SW_MAXIMIZE`	Maximizes specified window.
`SW_MINIMIZE`	Minimizes specified window and activates the next top-level window.
`SW_RESTORE`	Activates and displays the window.
`SW_SHOW`	Activates the window and displays it in its current size and position.
`SW_SHOWMAXIMIZED`	Activates window and displays it as a maximized window.
`SW_SHOWMINIMIZED`	Activates window and displays it as a minimized window.
`SW_SHOWMINNOACTIVE`	Displays the window as a minimized window. The active window remains active.
`SW_SHOWNA`	Displays the window in its current state. The active window remains active.
`SW_SHOWNOACTIVATE`	Displays a window in its most recent size and position. The active window remains active.
`SW_SHOWNORMAL`	Activates and displays a window. If the window is minimized or maximized, Windows restores it to its original size and position.

30.3.8 Windows procedure

The Windows procedure is called when an event occurs within a window. Information is passed into this procedure by messaging. The standard format for the Windows procedure is:

LRESULT CALLBACK *WndProc*(HWND *hWnd*, UINT *message*,
                                      WPARAM *wParam*, LPARAM *lParam*)

where

message   Specifies the Windows message to be processed.

wParam   Provides additional information used in processing the message.

lParam   Provides additional information used in processing the message.

These values can be tested with the following:

```
wmId    = LOWORD(wParam);
wmEvent = HIWORD(wParam);
```

where

wmEvent   The high-order word of *wParam* value specifies the notification code if the message is from a control. It is a 1 if the message is from an accelerator key, else it is from a menu option it is a 0. Example events are WM_COMMAND (which is sent when the user selects a command item from a menu, or when an accelerator keystroke is translated) and WM_PAINT (which is sent when an application makes a request to paint a portion of an application's window.).

wID   The low-order word of *wParam* specifies the identifier of the menu item, control or accelerator. This value is specified by the resources file.

For example, two event messages are:

```
int wmId, wmEvent;

switch (message)
{
    case WM_COMMAND: // Command event

        wmId    = LOWORD(wParam);
        wmEvent = HIWORD(wParam);

        switch (wmId)
        {
            case IDM_EXIT: DestroyWindow (hWnd); break;
        }
        break;

    case WM_PAINT: break;    // Paint event
}
```

30.3.9 DestroyWindow

The DestroyWindow function is used to destroy a window. It sends the message

`WM_DESTROY` and `WM_NCDESTROY` to the Windows procedure to deactivate it. Its syntax is:

`BOOL DestroyWindow( HWND` *hWnd* `);`

where

hWnd   Identifies the window to be destroyed.

30.3.10   *UpdateWindow*

The `UpdateWindow` function updates a window by sending a `WM_PAINT` message to the Windows procedure. Its syntax is:

`BOOL UpdateWindow(HWND` *hWnd* `);`

where

hWnd   Identifies the window to be updated.

30.3.11   *GetMessage, TranslateMessage and DispatchMessage*

See the next chapter.

30.4 Sample application

This section gives an example of creating a simple window.

30.4.1 *RC file*

The RC file, in Visual C++ Version 4, is designed by selecting ResourceView then selecting Insert → Resource → Menu, as shown in Figure 30.5 and Figure 30.6. In Visual C++ Version 5 a new project is created with Project → New → Project then selecting Win32 Application. Next the RC file is added with Insert → Resource → Menu. The menu options:

File → New, Open, Save, Save As, Print, Print Setup and Exit.
Edit → Undo, Cut, Copy, Paste, Paste Link, Links.

are added. Figure 30.7 shows an example of a menu item. The defined ID code for these menu items is:

```
IDM_NEW, IDM_OPEN,  IDM_SAVE, IDM_SAVEAS,
IDM_PRINT, IDM_PRINTSETUP, IDM_EXIT.
IDM_UNDO,IDM_CUT, IDM_COPY,   IDM_PASTE,
IDM_LINK, IDM_LINKS.
```

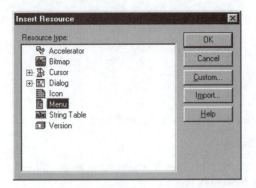

Figure 30.5   Adding a menu resource.

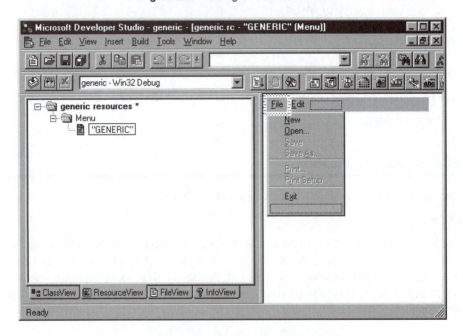

Figure 30.6   Adding a menu.

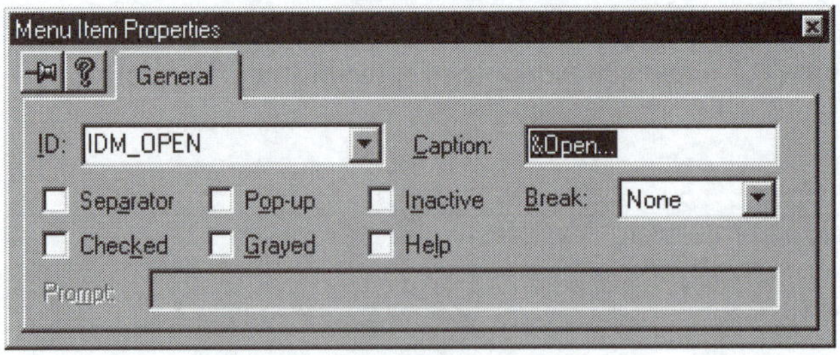

Figure 30.7   Adding menu item.

The resulting RC file is:

```
GENERIC MENU DISCARDABLE
BEGIN
    POPUP "&File"
    BEGIN
        MENUITEM "&New",               IDM_NEW
        MENUITEM "&Open...",           IDM_OPEN
        MENUITEM "&Save",                IDM_SAVE, GRAYED
        MENUITEM "Save &As...",        IDM_SAVEAS, GRAYED
        MENUITEM SEPARATOR
        MENUITEM "&Print...",            IDM_PRINT, GRAYED
        MENUITEM "P&rint Setup...",    IDM_PRINTSETUP, GRAYED
        MENUITEM SEPARATOR
        MENUITEM "E&xit",                IDM_EXIT
    END
    POPUP "&Edit"
    BEGIN
        MENUITEM "&Undo\tCtrl+Z",         IDM_UNDO, GRAYED
        MENUITEM SEPARATOR
        MENUITEM "Cu&t\tCtrl+X",          IDM_CUT, GRAYED
        MENUITEM "&Copy\tCtrl+C",         IDM_COPY, GRAYED
        MENUITEM "&Paste\tCtrl+V",        IDM_PASTE, GRAYED
        MENUITEM "Paste &Link",         IDM_LINK, GRAYED
        MENUITEM SEPARATOR
        MENUITEM "Lin&ks...",             IDM_LINKS, GRAYED
    END
END
```

30.4.2 Source file

The C file, in Visual C++ Version 4, is added by selecting ClassView then selecting Insert → File. Next, the C++ file is added with File → New → C++ Source File.

```c
#include <windows.h>
#include "generic.h"

char AppName[] = "Sample App."; // The name of this application
char AppTitle[]= "Sample App." // The title bar text

BOOL InitApplication(HINSTANCE);
BOOL InitInstance(HINSTANCE, int);
LRESULT CALLBACK WndProc(HWND, UINT, WPARAM, LPARAM);

//   FUNCTION: WinMain(HANDLE, HANDLE, LPSTR, int)
//
//   PURPOSE: Entry point for the application.
//
//   COMMENTS:
//
//     This function initializes the application and processes the
//     message loop.
//
int APIENTRY WinMain(HINSTANCE hInstance, HINSTANCE hPrevInstance, LPSTR
lpCmdLine, int nCmdShow)
{
    MSG msg;
    HANDLE hAccelTable;

    if (!hPrevInstance)
    {
        if (!InitApplication(hInstance)) {
            return (FALSE);
        }
    }

    if (!InitInstance(hInstance, nCmdShow))
    {
```

```
            return (FALSE);
    }

    while (GetMessage(&msg, NULL, 0, 0))
    {
            TranslateMessage(&msg);
            DispatchMessage(&msg);
    }

    return (msg.wParam);
}
//    FUNCTION: InitApplication(HANDLE)
//
//    PURPOSE: Initializes window data and registers window class
//
//    COMMENTS:
//
//       In this function, we initialize a window class by filling out a data
//       structure of type WNDCLASS and calling either RegisterClass or
//       the internal MyRegisterClass.
//
BOOL InitApplication(HINSTANCE hInstance)
{
    WNDCLASS  wc;

    // Fill in window class structure with parameters that describe
    // the main window.
    wc.style         = CS_HREDRAW | CS_VREDRAW;
    wc.lpfnWndProc   = (WNDPROC)WndProc;
    wc.cbClsExtra    = 0;
    wc.cbWndExtra    = 0;
    wc.hInstance     = hInstance;
    wc.hIcon         = LoadIcon (hInstance, AppName);
    wc.hCursor       = LoadCursor(NULL, IDC_ARROW);
    wc.hbrBackground = (HBRUSH)(COLOR_WINDOW+1);
    wc.lpszMenuName  = AppName;
    wc.lpszClassName = AppName;

     return RegisterClass(&wc);
}
//    FUNCTION: InitInstance(HANDLE, int)
//
//    PURPOSE: Saves instance handle and creates main window
//
//    COMMENTS:
//
//    In this function, we save the instance handle in a global variable and
//    create and display the main program window.
//
BOOL InitInstance(HINSTANCE hInstance, int nCmdShow)
{
    HWND hWnd;

    hWnd = CreateWindow(AppName, AppTitle, WS_OVERLAPPEDWINDOW,
        CW_USEDEFAULT, 0, CW_USEDEFAULT, 0,
        NULL, NULL, hInstance, NULL);

    if (!hWnd) {
       return (FALSE);
    }

    ShowWindow(hWnd, nCmdShow);
    UpdateWindow(hWnd);

    return (TRUE);
```

```
}
// FUNCTION: WndProc(HWND, unsigned, WORD, LONG)
//
// PURPOSE:  Processes messages for the main window.

LRESULT CALLBACK WndProc(HWND hWnd, UINT message, WPARAM wParam,
                  LPARAM lParam)
{
    int wmId, wmEvent;

    switch (message)
    {
        case WM_COMMAND:
            wmId    = LOWORD(wParam);
            wmEvent = HIWORD(wParam);

            // Determine menu option
            switch (wmId)
            {
                case IDM_EXIT:DestroyWindow (hWnd);        break;
                case IDM_NEW:
                   MessageBox(GetFocus(),"New",AppName, MB_OK|MB_ICONHAND);
                   break;
                case IDM_OPEN:
                   MessageBox(GetFocus(),"Open",AppName, MB_OK|MB_ICONHAND);
                   break;
                // The following are other options:
                case IDM_SAVE:
                case IDM_SAVEAS:
                case IDM_UNDO:
                case IDM_CUT:
                case IDM_COPY:
                case IDM_PASTE:
                case IDM_LINK:
                case IDM_LINKS:
                default: return (DefWindowProc(hWnd, message, wParam,
lParam));
            }
            break;
        default:return (DefWindowProc(hWnd, message, wParam, lParam));
    }
    return (0);
}
```

30.4.3 Header file

The associated header file `generic.h` is:

```
#define IDM_NEW              100
#define IDM_OPEN             101
#define IDM_SAVE             102
#define IDM_SAVEAS           103
#define IDM_PRINT            104
#define IDM_PRINTSETUP       105
#define IDM_EXIT             106
#define IDM_UNDO             200
#define IDM_CUT              201
#define IDM_COPY             202
#define IDM_PASTE            203
#define IDM_LINK             204
#define IDM_LINKS            205
```

30.4.4 Sample run

Figure 30.8 shows a sample run.

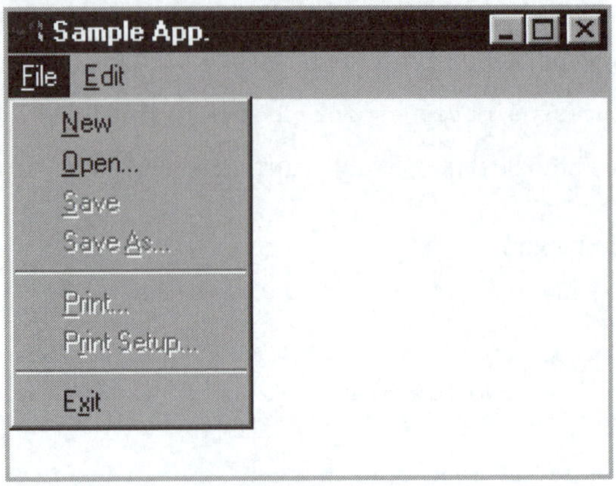

Figure 30.8 Sample run.

30.5 Other Windows support functions

The Windows support functions allow the manipulation of windows.

30.5.1 CloseWindow

The `CloseWindow` function minimizes the specified window to an icon. If it is successful then a TRUE is return, else a FALSE is returned. It differs from the `DestroyWindow` in that `CloseWindow` does not destroy the window. Its syntax is:

```
BOOL CloseWindow( HWND hWnd );
```

where

hWnd   Identifies the window to be minimized.

30.5.2 GetFocus

The `GetFocus` function retrieves the handle of the keyboard focus window associated with the thread that called the function. If successful then the return value is the handle of the keyboard focus window associated with the calling thread, else a NULL is return. Its syntax is:

```
HWND GetFocus(VOID)
```

30.5.3 GetParent

The `GetParent` function retrieves the handle of the parent window of the specified child window. If sucessful then the return value is the handle of the parent window, else a NULL is return. It syntax is:

```
HWND GetParent( HWND hWnd );
```

where

hWnd   Identifies the window whose parent window handle is to be retrieved.

30.5.4 GetWindow

The GetWindow function retrieves the handle of a window that has the specified relationship to the specified window. Windows organizes windows with the Z order which indicates a window's position in a stack of overlapping windows (the z-axis is an imaginary axis which extends outwards from the screen). The top of the Z order is the window that is foremost on the screen and the bottom is a window which is overlapped by all other windows.

The GetWindow function syntax is:

```
HWND GetWindow( HWND hWnd,UINT uCmd );
```

where

hWnd   Identifies a window. The window handle retrieved is relative to this window, based on the value of the *uCmd* parameter.

uCmd   Specifies the relationship between the specified window and the window whose handle is to be retrieved. This parameter can be one of the following values:

GW_CHILD
The retrieved handle identifies the child window at the top of the Z order, if the specified window is a parent window; otherwise, the retrieved handle is NULL. The function examines only child windows of the specified window. It does not examine descendant windows.

GW_HWNDFIRST
The retrieved handle identifies the window at the top of the Z order. If the specified window is a topmost window, the handle identifies the topmost window at the top of the Z order.

GW_HWNDLAST
The retrieved handle identifies the window at the bottom of the Z order. If the specified window is a topmost window, the handle identifies the topmost window at the bottom of the Z order.

GW_HWNDNEXT
The retrieved handle identifies the window below the specified window in the Z order. If the specified window is a topmost window, the handle identifies the topmost window below the specified window.

GW_HWNDPREV
The retrieved handle identifies the window above the specified window in the Z order. If the specified window is a topmost window, the handle identifies the topmost window above the specified window.

30.5.5 *SetActiveWindow*

The `SetActiveWindow` function makes the specified top-level window associated with the thread, calling this function the active window. If the function succeeds, the return value is the handle of the window that was previously active.

`HWND SetActiveWindow(` `HWND` *hWnd* `);`

where

hWnd   Identifies the top-level window to be activated.

30.5.6 *SetParent*

The `SetParent` function changes the parent window of the specified child window. If the function succeeds, the return value is the handle of the previous parent window. If the function fails, the return value is NULL. An application can use the `SetParent` function to set the parent window of a pop-up, overlapped, or child window. The new parent window and the child window must belong to the same application. If the window identified by the *hWndChild* parameter is visible, Windows performs the appropriate redrawing and repainting.

`HWND SetParent(` `HWND` *hWndChild,* `HWND` *hWndNewParent* `);`

where

hWndChild   Identifies the child window.

HWndNewParent   Identifies the new parent window. If this parameter is NULL, the desktop window becomes the new parent window.

30.6 Exercises

30.6.1   Create a message box with an icon question mark and the message 'Hello' with the following buttons:

> (i)   OK button   (ii) OK and Cancel
> (iii)   Abort, Retry and Ignore   (iv)   Yes, No and Cancel
> (iv)   Yes and No   (v)   Retry and Cancel

30.6.2   Write a Visual Basic program with the following menu system:

```
File          Edit          View                  Help
  Open          Copy          Normal
  Save          Paste         Full Screen
  Close         Select All
```

30.6.3   Modify the menu system in Exercise 30.6.2 so that if the user selects the Close option a message box appears which asks the user if they want to exit or not. If the user selects Yes then the program will exit, else it will not.

30.6.4   Modify the menu system in Exercise 30.6.2 so that message box appears which describes the function of the menu option.

30.6.5   Modify the menu system in Exercise 30.6.2 so that the Copy and Paste options in the Edit menu are greyed-out.

30.6.6   Modify the menu system in Exercise 30.6.2 so that the following hot-keys are implemented:

Alt-F	File	Alt-E	Edit	Alt-V	View
Cntrl-O	Open	Cntrl-S	Save	Cntrl-X	Close
Cntrl-C	Copy	Cntrl-V	Paste	Cntrl-A	Select all

30.6.7   Investigate different cursor types, such as a crosshair, an I-beam, a slashed circle and an hourglass.

31 Windows Messaging

31.1 Introduction

Each application can have multiple threads of execution, and each thread can create windows. Messaging is the method that Windows uses to react to hardware events that occur in a program. These messages are sent to the threads message queue. For example:

- WM_QUIT message indicates that there is a request to terminate an application.
- WM_DESTROY message indicates that a window is being destroyed.
- WM_ACTIVATE message indicates that a window is being activated or deactivated.
- WM_PAINT message indicates when Windows or another application makes a request to paint a portion of an application's window.
- WM_COMMAND message indicates that the user has selected a command item from a menu.
- WM_KEYUP message indicates that a non-system key has been released.
- WM_TIMECHANGE message indicates that the system time has been changed.

Appendix C.3 lists the complete set of messages.

31.2 Message structure

The MSG structure contains message information from a threads message queue.

```
typedef struct tagMSG {
    HWND    hwnd;         UINT   message;
    WPARAM wParam;        LPARAM lParam;
    DWORD   time;         POINT  pt;
} MSG;
```

where

hwnd	Identifies the window whose window procedure receives the message.
message	Specifies the message number.
wParam	Specifies additional information about the message. The exact meaning depends on the value of the *message* member.
lParam	Specifies additional information about the message. The exact meaning depends on the value of the *message* member.
time	Specifies the time at which the message was posted.
pt	Specifies the cursor position, in screen coordinates, when the message was posted.

31.3 Message functions

This section discusses the main functions used to get and process messages.

31.3.1 GetMessage

The `GetMessage` function retrieves messages from the message queue of the calling thread and places it into the message structure (`MSG`). Its syntax is:

```
BOOL GetMessage( LPMSG  lpMsg,   HWND  hWnd,
     UINT  wMsgFilterMin, UINT  wMsgFilterMax);
```

where

lpMsg	Points to an `MSG` structure that receives message information from the thread's message queue.
hWnd	Identifies the window whose messages are to be retrieved. A value of NULL retrieves messages for any window that belongs to the calling thread.
WMsgFilterMin	Is the Lowest message value to be retrieved.
WMsgFilterMax	Specifies the integer value of the highest message value to be retrieved. If the function retrieves a message other than `WM_QUIT`, the return value is TRUE, else `WM_QUIT` returns a FALSE. If there is an error then the return value is –1.

An example of the processing the messages is:

```
while (GetMessage(&msg, NULL, 0, 0)) // repeat until WM_QUIT
{
     TranslateMessage(&msg);
     DispatchMessage(&msg);
}
```

31.3.2 TranslateMessage

The `TranslateMessage` function changes virtual-key messages into actual character messages. Its syntax is:

```
BOOL TranslateMessage(CONST MSG *lpMsg);
```

where

lpMsg	Is a `MSG` structure which stores the message information from the `GetMessage` function.

31.3.3 DispatchMessage

The `DispatchMessage` function dispatches a message received by the `GetMessage` function to a window procedure. Its syntax is:

```
LONG DispatchMessage(CONST MSG  *lpmsg);
```

where

lpmsg   Is a MSG structure that contains the message.

31.3.4 ExitWindows

The `ExitWindows` function allows the user to quit from Windows. Its syntax is:

```
BOOL ExitWindows( DWORD dwReserved, UINT uReserved );
```

where

dwReserved   Is reserved and must be zero.
uReserved   Is reserved and must be zero.

31.3.5 PostMessage

The `PostMessage` function allows a message to be placed in a specified window. Messages in a message queue are retrieved by calls to the `GetMessage` function. It syntax is:

```
BOOL PostMessage( HWND hWnd, UINT Msg, WPARAM wParam, LPARAM lParam );
```

where

hWnd   Identifies the window.
Msg   Is the message to be posted.
wParam   Is additional message-specific information.
lParam   Is additional message-specific information.

31.3.6 SendMessage

The `SendMessage` function sends a message to a window. It calls the window procedure and does not return until the window procedure has processed the message. This differs from the `PostMessage` function which immediately returns without waiting. Its syntax is:

```
LRESULT SendMessage( HWND hWnd, UINT Msg,  WPARAM wParam, LPARAM lParam );
```

where

hWnd   Identifies the window.
Msg   Is the message to be sent.
wParam   Is additional message-specific information.
lParam   Is additional message-specific information.

31.3.7 ReplyMessage

The `ReplyMessage` function allows for a reply to a message which was posted by the `SendMessage` function. Its syntax is:

```
BOOL ReplyMessage( LRESULT lResult );
```

where

lResult   Is the result of the message processing.

31.3.8 WaitMessage

The `WaitMessage` function yields control and waits until a new message is placed in the message queue. Its syntax is:

```
BOOL WaitMessage(VOID)
```

31.4 Messages

Appendix C.3 gives a listing of the messages. This section outlines some of the most used messages. An outline windows procedure is shown below. Refer to the previous chapter for a full program.

```
LRESULT CALLBACK WndProc(HWND hWnd, UINT message, WPARAM wParam, LPARAM
lParam)
{
     int wmId, wmEvent,nWidth,nHeight,fwSizeType, nVirtKey, lKeyData;
     char  str[100];

     switch (message)
     {

       case WM_COMMAND:
          wmId   = LOWORD(wParam);
          wmEvent = HIWORD(wParam);
          break;
       case WM_SIZE:
          fwSizeType = wParam;       // resizing flag
          nWidth = LOWORD(lParam);   // width of client area
          nHeight = HIWORD(lParam); // height of client area
          wsprintf(str,"Width=%d Height=%d Flag=%d",
                        nWidth,nHeight,fwSizeType);
          MessageBox(GetFocus(),str,"Size", MB_OK|MB_ICONHAND);
          break;

       case WM_QUIT:
       case WM_CLOSE:
          MessageBox(GetFocus(),"Closing Window",
                        "Close",MB_OK|MB_ICONHAND);
          DestroyWindow(hWnd);
          break;

       case WM_KEYDOWN:
          nVirtKey = (int) wParam;    // virtual-key code
          lKeyData = lParam;          // key data
          wsprintf(str,"Key=%d Data=%d",nVirtKey,lKeyData);
          MessageBox(GetFocus(),str,"KeyDown", MB_OK|MB_ICONHAND);
          break;

       default:
          return (DefWindowProc(hWnd, message, wParam, lParam));
     }

     return (0);
}
```

31.4.1 WM_CREATE

The WM_CREATE message is sent when an application requests that a window be created by calling the CreateWindow function. The windows procedure of the new window receives this message after the window is created, but before the window becomes visible. The message is sent before the CreateWindow function returns.

31.4.2 WM_DESTROY

The WM_DESTROY message is sent when a window is being destroyed. It is sent to the windows procedure of the window being destroyed after the window is removed from the screen. This message is sent first to the window being destroyed and then to the child windows (if any) as they are destroyed. During the processing of the message, it can be assumed that all child windows still exist.

31.4.3 WM_MOVE

The WM_MOVE message is sent after a window when it is moved. In the windows procedure the following give the required information:

```
xPos = (int) LOWORD(lParam);    // horizontal position
yPos = (int) HIWORD(lParam);    // vertical position
```

where

xPos   Is the low-order word of *lParam* and specifies the x-coordinate of the upper-left corner of the window.

yPos   Is the high-order word of *lParam* and specifies the y-coordinate of the upper-left corner of the window.

31.4.4 WM_SIZE

The WM_SIZE message is sent to a window that has changed its size. In the windows procedure the following give the required information:

```
fwSizeType = wParam;        // resizing flag
nWidth = LOWORD(lParam);    // width of client area
nHeight = HIWORD(lParam);   // height of client area
```

where

fwSizeType   Specifies resizing type, such as:

SIZE_MAXIMIZED   Window has been maximized.
SIZE_MINIMIZED   Window has been minimized.
SIZE_RESTORED   Window has been resized, but neither the
                            SIZE_MINIMIZED nor SIZE_MAXIMIZED value applies.

NWidth   Is the low-order word of *lParam* and specifies the width of the window.
nHeight   Is the high-order word of *lParam* and specifies the height of the window.

The following example code shows how the WM_SIZE message is used and Figure 31.1

shows an example run. In this case it can be seen that the flag is set to 0, the width of the window is 270 pixels and its height is 176 pixels. Figure 31.2 shows an example of a minimized window. In this case the width and height are zero, and the flag is set to a 1 (SIZE_MINIMIZED).

```
LRESULT CALLBACK WndProc(HWND hWnd, UINT message,
                         WPARAM wParam, LPARAM lParam)
{
int    wmId, wmEvent,nWidth,nHeight,fwSizeType, nVirtKey, lKeyData;
char   str[100];

    switch (message)
    {

      case WM_COMMAND:
        wmId    = LOWORD(wParam);
        wmEvent = HIWORD(wParam);
        break;
      case WM_SIZE:
        fwSizeType = wParam;        // resizing flag
        nWidth = LOWORD(lParam);    // width of client area
        nHeight = HIWORD(lParam);   // height of client area
        wsprintf(str,"Width=%d Height=%d Flag=%d",
                    nWidth,nHeight,fwSizeType);
        MessageBox(GetFocus(),str,"Size", MB_OK|MB_ICONHAND);
        break;
      case WM_QUIT:
      case WM_CLOSE:
        MessageBox(GetFocus(),"Closing Window",
                              "Close",MB_OK|MB_ICONHAND);
        DestroyWindow(hWnd);
        break;

      case WM_KEYDOWN:
        nVirtKey = (int) wParam;    // virtual-key code
        lKeyData = lParam;          // key data
        wsprintf(str,"Key=%d Data=%d",nVirtKey,lKeyData);
        MessageBox(GetFocus(),str,"KeyDown", MB_OK|MB_ICONHAND);
        break;

      default:
        return (DefWindowProc(hWnd, message, wParam, lParam));
    }
    return (0);
}
```

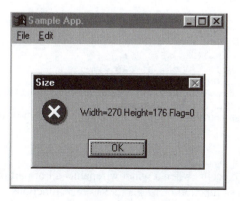

Figure 31.1 Sample run.

Figure 31.2 Sample run with the window minimized.

31.4.5 WM_ACTIVATE

The WM_ACTIVATE message occurs when a window is either activated or deactivated. In the windows procedure the following give the required information:

```
fActive = LOWORD(wParam);              // activation flag
fMinimized = (BOOL) HIWORD(wParam);    // minimized flag
hwnd = (HWND) lParam;                  // window handle
```

where

fActive   Is the low-order word of *wParam* and specifies whether the window is being activated or deactivated. It can have one of the following values:

WA_CLICKACTIVE Activated by a mouse click.

WA_ACTIVE   Activated by a method other than a mouse click.

WA_INACTIVE   Deactivated.

FMinimized   Is the high-order word of *wParam* which specifies the minimized state of the window being activated or deactivated. A non-zero value indicates the window is minimized.

hwnd   Is the value of *lParam* and identifies the window being activated or deactivated.

The following gives an example message handler. In this case an activated window displays a message box with the message "Hello". When the window is deactivated the message is "Goodbye".

```
case WM_SIZE:
    fActive = LOWORD(wParam);
    fMinimized = (BOOL) HIWORD(wParam);
    hwnd = (HWND) lParam;
    if (fActive==WA_ACTIVE) wsprintf(str,"Hello");
    else wsprintf(str,"Goodbye");
    MessageBox(GetFocus(),str,"Size", MB_OK|MB_ICONHAND);
    break;
```

31.4.6 WM_PAINT

The WM_PAINT message occurs when a window repaints all or part of a window. It is sent when the UpdateWindow function or DispatchMessage functions are called. In the windows procedure the following gives the required information:

```
hdc = (HDC) wParam; // the device context to draw in
```

where

`hdc`   Identifies the window.

31.4.7 WM_CLOSE

The `WM_CLOSE` message occurs when an application is to be closed.

31.4.8 WM_QUIT

The `WM_QUIT` message occurs when an application is to be exited. In the windows procedure the following parameter is used:

```
nExitCode = (int) wParam;   // exit code
```

where

`nExitCode`   Specifies exit code.

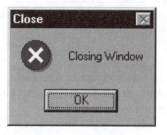

Figure 31.3   Sample run when Close Window is selected.

31.4.9 WM_SHOWWINDOW

The `WM_SHOWWINDOW` message occurs when a window is about to be either hidden or
shown. In the windows procedure the following are the parameters used:

```
fShow = (BOOL) wParam;      // show/hide flag
fnStatus = (int) lParam;    // status flag
```

where

`fShow`   Specifies whether a window is being shown. A TRUE indicates that the
windows is being shown else a window is being hidden.

`fnStatus`   Specifies the status of the window being shown, such as:

        `SW_OTHERUNZOOM`
        Window is being uncovered because a maximize window was restored or
        minimized.

```
SW_OTHERZOOM
```
Window is being covered by another window that has been maximized.
```
SW_PARENTCLOSING
```
Window's owner window is being minimized.
```
SW_PARENTOPENING
```
Window's owner window is being restored.

31.4.10   WM_MOUSEACTIVATE

The `WM_MOUSEACTIVATE` message occurs when a cursor is in an inactive window and the user presses a mouse button. In the windows procedure the following are the parameters used:

```
hwndTopLevel = (HWND) wParam;         // handle of top-level parent
nHittest = (INT) LOWORD(lParam);      // hit-test value
uMsg =     (UINT) HIWORD(lParam);     // mouse message
```

where

hwndTopLevel	Identifies the top-level window.
nHittest	Specifies the hit-test value.
uMsg	Specifies the identifier of the mouse message generated when the user pressed a mouse button.

31.4.11   WM_KEYDOWN

The `WM_KEYDOWN` message occurs with keyboard focus when a non-system key is pressed. A non-system key is a key that is pressed when the Alt key is *not* pressed. In the windows procedure the following are the parameters used:

```
nVirtKey = (int) wParam;     // virtual-key code
lKeyData = lParam;           // key data
```

where

`nVirtKey`	Specifies the virtual-key code of the non-system key.
`lKeyData`	Specifies the repeat count, scan code, extended-key flag, context code, previous key-state flag, and transition-state flag, as shown in the following table:

0–15	Specifies the repeat count (the number of times the keystroke is repeated as a result of the user holding down the key).
16–23	Specifies the scan code.
24	Specifies whether the key is an extended key, such as the right-hand Alt and Ctrl keys that appear on an enhanced 101- or 102-key keyboard. The value is 1 if it is an extended key; otherwise, it is 0.
25–28	Reserved.
29	Context code. The value is always 0 for a `WM_KEYDOWN` message.

| 30 | Previous key state. The value is 1 if the key is down before the message is sent, or it is 0 if the key is up. |
| 31 | Transition state. The value is always 0 for a WM_KEYDOWN message. |

The following program gives an example of a message event for key down press event. Figure 31.4 shows a run when the user presses the 'a' and also a 'b'.

```
LRESULT CALLBACK WndProc(HWND hWnd, UINT message,
          WPARAM wParam, LPARAM lParam)
{
int   nVirtKey, lKeyData;
char  str[100];

    switch (message)
    {
      case WM_QUIT:
      case WM_CLOSE:
          MessageBox(GetFocus(),"Closing Window",
            "Close",MB_OK|MB_ICONHAND);
          DestroyWindow(GetFocus);
          break;

      case WM_KEYDOWN:
          nVirtKey = (int) wParam;    // virtual-key code
          lKeyData = lParam;          // key data
          wsprintf(str,"Key=%d Data=%d",nVirtKey,lKeyData);
          MessageBox(GetFocus(),str,"KeyDown", MB_OK|MB_ICONHAND);
          break;
      default:
          return (DefWindowProc(hWnd, message, wParam, lParam));
    }
    return (0);
}
```

Figure 31.4 Sample run with the 'a' and 'b' key pressed.

31.4.12 WM_KEYUP

The WM_KEYUP message occurs with keyboard focus when a non-system key is pressed. A non-system key is a key that is pressed when the Alt key is *not* pressed. In the windows procedure the following are the parameters used:

```
nVirtKey = (int) wParam;    // virtual-key code
lKeyData = lParam;          // key data
```

where

nVirtKey   Value of *wParam*. Specifies the virtual-key code of the non-system key.
lKeyData   Value of *lParam*. Specifies the repeat count, scan code, extended-key flag, context code, previous key-state flag, and transition-state flag, as shown in the following table (see WM_KEYDOWN section, but replace WM_KEYDOWN with WM_KEYUP).

31.4.13   WM_CHAR

The WM_CHAR message occurs with keyboard focus when a WM_KEYDOWN message is translated by the TranslateMessage function. WM_CHAR contains the character code of the key that was pressed. In the windows procedure the following are the parameters used:

```
chCharCode = (TCHAR) wParam;    // character code
lKeyData = lParam;              // key data
```

where

chCharCode   Specifies the character code of the key.
lKeyData   Specifies the repeat count, scan code, extended-key flag, context code, previous key-state flag, and transition-state flag (see section 31.4.11).

31.4.14   WM_COMMAND

The WM_COMMAND message occurs when the user selects a command item from a menu, when a control sends a notification message to its parent window, or when an accelerator keystroke is translated. In the windows procedure the following are the parameters used:

```
wNotifyCode = HIWORD(wParam);// notification code
wID = LOWORD(wParam);
                // item, control, or accelerator identifier
hwndCtl = (HWND) lParam; // handle of control
```

where

wNotifyCode   Specifies the notification code if the message is from a control. If the message is from an accelerator, this parameter is 1. If the message is from a menu, this parameter is 0.
WID   Specifies the identifier of the menu item, control, or accelerator.
hwndCtl   Identifies the control sending the message if the message is from a control. Otherwise, this parameter is NULL.

31.4.15   WM_SYSCOMMAND

A window receives this message when the user chooses a command from the System menu (also known as Control menu) or when the user chooses the Maximize button or Minimize button. In the windows procedure the following are the parameters used:

```
uCmdType = wParam;    // type of system command requested
xPos = LOWORD(lParam);// horizontal position, in screen co-ordinates
yPos = HIWORD(lParam);// vertical position, in screen co-ordinates
```

where

`uCmdType`	Specifies the type of system command requested. This can be one of these values:
`SC_CLOSE`	Closes the window.
`SC_CONTEXTHELP`	Changes the cursor to a question mark with a pointer. If the user then clicks a control in the dialog box, the control receives a `WM_HELP` message.
`SC_DEFAULT`	Selects the default item; the user double-clicked the System menu.
`SC_HOTKEY`	Activates the window associated with the application-specified hot key. The low-order word of *lParam* identifies the window to activate.
`SC_HSCROLL`	Scrolls horizontally.
`SC_KEYMENU`	Retrieves the System menu as a result of a keystroke.
`SC_MAXIMIZE`	Maximizes the window.
`SC_MINIMIZE`	Minimizes the window.
`SC_MOUSEMENU`	Retrieves the System menu as a result of a mouse click.
`SC_MOVE`	Moves the window.
`SC_NEXTWINDOW`	Moves to the next window.
`SC_PREVWINDOW`	Moves to the previous window.
`SC_RESTORE`	Restores the window to its normal position and size.
`SC_SCREENSAVE`	Executes the screen saver application specified in the [boot] section of the SYSTEM.INI file.
`SC_SIZE`	Sizes the window.
`SC_TASKLIST`	Executes or activates Windows Task Manager.
`SC_VSCROLL`	Scrolls vertically.
xPos	Specifies the horizontal position of the cursor, in screen coordinates, if a System menu command is chosen with the mouse. Otherwise, the *xPos* parameter is not used.
yPos	Specifies the vertical position of the cursor, in screen coordinates, if a System menu command is chosen with the mouse. This parameter is -1 if the command is chosen using a system accelerator, or zero if using a mnemonic.

31.4.16   *WM_HSCROLL*

The `WM_HSCROLL` message occurs when a scroll event occurs in the window's standard horizontal scroll bar. In the windows procedure the following are the parameters used:

```
nScrollCode = (int) LOWORD(wParam);    // scroll bar value
nPos = (short int) HIWORD(wParam);     // scroll box position
hwndScrollBar = (HWND) lParam;         // handle of scroll bar
```

where

nScrollCode   Specifies a scroll bar value that indicates the user's scrolling request. Its settings can be:

SB_BOTTOM	Scrolls to the lower right.
SB_ENDSCROLL	Ends scroll.
SB_LINELEFT	Scrolls left by one unit.
SB_LINERIGHT	Scrolls right by one unit.
SB_PAGELEFT	Scrolls left by the width of the window.
SB_PAGERIGHT	Scrolls right by the width of the window.
SB_THUMBPOSITION	Scrolls to the absolute position. The current position is specified by the *nPos* parameter.
SB_THUMBTRACK	Drags scroll box to the specified position. The current position is specified by the *nPos* parameter.
SB_TOP	Scrolls to the upper left.

nPos   Specifies the current position of the scroll box if the *nScrollCode* parameter is SB_THUMBPOSITION or SB_THUMBTRACK; otherwise, *nPos* is not used.

HwndScrollBar
              Identifies the control if WM_HSCROLL is sent by a scroll bar control. If WM_HSCROLL is sent by a window's standard scroll bar, *hwndScrollBar* is not used.

31.4.17   *WM_VSCROLL*

The WM_VSCROLL message occurs when a scroll event occurs in the window's standard vertical scroll bar. In the windows procedure the following are the parameters used:

```
nScrollCode = (int) LOWORD(wParam); // scroll bar value
nPos = (short int) HIWORD(wParam);  // scroll box position
hwndScrollBar = (HWND) lParam;      // handle of scroll bar
```

where

nScrollCode
              Specifies a scroll bar value that indicates the user's scrolling request. This parameter can be one of the values defined in the previous section.

nPos   Specifies the current position of the scroll box if the *nScrollCode* parameter is SB_THUMBPOSITION or SB_THUMBTRACK; otherwise, *nPos* is not used.

hwndScrollBar
              Identifies the control if WM_VSCROLL is sent by a scroll bar control. If WM_VSCROLL is sent by a window's standard scroll bar, *hwndScrollBar* is not used.

31.5 Exercises

31.5.1   What is the purpose of the `WinProc` function?

31.5.2   What is the difference between the `WM_QUIT` and `WM_DESTROY` messages? Write a program which investigates their usage.

31.5.3   Write a program which reacts to the mouse up message (`WM_KEYUP`). The program should display the key pressed.

31.5.4   Write a program which minimizes or maximizes a window.

31.5.5   Write a program which uses the `WM_DESTROY` message. Before the window is closed a message should be displayed that says:

```
GOODBYE FOR EVER
```

32 Windows Output

32.1 Introduction

The graphic device interface (GDI) is the layer between the application and the output hardware. This layer is important in that it isolates the application from the specific type of hardware. Thus, the programmer does not need to worry about the operation of output devices such as the video adapter and printer.

32.2 Device context

The device context (or DC) is the method that Windows uses to create device independence. It is used by Windows to store information on the output device. Thus instead of an application sending information directly to the hardware the application simply sends it to Windows which then controls the hardware.

32.2.1 GetDC

The GetDC function gets a handle of a display device context for a specified window. Once it has been generated successfully, it can be used to output text or paint functions to the window. After the output operation has been performed, the ReleaseDC function must be called to release the device context.

The GetDC function's syntax is:

```
HDC GetDC( HWND hWnd);
```

where

hWnd   Specifies window.

32.2.2 ReleaseDC

The ReleaseDC function releases the device context so that the window can be used by other applications. Its syntax is:

```
int ReleaseDC( HWND hWnd, HDC hDC );
```

where

hWnd   Specifies window.
hDC   Specifies device context.

32.3 Text output

32.3.1 TextOut

The `TextOut` function is used to output text to a specified location using the currently selected font. Its syntax is:

> BOOL TextOut(HDC *hdc*, int *nXStart*, int *nYStart*, LPCTSTR *lpString*, int *cbString*);

where

hdc	Specifies window.
nXStart	Specifies the x-coordinate of the text.
nYStart	Specifies the y-coordinate of the text.
lpString	Is the text string to be outputted.
cbString	Is the length of string.

The following windows procedure shows how the `TextOut` function can be used to output text. In this program when a window is resized the text displayed in the window changes with the size of the window (a sample run is given in Figure 32.1). It also reacts to a keypress.

```
LRESULT CALLBACK WndProc(HWND hWnd, UINT message,
                WPARAM wParam, LPARAM lParam)
{
int   wmId, wmEvent,nWidth,nHeight,fwSizeType, nVirtKey, lKeyData;
char  str[100];
HDC   hdc;
    switch (message)
    {
       case WM_COMMAND:
          wmId    = LOWORD(wParam);
          wmEvent = HIWORD(wParam);
          break;
       case WM_SIZE:
          fwSizeType = wParam;       // resizing flag
          nWidth = LOWORD(lParam);   // width of client area
          nHeight = HIWORD(lParam);  // height of client area
          wsprintf(str,"Width=%d Height=%d Flag=%d",
                     nWidth,nHeight,fwSizeType);
          hdc=GetDC(hWnd);
          TextOut(hdc, 0,0, str, strlen(str));
          ReleaseDC(hWnd,hdc);
          break;
       case WM_QUIT:
       case WM_CLOSE:DestroyWindow(hWnd); break;
       case WM_KEYDOWN:
          nVirtKey = (int) wParam;    // virtual-key code
          lKeyData = lParam;          // key data
          wsprintf(str,"Key=%d Data=%x",nVirtKey,lKeyData);
          hdc=GetDC(hWnd);
          TextOut(hdc, 0,0, str, strlen(str));
          ReleaseDC(hWnd,hdc);
          break;
       default:
          return (DefWindowProc(hWnd, message, wParam, lParam));
    }
```

```
        return (0);
}
```

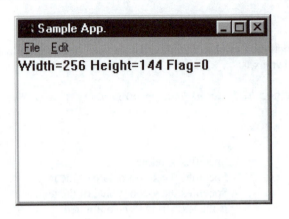

Figure 32.1   Sample run.

32.4 Various GDI functions

This section introduces some of the supported GDI functions in Win32.

32.4.1 GetSystemMetrics

The `GetSystemMetrics` function gets various system metrics (window heights and widths, in pixels) and system configuration settings. Its syntax is:

```
int GetSystemMetrics( int nIndex );
```

where

nIndex   Specifies the system metric or configuration setting to retrieve. The de-
                  fined values are:

SM_CMOUSEBUTTONS
Number of buttons on mouse, or zero if no mouse is installed.

SM_CXFULLSCREEN, SM_CYFULLSCREEN
Width and height of the client area for a full-screen window.

SM_CXHSCROLL, SM_CYHSCROLL
Width and height of arrow bitmap on horizontal scrollbar.

SM_CXHTHUMB   Width of horizontal scrollbar thumb box.

SM_CXICON, SM_CYICON
Default width and height of an icon (normally 32×32).

SM_CXMINSM_CYMIN   Minimum width and height of a window.

SM_CXMINTRACK, SM_CYMINTRACK
Minimum tracking width and height of a window.

SM_CXSCREEN,   SM_CYSCREEN   Width and height of the screen.

SM_CYVTHUMB	Height of vertical scrollbar thumb.
SM_CYCAPTION	Height of normal caption area.
SM_CYMENU	Height of single-line menu bar.

SM_MENUDROPALIGNMENT
Function returns a non-zero (or TRUE) if pop-up menus are right-aligned, else a zero (or FALSE) value is returned.

SM_MOUSEPRESENT
Function returns a non-zero (or TRUE) if a mouse is installed, else a zero (or FALSE) value is returned.

SM_PENWINDOWS
Function returns a non-zero (or TRUE) if Microsoft Windows for Pen computing extensions are installed, else a zero (or FALSE) value is returned.

SM_SWAPBUTTON
Function returns a non-zero (or TRUE) if the meanings of the left and right mouse buttons are swapped, else a zero value (or FALSE).

The return value from the function is the requested system metric or configuration setting. Program 32.1 uses the GetSystemMetrics function to determine the number of mouse buttons, width of the screen and the height of the screen. Figure 32.2 gives a sample run.

📖 Program 32.1

```
#include <windows.h>

LRESULT CALLBACK WinProc(HWND, UINT, WPARAM, LPARAM);

int WINAPI WinMain(HINSTANCE hInst, HINSTANCE hPrev, LPSTR lpCmd, int nShow)
{
    HWND hWnd;
    HDC hdc;
    WNDCLASS wc;
    BOOL rtn;
    int mb,mx,my;
    MSG message;
    char str[128];

    wc.style=CS_HREDRAW | CS_VREDRAW;
    wc.lpfnWndProc=(WNDPROC)WinProc;
    wc.cbClsExtra=0;
    wc.cbWndExtra=0;
    wc.hInstance=hInst;
    wc.hIcon=LoadIcon(hInst,"test");
    wc.hCursor=LoadCursor(NULL,IDC_ARROW);
    wc.hbrBackground=(HBRUSH)(COLOR_WINDOW+1);
    wc.lpszMenuName=NULL;
    wc.lpszClassName="test";
    rtn=RegisterClass(&wc);

    hWnd= CreateWindow("test", "Main", WS_OVERLAPPEDWINDOW,
        0, 0 , 300, 200 , NULL, NULL, hInst, NULL);

    ShowWindow(hWnd,nShow);
    UpdateWindow(hWnd);
    mb=GetSystemMetrics(SM_CMOUSEBUTTONS);
```

```
mx=GetSystemMetrics(SM_CXFULLSCREEN);
my=GetSystemMetrics(SM_CYFULLSCREEN);
wsprintf(str,"Mouse buttons=%d MaxX=%d MaxY=%d",mb,mx,my);
hdc=GetDC(hWnd);
TextOut(hdc,0,0,str,strlen(str));
ReleaseDC(hWnd,hdc);
while (GetMessage(&message,NULL,0,0))
{
        TranslateMessage(&message);
        DispatchMessage(&message);
}
return(0);
}

LRESULT CALLBACK WinProc(HWND hWnd, UINT message,
                   WPARAM wParam, LPARAM lParam)
{
      switch (message)
      {
      case WM_COMMAND: break;
      case WM_DESTROY: PostQuitMessage(0); break;
      default: return(DefWindowProc(hWnd, message,wParam,lParam));
      }
      return(0);
}
```

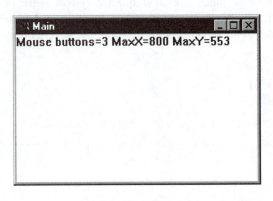

Figure 32.2   Sample run.

32.4.2 CreateFont

The `CreateFont` function is a powerful technique to create a font with given characteristics. Once specified the font can be used on any device. Its format is:

```
HFONT CreateFont(  int nHeight,  // logical height of font
     int nWidth, // logical average character width
     int nEscapement, // angle of escapement
     int nOrientation, // base-line orientation angle
     int fnWeight, // font weight
     DWORD fdwItalic, // italic attribute flag
     DWORD fdwUnderline, // underline attribute flag
     DWORD fdwStrikeOut, // strikeout attribute flag
     DWORD fdwCharSet, // character set identifier
     DWORD fdwOutputPrecision, // output precision
     DWORD fdwClipPrecision, // clipping precision
```

```
DWORD fdwQuality, // output quality
DWORD fdwPitchAndFamily, // pitch and family
LPCTSTR lpszFace // pointer to typeface name string );
```

where

nHeight	Specifies the height (in logical units) for the character. A value which is greater than zero transforms the value into device units and matches it against the cell height of the available fonts. If the value is zero then the default height value is used.
nWidth	Specifies the average width (in logical units) for the characters. A zero value will choose the closest matching width.
nEscapement	Specifies the angle (in tenths of degrees) between the base line of the text and the x-axis of the device.
nOrientation	Specifies the angle (in tenths of degrees) between the base line of the character and the x-axis of the device.
FnWeight	Specifies font weight between 0 and 1000. The following values are defined for convenience:

```
FW_DONTCARE    FW_THIN     FW_EXTRALIGHT  FW_ULTRALIGHT  FW_LIGHT
FW_NORMAL      FW_REGULAR  FW_MEDIUM      FW_SEMIBOLD    FW_DEMIBOLD
FW_BOLD        FW_EXTRABOLDFW_ULTRABOLD  FW_HEAVY       FW_BLACK
```

fdwItalic	If TRUE specifies italic font.
fdwUnderline	If TRUE specifies underlined font.
fdwStrikeOut	If TRUE specifies strikeout font.
fdwCharSet	Specifies character set. The following have been predefined:

```
ANSI_CHARSET   DEFAULT_CHARSET   SYMBOL_CHARSET   OEM_CHARSET
```

fdwOutputPrecision

Specifies output precision which defines how closely the font matches its output. The following have been predefined:

```
OUT_CHARACTER_PRECIS    OUT_DEFAULT_PRECIS      OUT_DEVICE_PRECIS
OUT_OUTLINE_PRECIS      OUT_RASTER_PRECIS OUT_STRING_PRECIS
OUT_STROKE_PRECIS       OUT_TT_ONLY_PRECIS      OUT_TT_PRECIS
```

fdwClipPrecision

Specifies clipping precision. The following have been predefined:

```
CLIP_DEFAULT_PRECIS CLIP_CHARACTER_PRECIS   CLIP_STROKE_PRECIS
CLIP_MASK           CLIP_EMBEDDED           CLIP_TT_ALWAYS
```

fdwQuality	Specifies output quality. The following are predefined:

```
DEFAULT_QUALITY   DRAFT_QUALITY  PROOF_QUALITY
```

fdwPitchAndFamily

Specifies pitch and family of the font. The two low-order bits define font pitch and can be one of the following:

```
DEFAULT_PITCH FIXED_PITCH VARIABLE_PITCH
```

The next four high-order bits define the font family, and can be:

```
FF_DECORATIVE FF_DONTCARE FF_MODERN FF_ROMAN FF_SCRIPT FF_SWISS
```

lpszFace   String which defines the font name, such as 'Times New Roman', 'Arial', 'Courier New' and so on.

Program 32.2 uses the `CreateFont` function to create a font which has a default height, a default width, is bold, italic and has strikethrough, and the font family is Arial. The `SelectObject` function assigns the newly created font (`nFont`) to the output device. Figure 32.3 shows a sample run.

📖 Program 32.2

```c
#include <windows.h>

LRESULT CALLBACK WinProc(HWND, UINT, WPARAM, LPARAM);

int WINAPI WinMain(HINSTANCE hInst, HINSTANCE hPrev, LPSTR lpCmd, int nShow)
{
    HWND hWnd;
    HDC hdc;
    WNDCLASS wc;
    BOOL rtn;
    int mb,mx,my;
    MSG message;
    char str[128];
    HFONT nFont;
    wc.style=CS_HREDRAW | CS_VREDRAW;
    wc.lpfnWndProc=(WNDPROC)WinProc;
    wc.cbClsExtra=0;
    wc.cbWndExtra=0;
    wc.hInstance=hInst;
    wc.hIcon=LoadIcon(hInst,"test");
    wc.hCursor=LoadCursor(NULL,IDC_ARROW);
    wc.hbrBackground=(HBRUSH)(COLOR_WINDOW+1);
    wc.lpszMenuName=NULL;
    wc.lpszClassName="test";
    rtn=RegisterClass(&wc);

    hWnd= CreateWindow("test", "Main", WS_OVERLAPPEDWINDOW,
        0, 0 , 500, 200 ,
        NULL, NULL, hInst, NULL);

    ShowWindow(hWnd,nShow);
    UpdateWindow(hWnd);

    mb=GetSystemMetrics(SM_CMOUSEBUTTONS);
    mx=GetSystemMetrics(SM_CXFULLSCREEN);
    my=GetSystemMetrics(SM_CYFULLSCREEN);

    wsprintf(str,"Mouse buttons=%d MaxX=%d MaxY=%d",mb,mx,my);

    nFont=CreateFont(0,0,0,0,FW_BOLD,TRUE, TRUE, TRUE,
        ANSI_CHARSET, OUT_DEFAULT_PRECIS, CLIP_DEFAULT_PRECIS,
        DEFAULT_QUALITY,FF_DECORATIVE,"Courier New");
    hdc=GetDC(hWnd);
    SelectObject(hdc,nFont);   // assign font to DC
    TextOut(hdc,0,0,str,strlen(str));
```

```
        ReleaseDC(hWnd,hdc);
        while (GetMessage(&message,NULL,0,0))
        {
                TranslateMessage(&message);
                DispatchMessage(&message);
        }
        return(0);
}

LRESULT CALLBACK WinProc(HWND hWnd, UINT message,
                    WPARAM wParam, LPARAM lParam)
{
        switch (message)
        {
        case WM_COMMAND: break;
        case WM_DESTROY: PostQuitMessage(0); break;
        default: return(DefWindowProc(hWnd, message,wParam,lParam));
        }
        return(0);
}
```

Figure 32.3 Sample run.

32.5 Exercises

32.5.1 What is the usage of the device context? What advantages does it have over output to a printer or a monitor?

32.5.2 Write a program which displays all of the system metrics, including:

- Number of mouse buttons.
- Width and height of full screen.
- and so on.

32.5.3 Write a program which displays all of the available system fonts.

32.5.4 Write a program which uses a Times Roman font for a font size of 8, 12, 16, 24 and 36.

32.5.5 Write a program which uses different font weightings, such as FW_LIGHT, FW_BOLD, and so on.

33 Drawing and Painting

33.1 Introduction

Win32 has a great deal of graphics related functions. This chapter discusses some of them.

33.2 Colours

Colours in Windows are represented by a 32-bit value which defines the strength of the red, green and blue. The structure used to define the colour is COLORREF.

33.2.1 COLORREF

Colours in Win32 are defined in the RGB (red/green/blue) strength and use the data type COLORREF. The format is 0xbbggrr, where rr is the hexadecimal equivalent for the red component, gg the hexadecimal equivalent for the green component and bb the hexadecimal equivalent for the blue component. Table 33.1 lists some of the colour codes.

Individual hexadecimal numbers use base 16 and range from 0 to F (in decimal this ranges from 0 to 15). A 2-digit hexadecimal number ranges from 00 to FF (in decimal this ranges from 0 to 255).

C++ uses percentage strengths for the colours. For example, FF represents full strength (100%) and 00 represents no strength (0%). Thus, white is made from FF (red), FF (green) and FF (blue) and black is made from 00 (red), 00 (green) and 00 (blue). Grey is made from equal weighting of each of the colours, such as 43, 43, 43 for dark grey (0x434343) and D4, D4 and D4 for light grey (0xD4D4D4). Thus, pure red with be #0000FF, pure green will be 0x00FF00 and pure blue with be #FF0000.

Each colour is represented by 8 bits, thus the colour is defined by 24 bits. This gives 16 777 216 colours (2^{24} different colours). Note that some video displays will not have enough memory to display 16.777 million colours in the certain mode so that colours may differ depending on the graphics adapter mode.

Table 33.1 Hexadecimal colours.

Colour	Code	Colour	Code
White	0xFFFFFF	Dark red	0x161FC9
Light red	0x0D64DC	Orange	0x0AA6F1
Yellow	0x03E5FC	Light green	0x0FD2BE
Dark green	0x438308	Light blue	0xBE9D00
Dark blue	0x81390D	Purple	0x590B3A
Pink	0xE3D7F3	Nearly black	0x434343
Dark grey	0x777777	Grey	0xA7A7A7
Light grey	0xD4D4D4	Black	0x000000

33.2.2 RGB

The RGB macro mixes a red, green and blue colours and fills a COLORREF value. Its syntax is:

```
COLORREF RGB( BYTE bRed, BYTE bGreen, BYTE bBlue);
```

where

bRed	Intensity of the red colour.
bGreen	Intensity of the green colour.
bBlue	Intensity of the blue colour.

33.3 Painting and drawing functions

Win32 has a large number of painting and drawing functions. Most of these return a TRUE when they successfully complete, else they return a FALSE. The outline program that will be used in this section is similar to the program used in the previous. The painting and drawing functions are contained within the resize message with the windows procedure. Thus every time the user resizes the window then the graphics will be redrawn. The basic outline is:

```
#include <windows.h>
#include "generic.h"

char AppName[] = "Generic";
char AppTitle[]  = "Sample App.";

BOOL     InitApplication(HINSTANCE);
BOOL     InitInstance(HINSTANCE, int);
LRESULT CALLBACK WndProc(HWND, UINT, WPARAM, LPARAM);

int APIENTRY WinMain(HINSTANCE hInstance, HINSTANCE hPrevInstance,
        LPSTR lpCmdLine, int nCmdShow)
{
MSG msg;
HANDLE hAccelTable;

    if (!hPrevInstance) {
        // Perform instance initialization:
        if (!InitApplication(hInstance)) {
            return (FALSE);
        }
    }

    if (!InitInstance(hInstance, nCmdShow)) {
        return (FALSE);
    }

    while (GetMessage(&msg, NULL, 0, 0))
    {
            TranslateMessage(&msg);
            DispatchMessage(&msg);
    }
    return (msg.wParam);
}
```

```
BOOL InitApplication(HINSTANCE hInstance)
{
    WNDCLASS  wc;

    wc.style           = CS_HREDRAW | CS_VREDRAW;
    wc.lpfnWndProc     = (WNDPROC)WndProc;
    wc.cbClsExtra      = 0;
    wc.cbWndExtra      = 0;
    wc.hInstance       = hInstance;
    wc.hIcon           = LoadIcon (hInstance, AppName);
    wc.hCursor         = LoadCursor(NULL, IDC_ARROW);
    wc.hbrBackground   = (HBRUSH)(COLOUR_WINDOW+1);
    wc.lpszMenuName    = AppName;
    wc.lpszClassName   = AppName;

    return RegisterClass(&wc);
}
BOOL InitInstance(HINSTANCE hInstance, int nCmdShow)
{
    HWND hWnd;

    hWnd = CreateWindow(AppName, AppTitle, WS_OVERLAPPEDWINDOW,
        CW_USEDEFAULT, 0, CW_USEDEFAULT, 0,
        NULL, NULL, hInstance, NULL);

    if (!hWnd) {
        return (FALSE);
    }

    ShowWindow(hWnd, nCmdShow);
    UpdateWindow(hWnd);
    return (TRUE);
}

LRESULT CALLBACK WndProc(HWND hWnd, UINT message, WPARAM wParam, LPARAM
lParam)
{
int wmId, wmEvent;
HDC   hdc;
POINT lp[17]={ {10,50}, {30,50}, {30,30}, {90,30},
    {100,50}, {140,50}, {140,70}, {110,70},
    {110,60}, {90,60}, {90,70}, {40,70},
    {40,60}, {20,60}, {20,70}, {10,70}, {10,50}};

    switch (message) {

        case WM_COMMAND:
            wmId    = LOWORD(wParam);
            wmEvent = HIWORD(wParam);
            if (wmId==IDM_EXIT) DestroyWindow(hWnd);
            break;
        case WM_QUIT:
        case WM_CLOSE:
            DestroyWindow(hWnd);
            break;
        case WM_SIZE:
            hdc=GetDC(hWnd);
            TextOut    (hdc,0,0,"My First Car",14);
            Polygon(hdc,lp,17);
            ReleaseDC(hWnd,hdc);
            break;
        default:
            return (DefWindowProc(hWnd, message, wParam, lParam));
    }
    return (0);
}
```

33.3.1 Arc

The Arc function draws an elliptical arc. It specifies a bounding rectangle with the points (*nLeftRect, nTopRect*) and (*nRightRect, nBottomRect*). These ellipses define the bounding area of the curve of the arc. The arc extends from the point where it intersects the radial from the centre of the bounding rectangle to the *(nXStartArc, nYStartArc)* point and ends where it intersects the radial from the centre of the bounding rectangle to the *(nXEndArc, nYEndArc)* point. There is no change in the graphic's current position. Its syntax is:

```
BOOL Arc(HDC hdc, int nLeftRect, int nTopRect, int nRightRect,  int nBottomRect,
         int nXStartArc, int nYStartArc, int nXEndArc,  int nYEndArc);
```

where

hdc	Device context.
nLeftRect	Upper-left corner x-coordinate of bounding rectangle.
nTopRect	Upper-left corner y-coordinate of bounding rectangle.
nRightRect	Lower-right corner x-coordinate of bounding rectangle.
nBottomRect	Lower-right corner y-coordinate of bounding rectangle.
nXStartArc	Start point x-coordinate of the radial line defining the starting point of the arc.
nYStartArc	Start point y-coordinate of the radial line defining the starting point of the arc.
nXEndArc	End point y-coordinate of the radial line defining the starting point of the arc.
nYEndArc	End point y-coordinate of the radial line defining the starting point of the arc.

The following windows procedure shows an example of using the Arc function to draw a face. In this, the Arc function is used to draw four circles. These are arcs with the same start and end point. Figure 33.1 shows how the points on the face are defined and also shows a sample run.

```
LRESULT CALLBACK WndProc(HWND hWnd, UINT message,
          WPARAM wParam, LPARAM lParam)
{
int wmId, wmEvent;
HDC   hdc;

    switch (message) {

       case WM_COMMAND:
           wmId    = LOWORD(wParam);
           wmEvent = HIWORD(wParam);
           if (wmId==IDM_EXIT) DestroyWindow(hWnd);
           break;
       case WM_QUIT:
       case WM_CLOSE:
           DestroyWindow(hWnd);
           break;
```

```
            case WM_SIZE:
               hdc=GetDC(hWnd);
               TextOut    (hdc,0,0,"My First Face",13);
               Arc(hdc,0,0,120,120,0,50,0,50);
               Arc(hdc,25,25,35,35,25,30,25,30);
               Arc(hdc,85,25,95,35,85,30,85,30);
               Arc(hdc,55,45,65,55,55,50,55,50);
               ReleaseDC(hWnd,hdc);
               break;

         default:
            return (DefWindowProc(hWnd, message, wParam, lParam));
      }
      return (0);
}
```

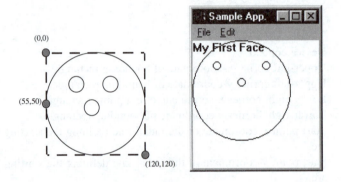

Figure 33.1 Sample run.

33.3.2 ArcTo

The `ArcTo` function draws an elliptical arc. It differs from `Arc` in that the `ArcTo` function updates the current graphics position.

33.3.3 BeginPaint

The `BeginPaint` function prepares the specified window for painting and fills a `PAINTSTRUCT` structure with painting information. Each call to `BeginPaint` must have a corresponding `EndPaint` call. The `BeginPaint` function syntax is:

```
   HDC BeginPaint(HWND  hwnd,   LPPAINTSTRUCT  lpPaint);
```

where

hwnd	Identifies the window to be repainted.
lpPaint	Is the pointer to the `PAINTSTRUCT` structure that will receive painting information.

33.3.4 BeginPath

The `BeginPath` function allows the path to be defined for the specified device context (DC). Once open the application can define the points path. The `EndPath` ends the path definition. Its syntax is:

```
BOOL BeginPath( HDC hdc);
```

where

hdc　　　　Identifies the DC.

33.3.5 Chord

The Chord function draws a chord. As with the Arc, the curve of the chord is defined by an ellipse that is contained within a bounding rectangle. The beginning point of the curve starts where the ellipse intersects the first radial and then goes counterclockwise to the point where it intersects a second radial. There is no change in the graphic's current position. Its syntax is:

```
BOOL Chord( HDC hdc, int nLeftRect, int nTopRect, int nRightRect,
   int nBottomRect, int nXRadial1, int nYRadial1,  int nXRadial2, int nYRadial2 );
```

where

hdc	Device context.
nLeftRect	Upper-left corner x-coordinate of bounding rectangle.
nTopRect	Upper-left corner y-coordinate of bounding rectangle.
nRightRect	Lower-right corner x-coordinate of bounding rectangle.
nBottomRect	Lower-right corner y-coordinate of bounding rectangle.
nXRadial1	End point radial x-coordinate for beginning of the chord.
nYRadial1	End point radial y-coordinate for beginning of the chord.
nXRadial2	End point radial x-coordinate for end of the chord.
nYRadial2	End point radial y-coordinate for end of the chord.

33.3.6 CopyRect

The CopyRect function copies the coordinates of one rectangle to another. Its syntax is:

```
BOOL CopyRect(LPRECT lprcDst, CONST RECT *lprcSrc);
```

where

lprcDst	RECT structure that will be filled with the points.
lprcSrc	RECT structure that will be used to fill the points.

33.3.7 CreatePen

The CreatePen function creates a pen that has a specified style, width and colour. Its syntax is:

```
HPEN CreatePen(int fnPenStyle, int nWidth, COLORREF crColour);
```

where

fnPenStyle   Specifies the pen style. It can be any one of the following values:

PS_SOLID	Solid pen.	PS_DASH	Dashed pen.
PS_DOT	Dotted pen.	PS_DASHDOT	Dashed/dotted pen.
PS_DASHDOTDOT	Dashed/dot/dot pen.	PS_NULL	Invisible pen.

nWidth   Pen width in logical units.
crColor   Pen colour reference.

33.3.8 *CreatePolygonRgn*

The CreatePolygonRgn function creates a polygonal region. Its syntax is:

    HRGN CreatePolygonRgn(CONST POINT *lppt, int cPoints, int fnPolyFillMode);

where

lppt   POINT structures that define the vertices of the polygon.
cPoints   Number of points in the array.
fnPolyFillMode
              Fill mode which can be one of the following:

ALTERNATE   Selects alternate mode which fills area between odd-numbered and even-numbered polygon sides on each scan line.
WINDING   Selects winding mode which fills any region with a non-zero winding value.

33.3.9 *CreateRectRgn*

The CreateRectRgn function creates a rectangular region. Its syntax is:

    HRGN CreateRectRgn(int nLeftRect, int nTopRect, int nRightRect, int nBottomRect);

where

nLeftRect   Upper-left corner x-coordinate of region.
nTopRect   Upper-left corner y-coordinate of region.
nRightRect   Lower-right corner x-coordinate of region.
nBottomRect Lower-right corner y-coordinate of region.

33.3.10   *DeleteObject*

The DeleteObject function deletes objects, such as a logical pen, a brush, a font, a bitmap, a region, or a palette. Its syntax is:

    BOOL DeleteObject(HGDIOBJ hObject);

where

hObject   Logical pen, brush, font, bitmap, region or palette.

33.3.11   *DrawIcon*

The `DrawIcon` function draws an icon in the client area of the window of the specified device context. Its syntax is:

```
BOOL DrawIcon( HDC hdc, int X, int Y, HICON hIcon);
```

where

hdc	Device context.
X	Upper-left x-coordinate corner of the icon.
Y	Upper-left y-coordinate corner of the icon.
hIcon	Identifies the icon to be drawn.

33.3.12   *DrawText*

The `DrawText` function draws formatted text in the specified rectangle and formats the text according to the specified method. Its syntax is:

```
int DrawText( HDC hdc, LPCTSTR lpString, int nCount,
    LPRECT lpRect,   UINT uFormat );
```

where

hdc	Device context.
lpString	Points to the string to be drawn. If the *nCount* parameter is −1, the string must be null-terminated.
nCount	Specifies the number of characters in the string (a −1 value defines a NULL-terminated string).
lpRect	RECT structure that contains the rectangle in which the text is to be formatted.
uFormat	Method of text formatting, such as:

DT_BOTTOM	Bottom-justifies text.
DT_CALCRECT	Determines the width and height of the rectangle.
DT_CENTER	Centres text horizontally.
DT_LEFT	Aligns text to the left.
DT_RIGHT	Aligns text to the right.
DT_SINGLELINE	Displays text on a single line only.
DT_TOP	Top-justifies text.
DT_VCENTER	Centres text vertically.

33.3.13   *Ellipse*

The `Ellipse` function draws an ellipse, where the centre of the ellipse is at the centre of the specified bounding rectangle. There is no change in the graphic's current position. Its syntax is:

```
BOOL Ellipse(HDC hdc,   int nLeftRect, int nTopRect,
    int nRightRect,   int nBottomRect );
```

where

hdc	Device context.
nLeftRect	Upper-left corner x-coordinate of bounding rectangle.
nTopRect	Upper-left corner y-coordinate of bounding rectangle.
nRightRect	Lower-right corner x-coordinate of bounding rectangle.
nBottomRect	Lower-right corner y-coordinate of bounding rectangle.

33.3.14   EndPaint

The `EndPaint` function marks the end of painting in the specified window. This function is required for each call to the `BeginPaint` function, but only after painting is complete. Its syntax is:

```
BOOL EndPaint(HWND hWnd, CONST PAINTSTRUCT *lpPaint );
```

where

hWnd	Identifies the window that has been repainted.
lpPaint	Points to a `PAINTSTRUCT` structure that contains the painting information retrieved by `BeginPaint`.

33.3.15   FillRect

The `FillRect` function fills a rectangle with the specified brush. Its syntax is:

```
int FillRect(HDC hdc, CONST RECT *lprc, BRUSH hbr );
```

where

hdc	Device context.
lprc	`RECT` structure that contains the coordinates of the rectangle to be filled.
hbr	Brush to fill the rectangle.

33.3.16   FillRgn

The `FillRgn` function fills a region by using the specified brush. Its syntax is:

```
BOOL FillRgn(HDC hdc, HRGN hrgn, HBRUSH hbr );
```

where

hdc	Device context.
hrgn	Identifies the region to be filled. The coordinates of the region are presumed to be in logical units.
hbr	Identifies the brush to be used to fill the region.

33.3.17   Floodfill

The `FloodFill` function fills a specified area with the current brush. Its syntax is:

```
BOOL FloodFill(HDC hdc,    int nXStart, int nYStart, COLORREF crFill );
```

where

nXStart	Starting x-coordinate where filling is to begin.
nYStart	Starting y-coordinate where filling is to begin.
crFill	Boundary colour to fill to.

33.3.18   *GetBkColor*

The GetBkColor function gets the current background colour for the specified device context. Its syntax is:

```
COLORREF GetBkColor(HDC hdc);
```

33.3.19   *GetPixel*

The GetPixel function gets the RGB colour value of a pixel. Its syntax is:

```
COLORREF GetPixel(HDC hdc,  int nXPos, int nYPos);
```

where

nXPos	Pixel x-coordinate.
nYPos	Pixel y-coordinate.

33.3.20   *InvertRect*

The InvertRect function inverts a rectangle in a window using a logical NOT operation on the colour values for each pixel in a rectangle. Its syntax is:

```
BOOL InvertRect( HDC hdc, CONST RECT * lprc);
```

where

lprc	RECT structure that contains the logical coordinates of the rectangle to be inverted.

33.3.21   *InvertRgn*

The InvertRgn function inverts the colours in the specified region. Its syntax is:

```
BOOL InvertRgn(HDC hdc,   HRGN hrgn);
```

where

hrgn	Region to be inverted (the HRGN structure is the same as the POINTS structure).

33.3.22   *LineTo*

The LineTo function draws a line from the current position to the specified end position, using the current pen. Its syntax is:

```
BOOL LineTo( HDC hdc, int nXEnd, int nYEnd);
```

where

hdc	Device context.
nXEnd	Line ending x-coordinate.
nYEnd	Line ending y-coordinate.

33.3.23   *MoveToEx*

The `MoveToEx` function updates the current position to the specified point and optionally returns the previous position.

```
BOOL MoveToEx( HDC hdc, int X, int Y, LPPOINT lpPoint );
```

where

X	New position x-coordinate.
Y	New position y-coordinate.
lpPoint	POINT structure which stores the previous current position. If it is a NULL pointer then the previous position is not returned.

33.3.24   *Polygon*

The `Polygon` function draws a polygon with two or more vertices connected by straight lines. Each line is drawn with the current pen and a line is drawn between consecutive points. The end and start points are automatically joined. Its syntax is:

```
BOOL Polygon( HDC hdc, CONST POINT *lpPoints, int cPoints);
```

where

lpPoints	Array of POINT structures where each element represents a single point.
cPoints	Number of points in the array.

The following windows procedure uses the Polygon to draw the outline graphic of a car. Figure 33.2 shows how the points on the polygon are defined and also shows a sample run.

```
LRESULT CALLBACK WndProc(HWND hWnd, UINT message, WPARAM wParam, LPARAM lParam)
{
    int wmId, wmEvent;
    HDC   hdc;
    POINT lp[17];

    lp[0].x=10; lp[0].y=50; lp[1].x=30; lp[1].y=50;
    lp[2].x=30; lp[2].y=30; lp[3].x=90; lp[3].y=30;
    lp[4].x=100; lp[4].y=50; lp[5].x=140; lp[5].y=50;
    lp[6].x=140; lp[6].y=70; lp[7].x=110; lp[7].y=70;
    lp[8].x=110; lp[8].y=60;  lp[9].x=90; lp[9].y=60;
    lp[10].x=90; lp[10].y=70; lp[11].x=40; lp[11].y=70;
    lp[12].x=40; lp[12].y=60; lp[13].x=20; lp[13].y=60;
    lp[14].x=20; lp[14].y=70; lp[15].x=10; lp[15].y=70;
```

```
lp[16].x=10; lp[16].y=50;

switch (message) {

    case WM_COMMAND:
        wmId    = LOWORD(wParam);
        wmEvent = HIWORD(wParam);
        if (wmId==IDM_EXIT) DestroyWindow(hWnd);
        break;
    case WM_QUIT:
    case WM_CLOSE:
        DestroyWindow(hWnd);
        break;

    case WM_SIZE:
        hdc=GetDC(hWnd);
        TextOut    (hdc,0,0,"My First Car",12);
        Polygon(hdc,lp,17);
        ReleaseDC(hWnd,hdc);
        break;

    default:
        return (DefWindowProc(hWnd, message, wParam, lParam));
    }
    return (0);
}
```

Note that an improved method of definition of the polygon array is to define the points in the structure when it is declared:

```
POINT lp[17]={ {10,50}, {30,50}, {30,30}, {90,30},
    {100,50}, {140,50}, {140,70}, {110,70},
    {110,60}, {90,60}, {90,70}, {40,70},
    {40,60}, {20,60}, {20,70}, {10,70}, {10,50}};
```

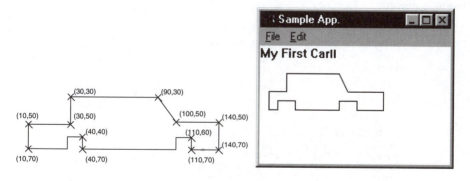

Figure 33.2   Sample run.

33.3.25   *Polyline*

The `Polyline` function draws a series of line segments as defined in an array of points. Each line is drawn with the current pen and a line is drawn between consecutive points. Its syntax is:

BOOL Polyline(HDC *hdc*, CONST POINT *lppt*, int *cPoints*);

where

hdc	Device context.
lppt	Array of POINT structures where each element represents a single point.
cPoints	Number of points in the array.

33.3.26   *Rectangle*

The Rectangle function draws a rectangle which is outlined with the current pen and filled using the current brush. There is no change in the graphic's current position. Its syntax is:

```
BOOL Rectangle(HDC hdc, int nLeftRect,  int nTopRect,
                    int nRightRect,  int nBottomRect );
```

where

hdc	Device context.
nLeftRect	Upper-left corner x-coordinate of rectangle.
nTopRect	Upper-left corner y-coordinate of rectangle.
nRightRect	Lower-right corner x-coordinate of rectangle.
nBottomRect	Lower-right corner y-coordinate of rectangle.

The following is an example window procedure which draws the simple graphic of a robot. It contains two rectangles and four lines, as illustrated in Figure 33.3. The Line-ToEx function is used to define each of the start points for the four lines and the Line function defines the end of the line. The robot graphic is updated every time that the window is resized.

```
LRESULT CALLBACK WndProc(HWND hWnd, UINT message,
                WPARAM wParam, LPARAM lParam)
{
int wmId, wmEvent;
HDC   hdc;

    switch (message)
    {
        case WM_COMMAND:
            wmId    = LOWORD(wParam);
            wmEvent = HIWORD(wParam);
            if (wmId==IDM_EXIT) DestroyWindow(hWnd);
            break;
        case WM_QUIT:
        case WM_CLOSE:
            DestroyWindow(hWnd);
            break;

        case WM_SIZE:
            hdc=GetDC(hWnd);
            TextOut   (hdc,0,0,"My First Robot",14);
            Rectangle(hdc, 50,50, 100, 100);
            Rectangle(hdc,60,30,90,50);
            MoveToEx(hdc,30,75,NULL);
            LineTo(hdc,50,75);
            MoveToEx(hdc,100,75,NULL);
            LineTo(hdc,120,75);
```

```
            MoveToEx(hdc,60,100,NULL);
            LineTo(hdc,60,120);
            MoveToEx(hdc,90,100,NULL);
            LineTo(hdc,90,120);
            ReleaseDC(hWnd,hdc);
            break;

      default:
            return (DefWindowProc(hWnd, message, wParam, lParam));
   }
   return (0);
}
```

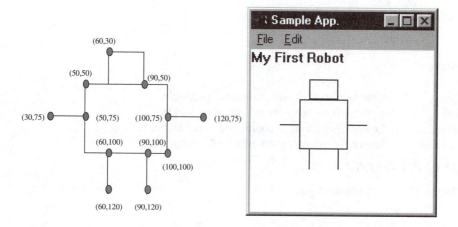

Figure 33.3   Sample run.

33.3.27   *SetBkColor*

The `SetBkColor` function sets the current background colour. Its syntax is:

    COLORREF SetBkColor(HDC *hdc*, COLORREF *crColor*);

where

crColor   New background colour.

33.3.28   *SetRect*

The `SetRect` function sets the coordinates of the specified rectangle. Its syntax is:

    BOOL SetRect(LPRECT *lprc*, int *xLeft*, int *yTop*, int *xRight*, int *yBottom*);
where

lprc	Points to the `RECT` structure that contains the rectangle to be set.
xLeft	Upper-left corner x-coordinate of rectangle.
yTop	Upper-left corner y-coordinate of rectangle.
xRight	Lower-right corner x-coordinate of rectangle.
yBottom	Lower-right corner y-coordinate of rectangle.

33.4 Structures

33.4.1 RECT

The RECT structure defines the coordinates of a rectangle, it is defined as:

```
typedef struct _RECT {
    LONG left;
    LONG top;
    LONG right;
    LONG bottom;
} RECT;
```

where

left	Upper-left corner x-coordinate of rectangle.
top	Upper-left corner y-coordinate of rectangle.
right	Lower-right corner x-coordinate of rectangle.
bottom	Lower-right corner y-coordinate of rectangle.

33.4.2 PAINTSTRUCT

The PAINTSTRUCT has the form:

```
typedef struct tagPAINTSTRUCT
{
    HDC   hdc;         BOOL fErase;
    RECT  rcPaint;     BOOL fRestore;
    BOOL  fIncUpdate;  BYTE rgbReserved[32];
} PAINTSTRUCT;
```

where

fErase	Specifies whether the background must be erased. A non-zero value erases the background.
rcPaint	RECT structure for the upper-left and lower-right corners of the rectangle in which the painting is requested.
fRestore	Reserved.
fIncUpdate	Reserved.
rgbReserved	Reserved.

33.4.3 POINTS

The POINTS structure defines the coordinates of a point. Its form is:

```
typedef struct tagPOINTS {
    SHORT x;
    SHORT y;
} POINTS;
```

where

x   Point x-coordinate.
y   Point y-coordinate.

33.5 Exercises

33.5.1   Write a program which draws a circle in the centre of the screen. The program then draws ever-increasing circles, each of which is 50% larger than the previous.

33.5.2   Write a program which draws six arcs which make up a circle. Each of the arcs should have a different colour.

33.5.3   Write separate Java applets, using simple rectangles and circles, to display the following graphics:

(a)   a television (a sample graphic is shown in Figure 33.4).
(b)   a face.
(c)   a house.
(d)   a robot.

Figure 33.4

33.5.4   Modify the program in Section 33.3.24 so that the car has wheels.

33.5.5   Modify the program in Exercise 33.5.3 so that the user can move them around the screen with the arrowkeys.

33.5.6   Write an applet which displays two faces. One of the faces is moved with the arrowkeys, and the other is moved by the 'A' (LEFT), 'W' (UP), 'X' (DOWN) and 'D' (RIGHT).

33.5.7   Write a program which displays the text TEST TEXT, determine the approximate colour of the following colour settings:

(a)   RGB(100, 50, 10)
(b)   RGB(200,200,0)
(c)   RGB(10,100,100)
(d)   RGB(200,200,200)
(e)   RGB(10,10,100)

33.5.8   Write an applet using a polygon for the following shapes:

    (a)   a ship (a sample is shown in Figure 33.5)
    (b)   a tank
    (c)   a plane

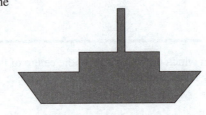

Figure 33.5

33.5.9   Investigate the `InvertRgn` function.

Networking

34.1 Introduction

The interconnection of PCs over a network is becoming more important especially as more hardware is accessed remotely and PCs intercommunicate with each other. This chapter gives an introduction to networking technology.

Computers communicate with other digital equipment over a local area network (LAN). A LAN is defined as a collection of computers within a single office or building that connect to a common electronic connection – commonly known as a network backbone. A LAN can be connected to other networks either directly or through a wide area network (WAN), as illustrated in Figure 34.1.

A WAN normally connects networks over a large physical area, such as in different buildings, towns or even countries. Figure 34.1 shows three local area networks, LAN A, LAN B and LAN C, some of which are connected by the WAN. A modem connects a LAN to a WAN when the WAN connection is an analogue line. For a digital connection a gateway connects one type of LAN to another LAN, or WAN, and a bridge connects a LAN to similar types of LAN.

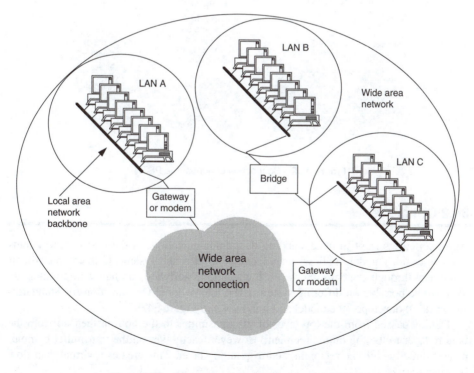

Figure 34.1   Interconnection of LANs to make a WAN.

The public switched telecommunications network (PSTN) provides long-distance analogue lines. These public telephone lines can connect one network line to another using circuit switching. Unfortunately, they have a limited bandwidth and can normally only transmit frequencies from 400 to 3 400 Hz. For a telephone line connection, a modem is used to convert the digital data into a transmittable form. Figure 34.2 illustrates the connection of computers to a PSTN. These computers can connect to the WAN through a service provider (such as CompuServe) or through another network which is connected by modem. The service provider has the required hardware to connect to the WAN.

A public switched data network (PSDN) allows the direct connection of digital equipment to a digital network. This has the advantage of not requiring the conversion of digital data into an analogue form. The integrated services digital network (ISDN) allows the transmission of many types of digital data into a truly global digital network. Transmittable data types include digitized video, digitized speech and computer data. Since the switching and transmission are digital, fast access times and relatively high bit rates are possible. Typical base bit rates may be 64 kbps. All connections to the ISDN require network termination equipment (NTE).

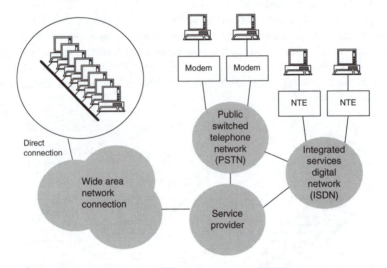

Figure 34.2   Connection of nodes to a PSTN.

34.2 OSI model

An important concept in understanding data communications is the OSI (open systems interconnection) model. It allows manufacturers of different systems to interconnect their equipment through standard interfaces. It also allows software and hardware to integrate well and be portable on differing systems. The International Organization for Standardization (ISO) developed the model and it is shown in Figure 34.3.

Data is passed from the top layer of the transmitter to the bottom then up from the bottom layer to the top on the recipient. However, each layer on the transmitter communicates directly with the recipient's corresponding layer. This creates a virtual data flow between layers.

The top layer (the application layer) initially gets data from an application and appends it with data that the recipient's application layer will read. This appended data passes to the next layer (the presentation layer). Again, it appends its own data, and so on, down to the physical layer. The physical layer is then responsible for transmitting the data to the recipient. The data sent can be termed a data packet or data frame.

Figure 34.4 shows the basic function of each of the layers. The physical link layer defines the electrical characteristics of the communications channel and the transmitted signals. This includes voltage levels, connector types, cabling, and so on.

The data link layer ensures that the transmitted bits are received in a reliable way. This includes adding bits to define the start and end of a data frame, adding extra error detection/correction bits and ensuring that multiple nodes do not try to access a common communications channel at the same time.

The network layer routes data frames through a network. If data packets require to go out of a network then the transport layer routes them through interconnected networks. Its task may involve splitting up data for transmission and reassembling it upon reception.

The session layer provides an open communications path to the other system. It involves setting up, maintaining and closing down a session. The communications channel and the internetworking of the data should be transparent to the session layer.

The presentation layer uses a set of translations that allow the data to be interpreted properly. It may have to carry out translations between two systems if they use different presentation standards such as different character sets or different character codes. For example, on a UNIX system a text file uses a single ASCII character for new line (the carriage return), whereas on a DOS-based system there are two, the line feed and the carriage return. The presentation layer would convert from one computer system to another so that the data could be displayed correctly, in this case by either adding or taking away a character. The presentation layer can also add data encryption for security purposes.

The application layer provides network services to application programs such as file transfer and electronic mail.

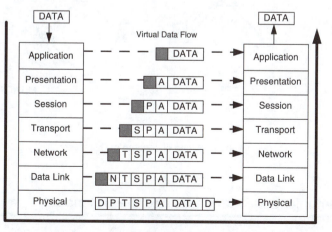

Figure 34.3 Seven-layer OSI model.

Figure 34.5 shows an example with two interconnected networks, Network A and Network B. Network A has four nodes N1, N2, N3 and N4, and Network B has nodes N5, N6, N7 and N8. If node N1 were to communicate with node N7 then a possible path would be via N2, N5 and N6. The data link layer ensures that the bits transmitted between nodes N1 and N2, nodes N2 and N5, and so on, are transmitted in a reliable way.

The network layer would then be responsible for routing the data packets through Network A and through Network B. The transport layer routes the data through interconnections between the networks. In this case, it would route data packets from N2 to N5. If other routes existed between N1 and N7 it might use another route.

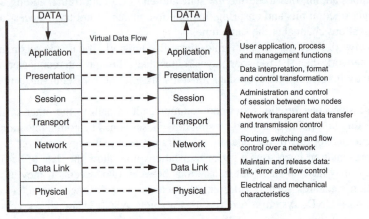

Figure 34.4   ISO open systems interconnection (OSI) model.

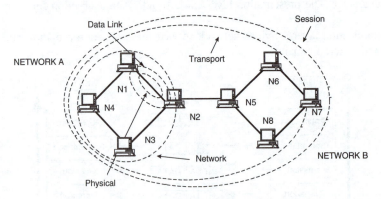

Figure 34.5   Scope of concern of OSI layers.

34.3 Communications standards and the OSI model

The following sections look at practical examples of data communications and networks, and how they fit into the layers of the OSI model. Unfortunately, many currently available technologies do not precisely align with the layers of this model. For example, RS-

232 provides a standard for a physical layer but it also includes some data link layer functions, such as adding error detection and framing bits for the start and end of a packet.

Figure 34.6 shows the main technologies. These are split into three basic sections: asynchronous data communication, local area networks (LANs) and wide area networks (WANs).

The most popular types of LAN are Ethernet and Token Ring. Standards for Ethernet include Ethernet 2.0 and IEEE 802.3 (with IEEE 802.2). For Token Ring the standards are IBM Token Ring and IEEE 802.5 (with IEEE 802.2). Ethernet uses carrier sense multiple access/collision detect (CMSA/CD) technology which is why the IEEE standard includes the name CSMA/CD.

One of the main standards for the interconnection of networks is the Transport Control Protocol/Internet Protocol (TCP/IP). IP routes data packets through a network and TCP routes data packets between interconnected networks. An equivalent to the TCP/IP standard used in some PC networks; is called SPX/IPX.

For digital connections to WANs the main standards are CCITT X.21, HDLC and CCITT X.25.

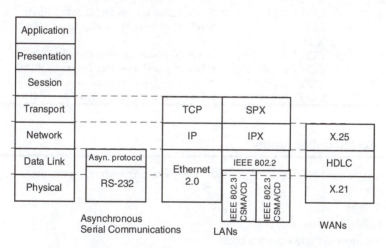

Figure 34.6 ISO open systems interconnection (OSI) model.

34.4 Standards agencies

There are six main international standards agencies that define standards for data communications systems. They are the International Organization for Standardization (ISO), the Comité Consultatif International Télégraphique et Telecommunications (CCITT), the Electrical Industries Association (EIA), the International Telecommunications Union (ITU), the American National Standards Institute (ANSI) and the Institute of Electrical and Electronic Engineers (IEEE).

The ISO and the IEEE have defined standards for the connection of computers to local area networks and the CCITT (now know as the ITU) has defined standards for the interconnection of national and international networks. The CCITT standards covered in this book split into three main sections: these are asynchronous communications (V.xx standards), PSDN connections (X.xxx standards) and ISDN (I.4xx standards). The main standards are given in Table 34.1. The EIA has defined standards for the interconnection of computers using serial communications. The original standard was RS-232-C; this gives a maximum bit rate of 20 kbps over 20 m. It has since defined several other standards, including RS-422 and RS-423, which provide a data rate of 10 Mbps.

Table 34.1   Typical standards.

Standard	Equivalent ISO/CCITT	Description
EIA RS-232C	CCITT V.28	Serial transmission up to 20 kps/20 m
EIA RS-422	CCITT V.11	Serial transmission up to 10 Mbps/1200 m
EIA RS-423	CCITT V.10	Serial transmission up to 300 Kbps/1200 m
ANSI X3T9.5		LAN: Fibre-optic FDDI standard
IEEE 802.2	ISO 8802.2	LAN: IEEE standard for logical link control
IEEE 802.3	ISO 8802.3	LAN: IEEE standard for CSMA/CD
IEEE 802.4	ISO 8802.4	LAN: Token passing in a Token Ring network
IEEE 802.5	ISO 8802.5	LAN: Token Ring topology
	CCITT X.21	WAN: Physical layer interface to a PSDN
HDLC	CCITT X.212/ 222	WAN: Data layer interfacing to a PSDN
	CCITT X.25	WAN: Network layer interfacing to a PSDN
	CCITT I430/1	ISDN: Physical layer interface to an ISDN
	CCITT I440/1	ISDN: Data layer interface to an ISDN
	CCITT I450/1	ISDN: Network layer interface to an ISDN

34.5 Network cable types

The cable type used on a network depends on several parameters, including:

- The data bit rate.
- The reliability of the cable.
- The maximum length between nodes.
- The possibility of electrical hazards.
- Power loss in the cables.
- Tolerance to harsh conditions.
- Expense and general availability of the cable.
- Ease of connection and maintenance.
- Ease of running cables, and so on.

The main types of cables used in networks are twisted-pair, coaxial and fibre-optic, they are illustrated in Figure 34.7. Twisted-pair and coaxial cables transmit electric signals, whereas fibre-optic cables transmit light pulses. Twisted-pair cables are not shielded and thus interfere with nearby cables. Public telephone lines generally use twisted-pair cables. In LANs they are generally used up to bit rates of 10 Mbps and with maximum lengths of 100 m.

Coaxial cable has a grounded metal sheath around the signal conductor. This limits the amount of interference between cables and thus allows higher data rates. Typically they are used at bit rates of 100 Mbps for maximum lengths of 1 km.

The highest specification of the three cables is fibre-optic. This type of cable allows extremely high bit rates over long distances. Fibre-optic cables do not interfere with nearby cables and give greater security, more protection from electrical damage by external equipment and greater resistance to harsh environments; they are also safer in hazardous environments.

A typical bit rate for a LAN using fibre-optic cables is 100 Mbps; in other applications this reaches several gigabits per second. The maximum length of the fibre-optic cable depends on the electronics in the transmitter and receiver, but a single length of 20 km is possible.

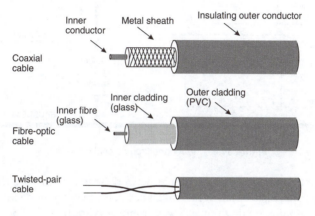

Figure 34.7 Types of network cable.

34.6 LAN topology

Computer networks are ever expanding, and a badly planned network can be inefficient and error prone. Unfortunately networks tend to undergo evolutionary change instead of revolutionary change and they can become difficult to manage if not planned properly. Most modern networks have a backbone, which is a common link to all the networks within an organization. This backbone allows users on different network segments to communicate and also allows data into and out of the local network. Figure 34.8 shows that a local area network contains various segments: LAN A, LAN B, LAN C, LAN D, LAN E and LAN F. These are connected to the local network via the BACKBONE1. Thus if LAN A talks to LAN E then the data must travel out of LAN A, onto BACKBONE1, then into LAN C and through onto LAN E.

Networks are partitioned from other networks using a bridge, a gateway or a router. A bridge links two networks of the same type, such as Ethernet to Ethernet, or Token Ring to Token Ring. A gateway connects two networks of dissimilar type. Routers operate rather like gateways and can either connect two similar networks or two dissimilar networks. The key operation of a gateway, bridge or router is that it only allows data traffic through itself when the data is intended for another network which is outside the connected network. This filters traffic and stops traffic not intended for the network from clogging up the backbone. Modern bridges, gateways and routers are intelligent and can determine the network topology.

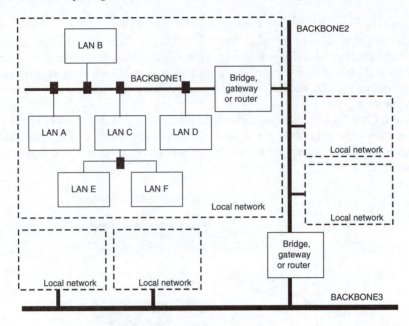

Figure 34.8   Interconnection of local networks.

A spanning-tree bridge allows multiple network segments to be interconnected. If more than one path exists between individual segments then the bridge finds alternative routes. This is useful in routing frames away from heavy traffic routes or around a faulty route. Conventional bridges can cause frames to loop around forever. Spanning-tree bridges have built-in intelligence and can communicate with other bridges. This allows them to build up a picture of the complete network and thus to make decisions on where frames are routed.

34.7 Internetworking connections

Networks connect to other networks through repeaters, bridges or routers. A repeater corresponds to the physical layer and always routes signals from one network segment to another. Bridges route using the data link layer and routers route using the network layer. Figure 34.9 illustrates the three interconnection types.

34.7.1 Repeaters

All types of network connections suffer from attenuation and pulse distortion; for a given cable specification and bit rate, each has a maximum length of cable. Repeaters can be used to increase the maximum interconnection length and will do the following:

- Clean signal pulses.
- Pass all signals between attached segments.
- Boost signal power.
- Possibly translate between two different media types (e.g. fibre-optic to twisted-pair cable).

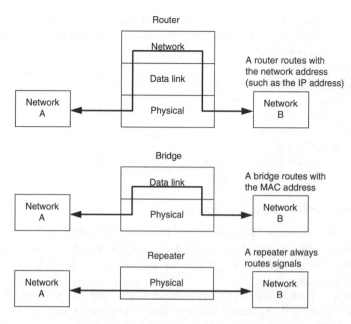

Figure 34.9   Repeaters, bridges and routers.

34.7.2 Bridges

Bridges filter input and output traffic so that only packets intended for a network are actually routed into the network and only packets intended for the outside are allowed out of the network.

The performance of a bridge is governed by two main factors (which are measured in packets per second or frames per second):

- The filtering rate – the bridge reads the MAC address of the Ethernet/Token Ring/FDDI node and then decides if it should forward the packet into the internetwork. When a bridge reads the destination address on an Ethernet frame or Token Ring packet and decides whether that packet should be allowed access to the internetwork. Filter rates for bridges range from around 5000 to 70 000 pps (packets per second). A typical bridge has a filtering rate of 17 500 pps.
- The forward rate – once the bridge has decided to route the packet into the internetwork then the bridge must forward the packet onto the internetwork media. This is a forwarding operation and typical rates range from 500 to 140 000 pps. A typical forwarding rate is 90 000 pps.

A typical Ethernet bridge has the following specifications:

Bit rate: 10 Mbps
Filtering rate: 17 500 pps
Forwarding rate: 11 000 pps
Connectors: 2 DB15 AUI (female), 1 DB9 male console port, 2 BNC
                   (for 10BASE2) or 2 RJ-45 (for 10BASE-T)

Algorithm: Spanning-tree protocol. It automatically learns the addresses of all de-
                  vices on both interconnected networks and builds a separate table for
                  each network

And for a Token Ring bridge:

Bit rate: 4/16 Mbps
Filtering rate: 120 000 pps
Forwarding rate: 3400 pps
Connectors: 1 DB9 male console port, 2 DB9 connectors
Algorithm: Source routing transparent

Spanning-tree architecture (STA) bridges

The spanning-tree algorithm has been defined by the standard IEEE 802.1. It is normally
implemented as software on STA-compliant bridges. On power-up they automatically
learn the addresses of all nodes on both interconnected networks and build a separate
table for each network.

They can also have two connections between two LANs so that when the primary
path becomes disabled, the spanning-tree algorithm can re-enable the previously disabled
redundant link. The path management is achieved by each bridge communicating using
configuration bridge protocol data units (configuration BPDU).

Source route bridging

With source route bridging a source device, not the bridge, is used to send special explorer packets which are then used to determine the best path to the destination. Explorer
packets are sent out from the source routing bridges until they reach their destination
workstation. Then each source routing bridge along the route enters its address in the
routing information field of the explorer packet. The destination node then sends back
the completed RIF field to the source node. When the source device (normally a PC) has
determined the best path to the destination, it sends the data message along with the path
instructions to the local bridge. It then forwards the data message according to the received path instructions.

Although the source routing bridge receives the data, there is a 7-hop limit on the
number of internetwork connections. This is because of the limited space in the router
information field (RIF) of the explorer packet.

34.7.3 Routers

Routers examine the network address field (such as IP or IPX) and determine the best
route for the packet. They have the great advantage that they normally support several
different types of network layer protocol.

Normally routers which only read one type of protocol have high filtering and forwarding rates. If they support multiple protocols then there is normally an overhead in
that the router must detect the protocol and look in the correct place for the destination
address.

Typical network layer protocols and their associated network operating systems or
upper layer protocols are:

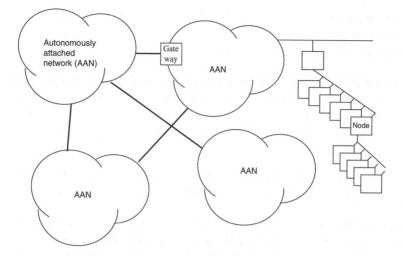

Figure 34.14 Autonomously attached networks.

BGP differs in that it tries to find any paths through the network. Thus, the main goal is reachability instead of the number of hops to the destination. So finding a path which is nearly optimal is a good achievement. The AAN administrator selects at least one node to be a BGP speaker and also one or more border gateways. These gateways simply route the packet into and out of the AAN. The border gateways are the routers through which packets reach the AAN. Most routing algorithms try to find the quickest way through the network.

The speaker on the AAN broadcasts its reachability information to all the networks within its AAN. This information states only whether a destination AAN can be reached; it does not describe any other metrics.

The BGP update packet also contains information on routes which cannot be reached (withdrawn routes). The content of the BGP-4 update packet is:

- Unfeasible routes length (2 bytes).
- Withdrawn routes (variable length).
- Total path attribute length (2 bytes).
- Path attributes (variable length).
- Network layer reachability information (variable length).

The network layer reachability information can contain extra information, such as 'use AAN 1 in preference to AAN 2'.

An important point is that BGP is not a distance vector or link state protocol because it transmits complete routing information instead of partial information.

34.9 Network topologies

There are three basic topologies for LANs, which are shown in Figure 34.15, these are:

- A star network.
- A ring network.
- A bus network.

There are other topologies which are either a combination of two or more topologies or are derivatives of the main types. A typical topology is a tree topology that is essentially a star and a bus network combined, as illustrated in Figure 34.16. A concentrator (or hub) is used to connect the nodes onto the network.

34.9.1 Star network

In a star topology, a central server switches data around the network. Data traffic between nodes and the server will thus be relatively low. Its main advantages are:

- Since the data rate is relatively low between central server and the node, a low-specification twisted-pair cable can be used connect the nodes to the server.
- A fault on one of the nodes will not affect the rest of the network. Typically, mainframe computers use a central server with terminals connected to it.

The main disadvantage of this type of topology is that the network is highly dependent upon the operation of the central server. If it were to slow down significantly then the network becomes slow. In addition, if it were to become un-operational then the complete network would shut down.

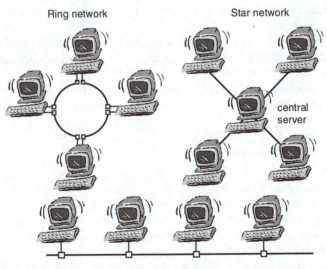

Figure 34.15   Network topologies.

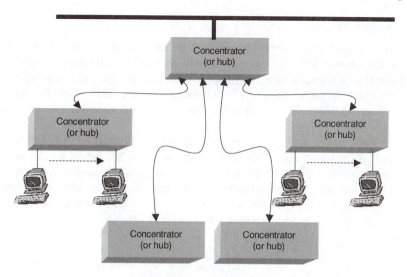

Figure 34.16   Tree topology.

34.9.2 Ring network

In a ring network the computers link together to form a ring. To allow an orderly access to the ring a single electronic token is passed from one computer to the next around the ring, as illustrated in Figure 34.17. A computer can only transmit data when it captures a token. In a manner similar to the star network each link between nodes is a point-to-point link and allows almost any transmission medium to be used. Typically, twisted-pair cables allow a bit rate of up to 16 Mbps, but coaxial and fibre-optic cables are normally used for extra reliability and higher data rates.

A typical ring network is IBM Token Ring. The main advantage of token ring networks is that all nodes on the network have an equal chance of transmitting data. Unfortunately it suffers from several problems, the most severe is that if one of the nodes goes down then the whole network may go down.

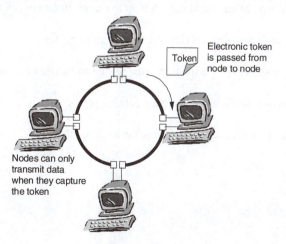

Figure 34.17   Token passing ring network.

34.9.3 Bus network

A bus network uses a multi-drop transmission medium, as shown in Figure 34.18. All nodes on the network share a common bus and all share communications. This allows only one device to communicate at a time. A distributed medium access protocol determines which station is to transmit. As with the ring network, data packets contain source and destination addresses. Each station monitors the bus and copies frames addressed to itself.

Twisted-pair cables give data rates up to 100 Mbps. Coaxial and fibre-optic cables give higher bit rates and longer transmission distances. A bus network is a good compromise over the other two topologies as it allows relatively high data rates. Also, if a node goes down then it does not affect the rest of the network. The main disadvantage of this topology is that it requires a network protocol to detect when two nodes are transmitting at the same time. A typical bus network is Ethernet 2.0.

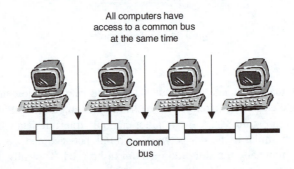

Figure 34.18   Bus topology.

34.10 Exercises

34.10.1   Explain why bridges and routers help to reduce internetwork traffic.

34.10.2   Distinguish between a repeater, a bridge and a router.

34.10.3   Distinguish between a spanning-tree bridge and a source route bridge.

34.10.4   Outline pros and cons of the main routing protocols.

34.10.5   Discuss the pros and cons of main network topologies.

35 Ethernet

35.1 Introduction

Ethernet is the most widely used networking technology used in LANs (local area networks). On its own, Ethernet cannot make a network; it needs some other protocol such as TCP/IP to allow nodes to communicate. Unfortunately, Ethernet in its standard form does not cope well with heavy traffic, but has many advantages, including:

- Its networks are easy to plan and cheap to install.
- Its network components are cheap and well supported.
- It is well-proven technology which is fairly robust and reliable.
- It is simple to add and delete computers on the network.
- It is supported by most software and hardware systems.

A major problem with Ethernet is that because computers compete for access to the network there is no guarantee that a particular computer will get access within a given time. And contention causes problems when two computers try to communicate at the same time; they must both back off and no data can be transmitted. In its standard form Ethernet allows a bit rate of 10 Mbps. New standards for fast Ethernet systems minimize the problems of contention and also increase the bit rate to 100 Mbps. Ethernet uses co-axial or twisted-pair cable.

DEC, Intel and the Xerox Corporation initially developed Ethernet, and the IEEE 802 committee have since defined standards for it. The most common standards for Ethernet are Ethernet 2.0 and IEEE 802.3. It uses a shared-media, bus-type network topology where all nodes share a common bus. It is a contention-type network where only one node communicates at a time. Data is transmitted in frames which contain the MAC (media access control) source and destination addresses of the sending and receiving node, respectively. The local shared-media is known as a segment. Each node on the network monitors the segment and copies any frames addressed to itself.

Ethernet uses carrier sense multiple access with collision detection (CSMA/CD). On a CSMA/CD network, nodes monitor the bus (or Ether) to determine if it is busy. A node wishing to send data waits for an idle condition then transmits its message. Unfortunately collision can occur when two nodes transmit at the same time, thus nodes must monitor the cable when they transmit. When this happens both nodes stop transmitting frames and transmit a jamming signal. This informs all nodes on the network that a collision has occurred. Each of the nodes then waits a random period before attempting a retransmission. As each node has a random delay time, there can be a prioritization of the nodes on the network. Nodes thus contend for the network and are not guaranteed access to it. Collisions generally slow down the network. Each node on the network must be able to detect collisions and must be capable of transmitting and receiving simultaneously.

35.2 IEEE standards

The IEEE is the main standards organization for LANs; it calls the standard for Ethernet CSMA/CD (carrier sense multiple access/collision detect). Figure 35.1 shows how the IEEE standards for Token Ring and CSMA/CD fit into the OSI model. The two layers of the IEEE standards correspond to the physical and data link layers of the OSI model. A Token Ring network uses IEEE 802.5 (ISO 8802.5) and a CSMA/CD network uses IEEE 802.3 (ISO 8802.3). On Ethernet networks, most hardware will comply with the IEEE 802.3 standard. The object of the MAC layer is to allow many nodes to share a single communication channel. It also adds start and end frame delimiters, error detection bits, access control information and source and destination addresses.

The IEEE 802.2 (ISO 8802.2) logical link control (LLC) layer conforms to the same specification for both types of network.

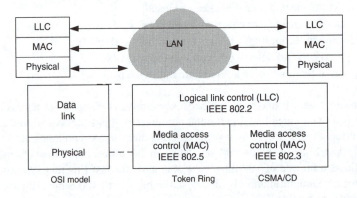

Figure 35.1   Standards for IEEE 802 LANs.

35.3 Ethernet – media access control (MAC) layer

When sending data the MAC layer takes the information from the LLC link layer. Figure 35.2 shows the IEEE 802.3 frame format. It contains 2 or 6 bytes for the source and destination addresses (16 or 48 bits each), 4 bytes for the CRC (32 bits), and 2 bytes for the LLC length (16 bits). The LLC part may be up to 1500 bytes long. The preamble and delay components define the start and end of the frame. The initial preamble and start delimiter are, in total, 8 bytes long and the delay component is a minimum of 96 bytes long.

A 7-byte preamble precedes the Ethernet 802.3 frame. Each byte has a fixed binary pattern of 10101010 and each node on the network uses it to synchronize their clocks and transmission timings. It also informs nodes that a frame is to be sent and for them to check the destination address in the frame.

The end of the frame is a 96-byte delay period which provides the minimum delay between two frames. This slot time delay allows for the worst-case network propagation delay.

The start delimiter field (SDF) is a single byte (or octet) of 10101011. It follows the preamble and identifies that there is a valid frame being transmitted. Most Ethernet systems use a 48-bit MAC address for the sending and receiving nodes. Each Ethernet node has a unique MAC address, which is normally defined using hexadecimal digits, such as:

```
4C - 31 - 22 - 10 - F1 - 32
or    4C31 : 2210: F132
```

A 48-bit address field allows 2^{48} different addresses (or approximately 281 474 976 710 000 different addresses).

The LLC length field defines whether the frame contains information or whether it can be used to define the number of bytes in the logical link field. The logical link field can contain up to 1500 bytes of information and has a minimum of 46 bytes; its format is given in Figure 35.2. If the information is greater than the upper limit then multiple frames are sent. Also, if the field is less than the lower limit then it is padded with extra redundant bits.

The 32-bit frame check sequence (FCS) is an error detection scheme. It is used to determine transmission errors and is often called a cyclic redundancy check (CRC) or simply a checksum.

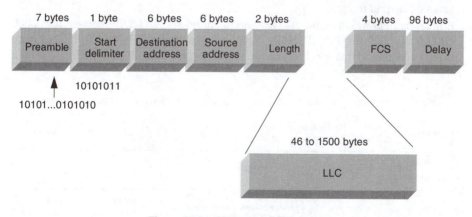

Figure 35.2 IEEE 802.3 frame format.

35.3.1 Ethernet II

The first standard for Ethernet was Ethernet I. Most currently available systems implement either Ethernet II or IEEE 802.3 (although most networks are now defined as being IEEE 802.3 compliant). An Ethernet II frame is similar to the IEEE 802.3 frame; it consists of 8 bytes of preamble, 6 bytes of destination address, 6 bytes of source address, 2 bytes of frame type, between 46 and 1500 bytes of data, and 4 bytes of the frame check sequence field.

When the protocol is IPX/SPX the type field contains the bit pattern 1000 0001 0011 0111, but when the protocol is TCP/IP the type field contains 0000 1000 0000 0000.

35.4 IEEE 802.2 and Ethernet SNAP

The LLC is embedded in the Ethernet frame and is defined by the IEEE 802.2 standard.

Figure 35.3 illustrates how the LLC fields are inserted into the IEEE 802.3 frame. The DSAP and SSAP fields define the types of network protocol used. A SAP code of 1110 0000 identifies the network operating system layer as NetWare, whereas 0000 0110 identifies the TCP/IP protocol. These SAP numbers are issued by the IEEE. The control field is, among other things, for the sequencing of frames.

In some cases it was difficult to modify networks to be IEEE 802-compliant. Thus an alternative method was to identify the network protocol, known as Ethernet SNAP (Sub-network Access Protocol). This was defined to ease the transition to the IEEE 802.2 standard and is illustrated in Figure 35.4. It simply adds an extra two fields to the LLC field to define an organization ID and a network layer identifier. NetWare allows for either Ethernet SNAP or Ethernet 802.2 (as Novell used Ethernet SNAP to translate to Ethernet 802.2).

Non-compliant protocols are identified with the DSAP and SSAP code of 1010 1010, and a control code of 0000 0011. After these fields:

- Organization ID which indicates where the company that developed the embedded protocol belongs. If this field contains all zeros it indicates a non-company-specific generic Ethernet frame.
- EtherType field which defines the networking protocol. A TCP/IP protocol uses 0000 1000 0000 0000 for TCP/IP, while NetWare uses 1000 0001 0011 0111. NetWare frames adhering to this specification are known as NetWare 802.2 SNAP.

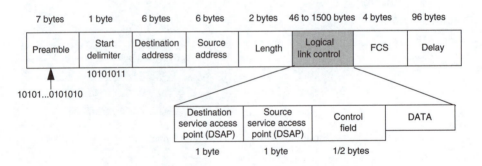

Figure 35.3 Ethernet IEEE 802.3 frame with LLC.

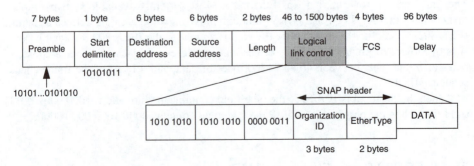

Figure 35.4 Ethernet IEEE 802.3 frame with LLC containing SNAP header.

35.4.1 LLC protocol

The 802.3 frame provides some of the data link layer functions, such as node addressing (source and destination MAC addresses), the addition of framing bits (the preamble) and error control (the FCS). The rest of the functions of the data link layer are performed with the control field of the LLC field; these functions are:

- Flow and error control. Each data frame sent has a frame number. A control frame is sent from the destination to a source node informing that it has or has not received the frames correctly.
- Sequencing of data. Large amounts of data are sliced and sent with frame numbers. The spliced data is then reassembled at the destination node.

Figure 35.5 shows the basic format of the LLC frame. There are three principal types of frame: information, supervisory and unnumbered. An information frame contains data, a supervisory frame is used for acknowledgment and flow control, and an unnumbered frame is used for control purposes. The first 2 bits of the control field determine which type of frame it is. If they are 0X (where X is a don't care) then it is an information frame, 10 specifies a supervisory frame and 11 specifies an unnumbered frame.

An information frame contains a send sequence number in the control field which ranges from 0 to 127. Each information frame has a consecutive number, N(S) (note that there is a roll-over from frame 127 to frame 0). The destination node acknowledges that it has received the frames by sending a supervisory frame. The function of the supervisory frame is specified by the 2-bit S-bit field. This can either be set to Receiver Ready (RR), Receiver Not Ready (RNR) or Reject (REJ). If an RNR function is set then the destination node acknowledges that all frames up to the number stored in the receive sequence number N(R) field were received correctly. An RNR function also acknowledges the frames up to the number N(R), but informs the source node that the destination node wishes to stop communicating. The REJ function specifies that frame N(R) has been rejected and all other frames up to N(R) are acknowledged.

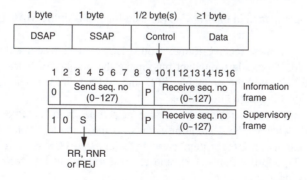

Figure 35.5   LLC frame format.

35.5 OSI and the IEEE 802.3 standard

Ethernet fits into the data link and the physical layer of the OSI model. These two layers only deal with the hardware of the network. The data link layer splits into two parts: the LLC and the MAC layer.

The IEEE 802.3 standard splits into three sublayers:

- MAC (media access control).
- Physical signalling (PLS).
- Physical media attachment (PMA).

The interface between PLS and PMA is called the attachment unit interface (AUI) and the interface between PMA and the transmission media is called the media dependent interface (MDI). This grouping into modules allows Ethernet to be very flexible and to support a number of bit rates, signalling methods and media types. Figure 35.6 illustrates how the layers interconnect.

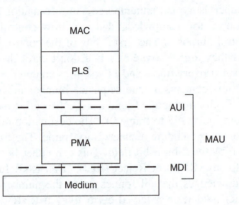

Figure 35.6   Organization of the IEEE 802.3 standard.

35.5.1 Media access control (MAC)

CSMA/CD is implemented in the MAC layer. The functions of the MAC layers are:

- When sending frames: receive frames from LLC; control whether the data fills the LLC data field, if not add redundant bits; make the number of bytes an integer, and calculate the FCS; add the preamble, SFD and address fields to the frame; send the frame to the PLS in a serial bit stream.
- When receiving frames: receive one frame at a time from the PLS in a serial bit stream; check whether the destination address is the same as the local node; ensure the frame contains an integer number of bytes and the FCS is correct; remove the preamble, SFD, address fields, FCS and remove redundant bits from the LLC data field; send the data to the LLC.
- Avoid collisions when transmitting frames and keep the right distance between frames by not sending when another node is sending; when the medium gets free, wait a specified period of time before starting to transmit.
- Handle any collision that appears by sending a jam signal; generate a random number and back off from sending during that random time.

35.5.2 Physical signalling (PLS) and physical medium attachment (PMA)

PLS defines transmission rates, types of encoding/decoding and signalling methods. In PMA a further definition of the transmission media is accomplished, such as coaxial, fibre or twisted-pair. PMA and MDI together form the media attachment unit (MAU), often known as the transceiver.

35.6 Ethernet transceivers

Ethernet requires a minimal amount of hardware. The cables used to connect it are either unshielded twisted-pair cable (UTP) or coaxial cables. These cables must be terminated with their characteristic impedance, which is $50\,\Omega$ for coaxial cables and $100\,\Omega$ for UTP cables.

Each node has transmission and reception hardware to control access to the cable and also to monitor network traffic. The transmission/reception hardware is called a transceiver (short for *trans*mitter/re*ceiver*) and a controller builds up and strips down the frame. The transceiver builds transmit bits at a rate of 10 Mbps and thus the time for one bit is $1/10 \times 10^6$ which is $0.1\,\mu s$.

The Ethernet transceiver transmits onto a single Ether. When none of the nodes are transmitting then the voltage on the line is +0.7 V. This provides a carrier sense signal for all nodes on the network; it is also known as the heartbeat. If a node detects this voltage then it knows that the network is active and that no nodes are currently transmitting.

Thus when a node wishes to transmit a message it listens for a quiet period. Then if two or more transmitters transmit at the same time, a collision results. When they detect the signal, each node transmits a 'jam' signal. The nodes involved in the collision then wait for a random period of time (ranging from 10 to 90 ms) before attempting to transmit again. Each node on a network also awaits a retransmission. Thus collisions are inefficient in a network as they stop nodes from transmitting. Transceivers normally detect a collision by monitoring the dc (or average) voltage on the line.

When transmitting, a transceiver unit transmits the preamble of consecutive 1s and 0s. The coding used is a Manchester code which represents a 0 as a high-to-low voltage transition and a 1 as a low-to-high voltage transition. A low voltage is –0.7 V and a high is +0.7 V. Thus when the preamble is transmitted the voltage will change between +0.7 and –0.7 V; this is illustrated in Figure 35.7. If after the transmission of the preamble no collisions are detected then the rest of the frame is sent.

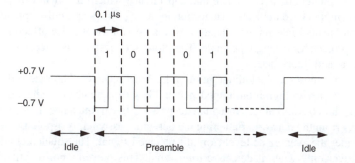

Figure 35.7 Ethernet digital signal.

35.7 NIC

When receiving data, the function of the NIC is to copy all data transmitted on the network, decode it and transfer it to the computer. An Ethernet NIC contains three parts:

- Physical medium interface. The physical medium interface corresponds to the PLS and PMA in the standard and is responsible for the electrical transmission and reception of data. It consists of two parts: the transceiver, which receivers and transmits data from or onto the transmission media; and a code converter that encodes/decodes the data. It also recognizes a collision of the media.
- Data link controller. The controller corresponds to the MAC layer.
- Computer interface.

It can be split into four main functional blocks:

- Network interface.
- Manchester decoder.
- Memory buffer.
- Computer interface.

35.7.1 Network interface

The network interface function is to listen, recreate the waveform transmitted on the cable into a digital signal and transfer the digital signal to the Manchester decoder. The network interface consists of three parts:

- BNC/RJ-45 connector.
- Reception hardware. The reception hardware translates the waveforms transmitted on the cable to digital signals then copies them to the Manchester decoder.
- Isolator. The isolator is connected directly between the reception hardware and the rest of the Manchester decoder; it guarantees that no noise from the network affects the computer, and vice-versa.

The reception hardware is called a receiver and is the main component in the network interface. Basically it has the function of an earphone, listening and copying the traffic on the cable. Unfortunately, the Ether and transceiver electronics are not perfect. The transmission line contains resistance and capacitance which distort the shape of the bit stream transmitted onto the Ether. Distortion in the system causes pulse spreading, which leads to intersymbol interference. There is also a possibility of noise affecting the digital pulse as it propagates through the cable. Therefore, the receiver also needs to recreate the digital signal and filter noise.

Figure 35.8 shows a block diagram of an Ethernet receiver. The received signal goes through a buffer with high input impedance and low capacitance to reduce the effects of loading on the coaxial cable. An equalizer passes high frequencies and attenuates low frequencies from the network, flattening the network passband. A 4-pole Bessel low-pass filter provides the average dc level from the received signal. The squelch circuit activates the line driver only when it detects a true signal. This prevents noise activating the receiver.

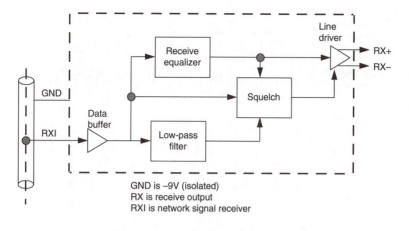

Figure 35.8 Ethernet receiver block diagram.

35.7.2 Manchester decoder

Manchester coding has the advantage of embedding timing (clock) information within the transmitted bits. A positively edged pulse (low → high) represents a 1 and a negatively edged pulse (high → low) a 0, as shown in Figure 35.9. Another advantage of this coding method is that the average voltage is always zero when used with equal positive and negative voltage levels.

Figure 35.10 is an example of transmitted bits using Manchester encoding. The receiver passes the received Manchester-encoded bits through a low-pass filter. This extracts the lowest frequency in the received bit stream, i.e., the clock frequency. With this clock the receiver can then determine the transmitted bit pattern.

For Manchester decoding, the Manchester-encoded signal is first synchronized to the receiver (called bit synchronization). A transition in the middle of each bit cell is used by a clock recovery circuit to produce a clock pulse in the centre of the second half of the bit cell. In Ethernet the bit synchronization is achieved by deriving the clock from the preamble field of the frame using a clock and data recovery circuit. Many Ethernet decoders used the SEEQ 8020 Manchester code converter, which uses a phase-locked loop (PLL) to recover the clock. The PLL is designed to lock onto the preamble of the incoming signal within 12-bit cells. Figure 35.11 shows a circuit schematic of bit synchronization using Manchester decoding and a PLL.

The PLL is a feedback circuit which is commonly used for the synchronization of digital signals. It consists of a phase detector (such as an EX-OR gate) and a voltage-controlled oscillator (VCO) which uses a crystal oscillator as a clock source.

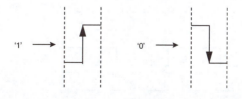

Figure 35.9 Manchester encoding.

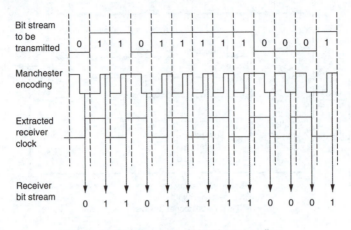

Figure 35.10   Example of Manchester coding.

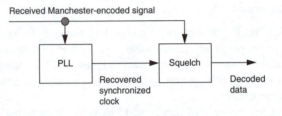

Figure 35.11   Manchester decoding with bit synchronization.

The frequency of the crystal is twice the frequency of the received signal. It is so constant that it only needs irregular and small adjustments to be synchronized to the received signal. The function of the phase detector is to find irregularities between the two signals and adjusts the VCO to minimize the error. This is accomplished by comparing the received signals and the output from the VCO. When the signals have the same frequency and phase the PLL is locked. Figure 35.12 shows the PLL components and the function of the EX-OR.

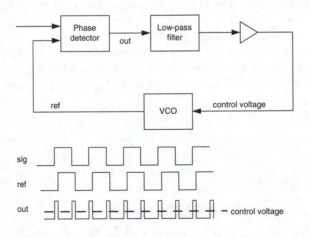

Figure 35.12   PLL and example waveform for the phase detector.

35.7.3 Memory buffer

The rate at which data is transmitted on the cable differs from the data rate used by the receiving computer, and the data appears in bursts. To compensate for the difference between the data rate, a first-in first-out (FIFO) memory buffer is used to produce a constant data rate. An important condition is that the average data input rate should not exceed the frequency of the output clock; if this is not the case the buffer will be filled up regardless of its size.

A FIFO is a RAM that uses a queuing technique where the output data appears in the same order that it went in. The input and output are controlled by separate clocks, and the FIFO keeps track of the data that has been written and the data that has been read and can thus be overwritten. This is achieved with a pointer. Figure 35.13 shows a block diagram of the FIFO configuration. The FIFO status is indicated by flags, the empty flag (EF) and the full flag (FF), which show whether the FIFO is either empty or full.

35.7.4 Ethernet implementation

The completed circuit for the Ethernet receiver is given in on the WWW page given in the Preface and is outlined in Figure 35.14. It uses the SEEQ Technologies 82C93A Ethernet transceiver as the receiver and the SEEQ 8020 Manchester code converter which decodes the Manchester code. A transformer and dc-to-dc converter isolates the SEEQ 82C92A and the network cable from the rest of the circuit (and the computer). The isolated dc-to-dc converter converts a 5 V supply to the −9 V needed by the transceiver.

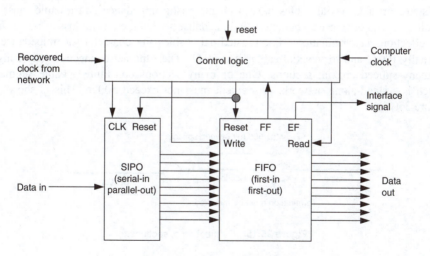

Figure 35.13 Memory buffering.

The memory buffer used is the AMD AM7204 FIFO which has 4096 data words with 9-bit words (but only 8 bits are actually used). The output of the circuit is 8 data lines, the control lines $\overline{FF}$, $\overline{EF}$, $\overline{RS}$, $\overline{R}$ and $\overline{W}$, and the +5 V and GND supply rails.

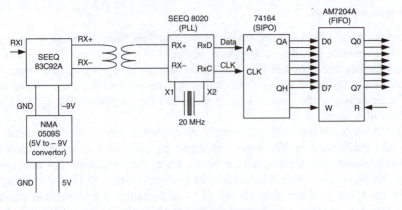

Figure 35.14   Ethernet receiver.

35.8 Standard Ethernet limitations

The standard Ethernet CSMA/CD specification places various limitations on maximum cable lengths. This limitation is due to maximum signal propagation times and the clock period.

35.8.1 Length of segments

Twisted-pair and coaxial cables have a characteristic impedance and a cable must be terminated with the correct characteristic impedance so that there is no loss of power and no reflections at terminations. For twisted-pair cables the characteristic impedance is normally $100\,\Omega$ and for coaxial cables it is $50\,\Omega$. The Ethernet connection may consist of many spliced coaxial sections. One or many sections constitute a cable segment, which is a stand-alone network. A segment must not exceed 500 m. This is shown in Figure 35.15.

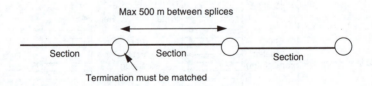

Figure 35.15   Connection of sections.

35.8.2 Repeater lengths

A repeater is added between segments to boost the signal. A maximum of two repeaters can be inserted into the path between two nodes. The maximum distance between two nodes connected via repeaters is 1500 m; this is illustrated in Figure 35.16.

35.8.3 Maximum links

The maximum length of a point-to-point coaxial link is 1500 m. A long run such as this is typically used as a link between two remote sites within a single building.

35.8.4 Distance between transceivers

Transceivers should not be placed closer than 2.5 m. Additionally, each segment should not have more than 100 transceiver units, as illustrated in Figure 35.17. Transceivers which are placed too close to each other can cause transmission interference and also an increased risk of collision.

Each node transceiver lowers network resistance and dissipates the transmission signal. A sufficient number of transceivers reduces the electrical characteristic of the network below the specified operation threshold.

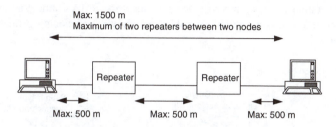

Figure 35.16 Maximum number of repeaters between two nodes.

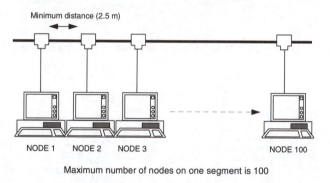

Figure 35.17 Connection of sections.

35.9 Ethernet types

The five main types of standard Ethernet are:

- Standard, or thick-wire, Ethernet (10BASE5).
- Thinnet, or thin-wire Ethernet, or Cheapernet (10BASE2).
- Twisted-pair Ethernet (10BASE-T).
- Optical fibre Ethernet (10BASE-FL).
- Fast Ethernet (100BASE-TX or 100VG-Any LAN).

The thin- and thick-wire types connect directly to an Ethernet segment, these are shown in Figure 35.18 and Figure 35.19. Standard Ethernet, 10BASE5, uses a high specification cable (RG-50) and N-type plugs to connect the transceiver to the Ethernet segment. A node connects to the transceiver using a 9-pin D-type connector. A vampire (or bee-sting) connector can be used to clamp the transceiver to the backbone cable.

Thin-wire, or Cheapernet, uses a lower specification cable (it has a smaller inner conductor diameter). The cable connector required is also of a lower specification, that is, BNC rather than N-type connectors. In standard Ethernet the transceiver unit is connected directly onto the backbone tap. On a Cheapernet network the transceiver is integrated into the node.

Many modern Ethernet connections are to a 10BASE-T hub, which connects UTP cables to the Ethernet segment. An RJ-45 connector is used for 10BASE-T. The fibre-optic type, 10BASE-FL, allows long lengths of interconnected lines, typically up to 2 km. They use either SMA connectors or ST connectors. SMA connectors are screw-on types while ST connectors are push-on. Table 35.1 shows the basic specifications for the different types.

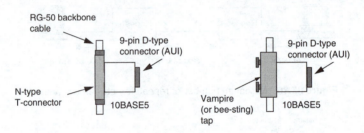

Figure 35.18   Ethernet connections for Thick Ethernet.

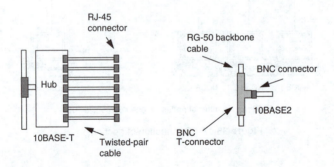

Figure 35.19   Ethernet connections for Thin Ethernet and 10BASE-T.

35.10 Twisted-pair hubs

Twisted-pair Ethernet (10BASE-T) nodes normally connect to the backbone using a hub, as illustrated in Figure 35.20. Connection to the twisted-pair cable is via an RJ-45 connector. The connection to the backbone can either be to thin- or thick-Ethernet. Hubs can also be stackable where one hub connects to another. This leads to concentrated area networks (CANs) and limits the amount of traffic on the backbone. Twisted-pair hubs normally improve network performance.

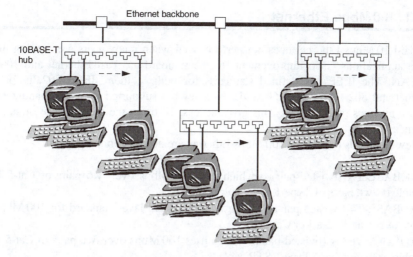

Figure 35.20 10BASE-T connection.

10BASE-T uses 2 twisted-pair cables, one for transmit and one for receive. A collision occurs when the node (or hub) detects that it is receiving data when it is currently transmitting data.

Table 35.1 Ethernet network parameters.

Parameter	10BASE5	10BASE2	10BASE-T
Common name	Standard or thick-wire Ethernet	Thinnet or thin-wire Ethernet	Twisted-pair Ethernet
Data rate	10 Mbps	10 Mbps	10 Mbps
Maximum segment length	500 m	200 m	100 m
Maximum nodes on a segment	100	30	3
Maximum number of repeaters	2	4	4
Maximum nodes per network	1024	1024	
Minimum node spacing	2.5 m	0.5 m	No limit
Location of transceiver electronics	Cable connection	Integrated into node	In a hub
Typical cable type	RG-50	RG-6	UTP cables
Connectors	N-type	BNC	RJ-45/Telco
Cable impedance	50 Ω	50 Ω	100 Ω

35.11 100Mbps Ethernet

Standard 10 Mbps Ethernet does not perform well when many users are running multi-media applications. Two improvements to the standard are Fast Ethernet and 100VG-AnyLAN. The IEEE has defined standards for both of them, IEEE 802.3u for Fast Ethernet and 802.12 for 100VG-AnyLAN. They are supported by many manufacturers and use bit rates of 100 Mbps. This gives at least 10 times the performance of standard Ethernet.

New standards relating to 100 Mbps Ethernet are now becoming popular:

- 100BASE-TX (twisted-pair) – which uses 100 Mbps over two pairs of Cat-5 UTP cable or two pairs of Type 1 STP cable.
- 100BASE-T4 (twisted-pair) – which is the physical layer standard for 100 Mbps bit rate over Cat-3, Cat-4 or Cat-5 UTP.
- 100VG-AnyLAN (twisted-pair) – which uses 100 Mbps over two pairs of Cat-5 UTP cable or two pairs of Type 1 STP cable.
- 100BASE-FX (fibre-optic cable) – which is the physical layer standard for 100 Mbps bit rate over fibre-optic cables.

Fast Ethernet, or 100BASE-T, is simply 10BASE-T running at 10 times the bit rate. It is a natural progression from standard Ethernet and thus allows existing Ethernet networks to be easily upgraded. Unfortunately, as with standard Ethernet, nodes contend for the network, reducing the network efficiency when there are high traffic rates. Also, as it uses collision detect, the maximum segment length is limited by the amount of time for the farthest nodes on a network to properly detect collisions. On a Fast Ethernet network with twisted-pair copper cables this distance is 100 m and for a fibre-optic link it is 400 m. Table 35.2 outlines the main network parameters for Fast Ethernet.

Since 100BASE-TX standards are compatible with 10BASE-TX networks then the network allows both 10 Mbps and 100 Mbps bit rates on the line. This makes upgrading simple, as the only additions to the network are dual-speed interface adapters. Nodes with the 100 Mbps capabilities can communicate at 100 Mbps, but they can also communicate with slower nodes, at 10 Mbps.

Table 35.2 Fast Ethernet network parameters.

	100BASE-TX	*100VG-AnyLAN*
Standard	IEEE 802.3u	IEEE 802.12
Bit rate	100 Mbps	100 Mbps
Actual throughput	Up to 50 Mbps	Up to 96 Mbps
Maximum distance (hub to node)	100 m (twisted-pair, Cat-5) 400 m (fibre)	100 m (twisted-pair, Cat-3) 200 m (twisted-pair, Cat-5) 2 km (fibre)
Scaleability	None	Up to 400 Mbps
Advantages	Easy migration from 10BASE-T	Greater throughput, greater distance

The basic rules of a 100BASE-TX network are:

- The network topology is a star network and there must be no loops.
- All four pairs are required in a four-pair UTP network. In other words, do not use the remaining two pairs in 100Base-TX for anything else.
- Cat-5 cable is used.
- Up to two hubs can be cascaded in a network.
- Each hub is equivalent of 5 metres in latency.
- Segment length is limited to 100 metres.
- Network diameter must not exceed 205 metres.

35.11.1 100BASE-4T

100BASE-4T allows the use of standard Cat-3 cables. These contain eight wires made up of four twisted pairs. 100BASE-4T uses all of the pairs to transmit at 100 Mbps. This differs from 10BASE-T in that 10BASE-T uses only two pairs, one for transmit and one for receive. 100BASE-T allows compatibility with 10BASE-T in that the first two pairs (Pair 1 and Pair 2) are used in the same way as 10BASE-T connections. 100BASE-T then uses the other two pairs (Pair 3 and Pair 4) with half-duplex links between the hub and the node. The connections are illustrated in Figure 35.21.

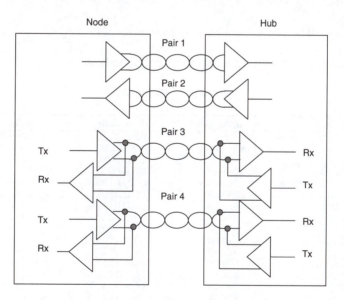

Figure 35.21   100BASE-4T connections.

8B6T

100BASE-4T uses four separate Cat-3 twisted-pair wires. The maximum clock rate that can be applied to Cat-3 cable is 30 Mbps. Thus, some mechanism must be devised which can reduce the line bit rate to under 30 Mbps but give a symbol rate of 100 Mbps. This is achieved with a 3-level code (+, − and 0) and is known as 8B6T. The code converts eight binary digits into six ternary symbols. Table 35.3 gives the part of the code table. Thus, the bit sequence 00000000 will be coded as a positive voltage, a negative voltage, a zero voltage, a zero voltage, a positive voltage and a negative voltage.

Apart from reducing the frequencies with the digital signal, the 8B6T code has the advantage of reducing the dc content of the signal. Most of the codes contain the same number of positive and negative voltages. This is because only 256 of the possible 729 (3^6) codes are actually used. The codes have also chosen to have at least two transitions in every code word, so that clock information is embedded into the signal.

Unfortunately, it is not possible to have all codes with the same number of negative voltages as positive voltages. Thus there are some codes which have a different number of negatives and positives, these include:

```
0100 0001      +0-00++
0111 1001      +++-0-
```

The technique used to overcome this is to invert consecutive codes which have a weighting of +1. For example, suppose the line code were:

```
+0++--     ++0+--     +++--0 +++--0
```

it would actually be coded as:

```
+0++--     --0-++     +++--0 ---++0
```

The receiver detects the −1 weighted codes as an inverted pattern.

Table 35.3   8B6T code.

8-bit data	Encoded data	8-bit data	Encoded data
00000000	+-00+-	00010000	+0+--0
00000001	0+-+-+	00010001	++0-0
00000010	+-0+-0	00010010	+0+-0-
00000011	-0++-0	00010011	0++-0-
00000100	-0+0+-	00010100	0++--0
00000101	0+--0+	00010101	++00--
00000110	+-0-0+	00010110	+0+0--
00000111	-0+-0+	00010111	0++0--
00001000	-+00+-	00011000	0+-0+-
00001001	0-++-0	00011001	0+-0-+
00001010	-+0+-0	00011010	0+-++-
00001011	+0-+-0	00011011	0+-00+
00001100	+0-0+-	00011100	0-+00+
00001101	0-+-0+	00011101	0-+++-
00001110	-+0-0+	00011110	0-+0-+
00001111	+0--0+	00011111	0-+0+-

35.11.2 100VG-AnyLAN

The 100VG-AnyLAN standard (IEEE 802.12) was developed mainly by Hewlett Packard and overcomes the contention problem by using a priority-based round-robin arbitration method, known as the demand priority access method (DPAM). Unlike Fast Ethernet, nodes always connect to a hub which regularly scans its input ports to determine whether any nodes have requests pending.

100VG-AnyLAN has the great advantage that it supports both IEEE 802.3 (Ethernet) and IEEE 802.5 (Token Ring) frames and can thus integrate well with existing 10BaseT and Token Ring networks.

100VG-AnyLAN has an in-built priority mechanism with two priority levels: a high-priority request and a normal-priority request. A normal-priority request is used for non-real-time data, such as data files, and so on. High-priority requests are used for real-time data, such as speech or video data. At present, there is limited usage of this feature and there is no support mechanism for this facility after the data has left the hub.

100VG-AnyLAN allows up to seven levels of hubs (i.e. one root and six cascaded hubs) with a maximum distance of 150 m between nodes. Unlike other forms of Ethernet, it allows any number of nodes to be connected to a segment.

5B6B

The 100VG-AnyLAN standard uses 5B6B to transmit an Ethernet frame between the hub and the node. This code is used so that there is an increase the number of transitions in the transmitted waveform.

In 100VG-AnyLAN, a 100 Mbps bit stream is multiplexed onto four 25 Mbps streams and transmitted over the four twisted-pair cables. The encoding process thus increases the bit rate on each twisted pair cable to 30 Mbps (as six encoded bits are sent for every five bit stream bits). Figure 35.22 illustrated this and Table 35.4 gives the 5B/6B encoding.

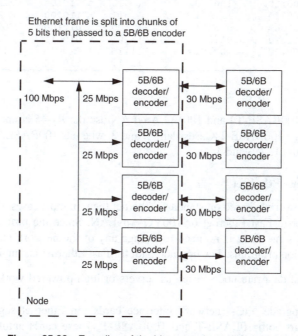

Figure 35.22   Encoding of the bit stream in 100VG-AnyLAN.

Unfortunately, it is not possible to code each one of the 6-bit encoded values with an equal number of 0s and 1s as there are only 20 encoded values which have an equal number of 0s and 1s, these are highlighted in Table 35.3. Thus, two modes are used with the other 12 values having either two 0s and four 1s or four 0s and two 1s. The data is then transmitted in two modes:

- Mode 2. Where the encoded data has either an equal number of 0s and 1s or has four 1s and two 0s.
- Mode 4. Where the encoded data has either an equal number of 1s and 0s or has four 0s and two 1s.

These modes alternate and this gives, on average, digital sum value (DSV) of zero.

Table 35.4   5B/6B encoding.

5-bit data	Mode 2 encoding	Mode 4 encoding	5-bit data	Mode 2 encoding	Mode 4 encoding
00000	001100	110011	10000	000101	111010
00001	101100	101100	10001	100101	100101
00010	100010	101110	10010	001001	110110
00011	001101	001101	10011	010110	010110
00100	001010	110101	10100	111000	111000
00101	010101	010101	10101	011000	100111
00110	001110	001110	10110	011001	011001
00111	001011	001011	10111	100001	011110
01000	000111	000111	11000	110001	110001
01001	100011	100011	11001	101010	101010
01010	100110	100110	11010	010100	101011
01011	000110	111001	11011	110100	110100
01100	101000	010111	11100	011100	011100
01101	011010	011010	11101	010011	010011
01110	100100	100100	11110	010010	101101
01111	101001	101001	11111	110010	110010

Connections

100BASE-TX, 100BASE-T4 and 100VG-AnyLAN use the RJ-45 connector, which has eight connections. 100BASE-TX uses Pairs 2 and 3, whereas 100BASE-T4 and 100VG-AnyLAN use Pairs 1, 2, 3 and 4.

Migration to Fast Ethernet

If an existing network is based on standard Ethernet then, in most cases, the best network upgrade is either to Fast Ethernet or 100VG-AnyLAN. Since the protocols and access methods are the same there is no need to change any of the network management software or application programs. The upgrade path for Fast Ethernet is simple and could be:

- Upgrade high data rate nodes, such as servers or high-powered workstations to Fast Ethernet.
- Gradually upgrade NICs (network interface cards) on Ethernet segments to cards which support both 10BASE-T and 100BASE-T. These cards automatically detect the transmission rate to give either 10 or 100 Mbps.

The upgrade path to 100VG-AnyLAN is less easy as it relies on hubs and, unlike Fast Ethernet, most NICs have different network connectors, one for 10BASE-T and the other for 100VG-AnyLAN (although it is likely that more NICs will have automatic detection). A possible path could be:

- Upgrade high data rate nodes, such as servers or high-powered workstations to 100VG-AnyLAN.
- Install 100VG-AnyLAN hubs.
- Connect nodes to 100VG-AnyLAN hubs and change over connectors.

It is difficult to assess the performance differences between Fast Ethernet and 100VG-AnyLAN. Fast Ethernet uses a well-proven technology but suffers from network contention. 100VG-AnyLAN is a relatively new technology and the handshaking with the hub increases delay time. The maximum data throughput of a 100BASE-TX network is limited to around 50 Mbps, whereas 100VG-AnyLAN allows rates up to 96 Mbps.

The 100BASE-TX standard does not allow future upgrading of the bit rate, whereas 100VG-AnyLAN allows possible upgrades to 400 Mbps.

35.12 Switches and switching hubs

A switch is a very fast, low-latency, multiport bridge that is used to segment LANs. They are typically also used to increase communication rates between segments with multiple parallel conversations and also between technologies (such as between FDDI and 100Base-TX).

A switching hub is a repeater that contains a number of network segments (typically 4, 8 or 16). Through software, any of the ports on the hub can directly connect to any of the four segments, at any time. Thus, for a 4-port switching hub connected to 10 Mbps segments, gives a maximum capacity of 40 Mbps in a single hub.

Ethernet switches overcome the contention problem of normal CSMA/CD networks. They segment traffic by giving each connection a guaranteed bandwidth allocation. Figure 35.23 and Figure 35.24 show the two types of switches, their main features are:

- Desktop switch (or workgroup switch). These connect directly to nodes. They are economical with fixed configuration for end-node connections and are designed for stand-alone networks or distributed workgroups in a larger network.
- Segment switch. These connect both 10 Mbps workgroup switches and 100 Mbps interconnect (backbone) switches that are used to interconnect hubs and desktop switches. They are modular, high-performance switches for interconnecting workgroups in mid- to large-size networks.

35.12.1 Segment switch

A segment switch allows simultaneous communication between any client and any server. These switches can simply replace existing Ethernet hubs. Figure 35.24 shows a switch with five ports, each transmitting at 10 Mbps. This allows up to five simultaneous connections giving a maximum aggregated bandwidth of 50 Mbps. If the nodes support 100 Mbps communication then the maximum aggregated bandwidth will be 500 Mbps. To optimize the network nodes should be connected to the switch that connects to the server that they most often communicate with. This allows for a direct connection with that server.

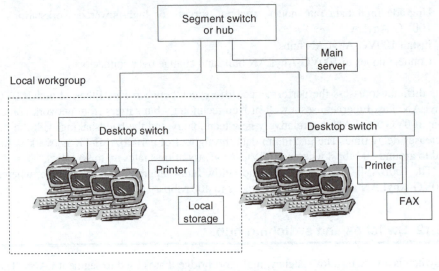

Figure 35.23   Desktop switch.

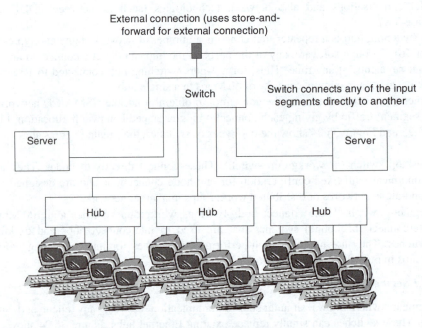

Figure 35.24   Segment switch.

35.12.2 Desktop switch

A desktop switch can simply replace an existing 10BASE-T/100BASE-T hubs. It has the advantage that any of the ports can connect directly to another. In the network in Figure 35.23 any of the computers in the local workgroup can connect directly to any others, or to the printer or to the local disk drive. This type of switch works well if there is a lot of local traffic, typically between a local server and local peripherals.

35.12.3 Store-and-forward switching

Store-and-forwarding techniques have been used extensively in bridges and routers, and they are now being used with switches. It involves reading the entire Ethernet frame, before forwarding it, with the required protocol and at the correct speed, to the destination port. This has the advantages of:

- Improved error checking. Bad frames are blocked from entering a network segment.
- Protocol filtering. Store-and-forwarding allows the switch to convert from one protocol to another.
- Speed matching. Typically, for Ethernet, reading at 10 Mbps or 100 Mbps and transmitting at 100 Mbps or 10 Mbps. Also a matching between ATM (155 Mbps), FDDI (100 Mbps), Token Ring (4/16 Mbps) and Ethernet (10/100 Mbps).

The main disadvantage is:

- System delay. As the frame must be totally read before it is transmitted there is a delay in the transmission. The improvement in error checking normally overcomes this disadvantage.

35.12.4 Switching technology

A switch uses store-and-forward packets to switch between ports. The main technologies used are:

- Shared bus. This method uses a high-speed backplane to interconnect the switched ports. It is frequently used to build modular switches that give a large number of ports and to interconnect multiple LAN technologies, such as FDDI, 100VG-AnyLAN, 100Base-T, and ATM.
- Shared memory. These use a common memory area (several MBs) in which data is passed between the ports. It is very common in low-cost, small-scale switches and has the advantage that it can cope with different types of network, which may be operating at different speeds. The main types of memory allocation are:

  - Pooled memory. Memory is allocated as it is need by the ports from a common memory pool.
  - Dedicated shared memory. Memory is fixed for each shared port pair.
  - Distributed memory. Memory is fixed and dedicated to each port.

35.13 Comparison of Fast Ethernet

Table 35.5 compares Fast Ethernet with other types of networking technologies.

Table 35.5   Comparison of Fast Ethernet.

	100VG-AnyLAN (Cat 3, 4, or 5)	100Base-T (TX/FX/T4)	Gigabit Ethernet (802.3z)
Maximum segment length	100 m	100m (Cat-5) 412m (Fibre)	100 m (Cat 5) 1000m (Fibre)
Maximum network diameter with repeater(s)	6000 m	320 m	To be determined by the standard
Bitrate	100 Mbps	100 Mbps	1 Gbps
Media access method	Demand Priority	CSMA/CD	CSMA/CD
Maximum nodes on each domain	1024	Limited by hub	To be determined
Frame type	Ethernet and Token Ring	Ethernet	Ethernet
Multimedia support	✓	✗	YES (with 802.1 p)
Integration with 10BASE2	YES with bridges, switches and routers	YES with switches	YES with 10/100 Mbps switching
Relative cost	Low	Low	Medium
Relative complexity	Low	Low	Low

35.14 Exercises

35.14.1   Discuss the main reasons for the preamble in an Ethernet frame.

35.14.2   Discuss the limitations of the different types of Ethernet.

35.14.3   Discuss 100 Mbps Ethernet technologies with respect to how they operate and their typical parameters.

35.14.4   A node has a binary network address of 0011 1111 0101 1111 1000 1000 0101 0000 0000 1000 0111 1111. Determine its hexadecimal address; that is, the address in the form xxxx:xxxx:xxxx. Table 35.6 shows the conversion of binary digits into hexadecimal.

The binary number `011101011100000` is converted into hexadecimal by the following:

Binary	0111	0101	1100	0000
Hex	7	5	C	0

35.14.5 Explain the usage of Ethernet SNAP.

35.14.6 State the main advantage of Manchester coding and show the bit pattern for the bit sequence:

01111010101101010001011010

35.14.7 Explain the main functional differences between 100BASE-T, 100BASE-4T and 100VG-AnyLAN.

Table 35.6 Decimal, binary and hexadecimal conversions.

Decimal	Binary	Hex	Decimal	Binary	Hex
0	0000	0	8	1000	8
1	0001	1	9	1001	9
2	0010	2	10	1010	A
3	0011	3	11	1011	B
4	0100	4	12	1100	C
5	0101	5	13	1101	D
6	0110	6	14	1110	E
7	0111	7	15	1111	F

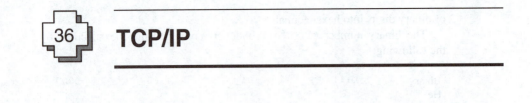

36 TCP/IP

36.1 Introduction

Networking technologies, such as Ethernet, Token Ring and FDDI provide a data link layer function, that is, they allow a reliable connection between one node and another on the same network. They do not provide for inter-networking where data can be transferred from one network to another or one network segment to another. For data to be transmitted across networks requires an addressing scheme which is read by a bridge, gateway or router. The interconnection of networks is known as internetworking (or internet). Each part of an internet is a subnetwork (or subnet).

The Transmission Control Protocol (TCP) and Internet Protocol (IP are a pair of protocols that allow one subnet to communicate with another. A protocol is a set of rules that allow the orderly exchange of information. The IP part corresponds to the Network layer of the OSI model and the TCP part to the Transport layer. As prevously mentioned their operation should be transparent to the Physical and Data Link layers and can thus be used on Ethernet, FDDI or Token Ring networks. This is illustrated in Figure 36.1. The address of the Data Link layer corresponds to the physical address of the node, such as the MAC address (in Ethernet and Token Ring) or the telephone number (for a modem connection). The IP address is assigned to each node on the internet and is used to identify the location of the network and any subnets.

TCP/IP was originally developed by the US Defense Advanced Research Projects Agency (DARPA). Their objective was to connect a number of universities and other research establishments to DARPA. The resultant internet is now known as the Internet. It has since outgrown this application and many commercial organizations and home users now connect to the Internet. The Internet uses TCP/IP as a standard to transfer data. Each node on the Internet is assigned a unique network address, called an IP address. Note that any organization can have its own internets, but if it they want to connect these to the Internet then their addresses must conform to the Internet addressing format.

The ISO have adopted TCP/IP as the basis for the standards relating to the network and transport layers of the OSI model. This standard is known as ISO-IP. Most currently available systems conform to the IP addressing standard.

Common applications that use TCP/IP communications are remote login and file transfer. Typical programs used in file transfer and log-in over TCP communication are `ftp` for file transfer program and `telnet` that allows remote login into another computer. The `ping` program determines if a node is responding to TCP/IP communications.

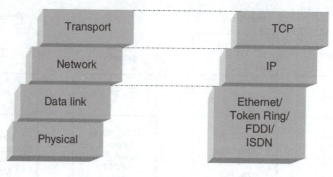

Figure 36.1   TCP/IP and the OSI model.

36.2 TCP/IP gateways and hosts

TCP/IP hosts are nodes which communicate over interconnected networks using TCP/IP communications. A TCP/IP gateway node connects one type of network to another. It contains hardware to provide the physical link between the different networks and the hardware and software to convert frames from one network to the other. Typically, it converts a Token Ring MAC layer to an equivalent Ethernet MAC layer, and vice versa.

A router connects a network to another of the same kind through a point-to-point link. The main operational difference between a gateway, a router, and a bridge, is that, for a Token Ring and Ethernet network, the bridge uses the 48-bit MAC address to route frames, whereas the gateway and router use the IP network address. As an analogy to the public telephone system, the MAC address is equivalent to a randomly assigned telephone number, whereas the IP address would contain the information on the logical located of the telephone, such as which country, area code, and so on.

Figure 36.2 shows how a gateway routes information. The gateway reads the frame from the computer on network A. It then reads the IP address contained in the frame and makes a decision as to whether it is routed out of network A to network B. If it does then it relays the frame to network B.

36.3 Function of the IP protocol

The main functions of the IP protocol are to:

- Route IP data frames – which are called internet datagrams – around an internet. The IP protocol program running on each node knows the location of the gateway on the network. The gateway must then be able to locate the interconnected network. Data then passes from node to gateway through the internet.
- Fragment the data into smaller units if it is greater than a given amount (64 kB).
- Report errors. When a datagram is being routed or is being reassembled an error can occur. If this happen then the node that detects the error reports back to the source node. Datagrams are deleted from the network if they travel through the network for more than a set time. Again, an error message is returned to the source node to inform it that the internet routing could not find a route for the datagram or that the destination node, or network, does not exist.

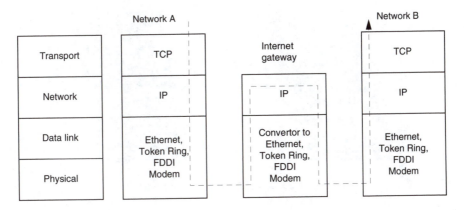

Figure 36.2   Internet gateway layers.

36.4 Internet datagram

The IP protocol is an implementation of the OSI network layer. It adds a data header onto the information passed from the transport layer, the resultant data packet is known as an internet datagram. The header contains information such as the destination and source IP addresses, the version number of the IP protocol and so on. Figure 36.3 shows its format.

The datagram contains up to 65 536 bytes (64 kB) of data. If the data to be transmitted is less than, or equal to, 64 kB, then it is sent as one datagram. If it is more than this then the sender splits the data into fragments and sends multiple datagrams. When transmitted from the source each datagram is routed separately through the internet and the received fragments are finally reassembled at the destination.

The fields in the IP datagram are:

- **Version**. The TCP/IP `version number` helps gateways and nodes correctly interpret the data unit. Differing versions may have a different format or the IP protocol interprets the header differently.
- **Type of service**. The `type of service` bit field is an 8-bit bit pattern in the form `PPPDTRXX`, where `PPP` defines the priority of the datagram (from 0 to 7), `D` sets a low delay service, `T` sets high throughput, `R` sets high reliability and `XX` are currently not used.
- **Header length**. The `header length` defines the size of the data unit in multiplies of 4 bytes (32 bits). The minimum length is 5 bytes and the maximum is 65 536 bytes. Padding bytes fill any unused spaces.
- **D and M bits**. A gateway may route a datagram and split it into smaller fragments. The `D` bit informs the gateway that it should not fragment the data and thus signifies that a receiving node should receive the data as a single unit or not at all. The `M` bit is the more fragments bit and identifies data fragments. The `fragment offset` contains the fragment number.

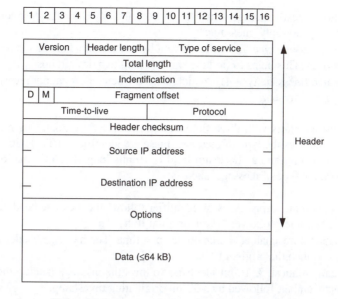

Figure 36.3   Internet datagram format and contents.

- **Time-to-live**. A datagram could propagate through the internet indefinitely. To prevent this, the 8-bit `time-to-live` value is set to the maximum transit time in seconds and is set initially by the source IP. Each gateway then decrements this value by a defined amount. When it becomes zero the datagram is discarded. It also defines the maximum amount of time that a destination IP node should wait for the next datagram fragment.

- **Protocol**. Different IP protocols can be used on the datagram. The 8-bit `protocol` field defines the type to be used.

- **Header checksum**. The `header checksum` contains a 16-bit pattern for error detection.

- **Source and destination IP addresses**. The `source` and `destination IP addresses` are stored in the 32-bit source and destination IP address fields.

- **Options**. The `options` field contains information such as debugging, error control and routing information.

36.5 ICMP

Messages, such as control data, information data and error recovery data, are carried between Internet hosts using the Internet Control Message Protocol (ICMP). These messages are sent with a standard IP header. Typical messages are:

- Destination unreachable (message type 3) – which is sent by a host on the network to say that the destination host is unreachable. It can also include the reason the host cannot be reached.

- Echo request/echo reply (message type 8 or 0) – which are used to check the connectivity between two hosts. The ping command uses this message, where it sends an

ICMP 'echo request' message to the target host and waits for the destination host to reply with an 'echo reply' message.
- Redirection (message type 5) – which is sent by a router to a host that is requesting its routing services. This helps to find the shortest path to a desired host.
- Source quench (message type 4) – which is used when a host cannot receive anymore IP packets at the present.

The ICMP message starts with three fields, as shown in Figure 36.4. The message type has 8 bits and identifies the type of message, these are identified in Table 36.1. The code field is also 8 bits long and a checksum field is 16 bits long. The information after this field depends on the type of message, such as:

- For echo request and reply. An 8-bit identifier follows the message header, then an 8-bit sequence number, followed by the original IP header.
- For destination unreachable, source quelch and time. The message header is followed by 32-bits and then the original IP header.
- For timestamp request. A 16-bit identifier follows the message header, then by a 16-bit sequence number, followed by a 32-bit originating timestamp.

Table 36.1   Message type field value.

Value	Message type	Value	Message type
0	Echo reply	12	Parameter problem
3	Destination unreachable	13	Timestamp request
4	Source quench	14	Timestamp reply
5	Redirect	17	Address mask request
8	Echo request	18	Address mask reply
11	Time-to-live exceeded		

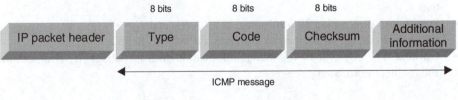

Figure 36.4   ICMP message format.

36.6 TCP/IP internets

Figure 36.5 illustrates a sample TCP/IP implementation. A gateway MERCURY provides a link between a token ring network (NETWORK A) and an Ethernet network (ETHER C). Another gateway PLUTO connects NETWORK B to ETHER C. The TCP/IP protocol thus allows a host on NETWORK A to communicate with VAX01.

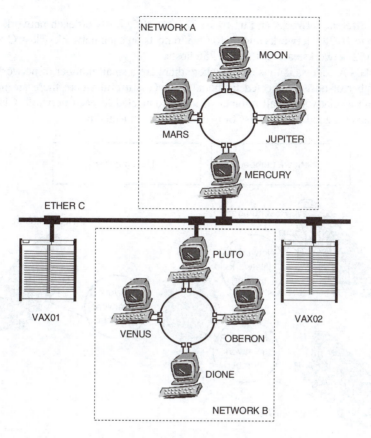

Figure 36.5 Example internet.

36.6.1 Selecting internet addresses

Each node using TCP/IP communications requires an IP address which is then matched to its Token Ring or Ethernet MAC address. The MAC address allows nodes on the same segment to communicate with each other. In order for nodes on a different network to communicate, each must be configured with an IP address.

Nodes on a TCP/IP network are either hosts or gateways. Any nodes that run application software or are terminals are hosts. Any node that routes TCP/IP packets between networks is called a TCP/IP gateway node. This node must have the necessary network controller boards to physically interface to the other networks it connects with.

36.6.2 Format of the IP address

A typical IP address consists of two fields: the left field (or the network number) identifies the network, and the right number (or the host number) identifies the particular host within that network. Figure 36.6 illustrates this.

The IP address is 32 bits long and can address over four billion physical addresses (2^{32} or 4 294 967 296 hosts). There are three main address formats; as shown in Figure 36.7.

Each of these types is applicable to certain types of networks. Class A allows up to

128 (2^7) different networks and up to 16 777 216 (2^{24}) hosts on each network. Class B allows up to 16 384 networks and up to 65 536 hosts on each network. Class C allows up to 2 097 152 networks each with up to 256 hosts.

The class A address is thus useful where there are a small number of networks with a large number of hosts connected to them. Class C is useful where there are many networks with a relatively small number of hosts connected to each network. Class B addressing gives a good compromise of networks and connected hosts.

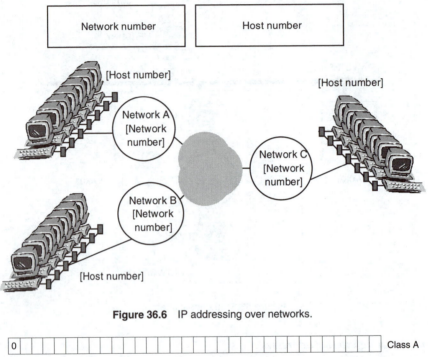

Figure 36.6   IP addressing over networks.

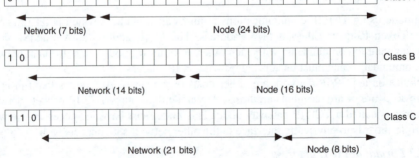

Figure 36.7   Type A, B and C IP address classes.

When selecting internet addresses for the network, the address can be specified simply with decimal numbers within a specific range. The standard DARPA IP addressing format is of the form:

```
W.X.Y.Z
```

where w, x, y and z represent 1 byte of the IP address. As decimal numbers they range from 0 to 255. The 4 bytes together represent both the network and host address.

Figure 36.7 gives the valid range of the different IP addresses is given and Table 36.2 defines the valid IP addresses. Thus for a class A type address there can be 127 networks and 16 711 680 (256×256×255) hosts. Class B can have 16 320 (64×255) networks and class C can have 2 088 960 (32×256×255) networks and 255 hosts.

Addresses above 223.255.254 are reserved, as are addresses with groups of zeros.

Table 36.2   Ranges of addresses for type A, B and C internet address.

Type	*Network portion*	*Host portion*
A	1 - 126	0.0.1 - 255.255.254
B	128.1 - 191.254	0.1 - 255.254
C	192.0.1 - 223.255.254	1 - 254

36.6.3 Creating IP addresses with subnet numbers

Besides selecting IP addresses of internets and host numbers, it is also possible to designate an intermediate number called a subnet number. Subnets extend the network field of the IP address beyond the limit defined by the type A, B, C scheme. They allow a hierarchy of internets within a network. For example, it is possible to have one network number for a network attached to the internet, and various subnet numbers for each subnet within the network. Figure 36.8 illustrated this.

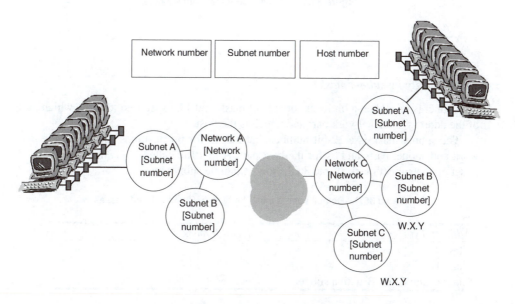

Figure 36.8   IP addresses with subnets.

For an address w.x.y.z, and for a type A, the address w specifies the network and x the subnet. For type B the y field specifies the subnet, as illustrated in Figure 36.9.

To connect to a global network a number is normally assigned by a central authority.

For the Internet network it is assigned by the Network Information Center (NIC). Typically, on the Internet an organization is assigned a type B network address. The first two fields of the address specify the organization network, the third specifies the subnet within the organization and the final specifies the host.

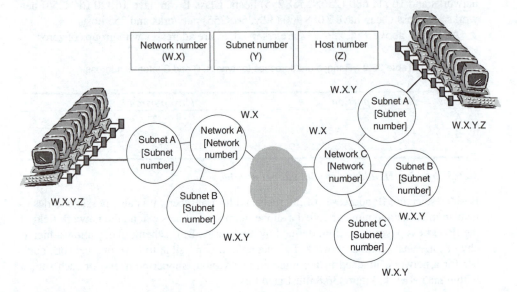

Figure 36.9   Internet addresses with subnets.

36.6.4 Specifying subnet masks

If a subnet is used then a bit mask, or subnet mask, must be specified to show which part of the address is the network part and which is the host.

The subnet mask is a 32-bit number that has 1s for bit positions specifying the network and subnet parts and 0s for the host part. A text file called *hosts* is normally used to set up the subnet mask. Table 36.3 shows example subnet masks.

Table 36.3   Default subnet mask for type A, B and C IP addresses.

Address Type	Default mask
Class A	255.0.0.0
Class B	255.255.0.0
Class C and Class B with a subnet	255.255.255.0

To set up the default mask the following line is added to the *hosts* file.

```
Hosts file
255.255.255.0  defaultmask
```

36.7 Domain name system

An IP address can be defined in the form www.xxx.yyy.zzz, where xxx, yyy, zzz and www are integer values in the range 0 to 255. On the Internet it is www.xxx.yyy that normally defines the subnet and www that defines the host. Such names may be difficult to remember. A better method is to use symbolic names rather than IP addresses.

Users and application programs can then use symbolic names rather than IP addresses. The directory network services on the Internet determines the IP address of the named destination user or application program. This has the advantage that users and application programs can move around the Internet and are not fixed to an IP address.

An analogy relates to the public telephone service. A telephone directory contains a list of subscribers and their associated telephone number. If someone looks for a telephone number, first the user name is looked up and their associated telephone number found. The telephone directory listing thus maps a user name (symbolic name) to an actual telephone number (the actual address).

Table 36.4 lists some Internet domain assignments for World Wide Web (WWW) servers. Note that domain assignments are not fixed and can change their corresponding IP addresses, if required. The binding between the symbolic name and its address can thus change at any time.

Table 36.4   Internet domain assignments for web servers.

Web server	Internet domain names	Internet IP address
NEC	web.nec.com	143.101.112.6
Sony	www.sony.com	198.83.178.11
Intel	www.intel.com	134.134.214.1
IEEE	www.ieee.com	140.98.1.1
University of Bath	www.bath.ac.uk	136.38.32.1
University of Edinburgh	www.ed.ac.uk	129.218.128.43
IEE	www.iee.org.uk	193.130.181.10
University of Manchester	www.man.ac.uk	130.88.203.16

36.8 Internet naming structure

The Internet naming structure uses labels separated by periods (full stops); an example is eece.napier.ac.uk. It uses a hierarchical structure where organizations are grouped into primary domain names. These are com (for commercial organizations), edu (for educational organizations), gov (for government organizations), mil (for military organizations), net (Internet network support centres) or org (other organizations). The primary domain name may also define the country in which the host is located, such as uk (United Kingdom), fr (France), and so on. All hosts on the Internet must be registered to one of these primary domain names.

The labels after the primary field describe the subnets within the network. For example in the address eece.napier.ac.uk, the ac label relates to an academic institution within the uk, napier to the name of the institution and eece the subnet with that organization. Figure 36.10 gives an example structure.

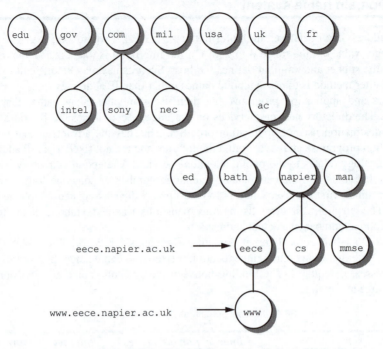

Figure 36.10   Example domain naming.

36.9 Domain name server

Each institution on the Internet has a host that runs a process called the domain name server (DNS). The DNS maintains a database called the directory information base (DIB) which contains directory information for that institution. On adding a new host, the system manager adds its name and its IP address. After this it can then access the Internet.

36.9.1 DNS program

The DNS program is typically run on a Lynx-based PC with a program called `named` (located in `/usr/sbin`) with an information file of `named.boot`. To run the program the following is used:

```
/usr/bin/named -b /usr/local/adm/named/named.boot
```

The following shows that the DNS program is currently running.

```
$ ps -ax
  PID TTY STAT   TIME COMMAND
  295 con S     0:00 bootpd
   35 con S     0:00 /usr/sbin/lpd
  272 con S     0:00 /usr/sbin/named -b /usr/local/adm/named/named.boot
  264 p 1 S     0:01 bash
  306 pp0 R     0:00 ps -ax
```

In this case the data file `named.boot` is located in the `/usr/local/adm/named` directory.

A sample `named.boot` file is:

```
/usr/local/adm/named - soabasefile
            eece.napier.ac.uk -main record of computer names
            net/net144   -reverse look-up database
            net/net145        "         "
            net/net146        "         "
            net/net147        "         "
            net/net150        "         "
            net/net151        "         "
```

This file specifies that the reverse look-up information on computers on the subnets 144, 145, 146, 147, 150 and 150 is contained in the `net144`, `net145`, `net146`, `net147`, `net150` and `net151` files, respectively. These are stored in the `net` subdirectory. The main file which contains the DNS information is, in this case, `eece.napier.ac.uk`.

Whenever a new computer is added onto a network, in this case, the `eece.napier.ac.uk` file and the `net/net1**` (where ** is the relevant subnet name) are updated to reflect the changes. Finally, the serial number at the top of these data files is updated to reflect the current date, such as 19970321 (for 21st March 1997).

The DNS program can then be tested using `nslookup`. For example:

```
$ nslookup
Default Server: ees99.eece.napier.ac.uk
Address:  146.176.151.99

> src.doc.ic.ac.uk
Server:  ees99.eece.napier.ac.uk
Address:  146.176.151.99

Non-authoritative answer:
Name:     swallow.doc.ic.ac.uk
Address:  193.63.255.4
Aliases:  src.doc.ic.ac.uk
```

36.10 Bootp protocol

The bootp protocol allocates IP addresses to computers based on a table of network card MAC addresses. When a computer is first booted, the bootp server interrogates its MAC address and then looks up the bootp table for its entry. The server then grants the corresponding IP address to the computer. The computer then uses it for connections. This is one method of limiting access to the Internet.

36.10.1 Bootp program

The bootp program is typically run on a Lynx-based PC with the `bootp` program. The following shows that the `bootp` program is currently running on a computer:

```
$ ps -ax
  PID TTY STAT   TIME COMMAND
    1 con S    0:06 init
   31 con S    0:01 /usr/sbin/inetd
14142 con S    0:00 bootpd -d 1
   35 con S    0:00 /usr/sbin/lpd
   49 p 3 S    0:00 /sbin/agetty 38400 tty3
14155 pp0 R    0:00 ps -ax
10762 con S    0:18 /usr/sbin/named -b /usr/local/adm/named/named.boot
```

For the bootp system to operate then it must use a table to reconciles the MAC addresses of the card to an IP address. In the previous example this table is contained in the bootptab file which is located in the /etc directory. The following file gives an example bootptab:

🗎 Contents of bootptab file

```
# /etc/bootptab: database for bootp server
# Blank lines and lines beginning with '#' are ignored.
#
# Legend:
#
#       first field -- hostname
#               (may be full domain name and probably should be)
#
#       hd -- home directory
#       bf -- bootfile
#       cs -- cookie servers
#       ds -- domain name servers
#       gw -- gateways
#       ha -- hardware address
#       ht -- hardware type
#       im -- impress servers
#       ip -- host IP address
#       lg -- log servers
#       lp -- LPR servers
#       ns -- IEN-116 name servers
#       rl -- resource location protocol servers
#       sm -- subnet mask
#       tc -- template host (points to similar host entry)
#       to -- time offset (seconds)
#       ts -- time servers
#
#hostname:ht=1:ha=ether_addr_in_hex:ip=ip_addr_in_dec:tc=allhost:
.default150:\
        :hd=/tmp:bf=null:\
        :ds=146.176.151.99 146.176.150.62 146.176.1.5:\
        :sm=255.255.255.0:gw=146.176.150.253:\
        :hn:vm=auto:to=0:
.default151:\
        :hd=/tmp:bf=null:\
        :ds=146.176.151.99 146.176.150.62 146.176.1.5:\
        :sm=255.255.255.0:gw=146.176.151.254:\
        :hn:vm=auto:to=0:
pc345:   ht=ethernet:   ha=0080C8226BE2:  ip=146.176.150.2:  tc=.default150:
pc307:   ht=ethernet:   ha=0080C822CD4E:  ip=146.176.150.3:  tc=.default150:
pc320:   ht=ethernet:   ha=0080C823114C:  ip=146.176.150.4:  tc=.default150:
pc331:   ht=ethernet:   ha=0080C823124B:  ip=146.176.150.5:  tc=.default150:
:        :
pc460:   ht=ethernet:   ha=0000E8C7BB63:  ip=146.176.151.142: tc=.default151:
pc414:   ht=ethernet:   ha=0080C8246A84:  ip=146.176.151.143: tc=.default151:
pc405:   ht=ethernet:   ha=0080C82382EE:  ip=146.176.151.145: tc=.default151:
```

The format of the file is:

```
#hostname:ht=1:ha=ether_addr_in_hex:ip=ip_addr_in_dec:tc=allhost:
```

where `hostname` is the hostname, the value defined after `ha=` is the Ethernet MAC address, the value after `ip=` is the IP address and the name after the `tc=` field defines the host information script. For example:

```
pc345:    ht=ethernet:    ha=0080C8226BE2:  ip=146.176.150.2: tc=.default150:
```

defines the hostname of `pc345`, indicates it is on an Ethernet network, and shows its IP address is `146.176.150.2`. The MAC address of the computer is `00:80:C8: 22:6B:E2` and it is defined by the script `.default150`. This file defines a subnet of 255.255.255.0 and has associated DNS of

```
146.176.151.99 146.176.150.62 146.176.1.5
```

and uses the gateway at:

```
146.176.150.253
```

36.11 Example network

A university network is shown in Figure 36.11. The connection to the outside global Internet is via the Janet gateway node and its IP address is `146.176.1.3`. Three subnets, `146.176.160`, `146.176.129` and `146.176.151`, connect the gateway to departmental bridges. The Computer Studies bridge address is `146.176.160.1` and the Electrical Department bridge has an address `146.176.151.254`.

The Electrical Department bridge links, through other bridges, to the subnets `146.176.144`, `146.176.145`, `146.176.147`, `146.176.150` and `146.176.151`.

The topology of the Electrical Department network is shown in Figure 36.12. The main bridge into the department connects to two Ethernet networks of PCs (subnets `146.176.150` and `146.176.151`) and to another bridge (`Bridge 1`). `Bridge 1` connects to the subnet `146.176.144`. Subnet `146.176.144` connects to workstations and X-terminals. It also connects to the gateway `Moon` that links the Token Ring subnet `146.176.145` with the Ethernet subnet `146.176.144`. The gateway `Oberon`, on the `146.176.145` subnet, connects to an Ethernet link `146.176.146`. This then connects to the gateway `Dione` that is also connected to the Token Ring subnet `146.176.147`.

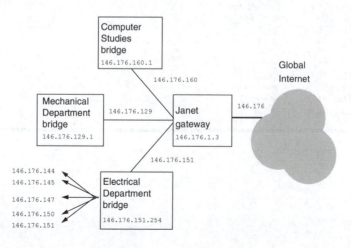

Figure 36.11   A university network.

Each node on the network is assigned an IP address. The *hosts* file for the setup in Figure 36.12 is shown next. For example, the IP address of Mimas is 146.176.145.21 and for miranda it is 146.176.144.14. Notice that the gateway nodes: Oberon, Moon and Dione all have two IP addresses.

🖹 Contents of host file

```
146.176.1.3          janet
146.176.144.10       hp
146.176.145.21       mimas
146.176.144.11       mwave
146.176.144.13       vax
146.176.144.14       miranda
146.176.144.20       triton
146.176.146.23       oberon
146.176.145.23       oberon
146.176.145.24       moon
146.176.144.24       moon
146.176.147.25       uranus
146.176.146.30       dione
146.176.147.30       dione
146.176.147.31       saturn
146.176.147.32       mercury
146.176.147.33       earth
146.176.147.34       deimos
146.176.147.35       ariel
146.176.147.36       neptune
146.176.147.37       phobos
146.176.147.39       io
146.176.147.40       titan
146.176.147.41       venus
146.176.147.42       pluto
146.176.147.43       mars
146.176.147.44       rhea
146.176.147.22       jupiter
146.176.144.54       leda
146.176.144.55       castor
146.176.144.56       pollux
146.176.144.57       rigel
146.176.144.58       spica
146.176.151.254      cubridge
146.176.151.99       bridge_1
146.176.151.98       pc2
146.176.151.97       pc3
              :::::
146.176.151.71       pc29
146.176.151.70       pc30
146.176.151.99       ees99
146.176.150.61       eepc01
146.176.150.62       eepc02
255.255.255.0        defaultmask
```

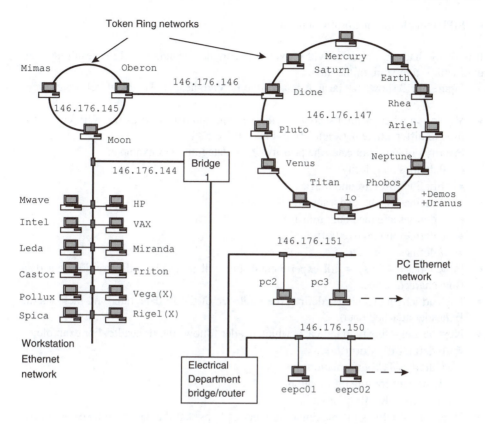

Figure 36.12   Network topology for the Department network.

36.12 IP Ver6

TCP and IP are extremely important protocols as they allow hosts to communicate over the Internet in a reliable way. TCP provides a connection between two hosts and supports error handling. This section discusses TCP in more detail and shows how a connection is established then maintained. An important concept of TCP/IP communications is the usage of ports and sockets. A port identifies the process type (such as FTP, TELNET, and so on) and the socket identifies a unique connection number. In this way TCP/IP can support multiple simultaneous connections of applications over a network.

The IP header (IP Ver4) is added to higher-level data. This header contains a 32-bit IP address of the destination node. Unfortunately, the standard 32-bit IP address is not large enough to support the growth in nodes connecting to the Internet. Thus a new standard, IP Version 6 (IP Ver6), has been developed to support a 128-bit address, as well as additional enhancements, such as authentication and encryption of data.

The main techniques being investigated are:

- TUBA (TCP and UDP with bigger addresses).
- CATNIP (common architecture for the Internet).

- SIPP (simple Internet protocol plus).

It is likely that none of these will provide the complete standard and the resulting standard will be a mixture of the three.

Figure 36.13 shows the basic format of the IP Ver6 header. The main fields are:

- Version number (4 bits) – contains the version number, such as 6 for IP Ver6. It is used to differentiate between IP Ver4 and IP Ver6.
- Priority (4 bits) – indicates the priority of the datagram. For example:
  - 0 defines no priority.
  - 1 defines background traffic.
  - 2 defines unattended transfer.
  - 4 defines attended bulk transfer.
  - 6 defines interactive traffic.
  - 7 defines control traffic.
- Flow label (24 bits) – still experimental, but will be used to identify different data flow characteristics.
- Payload length (16 bits) – defines the total size of the IP datagram (and includes the IP header attached data).
- Next header – this field indicates which header follows the IP header. For example:
  - 0 defines IP information.
  - 6 defines TCP information.
  - 43 defines routing information.
  - 58 defines ICMP information.
- Hop limit – defines the maximum number of hops that the datagram takes as it traverses the network. Each router decrements the hop limit by 1; when it reaches 0 it is deleted.

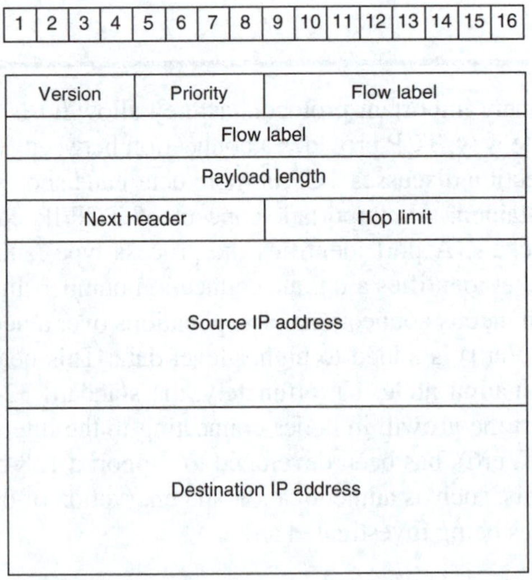

1	2	3	4	5	6	7	8	9	10	11	12	13	14	15	16

Version	Priority	Flow label
Flow label		
Payload length		
Next header		Hop limit

Source IP address

Destination IP address

Figure 36.13   IP Ver6 header format.

- IP addresses (128 bits) – defines IP address. There will be three main groups of IP addresses: unicast, multicast and anycast. A unicast address identifies a particular host, a multicast address enables the hosts with a particular group to receive the same packet, and the anycast address will be addressed to a number of interfaces on a single multicast address.

36.13 Transmission control protocol

In the OSI model, TCP fits into the transport layer and IP fits into the network layer. TCP thus sits above IP, which means that the IP header is added onto the higher-level information (such as transport, session, presentation and application). The main functions of TCP are to provide a robust and reliable transport protocol. It is characterised as a reliable, connection-oriented, acknowledged and data stream-oriented server. IP, itself, does not support the connection of two nodes, whereas TCP does. With TCP, a connection is initially established and is then maintained for the length of the transmission.

The TCP information contains simple acknowledgement messages and a set of sequential numbers. It also supports multiple simultaneous connections using destination and source port numbers, and manages them for both transmission and reception. As with IP, it supports data fragmentation and reassembly, and data multiplexing/demultiplexing.

The setup and operation of TCP is as follows:

1. When a host wishes to make a connection, TCP sends out a request message to the destination machine that contains a unique number, called a socket number and a port number. The port number has a value which is associated with the application (for example a TELNET connection has the port number 23 and an FTP connection has the port number 21). The message is then passed to the IP layer, which assembles a datagram for transmission to the destination.
2. When the destination host receives the connection request, it returns a message containing its own unique socket number and a port number. The socket number and port number thus identify the virtual connection between the two hosts.
3. After the connection has been made the data can flow between the two hosts (called a data stream).

After TCP receives the stream of data, it assembles the data into packets, called TCP segments. After the segment has been constructed, TCP adds a header (called the protocol data unit) to the front of the segment. This header contains information such as a checksum, port number, destination and source socket numbers, socket number of both machines and segment sequence numbers. The TCP layer then sends the packaged segment down to the IP layer, which encapsulates it and sends it over the network as a datagram.

36.13.1 Ports and sockets

As previously mentioned, TCP adds a port number and socket number for each host. The port number identifies the required service, whereas the socket number is a unique number for that connection. Thus, a node can have several TELNET connections with the same port number but each connection will have a different socket number. A port number can be any value but there is a standard convention that most systems adopt. Table

36.5 defines some of the most common values. Standard applications normally use port values from 0 to 255, while unspecified applications can use values above 255.

Table 36.5   Typical TCP port numbers.

Port	Process name	Notes
20	FTP-DATA	File Transfer Protocol - data
21	FTP	File Transfer Protocol - control
23	TELNET	Telnet
25	SMTP	Simple Mail Transfer Protocol
49	LOGIN	Login Protocol
53	DOMAIN	Domain Name Server
79	FINGER	Finger
161	SNMP	SNMP

36.13.2 TCP header format

The sender's TCP layer communicates with the receiver's TCP layer using the TCP protocol data unit. It defines parameters such as the source port, destination port, and so on, and is illustrated in Figure 36.14. The fields are:

- Source and destination port number – which are 16-bit values that identify the local port number (source number and destination port number or destination port).
- Sequence number – which identifies the current sequence number of the data segment. This allows the receiver to keep track of the data segments received. Any segments that are missing can be easily identified.
- Data offset – which is a 32-bit value that identifies the start of the data.
- Flags – the flag field is defined as UAPRSF, where U is the urgent flag, A the acknowledgement flag, P the push function, R the reset flag, S the sequence synchronize flag and F the end-of-transmission flag.

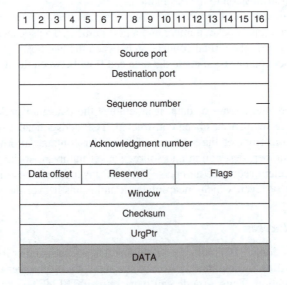

Figure 36.14   TCP header format.

- Windows – which is a 16-bit value and gives the number of data blocks that the receiving host can accept at a time.
- Checksum – which is a 16-bit checksum for the data and header.
- UrgPtr – which is the urgent pointer and is used to identify an important area of data (most systems do not support this facility).

36.14 TCP/IP commands

There are several standard programs available over TCP/IP connections. The example sessions is this section relate to the network outlined in Figure 36.12. These applications may include:

- FTP (File Transfer Protocol) – transfers file between computers.
- HTTP (Hypertext Transfer Protocol) – which is the protocol used in the World Wide Web (WWW) and can be used for client–server applications involving hypertext.
- MIME (Multipurpose Internet Mail Extension) – gives enhanced electronic mail facilities over TCP/IP.
- SMTP (Simple Mail Management Protocol) – gives simple electronic mail facilities.
- TELNET – allows remote login using TCP/IP.
- PING – determines if a node is responding to TCP/IP communications.

36.14.1 ping

The ping program (Packet Internet Gopher) determines whether a node is responding to TCP/IP communication. It is typically used to trace problems in networks and uses the Internet Control Message Protocol (ICMP) to send a response request from the target node. Sample run 36.1 shows that miranda is active and ariel isn't.

⌨ Sample run 36.1: Using PING command

```
C:\WINDOWS>ping miranda
miranda (146.176.144.14) is alive
C:\WINDOWS>ping ariel
no reply from ariel (146.176.147.35)
```

The ping program can also be used to determine the delay between one host and another, and also if there are any IP packet losses. In Sample run 36.2 the local host is pc419.eece.napier.ac.uk (which is on the 146.176.151 segment); the host miranda is tested (which is on the 146.176.144 segment). It can be seen that, on average, the delay is only 1 ms and there is no loss of packets.

⌨ Sample run 36.2: Using PING command

```
225 % ping miranda
PING miranda.eece.napier.ac.uk: 64 byte packets
64 bytes from 146.176.144.14: icmp_seq=0. time=1. ms
64 bytes from 146.176.144.14: icmp_seq=1. time=1. ms
64 bytes from 146.176.144.14: icmp_seq=2. time=1. ms
3 packets transmitted, 3 packets received, 0% packet loss
round-trip (ms)  min/avg/max = 1/1/1
```

In Sample run 36.3 the destination node (www.napier.ac.uk) is located within the same building but is on a different IP segment (147.176.2). It is also routed through a bridge. It can be seen that the packet delay has increased to between 9 and 10 ms. Again, there is no packet loss.

🖥 Sample run 36.3: Using PING command

```
226 % ping www.napier.ac.uk
PING central.napier.ac.uk: 64 byte packets
64 bytes from 146.176.2.3: icmp_seq=0. time=9. ms
64 bytes from 146.176.2.3: icmp_seq=1. time=9. ms
64 bytes from 146.176.2.3: icmp_seq=2. time=10. ms
3 packets transmitted, 3 packets received, 0% packet loss
round-trip (ms)  min/avg/max = 9/9/10
```

Sample run 36.4 shows a connection between Edinburgh and Bath in the UK (www.bath.ac.uk has an IP address of 138.38.32.5). This is a distance of approximately 500 miles and it can be seen that the delay is now between 30 and 49 ms. This time there is 25% packet loss.

🖥 Sample run 36.4: Using PING command

```
222 % ping www.bath.ac.uk
PING jess.bath.ac.uk: 64 byte packets
64 bytes from 138.38.32.5: icmp_seq=0. time=49. ms
64 bytes from 138.38.32.5: icmp_seq=2. time=35. ms
64 bytes from 138.38.32.5: icmp_seq=3. time=30. ms
4 packets transmitted, 3 packets received, 25% packet loss
round-trip (ms)  min/avg/max = 30/38/49
```

Finally, in Sample run 36.5 the ping program tests a link between Edinburgh, UK, and a WWW server in the USA (home.microsoft.com , which has the IP address of 207.68.137.51). It can be seen that in this case, the delay is between 447 and 468 ms, and the loss is 60%.

A similar utility program to ping is spray which uses Remote Procedure Call (RPC) to send a continuous stream of ICMP messages. It is useful when testing a network connection for its burst characteristics. This differs from ping, which waits for a predetermined amount of time between messages.

🖥 Sample run 36.5: Ping command with packet loss

```
224 % ping home.microsoft.com
PING home.microsoft.com: 64 byte packets
64 bytes from 207.68.137.51: icmp_seq=2. time=447. ms
64 bytes from 207.68.137.51: icmp_seq=3. time=468. ms
----home.microsoft.com PING Statistics----
5 packets transmitted, 2 packets received, 60% packet loss
```

36.14.2 ftp (file transfer protocol)

The ftp program uses the TCP/IP protocol to transfer files to and from remote nodes. If necessary, it reads the *hosts* file to determine the IP address. Once the user has logged into the remote node, the commands that can be used are similar to DOS commands such as cd (change directory), dir (list directory), open (open node), close (close node), pwd (present working directory). The `get` command copies a file from the remote node and the `put` command copies it to the remote node.

The type of file to be transferred must also be specified. This file can be ASCII text (the command `ascii`) or binary (the command `binary`).

36.14.3 telnet

The `telnet` program uses TCP/IP to remotely log in to a remote node.

36.14.4 nslookup

The `nslookup` program interrogates the local `hosts` file or a DNS server to determine the IP address of an Internet node. If it cannot find it in the local file then it communicates with gateways outside its own network to see if they know the address. Sample run 36.6 shows that the IP address of `www.intel.com` is `134.134.214.1`.

🖳 Sample run 36.6: Example of nslookup

```
C:\> nslookup
Default Server:  ees99.eece.napier.ac.uk
Address:  146.176.151.99
> www.intel.com
Server:  ees99.eece.napier.ac.uk
Address:  146.176.151.99
Name:    web.jf.intel.com
Address:  134.134.214.1
Aliases:  www.intel.com
230 % nslookup home.microsoft.com
Non-authoritative answer:
Name:    home.microsoft.com
Addresses:  207.68.137.69, 207.68.156.11, 207.68.156.14, 207.68.156.56
207.68.137.48, 207.68.137.51
```

36.14.5 netstat (network statistics)

On a UNIX system the command `netstat` can be used to determine the status of the network. The `-r` option shown in Sample run 36.7 shows that this node uses `moon` as a gateway to another network.

🖳 Sample run 36.7: Using Unix netstat command

```
[54:miranda :/net/castor_win/local_user/bill_b ] % netstat -r
```

Destination	Gateway	Flags	Refs	Use	Interface
localhost	localhost	UH	0	27306	lo0
default	moon	UG	0	1453856	lan0
146.176.144	miranda	U	8	6080432	lan0
146.176.1	146.176.144.252	UGD	0	51	lan0
146.176.151	146.176.144.252	UGD	11	5491	lan0

36.14.6 traceroute

The `traceroute` program traces the route of an IP packet through the Internet. It uses the IP protocol time-to-live field and attempts to get an ICMP TIME_EXCEEDED response from each gateway along the path to a defined host. The default probe datagram length is 38 bytes (although the sample runs use 40 byte packets by default). Sample run 36.8 shows an example of `traceroute` from a PC (`pc419.eece.napier.ac.uk`). It can be seen that initially it goes through a bridge (`pcbridge.eece.napier.ac.uk`) and then to the destination (`miranda.eece.napier.ac.uk`).

🖥 Sample run 36.8: Example traceroute

```
www:~/www$ traceroute miranda
traceroute to miranda.eece.napier.ac.uk (146.176.144.14), 30 hops max,
      40 byte packets
1   pcbridge.eece.napier.ac.uk (146.176.151.252)   2.684 ms   1.762 ms
                                                    1.725 ms
2   miranda.eece.napier.ac.uk (146.176.144.14)   2.451 ms   2.554 ms
                                                    2.357 ms
```

Sample run 36.9 shows the route from a PC (pc419.eece.napier.ac.uk) to a destination node (www.bath.ac.uk). Initially, from the originator, the route goes through a gateway (146.176.151.254) and then goes through a routing switch (146.176.1.27) and onto EaStMAN ring via 146.176.3.1. The route then goes round the EaStMAN to a gateway at the University of Edinburgh (smds-gw.ed.ja.net). It is then routed onto the SuperJanet network and reaches a gateway at the University of Bath (smds-gw.bath.ja.net). It then goes to another gateway (jips-gw.bath.ac.uk) and finally to its destination (jess.bath.ac.uk). Figure 36.15 shows the route the packet takes.

Note that gateways 4 and 8 hops away either don't send ICMP 'time exceeded' messages or send them with time-to-live values that are too small to be returned to the originator.

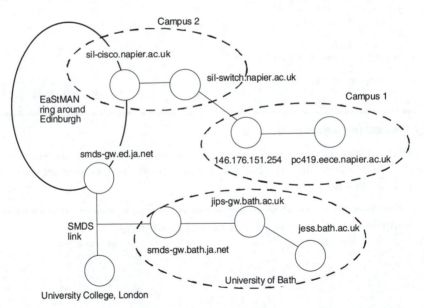

Figure 36.15   Route between local host and the University of Bath.

Sample run 36.10 shows an example route from a local host at Napier University, UK, to the USA. As before, it goes through the local gateway (146.176.151.254) and then goes through three other gateways to get onto the SMDS SuperJANET connection. The data packet then travels down this connection to University College, London (gw5.ulcc.ja.net). It then goes onto high speed connects to the USA and arrives at a US gateway (mcinet-2.sprintnap.net). Next it travels to core2-hssi2-0.WestOrange.mci.net before reaching the Microsoft Corporation gateway in Seattle (`microsoft.Seattle.mci.net`). It finally finds it way to the destination (`207.68.145.53`). The total journey time is just less than half-a-second.

🖳 Sample run 36.9: Example traceroute

```
www:~/www$ traceroute www.bath.ac.uk
traceroute to jess.bath.ac.uk (138.38.32.5), 30 hops max, 40 byte
packets
1   146.176.151.254 (146.176.151.254)  2.806 ms  2.76 ms  2.491 ms
2   sil-switch.napier.ac.uk (146.176.1.27)  19.315 ms  11.29 ms  6.285 ms
3   sil-cisco.napier.ac.uk (146.176.3.1)  6.427 ms  8.407 ms  8.872 ms
4   * * *
5   smds-gw.ed.ja.net (193.63.106.129)  8.98 ms  30.308 ms  398.623 ms
6   smds-gw.bath.ja.net (193.63.203.68)  39.104 ms  46.833 ms  38.036 ms
7   jips-gw.bath.ac.uk (146.97.104.2)  32.908 ms  41.336 ms  42.429 ms
8   * * *
9   jess.bath.ac.uk (138.38.32.5)  41.045 ms *  41.93 ms
```

🖳 Sample run 36.10: Example traceroute

```
> traceroute home.microsoft.com
 1   146.176.151.254 (146.176.151.254)  2.931 ms  2.68 ms  2.658 ms
 2   sil-switch.napier.ac.uk (146.176.1.27)  6.216 ms  8.818 ms  5.885 ms
 3   sil-cisco.napier.ac.uk (146.176.3.1)  6.502 ms  6.638 ms  10.218 ms
 4   * * *
 5   smds-gw.ed.ja.net (193.63.106.129)  18.367 ms  9.242 ms  15.145 ms
 6   smds-gw.ulcc.ja.net (193.63.203.33)  42.644 ms  36.794 ms  34.555 ms
 7   gw5.ulcc.ja.net (128.86.1.80)  31.906 ms  30.053 ms  39.151 ms
 8   icm-london-1.icp.net (193.63.175.53)  29.368 ms  25.42 ms  31.347 ms
 9   198.67.131.193 (198.67.131.193)  119.195 ms  120.482 ms  67.479 ms
10   icm-pen-1-H2/0-T3.icp.net (198.67.131.25)  115.314 ms  126.152 ms
149.982 ms
11   icm-pen-10-P4/0-OC3C.icp.net (198.67.142.69)  139.27 ms  197.953 ms
195.722 ms
12   mcinet-2.sprintnap.net (192.157.69.48)  199.267 ms  267.446 ms
287.834 ms
13   core2-hssi2-0.WestOrange.mci.net (204.70.1.49)  216.006 ms  688.139
ms  228.968 ms
14   microsoft.Seattle.mci.net (166.48.209.250)  310.447 ms  282.882 ms
313.619 ms
15   * microsoft.Seattle.mci.net (166.48.209.250)  324.797 ms  309.518 ms
16   * 207.68.145.53 (207.68.145.53)  435.195 ms *
```

36.14.7 arp

The `arp` program displays the IP to Ethernet MAC address mapping. It can also be used to delete or manually change any included address table entries. Within a network, a router forwards data packets depending on the destination IP address of the packet. Each connection must also specify a MAC address to transport the packet over the network, thus the router must maintain a list of MAC addresses. The `arp` protocol thus maintains this mapping. Addresses within this table are added on an as-needed basis. When a MAC address is required an `arp` message is sent to the node with an `arp` REQUEST packet which contains the IP address of the requested node. It will then reply with an `arp` RESPONSE packet which contains its MAC address and its IP address.

36.15 Exercises

36.15.1 Determine the IP addresses, and their type (i.e. class A, B or C), of the following 32-bit addresses:

(i)   10001100.01110001.00000001.00001001
(ii)   01000000.01111101.01000001.11101001
(iii)   10101110.01110001.00011101.00111001

36.15.2 Explain how an IP address is classified.

36.15.3 Explain the functions of the IP protocol.

36.15.4 Explain the function of the `time-to-live` field in an IP packet.

36.15.5 Explain the function of ICMP.

36.15.6 If possible, determine some IP addresses and their corresponding Internet domain names.

36.15.7 Determine the countries which use the following primary domain names:

(a) de   (b) nl   (c) it   (d) se   (e) dk   (f) sg
(g) ca   (h) ch   (i) tr   (j) jp   (k) au

Determine some other domain names.

36.15.8 Explain why gateway nodes require two IP addresses.

36.15.9 Explain the operation of the DNS and Bootp programs.

36.15.10 For a known TCP/IP network determine the names of the nodes and their Internet addresses.

36.15.11 For a known TCP/IP network determine how the DNS is implemented and how IP addresses are granted.

37 WinSock Programming

37.1 Introduction

The Windows Sockets specification describes a common interface for networked Windows programs. WinSock uses TCP/IP communications and provides for binary and source code compatibility for different network types.

The Windows Sockets API (WinSock API) is a library of functions that implement the socket interface by the Berkley Software Distribution of UNIX. WinSock augments the Berkley socket implementation by adding Windows-specific extensions to support the message-driven nature of the Windows system.

37.2 Windows Sockets

The main WinSock API calls are:

`socket()`.	Creates a socket.
`accept()`.	Accepts a connection on a socket.
`connect()`.	Establishes a connection to a peer.
`bind()`.	Associates a local address with a socket.
`listen()`.	Establishes a socket to listen for incoming connection.
`send()`.	Sends data on a connected socket.
`recv()`.	Receives data from a socket.
`shutdown()`.	Disables send or receive operations on a socket.
`closesocket()`.	Closes a socket.

Figure 37.1 shows the operation of a connection of a client to a server. The server is defined as the computer which waits for a connection, the client is the computer which initially makes contact with the server.

On the server the computer initially creates a socket with the `socket()` function, and this is bound to a name with the `bind()` function. After this the server listens for a connection with the `listen()` function. When the client calls the `connection()` function the server then accepts the connection with `accept()`. After this the server and client can send and receive data with the `send()` or `recv()` functions. When the data transfer is complete the `closesocket()` is used to close the socket.

37.2.1 socket()

The `socket()` function creates a socket. Its syntax is:

```
SOCKET socket ( int af, int type, int protocol)
```

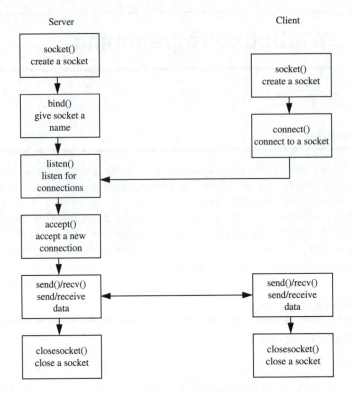

Figure 37.1 WinSock connection.

where

af   A value of `PF_INET` specifies the ARPA Internet address format specification.

type   Socket specification, which is either `SOCK_STREAM` or `SOCK_DGRAM`. The `SOCK_STREAM` uses TCP and provides a sequenced, reliable, two-way, connection-based stream. `SOCK_DGRAM` uses UDP and provides for connectionless datagrams. This type of connection is not recommended.

protocol   Defines the protocol to be used with the socket. If it is zero then the caller does not wish to specify a protocol.

If the `socket` function succeeds then the return value is a descriptor referencing the new socket. Otherwise, it returns `SOCKET_ERROR`, and the specific error code can be tested with `WSAGetLastError`. An example creation of a socket is given next:

```
SOCKET s;

    s=socket(PF_INET,SOCK_STREAM,0);
    if (s == INVALID_SOCKET)
    {
        cout << "Socket error"
    }
```

37.2.2 bind()

The `bind()` function associates a local address with a socket. It is before calls to the `connect` or `listen` functions. When a socket is created with `socket`, it exists in a name space (address family), but it has no name assigned. The `bind` function gives the socket a local association (host address/port number). Its syntax is:

```
int bind(SOCKET s, const struct sockaddr FAR * addr, int namelen);
```

where

s	A descriptor identifying an unbound socket.
namelen	The length of the *addr*.
addr	The address to assign to the socket. The `sockaddr` structure is defined as follows:

```
struct sockaddr
{
    u_short    sa_family;
    char       sa_data[14];
};
```

In the Internet address family, the `sockadd_in` structure is used by Windows Sockets to specify a local or remote endpoint address to which to connect a socket. This is the form of the `sockaddr` structure specific to the Internet address family and can be cast to `sockaddr`. This structure can be filled with the `sockaddr_in` structure which has the following form:

```
struct SOCKADDR_IN
{
    short              sin_family;
    unsigned short     sin_port;
    struct   in_addr sin_addr;
    char               sin_zero[8];
}
```

where

`sin_family`	must be set to `AF_INET`.
`sin_port`	IP port.
`sin_addr`	IP address.
`sin_zero`	Padding to make structure the same size as `sockaddr`.

If an application does not care what address is assigned to it, it may specify an Internet address equal to `INADDR_ANY`, a port equal to 0, or both. An Internet address equal to `INADDR_ANY` causes any appropriate network interface be used. A port value of 0 causes the Windows Sockets implementation to assign a unique port to the application with a value between 1024 and 5000.

If no error occurs then it returns a zero value. Otherwise, it returns `INVALID_SOCKET`, and the specific error code can be tested with `WSAGetLastError`.

If an application needs to bind to an arbitrary port outside of the range 1024 to 5000 then the following outline code can be used:

```
#include <windows.h>
#include <winsock.h>

int main(void)
{
SOCKADDR_IN   sin;
SOCKET        s;
    s = socket(AF_INET,SOCK_STREAM,0);

    if (s == INVALID_SOCKET)
    {
       // Socket failed
    }

    sin.sin_family = AF_INET;
    sin.sin_addr.s_addr = 0;

    sin.sin_port = htons(100); // port=100

    if (bind(s, (LPSOCKADDR)&sin, sizeof (sin)) == 0)
    {
     // Bind failed
    }
    return(0);
}
```

The Windows Sockets `htons` function converts an unsigned short (`u_short`) from host byte order to network byte order.

37.2.3 connect()

The `connect()` function establishes a connection with a peer. If the specified socket is unbound then unique values are assigned to the local association by the system and the socket is marked as bound. Its syntax is:

```
int connect (SOCKET s, const struct sockaddr FAR * name,
             int namelen)
```

where

s	Descriptor identifying an unconnected socket.
name	Name of the peer to which the socket is to be connected.
namelen	Name length.

If no error occurs then it returns a zero value. Otherwise, it returns `SOCKET_ERROR`, and the specific error code can be tested with `WSAGetLastError`.

37.2.4 listen()

The `listen()` function establishes a socket which listens for an incoming connection. The sequence to create and accept a socket is:

- `socket()`. Creates a socket.
- `listen()`. This creates a queue for incoming connections and is typically used by a

server that can have more than one connection at a time.

- `accept()`. These connections are then accepted with accept.

The syntax of `listen()` is:

```
int listen (SOCKET s, int backlog)
```

where

s   Describes a bound, unconnected socket.

backlog   Defines the queue size for the maximum number of pending connections
            may grow (typically a maximum of 5).

If no error occurs then it returns a zero value. Otherwise, it returns `SOCKET_ERROR`, and
the specific error code can be tested with `WSAGetLastError`.

```c
#include <windows.h>
#include <winsock.h>

int main(void)
{

SOCKADDR_IN    sin;
SOCKET         s;

     s = socket(AF_INET,SOCK_STREAM,0);
     if (s == INVALID_SOCKET)
     {
        // Socket failed
     }

     sin.sin_family = AF_INET;
     sin.sin_addr.s_addr = 0;

     sin.sin_port = htons(100); // port=100

     if (bind(s, (struct sockaddr FAR *)&sin, sizeof (sin)) == SOCKET_ERROR)
     {
       // Bind failed
   }

     if (listen(s,4)==SOCKET_ERROR)
     {
        // Listen failed
     }
     return(0);
}
```

37.2.5 accept()

The `accept()` function accepts a connection on a socket. It extracts any pending connections from the queue and creates a new socket with the same properties as the specified socket. Finally, it returns a handle to the new socket. Its syntax is:

```
SOCKET accept(SOCKET s, struct sockaddr FAR *addr, int FAR *addrlen );
```

where

s	Descriptor identifying a socket that is in listen mode.
addr	Pointer to a buffer that receives the address of the connecting entity, as known to the communications layer.
addrlen	Pointer to an integer which contains the length of the address *addr*.

If no error occurs then it returns a zero value. Otherwise, it returns INVALID_SOCKET, and the specific error code can be tested with WSAGetLastError.

```c
#include <windows.h>
#include <winsock.h>

int main(void)
{

SOCKADDR_IN    sin;
SOCKET         s;
int            sin_len;

    s = socket(AF_INET,SOCK_STREAM,0);
    if (s == INVALID_SOCKET)
    {
        // Socket failed
    }

    sin.sin_family = AF_INET;
    sin.sin_addr.s_addr = 0;
    sin.sin_port = htons(100); // port=100

    if (bind(s, (struct sockaddr FAR *)&sin, sizeof (sin)) == SOCKET_ERROR)
    {
        // Bind failed
    }

    if (listen(s,4)<0)
    {
        // Listen failed
    }
    sin_len = sizeof(sin);
    s=accept(s,(struct sockaddr FAR *) & sin,(int FAR *) &sin_len);
    if (s==INVALID_SOCKET)
    {
        // Accept failed
    }
    return(0);
}
```

37.2.6 send()

The send() function sends data to a connected socket. Its syntax is:

int send (SOCKET *s*, const char FAR *buf*, int *len*, int *flags*)

where

s	Connected socket descriptor.
buf	Transmission data buffer.
len	Buffer length.
flags	Calling flag.

37.3 Practical Win32 program

Refer to WWW page given in the Preface for a practical WinSock program, details of the `winsock.h` header file and the full range of WinSock APIs. Note that the `wsock32.lib` should be included in the project (in Visual C++ it is added in the Build → Settings → Object/library modules).

37.4 Exercises

37.4.1 Connect to a WWW server using port 13. This port should return the current date and time. Refer to Sample run 40.4.

37.4.2 Connect to a WWW server using port 19. This port should return the current date and time. Refer to Sample run 40.5.

37.4.3 Connect two computers over a network and set up a chat connection. One of the computers should be the chat server and the other the chat client. Modify it so that the server accepts calls from one or many clients.

The *flags* parameter influences the behaviour of the function. These can be:

`MSG_DONTROUTE`
        Specifies that the data should not be subject to routing.

`MSG_OOB`   Send out-of-band data.

If `send()` succeeds then the return value is the number of characters set (which can be less than the number indicated by *len*). Otherwise, it returns `SOCKET_ERRO`, and the specific error code can be tested with `WSAGetLastError`.

```
#include <windows.h>
#include <winsock.h>
#include <string.h>
#define  STRLENGTH 100

int main(void)
{

SOCKADDR_IN    sin;
SOCKET         s;
int sin_len;
char  sendbuf[STRLENGTH];

        s = socket(AF_INET,SOCK_STREAM,0);
        if (s == INVALID_SOCKET)
        {
           // Socket failed
        }
        sin.sin_family = AF_INET;
        sin.sin_addr.s_addr = 0;
        sin.sin_port = htons(100); // port=100
        if (bind(s, (struct sockaddr FAR *)&sin, sizeof (sin)) == SOCKET_ERROR)
        {
          // Bind failed
        }

        if (listen(s,4)<0)
        {
           // Listen failed
        }
        sin_len = sizeof(sin);

        s=accept(s,(struct sockaddr FAR *) & sin,(int FAR *) &sin_len);

        if (s<0)
        {
           // Accept failed
        }

        while (1)
        {
           // get message to send and put into sendbuff
           send(s,sendbuf,strlen(sendbuf),80);
        }
        return(0);
}
```

37.2.7 recv()

The `recv()` function receives data from a socket. It waits until data arrives and its syntax is:

```
int recv(SOCKET s, char FAR *buf, int len, int flags)
```

where

s	Connected socket descriptor.
buf	Incoming data buffer.
len	Buffer length.
flags	Specifies the method by which the data is received.

If `recv()` succeeds then the return value is the number of bytes received (a zero identifies that the connection has been closed). Otherwise, it returns `SOCKET_ERROR`, and the specific error code can be tested with `WSAGetLastError`.

The flags parameter may have one of the following values:

MSG_PEEK	Peek at the incoming data. Any received data is copied into the buffer, but not removed from the input queue.
MSG_OOB	Process out-of-band data.

```
#include <windows.h>
#include <winsock.h>

#define  STRLENGTH 100

int main(void)
{

SOCKADDR_IN    sin;
SOCKET         s;
int            sin_len,status;
char           recmsg[STRLENGTH];

    s = socket(AF_INET,SOCK_STREAM,0);

    if (s == INVALID_SOCKET)
    {
        // Socket failed
    }

    sin.sin_family = AF_INET;
    sin.sin_addr.s_addr = 0;

    sin.sin_port = htons(100); // port=100

    if (bind(s, (struct sockaddr FAR *)&sin, sizeof (sin)) == SOCKET_ERROR)
    {
        // Bind failed
    }

    if (listen(s,4)<0)
    {
        // Listen failed
    }
    sin_len = sizeof(sin);

    s=accept(s,(struct sockaddr FAR *) & sin,(int FAR *) &sin_len);

    if (s<0)
    {
```

```
        // Accept failed
    }
    while (1)
    {
        status=recv(s,recmsg,STRLENGTH,80);

        if (status==SOCKET_ERROR)
        {
            // no socket
            break;
        }

        recmsg[status]=NULL; // terminate string
        if (status)
        {
            // szMsg contains received string
        }
        else
        {
            break;
            // connection broken
        }
    }
    return(0);
}
```

37.2.8 *shutdown()*

The `shutdown()` function disables send or receive operations on a socket and close any opened sockets. Its syntax is:

```
int shutdown(SOCKET s, int how);
```

where

s	Socket descriptor.
how	Flag that identifies operation types that will no longer be allowed are:
	0 – Disallows subsequent receives.
	1 – Disallows subsequent sends.
	2 – Disables send and receive.

If no error occurs then it returns a zero value. Otherwise, it returns `INVALID_SOCP` the specific error code can be tested with `WSAGetLastError`.

37.2.9 *closesocket()*

The `closesocket()` function closes a socket. Its syntax is:

```
int closesocket (SOCKET s);
```

where

s	Socket descriptor.

If no error occurs then it returns a zero value. Otherwise, it returns `INVALID_SOCK` the specific error code can be tested with `WSAGetLastError`.

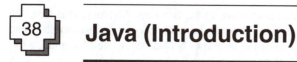

38 Java (Introduction)

38.1 Introduction

Java 1.0 was first released in 1995 and was quickly adopted as it fitted well with Internet-based programming. It was followed by Java 1.1 which gave faster interpretation of Java applets and included many new features. This book documents the basic features of Java 1.0 and the enhancements that have been made in Java 1.1.

It is a general-purpose, concurrent, class-based, object-oriented language and has been designed to be relatively simple to build complex applications. Java is developed from C and C++, but some parts of C++ have been dropped and others added.

Java has the great advantage over conventional software languages in that it produces code which is computer hardware independent. This is because the compiled code (called bytecodes) is interpreted by the WWW browser. Unfortunately this leads to slower execution, but, as much of the time in a graphical user interface program is spent updating the graphics display, then the overhead is, as far as the user is concerned, not a great one.

The other advantages that Java has over conventional software languages include:

- It is a more dynamic language than C/C++ and Pascal, and was designed to adapt to an evolving environment. It is extremely easy to add new methods and extra libraries without affecting existing applets and programs. It is also useful in Internet applications as it supports most of the standard compressed image, audio and video formats.
- It has networking facilities built into it. This provides support for TCP/IP sockets, URLs, IP addresses and datagrams.
- While Java is based on C and C++ it avoids some of the difficult areas of C/C++ code (such as pointers and parameter passing).
- It supports client-server applications where the Java applet runs on the server and the client receives the updated graphics information. In the most extreme case the client can simply be a graphics terminal which runs Java applets over a network. The small 'black-box' networked computer is one of the founding principles of Java, and it is hoped in the future that small Java-based computers could replace the complex PC/workstation for general-purpose applications, like accessing the Internet or playing network games. This 'black-box' computer concept is illustrated in Figure 38.1.

Most existing Web browsers are enabled for Java applets (such as Internet Explorer 3.0 and Netscape 2.0 and later versions). Figure 38.2 shows how Java applets are created. First the source code is produced with an editor, next a Java compiler compiles the Java source code into bytecode (normally appending the file name with `.class`). An HTML page is then constructed which has the reference to the applet. After this a Java-enabled browser or applet viewer can then be used to run the applet.

The Java Development Kit (JDK) is available, free, from Sun Microsystems from the WWW site `http://www.javasoft.com`. This can be used to compile Java applets and standalone programs. There are versions for Windows NT/95/98, Apple Mac and UNIX-based systems with many sample applets.

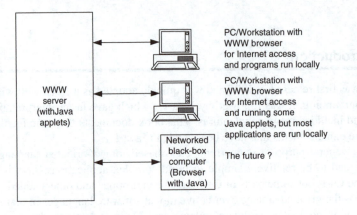

Figure 38.1   Internet accessing

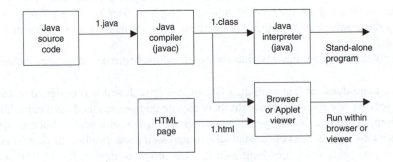

Figure 38.2   Constructing Java applets and standalone programs

Table 38.1 shows the main files used in the PC version and Figure 38.3 shows the directory structure of the JDK tools. The Java compiler, Java interpreter and applet viewer programs are stored in the `bin` directory. On the PC, this directory is normally set up in the PATH directory, so that the Java compiler can be called while the user is in another directory. The following is a typical setup (assuming that the home directory is `c:\`*javahome*):

```
PATH=C:\WINDOWS;C:\WINDOWS\COMMAND;C:\javahome\BIN
CLASSPATH=C:\javahome\LIB;.;C:\javahome
```

The `lib` directory contains the `classes.zip` file which is a zipped-up version of the Java class files. These class files are stored in the directories below the `src/java` directory. For example, the `io` classes (such as `File.java` and `InputStream.java`) are used for input/output in Java, the `awt` classes (such as `Panel.java` and `Dialog.java`) are used to create and maintain windows. These and other classes will be discussed later.

The `include` directory contains header files for integrating C/C++ programs with Java applets and the `demo` directory contains some sample Java applets.

Table 38.1 JDK programs.

File	Description
javac.exe	Java compiler
java.exe	Java interpreter
appletViewer.exe	Applet viewer for testing and running applets
classes.zip	It is needed by the compiler and interpreter
javap.exe	Java class disassembler
javadoc.exe	Java document generator
javah.exe	C Header and Stub File Generator
jar.exe	Java Archive Tool which combines class files and other resources into a single jar file.
jbd.exe	Java debugger

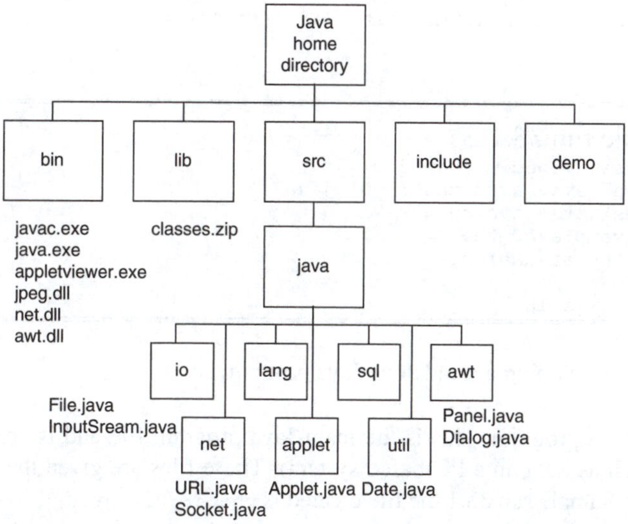

Figure 38.3 Sample directory structure of JDK for a PC-based system.

38.2 Standalone programs

A Java program can be run as a standalone program or as an applet. A standalone program allows the Java program to be run without a browser and is normally used when testing the Java applet. The method of output to the screen is:

```
System.out.println("message");
```

which prints a message (message) to the display. This type of debugging is messy as these statements need to be manually inserted in the program. It is likely that later versions of the JDK toolkit will contain a run-time debugger which will allow developers to view the execution of the program.

To run a standalone program the java.exe program is used and the user adds output statements with the System.out.println() method. Note that there is no output to the main graphics applet screen with this method.

Java program 38.1 gives a simple example of a standalone program. The `public static void main(Strings[] args)` defines the main method. Sample run 38.1 shows how the Java program is created (with `edit`) and then compiled (with `javac.exe`), and then finally run (with `java.exe`).

📖 **Java program 38.1** (chap38_1.java)
```
public class chap38_1
{
    public static void main(String[] args)
    {
    int i;
       i=10;
       System.out.println("This is an example of the ");
       System.out.println("output from the standalone");
       System.out.println("program");
       System.out.println("The value of i is " + i);
    }
}
```

🖥 **Sample run 38.1**
```
C:\DOCS\notes\java>edit chap38_01.java
C:\DOCS\notes\java>javac chap38_01.java
C:\DOCS\notes\java>java chap38_01
This is an example of the
output from the standalone
program
The value of i is 10
```

The process of developing a standalone Java program is:

*   Create a Java program. This is the main Java program file and is created by a text editor (such as `edit` in a PC-based system). These files are given the `.java` file extension. In Sample run 38.1 the file created is `chap38_01.java`.
*   Compile program to a class file. This is created by the Java compiler (`javac.exe`) when there is a successful compilation. By default, the file produced has the same filename as the source file and the `.class` file extension. In Sample run 38.1 the file created is `chap38_01.class`.
*   Run program with the Java interpreter. The Java interpreter (`java.exe`) reads from the class file (which contains the bytecode) and gives the required output.

38.3 Data types

Variables within a program can be stored as either boolean values, numbers or as characters. For example, the resistance of a copper wire would be stored as a number (a real value), whether it exists or not (as a boolean value) and the name of a component (such as "R1") would be stored as characters.

An integer is any value without a decimal point. Its range depends on the number of bytes used to store it. A floating-point value is any number and can include a decimal point. This value is always in a signed format. Again, the range depends on the number of bytes used.

Integers either take up 1, 2, 4 or 8 bytes in memory for a `byte`, `short`, `int` and `long`, respectively. These are all represented in 2's complement notation and thus can store positive and negative integer values. Table 38.2 gives some typical ranges for data types.

Table 38.2 Typical ranges for data types.

Type	Storage (bytes)	Range
boolean	1-bit	True or False
byte	1	−128 to 127
short	2	−32 768 to 32 767
int	4	−2 147 483 648 to 2 147 483 647
long	8	2 223 372 036 854 775 808 to −2 223 372 036 854 775 809
char	2	16-bit unsigned integers representing Unicode characters
float	4	$\pm 3.4 \times 10^{-38}$ to $\pm 3.4 \times 10^{38}$
double	8	$\pm 1.7 \times 10^{-308}$ to $\pm 1.7 \times 10^{308}$

38.4 Characters and strings

Typically, characters are stored using either ASCII or EBCDIC codes. ASCII is an acronym for American Standard Code for Information Interchange and EBCDIC for Extended Binary Coded Decimal Interchange Code.

ASCII characters from decimal 0 to 32 are non-printing characters that are used either to format the output or to control the hardware. Program 38.2 displays an ASCII character for an entered decimal value. The print() method displays the ASCII character. Sample run 38.2 shows a sample run (note that some of the displayed characters are non-printing).

📖 Java program 38.2 (chap38_2.java)

```
public class chap38_2
{
 public static void main (String args[])
 {
 char ch;
     for (ch=0;ch<256;ch++)
        System.out.print(" " + ch); // print from 0 to 255
 }
}
```

💻 Sample run 38.2
```
□ □ □ □ □ □ □ □        □
□ □ □ □ □ □ □ □ □ □ □ □ □ □  -     !  "  #  $  %  &  '  (  )  *  +  ,  -  .  /  0  1  2
3  4  5  6  7  8  9  :  ;  <  =  >  ?  @  A  B  C  D  E  F  G  H  I  J  K  L  M  N  O  P  Q  R  S  T  U  V
W  X  Y  Z  [  \  ]  ^  _  `  a  b  c  d  e  f  g  h  i  j  k  l  m  n  o  p  q  r  s  t  u  v  w  x  y  z
{  |  }  ~  □  □  □  ,  ƒ  „  …  †  ‡  ^  ‰  Š  ‹  Œ  □  □  □  □  '  '  "  "  •  –  —  ˜  ™  š  ›  œ  □  □
Ÿ   ¡  ¢  £  ¤  ¥  ¦  §  ¨  ©  ª  «  ¬  -  ®  ‾  °  ±  ²  ³  ´  µ  ¶  ·  ¸  ¹  º  »  ¼  ½  ¾  ¿  À  Á  Â
Ã  Ä  Å  Æ  Ç  È  É  Ê  Ë  Ì  Í  Î  Ï  Ð  Ñ  Ò  Ó  Ô  Õ  Ö  ×  Ø  Ù  Ú  Û  Ü  Ý  Þ  ß  à  á  â  ã  ä  å  æ
ç  è  é  ê  ë  ì  í  î  ï  ð  ñ  ò  ó  ô  õ  ö  ÷  ø  ù  ú  û  ü  ý  þ  ÿ
```

Characters of type char are stored as 2-byte Unicode characters (0x0000 to 0xFFFF). This allows for internationalization of the character set. The characters from 0 to 255 (0x0000 to 0x00FF) are standard extended ASCII character set (ISO8859-1, or Latin-1), where the characters are stored as the binary digits associated with the character. For example, the ASCII code for the character 'A' is 65 decimal (0x41); the binary storage for this character is thus 0100 0001.

The println() method sends a formatted string to the standard output (the display). This string can include special control characters, such as new lines ('\n'), backspaces ('\b') and tabspaces ('\t'); these are listed in Table 38.3.

The println() method writes a string of text to the standard output and at the end of the text a new line is automatically appended, whereas the print() method does not append the output with a new line.

Special control characters use a backslash to inform the program to escape from the way they would be normally be interpreted. The carriage return ('\r') is used to return the current character pointer on the display back to the start of the line (on many displays this is the leftmost side of the screen). A form-feed control character ('\f') is used to feed line printers on a single sheet and the horizontal tab ('\t') feeds the current character position forward one tab space.

Quotes enclose a single character, for example 'a', whereas inverted commas enclose a string of characters, such as "Java programming". Java has a special String object (String). Java program 38.3 shows an example of declaring two strings (name1 and name2) and Sample run 38.3 shows a sample run. The '\"' character is used to display inverted commas and the backspace character has been used to delete an extra character in the displayed string. The BELL character is displayed with the '\007' and '\u0007' escape sequence characters. Other escape characters used include the horizontal tab ('\t') and the new line character ('\n').

Strings can be easily concatenated using the '+' operator. For example to build a string of two strings (with a space in-between) then following can be implemented:

```
String name1, name2, name3;

name3=name1+" " + name2;
```

Table 38.3   Special control (or escape sequence) characters.

Characters	Function
\"	Double quotes (")
\'	Single quote (')
\\	Backslash (\ )
\u*nnnn*	Unicode character in hexadecimal code, e.g. \u041 gives '!'
\0*nn*	Unicode character in octal code, e.g. \041 gives '!'
\b	Backspace (move back one space)
\f	Form-feed
\n	New line (line-feed)
\r	Carriage return
\t	Horizontal tab spacing

📖 Java program 38.3 (`chap38_3.java`)

```
public class chap38_3
{

  public static void main (String args[])
  {

  String name1="Bill", name2="Buchanan";

      System.out.println("Ring the bell 3 times \u0007\007\007");
      System.out.print("\"My name is Bill\"\n");
      System.out.println("\t\"Buchh\banan\"");

      System.out.println(name1 + " " + name2);
  }
}
```

🖥 Sample run 38.3

```
C:\java\src\chap1>java chap1_04
Ring the bell 3 times
"My name is Bill"
        "Buchanan"
Bill Buchanan
```

38.5 Java operators

Java has a rich set of operators, of which there are four main types:

- Arithmetic
- Logical
- Bitwise
- Relational

38.5.1 Arithmetic

Arithmetic operators operate on numerical values. The basic arithmetic operations are add (+), subtract (-), multiply (*), divide (/) and modulus division (%). Modulus division gives the remainder of an integer division.

The assignment operator (=) is used when a variable 'takes on the value' of an operation. Other short-handed operators are used with it, including add equals (+=), minus equals (-=), multiplied equals (*=), divide equals (/=) and modulus equals (%=).

Table 38.4 summarizes the arithmetic operators.

38.5.2 Relationship

The relationship operators determine whether the result of a comparison is TRUE or FALSE. These operators are greater than (>), greater than or equal to (>=), less than (<), less than or equal to (<=), equal to (==) and not equal to (!=). Table 38.5 lists the relationship operators.

Table 38.4   Arithmetic operators.

Operator	Operation	Example
–	subtraction or minus	5-4→1
+	addition	4+2→6
*	multiplication	4*3→12
/	division	4/2→2
%	modulus	13%3→1
+=	add equals	x += 2 is equivalent to x=x+2
-=	minus equals	x -= 2 is equivalent to x=x-2
/=	divide equals	x /= y is equivalent to x=x/y
*=	multiplied equals	x *= 32 is equivalent to x=x*32
=	assignment	x = 1
++	increment	Count++ is equivalent to Count=Count+1
--	decrement	Sec-- is equivalent to Sec=Sec-1

38.5.3 Logical (TRUE or FALSE)

A logical operation is one in which a decision is made as to whether the operation performed is TRUE or FALSE. If required, several relationship operations can be grouped together to give the required functionality. Java assumes that a numerical value of 0 (zero) is FALSE and that any other value is TRUE. Table 38.6 lists the logical operators.

Table 38.5   Relationship operators.

Operator	Function	Example	TRUE Condition
>	greater than	(b>a)	when b is greater than a
>=	greater than or equal	(a>=4)	when a is greater than or equal to 4
<	less than	(c<f)	when c is less than f
<=	less than or equal	(x<=4)	when x is less than or equal to 4
==	equal to	(x==2)	when x is equal to 2
!=	not equal to	(y!=x)	when y is not equal to x

Table 38.6   Logical operators.

Operator	Function	Example	TRUE condition
&&	AND	((x==1) && (y<2))	when x is equal to 1 *and* y is less than 2
||	OR	((a!=b) || (a>0))	when a is not equal to b *or* a is greater than 0
!	NOT	(!(a>0))	when a is *not* greater than 0

For example, if a has the value 1 and b is also 1, then the following relationship statements would apply:

Statement	Result
(a==1) && (b==1)	TRUE
(a>1) && (b==1)	FALSE
(a==10) || (b==1)	TRUE
!(a==12)	TRUE

Java program 38.4 shows a Java program which proves the above table and Sample run 38.4 shows a sample run.

Java program 38.4 (chap38_4.java)

```
public class chap38_4
{
 public static void main (String args[])
 {
 int a=1,b=1;
     if ((a==1) && (b==1)) System.out.println("TRUE");
     else System.out.println("FALSE");
     if ((a>1) && (b==1)) System.out.println("TRUE");
     else System.out.println("FALSE");
     if ((a==10) || (b==1)) System.out.println("TRUE");
     else System.out.println("FALSE");
     if (!(a==10)) System.out.println("TRUE");
     else System.out.println("FALSE");
 }
}
```

Sample run 38.4

```
C:\java\src\chap38>java chap38_4
TRUE
FALSE
TRUE
TRUE
```

38.5.4 Bitwise

The bitwise operators are similar to the logical operators but they should not be confused as their operation differs. Bitwise operators operate directly on the individual bits of an operand(s), whereas logical operators determine whether a condition is TRUE or FALSE.

Numerical values are stored as bit patterns in either an unsigned integer format, signed integer (2's complement) or floating-point notation (an exponent and mantissa). Characters are normally stored as ASCII characters.

The basic bitwise operations are AND ($\&$), OR ($|$), 1's complement or bitwise inversion ($\sim$), XOR ($\wedge$), shift left (<<), shift right with sign (>>) and right shift without sign (>>>). Table 38.7 gives the results of the AND, OR and XOR bitwise operations on two values. It also gives other bitwise operators.

The bitwise operators operate on each of the individual bits of the operands. For example, if two decimal integers 58 and 41 (assuming 8-bit unsigned binary values) are operated on using the AND, OR and EX-OR bitwise operators, then the following applies:

	AND	OR	EX-OR
58	00111010b	00111010b	00111010b
41	00101001b	00101001b	00101001b
Result	00101000b	00111011b	00010011b

The results of these bitwise operations are as follows:

```
58 & 41 = 40      (that is, 00101000b)
58 | 41 = 59      (that is, 00111011b)
58 ^ 41 = 19      (that is, 00010011b)
```

Java Program 38.5 shows a program which tests these operations and Sample run 38.5 shows a test run.

The 1's complement operator operates on a single operand. For example, if an operand has the value of 17 (00010001b) then the 1's complement of this, in binary, will be 11101110b.

📖 **Java program 38.5** (chap38_5.java)

```java
public class chap38_5
{
 public static void main (String args[])
 {
 int a=58,b=41,val;
       val=a&b; System.out.println("AND "+ val);
       val=a|b; System.out.println("OR "+ val);
       val=a^b; System.out.println("X-OR "+ val);
 }
}
```

💻 **Sample run 38.5**

```
C:\java\src\chap1>java chap1_08
AND 40
OR 59
X-OR 19
```

To perform bit shifts, the <<, >> and >>> operators are used. These operators shift the bits in the operand by a given number defined by a value given on the right-hand side of the operation. The left-shift operator (<<) shifts the bits of the operand to the left and zeros fill the result on the right. The right-shift operator (>>) shifts the bits of the operand to the right and zeros fill the result if the integer is positive; otherwise it will fill with 1s. The right shift with sign (>>>) shifts the bits and ignores the sign flag; it thus treats signed integers as unsigned integers. The standard format for the three shift operators is:

```
operand >> no_of_bit_shift_positions
operand << no_of_bit_shift_positions
operand >>> no_of_bit_shift_positions
```

For example, if y = 59 (00111011), then y >> 3 will equate to 7 (00000111) and y<<2 to 236 (11101100). Table 38.7 gives a summary of the basic bitwise operators.

Table 38.7 Bitwise operators.

Operator	Function	Example
&	AND	c = A & B
|	OR	f = Z | y
^	XOR	h = 5 ^ f
~	1's complement	x = ~y
>>	shift right	x = y >> 1
<<	shift left	y = y << 2

38.6 Selection statements

38.6.1 if...else

A decision is made with the `if` statement. It logically determines whether a conditional expression is TRUE or FALSE. For a TRUE, the program executes one block of code; a FALSE causes the execution of another (if any). The keyword `else` identifies the FALSE block. In Java, braces (`{}`) are used to define the start and end of the block.

Relationship operators, include:

- Greater than (>).
- Less than (<).
- Greater than or equal to (>=).
- Less than or equal to (<=).
- Equal to (==).
- Not equal to (!=).

These operations yield a TRUE or FALSE from their operation. Logical statements (`&&`, `||`, `!`) can then group these together to give the required functionality. These are:

- AND (`&&`)
- OR (`||`)
- NOT (`!`)

If the operation is not a relationship, such as a bitwise or an arithmetic operation, then any non-zero value is TRUE and a zero is FALSE. The following is an example syntax of the `if` statement. If the statement block has only one statement then the braces (`{ }`) can be excluded.

```
if (expression)
{
    statement block
}
```

The following is an example format with an `else` extension.

```
if (expression)
{
```

```
    statement block1
}
else
{
    statement block2
}
```

It is possible to nest `if..else` statements to give a required functionality. In the next example, *statement block1* is executed if `expression1` is TRUE. If it is FALSE then the program checks the next expression. If this is TRUE the program executes *statement block2*, else it checks the next expression, and so on. If all expressions are FALSE then the program executes the final `else` statement block, in this case, *statement block4*:

```
if (expression1)
{
    statement block1
}
else if (expression2)
{
    statement block2
}
else if (expression3)
{
    statement block3
}
else
{
    statement block4
}
```

Java program 38.6 gives an example of a program which uses the if...else statement. In this case the variable `col` is tested for its value. When it matches a value from 0 to 6 the equivalent colour code is displayed. If it is not between 0 and 6 then the default message is displayed (`"Not Defined Yet!"`). Sample run 38.6 shows a sample run.

📖   Java program 38.6 (chap38_6.java)
```java
public class chap38_6
{
    public static void main (String args[])
    {
    int col;
        col=4;
        if (col==0) System.out.println("BLACK");
        else if (col==1) System.out.println("BROWN");
        else if (col==2) System.out.println("RED");
        else if (col==3) System.out.println("ORANGE");
        else if (col==4) System.out.println("YELLOW");
        else if (col==5) System.out.println("GREEN");
        else System.out.println("Not Defined Yet!");
    }
}
```

🖳🖳   Sample run 38.6
```
C:\java\src\chap2> edit chap2_01.java
C:\java\src\chap2> javac chap2_01.java
C:\java\src\chap2> java chap2_01
YELLOW
```

38.6.2 `switch`

The `switch` statement is used when there is a multiple decision to be made. It is normally used to replace the `if` statement when there are many routes of execution the program execution can take. The syntax of `switch` is as follows.

```
switch (expression)
{
    case const1:    statement(s) : break;
    case const2:    statement(s) ; break;
    :       :
    default:        statement(s) ; break;
}
```

The `switch` statement checks the `expression` against each of the constants in sequence (the constant must be an integer or character data type). When a match is found the statement(s) associated with the constant is (are) executed. The execution carries on to all other statements until a `break` is encountered or to the end of `switch`, whichever is sooner. If the `break` is omitted, the execution continues until the end of `switch`. If none of the constants matches the `switch` expression a set of statements associated with the default condition (`default:`) is executed. The data type of the `switch` constants can be either `byte`, `char`, `short`, `int` or `long`.

Java program 38.7 is the equivalent of Java program 38.6 but using a `switch` statement. Sample run 38.7 shows a sample run.

📖 Java program 38.7 (chap38_7.java)
```
import java.lang.Math;

public class chap38_7
{
    public static void main (String args[])
    {
    int col;
        col=4;
        switch (col)
        {
        case 0:  System.out.println("BLACK"); break;
        case 1:  System.out.println("BROWN"); break;
        case 2:  System.out.println("RED");      break;
        case 3:  System.out.println("ORANGE");   break;
        case 4:  System.out.println("YELLOW");   break;
        case 5:  System.out.println("GREEN"); break;
        default:    System.out.println("Not defined yet!");
        }
    }
}
```

🖥 Sample run 38.7
```
C:\java\src\chap2>java chap2_03
YELLOW
```

38.7 Loops

38.7.1 for()

Many tasks within a program are repetitive, such as prompting for data, counting values, and so on. The `for` loop allows the execution of a block of code for a given control function. The following is an example format; if there is only one statement in the block then the braces can be omitted.

```
for (starting condition;test condition;operation)
{
      statement block
}
```

where

`starting condition`	–	the starting value for the loop;
`test condition`	–	if `test condition` is TRUE the loop will continue execution;
`operation`	–	the operation conducted at the end of the loop.

Program 38.8 displays ASCII characters for entered start and end decimal values. Sample run 38.8 displays the ASCII characters from decimal 40 ('(') to 50 ('2'). The type conversion `(char)` is used to convert an integer to a `char`.

📖   Java program 38.8 (chap38_8.java)

```
public class chap38_8
{
   public static void main (String args[])
   {
   int start,end,ch;
      start=40; end=50;
      for (ch=start;ch<=end;ch++)
         System.out.println((int)ch+" "+(char)ch);
   }
}
```

🖥 Sample run 38.8

```
C:\java\src\chap38>java chap38_8
40 (
41 )
42 *
43 +
44 ,
45 -
46 .
47 /
48 0
49 1
50 2
```

38.7.2 while( )

The `while()` statement allows a block of code to be executed while a specified condition is TRUE. It checks the condition at the start of the block; if this is TRUE the block is executed, else it will exit the loop. The syntax is:

```
while (condition)
{
    :         :
    statement block
    :         :
}
```

If the statement block contains a single statement then the braces may be omitted (although it does no harm to keep them).

38.7.3 do...while()

The `do...while()` statement is similar in its operation to `while()` except that it tests the condition at the bottom of the loop. This allows *statement block* to be executed at least once. The syntax is:

```
do
{
        statement block
} while (condition);
```

As with `for()` and `while()` loops the braces are optional. The `do...while()` loop requires a semicolon at the end of the loop, whereas the `while()` does not.

The following is an example of the usage of the `do...while()` loop. Octal numbers uses base eight. To convert a decimal value to an octal number the decimal value is divided by 8 recursively and each remainder noted. The first remainder gives the least significant digit and the final remainder the most significant digit. For example, the following shows the octal equivalent of the decimal number 55:

$$
\begin{array}{r|r}
8 & 55 \\
& 6 \quad \text{r 7} \quad <<< \text{LSD (least significant digit)} \\
& 0 \quad \text{r 6} \quad <<< \text{MSD (most significant digit)}
\end{array}
$$

Thus the decimal value 55 is equivalent to 67o (where the o represents octal). Program 38.9 shows a program which determines an octal value for an entered decimal value. Unfortunately, it displays the least significant digit first and the most significant digit last, thus the displayed value must be read in reverse. Sample run 38.9 shows a sample run.

📖 **Java program 38.9** (chap38_9.java)
```
public class chap38_9
{
    public static void main (String args[])
    {
    int val,remainder;

        val=55;
        System.out.println("Conversion to octal (in reverse)");
        do
        {
```

```
        remainder=val % 8;    // find remainder with modulus
        System.out.print(remainder);
        val=val / 8;
    } while (val>0);
  }
}
```

🖥 Sample run 38.9
```
Conversion to octal (in reverse)
76
```

38.8 Classes

Classes are a general form of structure, which are common in many languages. They basically gather together data members, and in object-oriented design, they also include methods (known as functions in C and procedures in Pascal) which operate on the class. Everything within Java is contained within classes.

In C a program is normally split into modules named functions. Typically, these functions have parameters passed to them or from them. In Java these functions are named methods and operate within classes. Java program 38.10 includes a `Circle` class which contains two methods:

- `public float area(double r)`. In which the value of r is passed into the method and the return value is equal to πr^2 (`return(3.14159*r*r)`). The preceding `public double` defines that this method can be accessed from another class (`public`) and the `double` defines that the return type is of type `double`.
- `public float circum(double r)`. In which the value of r is passed into the method and the return value is equal to $2\pi r$ (`return(2*3.14159*r)`). The preceding `public double` defines that this method can be accessed from another class (`public`) and the `double` defines that the return type is of type `double`.

In defining a new class the program automatically defines a new data type (in Program 38.10 this new data type is named `Circle`). An instance of a class must first be created, thus for the `Circle` it can be achieved with:

```
    Circle cir;
```

this does not create a `Circle` object, it only refers to it. Next the object can be created with the `new` keyword with:

```
    cir = new Circle();
```

These two lines can be merged together into a single line with:

```
    Circle cir = new Circle();
```

which creates an instance of a `Circle` and assigns a variable to it. The methods can then be used to operate on the object. For example to apply the `area()` method:

```
val=cir.area(10);
```

can be used. This passes the value of 10 into the `radius` variable in the `area()` method and the return value will be put into the `val` variable. Sample run 38.10 shows a sample run.

📖   **Java program 38.10** (chap38_10.java)
```
public class chap38_10
{
   public static void main(String[] args)
   {
      Circle cir=new Circle();
      System.out.println("Area is "+cir.area(10));
      System.out.println("Circumference is "+cir.circum(10));
   }
}
class Circle          // class is named Circle
{
   public double circum(double radius)
   {
      return(2*3.14159*radius);            // 2πr
   }
   public double area(double radius)
   {
      return(3.14159*radius*radius);       // πr²
   }
}
```

🖥 **Sample run 38.10**
```
C:\java\src\chap38>java chap38_01
Area is 314.159
Circumference is 62.8318
```

The data and methods within a class can either be:

- Private. These are variables (or methods) which can only be used within the class and have a preceding `private` keyword. By default variables (the members of the class) and methods are private (restricted).
- Public. These are variables (or methods) which can be accessed from other classes and have a preceding `public` keyword.

It is obvious that all classes must have a public content so that they can be accessed by external functions. In Program 38.11 the `Circle` class has three public parts:

- The methods `area()` and `circum()`, which determine the area and circumference of a circle.
- The `Circle` class variable `radius`.

Once the `Circle` class has been declared then the class variable `radius` can be accessed from outside the `Circle` class using:

```
cir.radius=10;
```

which sets the class variable (radius) to a value of 10. The methods then do not need to be passed the value of radius as it is now set within the class (and will stay defined until either a new value is set or the class is deleted).

📖   **Java program 38.11** (chap38_11.java)

```java
public class chap38_11
{
   public static void main(String[] args)
   {
   Circle cir=new Circle();
      cir.radius=10;
      System.out.println("Area is "+c.area());
      System.out.println("Circumference is "+c.circum());
   }
}
class Circle
{
public float radius;

   public double circum()
   {
      return(2*3.14159*radius);
   }
   public double area()
   {
      return(3.14159*radius*radius);
   }
}
```

Many instances of a class can be initiated and each will have their own settings for their class variables. For example, in Program 38.12, two instances of the Circle class have been declared (cir1 and cir2). These are circle objects. The first circle object (cir1) has a radius of 15 and the second (cir2) has a radius of 10. Sample run 38.11 shows a sample run.

📖   **Java program 38.12** (chap38_12.java)

```java
public class chap38_12
{
   public static void main(String[] args)
   {
   Circle cir1, cir2;

      cir1=new Circle();
      cir2=new Circle();

      cir1.radius=15;
      cir2.radius=10;

      System.out.println("Area1 is "+cir1.area());
      System.out.println("Area2 is "+cir2.area());

   }
}
class Circle
{
public float radius;

   public double circum()
   {
      return(2*3.14159*radius);
```

```
    }
    public double area()
    {
        return(3.14159*radius*radius);
    }
}
```

🖳 Sample run 38.11

```
C:\java\src\chap38>java chap38_03
Area1 is 706.85775
Area2 is 314.159
```

38.9 Constructors

Constructors allow for the initialization of a class. It is a special initialization method that is automatically called whenever a class is declared. The constructor always has the same name as the class name, and no data types are defined for the argument list or the return type.

Program 38.13 has a class which is named Circle. The constructor for this class is Circle(). Sample run 38.12 shows a sample run. It can be seen that initially when the program is run the message "Constructing a circle" is displayed when the object is created.

📖 Java program 38.13 (chap38_13.java)

```
public class chap38_13
{
    public static void main(String[] args)
    {
    Circle c1,c2;
    double area1,area2;
        c1=new Circle();  c2=new Circle();

        c1.radius=15;     area1=c1.area();
        c2.radius=10;        area2=c2.area();
        System.out.println("Area1 is "+area1);
        System.out.println("Area2 is "+area2);
    }
}
class Circle
{
public float radius;

    public Circle()      // constructor called when object created
    {
        System.out.println("Constructing a circle");
    }
    public double circum()
    {
        return(2*3.14159*radius);
    }
    public double area()
    {
        return(3.14159*radius*radius);
    }
}
```

Sample run 38.12

```
C:\java\src\chap38>java chap38_13
Constructing a circle
Constructing a circle
Area1 is 706.85775
Area2 is 314.159
```

C++ has also a destructor which is a member of a function and is automatically called when the class is destroyed. It has the same name as the class name but is preceded by a tilde (~). Normally a destructor is used to clean-up when the class is destroyed. Java normally has no need for destructors as it implements a technique known as garbage collection which gets rids of objects which are no longer needed. If a final clear-up is required then the `finalize()` method can be used. This is called just before the garbage collection. For example:

```
class Circle
{
    public Circle()      // constructor called when object created
    {
        System.out.println("Constructing a circle");
    }
    public finalize()    // called when object deleted
    {
        System.out.println("Goodbye. I'm out with the trash");
    }

    public double circum()
    {
        return(2*3.14159*radius);
    }

    public double area()
    {
        return(3.14159*radius*radius);
    }
}
```

38.10 Method overloading

Often the programmer requires to call a method in a number of ways but wants the same name for the different implementations. Java allows this with method overloading. With overloading the programmer defines a number of methods, each of which has the same name but which are called with a different argument list or return type. The compiler then automatically decides which one should be called. For example, in Java program 38.14 the programmer has defined two square methods named `sqr()` and two for `max()`, which is a maximum method. The data type of the argument passed is of a different type for each of the methods, that is, either an `int` or a `double`. The return type is also different. The data type of the parameters passed to these methods is tested by the compiler and it then determines which of the methods it requires to use. Sample run 38.13 shows a sample run.

Java program 38.14 (chap38_14.java)

```java
public class chap38_14
{
    public static void main(String[] args)
    {
    MyMath m;
    int val1=4;
    double val2=4.1;

        m=new MyMath();

        System.out.println("Sqr(4)="+m.sqr(val1));
        System.out.println("Sqr(4.1)="+m.sqr(val2));
        System.out.println("Maximum (3,4)="+m.max(3,4));
        System.out.println("Maximum (3.0,4.0)="+m.max(3.0,4.0));
    }
}
class MyMath
{
    public int sqr(int val)
    {
        return(val*val);
    }
    public double sqr(double val)
    {
        return(val*val);
    }
    public int max(int a, int b)
    {
        if (a>b) return(a);
        else return(b);
    }
    public double max(double a, double b)
    {
        if (a>b) return(a);
        else return(b);
    }
}
```

Sample run 38.13

```
C:\java\src\chap38>java chap38_05
Sqr(4)=16
Sqr(4.1)=16.81
Maximum (3,4)=4
Maximum (3.0,4.0)=4.0
```

The argument list of the overloaded function does not have to have the same number of arguments for each of the overloaded functions. Program 38.15 shows an example of an overloaded method which has a different number of arguments for each of the function calls. In this case the max() function can either be called with two integer values or by passing an array to it. Arrays will be covered in Section 38.16.

Java program 38.15 (chap38_15.java)

```java
public class chap38_15
{
    public static void main(String[] args)
    {
    MyMath   m;
    int      val1=4, arr[]={1,5,-3,10,4}; // array has 5 elements
    double   val2=4.1;
```

```
        m=new MyMath();

        System.out.println("Sqr(4)="+m.sqr(val1));
        System.out.println("Sqr(4.1)="+m.sqr(val2));
        System.out.println("Maximum (3,4)="+m.max(3,4));
        System.out.println("Maximum (array)="+m.max(arr));
    }
}

class MyMath
{
    public int sqr(int val)
    {
        return(val*val);
    }
    public double sqr(double val)
    {
        return(val*val);
    }
    public int max(int a, int b)
    {
        if (a>b) return(a);
        else return(b);
    }
    public int max(int a[])
    {
    int i,max;
        max=a[0];                         // set max to first element
        for (i=1;i<a.length;i++)          // a.length returns array size
            if (max<a[i]) max=a[i];
        return(max);
    }
}
```

🖥 Sample run 38.14

```
C:\java\src\chap38>java chap38_15
Sqr(4)=16
Sqr(4.1)=16.81
Maximum (3,4)=4
Maximum (array)=10
```

38.11 Static methods

Declaring an object to get access to the methods in the MyMath class is obviously not efficient as every declaration creates a new object. If we just want access to the methods in a class then the methods within the class are declared as static methods. The methods are then accessed by preceding the method with the class name. Static methods are associated with a class and not an object, thus there is no need to create an object with them. Thus in Program 38.16 the methods are accessed by:

```
    val=MyMath.sqr(val1);   val=MyMath.max(3,4);
    val=MyMath.max(arr);
```

Sample run 38.15 shows a sample run.

📖 Java program 38.16 (chap38_16.java)

```
public class chap38_16
{
    public static void main(String[] args)
    {
    int      val1=4, arr[]={1,5,-3,10,4};     // array has 5 elements
    double   val2=4.1;
        System.out.println("Sqr(val1) "+MyMath.sqr(val1));
        System.out.println("Sqr(arr) "+MyMath.sqr(val2));
        System.out.println("Max(3.0,4.0) "+MyMath.max(3,4));
        System.out.println("Max(arr) "+MyMath.max(arr));
    }
}
class MyMath
{
    public static int sqr(int val)
    {
        return(val*val);
    }
    public static double sqr(double val)
    {
        return(val*val);
    }
    public static int max(int a, int b)
    {
        if (a>b) return(a);
        else return(b);
    }
    public static int max(int a[])
    {
    int i,max;
        max=a[0];                        // set max to first element
        for (i=1;i<a.length;i++)    //a.length returns array size
            if (max<a[i]) max=a[i];
        return(max);
    }
}
```

💻 Sample run 38.15

```
C:\java\src\chap38>java chap38_06
Sqr(val1) 16
Sqr(arr) 16.81
Max(3.0,4.0) 4
Max(arr) 10
```

38.12 Constants

Classes can contain constants which are defined as `public static` class variables. Such as:

```
class MyMath
{
    public static final double E = 2.7182818284590452354;
    public static final double PI = 3.14159265358979323846;
    public int sqr(int val)
    {
        return(val*val);
    }
    public double sqr(double val)
    {
```

```
        return(val*val);
    }
}
```

In this case the value of π is referenced by:

```
omega=2*MyMath.PI*f
```

The static class variables are declared as final so that they cannot be modified when an object is declared. Thus the following is INVALID:

```
MyMath.PI=10.1;
```

Program 38.17 shows a sample program and Sample run 38.16 shows a sample run.

📖   **Java program 38.17** (chap38_17.java)
```
public class chap38_17
{
    public static void main(String[] args)
    {
        System.out.println("PI is "+m.PI);
        System.out.println("E is ="+m.E);
    }
}
class MyMath
{
    public static final double E = 2.7182818284590452354;
    public static final double PI = 3.14159265358979323846;
    public static int sqr(int val)
    {
        return(val*val);
    }
    public static double sqr(double val)
    {
        return(val*val);
    }
    public static int max(int a, int b)
    {
        if (a>b) return(a);
        else return(b);
    }
    public static int max(int a[])
    {
    int i,max;

        max=a[0];                        // set max to first element
        for (i=1;i<a.length;i++)   //a.length returns array size
           if (max<a[i]) max=a[i];
        return(max);
    }
}
```

💻 **Sample run 38.16**
```
C:\java\src\chap38>java chap_08
PI is 3.141592653589793
E is =2.718281828459045
```

38.13 Package statements

The `package` statement defines that the classes within a Java file are part of a given package. The full name of a class is:

package.classFilename

The fully qualified name for a method is:

package.classFilename.method_name ()

Each class file with the same package name is stored in the same directory. For example, the `java.applet` package contains several files, such as:

```
applet.java            appletcontent.java
appletstub.java        audioclip.java
```

Each has a first line of:

```
package java.applet;
```

and the fully classified names of the class files are:

```
java.applet.applet            java.applet.appletcontent
java.applet.appletstub        java.applet.audioclip
```

These can be interpreted as in the `java/applet` directory. An example listing from the class library given in next:

```
java/
java/lang/
java/lang/Object.class
java/lang/Exception.class
java/lang/Integer.class
```

Normally when a Java class is being developed it is not part of a package as it is contained in the current directory. The main packages are:

```
java.applet           java.awt               java.awt.datatransfer
java.awt.event        java.awt.image         java.awt.peer
java.beans            java.io                java.lang
java.lang             java.lang.reflect      java.math
java.net              java.rmi               java.rmi.dgc
java.rmi.registry     java.rmi.server        java.security
java.security.acl     java.security.interfaces
java.text             java.util              java.sql
                                             java.utils.zip
```

38.14 Import statements

The `import` statement allows previously written code to be included in the applet. This code is stored in class libraries (or packages), which are compiled Java code. For the

JDK tools, the Java source code for these libraries is stored in the `src/java` directory. For example, a Java program which uses maths methods will begin with:

```
import java.lang.Math;
```

This includes the `math` class libraries (which is in the `java.lang` package). The default Java class libraries are stored in the `classes.zip` file in the `lib` directory. This file is in a compressed form and should not be unzipped before it is used. The following is an outline of the file.

```
Searching ZIP: CLASSES.ZIP
Testing: java/
Testing: java/lang/
Testing: java/lang/Object.class
Testing: java/lang/Exception.class
Testing: java/lang/Integer.class
    ::            ::
Testing: java/lang/Win32Process.class
Testing: java/io/
Testing: java/io/FilterOutputStream.class
Testing: java/io/OutputStream.class
    ::            ::
Testing: java/io/StreamTenizer.class
Testing: java/util/
Testing: java/util/Hashtable.class
Testing: java/util/Enumeration.class
    ::            ::
Testing: java/util/Stack.class
Testing: java/awt/
Testing: java/awt/Toolkit.class
Testing: java/awt/peer/
Testing: java/awt/peer/WindowPeer.class
    ::            ::
Testing: java/awt/peer/DialogPeer.class
Testing: java/awt/Image.class
Testing: java/awt/MenuItem.class

Testing: java/awt/MenuComponent.class
Testing: java/awt/image/
    ::            ::
    ::            ::
Testing: java/awt/ImageMediaEntry.class
Testing: java/awt/AWTException.class
Testing: java/net/
Testing: java/net/URL.class
Testing: java/net/URLStreamHandlerFactory.class
    ::            ::
Testing: java/net/URLEncoder.class
Testing: java/applet/
Testing: java/applet/Applet.class
Testing: java/applet/AppletContext.class
Testing: java/applet/AudioClip.class
Testing: java/applet/AppletStub.class
```

The other form of the `import` statement is:

```
import package.*;
```

which will import all the classes within the specified package. Table 38.8 lists the main class libraries and some sample libraries.

It can be seen that upgrading the Java compiler is simple, as all that is required is to replace the class libraries with new ones. For example, if the basic language is upgraded then `java.lang.*` files is simply replaced with a new version. The user can also easily add new class libraries to the standard ones.

Table 38.8 Class libraries.

Class libraries	Description	Example libraries
java.lang.*	Java language	java.lang.Class java.lang.Number java.lang.Process java.lang.String
java.io.*	I/O routines	java.io.InputStream java.io.OutputStream
java.util.*	Utilities	java.util.BitSet java.util.Dictionary
java.awt.*	Windows, menus and graphics	java.awt.Point java.awt.Polygon java.awt.MenuComponent java.awt.MenuBar java.awt.MenuItem
java.net.*	Networking (such as sockets, URLs, ftp, telnet and HTTP)	java.net.ServerSocket java.net.Socket java.net.SocketImpl
java.applet.*	Code required to run an applet	java.applet.AppletContext java.applet.AppletStub java.applet.AudioClip

38.15 Mathematical operations

Java has a basic set of mathematics methods which are defined in the `java.lang.Math` class library. Table 38.9 outlines these methods. An example of a method in this library is `abs()` which can be used to return the absolute value of either a `double`, an `int` or a `long` value. Java automatically picks the required format and the return data type will be of the same data type of the value to be operated on.

As the functions are part of the `Math` class they are preceded with the `Math.` class method. For example:

```
val2=Math.sqrt(val1);
val3=Math.abs(val2);
z=Math.min(x,y);
```

Java program 38.18 shows a few examples of mathematical operations and Sample run 38.17 shows a sample compilation and run session.

Table 38.9   Methods defined in `java.lang.Math`

Method	Description
double **abs**(double a)	Absolute double value of a.
float **abs**(float a)	Absolute float value of a.
int **abs**(int a)	Absolute integer value of a.
long **abs**(long a)	Absolute long value of a.
double **acos**(double a)	Inverse cosine of a, in the range of 0.0 to Pi.
double **asin**(double a)	Inverse sine of a, in the range of −Pi/2 to Pi/2.
double **atan**(double a)	Inverse tangent of a, in the range of −Pi/2 to Pi/2.
double **atan2**(double a, double b)	Converts rectangular coordinates (a, b) to polar (r, theta).
double **ceil**(double a)	Smallest whole number greater than or equal to a.
double **cos**(double a)	Cosine of an angle.
double **exp**(double a)	Exponential number e (2.718…) raised to the power of a.
double **floor**(double a)	Largest whole number less than or equal to a.
double **IEEEremainder** (double f1, double f2)	Remainder of f1 divided by f2 as defined by IEEE 754.
double **log**(double a)	Natural logarithm (base e) of a.
double **max**(double a, double b)	Greater of two double values, a and b.
double **max**(float a, float b)	Greater of two float values, a and b.
int **max**(int a, int b)	Greater of two int values, a and b.
long **max**(long a,long b)	Greater of two long values, a and b.
double **min**(double a, double b)	Smaller of two double values, a and b.
float **min**(float a, float b)	Smaller of two float values, a and b.
int **min**(int a, int b)	Smaller of two int values, a and b.
long **min**(long a, long b)	Smaller of two long values, a and b.
double **pow**(double a, double b)	Value of a raised to the power of b.
double **random**()	Random number between 0.0 and 1.0.
double **rint**(double b)	Double value converted into an integer value.
long **round**(double a)	Rounded value of a.
int **round**(float a)	Rounded value of a.
double **sin**(double a)	Sine of a.
double **sqrt**(double a)	Square root of a.
double **tan**(double a)	Tangent of a.

📖 Java program 38.18 (chap38_18.java)

```java
import java.lang.Math;
public class chap38_18
{
    public static void main(String[] args)
    {
    double x,y,z;
    int i;
        i=10;
        y=Math.log(10.0);
        x=Math.pow(3.0,4.0);
        z=Math.random(); // random number from 0 to 1
        System.out.println("Value of i is " + i);
        System.out.println("Value of log(10) is " + y);
        System.out.println("Value of 3^4 is " + x);
        System.out.println("A random number is " + z);
        System.out.println("Square root of 2 is " +    Math.sqrt(2));
    }
}
```

🖥 Sample run 38.17

```
C:\java\src\chap38>javac chap38_18.java
C:\java\src\chap38>java chap38_18
Value of i is 10
Value of log(10) is 2.30259
Value of 3^4 is 81
A random number is 0.0810851
Square root of 2 is 1.41421
```

Java has also two predefined mathematical constants. These are:

- PI is equivalent to 3.14159265358979323846
- E is equivalent to 2.71828182845904523546

38.16 Arrays

An array stores more than one value, of a common data type, under a collective name. Each value has a unique slot and is referenced using an indexing technique. For example, a circuit with five resistor components could be declared within a program with five simple float declarations. If these resistor variables were required to be passed into a method then all five values would have to be passed through the parameter list. A neater way uses arrays to store all of the values under a common name (in this case R). Then a single array variable can then be passed into any method that uses it.

The declaration of an array specifies the data type, the array name and the number of elements in the array in brackets ([]). The following gives the standard format for an array declaration.

> *data_type array_name*[];

The array is then created using the new keyword. For example, to declare an integer array named new_arr with 200 elements then the following is used:

    int new_arr[];

```
new_arr=new int[200];
```

or, in a single statement, with:

```
int new_arr[]=new int[200];
```

Java program 38.19 gives an example of this type of declaration where an array (arr) is filled with 20 random numbers (Figure 38.18 shows a sample run).

Like C, the first element of the array is indexed 0 and the last element as size-1. The compiler allocates memory for the first element array_name[0] to the last array element array_name[size-1]. The number of bytes allocated in memory will be the number of elements in the array multiplied by the number of bytes used to store the data type of the array.

📖 **Java program 38.19** (chap38_19.java)

```
public class chap38_19
{
    public static void main(String[] args)
    {
        double arr[]=new double[20];
        int    i;

        for (i=0;i<20;i++)  arr[i]=Math.random();
        for (i=0;i<20;i++)  System.out.println(arr[i]);
    }
}
```

💻 **Sample run 38.18**

```
C:\java\src\chap38>java chap38_19
0.6075765411193292
0.7524300612559963
0.8100796233691735
0.45045015538577704
0.32390753542869755
0.34033464565015836
0.5079716192482706
0.6426253967106341
0.7691175624480434
0.6475110502592946
0.1416366173783874
0.21181433233783153
0.21758072702009412
0.24203490620407764
0.7587570097412505
0.4470154908107362
0.19823448357551965
0.7340429664182364
0.7402367706819387
0.8975606689180567
```

Another way to create and initialize an array is to define the elements within the array within curly brackets ({}). A comma separates each element in the array. The size of the array is then equal to the number of elements in the array. For example:

```
int     arr1[]={-3, 4, 10, 100, 30, 22};
String  menus[]={"File", "Edit", "View", "Insert", "Help"};
```

A particular problem in most programming languages (such as C and Pascal) exists when accessing array elements which do not exist, especially by accessing an array element which is greater than the maximum size of the array. Java overcomes this by being able to determine the size of the array. This is done with the `length` field. For example, the previous example can be modified with:

```
for (i=0;i<arr.length;i++)    arr[i]=Math.random();
for (i=0;i<arr.length;i++)    System.out.println(arr[i]);
```

Java Program 38.20 gives an example of an array of strings. In this case the array contains the names of playing cards. When run the program displays five random playing cards. Sample run 38.19 shows a sample run.

📖 **Java program 38.20** (chap38_20.java)
```
public class chap38_20
{
    public static void main(String[] args)
    {
    int cards,pick;
    String    Card[]={"Ace","King","Queen","Jack","10",
                "9", "8", "7", "6", "5", "4", "3", "2"};

        for (cards=0;cards<5;cards++)
        {
            pick=(int)Math.round((Card.length)*Math.random());
            System.out.print(Card[pick] + " ");
        }
    }
}
```

💻 **Sample run 38.19**
```
Ace   10   King   2   3
```

Multi-dimensional arrays are declared in a similar manner. For example an array with 3 rows and 4 columns is declared with either of the following:

```
int arr[][]=new int[3][4];
```

or if the initial values are known with:

```
int arr[][]= { {1,2,3,4},  {5,6,7,8},  {9,10,11,12} } ;
```

where `arr[0][0]` is equal to 1, `arr[1][0]` is equal to 5, `arr[2][3]` is equal to 12, and so on. This is proved with Java Program 38.21 and Sample run 38.20.

📖 **Java program 38.21** (chap38_21.java)
```
public class chap38_21
{
    public static void main(String[] args)
    {
    int    row,col;
    int    arr[][]={ {1,2,3,4},{5,6,7,8},  {9,10,11,12} };
```

```
    for (row=0;row<3;row++)
      for (col=0;col<4;col++)
        System.out.println("Arr["+row+"]["+col+"]="+arr[row][col]);
    }
}
```

🖳 Sample run 38.20

```
C:\java\src\chap38>java chap38_05
Arr[0][0]=1
Arr[0][1]=2
Arr[0][2]=3
Arr[0][3]=4
Arr[1][0]=5
Arr[1][1]=6
Arr[1][2]=7
Arr[1][3]=8
Arr[2][0]=9
Arr[2][1]=10
Arr[2][2]=11
Arr[2][3]=12
```

38.17 Exercises

38.17.1   Java program 38.22 allows answers in this question to be checked by replacing the 0x34 value with the required value.

📖   **Java program 38.22** (chap38_22.java)
```
public class chap38_22
{
 public static void main (String args[])
 {
 int val1=0x34;

   System.out.println(" Val1 is "+val1);
 }
}
```

Complete the following table, giving the equivalent decimal, hexadecimal or octal numbers.

Hexadecimal	Octal	Decimal
0x12		
0xA1		
0x1f0		
	013	
	027	
	0206	

38.17.2   Assuming x=1 and y=2, determine whether each of the following will result in a TRUE or a FALSE. Answers can be tested using the template of Program 38.23.

(i)   ((x==1) && (y!=2))   (ii)   ((x!=1) || (y==2))
(iii)   (!(x==2))   (iv)   (!((x==1) && (y==2)))

(v) `((x>0) && (y<2))`   **(vi)**   `(x<=1)`
(vii) `((y>1) || (x==1))`

📖   Java program 38.23 (chap38_23.java)
```java
public class chap38_23
{
 public static void main (String args[])
 {
 int x=1,y=1;

        if ((x==1) && (y!=2))  System.out.println("TRUE");
        else System.out.println("FALSE");
 }
}
```

38.17.3   Modify Java program 38.2 so that it displays the whole range of Unicode characters (Hint the loop should go from 0x0000 to 0xffff).

38.17.4   Write a program which determines whether an entered integer value is exactly divisible by 4. For example, the following outline code can be used to determine if a value is exactly divisible by 2.

📖   Java program 38.24 (chap38_24.java)
```java
public class chap38_24
{
    public static void main (String args[])
    {
    int val;

      val=3;

      if ((val % 2)==0)
         System.out.println("Value is even");
      else
         System.out.println("Value is odd");
    }
}
```

38.17.5   Modify the program developed in Exercise 38.17.4 so that it determines whether the entered value is exactly divisible by 10.

38.17.6   Write a program which determines whether an entered integer value is exactly divisible by 3 and 4. The following outline code can be used to determine whether a value is exactly divisible by 2 and 3:

```java
      if (((val % 2)==0) && ((val % 3)==0))
         System.out.println("Value is even");
      else
         System.out.println("Value is odd");
```

38.17.7   Modify the program developed in Exercise 38.17.6 (using the | operator) so that it displays whether the value is exactly divisible by 3 or 4.

38.17.8   Write a program which lists the square of the values from 1 to 10.
38.17.9   Java program 38.25 gives a program which displays the sine of a number

from 0° degrees to 90° in steps of 10° and Sample run 38.21 gives a sample run. Modify it so that it determines the cosine of an angle from 0° degrees to 90° in steps of 10°. (Hint: use `cos()` method instead of `sin()`).

📖 **Java program 38.25** (chap38_25.java)

```
import java.lang.Math;

public class chap38_25
{
   public static void main (String args[])
   {
   double val;

      System.out.println("Val\tSine");
      for (val=0;val<=90;val+=10)
      {
         System.out.println(val+"\t"+
            Math.sin(val*3.14/180)); // convert to radians
      }
   }
}
```

💻 **Sample run 38.21**

```
C:\java\src\chap3>java chap3_04
Val     Sine
0.0     0.0
10.0    0.17356104045380674
20.0    0.34185384854620343
   ::     ::
80.0    0.9846845901305833
90.0    0.9999996829318346
```

38.17.10 Write a program to convert from decimal to hexadecimal (base 16). A sample run for a value of 42 is shown in Sample run 38.22. Program 38.26 shows a sample outline of the program.

💻 **Sample run 38.22**

```
The value in hexadecimal is (in reverse) A2
```

📖 **Java program 38.26** (chap38_26.java)

```
public class chap38_26
{
   public static void main (String args[])
   {
   int val,remain;

      val=55;
      System.out.println("Conversion to octal (in reverse)");
      do
      {
         remain=val % 16;   // find remainder with modulus
         if (remain<10) System.out.print(remain);
         else if (remain==10) System.out.print('A');
         else if (remain==11) System.out.print('B');
                  etc
         val=val / 16;
      } while (val>0);
```

```
      }
}
```

38.17.11 Create a `Rectangle` class which contains the variables `base` and `height`. The class has the associated method called `area()`, which determines the area from one-half of the base times the height. The following is an outline of a usage of the class:

```
Rectangle rec1;
double area;

rect1=new Rectangle();

rect1.base=15;
rect1.height=15;
area=rect1.area();
```

Modify the program so that it creates several instances of rectangles.

38.17.12 Add the following methods to the `MyMath` class (Program 38.16):

(i)   `min(int a, int b);   // returns minimum of two values`
      `min(double a, double b); // returns minimum of two values`
      `min(int a[]); // return minimum of an integer array`
      `min(double a[];// return minimum of an double array`

(ii) `mean(int a, int b);   // returns mean of two values`
      `mean(double a, double b);// returns mean of two values`
      `mean(int a[]); // return mean of an integer array`
      `mean(double a[];// return mean of an double array`

(iii) `isodd(int a);   // returns true if value is odd, else false`
      `iseven(int a);   // returns true if value is even, else false`

(iv) `fact(int a);   // returns factorial of the value`

(v)   `stdev(int a[]);   // returns standard deviation`
      `stdev(double a[]);// returns standard deviation`

The formulas which can be used to the mean ($\bar{x}$), standard deviation (σ) and factorial ($n!$) are:

$$Mean = \bar{x} = \frac{1}{N} \sum_{i=1}^{N} x_i \quad Stdev = \sigma = \sqrt{\frac{1}{N} \sum_{i=1}^{N} \left(x_i - \bar{x}\right)^2}$$

$$n! = n \times (n-1) \times (n-2) \ldots 2 \times 1$$

38.17.13 The sine function can be calculated, from first principles, with:

$$\sin(x) = x - \frac{x^3}{3!} + \frac{x^5}{5!} - \frac{x^7}{7!} + \frac{x^9}{9!} - \ldots$$

where the value of x is in radians. Java program 38.27 determines the sine function using the above formula, where the series is stopped when an individual term in the equation is less than 1×10^{-6}. It also uses a factorial method (`fact`) and a standard method from the Math class (`pow`). Sample run 38.23

shows a sample run.

📖   **Java program 38.27** (chap38_27.java)

```java
import java.lang.Math; // required for the pow() method

public class chap38_27
{
   public static void main(String[] args)
   {

      System.out.println("Sin(1.2) is "+MyMath.sin(1.2));
   }
}
class MyMath
{
   public static double sin(double x)
   {
   double val, term;
   int n, sign;
      sign=1;
      val=x;
      n=3;
      do
      {
         term=Math.pow(x,n)/fact(n);
         n=n+2;
         sign=-sign;
         val=val+sign*term;

      } while (term>1e-6);
      return(val);
   }

   public static long fact(long n)
   {
      long i, result;

      result=1;
      for (i=2;i<=n;i++)
            result=result*i;
      return(result);
   }
}
```

💻 **Sample run 38.23**

```
C:\java\src>java chap38_24
Sin(1.2) is 0.9320390842607376
```

Using Program 38.27 as a basis, add a method for a cosine function. It can be calculated, from first principles, with:

$$\cos(x) = 1 - \frac{x^2}{2!} + \frac{x^4}{4!} - \frac{x^6}{6!} + \frac{x^8}{8!} - \dots$$

The error in the function should be less than 1×10^{-6}.

39 **Java (Events and Windows)**

39.1 Introduction

As has been previously discussed a Java program can either be run as an applet within a WWW browser (such as Microsoft Internet Explorer or Netscape Communicator) or can be interpreted as a standalone program. The basic code within each program is almost the same and they can be easily converted from one to the other (typically a Java program will be run through an interpreter to test its results and then converted to run as an applet).

39.2 Applet tag

An applet is called from within an HTML script with the `APPLET` tag, such as:

```
<applet code="Test.class" width=200 height=300></applet>
```

which loads an applet called `Test.class` and sets the applet size to 200 pixels wide and 300 pixels high. Table 39.1 discusses some optional parameters.

Table 39.1   Other applet HTML parameters.

Applet parameters	Description
`CODEBASE=`*codebaseURL*	Specifies the directory (*codebaseURL*) that contains the applet's code.
`CODE=`*appletFile*	Specifies the name of the file (*appletFile*) of the compiled applet.
`ALT=`*alternateText*	Specifies the alternative text that is displayed if the browser cannot run the Java applet.
`NAME=`*appletInstanceName*	Specifies a name for the applet instance (*appletInstanceName*). This makes it possible for applets on the same page to find each other.
`WIDTH=`*pixels* `HEIGHT=`*pixels*	Specifies the initial width and height (in *pixels*) of the applet.
`ALIGN=`*alignment*	Specifies the *alignment* of the applet. Possible values are: `left`, `right`, `top`, `texttop`, `middle`, `absmiddle`, `baseline`, `bottom` and `absbottom`.
`VSPACE=`*pixels* `HSPACE=`*pixels*	Specifies the number of *pixels* above and below the applet (`VSPACE`) and on each side of the applet (`HSPACE`).

39.2.1 Applet viewer

A useful part of the JDK tools is an applet viewer which is used to test applets before they are run within the browser. The applet viewer on the PC version is `Applet-Viewer.exe` and the supplied argument is the HTML file that contains the applet tag(s). It then runs all the associated applets in separate windows.

39.3 Creating an applet

Java applet 39.1 shows a simple Java applet which displays two lines of text and HTML script 39.1 shows how the applet integrates into an HTML script.

First the Java applet (`chap39_1.java`) is created. In this case the `edit` program is used. The directory listing below shows that the files created are `chap39_1.java` and `chap39_1.html` (note that Windows NT/95 displays the 8.3 filename format on the left-hand side of the directory listing and the long filename on the right-hand side).

📖 **Java applet 39.1** (`chap39_1.java`)

```
import java.awt.*;
import java.applet.*;

public class chap39_1 extends Applet
{
  public void paint(Graphics g)
  {
   g.drawString("This is my first Java",5,25);
   g.drawString("applet.....",5,45);
  }
}
```

📖 **HTML script 39.1** (`chap39_1.html`)

```
<HTML><TITLE>First Applet</TITLE>
<APPLET CODE=chap39_1.class WIDTH=200
HEIGHT=200></APPLET></HTML>
```

💻 **Sample run 39.1**

```
C:\java\src\chap39> edit chap39_1.java
C:\java\src\chap39> edit chap39_1.html
C:\java\src\chap39> dir
CHAP39_~1 HTM          111  14/05/98  18:40 chap39_1.html
CHAP39_~1 JAV          228  13/05/98  22:35 chap39_1.java
```

Next the Java applet is compiled using the `javac.exe` program. It can be seen from the listing that, if there are no errors, the compiled file is named `chap39_1.class`. This can then be used, with the HTML file, to run as an applet.

💻 **Sample run 39.2**

```
C:\java\src\chap39> javac chap39_1.java
C:\java\src\chap39> dir
CHAP3_~1 HTM          111  14/05/98  18:40 chap39_1.html
CHAP3_~1 JAV          228  14/05/98  18:43 chap39_1.java
CHAP3_~1 CLA          460  14/05/98  18:43 chap39_1.class
C:\java\src\chap39> appletviewer chap39_1.html
```

39.4 Applet basics

Java applet 39.1 recaps the previous Java applet. This section analyzes the main parts of this Java applet.

📖 **Java applet 39.1** (chap39_1.java)

```
import java.awt.*;
import java.applet.*;
public class chap39_1 extends Applet
{
  public void paint(Graphics g)
  {
   g.drawString("This is my first Java",5,25);
   g.drawString("applet.....",5,45);
  }
}
```

39.4.1 Applet class

The start of the applet code is defined in the form:

```
public class chap39_1 extends Applet
```

which informs the Java compiler to create an applet named chap39_1 that extends the existing Applet class. The public keyword at the start of the statement allows the Java browser to run the applet, while if it is omitted the browser cannot access the applet.

The class keyword is used to create a class object named chap39_1 that extends the applet class. After this the applet is defined between the left and right braces (grouping symbols).

39.4.2 Applet methods

Methods allow Java applets to be split into smaller sub-tasks (just as C uses functions). These methods have the advantage that:

- They allow code to be reused.
- They allow for top-level design.
- They make applet debugging easier as each method can be tested in isolation to the rest of the applet.

A method has the public keyword, followed by the return value (if any) and the name of the method. After this the parameters passed to the method are defined within rounded brackets. Recapping from the previous example:

```
public void paint(Graphics g)
{
   g.drawString("This is my first Java",5,25);
   g.drawString("applet.....",5,45);
}
```

This method has the public keyword which allows any user to execute the method. The void type defines that there is nothing returned from this method and the name of the method is paint(). The parameter passed into the method is g which has the data type of Graphics. Within the paint() method the drawString() method is called. This method is defined in `java.awt.Graphics` class library (this library has been included with the `import java.awt.*` statement. The definition for this method is:

```
public abstract void drawString(String str, int x, int y)
```

which draws a string of characters using the current font and colour. The x,y position is the starting point of the baseline of the string (`str`).

It should be noted that Java is case sensitive and the names given must be referred to in the case that they are defined as.

39.5 The paint() object

The `paint()` object is the object that is called whenever the applet is redrawn. It will thus be called whenever the applet is run and then it is called whenever the applet is re-displayed.

Java applet 39.2 shows how a `for()` loop can be used to display the square and cube of the values from 0 to 9. Notice that the final value of `i` within the `for()` loop is 9 because the end condition is `i<10` (while `i` is less than 10).

📖 Java applet 39.2 (chap39_2.java)

```
import java.awt.*;
import java.applet.*;
public class chap39_2 extends Applet
{
  public void paint(Graphics g)
  {
  int     i;

  g.drawString("Value Square Cube",5,10);
  for (i=0;i<10;i++)
    {
      g.drawString(""+ i,5,20+10*i);
      g.drawString(""+ i*i ,45,20+10*i);
      g.drawString(""+ i*i*i,85,20+10*i);
    }
  }
}
```

```
Applet Viewer: cha...  [_][□][X]
Applet
Value Square Cube
0     0      0
1     1      1
2     4      8
3     9      27
4     16     64
5     25     125
6     36     216
7     49     343
8     64     512
9     81     729

Applet started.
```

📖 HTML script 39.2 (chap39_2.html)

```
<HTML> <TITLE>First Applet</TITLE>
<APPLET CODE=chap39_2.class WIDTH=200 HEIGHT=200
</APPLET>
</HTML>
```

39.6 Java events

The previous chapters have discussed the Java programming language. This chapter investigates event-driven programs. Traditional methods of programming involve writing a program which flows from one part to the next in a linear manner. Most programs are designed using a top-down structured design, where the task is split into a number of sub-modules, these are then called when they are required. This means that it is relatively difficult to interrupt the operation of a certain part of a program to do another activity, such as updating the graphics display.

In general Java is event-driven where the execution of a program is not predefined and its execution is triggered by events, such as a mouse click, a keyboard press, and so on. The main events are:

- Initialization and exit methods (`init()`, `start()`, `stop()` and `destroy()`).
- Repainting and resizing (`paint()`).
- Mouse events (`mouseUp()`, `mouseDown()` and `mouseDrag()` for Java 1.0, and `mouse-Pressed()`, `mouseReleased()` and `mouseDragged()` for Java 1.1).
- Keyboard events (`keyUp()` and `keyDown()` for Java 1.0, and `keyPressed()` and `keyReleased()` for Java 1.1).

39.7 Java 1.0 and Java 1.1

There has been a big change between Java 1.0 and Java 1.1. The main change is to greatly improve the architecture of the AWT, which helps in compatibility. Java 1.0 programs will work with most browsers, but only upgraded browsers will work with Java 1.1. The main reasons to upgrade though are:

- Java 1.1 adds new features.
- Faster architecture with more robust implementations of the AWT.
- Support for older facilities will be phased out.

39.7.1 Deprecation

Older facilities are contained within Java 1.0 and are still supported by Java 1.1, but the Java compiler gives a deprecation warning. This warning means that the facility will eventually be phased-out. The warning is in the form of:

```
C:\jdk1.1.6\src\chap39>javac chap39_1.java
Note: chap39_1.java uses a deprecated API.  Recompile with "-
deprecation" for details.
1 warning
```

The full details on the deprecation can be found by using the –deprecation flag. For example:

```
C:\jdk1.1.6\src\chap39>javac -deprecation chap39_1.java
chap39_1.java:9: Note: The method boolean mouseUp(java.awt. Event, int,
int) in class java.awt.Component has been deprecated, and class chap39_1
(which is not deprecated) overrides it.

  public boolean mouseUp(Event event,
                 ^
Note: chap39_1.java uses a deprecated API.  Please consult the
documentation for a better alternative.
1 warning
```

39.8 Initialization and exit methods

Java applets have various reserved methods which are called when various events occur. Table 39.2 shows typical initialization methods and their events, and Figure 39.1 illustrates how they are called.

Table 39.2   Java initialization and exit methods.

Method	Description
public void **init**()	This method is called each time the applet is started. It is typically used to add user interface components.
public void **stop**()	This method is called when the user moves away from the page on which the applet resides. It is thus typically used to stop processing while the user is not accessing the applet. Typically it is used to stop animation or audio files, or mathematical processing. The start() method normally restarts the processing.
public void **paint**(Graphics g)	This method is called when the applet is first called and whenever the user resizes or moves the windows.
public void **destroy**()	This method is called when the applet is stopped and is normally used to release associated resources, such as freeing memory, closing files, and so on.

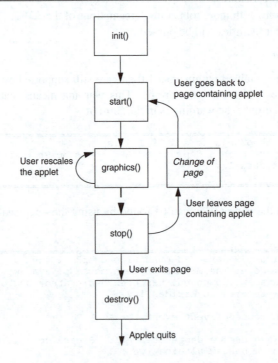

Figure 39.1   Java initialization and exit methods

Java applet 39.3 gives an example using the `init()` and `start()` methods. The variable i is declared within the applet and it is set to a value of 5 in the `init()` method. The `start()` method then adds 6 onto this value. After this the `paint()` method is called so that it displays the value of i (which should equal 11).

📖 **Java applet 39.3** (chap39_3.java)

```
import java.awt.*;
import java.applet.*;

public class chap39_3 extends Applet
{
int       i;
  public void init()
  {
    i=5;
  }
  public void start()
  {
    i=i+6;
  }
  public void paint(Graphics g)
  {
   g.drawString("The value of i is "
            + i,5,25);
  }
}
```

📖 **HTML script 39.3** (chap39_3.html)

```
<HTML>
<TITLE>Applet</TITLE>
<APPLET CODE=chap39_3.class
WIDTH=200 HEIGHT=200></APPLET></HTML>
```

39.9 Mouse events in Java 1.0

Most Java applets require some user interaction, normally with the mouse or from the keyboard. A mouse operation causes mouse events. The six basic mouse events which are supported in Java 1.0 are:

- `mouseUp(Event evt, int x, int y)`
- `mouseDown(Event evt, int x, int y)`
- `mouseDrag(Event evt, int x, int y)`
- `mouseEnter(Event evt, int x, int y)`
- `mouseExit(Event evt, int x, int y)`
- `mouseMove(Event evt, int x, int y)`

Java applet 39.4 uses three mouse events to display the current mouse cursor. Each of the methods must return a true value to identify that the event has been handled successfully (the return type is of data type boolean thus the return could only be a true or a false). In the example applet, on moving the mouse cursor with the left mouse key pressed down the `mouseDrag()` method is automatically called. The x and y coordinate of the cursor is stored in the x and y variable when the event occurs. This is used in the methods to build a message string (in the case of the drag event the string name is `MouseDragMsg`).

The `mouseEnter()` method is called when the mouse enters the component, `mouse-Exit()` is called when the mouse exits the component and `mouseMove()` when the mouse moves (the mouse button is up).

📖 Java applet 39.4 (chap39_4.java)

```
import java.awt.*;
import java.applet.*;
public class chap39_4 extends Applet
{
String  MouseDownMsg=null;
String  MouseUpMsg=null;
String  MouseDragMsg=null;

  public boolean mouseUp(Event event,
   int x, int y)
  {
    MouseUpMsg = "UP>" +x + "," + y;
    repaint();    // call paint()
    return(true);
  }
  public boolean mouseDown(Event event,
   int x, int y)
  {
    MouseDownMsg = "DOWN>" +x + "," + y;
    repaint();    // call paint()
    return(true);
  }

  public boolean mouseDrag(Event event,
   int x, int y)
  {
    MouseDragMsg = "DRAG>" +x + "," + y;
    repaint();    // call paint()
    return(true);
  }

  public void paint(Graphics g)
  {
    if (MouseUpMsg !=null)
      g.drawString(MouseUpMsg,5,20);
    if (MouseDownMsg !=null)
      g.drawString(MouseDownMsg,5,40);
    if (MouseDragMsg !=null)
      g.drawString(MouseDragMsg,5,60);
  }
}
```

📖 HTML script 39.4 (chap39_4.html)

```
<HTML>
<TITLE>Applet</TITLE>
<APPLET CODE=chap39_4.class WIDTH=200
HEIGHT=200></APPLET></HTML>
```

39.10 Mouse event handling in Java 1.1

Java 1.1 has changed the event handling. In its place is the concept of listeners. Each listener receivers notification about the types of events that it is interested in. For mouse handling the two listeners are:

- `MouseListener`. This has the associated methods of:
  - `mousePressed()` which is equivalent to `mouseDown()` in Java 1.0
  - `mouseReleased()` which is equivalent to `mouseUp()` in Java 1.0
  - `mouseEntered()` which is equivalent to `mouseEnter()` in Java 1.0
  - `mouseExited()` which is equivalent to `mouseExit()` in Java 1.0
  - `mouseClicked()`
- `MouseMotionListener`. This has the associated methods of:
  - `mouseDragged()` which is equivalent to `mouseDrag()` in Java 1.0
  - `mouseMoved()` which is equivalent to `mouseMove()` in Java 1.0

39.10.1 Mouse methods

The arguments passed to the methods have also changed, in that there are no `x` and `y` integers passed, and there is no return from them. Their syntax is as follows:

```
public void mousePressed(MouseEvent event) {};
public void mouseReleased(MouseEvent event) {};
public void mouseClicked(MouseEvent event) {};
public void mouseExited(MouseEvent event) {};
public void mouseEntered(MouseEvent event) {};
public void mouseDragged(MouseEvent event) {};
public void mouseMoved(MouseEvent event) {};
```

The x and y coordinates of the mouse event can be found by accessing the `getX()` and `getY()` methods of the event, such as:

```
x=event.getX();    y=event.getY();
```

39.10.2 Event class

The other main change to the Java program is to add the `java.awt.event` package, with:

```
import java.awt.event.*;
```

39.10.3 Class declaration

The class declaration is changed so that the appropriate listener is defined. If both mouse listeners are required then the class declaration is as follows:

```
public class class_name extends Applet
   implements MouseListener, MouseMotionListener
```

39.10.4 Defining components that generate events

The components which generate events must be defined. In the case of a mouse event these are added as:

```
        this.addMouseListener(this);
        this.addMouseMotionListener(this);
```

39.10.5 Updated Java program

Java applet 39.5 gives the updated Java program with Java 1.1 updates.

📖 Java applet 39.5 (chap39_5.java)

```java
import java.awt.*;
import java.applet.*;
import java.awt.event.*;

public class chap39_5 extends Applet
implements MouseListener, MouseMotionListener
{
String  MouseDownMsg=null;
String  MouseUpMsg=null;
String  MouseDragMsg=null;

  public void init()
  {
        this.addMouseListener(this);
        this.addMouseMotionListener(this);
  }

  public void paint(Graphics g)
  {
    if (MouseUpMsg !=null)  g.drawString(MouseUpMsg,5,20);
    if (MouseDownMsg !=null) g.drawString(MouseDownMsg,5,40);
    if (MouseDragMsg !=null) g.drawString(MouseDragMsg,5,60);
  }

  public void mousePressed(MouseEvent event)
  {
    MouseUpMsg = "UP>" +event.getX() + "," + event.getY();
    repaint();    // call paint()
  }
  public void mouseReleased(MouseEvent event)
  {
    MouseDownMsg = "DOWN>" +event.getX() + "," + event.getY();
    repaint();    // call paint()
  }
  public void mouseClicked(MouseEvent event) {};
  public void mouseExited(MouseEvent event) {};
  public void mouseEntered(MouseEvent event) {};

  public void mouseDragged(MouseEvent event)
  {
    MouseDragMsg = "DRAG>" +event.getX() + "," + event.getY();
    repaint();    // call paint()
  }
  public void mouseMoved(MouseEvent event) {};
}
```

39.11 Mouse selection in Java 1.0

In many applets the user is prompted to select an object using the mouse. To achieve this the x and y position of the event is tested to determine if the cursor is within the defined area. Java applet 39.6 is a program which allows the user to press the mouse button on the applet screen. The applet then uses the mouse events to determine if the cursor is within a given area of the screen (in this case between 10,10 and 100,50). If the user is within this defined area then the message displayed is HIT, else it is MISS. The graphics method g.drawRect(x1,y1,x2,y2) draws a rectangle from (x1,y1) to (x2,y2).

📖 **Java applet 39.6** (chap39_6.java)

```java
import java.awt.*;
import java.applet.*;
public class chap39_6 extends Applet
{
String  Msg=null;
int     x_start,y_start,x_end,y_end;

  public void init()
  {
    x_start=10;    y_start=10;
    x_end=100;     y_end=50;
  }

  public boolean mouseUp(Event event,
   int x, int y)
  {
    if ((x>x_start) && (x<x_end) &&
           (y>y_start) && (y<y_end))
               Msg = "HIT";
    else Msg="MISS";
    repaint();    // call paint()
    return(true);
  }

  public boolean mouseDown(Event event,
   int x, int y)
  {
    if ((x>x_start) && (x<x_end) &&
           (y>y_start) && (y<y_end))
               Msg = "HIT";
    else Msg="MISS";
    repaint();    // call paint()
    return(true);
  }

  public void paint(Graphics g)
  {

  g.drawRect(x_start,y_start,x_end,y_end);
    g.drawString("Hit",30,30);
    if (Msg !=null)
     g.drawString("HIT OR MISS: "
         + Msg,5,80);
  }
}
```

📖 **HTML script 39.5** (chap39_5.html)

```html
<HTML>
<TITLE>Applet</TITLE>
<APPLET CODE=chap39_6.class WIDTH=200
HEIGHT=200></APPLET></HTML>
```

Java applet 39.7 gives the updated Java program with Java 1.1 updates.

📖 **Java applet 39.7** (chap39_7.java)

```java
import java.awt.*;
import java.applet.*;
import java.awt.event.*;

public class chap39_7 extends Applet implements MouseListener
{
```

```
String  Msg=null;
int     x_start,y_start,x_end,y_end;

  public void init()
  {
    x_start=10;    y_start=10;
    x_end=100;     y_end=50;
    this.addMouseListener(this);
  }

  public void mousePressed(MouseEvent event)
  {
    int x,y;
    x=event.getX(); y=event.getY();

    if ((x>x_start) && (x<x_end) && (y>y_start) && (y<y_end))
           Msg = "HIT";
    else Msg="MISS";
    repaint();    // call paint()
  }

  public void mouseReleased(MouseEvent event)
  {
    int x,y;
    x=event.getX();  y=event.getY();
    if ((x>x_start) && (x<x_end) && (y>y_start) && (y<y_end))
           Msg = "HIT";
    else Msg="MISS";
    repaint();    // call paint()
  }
  public void mouseEntered(MouseEvent event) {};
  public void mouseExited(MouseEvent event) {};
  public void mouseClicked(MouseEvent event) {};

  public void paint(Graphics g)
  {
    g.drawRect(x_start,y_start,x_end,y_end);
    g.drawString("Hit",30,30);
    if (Msg !=null)
     g.drawString("HIT OR MISS: "
         + Msg,5,80);
  }
}
```

39.12 Keyboard input in Java 1.0

Java 1.0 provides for two keyboard events, these are:

- `keyUp(Event evt, int key)`. Called when a key has been released
- `keyDown(Event evt, int key)`. Called when a key has been pressed

The parameters passed into these methods are `event` (which defines the keyboard state) and an integer `Keypressed` which describes the key pressed.

The event contains an identification as to the type of event it is. When one of the function keys is pressed then the variable `event.id` is set to the macro `Event. KEY_ACTION` (as shown in Java applet 39.8). Other keys, such as the Cntrl, Alt and Shift keys, set bits in the `event.modifier` variable. The test for the Cntrl key is:

```
        if ((event.modifiers & Event.CTRL_MASK) !=0)
```

```
    Msg="CONTROL KEY "+KeyPress;
```

This tests the CTRL_MASK bit; if it is a 1 then the Cntrl key has been pressed. Java applet 39.8 shows its uses.

📖 **Java applet 39.8** (chap39_8.java)

```
import java.awt.*;
import java.applet.*;

public class chap39_8 extends Applet
{
String  Msg=null;

 public boolean keyUp(Event event,
  int KeyPress)
 {
   Msg="Key pressed="+(char)KeyPress;
   repaint();   // call paint()
   return(true);
 }
  public void paint(Graphics g)
  {
   if (Msg !=null)
          g.drawString(Msg,5,80);
  }
}
```

📖 **HTML script 39.6** (chap39_6.html)

```
<HTML><TITLE>Applet</TITLE>
<APPLET CODE=chap39_8.class WIDTH=200
HEIGHT=200></APPLET></HTML>
```

📖 **Java applet 39.9** (chap39_9.java)

```
import java.awt.*;
import java.applet.*;

public class chap39_9 extends Applet
{
String  Msg=null;
 public boolean keyDown(Event event, int KeyPress)
 {
 if (event.id == Event.KEY_ACTION)
   Msg="FUNCTION KEY "+KeyPress;
 else if ((event.modifiers & Event.SHIFT_MASK)!=0)
   Msg="SHIFT KEY "+KeyPress;
 else if ((event.modifiers & Event.CTRL_MASK)!=0)
   Msg="CONTROL KEY "+KeyPress;
 else if ((event.modifiers & Event.ALT_MASK)!=0)
   Msg="ALT KEY "+KeyPress;
 else Msg=""+(char)KeyPress;
 repaint();   // call paint()
 return(true);
 }
 public void paint(Graphics g)
 {
  if (Msg!=null)
    g.drawString(Msg,5,80);
 }
}
```

39.13 Keyboard events in Java 1.1

Java 1.1 has changed the event handling. In its place is the concept of listeners. Each listener receivers notification about the types of events that it is interested in. For keyboard handling the two listeners are:

- `KeyListener`. This has the associated methods of:
  - `keyPressed()` which is equivalent to `keyDown()` in Java 1.0
  - `keyReleased()` which is equivalent to `keyUp()` in Java 1.0
  - `keyTyped()`

39.13.1 Key methods

The arguments passed to the methods have also changed. Their syntax is as follows:

```
public void keyPressed(KeyEvent event) {}
public void keyReleased(KeyEvent event) {}
public void keyTyped(KeyEvent event) {}
```

39.13.2 Event class

Another change to the Java program is to add the `java.awt.event` package, with:

```
import java.awt.event.*;
```

39.13.3 Class declaration

The class declaration is changed so that the appropriate listener is defined. If the key listener is required then the class declaration is as follows:

```
public class class_name extends Applet implements KeyListener
```

39.13.4 Defining components that generate events

The components which generate events must be defined. In the case of a key event these are added as:

```
        compname.addKeyListener(this);
```

39.13.5 Updated Java program

Java applet 39.10 gives the updated Java program with Java 1.1 updates. In this case a `TextField` component is added to the applet (`text`). When a key is pressed on this component then the `keyPressed` event listener is called, when one is released the `keyReleased` is called. Figure 39.2 gives a sample run.

The `getKeyCode()` method is used to determine the key that has been activated. In the event method the `KeyEvent` defines a number of `VK_` constants, such as:

`VK_F1`	Function Key F1	`VK_A`	Character 'A'	`VK_ALT`	Alt key
`VK_CONTROL`	Control Key	`VK_0`	Character '0'	`VK_SHIFT`	Shift key

📖 Java applet 39.10 (chap39_10.java)

```
import java.awt.*;
import java.applet.*;
import java.awt.event.*;

public class chap39_10 extends Applet implements KeyListener
{
String  Msg=null;
TextField text;


    public void init()
    {
       text=new TextField(20);

       add(text);
       text.addKeyListener(this);
    }

    public void keyPressed(KeyEvent event)
    {
    int KeyPress;

       KeyPress=event.getKeyCode();

       if (KeyPress == KeyEvent.VK_ALT)  Msg="ALT KEY";
       else if (KeyPress == KeyEvent.VK_CONTROL)  Msg="Cntrl KEY ";
       else if (KeyPress == KeyEvent.VK_SHIFT) Msg="SHIFT KEY ";
       else if (KeyPress == KeyEvent.VK_RIGHT) Msg="RIGHT KEY ";
       else if (KeyPress == KeyEvent.VK_LEFT)  Msg="LEFT KEY ";
       else if (KeyPress == KeyEvent.VK_F1)    Msg="Function key F1";
       else Msg="Key:"+(char)KeyPress;

       text.setText(Msg);
    }
    public void keyReleased(KeyEvent event) { }
    public void keyTyped(KeyEvent event)  { }

}
```

Figure 39.2 Sample run.

39.14 Buttons and events

Java applet 39.11 creates three `Button` objects. These are created with the `add()` function which displays the button in the applet window.

📖 Java applet 39.11 (chap39_11.java)

```
import java.awt.*;
import java.applet.*;

public class chap39_11 extends Applet
{
  public void init()
  {
    add(new Button("Help"));
    add(new Button("Show"));
    add(new Button("Exit"));
  }
}
```

An alternative approach to creating buttons is to declare them using the Button type. For example the following applet is equivalent to Java applet 39.11. The names of the button objects, in this case, are `button1`, `button2` and `button3`.

```
import java.applet.*;
import java.awt.*;

public class chap39_11 extends Applet
{
Button button1= new Button("Help");
Button button2= new Button("Show");
Button button3= new Button("Exit");


    public void init()
    {
        add(button1);
        add(button2);
        add(button3);
    }
}
```

39.15 Action with Java 1.0

The action function is called when an event occurs, such as a keypress, button press, and so on. The information on the event is stored in the Event parameter. Its format is:

```
public boolean action(Event evt, Object obj)
```

where event is made with the specified target component, time stamp, event type, x and y coordinates, keyboard key, state of the modifier keys and argument. These are:

- `evt.target` is the target component.
- `evt.when` is the time stamp.
- `evt.id` is the event type.
- `evt.x` is the x coordinate.

- `evt.y` is the y coordinate.
- `evt.key` is the key pressed in a keyboard event.
- `evt.modifiers` is the state of the modifier keys.
- `evt.arg` is the specified argument.

Java applet 39.12 contains an example of the action method. It has two buttons (named New 1 and New 2). When any of the buttons is pressed the action method is called. Figure 39.3 shows the display when either of the buttons is pressed. In the left-hand side of Figure 39.3 the New 1 button is pressed and the right-hand side shows the display after the New 2 button is pressed. It can be seen that differences are in the `target`, `arg` parameter and the `x`, `y` coordinate parameters.

Java applet 39.12 (chap39_12.java)

```java
import java.applet.*;
import java.awt.*;

public class chap39_12 extends Applet
{

String Msg1=null, Msg2, Msg3, Msg4;

    public void init()
    {
        add (new Button("New 1"));
        add (new Button("New 2"));
    }

    public boolean action(Event evt, Object obj)
    {
        Msg1= "Target= "+evt.target;
        Msg2= "When= " + evt.when + " id=" + evt.id +
                " x= "+ evt.x + " y= " + evt.y;
        Msg3= "Arg= " + evt.arg + " Key= " + evt.key;
        Msg4= "Click= " + evt.clickCount;
        repaint();
        return true;
    }

    public void paint(Graphics g)
    {
        if (Msg1!=null)
        {
                g.drawString(Msg1,30,80);
                g.drawString(Msg2,30,100);
                g.drawString(Msg3,30,120);
                g.drawString(Msg4,30,140);
        }
    }
}
```

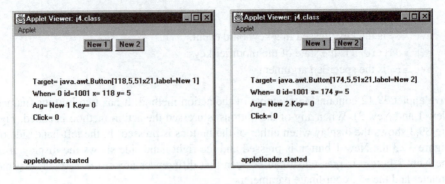

Figure 39.3   Sample runs.

Thus to determine the button that has been pressed the evt.arg string can be tested. Java applet 39.13 shows an example where the evt.arg parameter is tested for its string content.

📖   **Java applet 39.13** (chap39_13.java)

```
import java.applet.*;
import java.awt.*;

public class chap39_13 extends Applet
{

String Msg=null;

    public void init()
    {
        add (new Button("New 1"));
        add (new Button("New 2"));
    }

    public boolean action(Event evt, Object obj)
    {
        if (evt.arg=="New 1") Msg= "New 1 pressed";
        else if (evt.arg=="New 2") Msg= "New 2 pressed";
        repaint();
        return true;
    }

    public void paint(Graphics g)
    {
        if (Msg!=null)
        {
                g.drawString(Msg,30,80);
        }
    }
}
```

Java applet 39.14 uses the action function which is called when an event occurs. Within this function the event variable is tested to see if one of the buttons caused the event. This is achieved with:

```
if (event.target instanceof Button)
```

If this test is true then the Msg string takes on the value of the Object, which holds the name of the button that caused the event.

📖 Java applet 39.14 (chap39_14.java)

```
import java.awt.*;
import java.applet.*;

public class chap39_14 extends Applet
{
String  Msg=null;

  public void init()
  {
   add(new Button("Help"));
   add(new Button("Show"));
   add(new Button("Exit"));
  }
  public boolean action(Event event, Object object)
  {
   if (event.target instanceof Button)
   {
     Msg = (String) object;
     repaint();
   }
   return(true);
  }
  public void paint(Graphics g)
  {
   if (Msg!=null)
   g.drawString("Button:" + Msg,30,80);
  }
}
```

39.16 Action listener in Java 1.1

As with mouse events, buttons, menus and textfields are associated with an action lis-tener (named `ActionListener`). When an event associated with these occurs then the `actionPerformed` method is called. Its format is:

```
public void actionPerformed(ActionEvent evt)
```

where `evt` defines the event. The associated methods are:

- `getActionCommand()` is the action command.
- `evt.getModifiers()` is the state of the modifier keys.
- `evt.paramString()` is the parameter string.

Java applet 39.15 contains an example of the `action` method. It has two buttons (named `New1` and `New2`). When any of the buttons is pressed the action method is called. Each of the buttons has an associated listener which is initiated with:

```
button1.addActionListener(this);
button2.addActionListener(this);
```

Figure 39.4 shows the display when either of the buttons are pressed. In the left-hand side of Figure 39.4 the `New1` button is pressed and the right-hand side shows the display after the `New2` button is pressed.

Java applet 39.15 (chap39_15.java)

```
import java.applet.*;
import java.awt.*;
import java.awt.event.*;

public class chap39_15 extends Applet implements ActionListener
{
Button   button1, button2;
String   Msg1=null, Msg2, Msg3;

    public void init()
    {
        button1 = new Button("New 1");
        button2 = new Button("New 2");
        add(button1); add(button2);
        button1.addActionListener(this);
        button2.addActionListener(this);
    }

    public void actionPerformed(ActionEvent evt)
    {
        Msg1= "Command= "+evt.getActionCommand();
        Msg2= "Modifiers= " + evt.getModifiers();
        Msg3= "String= " + evt.paramString();
        repaint();
    }

    public void paint(Graphics g)
    {
        if (Msg1!=null)
        {
            g.drawString(Msg1,30,80);
            g.drawString(Msg2,30,100);
            g.drawString(Msg3,30,120);
        }
    }
}
```

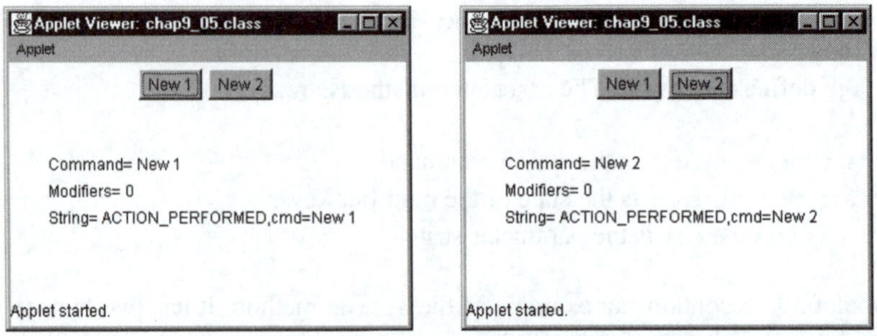

Figure 39.4   Sample run.

Thus to determine the button that has been pressed the getActionCommand() method is used. Java applet 39.16 shows an example where the getActionCommand() method is tested for its string content. Figure 39.5 shows a sample run.

Java applet 39.16 (⚡Java 1.1)

```java
import java.applet.*;
import java.awt.*;
import java.awt.event.*;

public class chap39_16 extends Applet implements ActionListener
{

Button button1, button2;
String Msg=null;

    public void init()
    {

        button1 = new Button("New 1");
        button2 = new Button("New 2");
        add(button1); add(button2);
        button1.addActionListener(this);
        button2.addActionListener(this);
    }

    public void actionPerformed(ActionEvent evt)
    {
    String command;

        command=evt.getActionCommand();

        if (command.equals("New 1")) Msg="New 1 pressed";
        if (command.equals("New 2")) Msg="New 2 pressed";

        repaint();
    }

    public void paint(Graphics g)
    {
        if (Msg!=null)
        {
                g.drawString(Msg,30,80);
        }
    }
}
```

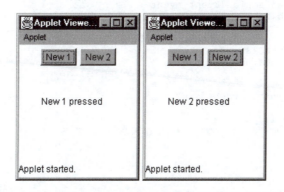

Figure 39.5 Sample run.

39.17 Checkboxes

Typically, checkboxes are used to select from a number of options. Java applet 39.17 shows how an applet can use checkboxes. As before, the `action` method is called when a checkbox changes its state and within the method the `event.target` parameter is tested for the checkbox with:

```
if (event.target instanceof Checkbox)
```

If this is true, then the method `DetermineCheckState()` is called which tests `event.target` for the checkbox value and its state (true or false).

Java applet 39.17 (⚡Java 1.0)

```
import java.awt.*;
import java.applet.*;
public class chap39_17 extends Applet
{
String  Msg=null;
Checkbox fax, telephone, email, post;

 public void init()
 {
  fax=new Checkbox("FAX");
  telephone=new Checkbox("Telephone");
  email=new Checkbox("Email");
  post=new Checkbox("Post",null,true);
  add(fax); add(telephone);
  add(email); add(post);
 }

 public void DetermineCheckState(
     Checkbox Cbox)
 {
  Msg=Cbox.getLabel()+" "+ Cbox.getState();
  repaint();
 }

 public boolean action(Event event,
     Object object)
 {
  if (event.target instanceof Checkbox)
    DetermineCheckState(
      (Checkbox)event.target);
  return(true);
 }
 public void paint(Graphics g)
 {
  if (Msg!=null)
    g.drawString("Check box:" + Msg,30,80);
 }
}
```

39.18 Item listener in Java 1.1

As with mouse events, checkboxes and lists are associated with an item listener (named `ItemListener`). When an event associated with these occur then the `itemStateChanged` method is called. Its format is:

```
        public void itemStateChanged(ItemEvent event)
```

where event defines the event. The associated methods are:

- getItem() is the item selected.
- getStateChange() is the state of the checkbox.
- paramString() is the parameter string.

Java applet 39.18 contains an example of checkboxes and Figure 39.6 shows a sample run. Each of the checkboxes has an associated listener which is initiated in the form:

> *chbox*.addItemListener(this);

📖   **Java applet 39.18 (↯Java 1.1)**

```
import java.awt.*;
import java.applet.*;
import java.awt.event.*;

public class chap39_18 extends Applet implements ItemListener
{
String      Msg1=null,Msg2,Msg3;
Checkbox    fax, telephone, email,post;

    public void init()
    {
        fax=new Checkbox("FAX");
        telephone=new Checkbox("Telephone");
        email=new Checkbox("Email");
        post=new Checkbox("Post",null,true);
        add(fax);
        add(telephone);
        add(email);
        add(post);

        fax.addItemListener(this);
        email.addItemListener(this);
        telephone.addItemListener(this);
        post.addItemListener(this);
    }

    public void itemStateChanged(ItemEvent event)
    {
        Msg1=""+event.getItem();
        Msg2=""+event.getStateChange();
        Msg3=event.paramString();
        repaint();
    }

    public void paint(Graphics g)
    {
        if (Msg1!=null)
        {
            g.drawString(Msg1,30,80);
            g.drawString(Msg2,30,110);
            g.drawString(Msg3,30,150);
        }
    }
}
```

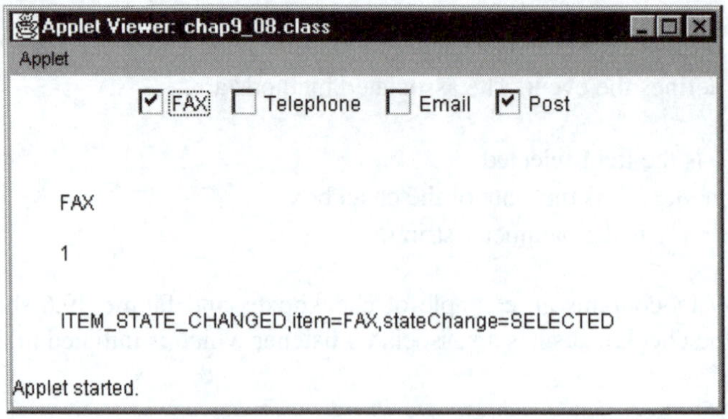

Figure 39.6 Sample run.

39.19 Radio buttons

The standard checkboxes allow any number of options to be selected. A radio button allows only one option to be selected at a time. The program is changed by:

- Adding checkbox names (such as fax, tele, email and post).
- Initializing the checkbox with CheckboxGroup() to a checkbox group identifier.
- Adding the identifier of the checkbox group to the Checkbox() method.
- Testing the target property of the event to see if it equals a checkbox name.

Java applet 39.19 shows how this is achieved with Java 1.1.

Java applet 39.19 (⚡Java 1.1)

```
import java.awt.*;
import java.awt.event.*;
import java.applet.*;

public class chap39_19 extends Applet implements ItemListener
{
String  Msg=null;
Checkbox fax, tele, email, post;

 public void init()
  {

      CheckboxGroup RadioGroup = new CheckboxGroup();

      add(fax=new Checkbox("FAX",RadioGroup,true));
      add(tele=new Checkbox("Telephone",RadioGroup,false));
      add (email=new Checkbox("Email",RadioGroup,false));
      add (post=new Checkbox("Post",RadioGroup,false));
         fax.addItemListener(this);
         tele.addItemListener(this);
         email.addItemListener(this);
         post.addItemListener(this);
  }

    public void itemStateChanged(ItemEvent event)
```

```
    {
Object obj;
        obj=event.getItem();

        if (obj.equals("FAX")) Msg="FAX";
        else if (obj.equals("Telephone")) Msg="Telephone";
        else if (obj.equals("Email")) Msg="Email";
        else if (obj.equals("Post")) Msg="Post";
        repaint();
    }

    public void paint(Graphics g)
    {
        if (Msg!=null)    g.drawString("Check box:" + Msg,30,80);
    }
}
```

This sets the checkbox type to `RadioGroup` and it can be seen that only one of the check-boxes is initially set (that is, 'FAX'). Figure 39.7 shows a sample run. It should be noted that grouped checkboxes use a round circle with a dot (⊙), whereas ungrouped check-boxes use a square box with a check mark (tick) (☑).

Figure 39.7   Sample run.

39.20 Pop-up menu choices

To create a pop-up menu the `Choice` object is initially created with:

```
Choice mymenu = new Choice();
```

After this the menu options are defined using the `addItem` method. Java applet 39.20 shows an example usage of a pop-up menu.

📖   Java applet 39.20 (♣Java 1.0)

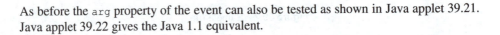

```java
import java.awt.*;
import java.applet.*;

public class chap39_20 extends Applet
{
String  Msg=null;
Choice  mymenu= new Choice();

  public void init()
  {
    mymenu.addItem("FAX");
    mymenu.addItem("Telephone");
    mymenu.addItem("Email");
    mymenu.addItem("Post");
    add(mymenu);
  }
  public void DetermineCheckState(
    Choice mymenu)
  {
    Msg=mymenu.getItem(
      mymenu.getSelectedIndex());
    repaint();
  }
  public boolean action(Event event,
      Object object)
  {
   if (event.target instanceof Choice)
    DetermineCheckState(
      (Choice)event.target);
   return(true);
  }

  public void paint(Graphics g)
  {
  if (Msg!=null)
   g.drawString("Menu select:"+Msg,30,120);
  }
}
```

As before the `arg` property of the event can also be tested as shown in Java applet 39.21.
Java applet 39.22 gives the Java 1.1 equivalent.

📖   Java applet 39.21 (♣Java 1.0)

```java
import java.awt.*;
import java.applet.*;

public class chap39_21 extends Applet
{
String  Msg=null;
Choice  mymenu= new Choice();

  public void init()
  {
    mymenu.addItem("FAX");
    mymenu.addItem("Telephone");
    mymenu.addItem("Email");
    mymenu.addItem("Post");
    add(mymenu);
  }
  public boolean action(Event event, Object object)
```

```
    {
      if (event.arg=="FAX") Msg="FAX";
      else if (event.arg=="Telephone") Msg="Telephone";
      else if (event.arg=="Email") Msg="Email";
      else if (event.arg == "Post") Msg="Post";
      repaint();
      return(true);
    }
    public void paint(Graphics g)
    {
      if (Msg!=null)
        g.drawString("Menu select:" + Msg,30,120);
    }
}
```

📖 Java applet 39.22 (⚡Java 1.1)

```
import java.awt.*;
import java.awt.event.*;
import java.applet.*;

public class chap39_22 extends Applet implements ItemListener
{
String  Msg=null;
Choice  mymenu= new Choice();

  public void init()
  {
    mymenu.addItem("FAX");
    mymenu.addItem("Telephone");
    mymenu.addItem("Email");
    mymenu.addItem("Post");
    add(mymenu);
    mymenu.addItemListener(this);
  }
  public void itemStateChanged(ItemEvent event)
  {
  Object obj;

    obj=event.getItem();

    if (obj.equals("FAX")) Msg="FAX";
    else if (obj.equals("Telephone")) Msg="Telephone";
    else if (obj.equals("Email")) Msg="Email";
    else if (obj.equals("Post")) Msg="Post";
    repaint();
  }
  public void paint(Graphics g)
  {
    if (Msg!=null)
      g.drawString("Menu select:" + Msg,30,120);
  }
}
```

39.21 Other pop-up menu options

The `java.awt.Choice` class allows for a pop-up menu. It includes the following methods:

`Public void` **addItem**`(String item);`   Adds a menu item to the end.

`Public void addNotify();`	Allows the modification of a list's appearance without changing its functionality.
`public int countItems();`	Returns the number of items in the menu.
`public String getItem(int index);`	Returns the string of the menu item at that index value.
`public int getSelectedIndex();`	Returns the index value of the selected item.
`public String getSelectedItem();`	Returns the string of the selected item.
`protected String paramString();`	Returns the parameter String of the list.
`public void select(int pos);`	Selects the menu item at a given index.
`public void select(String str);`	Selects the menu item with a given string name.

The `countItems` method is used to determine the number of items in a pop-up menu, for example:

```
Msg= "Number of items is " + mymenu.countItems()
```

The `getItem(int index)` returns the string associated with the menu item, where the first item has a value of zero. For example:

```
Msg= "Menu item number 2 is " + mymenu.getItem(2);
```

Java applet 39.23 uses the `select` method to display the second menu option as the default and the `getItem` method to display the name of the option.

📖 **Java applet 39.23 (⚡Java 1.1)**

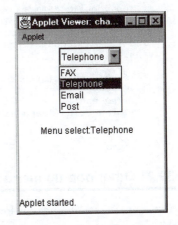

```
import java.awt.*;
import java.awt.event.*;
import java.applet.*;

public class chap39_23 extends Applet
      implements ItemListener
{
String  Msg=null;
Choice  mymenu= new Choice();

  public void init()
  {
    mymenu.addItem("FAX");
    mymenu.addItem("Telephone");
    mymenu.addItem("Email");
    mymenu.addItem("Post");
    add(mymenu);
    mymenu.addItemListener(this);
    mymenu.select(1);
        // Select item 1 (Telephone)
```

```
}
public void itemStateChanged(ItemEvent evt)
{
Object obj;

 obj=evt.getItem();

 if (obj.equals("FAX"))
     Msg=mymenu.getItem(0);
 else if (obj.equals("Telephone"))
     Msg=mymenu.getItem(1);
 else if (obj.equals("Email"))
     Msg=mymenu.getItem(2);
 else if (obj.equals("Post"))
     Msg=mymenu.getItem(3);
 repaint();
}
public void paint(Graphics g)
{
 if (Msg!=null)
   g.drawString("Menu select:"+Msg,30,120);
}
}
```

39.22 Multiple menus

Multiple menus can be created in a Java applet and the `action` event can be used to differentiate between the menus. Java applet 39.24 has two pull-down menus and two buttons (`age`, `gender`, `print` and `close`). The event method `getItem` is then used to determine which of the menus was selected. In this case the `print` button is used to display the options of the two pull-down menus and `close` is used to exit from the applet.

📖 **Java applet 39.24 (⚡Java 1.1)**

```
import java.applet.*;
import java.awt.*;
import java.awt.event.*;

public class chap39_24 extends Applet
   implements ItemListener, ActionListener
{
Choice age = new Choice();
Choice gender = new Choice();
Button print= new Button("Print");
Button close= new Button("Close");
String gendertype=null, agetype=null;

String Msg, Options[];

  public void init()
  {
      age.addItem("10-19");
      age.addItem("20-29");
      age.addItem("30-39");
      age.addItem("40-49");
      age.addItem("Other");
      add(age);

      gender.addItem("Male");
      gender.addItem("Female");
      add(gender);
```

```
        add(print);
        add(close);

        age.addItemListener(this);
        gender.addItemListener(this);
        print.addActionListener(this);
        close.addActionListener(this);
   }

public void itemStateChanged(ItemEvent evt)
{
 int i;
 Object obj;

     obj=evt.getItem();

 if (obj.equals("10-19")) agetype="10-19";
 else if (obj.equals("20-29"))
     agetype="20-29";
 else if (obj.equals("30-39"))
     agetype="30-39";
 else if (obj.equals("40-49"))
     agetype="40-49";
 else if (obj.equals("Other"))
     agetype="Other";
 else if (obj.equals("Male"))
     gendertype="Male";
 else if (obj.equals("Female"))
     gendertype="Female";
 }

public void actionPerformed(ActionEvent evt)
{
String str;

  str=evt.getActionCommand();
  if (str.equals("Print"))  repaint();
  else if (str.equals("Close"))
     System.exit(0);
}

public void paint(Graphics g)
{
 if ((agetype!=null) && (gendertype!=null))
  Msg="Your are " + agetype + " and a "
                 + gendertype;
 else Msg="Please select age and gender";

 if (Msg!=null) g.drawString(Msg,20,80);
 }
 }
```

39.23 Menu bar

Menu bars are now familiar in most GUIs (such as Microsoft Windows and Motif). They consist of a horizontal menu bar with pull-down submenus.

The `java.awt.MenuBar` class contains a constructor for a menu bar. Its format is:

```
        public MenuBar();
```

and the methods which can be applied to it are:

`Public Menu add(Menu m);`	Adds the specified menu to the menu bar.
`Public void addNotify();`	Allows a change of appearance of the menu bar without changing any of the menu bar's functionality.
`Public int countMenus();`	Counts the number of menus on the menu bar.
`Public Menu getHelpMenu();`	Gets the help menu on the menu bar.
`Public Menu getMenu(int i);`	Gets the specified menu.
`Public void remove(int index);`	Removes the menu located at the specified index from the menu bar.
`Public void remove( MenuComponent m);`	Removes the specified menu from the menu bar.
`Public void removeNotify();`	Removes notify.
`Public void setHelpMenu( Menu m);`	Sets the help menu to the specified menu on the menu bar.

Java program 39.25 gives an example of using a menu bar. Initially the menu bar is created with the `MenuBar()` constructor, and submenus with the `Menu` constructors (in this case, `mfile`, `medit` and `mhelp`). Items are added to the submenus with the `MenuItem` constructor (such as `New`, `Open`, and so on). A `handleEvent()` method has been added to catch a close window operation. The `addSeparator()` method has been added to add a line between menu items. Note that this program is not an applet so that it can be run directly with the Java interpreter (such as `java.exe`).

📖 Java program 39.25 (⚡Java 1.0)

```
import java.awt.*;

public class gomenu extends Frame
{
MenuBar mainmenu = new MenuBar();
Menu mfile = new Menu("File");
Menu medit = new Menu("Edit");
Menu mhelp = new Menu("Help");

    public gomenu()
    {
        mfile.add(new MenuItem("New"));
        mfile.add(new MenuItem("Open"));
        mfile.add(new MenuItem("Save"));
        mfile.add(new MenuItem("Save As"));
        mfile.add(new MenuItem("Close"));
        mfile.addSeparator();
        mfile.add(new MenuItem("Print"));
        mfile.addSeparator();
        mfile.add(new MenuItem("Exit"));
```

```
            mainmenu.add(mfile);

            medit.add(new MenuItem("Cut"));
            medit.add(new MenuItem("Copy"));
            medit.add(new MenuItem("Paste"));
            mainmenu.add(medit);

            mhelp.add(new MenuItem("Commands"));
            mhelp.add(new MenuItem("About"));
            mainmenu.add(mhelp);

            setMenuBar(mainmenu);
    }

    public boolean action(Event evt, Object obj)
    {
        if (evt.target instanceof MenuItem)
        {
            if (evt.arg=="Exit") System.exit(0);
        }
        return true;
    }

    public boolean handleEvent(Event evt)
    {
        if (evt.id == Event.WINDOW_DESTROY)
            System.exit(0);
        return true;
    }

    public static void main(String args[])
    {
        Frame f = new gomenu();
        f.resize(400,400);
        f.show();
    }
}
```

39.24 List box

A `List` component creates a scrolling list of options (where in a pull-down menu only one option can be viewed at a time). The `java.awt.List` class contains the `List` constructor which can be used to display a list component., which is in the form:

```
            public List();
            public List(int rows, boolean multipleSelections);
```

where `row` defines the number of rows in a list and `multipleSelections` is true when the user can select a number of selections, else it is false.

The methods that can be applied are:

`public void addItem(String item);`	Adds a menu item at the end.
`public void addItem(String item, int index);`	Add a menu item at the end.
`public void addNotify();`	Allows the modification of a list's appearance without changing its functionality.

`public boolean` **`allowsMultipleSelections`**`();`	Allows the selection of multiple selections.
`public void `**`clear`**`();`	Clears the list.
`public int `**`countItems`**`();`	Returns the number of items in the list.
`public void `**`delItem`**`(int position);`	Deletes an item from the list.
`public void `**`delItems`**`(int start,` `int end);`	Deletes items from the list.
`Public void `**`deselect`**`(int index);`	Deselects the item at the specified index.
`Public String `**`getItem`**`(int index);`	Gets the item associated with the specified index.
`public int `**`getRows`**`();`	Returns the number of visible lines in this list.
`public int `**`getSelectedIndex`**`();`	Gets the selected item on the list.
`public int[] `**`getSelectedIndexes`**`();`	Gets selected items on the list.
`public String `**`getSelectedItem`**`();`	Returns the selected item on the list as a string.
`public String[] `**`getSelectedItems`**`();`	Returns the selected items on the list as an array of strings.
`public int `**`getVisibleIndex`**`();`	Gets the index of the item that was last made visible by the method `makeVisible`.
`public boolean `**`isSelected`**`(` `int index);`	Returns true if the item at the specified index has been selected.
`public void `**`makeVisible`**`(int index);`	Makes a menu item visible.
`public Dimension `**`minimumSize`**`();`	Returns the minimum dimensions needed for the list.
`public Dimension `**`minimumSize`**`(int rows);`	Returns the minimum dimensions needed for the number of rows in the list.

`protected String paramString();`	Returns the parameter String of the list.
`public Dimension preferredSize();`	Returns the preferred size of the list.
`public Dimension preferredSize(int rows);`	Returns the preferred size of the list.
`public void removeNotify();`	Removes notify.
`public void replaceItem(String newValue, int index);`	Replaces the item at the given index.
`Public void select(int index);`	Selects the item at the specified index.
`Public void setMultipleSelections(boolean v);`	Allows multiple selections.

Java program 39.26 shows an example of a program with a list component. Initially the list is created with the `List` constructor. The `addItem` method is then used to add the four items ("Pop", "Rock", "Classical" and "Jazz"). Within `actionPerformed` the program uses the `Options` array of strings to build up a message string (`Msg`). The `Options.length` parameter is used to determine the number of items in the array.

📖   Java applet 39.26 (⚡Java 1.1)

```
import java.awt.*;
import java.awt.event.*;
import java.applet.*;

public class chap39_26 extends Applet
                    implements ActionListener
{
List lmenu = new List(4,true);
String Msg, Options[];

    public void init()
    {
        lmenu.addItem("Pop");
        lmenu.addItem("Rock");
        lmenu.addItem("Classical");
        lmenu.addItem("Jazz");
        add(lmenu);
        lmenu.addActionListener(this);
  }

    public void actionPerformed(
                        ActionEvent evt)
 {
    int i;
    String str;

    str=evt.getActionCommand();
    Options=lmenu.getSelectedItems();
    Msg="";
    for (i=0;i<Options.length;i++)
          Msg=Msg+Options[i] + " ";
    repaint();
 }
```

```
public void paint(Graphics g)
{

   if (Msg!=null) g.drawString(Msg,20,80);
 }
}
```

39.25 File dialog

The `java.awt.Filedialog` class contains the `FileDialog` constructor which can be used to display a dialog window. To create a dialog window the following can be used:

```
public FileDialog(Frame parent, String title);
public FileDialog(Frame parent, String title, int mode);
```

where the `parent` is the owner of the dialog, `title` is the title of the dialog window and the `mode` is defined as whether the file is to be loaded or save. Two fields are defined for the mode, these are:

```
public final static int LOAD;
public final static int SAVE;
```

The methods that can be applied are:

public void **addNotify**();	Allows applications to change the look of a file dialog window without changing its functionality.
public String **getDirectory**();	Gets the initial directory.
public String **getFile**();	Gets the file that the user specified.
Public FilenameFilter **getFilenameFilter**();	Sets the default file filter.
public int **getMode**();	Indicates whether the file dialog box is for file loading from or file saving.
protected String **paramString**();	Returns the parameter string representing the state of the file dialog window.
public void **setDirectory**(String dir);	Gets the initial directory.
public void **setFile**(String file);	Sets the selected file for this file dialog window to be the specified file.
public void setFilenameFilter(FilenameFilter filter);	Sets the filename filter for the file dialog window to the specified filter.

39.26 Exercises

39.26.1 Explain how the six mouse events occur in Java 1.0 and how they have been modified in Java 1.1.

39.26.2 Write a Java applet which displays all the mouse and keyboard events. Display the parameters passed to them (such as the x, y coordinate for the mouse and the key pressed for the keyboard events).

39.26.3 Write a Java applet which displays the message 'Move moving' and the x, y coordinate of the cursor when the mouse is moving.

39.26.4 Write a Java applet that contains a target which has areas with different point values. These point values are 50, 100 and 150. The program should accumulate the score so far. A sample screen is given in Figure 39.8.

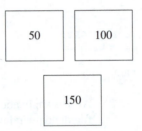

Points: 400

Figure 39.8   Exercise 39.26.4.

39.26.5 Modify the program in Exercise 39.26.4 so that a RESET button is displayed. When selected the points value should be reset to zero.

39.26.6 Write a Java applet which displays which function key or control key (Cntrl) has been pressed. The program should run continuously until the Cntrl-Z keystroke is pressed.

39.26.7 Implement the two Java applets in Figure 39.9. The Show button should display all the selected options.

39.26.8 Add a Reset button to the applets developed in Exercise 39.26.7. This button should set the selected items back to their initial values.

39.26.9 Implement a Java applet which displays the buttons on a basic calculator. An example is shown in Figure 39.10.

39.26.10 Implement a Java applet, with checkboxes, which prompts a user for their personal information such as height, weight, and so on.

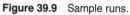

Figure 39.9 Sample runs.

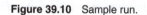

Figure 39.10 Sample run.

40 Java (Networking)

40.1 Introduction

Java is one of the fastest growing development languages and has the great advantage that it was developed after the Internet and WWW were created and thus has direct WWW/Internet support. This includes the use of HTTP and socket programming, and so on. This chapter provides an introduction to the usage of Java over a local or global area network.

40.2 HTTP protocol

The foundation protocol of the WWW is the Hypertext Transfer Protocol (HTTP) which can be used in any client-server application involving hypertext. It is used in the WWW for transmitting information using hypertext jumps and can support the transfer of plaintext, hypertext, audio, images, or any Internet-compatible information. The most recently defined standard is HTTP 1.1, which has been defined by the IETF standard.

HTTP is a stateless protocol where each transaction is independent of any previous transactions. The advantage of being stateless is that it allows the rapid access of WWW pages over several widely distributed servers. It uses the TCP protocol to establish a connection between a client and a server for each transaction then terminates the connection once the transaction completes.

HTTP also support many different formats of data. Initially a client issues a request to a server which may include a prioritized list of formats that it can handle. This allows new formats to be added easily and also prevents the transmission of unnecessary information.

A client's WWW browser (the user agent) initially establishes a direct connection with the destination server which contains the required WWW page. To make this connection the client initiates a TCP connection between the client and the server. After this is established the client then issues an HTTP request, such as the specific command (the method), the URL, and possibly extra information such as request parameters or client information. When the server receives the request, it attempts to perform the requested action. It then returns an HTTP response which includes status information, a success/error code, and extra information itself. After the client receives this, the TCP connection is closed.

40.2.1 Intermediate systems

The previous section discussed the direct connection of a client to a server. Many system organizations do not wish a direct connection to an internal network. Thus HTTP supports other connections which are formed through intermediate systems, such as:

- A proxy. A proxy connects to a number of clients; it acts on behalf of other clients and sends requests from the clients to a server. It thus acts as a client when it communicates with a server, but as a server when communicating with a client. A proxy is typically used for security purposes where the client and server are separated by a firewall. The proxy connects to the client side of the firewall and the server to the other side of the firewall. Thus the server must authenticate itself to the firewall before a connection can be made with the proxy. Only after this has been authenticated will the proxy pass requests through the firewall (see Figure 40.1).

- A gateway. Gateways are servers that act as if they are the destination server. They are typically used when clients cannot get direct access to the server, and typically for one of the security reasons where the gateway acts as a firewall so that the gateway communicates with the Internet and the server only communicates with the Internet through the gateway. The client must then authenticate itself to the proxy, which can then pass the request on to the server. They can also be used when the destination is a non-HTTP server. Web browsers have built into them the capability to contact servers for protocols other than HTTP, such as FTP and Gopher servers. This capability can also be provided by a gateway. The client makes an HTTP request to a gateway server. The gateway server than contacts the relevant FTP or Gopher server to obtain the desired result. This result is then converted into a form suitable for HTTP and transmitted back to the client.

- A tunnel. A tunnel does not perform any operation on the HTTP message; it passes messages onto the client or server unchanged. This differs from a proxy or a gateway, which modify the HTTP messages. Tunnels are typically used as firewalls, where the firewall authenticates the connection but simply relays the HTTP messages.

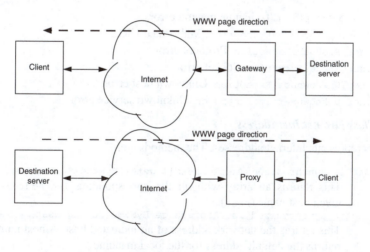

Figure 40.1 Usage of proxies and gateways.

40.2.2 Cache

In a computer system a cache is an area of memory that stores information likely to be accessed in a fast access memory area. For example, a cache controller takes a guess on which information the process is likely to access next. When the processor wishes to access the disk then, if it has guessed right it will load, the cache controller will load from the electronic memory rather than loading it from the disk. A WWW cache stores cacheable responses so that there is a reduction in network traffic and an improvement in access times.

40.3 Java networking functions

Java directly supports TCP/IP communications and has the following classes:

- `java.net.ContentHandler`. Class which reads data from a URLConnection and also supports MIME (Multipurpose Internet Mail Extension).
- `java.net.DatagramPacket`. Class representing a datagram packet which contains packet data, packet length, Internet addresses and the port number.
- `java.net.DatagramSocket`. Class representing a datagram Socket class.
- `java.net.InetAddress`. Class representing Internet addresses.
- `java.net.ServerSocket`. Class representing Socket server class.
- `java.net.Socket`. Class representing Socket client classes.
- `java.net.SocketImpl`. Socket implementation class.
- `java.net.URL`. Class URL representing a Uniform Reference Locator (URL) which is a reference to an object on the WWW.
- `java.net.URLConnection`. Class representing an active connection to an object represented by a URL.
- `java.net.URLEncoder`. Converts strings of text into URLEncoded format.
- `java.net.URLStreamHandler`. Class for opening URL streams.

When an error occurs in the connection or in the transmission and reception of data it causes an exception. The classes which handle these are:

- `java.io.IOException`. To handle general errors.
- `java.net.MalformedURLException`. Malformed URL.
- `java.net.ProtocolException`. Protocol error.
- `java.net.SocketException`. Socket error.
- `java.net.UnknownHostException`. Unknown host error.
- `java.net.UnknownServiceException`. Unknown service error.

40.3.1 Class java.net.InetAddress

This class represents Internet addresses. The methods are:

`public static synchronized InetAddress[] getAllByName(String host)`
> This returns an array with all the corresponding `InetAddresses` for a given host name (`host`).

`public static synchronized InetAddress getByName(String host)`
> This returns the network address of an indicated host. A host name of null returns the default address for the local machine.

`public String getHostAddress()`
> This returns the IP address string (`WW.XX.YY.ZZ`) in a string format.

`public byte[] getAddress()`
> This returns the raw IP address in network byte order. The array position 0 (`addr[0]`) contains the highest order byte.

`public String getHostName()`
> Gets the hostname for this address. If the host is equal to null, then this address refers to any of the local machine's available network addresses.

`public static InetAddress getLocalHost()`
> Returns the local host.

`public String toString()`   Converts the `InetAddress` to a String.

Java applet 40.1 uses the `getAllByName` method to determine all the IP addresses associated with an Internet host. In this case the host is named `www.microsoft.com`. It can be seen from the test run that there are 18 IP addresses associated with this domain name. It can be seen that the applet causes an exception error as the loop tries to display 30 such IP addresses. When the program reaches the 19th `InetAddress`, the exception error is displayed (`ArrayIndexOutOfBoundsException`).

Java applet 40.1 (chap40_1.java)

```
import java.net.*;
import java.awt.*;
import java.applet.*;
public class chap40_1 extends Applet
{
InetAddress[]  address;
int            i;
   public void start()
   {
      System.out.println("Started");
      try
      {
         address=InetAddress.getAllByName("www.microsoft.com");

         for (i=0;i<30;i++)
         {
            System.out.println("Address " + address[i]);
         }
      }
      catch (Exception e)
      {
         System.out.println("Error :" + e);
      }
   }
}
```

Sample run 40.1

```
C:\java\temp>appletviewer chap40_01.html
Started
Address www.microsoft.com/207.68.137.59
Address www.microsoft.com/207.68.143.192
Address www.microsoft.com/207.68.143.193
Address www.microsoft.com/207.68.143.194
Address www.microsoft.com/207.68.143.195
Address www.microsoft.com/207.68.156.49
Address www.microsoft.com/207.68.137.56
Address www.microsoft.com/207.68.156.51
Address www.microsoft.com/207.68.156.52
Address www.microsoft.com/207.68.137.62
Address www.microsoft.com/207.68.156.53
Address www.microsoft.com/207.68.156.54
Address www.microsoft.com/207.68.137.65
Address www.microsoft.com/207.68.156.73
Address www.microsoft.com/207.68.156.61
Address www.microsoft.com/207.68.156.16
Address www.microsoft.com/207.68.156.58
Address www.microsoft.com/207.68.137.53
Error :java.lang.ArrayIndexOutOfBoundsException: 18
```

Java applet 40.2 overcomes the problem of displaying the exception. In this case the exception is caught by inserting the address display within a `try {}` statement then having a catch statement which does nothing. Sample run 40.2 shows a test run.

📖   Java applet 40.2 (chap40_2.java)

```java
import java.net.*;
import java.awt.*;
import java.applet.*;
public class chap40_2 extends Applet
{
InetAddress[]  address;
int            i;
   public void start()
   {
      System.out.println("Started");
      try
      {
         address=InetAddress.getAllByName("www.microsoft.com");
         try
         {
            for (i=0;i<30;i++)
            {
                System.out.println("Address " + address[i]);
            }
         }
         catch(Exception e)
         { /* Do nothing about the exception, as it is not really
             an error */}
      }
      catch (Exception e)
      {
         System.out.println("Error :" + e);
      }
   }
}
```

💻 Sample run 40.2

```
C:\java\temp>appletviewer chap40_02.html
Started
Address www.microsoft.com/207.68.137.59
Address www.microsoft.com/207.68.143.192
Address www.microsoft.com/207.68.143.193
Address www.microsoft.com/207.68.143.194
Address www.microsoft.com/207.68.143.195
Address www.microsoft.com/207.68.156.49
Address www.microsoft.com/207.68.137.56
Address www.microsoft.com/207.68.156.51
Address www.microsoft.com/207.68.156.52
Address www.microsoft.com/207.68.137.62
Address www.microsoft.com/207.68.156.53
Address www.microsoft.com/207.68.156.54
Address www.microsoft.com/207.68.137.65
Address www.microsoft.com/207.68.156.73
Address www.microsoft.com/207.68.156.61
Address www.microsoft.com/207.68.156.16
Address www.microsoft.com/207.68.156.58
Address www.microsoft.com/207.68.137.53
```

Java applet 40.3 shows an example of displaying the local host name (getLocalHost), the host name (getHostName) and the host's IP address (getHostAddress). Sample run 40.3 shows a test run.

📖   Java applet 40.3 (chap40_3.java)

```
import java.net.*;
import java.awt.*;
import java.applet.*;

public class chap40_3 extends Applet
{
InetAddress host;
String str;
int i;
    public void start()
    {
        System.out.println("Started");

        try
        {
            host=InetAddress.getLocalHost();
            System.out.println("Local host " + host);

            str=host.getHostName();
            System.out.println("Host name: " + str);

            str=host.getHostAddress();
            System.out.println("Host address: " + str);
        }

        catch (Exception e)
        {
            System.out.println("Error :" + e);
        }
    }
}
```

💻 Sample run 40.3

```
C:\java\temp>appletviewer chap40_03.html
Started
Local host toshiba/195.232.26.125
Host name: toshiba
Host address: 195.232.26.125
```

The previous Java applets have all displayed their output to the output terminal (with System.out.println). Java applet 40.4 uses the drawString method to display the output text to the applet window. Figure 40.2 shows a sample run.

📖   Java applet 40.4 (chap40_4.java)

```
import java.net.*;
import java.awt.*;
import java.applet.*;

public class chap40_4 extends Applet
{
InetAddress[] address;
int i;

    public void paint(Graphics g)
    {
        g.drawString("Addresses for WWW.MICROSOFT.COM",5,10);
        try
        {
            address=InetAddress.getAllByName("www.microsoft.com");
```

```
        for (i=0;i<30;i++)
        {
            g.drawString(" "+address[i].toString(),5,20+10*i);
        }
    }
    catch (Exception e)
    {
        System.out.println("Error :" + e);
    }
  }
}
```

Figure 40.2   Sample run.

40.3.2 class java.net.URL

The URL (Uniform Reference Locator) class is used to reference to an object on the World Wide Web. The main constructors are:

```
public URL(String protocol, String host, int port, String file)
```
Creates an absolute URL from the specified protocol (protocol), host (host), port (port) and file (file).

```
public URL(String protocol, String host, String file)
```
Creates an absolute URL from the specified protocol (protocol), host (host) and file (file).

```
public URL(String spec)
```
Creates a URL from an unparsed absolute URL (spec).

```
public URL(URL context, String spec)
```
Creates a URL from an unparsed absolute URL (spec) in the specified context.

The methods are:

```
public int getPort()
```
Returns a port number. A return value of –1 indicates that the port is not set.

```
public String getProtocol()
```
Returns the protocol name.

```
public String getHost()
```
Returns the host name.

```
public String getFile()
```
Returns the file name.

```
public boolean equals(Object obj)
```
Compares two URLs, where `obj` is the URL to compare against.
```
public String toString()
```
Converts to a string format.
```
public String toExternalForm()
```
Reverses the URL parsing.
```
public URLConnection openConnection()
```
Creates a URLConnection object that contains a connection to the remote object referred to by the URL.
```
public final InputStream openStream()
```
Opens an input stream.

```
public final Object getContent()
```
Gets the contents from this opened connection.

40.3.3 class java.net.URLConnection

Represents an active connection to an object represented by a URL. The main methods are:

```
public abstract void connect()
```
URLConnection objects are initially created and then they are connected.
```
public URL getURL()
```
Returns the URL for this connection.
```
public int getContentLength()
```
Returns the content length, a -1 if not known.
```
public String getContentType()
```
Returns the content type, a null if not known.
```
public String getContentEncoding()
```
Returns the content encoding, a null if not known.
```
public long getExpiration()
```
Returns the expiration date of the object, a 0 if not known.
```
public long getDate()
```
Returns the sending date of the object, a 0 if not known.
```
public long getLastModified()
```
Returns the last modified date of the object, a 0 if not known.
```
public String getHeaderField(String name)
```
Returns a header field by name (`name`), a null if not known.
```
public Object getContent()
```
Returns the object referred to by this URL.
```
public InputStream getInputStream()
```
Used to read from objects.
```
public OutputStream getOutputStream()
```
Used to write to objects.
```
public String toString()
```
Returns the String URL representation.

40.3.4 class java.net.URLEncoder

This class converts text strings into x-www-form-urlencoded format.

```
public static String encode(String s)
```
Translates a string (s) into x-www-form-urlencoded format.

40.3.5 class java.net.URLStreamHandler

Abstract class for URL stream openers. Subclasses of this class know how to create streams for particular protocol types.

```
protected abstract URLConnection openConnection(URL u)
```
> Opens an input stream to the object referenced by the URL (u).
```
protected void parseURL(URL u, String spec, int start, int limit)
```
> Parses the string (spec) into the URL (u), where start and limit refer to the range of characters in spec that should be parsed.
```
protected String toExternalForm(URL u)
```
> Reverses the parsing of the URL.
```
protected void setURL(URL u,  String protocol,String host,
        int port, String file, String ref)
```
> Calls the (protected) set method out of the URL given.

40.3.6 java.applet.AppletContext

The AppletContext can be used by an applet to obtain information from the applet's environment, which is usually the browser or the applet viewer. Related methods are:

```
public abstract void showDocument(URL url)
```
> Shows a new document.
```
public abstract void showDocument(URL url,  String target)
```
> Shows a new document in a target window or frame.

40.4 Connecting to a WWW site

Java applet 40.5 shows an example of an applet that connects to a WWW site. In this case it connects to the www.microsoft.com site.

📖   Java applet 40.5 (chap40_5.java) (☕Java 1.1)
```java
import java.net.*;
import java.awt.*;
import java.awt.event.*;
import java.applet.*;

public class chap40_5 extends Applet implements ActionListener
{
URL       urlWWW;
Button    btn;

    public void init()
    {
        btn = (new Button("Connect to Microsoft WWW site"));
        add(btn);
        btn.addActionListener(this);
    }

    public void start()
    {
        //Check for valid URL
        try
        {
            urlWWW  = new URL("http://www.microsoft.com");
        }
        catch (MalformedURLException e)
        {
```

```
            System.out.println("URL Error: " + e);
        }
    }

    public void actionPerformed(ActionEvent evt)
    {

    if (evt.getActionCommand().equals(
            "Connect to Microsoft WWW site"))
    {
            getAppletContext().showDocument(urlWWW);
    }
  }
}
```

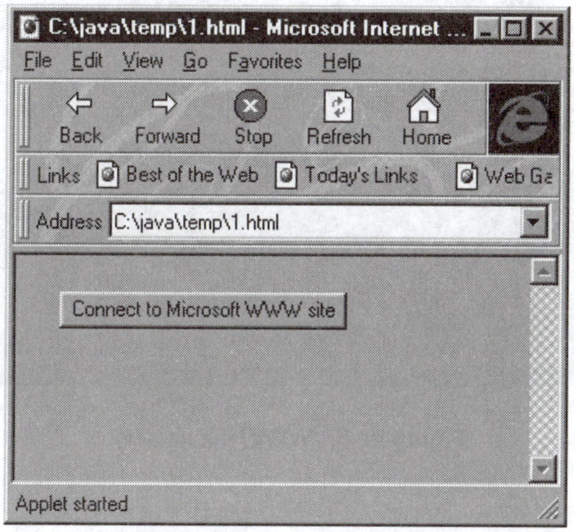

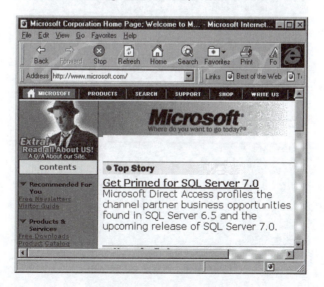

Figure 40.3 Sample run.

Figure 40.4 WWW connection.

Java applet 40.6 extends the previous applet by allowing the user to enter a URL and it also shows a status window (status). Figures 40.5, 40.6 and 40.7 show sample runs. In Figure 40.5 the user has added an incorrect URL (www.sun.com). The status windows shows that this is an error. In Figure 40.6 the user enters a correct URL (http://www.sun.com) and Figure 40.7 shows the result after the Connect button is pressed.

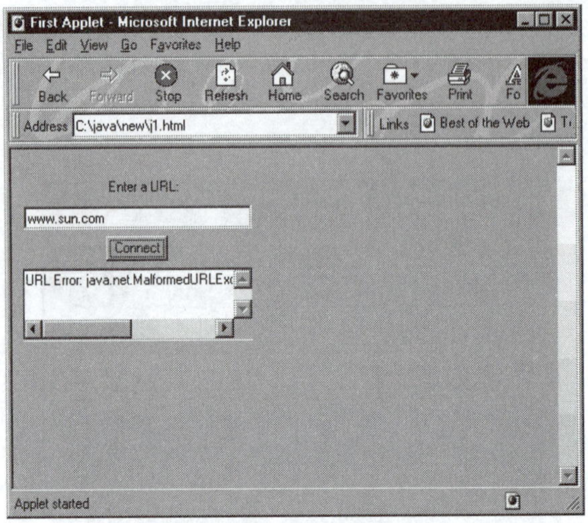

Figure 40.5   WWW connection.

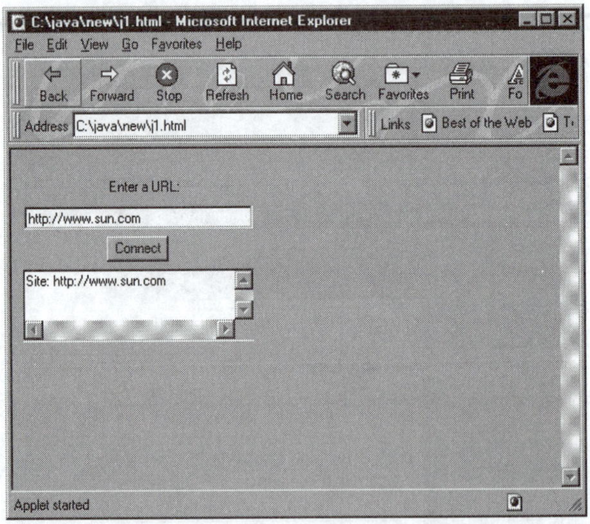

Figure 40.6   WWW connection.

Figure 40.7 WWW connection.

📖 **Java applet 40.6** (chap40_6.java)

```java
import java.net.*;
import java.awt.*;
import java.awt.event.*;
import java.applet.*;
public class chap40_06 extends Applet implements ActionListener
{
URL      urlWWW;
Button   btn;
Label    label = new Label("Enter a URL:");
TextField inURL = new TextField(30);
TextArea status = new TextArea(3,30);
   public void init()
   {
      add(label);
      add(inURL);
      btn = (new Button("Connect"));
      add(btn);
      add(status);
      btn.addActionListener(this);
   }
   public void getURL()//Check for valid URL
   {
      try
      {
      String str;
         str=inURL.getText();
         status.setText("Site: " + str);
         urlWWW  = new URL(str);
      }
      catch (MalformedURLException e)
      {
         status.setText("URL Error: " + e);
      }
   }
   public void actionPerformed(ActionEvent evt)
   {
String str;
      str=evt.getActionCommand();
```

```
        if (str.equals("Connect"))
        {
           status.setText("Connecting...\n");
           getURL();
           getAppletContext().showDocument(urlWWW);
        }
   }
}
```

40.5 Socket programming

The main calls in standard socket programming are:

socket() Creates a socket.
accept() Accepts a connection on a socket.
connect() Establishes a connection to a peer.
bind() Associates a local address with a socket.
listen() Establishes a socket to listen for incoming connection.
getInputStream()
          Gets an input data stream for a socket. This can be used to create a re-
          ceive() method.
getOutputStream()
          Gets an output data stream for a socket. This can be used to create a
          send() method.
close() Closes a socket.

Figure 40.8 shows the operation of a connection of a client to a server. The server is defined as the computer which waits for a connection, the client is the computer which initially makes contact with the server.

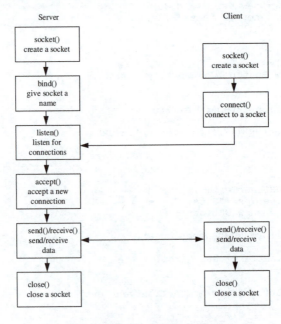

Figure 40.8   Socket connection.

On the server the computer initially creates a socket with the `socket()` method; this is bound to a name with the `bind()` method. After this the server listens for a connection with the `listen()` method. When the client calls the `connect()` method the server then accepts the connection with `accept()`. After this the server and client can send and receive data with the `send()` or `receive()` functions (these are created with the `getInputStream()` and `getOutputStream()` methods). When the data transfer is complete the `close()` method is used to close the socket.

The implementation for `send()` and `receive()` is:

```
public static void send(Socket client,String str)
{
 try
 {
  DataOutputStream send=new DataOutputStream(client.getOutputStream());
  send.writeUTF(str);
 }
 catch (IOException e)
 {
   //something
 }
}
public static String receive(Socket client)
{
 String str="";
 try
 {
  DataInputStream receive=new DataInputStream(client.getInputStream());
  str=receive.readLine();
 }
 catch (IOException e)
 {
      //something
 }
 return str;
}
```

40.5.1 class java.net.Socket

The TCP protocol links two computers using sockets and ports. The constructors for `java.net.Socket` are:

public **Socket**(InetAddress address, int port)
> Creates a stream socket and connects it to the specified address (`address`) on the specified port (`port`).

public **Socket**(InetAddress address, int port, boolean stream)
> Creates a socket and connects it to the specified address (`address`) on the specified port (`port`). The boolean value `stream` indicates whether this is a stream or datagram socket.

public **Socket**(String host, int port)
> Creates a stream socket and connects it to the specified port (`port`) on the specified host (`host`).

public **Socket**(String host, int port, boolean stream)
> Creates a socket and connects it to the specified port (`port`) on the specified host (`host`). The boolean value `stream` indicates whether this is a stream or datagram socket.

The methods are:

```
public synchronized void close()
```
           Closes the socket.

```
public InetAddress getInetAddress()
```
           Returns the address to which the socket is connected.

```
public InputStream getInputStream()
```
           Returns the `InputStream` for this socket.

```
public int getLocalPort()
```
Returns the local port to which the socket is connected.

```
public OutputStream getOutputStream()
```
           Returns an `OutputStream` for this socket.

```
public int getPort()
```
           Returns the remote port to which the socket is connected.

```
public String toString()
```
Converts the Socket to a String.

40.5.2 class java.net.SocketImpl

The `SocketImpl` class implements sockets. The methods are:

```
protected abstract void create(boolean stream)
```
           Creates a socket where `stream` indicates whether the socket is a stream or a datagram.

```
protected abstract void connect(String host, int port)
```
           Connects the socket to the specified port (`port`) on the specified host (`host`).

```
protected abstract void connect(InetAddress address, int port)
```
           Connects the socket to the specified address (`address`) on the specified port (`port`).

```
protected abstract void bind(InetAddress host, int port)
```
           Binds the socket to the specified port (`port`) on the specified host (`host`).

```
protected abstract void listen(int backlog)
```
           This specifies the number of connection requests (`backlog`) the system will queue up while waiting to execute `accept()`.

```
protected abstract void accept(SocketImpl s)
```
           Accepts a connection (`s`).

```
protected abstract InputStream getInputStream()
```
           Returns an `InputStream` for a socket.

```
protected abstract OutputStream getOutputStream()
```
           Returns an `OutputStream` for a socket.

```
protected abstract int available()
```
           Returns the number of bytes that can be read without blocking.

```
protected abstract void close()
```
           Closes the socket.

```
protected InetAddress getInetAddress()
protected int getPort()
protected int getLocalPort()
public String toString()
```
           Returns the address and port of this Socket as a String.

40.6 Creating a socket

Java applet 40.7 constructs a socket for www.sun.com using port 4001 (`Socket remote = new Socket("www.sun.com",4001)`). After this the data stream is created and assigned to `DataIn`. The `readln()` method is then used to get the text from the stream.

📖 Java applet 40.7 (`chap40_7.java`)

```java
import java.io.*;
import java.net.*;
import java.awt.*;
import jacva.applet.*;

public class chap40_7 extends Applet
{
    public void init()
    {

    String          Instr;
    InputStream     Instream;

        try
        {
            Socket remote = new Socket("www.sun.com",4001);
            Instream = remote.getInputStream();
            DataInputStream DataIn = new DataInputStream(Instream);
            do
            {

                Instr = DataIn.readLine();
                if (Instr!=null)  System.out.println(str);
            } while (Instr!=null);
        }
        catch (UnknownHostException err)
        {
            System.out.println("UNKNOWN HOST: "+err);
        }
        catch (IOException err)
        {
            System.out.println("Error" + err); }
        }
}
```

Java program 40.8 contacts a server on a given port and returns the local and remote port. It uses command line arguments where the program is run in the form:

```
java chap40_8 host port
```

where `java` is the Java interpreter, `chap40_8` is the name of the class file, *host* is the name of the host to contact and *port* is the port to use. The `args.length` parameter is used to determine the number of command line options, anything other than two will display the following message:

```
Usage : chap40_8 host port
```

📖 Java program 40.8 (`chap40_8.java`)

```java
import java.net.*;
import java.io.*;

public class chap40_8
{
 public static void main (String args[])
 {
  if (args.length !=2)
    System.out.println(" Usage : chap40_8 host port");

  else
```

```
{
 String inp;
 try
 {
  Socket sock = new Socket(args[0], Integer.valueOf(args[1]).intValue());
  DataInputStream is = new DataInputStream(sock.getInputStream());

  System.out.println("address : " + sock.getInetAddress());
  System.out.println("port : " + sock.getPort());
  System.out.println("Local address : " + sock.getLocalAddress());
  System.out.println("Localport : " + sock.getLocalPort());

  while((inp = is.readLine()) != null)
  { System.out.println(inp);}
 }
 catch (UnknownHostException e)
 {
  System.out.println(" Known Host : " + e.getMessage());
 }
 catch (IOException e)
 {
  System.out.println("error I/O : " + e.getMessage());
 }
 finally
 {
  System.out.println("End of program");
 }
 }
 }
}
```

Sample run 40.4 shows a test run which connects to port 13 on
www.eece.napier.ac.uk. It can be seen that the connection to this port causes the server
to return back the current date and time. Sample run 40.5 connects into the same server,
in this case on port 19. It can be seen that a connection to this port returns a sequence of
characters.

🖥 Sample run 40.4

```
>> java chap40_4 www.eece.napier.ac.uk 13
Host and IP address : www.eece.napier.ac.uk/146.176.151.139
port : 13
Local address :pc419.eece.napier.ac.uk
Localport : 1393
Fri May  8 13:19:59 1998
End of program
```

🖥 Sample run 40.5

```
>> java chap40_5 www.eece.napier.ac.uk 19
Host and IP address : www.eece.napier.ac.uk/146.176.151.139
port : 19
Local IP address :pc419.eece.napier.ac.uk
Localport : 1403
 !"#$%&'()*+,-./0123456789:;<=>?@ABCDEFGHIJKLMNOPQRSTUVWXYZ[\]^_`abcdefg
!"#$%&'()*+,-./0123456789:;<=>?@ABCDEFGHIJKLMNOPQRSTUVWXYZ[\]^_`abcdefgh
"#$%&'()*+,-./0123456789:;<=>?@ABCDEFGHIJKLMNOPQRSTUVWXYZ[\]^_`abcdefghi
#$%&'()*+,-./0123456789:;<=>?@ABCDEFGHIJKLMNOPQRSTUVWXYZ[\]^_`abcdefghij
$%&'()*+,-./0123456789:;<=>?@ABCDEFGHIJKLMNOPQRSTUVWXYZ[\]^_`abcdefghijk
%&'()*+,-./0123456789:;<=>?@ABCDEFGHIJKLMNOPQRSTUVWXYZ[\]^_`abcdefghijkl
&'()*+,-./0123456789:;<=>?@ABCDEFGHIJKLMNOPQRSTUVWXYZ[\]^_`abcdefghijklm
'()*+,-./0123456789:;<=>?@ABCDEFGHIJKLMNOPQRSTUVWXYZ[\]^_`abcdefghijklmn
()*+,-./0123456789:;<=>?@ABCDEFGHIJKLMNOPQRSTUVWXYZ[\]^_`abcdefghijklmno
```

```
)*+,-./0123456789:;<=>?@ABCDEFGHIJKLMNOPQRSTUVWXYZ[\]^_`abcdefghijklmnop
*+,-./0123456789:;<=>?@ABCDEFGHIJKLMNOPQRSTUVWXYZ[\]^_`abcdefghijklmnopq
+,-./0123456789:;<=>?@ABCDEFGHIJKLMNOPQRSTUVWXYZ[\]^_`abcdefghijklmnopqr
,-./0123456789:;<=>?@ABCDEFGHIJKLMNOPQRSTUVWXYZ[\]^_`abcdefghijklmnopqrs
-./0123456789:;<=>?@ABCDEFGHIJKLMNOPQRSTUVWXYZ[\]^_`abcdefghijklmnopqrst
./0123456789:;<=>?@ABCDEFGHIJKLMNOPQRSTUVWXYZ[\]^_`abcdefghijklmnopqrstu
/0123456789:;<=>?@ABCDEFGHIJKLMNOPQRSTUVWXYZ[\]^_`abcdefghijklmnopqrstuv
0123456789:;<=>?@ABCDEFGHIJKLMNOPQRSTUVWXYZ[\]^_`abcdefghijklmnopqrstuvw
123456789:;<=>?@ABCDEFGHIJKLMNOPQRSTUVWXYZ[\]^_`abcdefghijklmnopqrstuvwx
```

40.7 Client-server program

A server is a computer which runs a special program which waits for another computer (a client) to connect to it. This server normally performs some sort of special operation, such as:

- File Transfer Protocol. Transferring files.
- Telnet. Remote connection.
- WWW service.

Java program 40.9 acts as a server program and waits for a connection on port 1111. When a connection is received on this port it sends its current date and time back to the client. This program can be run with Java program 40.8 (which is running on a remote computer) with a connection to the server's IP address (or domain name) and using port 1111. When the client connects to the server, the server responds back to the client with its current date and time.

Sample run 40.6 shows a test run from the server (NOTE THE SERVER PROGRAM MUST BE RUN BEFORE THE CLIENT IS STARTED). It can be seen that it has received connection from the client with the IP address of 146.176.150.120 (Test run 40.7 shows the client connection).

📖 Java program 40.9 (chap40_9.java)

```java
import java.net.*;
import java.io.*;
import java.util.*;

class chap40_9
{
 public static void main( String arg[])
 {
  try
  {
   ServerSocket sock = new ServerSocket(1111);
   Socket sock1 = sock.accept();

   System.out.println(sock1.toString());
   System.out.println("address : " + sock1.getInetAddress());
   System.out.println("port     : " + sock1.getPort());

   DataOutputStream out = new DataOutputStream(sock1.getOutputStream());

   out.writeBytes("Welcome "+ sock1.getInetAddress().getHostName()+
          ". We are "+ new Date()+ "\n");

   sock1.close();
```

```
    sock.close();
  }
  catch(IOException err)
  {
    System.out.println(err.getMessage());
  }
  finally
  {
    System.out.println("End of the program");
  }
 }
}
```

🖥 **Sample run 40.6** (Server)
```
>> java chap14_03
address : pc419.eece.napier.ac.uk/146.176.151.130
port : 1111
End of program
```

🖥 **Sample run 40.7** (Client)
```
>> java chap14_02 146.176.150.120 1111
Host and IP address : pc419.eece.napier.ac.uk/146.176.151.130
port : 1111
Local address :pc419.eece.napier.ac.uk
Localport : 1393
Fri May  8 13:19:59 1998
End of program
```

40.8 Exercises

40.8.1   Write a Java applet in which the user selects from one of the following pop-up menu URLs. Theses are:

www.microsoft.com   www.ibm.com
www.intel.com   www.sun.com

40.8.2   Using Java program 40.7 connect to some WWW servers. Try different port values.

40.8.3   Find two computers which can be connected over TCP/IP. Determine their IP addresses (or DNS) and connect them over a network.

40.8.4   Connect two computers over a network and set up a chat connection. One of the computers should be the chat server and the other the chat client. Modify it so that the server accepts calls from one or many clients.

40.8.5   Develop a Java program which has send and receive text windows. The program should allow the user to specify the IP address (or DNS) of the server. The send and receive windows will then show the text sent and received.

A RS-232/Parallel Port

A.1 RS-232

A.1.1 The UART

The main device used to construct an RS-232 interface is the UART (universal asynchronous receiver and transmitter) which is a fully programmable device. It can be set-up to have a defined Baud rate, number of data bits, number of start bits, number of stop bits, type of parity, manipulation of the output and input handshaking lines. Figure A.1 shows a block diagram. The UART is fully compatible with TTL devices and has a +5 V and 0 V power supply. Typical UARTs are Intel's 8250, Motorola's MC8650, Motorola's MC68681 and National's INS 8250. The 8250/1 device is compatible with Intel's 80×86 microprocessors and is thus used in many PC applications. A 16-bit UART device is available and is named the 16450.

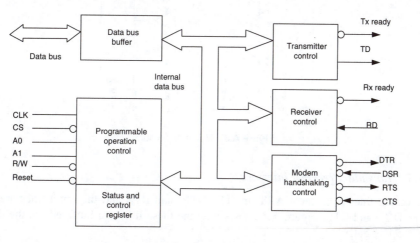

Figure A.1 UART.

A.1.2 Drivers and receivers

Driver ICs convert the TTL output/input of the UART to RS-232 voltage levels. The MC1488 quad line driver contains four NAND logic buffer gates and has supply lines of +/-12V and GND, as illustrated in Figure A.2. If the two inputs to the drivers are tied together to create an invertor function, a table of the conversion is shown next:

- 0 V input gives +12 V output.
- 5 V input gives –12 V output.

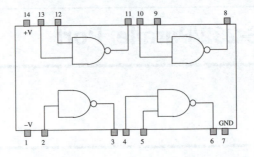

Figure A.2   MC1488 pin out.

The second input of the NAND gate can also be used to generate a Break signal on the transmit line, where a low input will cause a high output (+12 V).

The MC1489 is a line receiver that converts RS-232 line voltage back to TTL levels. This device is specially designed to receive pulses over a long and highly capacitive transmission line. Figure A.3 shows its pin connections.

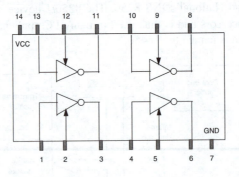

Figure A.3   MC1489 pin out.

A.1.3   Transmitter/receiver interface

The output lines from the UART are TD, DTR, and RTS and the input lines are RD, DSR, DCD and CTS. Figure A.4 shows how the these lines are buffered via the driver and receiver gates.

A.2   Parallel port

A.2.1   IEEE 1284 cables assemblies

The IEEE 1284 standard defined standards for computability between different platforms and peripherals. The most typical connector is a DB25 male on one end and a 36-pin Champ plug connector on the other. The cable has from 18 to 25 conductors and from one to eight ground wires. This cable is acceptable for low speed (10kB/sec) at a maximum distance of 2 m but will not operate properly for high bit rates (such as 2MB/sec) over relatively long runs (such as 10 m).

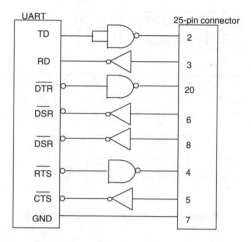

Figure A.4 Transmitter/receiver interface.

A 1284 connection complies with the following:

1. Signals connect to a twisted pair with a signal line and ground return.
2. Each signal has a characteristic unbalanced impedance of approx. 62 Ω.
3. Crosstalk is less than 10%.
4. 85% minimum coverage of braid over foil.
5. Cable shield connects to the connector backshell using a 360° concentric method (and no pigtail connections).
6. Cables are marked with the label: IEEE Std 1284-1994.

A.2.2 IEEE 1284 connectors

The 1284 standard defines the standard connectors to be used with the parallel port, for its both its mechanical and electrical specification. This ensures compatibility with existing and future applications.

The three connectors defined are:

- 1284 Type A. 25-pin DB25 connector.
- 1284 Type B. 36-pin, 0.085 centreline Champ connector with bale locks
- 1284 Type C. 36-pin, 0.050 centreline mini-connector with clip latches.

Figure A.5 illustrates these connectors. The best specification is the type C connector as:

- It has a smaller footprint than the others.
- It has a simple-to-use clip latch for cable retention.
- It has the easiest cable assembly with the optimal electrical properties.
- Its cable assembly has two extra signals, which are Peripheral Logic High and Host Logic High. These can be used to determine if the device at the other end of the cable is powered on. This allows for some degree of intelligent power management for 1284 interfaces.

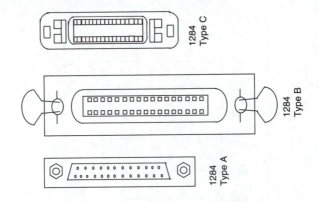

Figure A.5 1284 interface I/O connectors.

Typical assembly types are:

AMAM	Type A Male to Type A Male	AMAF	Type A Male to Type A Female
AB	Type A Male to Type B Plug	AC	Type A Male to Type C Plug
BC	Type B Plug to Type C Plug	CC	Type C Plug to Type C Plug

A.2.3 IEEE 1284 Electrical Interface

The 1284 standard defines two levels of interface compatibility:

- Level 1. Designed for low-speed applications, but which need the reverse channel capabilities.
- Level II. Design for advanced modes, high bit rates and long cables.

The electrical specifications for Level II drivers and receivers are defined at the connector interface. For drivers these are:

1. Open-circuit high-level output voltage: less than +5.5 V.
2. Open-circuit low-level output voltage: not less than –0.5 V.
3. DC steady-state, high-level output voltage: greater than +2.4 V with a source current of 14 mA.
4. DC steady-state, low-level output voltage: less than +0.4 V with a sink current of 14 mA.
5. Output impedance: 50 +/– 5 Ω.
6. Output slew rate: between 0.05 and 0.40 $V.ns^{-1}$.

For drivers these are:

1. Peak input voltage transients without damage: between –2.0 V and +7.0 V.
2. High-level input threshold: less than 2.0 V
3. Low-level input threshold: greater than 0.8 V.
4. Input hysteresis: at least 0.2 V, but not more than 1.2 V.
5. High-level sink current: less than 20 μA at +2.0 V.
6. Low-level input source current: less than 20 μA at +0.8 V.

7. Circuit and stray capacitance: less than 50 pF.

Figure A.6 shows the recommended termination for a driver/receiver pair, where R_0 is the output impedance at the connector. This should be matched to the impedance of the cable (Z_0) so that noise and reflections can be minimized. A series resistance (R_s) can thus be added to obtain a match.

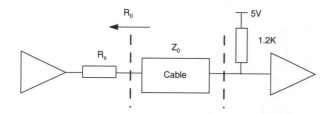

Figure A.6 Level II driver/receiver pair termination example.

A.3 PC connections

The 430HX motherboard uses the 82091AA (API) device. Thus incorporates two 8250 UARTs, a parallel port connection and a floppy disk interface. Refer to Figure 11.3 to pin out. It shows the connection between the AIP and the serial port interface. It shows the signal lines for COM1; these are fed into the GD75232SOP device which converts between 0/+5 V and +/–12 V. It then connects to a 10-pin header which is wired to the serial port.

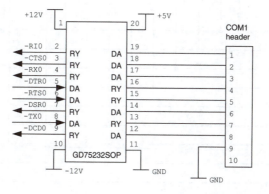

Figure A.7 COM1 connection.

A.4 Parallel port connection

Figure A.9 shows the connections from the AIP to the 26-pin parallel port header. The 33 Ω resistors on the output lines are the to protect against a short circuit on the output pins. This limits the short circuit current to less than 150 mA (5 V/33 Ω). The 1 kΩ pull-up resistor causes the input line to be a high input, if there is nothing connected to the port. Thus, when nothing is connected, the BUSY, SLCT and PE lines will be active, while ERR and ACK will be inactive. Note that the physical layout of the 26-pin header is:

1 (-STB)	2 (-AFD)
3 (PD0)	4 (-ERR)
5 (PD1)	6 (-INIT)
7 (PD2)	8 (-SLIN)
9 (PD3)	10 (GND)
11 (PD4)	12 (GND)
13 (PD5)	14 (GND)
15 (PD6)	16 (GND)
17 (PD7)	18 (GND)
19 (-ACK)	20 (GND)
21 (BUSY)	22 (GND)
23 (PE)	24 (GND)
25 (SLCT)	26 (N/C)

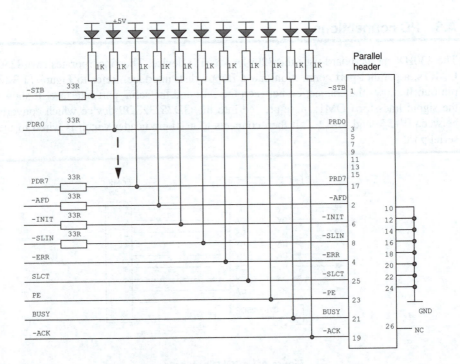

Figure A.8   Parallel port connection.

ASCII Character Codes

Binary	Decimal	Hex	Character	Binary	Decimal	Hex	Character
00000000	0	00	NUL	00010000	16	10	DLE
00000001	1	01	SOH	00010001	17	11	DC1
00000010	2	02	STX	00010010	18	12	DC2
00000011	3	03	ETX	00010011	19	13	DC3
00000100	4	04	EOT	00010100	20	14	DC4
00000101	5	05	ENQ	00010101	21	15	NAK
00000110	6	06	ACK	00010110	22	16	SYN
00000111	7	07	BEL	00010111	23	17	ETB
00001000	8	08	BS	00011000	24	18	CAN
00001001	9	09	HT	00011001	25	19	EM
00001010	10	0A	LF	00011010	26	1A	SUB
00001011	11	0B	VT	00011011	27	1B	ESC
00001100	12	0C	FF	00011100	28	1C	FS
00001101	13	0D	CR	00011101	29	1D	GS
00001110	14	0E	SO	00011110	30	1E	RS
00001111	15	0F	SI	00011111	31	1F	US

Binary	Decimal	Hex	Character	Binary	Decimal	Hex	Character
00100000	32	20	SPACE	00110000	48	30	0
00100001	33	21	!	00110001	49	31	1
00100010	34	22	"	00110010	50	32	2
00100011	35	23	#	00110011	51	33	3
00100100	36	24	$	00110100	52	34	4
00100101	37	25	%	00110101	53	35	5
00100110	38	26	&	00110110	54	36	6
00100111	39	27	'	00110111	55	37	7
00101000	40	28	(	00111000	56	38	8
00101001	41	29	)	00111001	57	39	9
00101010	42	2A	*	00111010	58	3A	:
00101011	43	2B	+	00111011	59	3B	;
00101100	44	2C	,	00111100	60	3C	<
00101101	45	2D	–	00111101	61	3D	=
00101110	46	2E	.	00111110	62	3E	>
00101111	47	2F	/	00111111	63	3F	?

Binary	Decimal	Hex	Character	Binary	Decimal	Hex	Character
01000000	64	40	@	01010000	80	50	P
01000001	65	41	A	01010001	81	51	Q
01000010	66	42	B	01010010	82	52	R
01000011	67	43	C	01010011	83	53	S
01000100	68	44	D	01010100	84	54	T
01000101	69	45	E	01010101	85	55	U
01000110	70	46	F	01010110	86	56	V
01000111	71	47	G	01010111	87	57	W
01001000	72	48	H	01011000	88	58	X
01001001	73	49	I	01011001	89	59	Y
01001010	74	4A	J	01011010	90	5A	Z
01001011	75	4B	K	01011011	91	5B	[
01001100	76	4C	L	01011100	92	5C	\
01001101	77	4D	M	01011101	93	5D	]
01001110	78	4E	N	01011110	94	5E	`
01001111	79	4F	O	01011111	95	5F	_

Binary	Decimal	Hex	Character	Binary	Decimal	Hex	Character
01100000	96	60		01110000	112	70	p
01100001	97	61	a	01110001	113	71	q
01100010	98	62	b	01110010	114	72	r
01100011	99	63	c	01110011	115	73	s
01100100	100	64	d	01110100	116	74	t
01100101	101	65	e	01110101	117	75	u
01100110	102	66	f	01110110	118	76	V
01100111	103	67	g	01110111	119	77	W
01101000	104	68	h	01111000	120	78	X
01101001	105	69	i	01111001	121	79	Y
01101010	106	6A	j	01111010	122	7A	z
01101011	107	6B	k	01111011	123	7B	{
01101100	108	6C	l	01111100	124	7C	:
01101101	109	6D	m	01111101	125	7D	}
01101110	110	6E	n	01111110	126	7E	~
01101111	111	6F	o	01111111	127	7F	DEL

Binary	Decimal	Hex	Character	Binary	Decimal	Hex	Character
10000000	128	80	Ç	10010000	144	90	É
10000001	129	81	ü	10010001	145	91	æ
10000010	130	82	é	10010010	146	92	Æ
10000011	131	83	â	10010011	147	93	ô
10000100	132	84	ä	10010100	148	94	ö
10000101	133	85	à	10010101	149	95	ò
10000110	134	86	å	10010110	150	96	û
10000111	135	87	ç	10010111	151	97	ù
10001000	136	88	ê	10011000	152	98	ÿ
10001001	137	89	ë	10011001	153	99	Ö
10001010	138	8A	è	10011010	154	9A	Ü
10001011	139	8B	ï	10011011	155	9B	¢
10001100	140	8C	î	10011100	156	9C	£
10001101	141	8D	ì	10011101	157	9D	¥
10001110	142	8E	Ä	10011110	158	9E	₧
10001111	143	8F	Å	10011111	159	9F	ƒ

Binary	Decimal	Hex	Character	Binary	Decimal	Hex	Character
10100000	160	A0	á	10110000	176	B0	
10100001	161	A1	í	10110001	177	B1	
10100010	162	A2	ó	10110010	178	B2	
10100011	163	A3	ú	10110011	179	B3	
10100100	164	A4	ñ	10110100	180	B4	
10100101	165	A5	Ñ	10110101	181	B5	
10100110	166	A6	ª	10110110	182	B6	
10100111	167	A7	º	10110111	183	B7	
10101000	168	A8	¿	10111000	184	B8	
10101001	169	A9	⌐	10111001	185	B9	
10101010	170	AA	¬	10111010	186	BA	
10101011	171	AB	½	10111011	187	BB	
10101100	172	AC	¼	10111100	188	BC	
10101101	173	AD	¡	10111101	189	BD	
10101110	174	AE	«	10111110	190	BE	
10101111	175	AF	»	10111111	191	BF	

Binary	Decimal	Hex	Character	Binary	Decimal	Hex	Character
11000000	192	C0		11010000	208	D0	
11000001	193	C1		11010001	209	D1	
11000010	194	C2		11010010	210	D2	
11000011	195	C3		11010011	211	D3	
11000100	196	C4		11010100	212	D4	
11000101	197	C5		11010101	213	D5	
11000110	198	C6		11010110	214	D6	
11000111	199	C7		11010111	215	D7	
11001000	200	C8		11011000	216	D8	
11001001	201	C9		11011001	217	D9	
11001010	202	CA		11011010	218	DA	
11001011	203	CB		11011011	219	DB	
11001100	204	CC		11011100	220	DC	
11001101	205	CD		11011101	221	DD	
11001110	206	CE		11011110	222	DE	
11001111	207	CF		11011111	223	DF	

Binary	Decimal	Hex	Character	Binary	Decimal	Hex	Character
11100000	224	E0	α	11110000	240	F0	Ξ
11100001	225	E1	ß	11110001	241	F1	±
11100010	226	E2	Γ	11110010	242	F2	≥
11100011	227	E3	π	11110011	243	F3	≤
11100100	228	E4	Σ	11110100	244	F4	⌠
11100101	229	E5	σ	11110101	245	F5	⌡
11100110	230	E6	µ	11110110	246	F6	÷
11100111	231	E7	τ	11110111	247	F7	≈
11101000	232	E8	Φ	11111000	248	F8	°
11101001	233	E9	Θ	11111001	249	F9	·
11101010	234	EA	Ω	11111010	250	FA	·
11101011	235	EB	δ	11111011	251	FB	√
11101100	236	EC	φ	11111100	252	FC	ⁿ
11101101	237	ED	ϕ	11111101	253	FD	²
11101110	238	EE	Ε	11111110	254	FE	■
11101111	239	EF	Λ	11111111	255	FF	

Win32

C.1 Window classes

C.1.1 Control class

The following predefined control classes can be specified in the *lpClassName* parameter:

BUTTON   Designates a small rectangular child window that represents a button the user can click to turn it on or off. Button controls can be used alone or in groups, and they can either be labelled or appear without text.

COMBOBOX   Designates a control consisting of a list box and a selection field similar to an edit control. When using this style, an application should either display the list box at all times or enable a drop-down list box.

EDIT   Designates a rectangular child window into which the user can type text from the keyboard. The user selects the control and gives it the keyboard focus by clicking it or moving to it by pressing the TAB key.

LISTBOX   Designates a list of character strings. Specify this control whenever an application must present a list of names, such as filenames, from which the user can choose. The user can select a string by clicking it.

MDICLIENT   Designates an MDI client window. This window receives messages that control the MDI application's child windows.

SCROLLBAR   Designates a rectangle that contains a scroll box and has direction arrows at both ends. The scrollbar sends a notification message to its parent window whenever the user clicks the control.

STATIC   Designates a simple text field, box, or rectangle used to label, box, or separate other controls. Static controls take no input and provide no output.

C.1.2 Window styles

The following window styles can be specified in the *dwStyle* parameter:

WS_BORDER   Creates a window that has a thin-line border.

WS_CAPTION   Creates a window that has a title bar.

WS_CHILD   Creates a child window.

WS_CLIPCHILDREN
    Excludes the area occupied by child windows when drawing occurs within the parent window.

WS_CLIPSIBLINGS
    Clips child windows relative to each other.

WS_DISABLED
    Creates a window that is initially disabled. A disabled window cannot receive input from the user.

WS_DLGFRAME   Creates a window that has a border of a style typically used with dialog boxes. A window with this style cannot have a title bar.

WS_GROUP   Specifies the first control of a group of controls. The user can change the keyboard focus from one control in the group to the next by using the direction keys.

WS_HSCROLL   Creates a window that has a horizontal scrollbar.

WS_ICONIC   Creates a window that is initially minimized. Same as the WS_MINIMIZE style.

WS_MAXIMIZE   Creates a window that is initially maximized.

WS_MAXIMIZEBOX
>Creates a window that has a Maximize button.

WS_MINIMIZE Creates a window that is initially minimized.

WS_MINIMIZEBOX
>Creates a window that has a Minimize button.

WS_OVERLAPPED
>Creates an overlapped window which has a title bar and a border.

WS_OVERLAPPEDWINDOW
>Creates an overlapped window.

WS_POPUP   Creates a pop-up window.

WS_POPUPWINDOW
>Creates a pop-up window with WS_BORDER, WS_POPUP, and WS_SYSMENU styles.

WS_SIZEBOX Creates a window that has a sizing border.

WS_SYSMENU Creates a window that has a System-menu box in its title bar.

WS_TABSTOP Specifies a control that can receive the keyboard focus when the user presses the TAB key. Pressing the TAB key changes the keyboard focus to the next control with the WS_TABSTOP style.

WS_THICKFRAME
>Creates a window that has a sizing border.

WS_TILED   Creates an overlapped window. An overlapped window has a title bar and a border.

WS_TILEDWINDOW
>Same as the WS_OVERLAPPEDWINDOW style.

WS_VISIBLE Creates a window that is initially visible.

WS_VSCROLL Creates a window that has a vertical scrollbar.

The definitionss for the window styles are:

```
#define WS_OVERLAPPED        0x00000000L
#define WS_POPUP             0x80000000L
#define WS_CHILD             0x40000000L
#define WS_MINIMIZE          0x20000000L
#define WS_VISIBLE           0x10000000L
#define WS_DISABLED          0x08000000L
#define WS_CLIPSIBLINGS      0x04000000L
#define WS_CLIPCHILDREN      0x02000000L
#define WS_MAXIMIZE          0x01000000L
#define WS_CAPTION           0x00C00000L
#define WS_BORDER            0x00800000L
#define WS_DLGFRAME          0x00400000L
#define WS_VSCROLL           0x00200000L
#define WS_HSCROLL           0x00100000L
#define WS_SYSMENU           0x00080000L
#define WS_THICKFRAME        0x00040000L
#define WS_GROUP             0x00020000L
#define WS_TABSTOP           0x00010000L
#define WS_MINIMIZEBOX       0x00020000L
#define WS_MAXIMIZEBOX       0x00010000L
```

C.1.3 Button

The following button styles (in the BUTTON class) can be specified in the *dwStyle* parameter:

BS_3STATE   Creates a button that is the same as a check box, except that the box can be greyed as well as checked or unchecked.

BS_AUTO3STATE
>Creates a button that is the same as a three-state check box, except that the box changes its state when the user selects it. The state cycles through checked, greyed, and unchecked.

BS_AUTOCHECKBOX
>Creates a button that is the same as a check box, except that the check state automatically toggles between checked and unchecked each time the user selects the check box.

BS_AUTORADIOBUTTON
>Creates a button that is the same as a radio button, except that when the user selects it. Windows automatically sets the button's check state to checked and automatically sets the check state for all other buttons in the same group to unchecked.

BS_CHECKBOX

Creates a small, empty check box with text. By default, the text is displayed to the right of the check box. To display the text to the left of the check box, combine this flag with the BS_LEFTTEXT style.

BS_DEFPUSHBUTTON

Creates a push button that behaves like a BS_PUSHBUTTON style button, but also has a heavy black border. If the button is in a dialog box, the user can select the button by pressing the ENTER key, even when the button does not have the input focus.

BS_GROUPBOX

Creates a rectangle in which other controls can be grouped. Any text associated with this style is displayed in the rectangle's upper left corner.

BS_LEFTTEXT

Places text on the left side of the radio button or check box when combined with a radio button or check box style.

BS_OWNERDRAW

Creates an owner-drawn button.

BS_PUSHBUTTON

Creates a push button that, when the user pushes the button, sends a command message to the owner window.

BS_RADIOBUTTON

Creates a small circle with text.

The definitions for the button styles are:

```
#define BS_PUSHBUTTON          0x00000000L
#define BS_DEFPUSHBUTTON       0x00000001L
#define BS_CHECKBOX            0x00000002L
#define BS_AUTOCHECKBOX        0x00000003L
#define BS_RADIOBUTTON         0x00000004L
#define BS_3STATE              0x00000005L
#define BS_AUTO3STATE          0x00000006L
#define BS_GROUPBOX            0x00000007L
#define BS_USERBUTTON          0x00000008L
#define BS_AUTORADIOBUTTON     0x00000009L
#define BS_OWNERDRAW           0x0000000BL
#define BS_LEFTTEXT            0x00000020L
```

C.1.4   Combo box

The following combo box styles (in the COMBOBOX class) can be specified in the *dwStyle* parameter:

CBS_AUTOHSCROLL

Automatically scrolls the text in an edit control to the right when the user types a character at the end of the line.

CBS_DISABLENOSCROLL

Shows a disabled vertical scrollbar in the list box when the box does not contain enough items to scroll.

CBS_DROPDOWN

Similar to CBS_SIMPLE, except that the list box is not displayed unless the user selects an icon next to the edit control.

CBS_DROPDOWNLIST

Similar to CBS_DROPDOWN, except that the edit control is replaced by a static text item that displays the current selection in the list box.

CBS_HASSTRINGS

Specifies that an owner-drawn combo box contains items consisting of strings.

CBS_LOWERCASE

Converts to lower case any upper case characters entered into the edit control of a combo box.

CBS_NOINTEGRALHEIGHT

Specifies that the size of the combo box is exactly the size specified by the application when it created the combo box.

CBS_OEMCONVERT

Converts text entered in the combo box edit control. The text is converted from the Windows character set to the OEM character set and then back to the Windows set.

CBS_OWNERDRAWFIXED

Specifies that the owner of the list box is responsible for drawing its contents and that the items in the list box are all the same height.

CBS_OWNERDRAWVARIABLE

Specifies that the owner of the list box is responsible for drawing its contents and that the items in the list box are variable in height.

CBS_SIMPLE   Displays the list box at all times. The current selection in the list box is displayed in the edit control.

CBS_SORT   Automatically sorts strings entered into the list box.

CBS_UPPERCASE

Converts to upper case any lower case characters entered into the edit control of a combo box.

The definitions for the combo box styles are:

```
#define CBS_SIMPLE              0x0001L
#define CBS_DROPDOWN            0x0002L
#define CBS_DROPDOWNLIST        0x0003L
#define CBS_OWNERDRAWFIXED      0x0010L
#define CBS_OWNERDRAWVARIABLE   0x0020L
#define CBS_AUTOHSCROLL         0x0040L
#define CBS_OEMCONVERT          0x0080L
#define CBS_SORT                0x0100L
#define CBS_HASSTRINGS          0x0200L
#define CBS_NOINTEGRALHEIGHT    0x0400L
#define CBS_DISABLENOSCROLL     0x0800L
```

C.1.5   *Edit control styles*

The following edit control styles (in the EDIT class) can be specified in the *dwStyle* parameter:

ES_AUTOHSCROLL

Automatically scrolls text to the right by 10 characters when the user types a character at the end of the line. When the user presses the ENTER key, the control scrolls all text back to position zero.

ES_AUTOVSCROLL

Automatically scrolls text up one page when the user presses the ENTER key on the last line.

ES_CENTER   Centres text in a multiline edit control.

ES_LEFT   Left-aligns text.

ES_LOWERCASE

Converts all characters to lower case as they are typed into the edit control.

ES_MULTILINE

Designates a multiline edit control. The default is single-line edit control. When the multiline edit control is in a dialog box, the default response to pressing the ENTER key is to activate the default button. To use the ENTER key as a carriage return, use the ES_WANTRETURN style.

ES_NOHIDESEL

Negates the default behaviour for an edit control. The default behaviour hides the selection when the control loses the input focus and inverts the selection when the control receives the input focus.

ES_OEMCONVERT

Converts text entered in the edit control. The text is converted from the Windows character set to the OEM character set and then back to the Windows set.

ES_PASSWORD

Displays an asterisk (*) for each character typed into the edit control.

ES_READONLY

Prevents the user from typing or editing text in the edit control.

ES_RIGHT   Right-aligns text in a multiline edit control.

ES_UPPERCASE

Converts all characters to upper case as they are typed into the edit control.

ES_WANTRETURN

Specifies that a carriage return be inserted when the user presses the ENTER key while entering text into a multiline edit control in a dialog box.

The definitions for the editor control styles are:
```
#define ES_LEFT            0x0000L
#define ES_CENTER          0x0001L
#define ES_RIGHT           0x0002L
#define ES_MULTILINE       0x0004L
#define ES_UPPERCASE       0x0008L
#define ES_LOWERCASE       0x0010L
#define ES_PASSWORD        0x0020L
#define ES_AUTOVSCROLL     0x0040L
#define ES_AUTOHSCROLL     0x0080L
#define ES_NOHIDESEL       0x0100L
#define ES_OEMCONVERT      0x0400L
#define ES_READONLY        0x0800L
#define ES_WANTRETURN      0x1000L
```

C.1.6   List box

The following list box control styles (in the LISTBOX class) can be specified in the *dwStyle* parameter:

LBS_DISABLENOSCROLL
Shows a disabled vertical scrollbar for the list box when the box does not contain enough items to scroll.

LBS_EXTENDEDSEL
Allows multiple items to be selected by using the SHIFT key and the mouse or special key combinations.

LBS_HASSTRINGS
Specifies that a list box contains items consisting of strings.

LBS_MULTICOLUMN
Specifies a multicolumn list box that is scrolled horizontally.

LBS_MULTIPLESEL
Turns string selection on or off each time the user clicks or double-clicks a string in the list box.

LBS_NODATA   Specifies a no-data list box. Specify this style when the count of items in the list box will exceed one thousand. A no-data list box must also have the LBS_OWNERDRAWFIXED style, but must not have the LBS_SORT or LBS_HASSTRINGS style.

LBS_NOINTEGRALHEIGHT
Specifies that the size of the list box is exactly the size specified by the application when it created the list box. Normally, Windows sizes a list box so that the list box does not display partial items.

LBS_NOREDRAW
Specifies that the list box's appearance is not updated when changes are made. You can change this style at any time by sending a WM_SETREDRAW message.

LBS_NOTIFY   Notifies the parent window with an input message whenever the user clicks or double-clicks a string in the list box.

LBS_OWNERDRAWFIXED
Specifies that the owner of the list box is responsible for drawing its contents and that the items in the list box are the same height.

LBS_OWNERDRAWVARIABLE
Specifies that the owner of the list box is responsible for drawing its contents and that the items in the list box are variable in height.

LBS_SORT   Sorts strings in the list box alphabetically.

LBS_STANDARD
Sorts strings in the list box alphabetically. The parent window receives an input message whenever the user clicks or double-clicks a string.

LBS_USETABSTOPS
Enables a list box to recognize and expand tab characters when drawing its strings. The default tab positions are 32 dialog box units. A dialog box unit is a horizontal or vertical distance.

LBS_WANTKEYBOARDINPUT

Specifies that the owner of the list box receives `WM_VKEYTOITEM` messages whenever the user presses a key and the list box has the input focus.

The definitions for the list box styles are:

```
#define LBS_NOTIFY              0x0001L
#define LBS_SORT                0x0002L
#define LBS_NOREDRAW            0x0004L
#define LBS_MULTIPLESEL         0x0008L
#define LBS_OWNERDRAWFIXED      0x0010L
#define LBS_OWNERDRAWVARIABLE   0x0020L
#define LBS_HASSTRINGS          0x0040L
#define LBS_USETABSTOPS         0x0080L
#define LBS_NOINTEGRALHEIGHT    0x0100L
#define LBS_MULTICOLUMN         0x0200L
#define LBS_WANTKEYBOARDINPUT   0x0400L
#define LBS_EXTENDEDSEL         0x0800L
#define LBS_DISABLENOSCROLL     0x1000L
#define LBS_NODATA              0x2000L
```

C.1.7   *Scrollbars*

The following scrollbar styles (in the SCROLLBAR class) can be specified in the *dwStyle* parameter:

SBS_BOTTOMALIGN
: Aligns the bottom edge of the scrollbar with the bottom edge of the rectangle defined by the `CreateWindow` parameters *x*, *y*, *nWidth*, and *nHeight*. The scrollbar has the default height for system scrollbars. Use this style with the SBS_HORZ style.

SBS_HORZ
: Designates a horizontal scrollbar. If neither the SBS_BOTTOMALIGN nor SBS_TOPALIGN style is specified, the scrollbar has the height, width, and position specified by the parameters of `CreateWindow`.

SBS_LEFTALIGN
: Aligns the left edge of the scrollbar with the left edge of the rectangle defined by the parameters of `CreateWindow`. The scrollbar has the default width for system scrollbars. Use this style with the SBS_VERT style.

SBS_RIGHTALIGN
: Aligns the right edge of the scrollbar with the right edge of the rectangle defined by the parameters of `CreateWindow`. The scrollbar has the default width for system scrollbars. Use this style with the SBS_VERT style.

SBS_SIZEBOX
: Designates a size box. If you specify neither the SBS_SIZEBOXBOTTOMRIGHTALIGN nor the SBS_SIZEBOXTOPLEFTALIGN style, the size box has the height, width, and position specified by the parameters of `CreateWindow`.

SBS_SIZEBOXBOTTOMRIGHTALIGN
: Aligns the lower-right corner of the size box with the lower-right corner of the rectangle specified by the parameters of `CreateWindow`. The size box has the default size for system size boxes. Use this style with the SBS_SIZEBOX style.

SBS_SIZEBOXTOPLEFTALIGN
: Aligns the upper-left corner of the size box with the upper-left corner of the rectangle specified by the parameters of `CreateWindow`. The size box has the default size for system size boxes. Use this style with the SBS_SIZEBOX style.

SBS_TOPALIGN
: Aligns the top edge of the scrollbar with the top edge of the rectangle defined by the parameters of `CreateWindow`. The scrollbar has the default height for system scrollbars. Use this style with the SBS_HORZ style.

SBS_VERT
: Designates a vertical scrollbar. If you specify neither the SBS_RIGHTALIGN nor the SBS_LEFTALIGN style, the scrollbar has the height, width, and position specified by the parameters of `CreateWindow`.

The definitions for the scrollbar styles are:

```
#define SBS_HORZ                0x0000L
#define SBS_VERT                0x0001L
```

```
#define SBS_TOPALIGN                    0x0002L
#define SBS_LEFTALIGN                   0x0002L
#define SBS_BOTTOMALIGN                 0x0004L
#define SBS_RIGHTALIGN                  0x0004L
#define SBS_SIZEBOXTOPLEFTALIGN         0x0002L
#define SBS_SIZEBOXBOTTOMRIGHTALIGN     0x0004L
#define SBS_SIZEBOX                     0x0008L
```

C.1.8   *Static control*

The following static control styles (in the STATIC class) can be specified in the *dwStyle* parameter. A static control can have only one of these styles:

SS_BITMAP   Specifies a bitmap is to be displayed in the static control. The error code text is the name of a bitmap (not a filename) defined elsewhere in the resource file. The style ignores the *nWidth* and *nHeight* parameters; the control automatically sizes itself to accommodate the bitmap.

SS_BLACKFRAME
Specifies a box with a frame drawn in the same colour as the window frames. This colour is black in the default Windows colour scheme.

SS_BLACKRECT
Specifies a rectangle filled with the current window frame colour. This colour is black in the default Windows colour scheme.

SS_CENTER   Specifies a simple rectangle and centres the error code text in the rectangle. The text is formatted before it is displayed. Words that extend past the end of a line are automatically wrapped to the beginning of the next centred line.

SS_CENTERIMAGE
Specifies that the midpoint of a static control with the SS_BITMAP or SS_ICON style is to remain fixed when the control is resized. The four sides are adjusted to accommodate a new bitmap or icon.

SS_GRAYFRAME
Specifies a box with a frame drawn with the same colour as the screen background (desktop). This colour is grey in the default Windows colour scheme.

SS_GRAYRECT Specifies a rectangle filled with the current screen background colour. This colour is grey in the default Windows colour scheme.

SS_ICON   Specifies an icon displayed in the dialog box. The given text is the name of an icon (not a filename) defined elsewhere in the resource file. The style ignores the *nWidth* and *nHeight* parameters; the icon automatically sizes itself.

SS_LEFT   Specifies a simple rectangle and left-aligns the given text in the rectangle. The text is formatted before it is displayed. Words that extend past the end of a line are automatically wrapped to the beginning of the next left-aligned line.

SS_LEFTNOWORDWRAP
Specifies a simple rectangle and left-aligns the given text in the rectangle. Tabs are expanded but words are not wrapped. Text that extends past the end of a line is clipped.

SS_METAPICT
Specifies a metafile picture is to be displayed in the static control. The given text is the name of a metafile picture (not a filename) defined elsewhere in the resource file.

SS_NOPREFIX Prevents interpretation of any ampersand (&) characters in the control's text as accelerator prefix characters. These are displayed with the ampersand removed and the next character in the string underlined. This static control style may be included with any of the defined static controls.

SS_NOTIFY   Sends the parent window STN_CLICKED and STN_DBLCLK notification messages when the user clicks or double-clicks the control.

SS_RIGHT   Specifies a simple rectangle and right-aligns the given text in the rectangle. The text is formatted before it is displayed. Words that extend past the end of a line are automatically wrapped to the beginning of the next right-aligned line.

SS_RIGHTIMAGE
Specifies that the bottom-right corner of a static control with the SS_BITMAP or SS_ICON style is to remain fixed when the control is resized. Only the top and left sides are adjusted to accommodate a new bitmap or icon.

SS_SIMPLE   Specifies a simple rectangle and displays a single line of left-aligned text in the rectangle. The text line cannot be shortened or altered in any way. The control's parent window or dialog box must not process the WM_CTLCOLORSTATIC message.

SS_WHITEFRAME
    Specifies a box with a frame drawn with the same colour as the window backgrounds. This colour is white in the default Windows colour scheme.

SS_WHITERECT
    Specifies a rectangle filled with the current window background colour. This colour is white in the default Windows colour scheme.

The definitions for the static control styles are:

```
#define SS_LEFT            0x00000000L
#define SS_CENTER          0x00000001L
#define SS_RIGHT           0x00000002L
#define SS_ICON            0x00000003L
#define SS_BLACKRECT       0x00000004L
#define SS_GRAYRECT        0x00000005L
#define SS_WHITERECT       0x00000006L
#define SS_BLACKFRAME      0x00000007L
#define SS_GRAYFRAME       0x00000008L
#define SS_WHITEFRAME      0x00000009L
#define SS_USERITEM        0x0000000AL
#define SS_SIMPLE          0x0000000BL
#define SS_LEFTNOWORDWRAP  0x0000000CL
#define SS_BITMAP          0x0000000EL
```

C.1.9 Dialog box

The following dialog box styles can be specified in the *dwStyle* parameter:

DS_ABSALIGN Indicates that the coordinates of the dialog box are screen coordinates; otherwise, Windows assumes they are client coordinates.

DS_CONTEXTHELP
    Includes a question mark in the title bar of the dialog box. When the user clicks the question mark, the cursor changes to a question mark with a pointer. If the user then clicks a control in the dialog box, the control receives a WM_HELP message.

DS_CONTROL   Creates a dialog box that works well as a child window of another dialog box, much like a page in a property sheet. This style allows the user to tab among the control windows of a child dialog box, use its accelerator keys, and so on.

DS_LOCALEDIT
    Applies to 16-bit applications only. This style directs edit controls in the dialog box to allocate memory from the application's data segment. Otherwise, edit controls allocate storage from a global memory object.

DS_MODALFRAME
    Creates a dialog box with a modal dialog box frame that can be combined with a title bar and System menu by specifying the WS_CAPTION and WS_SYSMENU styles.

DS_NOIDLEMSG
    Suppresses WM_ENTERIDLE messages that Windows would otherwise send to the owner of the dialog box while the dialog box is displayed.

DS_RECURSE   Dialog box style for control-like dialog boxes.

DS_SETFONT   Indicates that the dialog box template (the DLGTEMPLATE structure) contains two additional members specifying a font name and point size.

DS_SETFOREGROUND
    Does not apply to 16-bit versions of Microsoft Windows. This style brings the dialog box to the foreground.

DS_SYSMODAL Creates a system-modal dialog box. This style causes the dialog box to have the WS_EX_TOPMOST style, but otherwise has no effect on the dialog box or the behaviour of other windows in the system when the dialog box is displayed.

The definitions for the dialog control styles are:

```
#define DS_ABSALIGN        0x01L
```

```
#define DS_SYSMODAL        0x02L
#define DS_LOCALEDIT       0x20L
#define DS_SETFONT         0x40L
#define DS_MODALFRAME      0x80L
#define DS_NOIDLEMSG       0x100L
#define DS_SETFOREGROUND   0x200L
```

C.2 WNDCLASS

```
typedef struct _WNDCLASS {
    UINT     style;
    WNDPROC  lpfnWndProc;
    int      cbClsExtra;
    int      cbWndExtra;
    HANDLE   hInstance;
    HICON    hIcon;
    HCURSOR  hCursor;
    HBRUSH   hbrBackground;
    LPCTSTR  lpszMenuName;
    LPCTSTR  lpszClassName;
} WNDCLASS;
```

C.2.1 Style

CS_BYTEALIGNCLIENT

Aligns the window's client area on the byte boundary (in the x direction) to enhance performance during drawing operations. This style affects the width of the window and its horizontal position on the display.

CS_BYTEALIGNWINDOW

Aligns a window on a byte boundary (in the x direction) to enhance performance during operations that involve moving or sizing the window. This style affects the width of the window and its horizontal position on the display.

CS_CLASSDC Allocates one device context to be shared by all windows in the class. Because window classes are process specific, it is possible for multiple threads of a multithreaded application to create a window of the same class. It is also possible for the threads to attempt to use the device context simultaneously. When this happens, the operating system allows only one of the threads to successfully finish its drawing operation.

CS_DBLCLKS Sends double-click messages to the window procedure when the user double-clicks the mouse while the cursor is within a window belonging to the class.

CS_HREDRAW Redraws the entire window if a movement or size adjustment changes the width of the client area.

CS_NOCLOSE Disables the Close command on the System menu.

CS_OWNDC Allocates a unique device context for each window in the class.

CS_PARENTDC Specifies that child windows inherit their parent window's device context. Specifying CS_PARENTDC enhances an application's performance.

CS_SAVEBITS Saves, as a bitmap, the portion of the screen image obscured by a window. Windows uses the saved bitmap to recreate the screen image when the window is removed.

CS_VREDRAW Redraws the entire window if a movement or size adjustment changes the height of the client area.

C.2.2 Background brush

```
COLOR_ACTIVEBORDER        COLOR_ACTIVECAPTION
COLOR_APPWORKSPACE        COLOR_BACKGROUND
COLOR_BTNFACE             COLOR_BTNSHADOW
COLOR_BTNTEXT             COLOR_CAPTIONTEXT
COLOR_GRAYTEXT            COLOR_HIGHLIGHT
```

```
COLOR_HIGHLIGHTTEXT          COLOR_INACTIVEBORDER
COLOR_INACTIVECAPTION        COLOR_MENU
COLOR_MENUTEXT               COLOR_SCROLLBAR
COLOR_WINDOW                 COLOR_WINDOWFRAME
COLOR_WINDOWTEXT
```

C.3 Messages

```
WM_NULL                  WM_CREATE                WM_DESTROY
WM_MOVE                  WM_SIZE                  WM_ACTIVATE
WM_SETFOCUS              WM_KILLFOCUS             WM_ENABLE
WM_SETREDRAW             WM_SETTEXT               WM_GETTEXT
WM_GETTEXTLENGTH         WM_PAINT                 WM_CLOSE
WM_QUERYENDSESSION       WM_QUIT                  WM_QUERYOPEN
WM_ERASEBKGND            WM_SYSCOLORCHANGE        WM_ENDSESSION
WM_SHOWWINDOW            WM_WININICHANGE          WM_DEVMODECHANGE
WM_ACTIVATEAPP           WM_FONTCHANGE            WM_TIMECHANGE
WM_CANCELMODE            WM_SETCURSOR             WM_MOUSEACTIVATE
WM_CHILDACTIVATE         WM_QUEUESYNC             WM_GETMINMAXINFO
WM_PAINTICON             WM_ICONERASEBKGND        WM_NEXTDLGCTL
WM_SPOOLERSTATUS         WM_DRAWITEM              WM_MEASUREITEM
WM_DELETEITEM            WM_VKEYTOITEM            WM_CHARTOITEM
WM_SETFONT               WM_GETFONT               WM_SETHOTKEY
WM_GETHOTKEY             WM_QUERYDRAGICON         WM_COMPAREITEM
WM_COMPACTING            WM_WINDOWPOSCHANGING     WM_WINDOWPOSCHANGED
WM_POWER                 WM_COPYDATA              WM_CANCELJOURNAL
WM_NCCREATE              WM_NCDESTROY             WM_NCCALCSIZE
WM_NCHITTEST             WM_NCPAINT               WM_NCACTIVATE
WM_GETDLGCODE            WM_NCMOUSEMOVE           WM_NCLBUTTONDOWN
WM_NCLBUTTONUP           WM_NCLBUTTONDBLCLK       WM_NCRBUTTONDOWN
WM_NCRBUTTONUP           M_NCRBUTTONDBLCLK        WM_NCMBUTTONDOWN
WM_NCMBUTTONUP           WM_NCMBUTTONDBLCLK       WM_KEYFIRST
WM_KEYDOWN               WM_KEYUP                 WM_CHAR
WM_DEADCHAR              WM_SYSKEYDOWN            WM_SYSKEYUP
WM_SYSCHAR               WM_SYSDEADCHAR           WM_KEYLAST
WM_INITDIALOG            WM_COMMAND               WM_SYSCOMMAND
WM_TIMER                 WM_HSCROLL               WM_VSCROLL
WM_INITMENU              WM_INITMENUPOPUP         WM_MENUSELECT
WM_MENUCHAR              WM_ENTERIDLE             WM_CTLCOLORMSGBOX
WM_CTLCOLOREDIT          WM_CTLCOLORLISTBOX       WM_CTLCOLORBTN
WM_CTLCOLORDLG           WM_CTLCOLORSCROLLBAR     WM_CTLCOLORSTATIC
WM_MOUSEFIRST            WM_MOUSEMOVE             WM_LBUTTONDOWN
WM_LBUTTONUP             WM_LBUTTONDBLCLK         WM_RBUTTONDOWN
WM_RBUTTONUP             WM_RBUTTONDBLCLK
WM_MBUTTONDOWN           WM_MBUTTONUP             WM_MBUTTONDBLCLK
WM_MOUSELAST             WM_PARENTNOTIFY          WM_ENTERMENULOOP
WM_EXITMENULOOP          WM_SIZING                WM_CAPTURECHANGED
WM_MOVING                WM_POWERBROADCAST        WM_DEVICECHANGE
WM_MDICREATE             WM_MDIDESTROY            WM_MDIACTIVATE
WM_MDIRESTORE            WM_MDINEXT               WM_MDIMAXIMIZE
WM_MDITILE               WM_MDICASCADE            WM_MDIICONARRANGE
WM_MDIGETACTIVE          WM_MDISETMENU            WM_ENTERSIZEMOVE
WM_EXITSIZEMOVE          WM_DROPFILES             WM_MDIREFRESHMENU
WM_CUT                   WM_COPY                  WM_PASTE
WM_CLEAR                 WM_UNDO                  WM_RENDERFORMAT
WM_RENDERALLFORMATS      WM_DESTROYCLIPBOARD      WM_DRAWCLIPBOARD
WM_PAINTCLIPBOARD        WM_VSCROLLCLIPBOARD      WM_SIZECLIPBOARD
WM_ASKCBFORMATNAME       WM_CHANGECBCHAIN         WM_HSCROLLCLIPBOARD
WM_QUERYNEWPALETTE       WM_PALETTEISCHANGING     WM_PALETTECHANGED
WM_HOTKEY                WM_PENWINFIRST           WM_PENWINLAST
```

C.4   Win32 functions

C.4.1   *32-bit memory management functions*

GetWinMem32Version	Retrieves the version of the 32-bit memory API
Global16PointerAlloc	Converts a 16:32 pointer to a 16:16 pointer alias
Global16PointerFree	Frees a 16:16 pointer alias
Global32Alloc	Allocates a USE32 memory object
Global32CodeAlias	Creates a USE32 alias selector for 32-bit object
Global32CodeAliasFree	Frees a USE32 code-segment alias selector
Global32Free	Frees a USE32 memory object
Global32Realloc	Changes the size of a USE32 memory object

C.4.2   *Application-execution functions*

LoadModule	Loads and executes Windows application
WinExec	Runs the specified application
WinHelp	Invokes Windows Help

C.4.3   *Atom-management functions*

AddAtom	Adds a string to the local atom table
DeleteAtom	Decrements the reference count of a local atom
FindAtom	Retrieves a string atom from a local atom table
GetAtomHandle	Retrieves an atom handle
GetAtomName	Retrieves a local atom string
GlobalAddAtom	Adds a string to the system atom table
GlobalDeleteAtom	Decrements the reference count of a global atom
GlobalFindAtom	Retrieves a string atom from a global atom table
GlobalGetAtomName	Retrieves a global atom string
InitAtomTable	Sets the size of the local atom hash table

C.4.4   *Bitmap functions*

BitBlt	Copies a bitmap between device contexts
CreateBitmap	Creates a device-dependent memory bitmap
CreateBitmapIndirect	Creates a bitmap using a TBITMAP structure
CreateCompatibleBitmap	Creates a bitmap compatible with a device context
CreateDIBitmap	Creates a bitmap handle from a DIB specification
CreateDiscardableBitmap	Creates a discardable bitmap
GetBitmapBits	Copies bitmap bits into a buffer
GetBitmapDimension	Retrieves the width and height of a bitmap
GetBitmapDimensionEx	Retrieves the width and height of a bitmap
GetDIBits	Copies DIB bits into a buffer
GetPixel	Retrieves the RGB colour of a specified pixel
LoadBitmap	Loads a bitmap resource
PatBlt	Creates a bit pattern on a device
SetBitmapBits	Sets bitmap bits from an array of bytes
SetBitmapDimension	Sets the width and height of bitmap
SetBitmapDimensionEx	Sets the width and height of bitmap
SetDIBits	Sets the bits of a bitmap
SetDIBitsToDevice	Sets DIB bits to a device
SetPixel	Sets a pixel to a specified colour
StretchBlt	Sets the bitmap-stretching mode
StretchDIBits	Moves DIB from source to destination rectangle

C.4.5   *Brush functions*

CreateBrushIndirect	Creates a brush with the specified attributes
CreateHatchBrush	Creates a hatched brush
CreatePatternBrush	Creates a pattern brush from a bitmap
CreateSolidBrush	Creates a solid brush with a specified colour
GetBrushOrg	Retrieves the origin of the current brush
GetBrushOrgEx	Retrieves the origin of the current brush
GetStockObject	Retrieves the handle of a stock pen, brush, or font

SetBrushOrg	Sets the origin of the current brush

C.4.6   *Callback functions*

AbortProc	Processes a cancelled print job
CallWndProc	Filters messages sent by the SendMessage function
CBTProc	Allows a CBT application to prevent an operation
CPlApplet	Processes messages for a Control Panel DLL
DdeCallback	Processes DDEML transactions
DebugProc	Examines data before it is sent to a hook
DialogProc	Processes messages sent to a modeless dialog box
DriverProc	Processes messages for an installable driver
EnumChildProc	Receives child window handles during enumeration
EnumFontFamProc	Retrieves information about available fonts
EnumFontsProc	Retrieves information about available fonts
EnumMetaFileProc	Processes metafile data
EnumObjectsProc	Processes object data
EnumPropFixedProc	Receives enumerated property data for a window
EnumPropMovableProc	Receives enumerated property data for a window
EnumTaskWndProc	Processes task window handles during enumeration
EnumWindowsProc	Receives parent window handles during enumeration
GetMsgProc	Filters messages retrieved by the GetMessage function
GrayStringProc	Outputs text for the GrayString function
HardwareProc	Filters non-standard hardware messages
JournalPlaybackProc	Places recorded events into the system queue
JournalRecordProc	Records event messages
KeyboardProc	Filters keyboard messages
LibMain	Initializes a dynamic-link library
LineDDAProc	Processes line data
LoadProc	Receives and processes resource information
MessageProc	Filters dialog box, message box, or menu messages
MouseProc	Filters mouse messages
NotifyProc	Determines whether to discard a global memory object
ShellProc	Receives notifications from the system
SysMsgProc	Filters dialog box, message box, or menu messages
TimerProc	Processes WM_TIMER messages
WEP	Cleans up and exits a dynamic-link library
WindowProc	Processes messages sent to a window
WinMain	Initializes an application and processes message loop
WordBreakProc	Determines line breaks in an edit control

C.4.7   *Caret functions*

CreateCaret	Creates a new shape for the system caret
DestroyCaret	Destroys the current caret shape
GetCaretBlinkTime	Retrieves the caret blink rate
GetCaretPos	Retrieves the current caret position
HideCaret	Removes the caret from the screen
SetCaretBlinkTime	Sets the caret blink rate
SetCaretPos	Sets the caret position
ShowCaret	Shows (unhides) the caret on the screen

C.4.8   *Clipboard functions*

ChangeClipboardChain	Removes window from clipboard-viewer chain
CloseClipboard	Closes the clipboard
CountClipboardFormats	Retrieves the number of clipboard formats
EmptyClipboard	Empties the clipboard and frees data handles
EnumClipboardFormats	Returns the available clipboard formats
GetClipboardData	Retrieves a handle to clipboard data
GetClipboardFormatName	Retrieves the registered clipboard-format name
GetClipboardOwner	Retrieves clipboard-owner window handle
GetClipboardViewer	Retrieves first clipboard-viewer window handle
GetPriorityClipboardFormat	Retrieves first clipboard format in priority list

IsClipboardFormatAvailable	Determines whether format data is available
OpenClipboard	Opens the clipboard
RegisterClipboardFormat	Registers a new clipboard format
SetClipboardData	Sets the data in the clipboard
SetClipboardViewer	Adds a window to the clipboard-viewer chain

C.4.9   Clipping functions

ExcludeClipRect	Creates new clipping region, excluding rectangle
GetClipBox	Retrieves a rectangle for the clipping region
IntersectClipRect	Creates a clipping region from an intersection
OffsetClipRgn	Moves a clipping region
PtVisible	Queries whether a point is within the clipping region
RectVisible	Queries whether a rectangle is within the clipping region
SelectClipRgn	Selects a clipping region for the device context

C.4.10   Common-dialog box functions

CommDlgExtendedError	Retrieves error data for common dialog box procedure
ChooseColor	Creates a colour-selection dialog box
ChooseFont function	Creates a font-selection dialog box
FindText	Creates a find-text dialog box
GetFileTitle	Retrieves a filename
GetOpenFileName	Creates an open-filename dialog box
GetSaveFileName	Creates a save-filename dialog box
PrintDlg function	Creates a print-text dialog box
ReplaceText	Creates a replace-text dialog box

C.4.11   Communication functions

BuildCommDCB	Translates a device-definition string to a DCB
ClearCommBreak	Restores character transmission
CloseComm	Closes a communications device
EnableCommNotification	Enables or disables WM_COMMNOTIFY posting
EscapeCommFunction	Passes an extended function to a device
FlushComm	Flushes a transmission or receiving queue
GetCommError	Retrieves the communications-device status
GetCommEventMask	Retrieves the device event word
GetCommState	Retrieves the device control block
OpenComm	Opens a communications device
ReadComm	Reads from a communications device
SetCommBreak	Suspends character transmission
SetCommEventMask	Enables events in a device event word
SetCommState	Sets the communications-device state
TransmitCommChar	Places a character in the transmission queue
UngetCommChar	Puts a character back in the receiving queue
WriteComm	Writes to a communications device

C.4.12   Coordinate functions

ChildWindowFromPoint	Determines which child window contains a point
ClientToScreen	Converts client point to screen coordinates
DPtoLP	Converts device points to logical coordinates
GetCurrentPosition	Retrieves position in logical coordinates
GetCurrentPositionEx	Retrieves position in logical coordinates
LPtoDP	Converts logical points to device coordinates
MapWindowPoints	Converts points to another coordinate system
ScreenToClient	Converts screen points to client coordinates
WindowFromPoint	Returns the handle of a window containing a point

C.4.13   Cursor functions

ClipCursor	Confines the cursor to a specified rectangle
CreateCursor	Creates a cursor with specified dimensions
DestroyCursor	Destroys a cursor created by CreateCursor or LoadCursor
GetCursorPos	Retrieves the current cursor position in screen coordinates
LoadCursor	Loads a cursor resource

SetCursor	Changes the mouse cursor
SetCursorPos	Sets the mouse-cursor position in screen coordinates
ShowCursor	Shows or hides the mouse cursor

C.4.14 DDE functions

DdeAbandonTransaction	Abandons an asynchronous transaction
DdeAccessData	Accesses a DDE global memory object
DdeAddData	Adds data to a DDE global memory object
DdeClientTransaction	Begins a DDE data transaction
DdeCmpStringHandles	Compares two DDE string handles
DdeConnect	Establishes a conversation with a server application
DdeConnectList	Establishes multiple DDE conversations
DdeCreateDataHandle	Creates a DDE data handle
DdeCreateStringHandle	Creates a DDE string handle
DdeDisconnect	Terminates a DDE conversation
DdeDisconnectList	Destroys a DDE conversation list
DdeEnableCallback	Enables or disables one or more DDE conversations
DdeFreeDataHandle	Frees a global memory object
DdeFreeStringHandle	Frees a DDE string handle
DdeGetData	Copies data from a global memory object to a buffer
DdeGetLastError	Returns an error value set by a DDEML function
DdeInitialize	Registers an application with the DDEML
DdeKeepStringHandle	Increments the usage count for a string handle
DdeNameService	Registers or unregisters a service name
DdePostAdvise	Prompts a server to send advise data to a client
DdeQueryConvInfo	Retrieves information about a DDE conversation
DdeQueryNextServer	Obtains the next handle in a DDE conversation list
DdeQueryString	Copies string-handle text into a buffer
DdeReconnect	Re-establishes a DDE conversation
DdeSetUserHandle	Associates a user-defined handle with a transaction
DdeUnaccessData	Frees a DDE global memory object
DdeUninitialize	Frees DDEML resources associated with an application

C.4.15 Debugging functions

DebugBreak	Causes a breakpoint exception
DebugOutput	Sends messages to the debugging terminal
DirectedYield	Forces execution of a specified task
FatalAppExit	Terminates an application
FatalExit	Sends current state of Windows to the debugger
GetSystemDebugState	Returns system-state information to a debugger
GetWinDebugInfo	Retrieves current system-debugging information
LockInput	Locks input to all tasks except the current one
LogError	Identifies the most recent system error
LogParamError	Identifies a parameter validation error
OutputDebugString	Sends a character string to the debugger
QuerySendMessage	Determines whether a message originated in a task
SetWinDebugInfo	Sets the current system-debugging information
ValidateCodeSegments	Tests for random memory overwrites
ValidateFreeSpaces	Checks free memory for valid contents

C.4.16 Device-Context functions

CreateCompatibleDC	Creates a DC compatible with a specified device
CreateDC	Creates a device context
CreateIC	Creates an information context
DeleteDC	Deletes a device context
GetDC	Retrieves the handle of a device context
GetDCEx	Retrieves the handle of a device context
GetDCOrg	Retrieves the translation origin for a device context
ResetDC	Updates a device context
RestoreDC	Restores a device context
ReleaseDC	Frees a device context

SaveDC   Saves the current state of a device context

C.4.17   Dialog box functions

CheckDlgButton   Changes a check mark by a dialog box button
CheckRadioButton   Adds a check mark to a radio button
CreateDialog   Creates a modeless dialog box
CreateDialogIndirect   Creates modeless dialog box from memory template
CreateDialogIndirectParam   Creates modeless dialog box from memory template
CreateDialogParam   Creates a modeless dialog box
DefDlgProc   Provides default window message processing
DialogBox   Creates a modal dialog box
DialogBoxIndirect   Creates modal dialog box from memory template
DialogBoxIndirectParam   Creates modal dialog box from memory template
DialogBoxParam   Creates a modal dialog box
DlgDirList   Fills a directory list box
DlgDirListComboBox   Fills a directory list box
DlgDirSelect   Retrieves a selection from a directory list box
DlgDirSelectEx   Retrieves a selection from a directory list box
DlgDirSelectComboBox   Retrieves a selection from a directory list box
DlgDirSelectComboBoxEx   Retrieves a selection from a directory list box
EndDialog   Hides a modal dialog box
GetDialogBaseUnits   Returns dialog base units
GetDlgCtrlID   Returns the handle of a child window
GetDlgItem   Retrieves the handle of a dialog box control
GetDlgItemInt   Translates control text into an integer
GetDlgItemText   Retrieves control text or title
GetNextDlgGroupItem   Returns handle of previous or next group control
GetNextDlgTabItem   Returns the next or previous WS_TABSTOP control
IsDialogMessage   Determines if message is for modeless dialog box
IsDlgButtonChecked   Determines the state of a button
MapDialogRect   Maps dialog box units to pixels
SendDlgItemMessage   Sends a message to a dialog box control
SetDlgItemInt   Converts an integer to a dialog box string
SetDlgItemText   Sets title or text of a control

C.4.18   Display and movement functions

ArrangeIconicWindows   Arranges minimized child windows
BeginDeferWindowPos   Creates a window-position structure
BringWindowToTop   Uncovers an overlapped window
CloseWindow   Minimizes (but does not destroy) a window
DeferWindowPos   Updates a window-position structure
EndDeferWindowPos   Updates the position and size of multiple windows
GetClientRect   Retrieves a window's client coordinates
GetWindowRect   Retrieves a window's screen coordinates
GetWindowText   Copies window title or control text to a buffer
GetWindowTextLength   Returns length of window title or control text
IsIconic   Determines whether a window is minimized
IsWindowVisible   Determines the visibility state of a window
IsZoomed   Determines whether a window is maximized
MoveWindow   Changes the position and dimensions of a window
OpenIcon   Activates and displays a minimized window
SetWindowPos   Sets a window's size, position, and z-order
SetWindowText   Sets control text or window title
ShowOwnedPopups   Shows or hides pop-up windows
ShowWindow   Sets a window's visibility state

C.4.19   Drag-drop functions

DragAcceptFiles   Registers whether a window accepts dropped files
DragFinish   Releases memory allocated for dropping files
DragQueryFile   Retrieves the filename of a dropped file
DragQueryPoint   Retrieves the mouse position when a file is dropped

C.4.20   Drawing-attribute functions

GetBkColor	Retrieves the current background colour
GetBkMode	Retrieves the background mode
GetPolyFillMode	Retrieves the current polygon-filling mode
GetROP2	Retrieves the current drawing mode
GetStretchBltMode	Retrieves the current bitmap-stretching mode
GetTextColor	Retrieves the current text colour
SetBkColor	Sets the background colour
SetBkMode	Sets the background mode
SetPolyFillMode	Sets the polygon-filling mode
SetROP2	Sets the drawing mode
SetStretchBltMode	Sets the bitmap-stretching mode
SetTextColor	Sets the foreground colour of text

C.4.21   Drawing-tool functions

CreateBrushIndirect	Creates a brush with the specified attributes
CreateDIBPatternBrush	Creates a pattern brush from a DIB
CreateHatchBrush	Creates a hatched brush
CreatePatternBrush	Creates a pattern brush from a bitmap
CreatePen	Creates a pen with the specified attributes
CreatePenIndirect	Creates a pen using a TLOGPEN structure
CreateSolidBrush	Creates a solid brush with a specified colour
DeleteObject	Deletes an object from memory
EnumObjects	Enumerates the pens and brushes in a device context
GetBrushOrg	Retrieves the origin of the current brush
GetObject	Retrieves information about an object
GetStockObject	Retrieves the handle of a stock pen, brush, or font
IsGDIObject	Determines if handle is not handle of GDI object
SelectObject	Selects an object into a device context
SetBrushOrg	Sets the origin of the current brush
UnrealizeObject	Resets brush origins or logical palettes

C.4.22   Ellipse and polygon functions

Chord	Draws a chord
DrawFocusRect	Draws a rectangle in the focus style
Ellipse	Draws an ellipse
Pie	Draws a pie-shaped wedge
Polygon	Draws a polygon
PolyPolygon	Draws a series of polygons
Rectangle	Draws a rectangle
RoundRect	Draws a rectangle with rounded corners

C.4.23   Error functions

FlashWindow	Flashes a window once
MessageBeep	Generates a beep sound
MessageBox	Creates and displays a message-box window

C.4.24   File I/O functions

GetDriveType	Determines the drive type
GetSystemDirectory	Returns the path of the Windows system directory
GetTempDrive	Returns a disk drive letter for temporary files
GetTempFileName	Creates a temporary filename
GetWindowsDirectory	Returns the path of the Windows directory
_hread	Reads data from a file
_hwrite	Writes data to a file
_lclose	Closes an open file
_lcreat	Creates or opens a file
_llseek	Repositions the file pointer
_lopen	Opens an existing file
_lread	Reads data from a file
_lwrite	Writes data to a file

hmemcpy	Copies bytes from source to destination buffer
OpenFile	Creates, opens, reopens, or deletes a file
SetHandleCount	Changes the number of available file handles

C.4.25   Font functions

AddFontResource	Adds a font resource to the font table
CreateFont	Creates a logical font
CreateFontIndirect	Creates a font using the TLOGFONT structure
CreateScalableFontResource	Creates a resource file with font information
EnumFontFamilies	Enumerates fonts in a specified family
EnumFonts	Enumerates fonts on a specified device
GetAspectRatioFilter	Retrieves the current aspect-ratio filter
GetAspectRatioFilterEx	Retrieves the current aspect-ratio filter
GetCharABCWidths	Retrieves the widths of consecutive characters
GetCharWidth	Retrieves character widths
GetFontData	Retrieves font-metric information
GetGlyphOutline	Retrieves data for individual outline character
GetKerningPairs	Retrieves kerning pairs for the current font
GetOutlineTextMetrics	Retrieves metrics for TrueType fonts
GetRasterizerCaps	Retrieves status of TrueType fonts on system
RemoveFontResource	Removes an added font resource
SetMapperFlags	Sets the font-mapper flag

C.4.26   GDI functions

AbortDoc	Terminates a print job
AddFontResource	Adds a font to the font table
AnimatePalette	Replaces entries in a logical palette
Arc	Draws an arc
BitBlt	Copies a bitmap between device contexts
Chord	Draws a chord
CloseMetaFile	Closes a metafile DC and gets the handle
CombineRgn	Creates a region by combining two regions
CopyMetaFile	Copies a metafile
CreateBitmap	Creates a device-dependent memory bitmap
CreateBitmapIndirect	Creates a bitmap using TBITMAP structure
CreateBrushIndirect	Creates a brush with the specified attributes
CreateCompatibleBitmap	Creates a bitmap compatible with the DC
CreateCompatibleDC	Creates a DC compatible with the specified DC
CreateDC	Creates a device context
CreateDIBitmap	Creates bitmap handle from DIB specification
CreateDIBPatternBrush	Creates a pattern brush from a DIB
CreateDiscardableBitmap	Creates discardable bitmap
CreateEllipticRgn	Creates an elliptical region
CreateEllipticRgnIndirect	Creates an elliptical region
CreateFont	Creates a logical font
CreateFontIndirect	Creates a font using a TLOGFONT structure
CreateHatchBrush	Creates a hatched brush
CreateIC	Creates an information context
CreateMetaFile	Creates a metafile device context
CreatePalette	Creates a logical colour palette
CreatePatternBrush	Creates a pattern brush from a bitmap
CreatePen	Creates a pen
CreatePenIndirect	Creates a pen using a TLOGPEN structure
CreatePolygonRgn	Creates a polygonal region
CreatePolyPolygonRgn	Creates a region consisting of polygons
CreateRectRgn	Creates a rectangular region
CreateRectRgnIndirect	Creates a region using a TRECT structure
CreateRoundRectRgn	Creates a rectangular region with round corners
CreateScalableFontResource	Creates a resource file with font info
CreateSolidBrush	Creates a solid brush with a specified colour
DeleteDC	Deletes a device context

DeleteMetaFile	Invalidates a metafile handle
DeleteObject	Deletes an object from memory
DeviceCapabilities	Retrieves the capabilities of a device
DeviceMode	Displays a dialog box for printing modes
DPtoLP	Converts device points to logical points
Ellipse	Draws an ellipse
EndDoc	Ends a print job
EndPage	Ends a page
EnumFontFamilies	Retrieves fonts in a specified family
EnumFonts	Enumerates fonts on the specified device
EnumMetaFile	Enumerates metafile records
EnumObjects	Enumerates pens and brushes in a device context
EqualRgn	Compares two regions for equality
Escape	Allows access to capabilities device
ExcludeClipRect	Changes clipping region, excluding rectangle
ExtDeviceMode	Displays a dialog box for printing modes
ExtFloodFill	Fills an area with the current brush
ExtTextOut	Writes character string in rectangular region
FillRgn	Fills a region with the specified brush
FloodFill	Fills an area with the current brush
FrameRgn	Draws a border around a region
GetAspectRatioFilter	Retrieves setting of aspect-ratio filter
GetAspectRatioFilterEx	Retrieves setting of aspect-ratio filter
GetBitmapBits	Copies bitmap bits to a buffer
GetBitmapDimension	Retrieves the width and height of a bitmap
GetBitmapDimensionEx	Retrieves the width and height of a bitmap
GetBkColor	Retrieves the current background colour
GetBkMode	Retrieves the background mode
GetBoundsRect	Returns current accumulated bounding rectangle
GetBrushOrg	Retrieves the origin of the current brush
GetBrushOrgEx	Retrieves the origin of the current brush
GetCharABCWidths	Retrieves the widths of TrueType characters
GetCharWidth	Retrieves the character widths
GetClipBox	Retrieves a rectangle for the clipping region
GetCurrentPosition	Retrieves the current position, in logical units
GetCurrentPositionEx	Retrieves the current position, in logical units
GetDCOrg	Retrieves translation origin for device context
GetDeviceCaps	Retrieves the device capabilities
GetDIBits	Copies the DIB bits into a buffer
GetFontData	Retrieves font metric data
GetGlyphOutline	Retrieves data for individual outline character
GetKerningPairs	Retrieves kerning pairs for the current font
GetMapMode	Retrieves the mapping mode
GetMetaFile	Creates a handle to a specified metafile
GetMetaFileBits	Creates a global memory object from a metafile
GetNearestColor	Retrieves the closest available colour
GetNearestPaletteIndex	Retrieves the nearest match for a colour
GetObject	Retrieves information about an object
GetOutlineTextMetrics	Retrieves metrics for TrueType fonts
GetPaletteEntries	Retrieves a range of palette entries
GetPixel	Retrieves RGB colour value of specified pixel
GetPolyFillMode	Retrieves the current polygon-filling mode
GetRasterizerCaps	Retrieves status of TrueType fonts on system
GetRgnBox	Retrieves the bounding rectangle for a region
GetROP2	Retrieves the current drawing mode
GetStockObject	Retrieves handle of stock pen, brush, or font
GetStretchBltMode	Retrieves the current bitmap-stretching mode
GetSystemPaletteEntries	Retrieves entries from the system palette
GetSystemPaletteUse	Determines the use of an entire system palette
GetTextCharacterExtra	Retrieves the intercharacter spacing

GetTextAlign	Retrieves the text-alignment flags
GetTextColor	Retrieves the current text colour
GetTextExtent	Determines dimensions of specified text string
GetTextExtentPoint	Retrieves dimensions of specified text string
GetTextFace	Retrieves the typeface name of the current font
GetTextMetrics	Retrieves the metrics for the current font
GetViewportExt	Retrieves the viewport extent
GetViewportExtEx	Retrieves the viewport extent
GetViewportOrg	Retrieves the viewport origin
GetViewportOrgEx	Retrieves the viewport origin
GetWindowExt	Retrieves the window extents
GetWindowExtEx	Retrieves the window extents
GetWindowOrg	Retrieves the window origin
GetWindowOrgEx	Retrieves the window origin
IntersectClipRect	Creates a clipping region from an intersection
InvertRgn	Inverts the colours in a region
IsGDIObject	Determines if a handle is not a GDI object
LineDDA	Computes successive points in a line
LineTo	Draws a line from the current position
LPtoDP	Converts logical points to device points
MoveTo	Moves the current position
MoveToEx	Moves the current position
OffsetClipRgn	Moves a clipping region
OffsetRgn	Moves a region by a specified offset
OffsetViewportOrg	Moves the viewport origin
OffsetViewportOrgEx	Moves the viewport origin
OffsetWindowOrg	Moves the window origin
OffsetWindowOrgEx	Moves the window origin
PaintRgn	Fills region with brush in given device context
PatBlt	Creates a bitmap pattern
Pie	Draws a pie-shaped wedge
PlayMetaFile	Plays a metafile
PlayMetaFileRecord	Plays a metafile record
Polygon	Draws a polygon
Polyline	Draws line segments to connect specified points
PolyPolygon	Draws a series of polygons
PtInRegion	Determines whether a point is in a region
PtVisible	Determines whether point is in clipping region
QueryAbort	Determines whether to terminate a print job
Rectangle	Draws a rectangle
RectInRegion	Determines whether rectangle overlaps region
RectVisible	Determines whether rectangle is in clip region
RemoveFontResource	Removes an added font resource
ResetDC	Updates a device context
ResizePalette	Changes the size of a logical palette
RestoreDC	Restores the device context
RoundRect	Draws a rectangle with rounded corners
SaveDC	Saves the current state of a device context
ScaleViewportExt	Scales the viewport extents
ScaleViewportExtEx	Scales the viewport extents
ScaleWindowExt	Scales the window extents
ScaleWindowExtEx	Scales the window extents
SelectClipRgn	Selects clipping region for device context
SelectObject	Selects an object into a device context
SetAbortProc	Sets the abort function for a print job
SetBitmapBits	Sets the bitmap bits from an array of bytes
SetBitmapDimension	Sets the width and height of a bitmap
SetBitmapDimensionEx	Sets the width and height of a bitmap
SetBkColor	Sets the current background colour
SetBkMode	Sets the background mode

SetBoundsRect	Controls the bounding-rectangle accumulation
SetBrushOrg	Sets the origin of the current brush
SetDIBits	Sets the bits of a bitmap
SetDIBitsToDevice	Sets DIB bits to a device
SetMapMode	Sets the mapping mode
SetMapperFlags	Sets the font-mapper flag
SetMetaFileBits	Creates a memory object from the metafile
SetMetaFileBitsBetter	Creates a memory object from the metafile
SetPaletteEntries	Sets the colours and flags for a colour palette
SetPixel	Sets a pixel to the specified colour
SetPolyFillMode	Sets the polygon-filling mode
SetRectRgn	Changes a region into a specified rectangle
SetROP2	Sets the current drawing mode
SetStretchBltMode	Sets the bitmap-stretching mode
SetSystemPaletteUse	Sets the use of system-palette static colours
SetTextAlign	Sets the text-alignment flags
SetTextCharacterExtra	Sets the intercharacter spacing
SetTextColor	Sets the foreground colour for text
SetTextJustification	Sets the alignment for text output
SetViewportExt	Sets the viewport extents
SetViewportExtEx	Sets the viewport extents
SetViewportOrg	Sets the viewport origin
SetViewportOrgEx	Sets the viewport origin
SetWindowExt	Sets the window extents
SetWindowExtEx	Sets the window extents
SetWindowOrg	Sets the window origin
SetWindowOrgEx	Sets the window origin
SpoolFile	Puts a file in the spooler queue
StartDoc	Starts a print job
StartPage	Prepares a printer driver to receive data
StretchBlt	Copies a bitmap, transforming it if required
StretchDIBits	Moves DIB from source to destination rectangle
TextOut	Writes character string at specified location
UnrealizeObject	Resets brush origins and realizes palettes
UpdateColors	Updates colours in the client area

C.4.27 Hardware functions

EnableHardwareInput	Controls mouse and keyboard input queuing
GetAsyncKeyState	Determines the key state
GetInputState	Determines mouse, keyboard and timer queuing status
GetKeyboardState	Copies virtual-keyboard keys status to a buffer
GetKeyNameText	Retrieves the string representing the name of a key
GetKeyState	Retrieves the virtual-key state
GetKBCodePage	Returns the current Windows code page
OemKeyScan	Translates OEM ASCII to scan codes
SetKeyboardState	Sets the Windows keyboard-state table
MapVirtualKey	Translates a virtual-key code or scan code
VkKeyScan	Translates a Windows character to a virtual-key code

C.4.28 Hook functions

CallMsgFilter	Passes a message to a message-filter function
DefHookProc	Calls the next function in a hook-function chain
SetWindowsHook	Installs an application-defined hook function
SetWindowsHookEx	Installs an application-defined hook function
UnhookWindowsHook	Removes an application-defined hook function

C.4.29 Icon functions

ArrangeIconicWindows	Arranges minimized child windows
CopyIcon	Copies an icon
CreateIcon	Creates an icon with the specified dimensions
DestroyIcon	Destroys an icon created by CreateIcon or LoadIcon

DrawIcon	Draws an icon in the specified device context
IsIconic	Determines whether a window is minimized
LoadIcon	Loads an icon resource
OpenIcon	Activates and displays a minimized window

C.4.30   Information functions

AnyPopup	Indicates whether pop-up or overlapped window exists
ChildWindowFromPoint	Determines which child window contains a point
EnumChildWindows	Enumerates child windows
EnumTaskWindows	Enumerates windows associated with task on screen
EnumWindows	Enumerates parent windows
FindWindow	Returns window handle for class name and window name
GetNextWindow	Returns handle of window in window manager's list
GetParent	Returns parent window handle
GetTopWindow	Returns handle for top-level child of given window
GetWindow	Returns handle of window with specified relationship
GetWindowTask	Returns the task handle associated with a window
IsChild	Determines whether a window is a child
IsWindow	Determines whether a window handle is valid
SetParent	Changes a child's parent window
WindowFromPoint	Returns the handle of window containing a point

C.4.31   Initialization-file functions

GetPrivateProfileInt	Retrieves integer value from initialization file
GetPrivateProfileString	Retrieves a string from an initialization file
GetProfileInt	Retrieves an integer value from WIN.INI
GetProfileString	Retrieves a string from WIN.INI
WritePrivateProfileString	Writes a string to an initialization file
WriteProfileString	Writes a string to WIN.INI

C.4.32   Input functions

EnableWindow	Enables or disables input to a window or control
GetActiveWindow	Retrieves the handle of the active window
GetCapture	Returns the handle for the mouse-capture window
GetCurrentTime	Retrieves the elapsed time since Windows started
GetDoubleClickTime	Retrieves mouse double-click time
GetFocus	Returns handle of window with input focus
GetTickCount	Retrieves the amount of time Windows has been running
IsWindowEnabled	Determines whether a window accepts user input
KillTimer	Removes a timer
ReleaseCapture	Releases the mouse capture
SetActiveWindow	Makes a top-level window active
SetCapture	Sets the mouse capture to a window
SetDoubleClickTime	Sets the mouse double-click time
SetFocus	Sets the input focus to a window
SetSysModalWindow	Makes a window the system-modal window
SetTimer	Installs a system timer
SwapMouseButton	Reverses the meaning of mouse buttons

C.4.33   Installable-driver functions

CloseDriver	Closes an installable driver
DefDriverProc	Default processing of installable-driver messages
DriverProc	Processes installable-driver messages
GetDriverModuleHandle	Returns an installable-driver instance handle
GetDriverInfo	Retrieves installable-driver data
GetNextDriver	Enumerates installable-driver instances
OpenDriver	Opens an installable driver
SendDriverMessage	Sends a message to an installable driver

C.4.34   Lempel-Ziv encoding functions

CopyLZFile	Copies files and decompresses them if compressed
GetExpandedName	Retrieves the original filename of a compressed file

LZClose	Closes a file
LZCopy	Copies a file and decompresses it if compressed
LZDone	Frees buffers allocated by the LZStart function
LZInit	Initializes structures needed for decompression
LZOpenFile	Opens a file (both compressed and uncompressed)
LZRead	Reads a specified number of bytes from a compressed file
LZSeek	Repositions a pointer in a file
LZStart	Allocates buffers for the CopyLZFile function

C.4.35 Line-output functions

Arc	Draws an arc
LineDDA	Computes successive points in a line
LineTo	Draws a line from the current position
MoveTo	Moves the current position
MoveToEx	Moves the current position
Polyline	Draws line segments to connect specified points

C.4.36 Mapping functions

GetMapMode	Retrieves the mapping mode
GetViewportExt	Retrieves viewport extents
GetViewportExtEx	Retrieves viewport extents
GetViewportOrg	Retrieves the viewport origin
GetViewportOrgEx	Retrieves the viewport origin
GetWindowExt	Retrieves the window extents
GetWindowExtEx	Retrieves the window extents
GetWindowOrg	Retrieves the window origin
GetWindowOrgEx	Retrieves the window origin
OffsetViewportOrg	Moves the viewport origin
OffsetViewportOrgEx	Moves the viewport origin
OffsetWindowOrg	Moves the window origin
OffsetWindowOrgEx	Moves the window origin
ScaleViewportExt	Scales the viewport extents
ScaleViewportExtEx	Scales the viewport extents
ScaleWindowExt	Scales the window extents
ScaleWindowExtEx	Scales the window extents
SetMapMode	Sets the mapping mode
SetViewportExt	Sets the viewport extents
SetViewportExtEx	Sets the viewport extents
SetViewportOrg	Sets the viewport origin
SetViewportOrgEx	Sets the viewport origin
SetWindowExt	Sets the window extents
SetWindowExtEx	Sets the window extents
SetWindowOrg	Sets the window origin
SetWindowOrgEx	Sets the window origin

C.4.37 Memory-management functions

GetFreeSpace	Returns the number of free bytes in the global heap
GetFreeSystemResources	Returns the percentage of free system-resource space
GetSelectorBase	Retrieves the base address of a selector
GetSelectorLimit	Retrieves the limit of a selector
GetWinFlags	Returns the current system configuration flags
GlobalAlloc	Allocates memory from the global heap
GlobalCompact	Generates free global memory by compacting
GlobalDosAlloc	Allocates memory available to MS-DOS in real mode
GlobalDosFree	Frees global memory allocated by GlobalDosAlloc
GlobalFlags	Returns information about a global memory object
GlobalFree	Frees a global memory object
GlobalHandle	Retrieves the handle for a specified selector
GlobalLock	Locks global memory object and returns pointer
GlobalLRUNewest	Moves global memory object to newest LRU position
GlobalLRUOldest	Moves global memory object to oldest LRU position

GlobalNotify	Installs a notification procedure
GlobalReAlloc	Changes size or attributes of global memory object
GlobalSize	Returns the size of a global memory object
GlobalUnlock	Unlocks a global memory object
GlobalUnwire	Not used in Windows 3.1
GlobalWire	Not used in Windows 3.1
LimitEMSPages	Not used in Windows 3.1
LocalAlloc	Allocates memory from the local heap
LocalCompact	Generates free local memory by compacting
LocalFlags	Returns local memory object information
LocalFree	Frees a local memory object
LocalHandle	Returns the handle of a local memory object
LocalInit	Initializes the specified local heap
LocalLock	Locks local memory object and returns pointer
LocalReAlloc	Changes size or attributes of local memory object
LocalShrink	Shrinks the specified local heap
LocalSize	Returns the size of a local memory object
LocalUnlock	Unlocks a local memory object
LockSegment	Locks a discardable memory segment
SetSelectorBase	Sets the base address of a selector
SetSelectorLimit	Sets the limit of a selector
SetSwapAreaSize	Sets the amount of memory used for code segments
SwitchStackBack	Restores the current task stack
SwitchStackTo	Changes the location of the current task stack
UnLockSegment	Unlocks a discardable memory segment

C.4.38 Menu functions

AppendMenu	Appends a new item to the end of a menu
CheckMenuItem	Changes a check mark by a menu item
CreateMenu	Creates a menu
CreatePopupMenu	Creates an empty pop-up window
DeleteMenu	Deletes an item from a menu
DestroyMenu	Destroys a menu
DrawMenuBar	Redraws the menu bar of a window
EnableMenuItem	Enables, disables, or greys a menu item
GetMenu	Returns a menu handle for the specified window
GetMenuCheckMarkDimensions	Retrieves default check mark bitmap dimensions
GetMenuItemCount	Retrieves the number of items in a menu
GetMenuItemID	Returns the handle of a menu item
GetMenuState	Retrieves status flags for a menu item
GetMenuString	Copies a menu-item label into a buffer
GetSubMenu	Returns a pop-up menu handle
GetSystemMenu	Provides access to the System menu
HiliteMenuItem	Changes highlighting of top-level menu item
InsertMenu	Inserts a new item in a menu
LoadMenuIndirect	Returns a menu handle for a menu template
ModifyMenu	Changes an existing menu item
RemoveMenu	Deletes a menu item and pop-up menu
SetMenu	Sets the menu for a window
SetMenuItemBitmaps	Associates bitmaps with a menu item
TrackPopupMenu	Displays and tracks a pop-up menu

C.4.39 Message functions

CallWindowProc	Passes message information to a window procedure
DispatchMessage	Dispatches a message to a window
GetMessage	Retrieves a message from the message queue
GetMessagePos	Retrieves the cursor position for the last message
GetMessageTime	Retrieves the time for the last message
InSendMessage	Determines whether window is processing SendMessage
PeekMessage	Checks an application's message queue

PostAppMessage	Posts a message to an application (task)
PostMessage	Places a message in a window's message queue
PostQuitMessage	Informs Windows that an application is exiting
ReplyMessage	Replies to a message sent through SendMessage
SendMessage	Sends a message to a window
SetMessageQueue	Creates a new message queue
TranslateAccelerator	Processes accelerator keys for menu commands
TranslateMDISysAccel	Processes MDI keyboard accelerators
TranslateMessage	Translates virtual-key messages
WaitMessage	Suspends an application and yields control

C.4.40 Metafile functions

CloseMetaFile	Closes a metafile device context and creates a handle
CopyMetaFile	Copies a source metafile to a file
CreateMetaFile	Creates a metafile device context
DeleteMetaFile	Invalidates a metafile handle
EnumMetaFile	Enumerates the metafile records in a metafile
GetMetaFile	Creates a handle to a metafile
GetMetaFileBits	Creates a memory object from a metafile
PlayMetaFile	Plays a metafile
PlayMetaFileRecord	Plays a metafile record
SetMetaFileBits	Creates a memory object from a metafile
SetMetaFileBitsBetter	Creates a memory object from a metafile

C.4.41 Module-management functions

FreeLibrary	Frees a loaded library module
FreeModule	Frees a loaded module
FreeProcInstance	Frees a function instance
GetCodeHandle	Determines the location of a function
GetInstanceData	Copies data from previous instance to current one
GetModuleFileName	Returns the filename for a module
GetModuleHandle	Retrieves a handle for the specified module
GetModuleUsage	Retrieves the reference count of a module
GetProcAddress	Returns the address of an exported DLL function
GetVersion	Returns the current MS-DOS and Windows versions
LoadLibrary	Loads the specified library module
MakeProcInstance	Returns address of prolog code for function

C.4.42 OLE function groups

OleEnumObjects	Enumerates objects in a document
OleRegisterClientDoc	Registers a document with the library
OleRegisterServerDoc	Registers a document with the server library
OleRename	Informs the library that an object is renamed
OleRenameClientDoc	Informs the library that a document is renamed
OleRenameServerDoc	Informs the library that a document is renamed
OleRevertClientDoc	Informs library that document reverted to saved state
OleRevertServerDoc	Informs library that document is reset to saved state
OleRevokeClientDoc	Informs the library that a document is not open
OleRevokeServerDoc	Revokes the specified document
OleSavedClientDoc	Informs library that a document has been saved
OleSavedServerDoc	Informs library that a document has been saved
OleGetLinkUpdateOptions	Retrieves update options for an object
OleQueryLinkFromClip	Retrieves link data for clipboard object
OleQueryOutOfDate	Determines whether an object is out-of-date
OleSetLinkUpdateOptions	Sets link-update options for an object
OleUpdate	Updates the specified object
OleClone	Makes a copy of an object
OleCopyFromLink	Makes an embedded copy of a linked object
OleCreate	Creates an object of a specified class
OleCreateFromClip	Creates an object from the clipboard
OleCreateFromFile	Creates an object from a file

OleCreateFromTemplate	Creates an object from a template
OleCreateInvisible	Creates an object without displaying it
OleCreateLinkFromClip	Creates a link to an object from the clipboard
OleCreateLinkFromFile	Creates a link to an object in a file
OleLoadFromStream	Loads an object from the containing document
OleObjectConvert	Creates a new object using a specified protocol
OleQueryCreateFromClip	Retrieves protocol data for clipboard object
OleActivate	Opens an object for an operation
OleCopyToClipboard	Puts the specified object on the clipboard
OleDelete	Deletes an object
OleDraw	Draws an object into a device context
OleEnumFormats	Enumerates data formats for an object
OleEqual	Compares two objects for equality
OleGetData	Retrieves data from an object in a specified format
OleQueryBounds	Retrieves the bounding rectangle for an object
OleQueryClientVersion	Retrieves the version number of a client library
OleQueryName	Retrieves the name of an object
OleQueryProtocol	Determines whether an object supports a protocol
OleQuerySize	Retrieves the size of an object
OleQueryType	Determines if object is linked, embedded, or static
OleRelease	Releases an object from memory
OleSaveToStream	Saves an object to the stream
OleSetBounds	Sets the bounding rectangle for an object
OleSetColorScheme	Specifies the client's recommended object colours
OleSetData	Sends data in the specified format to the server
OleSetHostNames	Sets the client name and object name for server
OleSetTargetDevice	Specifies the target device for an object
OleClose	Closes the specified open object
OleExecute	Sends DDE execute commands to a server
OleLockServer	Keeps an open server application in memory
OleQueryOpen	Determines whether an object is open
OleQueryReleaseError	Determines the status of a released operation
OleQueryReleaseMethod	Determines which operation released
OleQueryReleaseStatus	Determines whether an operation released
OleReconnect	Reconnects to an open linked object
OleRequestData	Retrieves data from a server in a specified format
OleUnlockServer	Releases a server locked with OleLockServer

C.4.43 Painting functions

BeginPaint	Prepares a window for painting
DrawFocusRect	Draws a rectangle in the focus style
DrawIcon	Draws an icon in the specified device context
EndPaint	Marks the end of painting in the specified window
ExcludeUpdateRgn	Excludes an updated region from a clipping region
FrameRect	Draws a window border with the specified brush
GetDC	Returns a window device-context handle
GetUpdateRect	Retrieves window update-region dimensions
GetUpdateRgn	Retrieves the window update region
GetWindowDC	Retrieves the window device context
GrayString	Draws grey text at the specified location
InvalidateRect	Adds a rectangle to a window's update region
InvalidateRgn	Adds a region to a window's update region
InvertRect	Inverts a rectangular area
ReleaseDC	Frees a device context
UpdateWindow	Updates a window's client area
ValidateRect	Removes a rectangle from a window's update region
ValidateRgn	Removes a region from a window's update region

C.4.44 Palette functions

| AnimatePalette | Replaces entries in a logical palette |
| CreatePalette | Creates a logical colour palette |

GetNearestColor	Retrieves the closest available colour
GetNearestPaletteIndex	Retrieves the nearest match for a colour
GetPaletteEntries	Retrieves a range of palette entries
GetSystemPaletteEntries	Retrieves entries from the system palette
GetSystemPaletteUse	Determines access to the entire system palette
RealizePalette	Maps entries from logical to system palette
ResizePalette	Changes the size of a logical palette
SelectPalette	Selects a palette into a device context
SetPaletteEntries	Sets colours and flags for a logical palette
SetSystemPaletteUse	Sets the use of static colours in the system palette

C.4.45 Pen functions

CreatePen	Creates a pen with the specified attributes
CreatePenIndirect	Creates a pen using a TLOGPEN structure
GetStockObject	Retrieves the handle of a stock pen, brush, or font
LineTo	Draws a line from the current position

C.4.46 Pointer validation functions

IsBadCodePtr	Determines whether a code pointer is valid
IsBadHugeReadPtr	Determines whether a huge read pointer is valid
IsBadHugeWritePtr	Determines whether a huge write pointer is valid
IsBadReadPtr	Determines whether a read pointer is valid
IsBadStringPtr	Determines whether a string pointer is valid
IsBadWritePtr	Determines whether a write pointer is valid

C.4.47 Printer-control functions

AbortDoc	Terminates a print job
DeviceCapabilities	Retrieves the capabilities of a device
DeviceMode	Displays a dialog box for the printing modes
EndDoc	Ends a print job
EndPage	Ends a page
Escape	Allows access to device capabilities
ExtDeviceMode	Displays a dialog box for the printing modes
GetDeviceCaps	Retrieves the device capabilities
SetAbortProc	Sets the abort function for a print job
SpoolFile	Puts a file in the spooler queue
StartDoc	Starts a print job
StartPage	Prepares the printer driver to accept data
QueryAbort	Queries whether to terminate a print job

C.4.48 Property functions

EnumProps	Enumerates property-list entries
GetProp	Returns a data handle from a window property list
RemoveProp	Removes a property-list entry
SetProp	Adds or changes a property-list entry

C.4.49 Rectangle functions

CopyRect	Copies the dimensions of a rectangle
EqualRect	Determines whether two rectangles are equal
FrameRect	Draws a window border with the specified brush
FillRect	Fills a rectangle with the specified brush
GetBoundsRect	Returns current accumulated bounding rectangle
InflateRect	Changes rectangle dimensions
IntersectRect	Calculates the intersection of two rectangles
InvertRect	Inverts a rectangular area
IsRectEmpty	Determines whether a rectangle is empty
OffsetRect	Moves a rectangle by the specified offsets
PtInRect	Determines whether a point is in a rectangle
SetBoundsRect	Controls bounding-rectangle accumulation
SetRect	Sets rectangle coordinates
SetRectEmpty	Creates an empty rectangle
SubtractRect	Creates rectangle from difference of two others

UnionRect	Creates the union of two rectangles

C.4.50 Region functions

CombineRgn	Creates a region by combining two regions
CreateEllipticRgn	Creates an elliptical region
CreateEllipticRgnIndirect	Creates an elliptical region
CreatePolygonRgn	Creates a polygonal region
CreatePolyPolygonRgn	Creates a region consisting of polygons
CreateRectRgn	Creates a rectangular region
CreateRectRgnIndirect	Creates a region using a TRECT structure
CreateRoundRectRgn	Creates a rectangular region with round corners
EqualRgn	Compares two regions for equality
FillRgn	Fills a region with the specified brush
FrameRgn	Draws a border around a region
GetRgnBox	Retrieves the bounding rectangle for a region
InvertRgn	Inverts the colours in a region
OffsetRgn	Moves a region by the specified offsets
PaintRgn	Fills region with brush in device context
PtInRegion	Queries whether a point is in a region
RectInRegion	Queries whether a rectangle overlaps a region
SetRectRgn	Changes a region into the specified rectangle

C.4.51 Registration functions

RegCreateKey	Creates a specified key
RegDeleteKey	Deletes a specified key
RegEnumKey	Enumerates the subkeys of a specified key
RegOpenKey	Opens a specified key
RegQueryValue	Retrieves the text string for a specified key
RegSetValue	Associates a text string with a specified key

C.4.52 Resource-management functions

AccessResource	Opens an executable file and locates a resource
AllocResource	Allocates memory for a resource
FindResource	Locates a resource in a resource file
FreeResource	Frees a loaded resource
LoadAccelerators	Loads an accelerator table
LoadBitmap	Loads a bitmap resource
LoadCursor	Loads a cursor resource
LoadIcon	Loads an icon resource
LoadMenu	Loads a menu resource
LoadResource	Loads the specified resource in global memory
LoadString	Loads a string resource
LockResource	Locks a resource in memory
SetResourceHandler	Installs a callback function that loads resources
SizeofResource	Returns the size of a resource

C.4.53 Screen-saver functions

DefScreenSaverProc	Calls default screen-saver window procedure
DlgChangePassword	Changes the password for a screen-saver
DlgGetPassword	Retrieves the password for a screen-saver
DlgInvalidPassword	Warns of an invalid screen-saver password
HelpMessageFilterHookFunction	Posts a screen-saver help message
RegisterDialogClasses	Registers screen-saver dialog box classes
ScreenSaverConfigureDialog	Processes config. dialog box messages
ScreenSaverProc	Processes screen-saver window messages

C.4.54 Scrolling functions

GetScrollPos	Retrieves the current scrollbar thumb position
GetScrollRange	Retrieves the minimum and maximum scrollbar positions
ScrollDC	Scrolls a rectangle of bits horizontally and vertically
ScrollWindow	Scrolls the contents of a window's client area

ScrollWindowEx	Scrolls the contents of a window's client area
SetScrollPos	Sets the scrollbar thumb position
SetScrollRange	Sets minimum and maximum scrollbar positions
ShowScrollBar	Shows or hides a scrollbar

C.4.55 Segment functions

AllocDStoCSAlias	Translates a data segment to a code segment
AllocSelector	Allocates a new selector
FreeSelector	Frees an allocated selector
GetCodeInfo	Retrieves code-segment information
GlobalFix	Locks a global memory object in linear memory
GlobalPageLock	Increments the global memory page-lock count
GlobalPageUnlock	Decrements the global memory page-lock count
GlobalUnfix	Unlocks a global memory object in linear memory
LockSegment	Locks a discardable memory segment
PrestoChangoSelector	Converts a code or data selector
UnlockSegment	Unlocks a discardable memory segment

C.4.56 Shell functions

ExtractIcon	Retrieves the handle of an icon from an executable file
FindExecutable	Retrieves executable filename for a specified file
ShellExecute	Opens or prints the specified file

C.4.57 Stress functions

AllocDiskSpace	Creates a file to consume space on a disk partition
AllocFileHandles	Allocates up to 256 file handles
AllocGDIMem	Allocates memory in the GDI heap
AllocMem	Allocates global memory
AllocUserMem	Allocates memory in the USER heap
FreeAllGDIMem	Frees all memory allocated by the AllocGDIMem function
FreeAllMem	Frees all memory allocated by the AllocMem function
FreeAllUserMem	Frees all memory allocated by the AllocUserMem function
GetFreeFileHandles	Returns the number of free file handles
UnAllocDiskSpace	Deletes file created by AllocDiskSpace and frees space
UnAllocFileHandles	Frees file handles allocated by AllocFileHandles

C.4.58 String-manipulation functions

AnsiLower	Converts a string to lower case
AnsiLowerBuff	Converts a buffer string to lower case
AnsiNext	Moves to the next character in a string
AnsiPrev	Moves to the previous character in a string
AnsiToOem	Translates a Windows string to an OEM string
AnsiToOemBuff	Translates a Windows string to an OEM string
AnsiUpper	Converts a string to upper case
AnsiUpperBuff	Converts a buffer string to upper case
IsCharAlpha	Determines whether a character is alphabetic
IsCharAlphaNumeric	Determines whether a character is alphanumeric
IsCharLower	Determines whether a character is lower case
IsCharUpper	Determines whether a character is upper case
lstrcat	Appends one string to another
lstrcmp	Compares two character strings
lstrcmpi	Compares two character strings
lstrcpy	Copies a string to a buffer
lstrcpyn	Copies characters from a string to a buffer
lstrlen	Returns the length, in bytes, of a string
OemToAnsi	Translates an OEM string to a Windows string
OemToAnsiBuff	Translates an OEM string to a Windows string
ToAscii	Translates virtual-key code to Windows character
wvsprintf	Formats and stores a string in a buffer

C.4.59 System functions

GetSysColor	Retrieves the display-element colour

GetSystemMetrics	Retrieves the system metrics
GetTickCount	Retrieves the amount of time Windows has been running
SetSysColors	Sets one or more system colours

C.4.60 Task functions

Catch	Captures the current execution environment
ExitWindows	Restarts or terminates Windows
GetCurrentPDB	Returns the selector address of the current PDB
GetCurrentTask	Returns the current task handle
GetDOSEnvironment	Returns a far pointer to the current environment
GetNumTasks	Retrieves the current number of tasks
IsTask	Determines whether a task handle is valid
SetErrorMode	Controls Interrupt 24h error handling
Throw	Restores the execution environment
Yield	Stops the current task

C.4.61 Text functions

DrawText	
ExtTextOut	Writes a character string in a rectangular region
GetTabbedTextExtent	Determines the dimensions of a tabbed string
GetTextAlign	Retrieves the status of text-alignment flags
GetTextCharacterExtra	Retrieves the intercharacter spacing
GetTextExtent	Computes the dimensions of a string
GetTextExtentPoint	Computes the dimensions of a string
GetTextFace	Retrieves the typeface name of the current font
GetTextMetrics	Retrieves the metrics for the current font
SetTextAlign	Sets text-alignment flags for the device context
SetTextCharacterExtra	Sets the intercharacter spacing
SetTextJustification	Sets the justification for text output
TabbedTextOut	Writes a tabbed character string
TextOut	Writes a character string at the specified location

C.4.62 Toolhelp functions

ClassNext	Retrieves information about next class in class list
GlobalEntryHandle	Retrieves information about given global memory object
GlobalEntryModule	Retrieves information about specified module segment
GlobalFirst	Retrieves information about first global memory object
GlobalHandleToSel	Converts the given global handle to a selector
GlobalInfo function	Retrieves information about the global heap
GlobalNext	Retrieves information about next global memory object
InterruptRegister	Installs callback function to handle system interrupts
InterruptUnRegister	Removes function handling system interrupts
LocalFirst	Retrieves information about first local memory object
LocalInfo function	Fills structure with information about local heap
LocalNext	Retrieves information about next local memory object
MemManInfo function	Retrieves information about the memory manager
MemoryRead	Reads memory from an arbitrary global heap object
MemoryWrite	Writes memory to an arbitrary global heap object
ModuleFindHandle	Retrieves information about the given module
ModuleFindName	Retrieves information about module with specified name
ModuleFirst	Retrieves information about the first module
ModuleNext	Retrieves information about the next module
NotifyRegister	Installs a notification callback function
NotifyUnRegister	Removes a notification callback function
StackTraceCSIPFirst	Retrieves information about a stack frame
StackTraceFirst	Retrieves information about the first stack frame
StackTraceNext	Retrieves information about the next stack frame
SystemHeapInfo	Retrieves information about the USER and GDI heaps
TaskFindHandle	Retrieves information about a task
TaskFirst	Retrieves information about first task in task queue
TaskGetCSIP	Returns the next CS:IP value of a sleeping task

TaskNext	Retrieves information about next task on the task queue
TaskSetCSIP	Sets the CS:IP value of a sleeping task
TaskSwitch	Switches to a specific address within a new task
TerminateApp	Ends the given application instance (task)
TimerCount	Retrieves execution times of current task and VM

C.4.63 TrueType functions

CreateScalableFontResource	Creates a resource file with font information
GetCharABCWidths	Retrieves the widths of consecutive characters
GetFontData	Retrieves font-metric information
GetGlyphOutline	Retrieves data for individual outline character
GetKerningPairs	Retrieves kerning pairs for the current font
GetOutlineTextMetrics	Retrieves metric information for TrueType fonts
GetRasterizerCaps	Retrieves status of TrueType fonts on system

C.4.64 Version functions

GetFileResource	Copies a resource into a buffer
GetFileResourceSize	Returns the size of a resource
GetFileVersionInfo	Returns version information about a specified file
GetFileVersionInfoSize	Returns the size of version information for a file
GetSystemDir	Returns the path of the Windows system subdirectory
GetWindowsDir	Returns the path of the Windows directory
VerFindFile	Determines where to install a file
VerInstallFile	Installs a file and checks for errors
VerLanguageName	Converts a binary language identifier into a string
VerQueryValue	Returns version information about a block

C.4.65 Window-creation functions

AdjustWindowRect	Computes the required size of a window rectangle
AdjustWindowRectEx	Computes the required size of a window rectangle
CreateWindow	Creates an overlapped, pop-up, or child window
CreateWindowEx	Creates an overlapped, pop-up, or child window
DefDlgProc	Provides default window message processing
DefFrameProc	Provides default MDI frame window message processing
DefMDIChildProc	Provides default MDI child window message processing
DefWindowProc	Calls the default window procedure
DestroyWindow	Destroys a window
GetClassInfo	Returns window class information
GetClassLong	Retrieves a long value from extra class memory window class
GetClassName	Retrieves class name of a window
GetClassWord	Retrieves a word value from extra class memory window class memory word
GetLastActivePopup	Determines most recently active pop-up window
GetWindowLong	Retrieves a long value from extra window memory
GetWindowWord	Retrieves a word value from extra window memory
RegisterClass	Registers a window class
SetClassLong	Sets a long value in extra class memory
SetClassWord	Sets a word value in extra class memory
SetWindowLong	Sets a long value in extra window memory
SetWindowWord	Sets a word value in extra window memory
UnregisterClass	Frees a window class

Modem Codes

D.1   AT commands

The AT commands are preceded by the attention code AT. They are:

A   **Go on-line in answer mode**
                         Instructs the modem to go off-hook immediately and then make a connection with a remote
                         modem

Bn   **Select protocol to 300 bps to 1200 bps**
                         B0   Selects CCITT operation at 300 bps or 1200 bps
                         B1   Selects BELL operation at 300 bps or 1200 bps

D   **Go on-line in originate mode**
                         Instructs the modem to go off-hook and automatically dials the number contained in the dial
                         string which follows the D command

En   **Command echo**
                         E0   Disable command echo
                         E1   Enables command echo (default)

Fn   **Select line modulation**
                         F0   Select auto-detect mode
                         F1   Select V.21 or Bell 103
                         F4   Select V.22 or Bell 212A 1200 bps
                         F5   Select V.22bis line modulation
                         F6   Select V.32bis or V.32 4800 bps line modulation
                         F7   Select V.32bis or V.32 7200 bps line modulation
                         F8   Select V.32bis or V.32 9600 bps line modulation
                         F9   Select V.32bis 12000 line modulation
                         F10   Select V.32bis 14400 line modulation

Hn   **Hang-up**
                         H0   Go on-hook (hang-up connection)
                         H1   Goes off-hook

In   **Request product code or ROM checksum**
                         I0   Reports the product code
                         I1/I2   Reports the hardware ROM checksum
                         I3   Reports the product revision code
                         I4   Reports response programmed by an OEM
                         I5   Reports the country code number

Ln   **Control speaker volume**
                         L0   Low volume
                         L1   Low volume
                         L2   Medium volume (default)
                         L3   High volume

Mn   **Monitor speaker on/off**
                         M0/M   Speaker is always off
                         M1   Speaker is off while receiving carrier (default)
                         M2   Speaker is always on
                         M3   Speaker is on when dialling but is off at any other time

Nn   **Automode enable**
                         N0   Automode detection is disabled
                         N1   Automode detection is enabled

On   **Return to the on-line state**
                         O0   Enters on-line data mode with a retrain

	O1	Enters on-line data mode without a retrain
P	**Set pulse dial as default**	
Q	**Result code display**	
	Q0	Send result codes to the computer
	Q1	No return codes
Sn	**Reading and writing to S registers**	
	Sn?	Reads the Sn register
	Sn=val	Writes the value of val to the Sn register
T	**Set tone dial as default**	
Vn	**Select word or digit result code**	
	V0	Display result codes in a numeric form
	V1	Display result code in a long form (default)
Wn	**Error correction message control**	
	W0	When connected report computer connection speed
	W1	When connected report computer connection speed, error correcting protocol and line speed
	W2	When connected report modem connection speed
Xn	**Select result code**	
	X0	Partial connect message, dial-tone monitor off, busy tone monitor off
	X1	Full connect message, dial-tone monitor off, busy tone monitor off
	X2	Full connect message, dial-tone monitor on, busy tone monitor off
	X3	Full connect message, dial-tone monitor off, busy tone monitor on
	X4	Full connect message, dial-tone monitor on, busy tone monitor on
Yn	**Enables or disables long space disconnection**	
	Y0	Disables long space disconnect (default)
	Y1	Enables long space disconnect
Zn	**Reset**	
	Z0	Resets modem and load stored profile 0
	Z1	Resets modem and load stored profile 1
&Cn	**Select DCD options**	
	&C0	Sets DCD permanently on
	&C1	Use state of carrier to set DCD (default)
&Dn	**DTR option**	

This is used with the &Qn setting to determine the operation of the DTR signal

	&D0	&D1	&D2	&D3
&Q0	a	c	d	e
&Q1	b	c	d	e
&Q2	d	d	d	d
&Q3	d	d	d	d
&Q4	b	c	d	e
&Q5	a	c	d	e
&Q6	a	c	d	e

where

a – modem ignore DTR signal
b – modem disconnects and sends OK result code
c – modem goes into command mode and sends OK result code
d – modem disconnects and sends OK result code

&F	**Restore factory configuration**	
&Gn	**Set guard tone**	
	&G0	Disables guard tone (default)
	&G1	Disables guard tone
	&G2	Selects 1800 Hz guard tone
&Kn	**DTE/modem flow control**	
	&K0	Disables DTE/DCE flow control

	&K3	Enables RTS/CTS handshaking flow control (Default)
	&K4	Enables XON/XOFF flow control
	&K5	Enables transparent XON/XOFF flow control
	&K6	Enables RTS/CTS and XON/XOFF flow control
&L	**Line selection**	
	&L0	Selects dial-up line operation (Default)
	&L1	Selects leased line operation
&Mn	**Communications mode**	
&Pn	**Select pulse dialling make/break ratio**	
	&P0	Sets a 39/61 make-break ratio at 10 pps (Default)
	&P1	Sets a 33/67 make-break ratio at 10 pps (Default)
	&P2	Sets a 39/61 make-break ratio at 20 pps (Default)
	&P3	Sets a 33/67 make-break ratio at 20 pps (Default)
&Qn	**Asynchronous/synchronous mode selection**	
	&Q0	Set direct asynchronous operation
	&Q1	Set synchronous operation with asynchronous off-line
	&Q2	Set synchronous connect mode with asynchronous off-line
	&Q3	Set synchronous connect mode
	&Q5	Modem negotiation for error-corrected link
	&Q6	Set asynchronous operation in normal mode
&Rn	**RTS/CTS option**	
	&R0	In synchronous mode, CTS changes with RTS (the delay is defined by the S26 register)
	&R1	In synchronous mode, CTS is always ON
&Sn	**DSR option**	
	&S0	DSR is always ON (Default)
	&S1	DSR is active after the answer tone has been detected
&Tn	**Testing and diagnostics**	
	&T0	Terminates any current test
	&T1	Local analogue loopback test
	&T2	Local digital loopback test
&V	**View configuration profiles**	
&Wn	**Store the current configuration in non-volatile RAM**	
	&W0	Writes current settings to profile 0 in nonvolatile RAM
	&W1	Writes current settings to profile 1 in nonvolatile RAM
&Xn	**Clock source selection**	
	&X0	Selects internal timing, where the modem uses its own clock for transmitted data
	&X1	Selects external timing, where the modem gets its timing from the DTE (computer)
	&X2	Selects slave receive timing, where the modem gets its timing from the received signal
&Yn	**Select default profile**	
	&Y0	Use profile 0 on power-up (Default)
	&Y1	Use profile 1 on power-up
&Zn	**Store telephone numbers**	
	&Z0	Store telephone number 1
	&Z1	Store telephone number 2
	&Z2	Store telephone number 3
	&Z3	Store telephone number 4
\An	**Maximum MNP block size**	
	\A0	64 characters
	\A1	128 characters
	\A2	192 characters
	\A3	256 characters
\Bn	**Transmit break**	
	\B1	Break length 100 ms
	\B2	Break length 200 ms
	\B3	Break length 300 ms (Default) *and so on.*
\Gn	**Modem/modem flow control**	

	\G0	Disable (Default)	
	\G1	Enable	
\Jn		**Enable/disable DTE auto rate adjustment**	
	\J0	Disable	\J1 Enable
\Kn		**Break control**	
	\K0	Enter on-line command mode with no break signal	
	\K1	Clear data buffers and send a break to the remote modem	
	\K3	Send a break to the remote modem immediately	
	\K5	Send a break to the remote modem with transmitted data	
\Ln		**MNP block transfer control**	
	\L0	Use stream mode for MNP connection (Default)	
	\L1	Use interactive MNP block mode	

D.2 Result codes

After the modem has received an AT command it responds with a return code. A complete set of return codes are given in Table D.1.

Table D.1 Modem return codes.

Message	Digit	Description
OK	0	Command executed without errors
CONNECT	1	A connection has been made
RING	2	An incoming call has been detected
NO CARRIER	3	No carrier detected
ERROR	4	Invalid command
CONNECT 1200	5	Connected to a 1200 bps modem
NO DIAL-TONE	6	Dial-tone not detected
BUSY	7	Remote line is busy
NO ANSWER	8	No answer from remote line
CONNECT 600	9	Connected to a 600 bps modem
CONNECT 2400	10	Connected to a 2400 bps modem
CONNECT 4800	11	Connected to a 4800 bps modem
CONNECT 9600	13	Connected to a 9600 bps modem
CONNECT 14400	15	Connected to a 14 400 bps modem
CONNECT 19200	16	Connected to a 19200 bps modem
CONNECT 28400	17	Connected to a 28400 bps modem
CONNECT 38400	18	Connected to a 38400 bps modem
CONNECT 115200	19	Connected to a 115200 bps modem
FAX	33	Connected to a FAX modem in FAX mode
DATA	35	Connected to a data modem in FAX mode
CARRIER 300	40	Connected to V.21 or Bell 103 modem
CARRIER 1200/75	44	Connected to V.23 backward channel carrier modem
CARRIER 75/1200	45	Connected to V.23 forwards channel carrier modem
CARRIER 1200	46	Connected to V.22 or Bell 212 modem
CARRIER 2400	47	Connected to V.22 modem
CARRIER 4800	48	Connected to V.32bis 4800 bps modem
CONNECT 7200	49	Connected to V.32bis 7200 bps modem
CONNECT 9600	50	Connected to V.32bis 9600 bps modem
CONNECT 12000	51	Connected to V.32bis 12000 bps modem
CONNECT 14400	52	Connected to V.32bis 14400 bps modem
CONNECT 19200	61	Connected to a 19 200 bps modem
CONNECT 28800	65	Connected to a 28 800 bps modem
COMPRESSION: CLASS 5	66	Connected to modem with MNP Class 5 compression
COMPRESSION: V.42bis	67	Connected to a V.42bis modem with compression
COMPRESSION: NONE	69	Connection to a modem with no data compression
PROTOCOL: NONE	70	
PROTOCOL: LAPM	77	
PROTOCOL: ALT	80	

D.3   S-registers

The modem contains various status registers called the S-registers which store modem settings. Table D.2 lists these registers.

Table D.2   Modem registers.

Register	Function	Range [typical default]
S0	Rings to auto-answer	0–255 rings [0 rings]
S1	Ring counter	0–255 rings [0 rings]
S2	Escape character	[43]
S3	Carriage return character	[13]
S6	Wait time for dial-tone	2–255 s [2 s]
S7	Wait time for carrier	1–255 s [50 s]
S8	Pause time for automatic dialling	0–255 s [2 s]
S9	Carrier detect response time	1–255 in 0.1 s units [6]
S10	Carrier loss disconnection time	1–255 in 0.1 s units [14]
S11	DTMF tone duration	50–255 in 0.001 s units [95]
S12	Escape code guard time	0–255 in 0.02 s units [50]
S13	Reserved	
S14	General bitmapped options	[8Ah (1000 1010b)]
S15	Reserved	
S16	Test mode bitmapped options (&T)	[0]
S17	Reserved	
S18	Test timer	0–255 s [0]
S19–S20	Reserved	
S21	V.24/General bitmapped options	[04h (0000 0100b)]
S22	Speak/results bitmapped options	[75h (0111 0101b)]
S23	General bitmapped options	[37h (0011 0111b)]
S24	Sleep activity timer	0–255 s [0]
S25	Delay to DSR off	0–255 s [5]
S26	RTS–CTS delay	0–255 in 0.01 s [1]
S27	General bitmapped options	[49h (0100 1001b)]
S28	General bitmapped options	[00h]
S29	Flash dial modifier time	0–255 in 10 ms [0]
S30	Disconnect inactivity timer	0–255 in 10 s [0]
S31	General bitmapped options	[02h (0000 0010b)]
S32	XON character	[Cntrl–Q, 11h (0001 0001b)]
S33	XOFF character	[Cntrl–S, 13h (0001 0011b)]
S34–S35	Reserved	
S36	LAMP failure control	[7]
S37	Line connection speed	[0]
S38	Delay before forced hang-up	0–255 s [20]
S39	Flow control	[3]
S40	General bitmapped options	[69h (0110 1001b)]
S41	General bitmapped options	[3]
S42–S45	Reserved	
S46	Data compression control	[8Ah (1000 1010b)]
S48	V.42 negotiation control	[07h (0000 0111b)]
S80	Soft-switch functions	[0]
S82	LAPM break control	[40h (0100 0000b)]
S86	Call failure reason code	0–255
S91	PSTN transmit attenuation level	0–15 dBm [10]
S92	Fax transmit attenuation level	0–15 dBm [10]
S95	Result code message control	[0]
S99	Leased line transmit level	0–15 dBm [10]

S14	**Bitmapped options**		
		0	1
	Bit 0		
	Bit 1	E0	**E1**
	Bit 2	**Q0**	Q1
	Bit 3	V0	**V1**
	Bit 4	Reserved	
	Bit 5	**T** (tone dial)	P (pulse dial)
	Bit 6	Reserved	
	Bit 7	Answer mode	**Originate mode**

S16	**Modem test mode register**		
		0	1
	Bit 0	Local analogue loopback terminated	Local analogue loopback test in progress
	Bit 1	Unused	
	Bit 2	Local digital loopback terminated	Local digital loopback test in progress
	Bit 3	Remote modem analogue loopback test terminated	Remote modem analogue loopback test in progress
	Bit 4	Remote modem digital loopback test terminated	Remote modem digital loopback test in progress
	Bit 5	Remote modem digital self-test terminated	Remote modem digital self-test in progress
	Bit 6	Remote modem analogue self-test terminated	Remote modem analogue self-test in progress
	Bit 7	Unused	

S21	**Bitmapped options**		
		0	1
	Bit 0	**&J0**	&J1
	Bit 1		
	Bit 2	&R0	**&R1**
	Bit 5	&C0	**&C1**
	Bit 6	**&S0**	&S1
	Bit 7	**Y0**	Y1
	Bit 4, 3 = 00 &D0		
	Bit 4, 3 = 01 &D1		
	Bit 4, 3 = 10 **&D2**		
	Bit 4, 3 = 11 &D3		

S22	**Speaker/results bitmapped options**
	Bit 1, 0 = 00 L0
	Bit 1, 0 = 01 **L1**
	Bit 1, 0 = 10 L2
	Bit 1, 0 = 11 L3
	Bit 3, 2 = 00 M0
	Bit 3, 2 = 01 **M1**
	Bit 3, 2 = 10 M2
	Bit 3, 2 = 11 M3
	Bit 6, 5, 4 = 000 X0
	Bit 6, 5, 4 = 001 Reserved
	Bit 6, 5, 4 = 010 Reserved
	Bit 6, 5, 4 = 011 Reserved
	Bit 6, 5, 4 = 100 X1
	Bit 6, 5, 4 = 101 X2
	Bit 6, 5, 4 = 110 X3
	Bit 6, 5, 4 = 111 **X4**
	Bit 7 Reserved

S23	**Bitmapped options**		
		0	1
	Bit 0	&T5	**&T4**
	Bit 3, 2, 1 = 000	300 bps communications rate	

	Bit 3, 2, 1 = 001	600 bps communications rate
	Bit 3, 2, 1 = 010	1200 bps communications rate
	Bit 3, 2, 1 = 011	**2400 bps communications rate**
	Bit 3, 2, 1 = 100	4800 bps communications rate
	Bit 3, 2, 1 = 101	960 bps communications rate
	Bit 3, 2, 1 = 110	19200 bps communications rate
	Bit 3, 2, 1 = 111	Reserved
	Bit 5, 4 = 00	Even parity
	Bit 5, 4 = 01	**Not used**
	Bit 5, 4 = 10	Odd parity
	Bit 5, 4 = 11	No parity
	Bit 7, 6 = 00 **G0**	
	Bit 7, 6 = 01 G1	
	Bit 7, 6 = 10 G2	
	Bit 7, 6 = 11 G3	

S23 **Bitmapped options**

Bit 3, 1, 0 = 000 &M0 or &Q0
Bit 3, 1, 0 = 001 &M1 or &Q1
Bit 3, 1, 0 = 010 &M2 or &Q2
Bit 3, 1, 0 = 011 &M3 or &Q3
Bit 3, 1, 0 = 100 &Q3
Bit 3, 1, 0 = 101 &Q4
Bit 3, 1, 0 = 110 **&Q5**
Bit 3, 1, 0 = 111 &Q6

	0	1
Bit 2	**&L0**	&L1
Bit 6	B0	**B1**

Bit 5, 4 = 00 **X0**
Bit 5, 4 = 01 X1
Bit 5, 4 = 10 X2

S28 **Bitmapped options**

Bits 0, 1, 2 Reserved
Bit 4, 3 = 00 **&P0**
Bit 4, 3 = 01 &P1
Bit 4, 3 = 10 &P2
Bit 4, 3 = 11 &P3

S31 **Bitmapped options**

	0	1
Bit 1	**N0**	N1

Bit 3, 2 = 00 **W0**
Bit 3, 2 = 01 W1
Bit 3, 2 = 10 W2

S36 **LAPM failure control**

Bit 2, 1, 0 = 000 Modem disconnect
Bit 2, 1, 0 = 001 Modem stays on-line and a direct mode connection
Bit 2, 1, 0 = 010 Reserved
Bit 2, 1, 0 = 011 Modem stays on-line and normal mode connection is established
Bit 2, 1, 0 = 100 An MNP connection is made, if it fails then the modem disconnects
Bit 2, 1, 0 = 101 An MNP connection is made, if it fails then the modem makes a direct connection
Bit 2, 1, 0 = 110 Reserved
Bit 2, 1, 0 = 111 An MNP connection is made, if it fails then the modem makes a normal mode connection

S37 **Desired line connection speed**

Bit 3, 2, 1, 0 = 0000 **Auto mode connection (F0)**
Bit 3, 2, 1, 0 = 0001 Modem connects at 300 bps (F1)
Bit 3, 2, 1, 0 = 0010 Modem connects at 300 bps (F1)
Bit 3, 2, 1, 0 = 0011 Modem connects at 300 bps (F1)
Bit 3, 2, 1, 0 = 0100 Reserved
Bit 3, 2, 1, 0 = 0101 Modem connects at 1200 bps (F4)

	Bit 3, 2, 1, 0 = 0110 Modem connects at 2400 bps (F5)
	Bit 3, 2, 1, 0 = 0111 Modem connects at V.23 (F3)
	Bit 3, 2, 1, 0 = 1000 Modem connects at 4800 bps (F6)
	Bit 3, 2, 1, 0 = 1001 Modem connects at 9600 bps (F8)
	Bit 3, 2, 1, 0 = 1010 Modem connects at 12000 bps (F9)
	Bit 3, 2, 1, 0 = 1011 Modem connects at 144000 bps (F10)
	Bit 3, 2, 1, 0 = 1100 Modem connects at 7200 bps (F7)

S39   **Flow control**

Bit 2, 1, 0 = 000   No flow control
Bit 2, 1, 0 = 011   **RTS/CTS (&K3)**
Bit 2, 1, 0 = 100   XON/XOFF (&K4)
Bit 2, 1, 0 = 101   Transparent XON (&K5)
Bit 2, 1, 0 = 110   RTS/CTS and XON/XOFF (&K6)

S39   **General bitmapped options**

Bit 5, 4, 3 = 000   \K0
Bit 5, 4, 3 = 001   \K1
Bit 5, 4, 3 = 010   \K2
Bit 5, 4, 3 = 011   \K3
Bit 5, 4, 3 = 100   \K4
Bit 5, 4, 3 = 101   **\K5**
Bit 7, 6 = 00 MNP 64 character block size (\A0)
Bit 7, 6 = 01 **MNP 128 character block size (\A1)**
Bit 7, 6 = 10 MNP 192 character block size (\A2)
Bit 7, 6 = 11 MNP 256 character block size (\A3)

Quick Reference

Description	Page	Description	Page
80486 pin-out	32	LX motherboard	139
80486 registers	35	Memory I/O map	53
8088 pin-out	3	Memory reference	10
82091AA (AIP) pin-out	133	Modem registers	242
82344	111	Modem return codes	241
8250 pin-out	60	Parallel port	211
8254 (PTC) Control Register	79	PC bus	105
8254 (PTC) pin-out	78	PCI bus cycles	119
8255 (PPI) Control Register	71	PCI connections	117
8255 (PPI) pin-out	70	PCI system architecture	127
8259 (PIC) pin-out	68	PCMCIA pin-out	177
Assembly language	11	PCMCIA registers	178
AT task	147	Pentium connections	48
DRAM	134	PIIX3 pin-out	128
ECP registers	234	ES-232 (25-pin)	185
E-IDE	153	RS-232 (9-pin)	184
EPP mode signals	231	RS-232 connections	189
HX motherboard	127	SCSI messages	170
ICS9159 (Clock)	135	SCSI commands	172
IDE connections	146	SCSI status	174
IDE/ISA	136	SCSI-I connections	165
Interrupt handling	93	SCSI-II connections	166
ISA connections	107	TXC pin-out	128
LCR	66	VL-local bus connections	116
LSR	65		

Parallel port

Pin	Name	Pin	Name
1	Strobe	14	GND
2	Auto Feed	15	D6
3	D0	16	GND
4	Error	17	D7
5	D1	18	GND
6	INIT	19	ACK
7	D2	20	GND
8	SLCT IN	21	BUSY
9	D3	22	GND
10	GND	23	PE
11	D4	24	GND
12	GND	25	SLCT
13	D5		

Serial port

Pin	Name	Pin	Name
1	DCD	6	CTS
2	DSR	7	DTR
3	RX	8	RI
4	RTS	9	GND
5	TX		

IDE

Pin	Name	Pin	Name
1	Reset	2	GND
3	D7	4	D8
5	D6	6	D9
7	D5	8	D10
9	D4	10	D11
11	D3	12	D12
13	D2	14	D13
15	D1	16	D14
17	D0	18	D15
19	GND	20	Key
21	DRQ3	22	GND
23	-I/O W	24	GND
25	-I/O R	26	GND
27	IOCHRDY	28	BALE
29	-DACK3	30	GND
31	IRQ14	32	IOCS16
33	ADD 1	34	GND
35	ADD 0	36	ADD 2
37	-CS 0	38	CS 1
39	ACTIVITY	40	GND

Floppy disk

Pin	Name	Pin	Name
1	GND	2	FDHDIN
3	GND	4	Reserved
5	Key	6	FDEDIN
7	RTS	8	-Index
9	GND	10	Motor En A
11	GND	12	Drive Sel B
13	GND	14	Drive Sel A
15	GND	16	Motor En B
17	GND	18	DIR
19	GND	20	STEP
21	GND	22	Write Data
23	GND	24	Write Gate
25	GND	26	Track 00
27	GND	28	Write Protect
29	GND	30	Read Data
31	GND	32	Side 1 Sel
33	GND	34	Diskette

Typical IRQs

0	Internal Timer	1	Keyboard
2	Cascaded interrupt	3	COM2
4	COM1	5	(Soundcard)
6	Floppy disk	7	LPT1
8	Real-time clock	9	User available
10	User available	11	(PCI steering)
12	Serial bus mouse (if any)	13	Math coprocessor
14	Primary IDE	15	Secondary IDE

Typical DMA channels

0	Any
1	Any
2	Floppy disk
3	Parallel port
4	Cascaded DMA
5	Any
6	Any
7	Any

Example I/O map

0000–000F	Slave DMA controller	0376	Secondary IDE
0020–0021	Master PIC	0378–037A	LPT1
0040–0043	System timer	0388–03B8	Soundcard
0060	Keyboard	03B0–03BB	VGA
0061	Speaker	03C0–03DF	VGA
0064	Keyboard	03F6	Primary IDE
0070–0071	Real-time clock	03F8–03FF	COM1
0080–008F	DMA	0480–048F	PCI bus
00A0–00A1	Slave PIC	04D0–04D1	PCI bus
00F0–00FF	Numeric processor	0530–0537	Soundcard
0170–0177	Secondary H/D	0778–077A	ECP Port (LPT1)
0200–020F	Game port	0CF8–0CFF	PCI bus
0220–022F	Soundcard	4000–403F	PCI bus
0294–0297	PCI bus	5000–5018	PCI bus
02F8–02FF	COM2	D000–DFFF	AGP controller
0330–0331	Soundcard	E000–E01F	USB controller
0370–0371	Soundcard	E400–E4FF	VGA

Braces, 100, 529, 533–555
Bridges, 44, 46, 115, 118, 119, 121, 122, 124–126, 129, 245, 247, 439, 445–449, 456, 477, 482, 483, 495, 497, 502, 504
    example, 449
    filtering rate, 447
    forward rate, 447, 448
    source routing, 448
    spanning tree, 448
Brightness, 251
Browser, 517, 519, 553, 554, 555, 590, 598
B-tree, 154
Buffer, 64–67, 109, 118, 146, 147, 150, 174, 185–193, 201–204, 207–209, 226, 332–334, 336–344, 464, 467, 512–514
Bus arbitration, 121
Bus enumerator, 349, 350
Bus network, 454, 456
Bus network, 456
Bus-type network, 457
Button settings, 271
Buttons, 272
Byte enable, 31, 32, 47, 48, 108, 113, 118–120, 128
Byte enable signals, 31, 119
Bytecodes, 517
C program, 98, 221, 379
Cable impedance, 471
Cable type, 444, 471
Cabling, 441
Cache, 31, 42–45, 48, 49, 123, 126, 130, 141, 144, 352, 353, 591
    L-1, 42–44
    L-2, 42–44, 126
CANs, 470
Caption, 299
Caption property, 282, 289, 293, 295, 296
Carriage return, 200, 212, 240, 243, 441, 522
Carry flag, 11, 13, 14, 20
Cat-3, 472, 473
Cat-4, 472
Cat-5, 472, 473, 480
CATNIP, 498

CCITT, 239, 244, 443, 444
CD, 141, 157–160, 210, 244, 333, 337, 340, 341, 443, 444, 457, 458, 462, 468
    audio, 158
    pit, 141, 156–158
CD-DA, 158, 159
CD-E, 158, 160
CDFS, 344, 352, 353, 354
CD-I, 160
CD-R, 158, 159, 160
CD-ROM, 113, 141, 145, 157–162, 176, 210, 230, 232, 344, 349, 352, 353, 369
    disk format, 158
    lead in, 158, 159
    lead out, 158, 159
    program area, 158
CD-ROM-XA, 158, 160
CD-RW, 158
Centigrade, 289, 290
Centronics, 210, 211, 226, 228, 234
Characteristic impedance, 463, 468
Characters and numbers, 16
Cheapernet, 469, 470
Checkboxes, 576
Checksum, 501
Class code, 122
Class declaration, 562, 568
Classes, 366, 488, 518, 519, 535, 536, 543, 545, 546, 547, 592
Classes.zip, 518, 519, 546
Click, 313–315, 322, 324, 326, 327, 329
Client, 609, 610
Client–server, 501, 517, 590, 609
Clock doubler, 31
Clock period, 82, 468
Cls, 325, 330
CMC, 11
Coaxial, 183, 444, 455–457, 463, 464, 468
Collision, 443, 457, 458, 462, 463, 464, 469, 471, 472
Colour code, 275, 276
COM1, 63, 64, 67, 91, 93, 94, 96, 133, 138, 176, 184, 187, 191, 194, 199, 203–206, 214, 335, 341, 342

COM2, 63, 64, 91, 93, 94, 96, 99, 100, 133, 138, 176, 181, 184, 199, 204, 209, 214, 343, 344
Comments, 16
CommonDialog, 305, 308, 310
Communicator, 553
Compact, 157, 160, 161, 345, 361
Compatibility, 106, 110, 226, 236, 239, 376, 473, 507, 557
Compilation, 548
Compiler, 268, 518, 519, 520, 547, 551, 555
Compression, 152, 232, 236, 237, 239, 249–251, 377
Compression ratio, 232, 251
CompuServe, 194, 243, 440
Concatenated, 522
Concentrator, 454
Conditional jump, 22
Configuration Manager, 346, 348–350, 361
Connection-oriented, 499
Constants, 16, 308, 310, 317, 550, 543
Constructors, 538
Control field, 173, 460, 461
Controls, 255, 263
Core system components, 354
Correction, 45, 130, 140, 239, 250, 441
Cosine, 549, 557, 558
CPU, 18, 24, 26, 139
CR, 63, 65, 242
CRC, 458, 459
CSMA, 443, 444, 457, 458, 462, 468, 477, 480
CSMA/CD, 443, 444, 457, 458, 462, 468, 477, 480
Ctrl, 258, 566, 567
Ctrl-Alt-Del, 95
Ctrl-Break, 95
CTS, 63, 185, 186, 188, 190, 337, 338, 340, 341
Currency, 267, 268
Current, 257–261, 266, 278, 295, 296, 298, 308, 317, 319, 326, 327, 560
Cursor, 102
Cyclic redundancy check, 151, 459
Cylinders, 143, 151, 152

DA, 136
DARPA, 482, 488
DAS, 11
DAT, 141, 161, 362
Data compression, 239
Data definition, 25, 26
Data frame, 441, 461, 483
Data link layer, 441–443, 446, 449, 458, 461, 462, 482
Data rate, 471
Data segment, 25, 26
Data type, 267–269, 270, 547, 550, 551, 556, 560
Data type checking, 268
Data types, 266, 267, 520
Datastream-oriented, 499
Date, 102, 266–269, 279, 609
DB25S, 184
DB9S, 184
DC, 414, 421, 427, 463, 464, 467, 474
DCE, 184, 185, 188, 190
DD, 136, 142
Debugger, 27–30, 519
DEC, 12, 19, 180, 457
Decimal, 16, 17, 220, 268, 422, 533, 534, 556
Decimal, 11, 481, 521
Decisions and loops, 275
Decrement, 525
Degrees, 555
Del, 299, 373–375
Delphi, 253
Demand Priority Access Method, 474
Demand-paged, 350, 351
Demodulator, 237
Deprecation, 557, 558
Destination address, 16, 447, 448, 456–459, 462
Device driver, 344, 345, 347–350, 353, 355, 359–364, 369, 371
Dialog Box, 307
Dialog boxes, 376
DIB, 259, 356, 492
Digital, 72, 147, 150, 161, 248
Digital audio, 158
Digital modulation, 248
Digitized video, 440
DIMM, 46

DIO card, 72
Disassembler, 519
Discrete, 59
Disk
   automatic defect reallocation, 164
   capacity, 142, 152
   drives, 260
   duplexing, 155
   mirroring, 155, 156
   predictive failure analysis, 164
   striping with parity, 155
   striping, 155
   transfers, 114
Division, 11, 266, 267, 523, 525
DMA, 105, 106, 108, 129, 137, 139,
   147, 232, 359, 371
DNS, 492, 493, 495, 503, 507, 610
Do ... while loop, 278
Domain name system, 491
Domain names, 491, 507
DOS, 26, 89, 92, 102, 103, 152, 153,
   214, 253, 344, 345, 359, 441, 503
DOS-based, 201, 441
DPAM, *see* Demand Priority Access
            Method
DPSK, 249
Drag and drop, 319
DRAM, 45, 126, 130, 131, 134, 135,
   140, 141
Drive specifications, 143
DSR, 185, 186, 188, 337, 338, 340,
   341
DTE, 184, 185, 187, 188, 190, 244
DTR, 185, 186, 188, 244, 338, 340
D-type, 78, 184, 210, 238, 469
EaStMAN, 504
EBCDIC, 521
ECC, 46, 130, 140, 151
echo cancellation, 249, 250
ECP, 210
Edinburgh, 282, 288, 491, 502, 503,
   504
EDO, 134
Eece.napier.ac.uk, 491, 493, 502–504,
   608, 610
EGA/VGA, 51
EIA, 183, 251, 443, 444
E-IDE, 145, 148–152, 162

EISA, 46, 104, 110–115, 122, 144,
   348
Electronic mail, 441, 501
Electronic token, 455
Email, 576–579
EMF, 356
Encryption, 441, 498
End of interrupt, 97, 98, 203, 205, 207,
   221, 222, 225
Enhanced parallel port, 210, 226, 230,
   231, 234, 235
   byte mode, 226, 229, 230, 234
   nibble mode, 226, 227, 228
   protocol, 230
   registers, 230
Error
   control, 61, 461, 485
   detection, 44, 45, 61, 130, 158, 174,
      250, 441, 443, 458, 459, 485
Esc, 208
Escape sequence, 522
ESDI, 144, 145, 161, 354
Ether, 443, 463, 464, 494, 495
Ethernet, 112, 114, 122, 130, 443, 445,
   447, 450, 456–483, 486, 487, 495,
   506
   100BASE-4T, 473, 481
   100BASE-FX, 472
   100BASE-T, 472, 473, 476, 478,
      481
   100BASE-TX, 469, 472, 473, 476,
      477
   100 Mbps, 121, 472, 480
   100VG-Any LAN, 469
   100VG-AnyLAN, 472, 474–481
   10BASE2, 447, 469, 471, 480
   10BASE5, 469, 471
   10BASE-FL, 469, 470
   10BASE-T connections, 473
   10BASE-T, 447, 469–473, 476, 478
   AUI, 462
   cheapernet, 469, 470
   distance between transceivers, 469
   DSAP, 460
   fast ethernet, 469, 472, 474, 476,
      477, 479, 480
   II, 459
   implementation, 467

limitations, 468
LLC protocol, 461
MDI, 462
migration to fast ethernet, 476
PLS, 462, 463
repeater lengths, 468
segment lengths, 468
SNAP, 459, 460, 481
SSAP, 460
transceiver, 463, 467
types, 469
Event handling, 561, 567
Event-driven, 253, 313, 333, 567
Events, 174, 253, 255, 259, 263, 279,
    281, 300, 313–315, 319–321, 333,
    338–340, 355, 390, 400, 557, 558,
    560–568, 573, 577
Exabyte, 161
Exceptions, 355, 377
Explorer, 448, 517
Exponent, 526
Exponential, 549
Extended capability port, 182, 210,
    231–236, 356
    channel address, 231–233
    forward data, 233
    mode signals, 232
    protocol, 232
    register settings, 235
    registers, 234
Extended parallel port
    mode signals, 231
    register definitions, 231
Factorial, 277
Fahrenheit, 289, 290
FAT, 152–154, 162, 352
Fault tolerance, 155
FAX, 232, 239, 576, 578–583
Fax transmission, 251
FCS, 459, 461, 462
FDDI, 122, 444, 447, 477, 479, 482
    DAS, 11
    network, 122
FF, 18, 24, 26, 420–422, 467
Fibre optic, 444, 445, 455, 470, 472
File attributes, 153
File dialog, 590
File I/O, 141, 163

File system, 152–155, 158, 159, 162,
    344, 352, 353
    FAT, 152–154, 162, 352
    HPFS, 152, 154
    NTFS, 152, 154
File Transfer Protocol, 500, 501, 609
FINGER, 500
Firewall, 591
Fixed disks, 142
Floating-point, 43, 48, 266–270, 377,
    380, 521, 526
Floppy disks, 142
Flow, 461, 498
Flow control, 187, 461
Flying head, 142
Font
    courier, 281, 420, 421
    italic, 419, 420
    times roman, 280, 420, 422
For loop, 277, 533, 534, 556
Forms, 255, 281
Forms and code, 281
Fragment, 483
Fragmentation, 499
Frame, 60, 61, 239, 259, 441, 447,
    458–465, 475, 479, 480, 483, 598
Frame check sequence, 459
Frame format, 60, 185, 238
Framing bits, 443, 461
France, 282, 288, 491
Frequency, 31, 59, 66, 83, 104, 132,
    135, 140, 191–193, 248, 249, 251,
    465, 466, 467
Frequency-shift keying, 248
FSK, 248, 249
Ftp, 361, 482, 503, 498, 499, 500, 501,
    503, 547, 591
Full-duplex, 248, 344
Gateway, 50, 439, 445, 449, 453, 482–
    487, 494, 495, 496, 503–505, 507,
    591
GIF, 237
Gopher, 501, 591
Gradient, 299
Graphical Device Interface, 354, 355,
    376, 414, 416
Graphical User Interface, 112

Green Book, 160
Ground, 63, 184, 185, 190, 210, 214
Group III, 251
Group IV, 251
GUI, 112
HAL, 359
Half-duplex, 473
Handshaking, 59, 63, 67, 69, 71, 72,
    77, 108, 109, 118, 120, 129, 169,
    170, 185–190, 210, 211, 227–230,
    236, 237, 333, 337, 338, 344, 477
Hard disk/CD-ROM interfaces, 144
Hard disk, 148
Hardware, 89, 517, 521
Hardware handshaking, 186, 188
Hayes, 240
HD, 142
HDLC, 443, 444
Header files, 518
Helix, 161
Help manuals, 310
Hexadecimal, 16, 262, 324, 328, 363,
    380, 422, 459, 480, 481, 523, 556
HFS, 159
Hi-fi, 157, 161
High-level language, 16
Hosts, 483–491, 496, 497, 499, 500,
    503
Hot fixing, 154
HPFS, 152, 154
HTML script, 553, 554, 556, 559, 560,
    564, 566
HTTP, 501, 518, 547, 590, 591, 599,
    600
    message, 591
Hub, 126, 130, 140, 454, 470–480
Huffman, 251
    modified, 251
    coding, 251
HyperTerminal, 194, 195
Hypertext, 501, 590
Hz, 237, 248
I/O
    read, 47, 105, 119, 120, 177
    write, 47, 105, 119, 120, 177, 230
IBM, 106, 110, 210, 443, 455
ICMP, 485, 486, 498, 501, 503, 504,
    506

Icon, 322, 324, 373
ICP, 68
ICW, 97
IDC, 78, 385, 386, 388, 395, 417, 420,
    424
IDE, 108, 122, 126, 129, 136, 137,
    139, 141, 144–151, 161–165, 353
IDE/ISA interface, 137
IDI, 385
IEEE, 210, 226, 268, 443, 444, 448,
    457–462, 472, 474, 475, 491, 549
    1284, 210, 226
    802.12, 472, 474
    802.2, 443, 444, 458, 459, 460
    802.3, 443, 444, 457–462, 472, 475
    802.3 frame format, 458, 459
    802.3u, 472
    802.4, 444
    802.5, 443, 444, 458, 475
    standards, 458
IETF, 590
If..else, 529–531
Image scanner, 251
Images, 232, 237, 251, 255, 259, 260,
    332, 590
Import statements, 545
IMR, 68, 97, 98, 204, 205, 206, 221–
    224
Increment, 525
Indexing, 550
Inetd, 494
INF files, 369, 373
    format, 369
Initialization, 538, 558, 559
Initialization and exit methods, 557,
    558
Input/output, 518
Input/output supervisor, 353
Installable File System, 352
Integer division, 523
Intel, 42, 43, 97, 104, 115, 126, 345,
    457, 491
Intensity, 158
Interconnected networks, 441–443,
    448, 483
Interconnection length, 446
Interface, 253–255, 281, 517, 558

Interfacing
  isolated, 50
internet, 482, 483, 484, 485, 487, 488,
  489
Internet, 196, 237, 357, 443, 449, 450,
  452, 482, 484, 485, 490–509, 517,
  518, 553, 590–593
  addresses, 487, 488
  datagram, 484, 485
  example domain addresses, 491
  example, 487
  explorer, 517, 553
  naming structure, 491
  primary domain names, 491, 507
  protocol, 443, 482
  routing protocols, 450
Inter-networking, 482
Internetworking connections, 446
Interrupt, 12, 47, 51, 59, 68, 89–93,
  97, 98, 100, 106, 108, 138, 205,
  206, 222
  1Ch, 100
  edge-triggered, 96, 97
  handling, 89, 91, 93
  hardware, 59, 104, 205
  mask register, 97, 98
  processor, 92
  software, 89, 98
  vector, 51, 90, 93
Interrupt Control Port, 68, 205
Interrupt controller, 138
Interrupt Mask Register, 68, 97, 98,
  204, 205, 206, 221, 222, 223, 224
Interrupt request, 48, 88, 91–93, 96,
  106, 108
Interval timer, 138
IP, 345, 443, 448–450, 457, 459, 460,
  482–509, 517, 592, 593, 595, 608–
  610
  address format, 487
  class A, 487, 488, 490
  class B, 488, 489, 490
  class C, 488, 490
  time-to-live, 485, 504, 506
IP address, 450, 482–509, 517, 592,
  593, 595, 608–610
  addressing, 482, 488
  data frames, 483

  header, 485, 486, 498, 499
  protocol, 460, 483, 484–486, 503,
    504, 506
  Ver4, 498
  Ver6, 497–499
IPX, 348, 448–450, 459
IRQ, 91, 93–96, 108, 115, 124, 128,
  129, 162, 163, 186, 216, 221, 333,
  345, 371
  IRQ0, 91, 93, 94, 97, 98, 124, 130,
    138
  IRQ1, 91, 93, 95, 98, 128, 130, 140,
    354
  IRQ10, 93, 121, 128
  IRQ11, 93, 128
  IRQ12, 93, 128, 129, 130, 138, 140
  IRQ13, 93, 108, 130, 138
  IRQ14, 93, 108, 128–130, 138, 145,
    146, 150
  IRQ15, 93, 96, 108, 124, 128–130,
    138
  IRQ2, 91, 93, 94, 96, 98, 130, 138
  IRQ3, 91, 93, 96, 98, 104, 128, 132,
    133, 138
  IRQ4, 91, 93, 96, 98, 104, 128, 132,
    133, 138, 204–206
  IRQ5, 91, 93, 96, 128, 133
  IRQ6, 91, 93, 96, 98, 128, 133
  IRQ7, 91, 93, 94, 96, 98, 128, 133,
    221–225
  IRQ8, 93, 96
  IRQ9, 93, 96, 116, 128
ISA, 46, 104–115, 117, 122, 125, 126,
  128, 130, 133, 135, 136, 139, 141,
  144, 145, 174, 230, 348
ISDN, 237, 251, 440, 444
  system connections, 191
ISO, 158, 159, 353, 440, 442, 443,
  444, 458, 482
ISO 9660, 158, 159, 353
ISO-IP, 482
Isolator, 464
ISR, 88, 90, 92, 93, 101, 205–207,
  224, 225
Italic, 419, 420
ITU, 239, 249, 250, 251, 443
Jamming signal, 457
JANET, 505

Japan, 160
Java
   1.0 and 1.1, 557
   action listeners, 571
   checkboxes, 574
   compiler, 517–520, 547, 555, 557
   events and windows, 553–588
   file dialog, 587
   interpreter, 518–520, 586, 607
   item listener, 574
   keyboard, 564–566
   list box, 584
   menu bar, 582
   mouse events, 559–564
   networking, 590–608
   radio button, 576
Java.exe, 519, 520, 586
Javac.exe, 519, 520, 554
JDK, 518, 519, 546, 554
Joliet, 159
JPE, 12
JPG, 237
Key methods, 567
Keyboard, 91–95, 135, 369, 370, 373–
   375, 557, 560, 565–567
   data ready, 95
   events, 557, 567
   input, 565
KeyPress, 313–315, 319, 566, 567
Keystroke, 592
Keywords, 529
LAN, 112, 439, 443–445, 448, 450,
   453, 457, 458, 469, 477, 479
Laser, 141, 156, 158
LCR, 63, 65–67, 191, 192, 193, 200,
   205
LED, 83, 217
Lempel-Ziv, 250
Length, 268, 322
Lens, 156
Library, 305, 359, 507, 516, 545, 547,
   556
LIFO, 23
Light, 88, 156, 157, 422, 444
Line break, 183
Links, 392

List box, 389, 587
Listeners, 561, 562, 567, 568
   action, 573
   item, 577
Lists, 369
LLC, *see* Logical link control
Logical block address, 149, 151, 172
Logical link control, 444, 458–462
Logical operator, 525, 526
Logical unit number, 172
LOGIN, 500
Long integer, 267, 268
Loops, 533
Lost focus, 320
LPT1, 93, 94, 96, 133, 184, 213, 214,
   222, 224
LPT2, 93, 94, 96, 213
LSR, 63–67, 191–193, 200, 201, 203,
   205, 207, 208
Lynx, 492, 493
MAC, 122, 447, 457, 458, 459, 461,
   462, 464, 482, 483, 487, 493–495,
   506, 518
   address, 447, 459, 461, 482, 483,
      487, 493–495, 506
   layer, 458, 462, 464, 483
Machine code, 18
Macros, 25
Magnetic
   disk, 141
   fields, 141
   tape, 141, 160
Magneto-optical, 159
Manchester,
   code, 463, 465, 467
   coding, 465, 466, 481
   decoder, 464, 465
MANs, 439
M-ary, 249
   ASK, 249
   FSK, 249
   modulation, 249
   PSK, 249
MASM, 26
Math co-processor, 93
MAU, 463

Media access control, 457, 458, 462
Memory, 12–20, 24, 31, 32, 42–52,
    63, 64, 69, 78, 88, 90, 104–108,
    111–126, 130, 134, 135, 139, 140,
    141, 144, 150, 156, 157, 170, 174,
    176–180, 182, 185, 211, 214, 230,
    253, 344, 345, 348, 350–352, 354–
    356, 358–360, 371, 377, 380, 381,
    422, 467, 479, 521, 551, 558, 591
    addressable, 106, 124, 176
    addressing, 17
    mapped, 51
    models, 345
    paging, 350, 351
    segmented, 352
Menu, 256, 257, 261, 263, 279, 299,
    300, 301, 302, 303, 304, 306, 310,
    376, 580
    bar, 256, 585
    creating, 300
    editor, 299, 300
    multiple, 584
    pop-up, 417, 580, 582, 583
Messaging, 400–412
    structure, 400
    functions, 401
Metafile, 255, 260, 322, 356
Method overloading, 540
Methods, 555
Micro-ops, 43
Microprocessor, 50, 59, 67, 69, 77,
    112
Microsoft, 26, 31, 51, 52, 89, 93, 150,
    191, 231, 242, 253, 268, 305, 332,
    344, 346, 359, 373, 375, 379, 417,
    505, 585, 599
    Assembler, 26
    Visual C++, 253
    Windows, 31, 51, 52, 89, 93, 242,
        253, 268, 305, 344, 379, 417, 585
Migration, 472
Military, 491
MIME, 501, 592
Miniport, 353, 354
MIPs, 42
MMX, 44
MNP level 5, 249, 250
Modem, 62, 114, 176, 237–241, 244,

245, 248–250, 252
    AT commands, 240, 249, 648–650
    AT prefix, 240
    auto-answer, 237, 242, 244
    auto-dial, 237
    commands, 240, 242, 243
    connection, 189, 190, 246, 247, 482
    dialling, 243
    example return codes, 241, 651
    indicators, 244
    profile viewing, 244
    registers, 242, 652
    setups, 242
    S-registers, 242, 252, 652–656
    standards, 239
    test modes, 245
    typical, 249
    V.22bis, 239, 249, 250
    V.32, 239, 249, 250
    V.42bis, 239, 249, 250
Modulator, 237
Modulus, 523, 524, 525, 535
Mouse, 138, 140, 317, 348, 370, 418,
    421, 557, 560, 561, 563
    down, 316
    events, 557, 560
    function, 138
    selection, 563
    up, 316
MPEG, 157
MR, 244
MS-DOS, 152, 153, 344, 345, 347,
    350, 352, 354, 359, 360
MS-DOS Mode support, 350
Multi-dimensional arrays, 552
Multimedia, 377, 480
Multiple choice example, 282
Multiple file systems, 352
Multiplexing, 117, 210, 499
Multiplexing/demultiplexing, 499
Multiplication, 525
Multi-station access unit, 463
Multitasking, 43, 101, 209, 344, 347,
    350–352, 357, 361
    co-operative, 357
    pre-emptive, 345, 357
MUX, 136
Napier

electrical department, 491, 493,
    502–504, 608, 610
University, 289, 505
NDIS, 348
Netscape, 517, 553
Netstat, 504
NetWare, 155, 162, 163, 348, 449, 460
NetWare 4.1, 449
Network, 155, 196, 364, 377, 442,
    444, 450, 452–454, 457, 464, 473,
    476, 482, 489, 490, 497
    addresses, 491, 592
    cable types, 444
    layer, 441, 442, 446, 448, 449, 453,
        460, 484, 499
    management, 476
    statistics, 504
    topologies, 453, 454
    traffic, 450, 463, 591
Newline, 522
NFS
    RPC, 503
NIC, 464, 490
NLSP, 449
Noise, 248, 464
Nslookup, 493, 503
NT, 89, 152–155, 196, 197, 253, 344,
    345, 347, 350–352, 357, 359–361,
    376, 518, 554
NTE, 440
NTFS, 152, 154
N-type, 469–471
Object properties, 281
Object-oriented, 253, 517, 535
Objects, 255, 258, 260, 264, 297, 301,
    314, 322, 570
Octal, 16, 523, 534, 535, 554
OH, 244
OLE, 260, 288, 376, 377
Operating system, 43, 89, 112, 152,
    155, 159, 160, 201, 253, 344, 345,
    351, 352, 355, 356–362, 364, 369,
    376, 377, 448, 449, 460
Operators, 219, 266, 523–529
Optical disk, 141, 156, 159
Optical storage, 156
OR, 13, 19, 20, 216, 564
Orange Book, 158, 160

OR-tied, 166, 167, 174
OS/2, 152, 154, 155, 163
OSI, 440–443, 449, 458, 461, 482–
    484, 499
    model, 440–442, 458, 461, 482,
        483, 499
Packet, 159, 441, 443, 447, 448, 450,
    453, 484, 486, 499, 502–506, 592
Packet Internet Gopher, 501
Paint() object, 556
Parallel, 42, 43, 93, 96, 103, 106, 126,
    130, 132, 183, 184, 210, 211, 214,
    216, 219–227, 232, 236, 360, 477
Parallel port, 103, 210, 214, 216, 219
Parameter list, 550
Parameter passing, 517
Parameters, 270, 274, 315, 553, 555,
    566
Parentheses, 173
Parity, 61, 132, 140, 156, 164, 201,
    340, 341
    even, 48, 61, 99, 122, 191, 193, 335
    odd, 60, 61
Pascal, 50, 65, 86, 214, 255, 266–278,
    517, 535, 552
Password, 451
PATH, 518
PC bus, 104–106, 117
PC connectors, 184
PCI bus
    arbitration transaction, 46
    burst mode, 118
    data transaction, 47
    error transaction, 46
    interface, 139
    ISA bridge, 126
    man. ID, 122
    multiplexed mode, 117
    request transaction, 46
    response transaction, 46
    unit ID, 122
PCI bus cycles
    address phase, 119
    configuration address space, 122
    configuration read access, 119, 121
    configuration write access, 119, 121
    dual addressing, 119, 121
    multiple read, 119, 121

PCMCIA, 176, 177, 178, 181, 182, 365, 370
  interface controller, 178
  registers, 178
  type II, 176
  type III, 176
  type IV, 176
Peer-to-peer, 344
Pentium, 31, 42, 43, 44, 45, 46, 48, 108, 115, 117, 121, 126, 128, 141, 352
Pentium II, 42, 44, 45, 126, 128
Pentium Pro, 42–45
Phase shift keying, 248
Philips, 158, 159
Phone, 237, 240, 491
Physical layer, 441, 443, 446, 461, 472
PIIX3, 126–141
PIIX4, 126
Ping, 361, 482, 486, 501–503, 506
Pipeline, 43, 43, 45, 130
Pixels, 112, 251, 328, 329, 416, 431, 432, 553
PKZIP, 366
Plain text, 590
Platter, 143
Playing cards, 552
PLL, 465, 466
Plug-and-Play, 128, 129, 346, 348, 356, 358, 365
Pointer, 63, 64, 151, 258, 317–319, 381, 411, 419, 427, 432, 467, 501
  far, 63
Point-to-point protocol, 195, 197, 348, 484
Polarization, 157
Port driver, 353
Port number, 100, 334, 335, 343, 499, 500, 509, 592, 597
Ports and sockets, 500
POSIX, 155
Power management, 126, 139
PPI, 65, 69–74
Precedence, 266, 267
Pre-emptive, 344, 345, 350, 351, 361
Pre-emptive multitasking, 345
Presentation layer, 441
Print servers, 344

Priority, 163, 166, 175, 357, 358, 359, 360, 361, 474, 475, 484, 498
Prism, 157
Process scheduling, 350
Programmable Interrupt Controller, 43, 59, 67, 68, 88, 92, 93, 96, 97, 126, 129, 205, 206, 221, 224
Programmable Timer Controller, 77
Project files, 255
Proxy, 590, 591
PS, 110, 129, 130, 138, 139, 140, 428
PSK, 248, 249
PSTN, 440
PTC, 65, 69, 78, 79, 83–86
Public, 444, 536, 588, 589
Public switched data network, 440
Public switched telecommunications network, 440
Public telephone, 238, 440, 483, 491
QAM, 249
QIC, 161
Quadratic equation, 292, 293, 313
Quadratic roots, 292
Radians, 327
Radio, 255, 578
Radio button, 255, 280, 578
RAID, 155, 156
  level 0, 156
  level 5, 155, 156
RAM, 51, 112, 122, 126, 467
Random numbers, 551
RD, 59, 63, 67, 185, 187, 190–193, 244
Real-time, 209, 232, 360, 475
Receiver Not Ready, 461
Receiver Ready, 461
Recording, 112, 157
Red Book, 158, 159
Redundancy, 459
Reel-to-reel, 160
Register, 11–20, 24, 25, 31
Registry, 345, 362–373
Registry keys
  HKEY_CLASSES_ROOT, 363
  HKEY_CURRENT_CONFIG, 363, 365
  HKEY_CURRENT_USER, 363

HKEY_LOCAL_MACHINE, 365
HKEY_USERS, 363
REJ, 461
Reject, 461
Relationship, 524, 525, 529
Relationship operator, 524
Remote Procedure Call, 503
Repeater, 446, 447, 456, 468, 477, 480
Resistance, 278, 296, 445, 464, 469, 520
Resource arbitrators, 350
Return type, 379, 535, 538, 540, 560
Return value, 273, 555
Revision, 122
RG-50, 469, 471
RG-6, 471
RGB, 262, 279, 324, 326, 327, 422, 423, 431, 438
RI, 341
Ring
  three, 345
  zero, 345
Ring in, 59
Ring network, 122, 444, 454–458, 475, 482, 486
Ring topology, 444
RIP, 449, 450
  packet format, 450
RJ-45, 447, 464, 470, 471, 476
RLE, 232, 233, 235, 251, 322
RLE count, 233
RNR, 461
ROM, 46, 51, 89, 123, 141, 157, 159, 210
ROM BIOS, 51, 89
Root, 292, 549, 550
Routers, 445, 448, 449
Routing protocol
  BGP, 449
  EGP, 449
  NLSP, 449
  OSPF, 449–452
  RIP, 449, 450
RPC, 503
RR, 262, 461
RS-232, 59–63, 183–190, 194, 201, 205, 206, 237–239, 335, 343, 344, 358, 443, 444, 450

bit stream timings, 62
communications, 62, 63, 184, 189, 194, 238, 239
DTE-DCE connections, 189
frame format, 60, 185
programming, 63, 190
setup, 186
RS-328, 251
RS-422, 183, 444
RS-449, 183
RTS, 63, 185, 186, 188, 190, 333, 338
Run Length Count, 231, 233
Sampling, 112, 113
Sampling rate, 112
Scaleability, 472
SCSI, 104, 122, 141, 144, 145, 163–175, 353
  A-cable, 164
  B-cable, 164
  commands, 172
  host, 165
  interface, 165
  layer, 353
  logical unit number, 172
  message codes, 170
  message format, 170
  message system description, 170
  P-cable, 164
  pointers, 170
  SCSI-I connections, 165
  SCSI-I, 163–166, 174
  SCSI-II, 145, 163–166, 174
  SCSI-III, 163–166, 174
  tagged command queue, 163, 164
SCSI states
  arbitration, 167
  command, 168
  data, 168
  free-bus, 167
  message, 168
  selection, 167
  status, 168
SCSI-ID, 163, 166–168, 175
Seagate Technologies, 144
Search, 154, 160, 264, 482
Sectors, 141–143, 146, 148, 151–153, 158
Security permissions, 155

Segment, 13, 14, 17, 24–27, 90, 221, 352, 446, 457, 468–472, 475, 477, 479, 480, 482, 487, 500, 502
Selection statements, 529
Sensor, 157
Sequence number, 461, 486, 500
Sequencing of data, 461
Serial, 59, 64, 67, 91, 93, 112, 126, 130, 332, 348, 364, 444
Serial communications, 59, 63, 100, 104, 183, 184, 190, 194, 201, 214, 332, 333, 342, 444
Servers, 135, 155, 196, 197, 198, 344, 476, 477, 491, 493, 494, 500, 590, 591, 610
Session layer, 441
Seven-layer OSI model, 441
Shift instructions, 20
Shift/rotate, 20
SIMM, 134
Sine, 248, 549, 555
SIPP, 498
SMA, 470
SMARTDRV.EXE, 352
SMDS, 505
SMM, *see* System Management Mode
SMTP, 500, 501
SNMP, 500
Socket, 508, 510–516, 547, 592, 603–609
    connection, 604
    creating, 606
    number, 499, 500
Software handshaking, 186, 188
Sony, 158, 491
Source address, 459
Spanning-tree bridge, 446, 456
Speaker volume, 240
Speech, 237, 440, 475
SPX, 443, 449, 450, 459
SPX/IPX, 443
Square root, 549
Squares, 260
SRAM, 126, 130, 135, 141
ST connector, 470
ST-506, 144, 145, 161
Standalone, 251, 518–520, 553
Standards, 104, 114, 159, 440, 443,
458
Star network, 454, 455, 473
Start bit, 60–62, 238
Start delimiter, 458
Stateless protocol, 590
Static methods, 542
Stereo audio, 162
Stop bit, 60–62, 65, 99, 100, 187, 191, 193, 205, 238, 239, 335, 342, 344
STP, 472
Strings, 11, 266, 268, 276, 304, 370, 521, 522, 552, 588, 589, 592, 598
Striping with parity, 155
SUB, 14, 18, 19
Subnet, 450, 482, 489–495
    masks, 450, 490
Subroutine calls, 23
Sun, 518
Sun Microsystems, 518
SuperJANET, 505
Switch(), 531
Synchronized, 60, 238, 465, 466, 592, 605
Synchronous, 110, 113, 130, 163, 238
Synchronous modems, 238
System Management Mode, 43, 139
System policies, 347, 363, 364
System timer, 91, 93, 94
Tab, 134, 259, 522, 523
Tape backup, 348
TASM, 26
TCP, 197, 345, 348, 443, 449, 457, 459, 460, 482–484, 486, 487, 497–501, 503, 507, 508, 517, 590, 592, 605, 610
    header format, 500, 501
    rotocol Data Unit, 500
TCP/IP, 197, 345, 443, 449, 457, 459, 460, 482–484, 486, 487, 497, 501, 503, 507, 517, 592, 610
    class A, 487, 488, 490
    class B, 488, 489, 490
    class C, 488, 490
    gateway, 483, 487
    implementation, 486
    internets, 486
    ports and sockets, 500
    version number, 484

TD, 59, 63, 67, 185, 187–193

TDI, 117, 122

Telephone number, 194, 196, 241, 482, 483, 491

Television, 438

Telnet, 361, 482, 498–503, 547, 609

Temperature conversion, 290
program, 289

Terminal, 59, 106, 185, 186, 194, 202, 208, 242, 252

Text editor, 520

Thick-Ethernet, 470

Thick-wire, 469, 471

Thinnet, 469, 471

Thin-wire, 470

Thin-wire Ethernet, 469, 471

Throughput, 106, 112, 174, 351, 449, 472, 477, 484

Tilde, 539

Timestamp, 486

Token, 27

Token ring, 443–445, 447, 448, 455, 458, 475, 479, 480, 482, 483, 487, 495
data exchange, 377

Top-down, 253, 557

Topology, 444, 445, 452, 454–457, 473, 495, 497

TR, 244

Traceroute, 504, 505

Tracks, 141, 142

Traffic, 88, 445–447, 449–451, 454–457, 463, 464, 470, 472, 477–591

Transceiver, 45, 463, 464, 467, 469–471

Transfer length, 172

Transfer rates, 159

Transmission channel, 248

Transport, 443, 482

Transport Control Protocol, 443

Transport layer, 441, 442, 482, 484, 499

Tree topology, 455

Trellis, 250

TUBA, 498

Tunnel, 591

Turbo Pascal, 214

Twisted-pair, 183, 444–446, 454–457,

463, 468, 470–473, 475

Twisted-pair hubs, 470

TXC, 126–140

Types of roots, 292

UI, 462

UK, 502, 503, 505

Uncompressed, 157, 237

Unconditional jump, 22

Unicast, 499

Unicode, 521–523

University College, London, 505

University of Bath, 491, 504, 505

University of Edinburgh, 491, 504

UNIX, 152, 344, 441, 449, 504, 507, 518

URL, 517, 546, 547, 590, 592, 596–600, 602

USA, 503, 505

USB, 126, 129, 130, 135, 140

UTP, 463, 470, 471, 472, 473

V.21, 239, 248, 249

V.22bis, 239, 249, 250

V.32, 239, 249, 250

V.32bis, 239, 249, 250

V.42bis, 239, 249, 250

Vampire, 469

Variables, 25, 26, 266, 267, 268, 270, 550

VCO, 465, 466

VCR quality, 157

VDDs, *see* Virtual device driver

VESA, 114–116

VFAT, 344, 352

VGA, 112, 122

Video, 91, 103, 104, 115, 122, 141, 157, 160, 161, 232, 237, 414, 422, 440, 475, 517

Violation, 380

Virtual data flow, 440

Virtual device driver, 347, 348, 354, 360, 376

Virtual Machine Manager, 350, 361

Visual Basic, 253–258, 264, 266–269, 275, 281, 286, 297–299, 305, 311–313, 320–322, 325, 332, 333, 344, 382, 399
controls and events, 263
form window, 257, 258

menu bar, 256
object box, 261
project window, 257, 263, 265
properties window, 256, 258, 259,
    261, 262, 279
toolbox, 258, 261
files, 253
VL-local bus, 112, 114–117, 144
Voltage, 278, 295, 296, 297
VxD, 347, 348, 353, 354, 361, 375–
    376, 377
WAN, 439, 440, 443, 444, 449, 450
Waveform, 464, 466, 475
Web, 491, 501, 517, 591
While(), 278, 534
White Book, 160
White run length coding, 251
Win32, 201, 354, 359, 376, 377, 379,
    380, 392, 416, 422, 423, 516
APIs, 376
Win32s, 376, 377, 380
Winchester, 141
Windows,
    3.*x*, 153, 194, 242, 253, 344–348,
        350, 352, 353, 359, 361, 376, 377
    95/98, 43, 51, 52, 152–154, 186,
        194, 196, 197, 201, 242, 253,
        344, 345–348, 35–354, 356, 361–

365, 369, 370, 373, 376
messages, 400–412, 627, 628
NT, 43, 152–155, 162, 163, 196,
    197, 201, 253, 344, 345, 347,
    353, 357, 359, 360, 367, 368,
    376, 377, 381, 518, 554
output, 414–421
sockets, 377
WinSock, 348, 507, 508, 516
WMF, 255, 259, 260, 322
Workstation, 448, 517
WORM, 141, 157
WP, 180
WWW, 237, 491, 501, 503, 516–518,
    553, 590, 591, 592, 596, 598–602,
    609, 610
X.21, 443, 444
X.25, 443, 444
X3T9.5, 444
XD bus, 46
Xerox Corporation, 457
X-OFF, 187, 188
X-ON, 187, 188
XOR, 14, 19, 61, 155, 216, 527, 529
X-terminals, 495
Yellow Book, 158, 160
ZIF, 31
ZIP, 237, 366, 546